The Theory of Papal Monarchy in the Fourteenth Century : The *Tractatus de causa immediata ecclesiastice potestatis* of Guillaume de Pierre Godin, OP

edited by

Wm. D. McCready

The *Tractatus de causa immediata ecclesiastice potestatis* is an ecclesiological treatise of the early fourteenth century. Judging from the surviving manuscripts, it assumed particular importance in the fifteenth century, during the conciliar controversy, when the subject of the constitution of the church became an object of sustained debate. It provides a particularly extreme statement of the papal hierocratic point of view, that the pope is immune to human judgment because he is the source of all governmental or jurisdictional authority in the church. The author buttresses his convictions by appealing to canon law and to the Church Fathers. But much more significantly in view of the recent historiography, he attempts to meet the anti-papalists on their own ground, by basing his ecclesiology on the *ecclesia primitiva* of the New Testament. It is the work of a first-rate canonist and skilled publicist, but hitherto it has been available only in the relatively rare and defective edition of Jean Barbier, published in Paris in 1506. The present edition, accompanied by an *apparatus criticus* and *apparatus fontium*, has been based on an examination and collation of all thirty extant manuscripts.

The text is preceded by an introduction which discusses the problem of authorship and the date of the treatise. The introduction also contains a description of the extant manuscripts, and a discussion of the lines of filiation among the manuscripts and the principles governing the edition of the text. The discussion of authorship, which also serves as an introduction to the treatise itself, supports the argument that the *De causa* should be attributed to Guillaume de Pierre Godin rather than Pierre de la Palu, to whom it has often been ascribed.

STUDIES AND TEXTS 56

THE THEORY OF PAPAL MONARCHY IN THE FOURTEENTH CENTURY

GUILLAUME DE PIERRE GODIN, *TRACTATUS DE CAUSA IMMEDIATA ECCLESIASTICE POTESTATIS*

EDITED BY

WM. D. McCREADY

PONTIFICAL INSTITUTE OF MEDIAEVAL STUDIES

ACKNOWLEDGMENT

This book has been published with the help of a grant from the Canadian Federation for the Humanities, using funds provided by the Social Sciences and Humanities Research Council of Canada.

CANADIAN CATALOGUING IN PUBLICATION DATA

Tractatus de causa immediata ecclesiastice potestatis.
The theory of papal monarchy in the fourteenth century

(Studies and texts, ISSN 0082-5328 ; 56)
Manuscript variously attributed to Guillelmus Petri de Godino, and Petrus de Palude.
Bibliography: p.
Includes index.
ISBN 0-88844-056-1

1. Catholic church - Government - History - Sources. 2. Popes - Primacy - History - Sources. I. Guillelmus Petri de Godino, Cardinal, ca. 1260-1336. II. Petrus de Palude, Patriarch of Jerusalem, d. 1342. III. McCready, William D. (William David), 1943- IV. Pontifical Institute of Mediaeval Studies. V. Title. VI. Series: Studies and texts (Pontifical Institute of Mediaeval Studies) ; 56.

BX1800.T7 1982 262′.13′09023 C81-094503-7

Pontifical Institute of Mediaeval Studies
59 Queen's Park Crescent East
Toronto, Ontario, Canada M5S 2C4

PRINTED BY UNIVERSA, WETTEREN, BELGIUM

Valeriae carae

Contents

PROLEGOMENA

TRACTATUS DE CAUSA IMMEDIATA ECCLESIASTICE POTESTATIS

Preface

A work such as this, which is the product of several years of research, cannot be completed without accumulating debts to a great many individuals and institutions, without whose assistance it scarcely would have been possible. My greatest debt is owed to the librarians who provided me with microfilm or xerox copies of the manuscripts. The overwhelming majority of the people with whom I had to deal were prompt and courteous in replying to my queries and in providing me with copies, and for that I am most grateful indeed. I was not able to visit all the libraries personally, but when I chose to do so I was greatly encouraged by the welcome and the assistance I received. I am particularly indebted to those individuals who were kind enough to examine manuscripts on my behalf, to help me settle particular points, when a personal inspection on my part was not possible. Special thanks are owed to Teresa Santander of the Universidad Literaria de Salamanca; J. S. G. Simmons of All Souls' College, Oxford; Dr Breitenbruch of the Stadtbibliothek Ulm; Dr Eva Irblich of the Österreichische Nationalbibliothek in Vienna; Denise Bloch of the Bibliothèque nationale in Paris; and A. Paravicini Bagliani of the Biblioteca Apostolica Vaticana. Special thanks are also owed to a number of people who helped me settle other specific points in my research, above all, Justo García Morales of the Centro Nacional del Tesoro Documental y Bibliográfico in Madrid, Monique Cécile Garand of the Comité International de Paléographie in Paris, and Prof. P. T. Stella of the Università Pontificia Salesiana in Rome.

In the course of my research I did encounter one or two obstacles which might have become serious impediments had it not been for the efforts of individuals who offered valuable advice, or who were willing to intercede on my behálf. Not all the efforts were equally effective, but they were all very much appreciated nonetheless. In this regard I would like to thank Dr Julian G. Plante of the Hill Monastic Manuscript Library in Collegeville, Minnesota; Mr H. B. Singleton of the Department of External Affairs in Ottawa; the Most Rev. J. L. Wilhelm, Archbishop of Kingston; and a number of my colleagues at Queen's University in Kingston: Prof. N. J. P. Brown of the Department of Philosophy, Prof. John Walker of the Department of Spanish and Italian, and Prof. A. W.

Riley of the Department of German. I would also like to express my deep appreciation to those who were kind enough to read my manuscript at various stages and provide me with the benefit of their advice and criticism: Dr Paul J. Meyvaert of the Mediaeval Academy of America; Prof. Leonard Boyle of the Pontifical Institute of Mediaeval Studies; Prof. Ross Kilpatrick of the Department of Classics, Queen's University; and the anonymous readers appointed by the Canadian Federation for the Humanities and the Pontifical Institute of Mediaeval Studies. Their careful reading of the manuscript saved me the embarrassment of many errors and inadequacies in addition to those which doubtless remain.

Finally, although theirs was far from being the least important kind of assistance I received, I would like to thank the Advisory Research Committee of Queen's University for the financial support extended to me over a number of years; the Canada Council, for providing me with a Leave Fellowship and research award for the academic year, 1975-76, which enabled me to devote a year's uninterrupted effort to my research; and the Canadian Federation for the Humanities, for the generous provision of a grant in aid of publication.

Note: At a couple of points in the Prolegomena I refer to there being one extant manuscript of Pierre de la Palu's *Tractatus de potestate papae*. A recent article draws attention to an additional manuscript of qu. 1: Biblioteca Apostolica Vaticana, Vat. lat. 4134, fols. 1r-19v. Cf. Jürgen Miethke, "Eine unbekannte Handschrift von Petrus de Paludes Traktat 'De potestate papae' aus dem Besitz Juan de Torquemadas in der Vatikanischen Bibliothek," *Quellen und Forschungen aus Italienischen Archiven und Bibliotheken*, 59 (1979): 468-475.

A Select Bibliography

The following bibliography offers a selection of titles only, and hence makes no claim to be definitive. It does not include all the sources used in the preparation of this edition, and so can be supplemented by consulting the notes. Part one, a list of primary source literature, is restricted to a selection of publicistic literature of which the *Tractatus de causa immediata ecclesiastice potestatis* is an example. Part two, a list of secondary sources, is restricted to a selection of titles which fall into one of the following four categories: (1) basic reference works, (2) works which deal with the *De causa* or its author specifically, (3) works which focus on other outstanding examples of late medieval publicistic literature, or (4) works which deal with this publicistic literature or its intellectual background in more general terms.

Part 1: Primary Sources

Anonymous. *Compendium maius octo processuum papalium*, ed. Richard Scholz, *Unbekannte kirchenpolitische Streitschriften aus der Zeit Ludwigs des Bayern (1327-1354)* 2 (Rome: Loescher, 1914), pp. 169-187.

——. *De potestate ecclesie*, ed. Jean Leclercq, "Textes contemporains de Dante sur des sujets qu'il a traités," *Studi Medievali*, 3rd ser. 6, pt. 2 (1965): 507-517.

——. *Non ponant laici*, ed. Richard Scholz, *Die Publizistik zur Zeit Philipps des Schönen und Bonifaz VIII.* (Stuttgart: Enke, 1903), pp. 471-484.

——. *Quaestio in utramque partem*, ed. Gustavo Vinay, "Egidio Romano e la cosidetta 'Quaestio in utramque partem'," *Bullettino dell'Istituto Storico Italiano per il Medio Evo*, 53 (1939): 93-116.

Aegidius Romanus. *De ecclesiastica potestate*, ed. Richard Scholz. Weimar: Bohlaus Nachfolger, 1929.

——. *De regimine principum*. Rome: Apud Zanettum, 1607.

——. *De renunciatione papae*, ed. Juan Thomás Rocaberti de Perelada, *Bibliotheca maxima pontificia* 2.1 (Rome: Buagni, 1698), pp. 1-64.

Aegidius Spiritalis. *Libellus contra infideles*, ed. Scholz, *Unbekannte kirchenpolitische Streitschriften* 2, pp. 105-129.

Alexander de S. Elpidio. *De ecclesiastica potestate*, ed. Rocaberti, *Bibliotheca* 2.7, pp. 1-40.

Alvarus Pelagius. *Collirium adversus hereses novas*, ed. Scholz, *Unbekannte kirchenpolitische Streitschriften* 2, pp. 491-514.

——. *De planctu ecclesiae*, ed. Rocaberti, *Bibliotheca* 3, pp. 23-264.

——. *Speculum regum*, ed. Scholz, *Unbekannte kirchenpolitische Streitschriften* 2, pp. 514-529.

Augustinus Triumphus. *De potestate collegii mortuo papa*, ed. Scholz, *Die Publizistik*, pp. 501-508; ed. W. Mulder in *Studia catholica*, 5 (1928-29): 46-53.

——. *Summa de ecclesiastica potestate*. Augsburg: Johannes Schlüssler, 1473.

——. *Tractatus brevis de duplici potestate prelatorum et laicorum*, ed. Scholz, *Die Publizistik*, pp. 486-501.

Bertrand, Pierre. See Pierre Bertrand.

Capocci, Giacomo. See James of Viterbo.

Colonna, Egidio. See Aegidius Romanus.

Conrad of Megenberg. *De translatione Romani imperii*, ed. Scholz, *Unbekannte kirchenpolitische Streitschriften* 2, pp. 249-345.

Dante Alighieri. *De monarchia*, ed. Gustavo Vinay. Florence: Sansoni, 1950; trans. Donald Nicholl. London: Weidenfeld, 1954; Herbert W. Schneider, 2nd ed. New York: Liberal Arts Press, 1957.

Durandus de S. Porciano. *De iurisdictione ecclesiastica*, ed. Jean Barbier. Paris, 1506.

Franciscus Toti de Perusio. *Tractatus contra Bavarum*, ed. Scholz, *Unbekannte kirchenpolitische Streitschriften* 2, pp. 76-88.

François de Meyronnes. *De praelatura dominii spiritualis ad dominium temporale*, ed. Friedrich Baethgen, "Dante und Franz von Mayronis," *Deutsches Archiv für Erforschung des Mittelalters*, 15 (1959): 120-136.

——. *Quaestio de subiectione*, ed. P. de Lapparent, "L'œuvre politique de François de Meyronnes," *Archives d'histoire doctrinale et littéraire du moyen âge*, 13 (1940-42): 75-92.

——. *Tractatus de principatu regni Siciliae*, ed. Lapparent, "L'œuvre," pp. 93-116.

Guido Terreni. *Quaestio de magisterio infallibili Romani pontificis*, ed. Bartolomé-Maria Xiberta. Münster: Aschendorf, 1926.

Guido Vernani. *De reprobatione Monarchiae compositae a Dante*, ed. Thomas Kaeppeli, "Der Dantegegner Guido Vernani O.P. vom Rimini," *Quellen und Forschungen aus italienischen Archiven und Bibliotheken*, 28 (1937-1938): 123-146.

Guillelmus de Villana [Guillelmus Amidani de Cremona]. *Reprobatio errorum*, ed. Darach Mac Fhionnbhairr. Rome: Augustinianum, 1977.

Guillelmus de Sarzano. *Tractatus de potestate summi pontificis*, ed. Renato Del Ponte in *Studi Medievali*, 3rd ser. 12 (1971): 1020-1094.

Henry of Cremona. *De potestate papae*, ed. Scholz, *Die Publizistik*, pp. 459-471.

Hermannus de Scildis. *Tractatus contra haereticos negantes immunitatem et iurisdictionem sanctae Ecclesiae*, ed. Adolar Zumkeller. Würzburg: Augustinus-Verlag, 1970.

Herveus Natalis. *Tractatus de iurisdictione*, ed. Ludwig Hödl. Munich: Hueber, 1959.

——. *Tractatus de potestate papae*, appended to his *In quatuor libros Sententiarum commentaria*. Paris: Apud viduam Dyonisii Moreau, 1647.

James of Viterbo. *De regimine christiano*, ed. Henri-Xavier Arquillière, *Le plus ancien traité de l'église*. Paris: Beauchesne, 1926.

Johannes Branchazolus. *De principio et origine et potencia imperatoris et pape*, ed. Edmund E. Stengel, *Nova Alamanniae* 1 (Berlin: Weidmannsche Buchhandlung, 1921), pp. 44-52.

John of Naples. *Quaestiones variae Parisiis disputatae*. Naples: C. Vitalis, 1618; repr. Ridgewood, NJ: Gregg Press, 1966.

John of Paris. *Tractatus de regia potestate et papali*, ed. Fritz Bleienstein, *Johannes Quidort von Paris, Über königliche und päpstliche Gewalt*. Stuttgart: Klett, 1969; trans. John A. Watt. Toronto: Pontifical Institute of Mediaeval Studies, 1971; Arthur P. Monahan. New York: Columbia Univ. Press, 1974.

Lambertus Guerrici de Hoyo. *Liber de commendatione Iohannis XXII*, ed. Scholz, *Unbekannte kirchenpolitische Streitschriften* 2, pp. 154-168.

Marsilius of Padua. *Defensor minor*, ed. C. Kenneth Brampton. Birmingham: Cornish Bros., 1922.

——. *Defensor pacis*, ed. Charles William Previté-Orton. Cambridge: Cambridge Univ. Press, 1928; trans. Alan Gewirth, *Marsilius of Padua*, vol. 1: *The Defensor Pacis*. New York: Columbia Univ. Press, 1956.

——. *De translatione imperii*, ed. Melchior Goldast, *Monarchia Sancti Romani Imperii* 2 (Frankfurt: Conrad Biermann, 1614; repr. Graz: Akademische Druck- u. Verlagsanstalt, 1960), pp. 147-153.

Ockham, William. See William of Ockham.

Olivi, Pierre Jean. See Peter Olivi.

Opicinus de Canistris. *De preeminentia spiritualis imperii*, ed. Scholz, *Unbekannte kirchenpolitische Streitschriften* 2, pp. 89-104.

Peter Olivi. *De renunciatione papae*, ed. P. Livarius Oliger in *Archivum Franciscanum historicum*, 11 (1918): 340-366.

——. *Epistola ad Conradum de Offida*, ed. Oliger, *Archivum Fr. hist.* 11, pp. 366-373.

——. *Quaestio de infallibilitate Romani pontificis*, ed. Michele Maccarrone in *Rivista di storia della chiesa in Italia*, 3 (1949): 309-343.

Petrus de Palude. See Pierre de la Palu.

Pierre Bertrand. *De iurisdictione ecclesiastica et politica*, ed. Goldast, *Monarchia Sancti Romani Imperii* 2, pp. 1361-1383.

Pierre de la Palu. *Articuli ... circa materiam confessionum*, ed. Jean Barbier. Paris, 1506.

——. *Tractatus de potestate papae*, ed. Prospero T. Stella. Zürich: Pas-Verlag, 1966.

Ptolemy of Lucca. *Determinatio compendiosa de iurisdictione imperii*, ed. Marius Krammer, *MGH*, *Fontes iuris Germanici antiqui* 1. Hanover and Leipzig: Hahn, 1909.

Trionfo, Agostino. See Augustinus Triumphus.

William of Ockham, *Allegationes de potestate imperiali*, ed. Scholz, *Unbekannte kirchenpolitische Streitschriften* 2, pp. 417-431.

——. *An princeps pro suo succursu, scilicet guerrae, possit recipere bona ecclesiarum*, ed. H. S. Offler and R. H. Snape, *Guillelmi de Ockham Opera politica* 1 (Manchester: Manchester Univ. Press, 1940), pp. 223-271; revised edition, H. S. Offler, 1974, pp. 219-267.

——. *Breviloquium de principatu tyrannico*, ed. Richard Scholz, *Wilhelm von Ockham als politischer Denker und sein Breviloquium de principatu tyrannico*. Stuttgart: Hiersemann, 1944.

——. *De imperatorum et pontificum potestate*, ed. C. Kenneth Brampton. Oxford: Clarendon, 1927.

——. *Dialogus de imperio et pontificia potestate*, in *Guillelmus de Occam* O.F.M. *(†1349-50), Opera plurima* 1. Lyon, 1494; repr. London: Gregg Press, 1962.

——. *Octo quaestiones de potestate papae*, ed. J. G. Sikes, *Guillelmi de Ockham Opera politica* 1, pp. 1-221; revised edition, H. S. Offler, pp. 1-217.

Part 2: Secondary Sources

Alberigo, Giuseppe. *Cardinalato e collegialità: studi sull'ecclesiologia tra l'*XI *e il* XIV *secolo*. Florence: Vallecchi, 1969.

Arquillière, Henri Xavier. *L'Augustinisme politique: essai sur la formation des théories politiques du moyen âge*, 2nd ed. Paris: Vrin, 1955.

Baluze, Etienne. *Vitae paparum Avenionensium*, ed. G. Mollat. Paris: Letouzey, 1914-1927.

Benson, Robert Louis. *The Bishop Elect: A Study in Medieval Ecclesiastical Office*. Princeton: Princeton Univ. Press, 1968.

Buisson, Ludwig. *Potestas und Caritas: Die päpstliche Gewalt in Spätmittelalter*. Cologne: Böhlau, 1958.

Carlyle, Alex. James and Robt. Warand. *A History of Mediaeval Political Theory in the West*. 6 vols. Edinburgh: Blackwood, 1903-1936.

Congar, Yves Marie-Joseph. "Aspects ecclésiologiques de la querelle entre mendiants et séculiers dans la seconde moitié du XIIIe siècle et le début du XIVe," *Archives d'histoire doctrinale et littéraire du moyen âge*, 28 (1961): 35-151.

——. *L'Ecclésiologie du haut Moyen Âge*. Paris: Éditions du Cerf, 1968.

Costa, Pietro. *Iurisdictio: semantica del potere politico nella pubblicistica medievale (1100-1433)*. (Università di Firenze. Pubblicazioni della Facoltà di giurisprudenza, 1). Milan: Giuffrè, 1969.

Darricau, Raymond. "Le cardinal Bayonnais, Guillaume de Pierre Godin, des Frères Prêcheurs (1260-1336)," *Société des sciences, lettres et arts de Bayonne*, n.s. 129 (1973): 125-141.

Dempf, Alois. *Sacrum imperium: Geschichts- und Staatsphilosophie des Mittelalters und der politischen Renaissance*. Munich: Oldenbourg, 1962.

Dolcini, Carlo. *Il pensiero politico di Michele da Cesena, 1328-1338*. Faenza: Fratelli Lega, 1977.

Ercole, Francesco. *Il pensiero politico di Dante*. Milan: Alpes, 1927-1928.

Fournier, Paul. "Le cardinal Guillaume de Peyre Godin," *Bibliothèque de l'École des Chartes*, 86 (1925): 100-121.

——. "Guillaume de Peyre de Godin, cardinal," *Histoire littéraire de la France*, 37 (1938): 146-153.

——. "Pierre de la Palu, théologien et canoniste," *Histoire littéraire de la France*, 37 (1938): 39-84.

Ganzer, Klaus. *Papsttum und Bistumsbesetzungen in der Zeit von Gregor* IX. *bis Bonifaz* VIII. Cologne: Böhlau, 1968.

Gewirth, Alan. *Marsilius of Padua*, vol. 1: *Marsilius of Padua and Medieval Political Philosophy*. New York: Columbia Univ. Press, 1951.

——. "Philosophy and Political Thought in the Fourteenth Century," *The Forward Movement of the Fourteenth Century*, ed. Francis Lee Utley (Columbus, Ohio: Ohio State Univ. Press, 1961), pp. 125-164.

Gierke, Otto Friedrich von. *Political Theories of the Middle Age*. Boston: Beacon Press, 1958.

Glorieux, Palémon. *Répertoire des maîtres en théologie de Paris au* XIIIe *siècle*. 2 vols. Paris: Vrin, 1933.

Grabmann, Martin. "Kardinal Guillelmus Petri de Godino O.P. (†1336) und seine Lectura Thomasina," *Divus Thomas*, 4 (1926): 385-403; repr. *Mittelalterliches Geistesleben*, vol. 2 (München: Max Hueber, 1936), pp. 559-576.

Groppo, Giuseppe. "La teologia e il suo 'Subiectum' secondo il prologo del commento alle Sentenze di Pietro da Palude O.P. (†1342)," *Salesianum*, 23 (1961): 219-316.

Hendrix, S. H. "In Quest of the *vera ecclesia*: The Crises of Late Medieval Ecclesiology," *Viator*, 7 (1976): 347-378.

Iung, Nicolas. *Un franciscain, théologien du pouvoir pontifical au* XIVe *siècle: Alvaro Pelayo, évêque et pénitencier de Jean* XXII. Paris: Vrin, 1931.

Kaeppeli, Thomas. *Scriptores Ordinis Praedicatorum Medii Aevi*. 2 vols. Rome: Sabinae, 1970-1975.

Kantorowicz, Ernst Hartwig. *The King's Two Bodies: A Study in Mediaeval Political Theology*. Princeton: Princeton Univ. Press, 1957.

Koch, Joseph. "Der Prozeß gegen den Magister Johannes de Polliaco und seine Vorgeschichte (1312-1321)," *Recherches de théologie ancienne et médiévale*, 5 (1933): 391-422.

Kölmel, Wilhelm. "Über spirituale und temporale Ordnung," *Franziskanische Studien*, 36 (1954): 171-195.

——. *Wilhelm Ockham und seine kirchenpolitischen Schriften*. Essen: Ludgerus-Verlag, 1962.

——. "Einheit und Zweiheit der Gewalt im corpus mysticum: Zur Souveränitätslehre des Augustinus Triumphus," *Historisches Jahrbuch*, 83 (1963): 103-147.

——. "Paupertas und potestas: Kirche und Welt in der Sicht des Alvarus Pelagius," *Franziskanische Studien*, 46 (1964): 57-101.

——. "A Deo sed per homines: Zur Begründung des Staatsgewalt im Ordnungsverständnis des Mittelalters," *Franziskanische Studien*, 48 (1966): 308-335.

——. *Regimen Christianum: Weg und Ergebnisse des Gewaltenverhältnisses und des Gewaltenverständnisses (8. bis 14. Jahrhundert).* Berlin: de Gruyter, 1970.

Kuiters, Raphaël. "De ecclesiastica sive de summi pontificis potestate secundum Aegidium Romanum," *Analecta Augustiniana*, 20 (1946): 146-214.

——. "Was bedeuten die Ausdrücke 'directa' und 'indirecta potestas' papae in temporalibus bei Aegidius von Rom, (Jakobus von Viterbo) und Johannes von Paris?" *Archiv für katholisches Kirchenrecht*, 128 (1957-1958): 99-105.

——. "Aegidius Romanus and the Authorship of 'In utramque partem' and 'De ecclesiastica potestate'," *Augustiniana*, 8 (1958): 267-280.

Ladner, Gerhart B. "The Concepts of 'ecclesia' and 'christianitas' and their Relation to the Idea of Papal 'plenitudo potestatis' from Gregory VII to Boniface VIII," *Sacerdozio e Regno da Gregorio VII a Bonifacio VIII*, MHP, 18 (1954): 49-77.

Laehr, Gerhard. *Die Konstantinische Schenkung in der abendländischen Literatur des Mittelalters.* Berlin: Ebering, 1926.

Lagarde, Georges de. *La naissance de l'esprit laïque au déclin du Moyen Âge*, vol. 1: *Bilan du XIIIème siècle*, 3rd ed. Louvain: Nauwelaerts, 1956; vol. 2: *Secteur social de la scolastique*, 2nd ed. Louvain: Nauwelaerts, 1958; vol. 3: *Le Defensor pacis*. Louvain: Nauwelaerts, 1970; vol. 4: *Guillaume d'Ockham, Défense de l'empire.* Louvain: Nauwelaerts, 1962; vol. 5: *Guillaume d'Ockham, Critique des structures ecclésiales.* Louvain: Nauwelaerts, 1963.

Laurent, M.-H. "Le testament et la succession du cardinal dominicain Guillaume de Pierre Godin," *Archivum Fratrum Praedicatorum*, 2 (1932): 84-231.

Lecler, Joseph. "Pars corporis papae.... Le sacré collège dans l'ecclésiologie médiévale," in *L'homme devant Dieu: mélanges offerts au Père Henri de Lubac* 2 (Paris, 1964), pp. 183-198.

Leclercq, Jean. *Jean de Paris et l'ecclésiologie du XIIIe siècle.* Paris: Vrin, 1942.

——. *L'Idée de la royauté du Christ au moyen âge.* Paris: Éditions du Cerf, 1959.

Leff, Gordon. "The Apostolic Ideal in Later Medieval Ecclesiology," *Journal of Theological Studies*, n.s. 18 (1967): 58-82.

——. *William of Ockham: The Metamorphosis of Scholastic Discourse.* Manchester: Manchester Univ. Press, 1975.

Lewis, Ewart (Kellogg). *Medieval Political Ideas.* 2 vols. London: Routledge and Kegan Paul, 1954.

Maccarrone, Michele. *Vicarius Christi: storia del titolo papale.* Rome: Facultas Theologica Pontificii Athenaei Lateranensis, 1952.

——. "Potestas directa e potestas indirecta nei teologi del XII e XIII secolo," *Sacerdozio e Regno*, pp. 27-47.

Maffei, Domenico. *La Donazione di Costantino nei giuristi medievali.* Milan: Giuffrè, 1964.

Mariani, Ugo. *Chiesa e stato nei teologi agostiniani del secolo XIV.* (Uomini e dottrine, 5). Rome: Edizioni di Storia e Letteratura, 1957.

McCready, Wm. D. "Papal *plenitudo potestatis* and the Source of Temporal Authority in Late Medieval Papal Hierocratic Theory," *Speculum*, 48 (1973): 654-674.

——. "The Problem of the Empire in Augustinus Triumphus and Late Medieval Papal Hierocratic Theory," *Traditio*, 30 (1974): 325-349.

——. "Papalists and Anti-Papalists: Aspects of the Church/State Controversy in the Later Middle Ages," *Viator*, 6 (1975): 241-273.

——. "The Papal Sovereign in the Ecclesiology of Augustinus Triumphus," *Mediaeval Studies*, 39 (1977): 177-205.

McGrade, Arthur S. *The Political Thought of William of Ockham: Personal and Institutional Principles.* Cambridge: Cambridge Univ. Press, 1974.

McIlwain, Charles Howard. *The Growth of Political Thought in the West.* London: Macmillan, 1932.

Mochi Onory, Sergio. *Fonti canonistiche dell'idea moderna dello stato.* Milan: Vita e pensiero, 1951.

Moynihan, James M. *Papal Immunity and Liability in the Writings of the Medieval Canonists.* Rome: Gregorian Univ. Press, 1961.

Oakley, Francis. "Celestial Hierarchies Revisited: Walter Ullmann's Vision of Medieval Politics," *Past and Present*, 60 (August, 1973): 3-48.

Pacaut, Marcel. *La théocratie: l'Église et le pouvoir au moyen âge.* Paris: Aubier, 1957.

Passerin d'Entrèves, Alexander. *The Medieval Contribution to Political Thought.* Oxford: Oxford Univ. Press, 1939.

Pilati, Giovanni. *Chiesa e stato nei primi quindici secoli.* Rome: Desclée, 1961.

Post, Gaines. *Studies in Medieval Legal Thought.* Princeton: Princeton Univ. Press, 1964.

——. "Vincentius Hispanus, 'Pro ratione voluntas', and Medieval and Early Modern Theories of Sovereignty," *Traditio*, 28 (1972): 159-184.

Quétif, Jacques and Jacques Echard. *Scriptores Ordinis Praedicatorum.* 2 vols. Paris: J. B. C. Ballard, 1719-1721.

Quillet, Jeannine. *La philosophie politique de Marsile de Padoue.* Paris: Vrin, 1970.

Rivière, Jean. "Une première 'Somme' du pouvoir pontifical: le pape chez Augustin d'Ancône," *Revue des sciences religieuses*, 18 (1938): 149-183.

Roensch, Frederick J. *Early Thomistic School.* Dubuque, Iowa: Priory Press, 1964.

Scholz, Richard. *Die Publizistik zur Zeit Philipps des Schönen und Bonifaz VIII.* Stuttgart: Enke, 1903.

Segall, Hermann. *Der 'Defensor pacis' des Marsilius von Padua. Grundfragen der Interpretation.* Wiesbaden: Steiner, 1959.

Sikes, J. G. "John de Pouilli and Peter de la Palu," *English Historical Review*, 49 (1934): 219-240.

Stegmüller, Friedrich. *Repertorium commentariorum in Sententias Petri Lombardi*. 2 vols. Würzburg: Schöningh, 1947.

Stella, Prospero T. "A proposito della attribuzione a Pietro di La Palu del 'Tractatus de causa immediata ecclesiasticae potestatis'," *Salesianum*, 27 (1965): 382-409.

——. *Magistri Petri de Palude, O.P., Tractatus de potestate papae*. Zürich: Pas-Verlag, 1966.

Stickler, Alfons. "Sacerdozio e Regno nelle nuove ricerche attorno ai secoli XII e XIII nei decretisti e decretalisti fino alle decretali di Gregorio IX," *Sacerdozio e Regno*, pp. 1-26.

——. "Imperator vicarius papae: Die Lehren der französisch-deutschen Dekretistenschule des 12. und beginnenden 13. Jahrhunderts über die Beziehungen zwischen Papst und Kaiser," *Mitteilungen des Instituts für Österreichische Geschichtsforschung*, 62 (1954): 165-212.

Tabacco, Giovanni. *Le relazione fra i concetti di potere temporale e di potere spirituale nella tradizione cristiana fino al secolo XIV*. (Pubblicazioni della Facoltà di lettere e filosofia, v. 2, fasc. 5). Turin: Università di Torino, 1950.

Tierney, Brian. *Foundations of the Conciliar Theory*. Cambridge: Cambridge Univ. Press, 1955.

——. "The Continuity of Papal Political Theory in the Thirteenth Century: Some Methodological Considerations," *Mediaeval Studies*, 27 (1965): 227-245.

——. *Origins of Papal Infallibility, 1150-1350*. Leiden: Brill, 1972.

Ullmann, Walter. *Medieval Papalism: The Political Theories of the Medieval Canonists*. London: Methuen, 1949.

——. *The Medieval Papacy: St Thomas and Beyond*. London: Aquin Press, 1960.

——. *The Growth of Papal Government in the Middle Ages*, 2nd ed. London: Methuen, 1962.

——. *A History of Political Thought: The Middle Ages*. Harmondsworth, Middlesex: Penguin, 1965.

——. *Principles of Government and Politics in the Middle Ages*, 2nd ed. London: Methuen, 1966.

——. *The Individual and Society in the Middle Ages*. Baltimore: John Hopkins Press, 1966.

——. *A Short History of the Papacy in the Middle Ages*. London: Methuen, 1972.

——. "Die Bulle Unam Sanctam: Rückblick und Ausblick," *Römische Historische Mitteilungen*, 16 (1974): 45-77.

——. *Law and Politics in the Middle Ages*. Ithaca: Cornell Univ. Press, 1975.

——. "Boniface VIII and his Contemporary Scholarship," *Journal of Theological Studies*, n.s. 27 (1976): 58-87.

Schulte, Johann Friedrich, Ritter von. *Die Geschichte der Quellen und Literatur des canonischen Rechts von Gratian bis auf die Gegenwart*. Stuttgart: Enke, 1877.

Watt, John A. "The 'Quaestio in utramque partem' Reconsidered," *Studia Gratiana*, 13 (1967): 411-453.

——. "The Constitutional Law of the College of Cardinals: Hostiensis to Joannes Andreae," *Mediaeval Studies*, 33 (1971): 127-157.

——. *The Theory of Papal Monarchy in the Thirteenth Century*. New York: Fordham Univ. Press, 1965.

Wilks, Michael J. "*Papa est nomen iurisdictionis*: Augustinus Triumphus and the Papal Vicariate of Christ," *Journal of Theological Studies*, n.s. 8 (1957): 71-91, 256-271.

——. "The *apostolicus* and the Bishop of Rome," *Journal of Theological Studies*, n.s. 13 (1962): 290-317; 14 (1963): 311-354.

——. *The Problem of Sovereignty in the Later Middle Ages*. Cambridge: Cambridge Univ. Press, 1963.

Zeyen, Rainer. *Die theologische Disputation des Johannes de Polliaco zur kirchlichen Verfassung*. Berne: H. Lang, 1976. [I was unable to obtain a copy of this work until my manuscript had gone to the printer, and so I have not been able to refer to it in the pages which follow.]

Zimmermann, Harald. *Papstabsetzungen des Mittelalters*. Graz: Böhlau, 1968.

List of Abbreviations and Symbols

Act. – Actus Apostolorum
add. – *addit, addunt*
Apoc. – Apocalypsis
Barb. – J. Barbier ed., *Tractatus de causa immediata ecclesiastice potestatis* (Paris, 1506)
c. – capitulum, canon
Cant. – Canticum Canticorum
Cat. aur. in Luc. 22.9 (Theophylactus), 2: 289B (2: 316B) – Thomas Aquinas, *Catena aurea in quatuor Evangelia*, the gloss of Theophylactus on Luke 22, ed. P. A. Guarienti (Turin/Rome, 1953), 2: 289, col. B. (An alternate edition is that of Turin, 1925, in which the location for the passage in question is 2: 316, col. B.)
CCL 50: 224 – *Corpus Christianorum. Series Latina* (Turnholti, 1953 –). The reference here is to vol. 50, p. 224.
cet. mss. – *ceteri manuscripti*
Clem. 1.3.2 – Pope Clement V, *Constitutiones*, ed. E. A. Friedberg, *Corpus iuris canonici* 2 (Leipzig, 1881). The reference is to Liber 1, Titulus 3, Capitulum 2.
Cod. 3.13.3 – *Codex Iustinianus*, ed. P. Krueger, *Corpus iuris civilis* 2 (Berolini, Apud Weidmannos, 1954). The reference is to Liber 3, Titulus 13.3.
Contra er. Gr., p. 323 – Thomas Aquinas, *Contra errores Grecorum*, ed. R. P. Mandonnet in *Opuscula omnia* 3 (Paris, 1927), pp. 279-328 at p. 323
Cor. – ad Corinthios
corr. – *corrigit, corrigunt*
CSEL 67: 64 – *Corpus scriptorum ecclesiasticorum latinorum* (Vindobonae, 1866 –). The reference is to vol. 67, p. 64.
des. – *desinit, desinunt*
Deut. – Deuteronomium
Dig. 2.1.2 – *Iustiniani Digesta*, ed. T. Mommsen and P. Krueger, *Corpus iuris civilis* 1. The reference is to Liber 2, Titulus 1.2.
Eccli. – Ecclesiasticus
Eph. – ad Ephesios
Esdr. – Esdras
Ex. – Exodus
exp. – *expunxit*
expl. – *explicit*

fol. (fols.) – folio (folios)
Gal. – ad Galatas
Gen. – Genesis
Gratian, C.2 q.7 c.37 – Gratian of Bologna, *Decretum*, ed. E. A. Friedberg, *Corpus iuris canonici* 1 (Leipzig, 1879). The reference is to Pars Secunda, Causa 2, Questio 7, Capitulum 37.
Gratian, D.21 c.2 – Gratian of Bologna, *Decretum*, Prima Pars, Distinctio 21, Capitulum 2
Gratian, *De cons.* D.4 c.19 – Gratian of Bologna, *Decretum*, Pars Tertia (*De consecratione*), Distinctio 4, Capitulum 19
Gratian, *De poen.* D.1 c.60 – Gratian of Bologna, *Decretum*, Pars Secunda, Causa 33, Questio 3 (*De poenitentia*), Distinctio 1, Capitulum 60
Heb. – ad Hebraeos
hom. – homoeoteleuton
inc. – incipit
Inst. 1.2.6 – *Iustiniani Institutiones*, ed. P. Krueger, *Corpus iuris civilis* 1. The reference is to Liber 1, Titulus 2.6.
inv. – invertit, invertunt
Is. – Isaias
Jac. – epistola Jacobi
Joan. – Joannes, epistola Joannis
Lev. – Leviticus
Luc. – Lucas
Mansi – G. D. Mansi, *Sacrorum conciliorum nova et amplissima collectio* (repr. Graz, 1960 –)
Marc. – Marcus
marg. – margine
Matt. – Matthaeus
MGH – *Monumenta Germaniae historica* (Hanover, 1835 –)
MS (MSS) – *codex manuscriptus* (*codices manuscripti*)
Nov. 15.1.1 – *Iustiniani Novellae*, ed. R. Schoell and G. Kroll, *Corpus iuris civilis* 3. The reference is to Nov. 15, caput 1.1.
Num. – Numeri
om. – omittit, omittunt
Par. – Paralipomenon
Pet. – epistola Petri
PG 50: 727 – J. P. Migne ed., *Patrologiae cursus completus. Series Graeca* (Parisiis, 1857-1866). The reference is to vol. 50, col. 727.
PL 92: 986 – J. P. Migne ed., *Patrologiae cursus completus. Series Latina* (Parisiis, 1844-1864). The reference is to vol. 92, col. 986.
praem. – praemittit, praemittunt
Ps. – Psalmi
Reg. – liber Regum
rep. – repetit, repetunt

Rom. – ad Romanos

Sent. – Peter Lombard, *Quatuor libri sententiarum*, 2 vols. (Quaracchi, 1916). A reference such as Aquinas, 4 *Sent.* refers to Aquinas' commentary on the fourth book of the *Sentences*.

Sext. 3.17.1 – Pope Boniface VIII, *Liber sextus decretalium*, ed. Friedberg, *Corpus iuris canonici* 2. The reference is to Liber 3, Titulus 17, Capitulum 1.

Tim. – ad Timotheum

Tit. – ad Titum

X. 3.42.3 – Pope Gregory IX, *Decretales*, ed. Friedberg, *Corpus iuris canonici* 2. The reference is to Liber 3, Titulus 42, Capitulum 3.

Symbols

( ) Parentheses – These are used on a few occasions as punctuation. Words enclosed in parentheses belong to the text, but their meaning is parenthetical within the meaning of the sentence.

[ ] Square Brackets – These enclose words which, in the editor's judgment, do not belong to the text, but which are found in several important manuscripts nonetheless. In the Epilogus, Appendix C and apparatus they enclose explanations of the editor. In the *apparatus criticus* a single squared bracket is used to separate the lemma from the list of variants.

< > Angular Brackets – These enclose words which, in the editor's opinion, should be included in the text, but are not found in the manuscript sources.

§ Paragraph Sign – This is used to indicate a paragraph or subdivision of an ancient or medieval text.

List of Sigla

B^1	= Barcelona, Catedral 2
B^2	= Barcelona, Catedral 16
Bl	= Basel, Universitätsb. B II 24
Bm^1	= Bamberg, Staatsb. Patr. 152
Bm^2	= Bamberg, Staatsb. Theol. 227
Bo	= Burgo de Osma, Catedral 65
Br	= Berlin, Staatsb. Elect. lat. 475
O	= Oxford, All Souls' 47
P^1	= Paris, Bibl. nat. lat. 1514
P^2	= Paris, Bibl. nat. lat. 4232
P^3	= Paris, Bibl. nat. lat. 4233
P^4	= Paris, Bibl. nat. lat. 12467
Pr	= Prague, Metrop. Kap. O 50
R	= Reims, Bibl. mun. 493
S	= Salamanca, Bibl. Univ. 18
Sr	= Saint-Omer, Bibl. mun. 382
St	= Stuttgart, Landesbibl. theol. 4° 614
Sv	= Seville, Bibl. Colombina 7-4-11
Sz	= Salzburg, St. Peter b.XI.25
T	= Tortosa, Catedral 151
U	= Ulm, Stadtb. 6740-44
V^1	= Vatican, Ottob. lat. 641
V^2	= Vatican, Ottob. lat. 779
V^3	= Vatican, Ross. 466
V^4	= Vatican, Vat. lat. 4109
V^5	= Vatican, Vat. lat. 4139
V^6	= Vatican, Vat. lat. 6586
V^7	= Vatican, Vat. lat. 7188
Va	= Vienna, Öster. Nationalb. 2168
W	= Wrocław, Bibl. Uniw. IV F 64

Bamberg, Staatsb. Patr. 152	= Bm^1
——. Staatsb. Theol. 227	= Bm^2
Barcelona, Catedral 2	= B^1
——. Catedral 16	= B^2
Basel, Universitätsb. B II 24	= Bl
Berlin, Staatsb. Elect. lat. 475	= Br
Burgo de Osma, Catedral 65	= Bo
Oxford, All Souls' 47	= O
Paris, Bibl. nat. lat. 1514	= P^1
——. Bibl. nat. lat. 4232	= P^2
——. Bibl. nat. lat. 4233	= P^3
——. Bibl. nat. lat. 12467	= P^4

Prague, Metrop. Kap. O 50	= Pr
Reims, Bibl. mun. 493	= R
Saint-Omer, Bibl. mun. 382	= Sr
Salamanca, Bibl. Univ. 18	= S
Salzburg, St Peter b.XI.25	= Sz
Seville, Bibl. Colombina 7-4-11	= Sv
Stuttgart, Landesbibl. theol. 4° 614	= St
Tortosa, Catedral 151	= T
Ulm, Stadtb. 6740-44	= U
Vatican, Ottob. lat. 641	= V^1
——. Ottob. lat. 779	= V^2
——. Ross. 466	= V^3
——. Vat. lat. 4109	= V^4
——. Vat. lat. 4139	= V^5
——. Vat. lat. 6586	= V^6
——. Vat. lat. 7188	= V^7
Vienna, Öster. Nationalb. 2168	= Va
Wrocław, Bibl. Uniw. IV F 64	= W

In the apparatus groups of manuscripts are referred to by the symbols for their hyparchetypes. Hence:

α = $OV^1BoV^2V^5V^3P^3SvSStUBm^1PrWBlV^4B^2P^2V^7$
β = $P^4RP^1B^1TBm^2BrSzBarb.V^6SrVa$
γ = $StUBm^1PrWBlV^4B^2P^2V^7$
θ = $OV^1BoV^2V^5V^3P^3SvS$
  θ^1 = $BoV^2V^5V^3P^3SvS$
  θ^2 = OV^1
  θ^3 = BoV^2V^5
  θ^4 = V^3P^3SvS
π = $P^4RP^1B^1T$
  π^1 = P^4R
  π^2 = P^1B^1T
ρ = $Bm^2BrSzBarb.V^6$
  ρ^1 = Bm^2BrSz
  ρ^2 = BrSz
σ = SrVa
φ = $StUBm^1PrWBlV^4$
  φ^1 = $StUBm^1$
  φ^2 = $PrWBlV^4$
  φ^3 = StU
  φ^4 = BlV^4
  φ^5 = PrW
ψ = P^2V^7

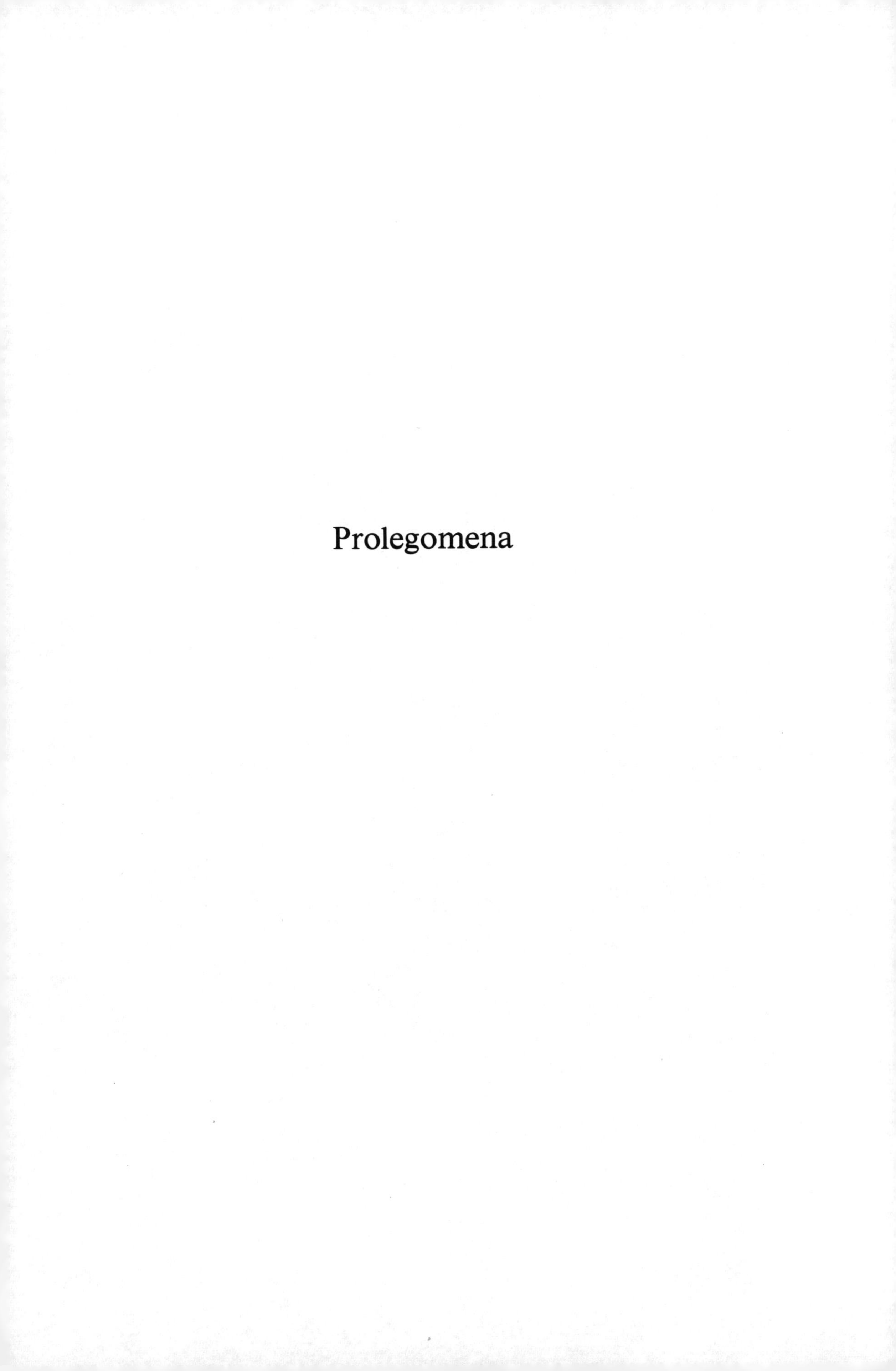

Prolegomena

1

The Character and Significance of the *De causa immediata ecclesiastice potestatis*

Judging from the nature of the surviving evidence, the *De causa immediata ecclesiastice potestatis* was a treatise of some considerable importance in the later Middle Ages. One indication of its significance is the fact that it survives in thirty extant manuscripts, whereas the *Defensor pacis* of Marsilius of Padua, regarded by many as the most significant political treatise of the fourteenth century, survives in twenty-seven. One cannot justify claims to prominence exclusively on such a basis, for among other things, it is usually extremely difficult to determine how many manuscripts have been lost in the intervening centuries. The reaction of contemporaries has to be taken into account as well, and when that is done it becomes difficult to maintain that the *Defensor pacis* does not deserve the scholarly attention which has been lavished upon it, or that the *De causa* must be regarded as having been equally significant. During the fourteenth century the *Defensor pacis* became the centre of a storm of controversy, whereas nothing similar seems to have happened in the case of the *De causa*. But even if one cannot maintain that the *De causa* rivals the *Defensor pacis* in importance, the surviving manuscripts of the *De causa*, which stretch from one end of Europe to the other, do seem to justify some more modest claims. The sheer number of them would seem to indicate that the *De causa* was widely read in the later Middle Ages, and that it undoubtedly exerted its influence, if only in a quieter fashion. The fact that most of the manuscripts come to us from the fifteenth century, and that some of them can be traced back to the Council of Basel, would seem to indicate that it was at the height of its fame during the conciliar controversy, when a good deal of doubt and confusion prevailed concerning the proper nature of church government.

Concrete evidence for its importance in the fifteenth century is provided by a short piece (transcribed in its entirety in our Appendix C) which was prepared by some anonymous protagonist for the Roman line of popes during the Great Schism. The author excerpts some passages from the *De causa*, which he then proceeds to apply directly to the circumstances of the Schism, declaring that nothing short of an act of Providence could account for the fact that the *De causa* should have been preserved for a century or more to help him and his contemporaries find the correct solution to their problems. This anonymous writer could have been impressed by the scholarship of the *De causa*. Although it dates from the early fourteenth century, and hence from the period before the constitution of the church became an object of heated and sustained debate, the *De causa* is still one of the most complete and systematic of the late medieval attempts to elucidate the nature of ecclesiastical government. But undoubtedly it was the argument of the *De causa* in which he took particular delight, for the author of the *De causa* is a champion of papal monarchy. In approaching ecclesiological problems from the papalists' perspective, the author of the *De causa* was representing the established opinion of his day, one shared by virtually all the other ecclesiological treatises produced in the early fourteenth century. Some, indeed, had sought to limit papal involvement in political concerns, to argue for a separation of spiritual and temporal authority, but not in most cases by attacking the monarchical structure of the church itself. Marsilius of Padua and the *Defensor pacis* notwithstanding, conciliar solutions were not the order of the day until the crisis produced by the Great Schism forced them into prominence. But the author of the *De causa* does more than echo the received orthodoxy. What makes him particularly noteworthy is that he is considerably more intent than most other late medieval papalists on exploring the implications of the church's monarchical structure, and perhaps even more significantly, much more conscientious than most in attempting to construct a firm foundation for papal monarchy from the evidence of Biblical sources.

The author of the *De causa* does not have too much to say about the issue receiving most of the attention at the time of his writing, the relationship of church and state. On this issue he is content to echo the moderate anti-papalism found in the *Tractatus de potestate papae* of Pierre de la Palu. The pope does not have any temporal authority *per se*, although he does have the right to intervene in the temporal order whenever the spiritual welfare of Christendom demands it.[1] However, on

[1] Cf. *De causa* **4**: 135-137: "papa est superior eo [principi] in spiritualibus, et per consequens in temporalibus quantum necesse est pro bono spirituali ipsius et aliorum, et adminus ratione delicti." The contents of the *De causa* are discussed more fully on pp. 21-33, and references are provided there.

the issue of the constitutional structure of the church itself, the author of the *De causa* could reasonably be described as a papal extremist. As the title of his work indicates, he is concerned with the immediate cause of ecclesiastical power, and he spares no effort in insisting that that cause must be the pope. He is prepared to admit that all bishops and priests receive their sacramental authority, their *potestas ordinis*, directly from Christ. But he goes on to argue that all jurisdictional authority, *potestas iurisdictionis*, must be derived from the pope, to whom a *plenitudo potestatis* has been entrusted by Christ himself. Hence the jurisdictional authority exercised by all bishops and priests in the church is something they possess only on papal licence, and the pope has the right to limit this authority, or even take it away, if it seems appropriate to him so to do. Others, of course, had argued for a position in its substance very much the same: Herveus Natalis, for example, by whom the author of the *De causa* may have been influenced. But the author of the *De causa* elaborates a particularly forceful statement of this doctrine, firmly buttressed by canon law; and what is even more significant, he attempts to meet the anti-papalists on their own ground by making the New Testament foundation of the doctrine as clear as possible.

The appeal to the apostolic simplicity of the *ecclesia primitiva* was one of the distinguishing characteristics of the anti-papal literature of the early fourteenth century. Leff regards the idea of the *ecclesia primitiva* as being of more importance for shaping anti-papal thought than the political doctrines of Aristotle, to which Ullmann and Wilks have attached a great deal of importance.[2] What is most striking about the *De causa* is that the appeal to the *ecclesia primitiva* can be found here as well, but pressed into the service of the papal monarchy. The author argues at some length that the ecclesiological doctrine which he defends was present in the original constitution of the church established by Christ himself. Christ made Peter and Peter alone a bishop and a pope. The other apostles, traditionally thought to be the original bishops, were simple priests who received their episcopal status only later. The seventy-two disciples, traditionally thought to be the original priests, were not such at all, for some of them

[2] Cf. G. Leff, "The Apostolic Ideal in Later Medieval Ecclesiology," *Journal of Theological Studies*, n.s. 18 (1967): 58-82. For the views of Ullmann and Wilks, cf. W. Ullmann, *A History of Political Thought: The Middle Ages* (Harmondsworth, Middlesex, 1965), pp. 159ff.; idem, *The Growth of Papal Government in the Middle Ages*, 2nd edition (London, 1962), pp. 447ff.; idem, *Principles of Government and Politics in the Middle Ages*, 2nd edition (London, 1966), pp. 231ff.; idem, *The Individual and Society in the Middle Ages* (Baltimore, 1966), esp. pp. 101ff.; and M. J. Wilks, *The Problem of Sovereignty in the Later Middle Ages* (Cambridge, 1963), esp. pp. 84ff.

were later ordained as deacons. Christ made the preeminent position of Peter absolutely clear by these provisions, and by investing him with a plenitude of jurisdictional authority for the governing of the church. Hence, just as the bishops and priests of the early church could have received their jurisdictional authority only from the hand of Peter, even so now authority in the church descends downwards from the pope to the other members of the ecclesiastical hierarchy.

At the time of his widest readership the author of the *De causa* appealed most strongly to those on the losing side. But conciliarism proved to be relatively short-lived, and it did not take long for the papal monarchy to reassert itself. To assess the reasons for this would take us beyond the limits of this introduction, and beyond the competence of its writer as well. But undoubtedly one of the major factors was that the papal monarchy had its staunch defenders, individuals like the author of the *De causa*. Today they are not as well known as they should be. The best known works, certainly those which have penetrated to the popular level of text-books, are those which are expressly anti-papal, or which seem to foreshadow the rise of modern liberal democracy. The best examples of this are the *Defensor pacis* of Marsilius of Padua, and the *Tractatus de potestate regia et papali* of John of Paris, both of which exist in good critical editions, and both of which have been translated in their entirety into English, the latter in two very recent translations. The papalists have not fared so well, most of them available only in manuscript form or in early printed editions. In view of the prevailing democratic orthodoxy, this is readily understandable. But it should not obscure the fact that, as an anonymous reader of an earlier draft of this introduction put it, "it is certainly in the best interests of historical scholarship that the other side be better known and not <be> assumed to be, in default of readily available evidence, a rear-guard obscurantist action in defence of a doomed cause." It is as a modest contribution to the "best interests of historical scholarship" so defined that the present edition has been prepared. The *De causa* is the product of a first-class scholar, hitherto available only in the relatively rare and defective edition of Jean Barbier, published in Paris in 1506. It deserves to be available in a modern edition.

2

The Author

Since Guillaume de Pierre Godin[1] is one of the major figures in the ecclesiastical history of the later Middle Ages, the main lines of his biography can be established fairly easily.[2] He was born about 1260, into one of the more distinguished families of Bayonne. At an early age he entered the convent of the Order of Preachers in his native city. In 1279 he was assigned to the Dominican convent at Béziers, where he studied the *Naturalia*. In the years immediately following he was entrusted with the office of *lector* in natural philosophy at various other Dominican convents: at Orthez in 1281, at Bordeaux in 1282, and at Condom in 1283. From 1284 to 1286 he studied theology at Montpellier, and in 1287 the Provincial Chapter of Bordeaux appointed him *lector* in theology at Bayonne, where he seems to have spent three years. Then in 1290 the Provincial Chapter of Pamiers transferred him to Condom, where he had the same responsibilities; and in 1291 the Provincial Chapter of Béziers assigned him to Montpellier.

[1] The Latin form of Guillaume's name, "Guillelmus Petri de Godino," has been translated into the vernacular in several different ways: "Guillaume de Peyre de Godin" and "Guillaume de Peyre Godin," for example. However, there now seems to be a consensus in favour of "Guillaume de Pierre Godin," and so that is the form I have chosen. Throughout this introduction I have adopted vernacular forms for Latin names whenever there is a consensus in their favour: hence "Jean de Pouilly" rather than "Joannes de Polliaco," but "Herveus Natalis" rather than "Hervé Nédélec." When confronted with a choice of vernacular forms, I have tried to adopt the form most commonly used in the English-speaking world: hence "John of Paris" rather than "Jean de Paris" or "Joannes Parisiensis," but "Pierre de la Palu" rather than "Peter de la Palu" or "Petrus de Palude."

[2] Several of the items listed in the bibliography contain biographical information. See, for example, R. Darricau, "Le cardinal Bayonnais, Guillaume de Pierre Godin, des Frères Prêcheurs (1260-1336)," *Société des sciences, lettres et arts de Bayonne*, n.s. 129 (1973): 125-141; P. Fournier, "Le cardinal Guillaume de Peyre Godin," *Bibliothèque de l'École des Chartes*, 86 (1925): 100-121; idem, "Guillaume de Peyre de Godin, cardinal," *Histoire littéraire de la France*, 37 (1938): 146-153; M.-H. Laurent, "Le testament et la succession du cardinal dominicain Guillaume de Pierre Godin," *Archivum Fratrum Praedicatorum*, 2 (1932): 84-231; and F. J. Roensch, *Early Thomistic School* (Dubuque, Iowa, 1964), pp. 120-124.

By this time Guillaume had already begun to make a name for himself, for he had been appointed Preacher General at the Provincial Chapter at Narbonne in 1289. This was only the first of a number of honours which distinguished his career. In 1292 he was sent to Paris, to the Dominican convent of St Jacques, so that he could continue his studies toward the baccalaureate in theology, and he seems to have been in Paris at least until 1296, when he was sent to Toulouse to lecture on the *Sentences*. Two years later, in 1298, he received his next major appointment by being named *definitor* for the General Chapter at Cahors, and three years after that – years in which he returned to Paris and, as a young bachelor, completed his commentary on the four books of the *Sentences*, the celebrated *Lectura Thomasina* – he was awarded an even greater distinction. In July of 1301, at the Provincial Chapter at Agen, he was chosen to succeed Bernard de Jusix as Prior Provincial of Provence. After the division of the province, he was elected the first Prior Provincial of the new province of Toulouse.

In the spring of 1304 the General Chapter at Toulouse released Guillaume from his responsibilities as Prior Provincial, and sent him back to Paris to pursue his mastership in theology. He obtained the license to incept in theology the same year. But very soon he was destined to leave the world of academe once again and pass into the service of the Holy See. After the death of Benedict XI (7 July 1304), the archbishop of Bordeaux, Bertrand de Got, assumed the papal throne with the name of Clement V, and he very soon demonstrated his interest in Guillaume by summoning him to Avignon. In 1306 he entrusted Guillaume with a position he would hold for the next six years, that of his personal theologian and teacher of theology at the papal court, succeeding Remigio de Girolami.[3] Since this was a position which made of him one of the most important papal advisers, it is not surprising that Clement V found other ways to make use of his services. Hence between 1308 and 1310 Guillaume was entrusted with various diplomatic missions to the French court, and in 1310 he was appointed to a cardinals' commission charged with investigating the teachings of the Spiritual Franciscans. His own appointment to the cardinalate was to follow shortly thereafter, in December 1312, when Clement V created him a cardinal priest with the title of St Cecilia. Guillaume continued to enjoy papal favour under Pope

[3] Darricau (p. 129, n. 32) explains that this person was described in a variety of ways: as *magister in theologia*, *magister curiae*, and then in 1342 as *lector sacri palatii*, and in 1343 as *magister sacri palatii*.

John XXII as well, who appointed him cardinal bishop of Sabina in 1317. John XXII entrusted him with a number of important responsibilities, such as the direction of the case against Hubert of Casals, who was accused of heresy in 1325. Most importantly, from 1320 to 1324 Guillaume served as papal legate *a latere* to Spain. In this capacity he concerned himself with internal Spanish political problems, and seems to have worked strenuously to establish peace; he organized Spanish resistance against the infidels; and he enacted several measures designed to achieve the reform of the Spanish clergy, the most important of which was his summoning of the Council of Valladolid in 1322, the Acts of which he drew up himself.

Guillaume's faithful service under both Clement V and John XXII was richly rewarded. He became a man of considerable influence, with a large number of clients who benefited from his patronage. He also accumulated a large number of benefices for himself, the revenues of which were sufficient to make him a man of very considerable wealth. He seems to have used his wealth unselfishly, and he was particularly generous towards the establishments of his own order. There were few Dominican convents in the south of France which did not experience his favour: Avignon, Bayonne, Toulouse, Montpellier and several others owed a significant portion of their property to his largesse. He died on 4 June 1336, only eighteen months after John XXII, and he was buried, according to the stipulations of his will, in the church of the Dominicans at Toulouse. His career had been a spectacular one: "Collaborateur intime de Clément V, le pape bordelais, et de Jean XXII, le pontife quercynois, il fut pendant plus de vingt ans au premier plan de toutes les grandes affaires européennes."[4] Paradoxically, however, in view of the influence he had attained in his life, controversy surrounded him in death, focusing on the alleged evils attendant upon his mismanagement of his benefices. The response of Benedict XII was to freeze the estate of the cardinal, placing all of it under the protection of the Roman church, and authorizing a series of enquiries to determine if the complaints were justified; and ultimately heavy restitutions were imposed upon Guillaume's heirs.

From this brief sketch of his career, it is clear that Guillaume de Pierre Godin's chief claim to fame was his political and administrative activity. However, he was also a scholar who enjoyed the respect of scholars, and he made his own significant contributions to the scholarly world. In this regard the *De causa* could well be considered his most important accomplishment. It is unfortunate, however, given the importance of the

[4] Ibid., p. 137.

De causa both for the intellectual history of the later Middle Ages and for a balanced assessment of Guillaume's career, that doubt should surround Guillaume's authorship. But doubt there has been, giving rise to a considerable amount of literature on the problem, although only one other candidate has emerged, Guillaume's fellow Dominican, Pierre de la Palu. In what follows we shall make no attempt to deal with all the literature on the subject: it tends to be rather repetitious. Instead we shall take as our point of departure the principal arguments in favour of each candidate. Although one of the most recent contributors to the discussion, P. T. Stella, has argued persuasively in favour of Guillaume, it would be premature as yet to suggest that the matter has been laid to rest once and for all.[5]

Stella was not the first to argue on behalf of Guillaume. Quétif and Echard were of the same opinion in the early eighteenth century,[6] as was Grabmann in the early twentieth,[7] and for essentially two reasons: (1) Guillaume is cited as the author in one of the extant manuscripts (Paris, Bibliothèque nationale, MS lat. 12467), and (2) Pierre Bertrand, the distinguished cardinal and canonist, and a contemporary of Guillaume, attributes the *De causa* to Guillaume in his *Apparatus* to the *Liber Sextus*. The testimony of Bertrand had already been noted by Baluze in his *Vitae paparum Avenionensium*, where he cites the

> tractatum *De potestate Ecclesie*, quem laudat Petrus Bertrandi cardinalis S. Clementis in proemium libri sixti *Decretalium* his verbis: *Predicta extraxi de quodam tractatu quem fecit dominus G. Petri episcopus Sabinensis cardinalis, quem tractatum intitulavit de causa potestatis Ecclesie.* Idem in cap. *Quoniam*, de renuntiat., in *Sexto*, ita scribit: *Circa autem materiam istam dicit dictus dominus G. Petri Sabinensis in dicto libello suo de potestate apostolorum sic dicendum, quod papa in nullo casu, quamdiu est papa, propter quodcumque crimen potest nec a concilio, nec a tota Ecclesia nec a toto mundo deponi, non solum quia est superior, sed quia est a Deo, qui sibi romani presulis, quamdiu presul est, judicium reservavit.*[8]

There can be no doubt that Bertrand is referring to the *De causa* here. The title he attributes to it is not that given in most of the manuscripts, to be

[5] Cf. P. T. Stella, "A proposito della attribuzione a Pietro di La Palu del 'Tractatus de causa immediata ecclesiasticae potestatis'," *Salesianum*, 27 (1965): 382-409; and Stella's introductory comments in *Magistri Petri de Palude* O.P. *Tractatus de potestate papae* (Zurich, 1966), pp. 27-35.

[6] J. Quétif and J. Echard, *Scriptores Ordinis Praedicatorum* 1 (Paris, 1719), p. 592.

[7] M. Grabmann, "Kardinal Guillelmus Petri de Godino (†1336) und seine Lectura Thomasina," *Mittelalterliches Geistesleben* 2 (München, 1936), pp. 563-567.

[8] E. Baluze, *Vitae paparum Avenionensium* 2 (Paris, 1927), pp. 160-161.

sure, but the manuscripts display a considerable variety in this regard. In addition to *Tractatus de causa immediata ecclesiastice potestatis*, we also find *Tractatus de potestate ecclesiastice dignitatis*, <*Tractatus*> *de potestate collata a Christo prelatis ecclesie militantis*, and <*Tractatus*> *de potestate ecclesiastica*, to give just a few. Perhaps significantly, the Paris manuscript which attributes the work to Guillaume gives the title: *Tractatus de pape et prelatorum ecclesie potestate.*[9] The important fact is that Bertrand quotes from the work he uses, and his quotation corresponds exactly to the *De causa* at our **4**: 177-180.

Whether the testimony of Bertrand should be accepted at face value is, of course, another question, and Koch, for one, has claimed that it should not be. Since Bertrand was not above claiming the work of another as his own, Koch maintains that he cannot be regarded as a reliable witness.[10] However, Stella has pointed out quite properly that practices which today would be regarded as plagiarism were common in the early fourteenth century.[11] If we were to apply our own standards of intellectual honesty in assessing the testimony of late medieval scholars, very few would be found to be above reproach. Besides, although one can see how someone might hope to gain in claiming for himself work written by someone else, it is difficult to understand what advantage a person might expect to derive from attributing the work of someone else to a third party. Given the fact then that Bertrand does not claim the *De causa* as his own, there is no reason to suspect his honesty in attributing it to Guillaume, just as he was being quite honest, and incidentally quite correct, in attributing to Durandus de S. Porciano the *De origine iurisdictionum.*[12] Of course, Bertrand might simply have been mistaken. But Stella has pointed out that Bertrand was in a unique position for checking the authenticity of the treatise. Bertrand was created a cardinal with the title of S. Clemente by Pope John xxii on 20 December 1331, and he died on 24 June 1348. Since Guillaume was created a cardinal with the title of S. Cecilia in January 1312 and died on 4 June 1336, there was a period of over four years in which they served together in the papal curia. Presumably Bertrand had

[9] Eleven of the thirty extant manuscripts provide no title at all. Of the remaining nineteen, ten provide the title adopted in this edition, or something very close to it, as does the edition of 1506. None of the other possibilities has the support of more than one or two manuscripts.

[10] J. Koch, "Der Prozeß gegen den Magister Johannes de Polliaco und seine Vorgeschichte (1312-1321)," *Recherches de théologie ancienne et médiévale*, 5 (1933): 404 n. 50.

[11] Stella, "A proposito," p. 408; *Tractatus*, p. 35.

[12] Stella, "A proposito," pp. 408-409; *Tractatus*, p. 35.

some opportunity to get to know Guillaume and to familiarize himself with the latter's work, and this must make his testimony worthy of some respect.[13]

On the other side, however, there is a considerable amount of evidence which suggests that Pierre de la Palu was the author of the *De causa*, evidence which some at least have considered conclusive. Of the thirty extant manuscripts, twenty-six attribute the *De causa* to Pierre, as does the edition of 1506, and three provide no attribution of authorship whatever. If the one remaining manuscript is correct in attributing the treatise to Guillaume, the surprising unanimity among the other manuscripts, which otherwise divide themselves into a number of different families with distinctive characteristics, requires some kind of explanation. Furthermore, of these thiry manuscripts, Koch has drawn particular attention to Vienna, Österreichische Nationalbibliothek, MS 2168,[14] since in addition to the *De causa*, this manuscript, which is the product of one scribe, contains a number of smaller treatises, all of which concern the inquiry into the doctrines of Jean de Pouilly, and all of which, with the exception of a *Responsio* written by Jean himself, are indisputably the work of Pierre de la Palu. Perhaps most significant, however, is the fact, first pointed out by Koch,[15] that the *De causa* itself contains a long polemic against the doctrines of Jean de Pouilly which alone would be enough to suggest that Pierre de la Palu was the author.

The story of the controversy between Jean de Pouilly and Pierre de la Palu has been told too often to require retelling here.[16] Briefly, the origins of the controversy can be traced back to Jean's fifth *Quodlibet* of Advent 1312. It was finally brought to a conclusion with his condemnation by the bull *Vas Electionis* of 24 July 1321. It was an ecclesiological controversy, occasioned by Jean's too vigorous defence of the rights of the parish clergy against what he perceived as the encroachments of the mendicants. His principal opponents were members of the mendicant orders, who wanted to ensure their rights of preaching and hearing confessions even at the expense of the parish clergy, and who therefore championed a conception of papal authority strong enough to enable the pope to be the guarantor of their privileges. Pierre de la Palu was not one of the principal

[13] Stella, "A proposito," p. 383; *Tractatus*, pp. 2-3. Cf. Grabmann, *Mittelalterliches Geistesleben* 2, pp. 565-566.

[14] Koch, "Der Prozeß," p. 404, n. 50.

[15] Ibid., p. 404 n. 50 and p. 405.

[16] Cf. Koch, "Der Prozeß," and J. G. Sikes, "John de Pouilli and Peter de la Palu," *English Historical Review*, 49 (1934): 219-240.

movers in lodging accusations against Jean's doctrines. Rather, this distinction must go to some members of the Franciscan convent at Paris, who drew up the initial charge against him in 1317. But Pierre had an important and active role to play in the controversy nonetheless, and since he was a Dominican, it is not surprising that, once he was drawn into the conflict, he came in on the side of Jean's opponents. Pierre's official position seems to have been that of a theological appraiser appointed by the papal curia.[17] In the course of things, however, the controversy took the form of a confrontation between Jean and Pierre himself, and Pierre wrote a number of short treatises in which Jean's doctrines are examined word for word and refuted point by point.

Perhaps significantly, the *De causa* displays a similar preoccupation with the doctrines of Jean de Pouilly. In the third conclusion of the sixth article, the author of the *De causa* adopts a point of view with which Jean definitely would not sympathize:

> Tertia conclusio principalis, de potestate curatorum per comparationem ad statum et ad ecclesias ipsorum, est quod omnes ecclesie parochiales et cure simplices, quidquid habent potestatis spiritualis in quantum huiusmodi, totum habent a papa sive ecclesia Romana.[18]

After offering some proof for this proposition, he goes on to consider possible objections ("Contra hoc autem arguunt alii sic dicentes...."[19]) which he then procedes to dismiss. The interesting point in all this is that the procedure adopted by the author of the *De causa* is that of Pierre de la Palu precisely. The objections are taken word for word from the fifth *Quodlibet* of Jean de Pouilly. Hence, as in the undisputed works of Pierre de la Palu, the doctrines of Jean de Pouilly are quoted verbatim; and again as in the undisputed works of Pierre de la Palu, they are answered point by point and at considerable length.

Significant as it may appear, however, this evidence for the authorship of Pierre de la Palu is certainly not decisive. The handling of Jean de Pouilly might incline one to suspect Pierre. But since Pierre was only one of many who opposed Jean's doctrines, there is no reason to believe that Guillaume de Pierre Godin could not have been equally concerned about taking Jean to task. Moreover, Guillaume, who was appointed a cardinal in 1312, was in an excellent position to familiarize himself with Jean's doctrines after the attention of the papal curia had been drawn towards

[17] Koch, "Der Prozeß," pp. 406-408.
[18] *De causa* **6**: 243-246.
[19] Ibid. **6**: 292.

them. It is interesting to speculate on how this might have occurred. In the spring of 1318 Pope John xxii sent Pierre de la Palu on a diplomatic mission to Flanders where he was to attempt to secure peace between the prince and the king of France. Largely because his efforts were unsuccessful, on his return to Avignon he was confronted with a charge of treachery against the French crown, and Guillaume de Pierre Godin was jointly commissioned along with Herveus Natalis, another Dominican, with the investigation. This led to Pierre's ultimate acquittal in July, and again in September 1318. Immediately thereafter, between June 1318 and September 1320, Pierre de la Palu was a member of the commission charged with the investigation of Olivi's *Postilla* on the *Apocalypse*, the same commission on which Guillaume served in 1318 and 1319.[20] Given this record of contact between Guillaume de Pierre Godin and Pierre de la Palu in 1318 and 1319, Guillaume may have learned of the views of Jean de Pouilly from Pierre de la Palu himself.

The manuscript tradition might be considered stronger evidence for Pierre's authorship. But genuine confusion could have arisen quite early from the fact that Guillaume and Pierre worked side by side at Avignon, and undoubtedly submitted their treatises to one another. Moreover, since Pierre de la Palu already had a solid reputation for having concerned himself with ecclesiological problems, whereas Guillaume had not, the learned audience of the day might have been expecting Pierre to produce a substantial treatise on ecclesiological problems. Hence, since the *De causa* comes closer to being considered a genuine ecclesiological treatise than Pierre's legitimate work, the *Tractatus de potestate papae*; and since the *Tractatus* itself, judging from the one surviving manuscript, does not seem to have been very well known in the later Middle Ages, it is not difficult to see how the confusion arising from their common interests and common residence at Avignon could have worked in Pierre's favour. But there is more direct evidence than any considered so far for the authorship of Guillaume de Pierre Godin: the fact, first pointed out by Stella, that the author of the *De causa* appears to borrow from the *Tractatus* of Pierre de la Palu, and that he does so in such a way as to suggest that he must have been someone other than Pierre himself.

Stella lists a number of passages which the *De causa* and the *Tractatus de potestate papae* of Pierre de la Palu share in common. Several more could be added, and all of them are identified in the *apparatus fontium* to the text. The mere existence of such common passages is not in itself very significant, for there are similar passages shared by the *De causa* and the

[20] Roensch, *Early Thomistic School*, pp. 121 and 125.

Iudicium of Pierre de la Palu. When these latter passages are analyzed carefully, two points emerge. First, it is extremely difficult to determine the precise nature of the relationship between the two treatises. One of them obviously copies the other, although which is the original and which the copy is by no means certain. Secondly, whether the *De causa* copies the *Iudicium* or the *Iudicium* the *De causa*, both treatises could still have been written by Pierre de la Palu, for a comparison of Pierre's *Quodlibet* and either his *Responsiones* or his *Articuli circa materiam confessionum* is sufficient to indicate that on other occasions Pierre was not beyond using his own material more than once. Hence the dependence of the *De causa* on the *Iudicium*, or of the *Iudicium* on the *De causa*, may simply be another case of Pierre de la Palu getting maximum usage out of material he had already written.

However, the relationship between the *De causa* and the *Tractatus* of Pierre de la Palu is qualitatively different, and does, I think, virtually eliminate the possibility of Pierre's authorship of the *De causa*. Several of the common passages yield firm conclusions when subjected to a close analysis, but the following one is perhaps the most instructive:

De causa immediata ecclesiastice potestatis **4**: 434-500.	Pierre de la Palu, *Tractatus de potestate papae* 1.3, pp. 188-190.[21]
Contra hoc autem arguitur dupliciter. Primo quia, secundum hoc, papa non posset sedem suam a Roma mutare et alibi transferre. Hoc autem est inconveniens. Ergo et primum. Quod autem hoc sit inconveniens, et quod papa ex causa rationabili *possit mutare sedem suam, dupliciter patet.* Primo quod ponat Rome alium episcopum, et ipse presideat omnibus ecclesiis universaliter et nulli specialiter. Secundo quod ipse sedem suam transferat ad aliam *specialem sedem episcopalem,* novam vel veterem.	*Quinto probandum est* quod papa ex causa rationabili *potest sedem suam mutare tripliciter.* Primo *modo,* quod ponat Rome alium episcopum, et ipse presideat omnibus ecclesiis universaliter et nulli specialiter. Secundo, quod ipse sedem suam transferat ad aliam *sedem specialem* novam vel veterem. *Tertio, quod ipse det ius eligendi papam aliis, quam cardinalibus.*

[21] This selection from the *Tractatus* is taken from Stella's edition of the one surviving manuscript: Toulouse, Bibliothèque de la Ville, MS 744. Readings in angular brackets are to be found in the original, but have been amended in Stella's edition.

Primum patet, quia in his que sunt iurisdictionis non minus potest papa quam Petrus in eo quod papa.

Sed Petrus usquequo venit Antiochiam fuit sine sede speciali, et ab illo tempore quo Antiochie Ignatium constituit quousque Rome sedit. Ergo et papa sic potest esse sine speciali sede.

Per idem patet secundum, quia et Petrus sedem suam de Antiochia Romam transtulit.

Quod autem illud sequatur patet, quia homo non potest destruere fundamentum Dei, dicente apostolo 2 ad Timotheum 2: "Firmum fundamentum Dei stat." Si ergo ecclesia Romana a Christo est fundata, ergo papa non potest sedem apostolicam alibi transferre nec aliquo modo mutare, quod esset Dei fundamentum destruere. Et confirmatur quod nec ipse Petrus potuisset mutare si vixisset, quia servus non potest tollere legem domini sui. Unde *id* quod Petrus fecit proprio capite papa successor potest tollere. Sed illud quod Petrus fecit divina iussione videtur quod nec ipsemet Petrus, et multo minus quicumque successor alius, possit revocare.

Sedes autem Petri electa est Rome de speciali Domini iussione. Ergo nullus purus homo potest *istam* sedem alibi transferre *nec aliter mutare.* Maior prmbata est. Minor patet per illud quod scribit Marcellus papa universis episcopis per Antiochiam constitutis, 24 q. 1 Rogamus: "Ipse est caput totius ecclesie cui ait Dominus: 'Tu es Petrus, et super hanc petram edificabo ecclesiam *meam.*' Eius enim sedes primitus fuit apud vos, que postea iubente Domino Romam translata est." Hunc autem iussum Domini exponit Innocentius, Qui filii *sint* legitimi c. Per

Primum patet, quia in his que sunt iurisdictionis non minus potest papa *quilibet*, quam Petrus in eo quod papa. Sed Petrus usquequo venit Antiochiam fuit sine sede speciali, et ab illo tempore quo Antiochie Ignatium constituit quousque Rome sedit. Ergo et papa sic potest esse sine speciali sede.

Per idem patet secundum, quia et Petrus sedem suam de Antiochia Romam transtulit.

Per idem patet tertium, quia per aliquem papam potestas eligendi cardinalibus collata fuit; ergo per alium papam equaliter potest auferri et aliis dari, quia par in parem non habet imperium, nec predecessor legem potest imponere successori, qui est per electionem et per consequens nihil habet a predecessore, C., De legibus, 1. Digna vox.

Sed contra hoc est quia servus non potest tollere legem domini sui; unde *illud* quod Petrus fecit proprio capite, papa successor potest tollere; sed illud quod Petrus fecit divina iussione, videtur quod nec ipsemet Petrus, et multo minus quicumque successor alius possit revocare; sedes, autem, Petri electa est Rome de speciali Domini iussione; ergo nullus purus homo potest *illam* sedem alibi transferre. – Maior probata est. – Minor patet per illud quod scribit Marcellus papa universis episcopis per Antiochiam constitutis, 24, q. 1, Rogamus, "Ipse est caput totius ecclesie, cui ait Dominus 'Tu es Petrus, et super hanc petram edificabo ecclesiam' *etc.* Eius, enim, sedes primitus fuit apud vos, que postea iubente Domino Romam translata est." Hunc, autem, iussum Domini exponit Innocentius, Qui filii *sunt* legitimi, c. Per venerabilem, ubi dicit sic: "Locus quem elegit Dominus apostolica sedes esse *dinoscitur.* Cum enim Petrus urbem fugiens exivisset, volens eum Dominus ad locum quem elegerat revocare, interrogatus ab eo: 'Domine quo vadis?' respondit: 'Venio Romam iterum crucifigi,' quod intelligens pro se dictum, ad locum pristinum est reversus." Motus enim Petrus lacrimis Christianorum, a facie Neronis fugiens aliam sedem *forte* eligere volebat, *secundum illud Matthei 10: "Cum autem persequentur vos in civitate ista, fugite in aliam."* Sed hoc Dominus prohibuit, volens ibi *sedem Petri finaliter* permanere. Unde non ex Petri sed ex Christi electione *facta est* sedes Petri; quare non potest etiam a Petro mutari. Sicut elegit Dominus Sion in templum, ut esset locus orationis, nec ex tunc licuit alibi templum facere, etiam summo sacerdoti. Unde peccavit Eliachim in Eliopoleos Egipti simile templum faciens illi Hierosolimorum, ut refert Josephus.

Ad hoc dicendum quod, sicut nutu Dei factus est serpens eneus quando *profuit* in deserto, *Numeri 21*; postea vero, quando in idolatriam versus est, destructus *est* iusto *iudicio regis* Ezechie, *4 Regum 18*; ita si nunc Romani in rebellione ecclesie existerent, vel alia civitas in mundo *appareret* communior et aptior ad universalis ecclesie regimen, posset papa, *forte de voluntate Dei interpretativa*, inde *sedem suam* mutare eadem ratione qua Petrus eam *Romam* transtulit, sicut Constantinus sedem imperii a Roma Constantinopolim *transtulit, ei Romana privilegia concedendo.* Argumentum ad hoc, 63 d. c. Quia sancta, ibi: "Sicut divina *Scriptura*" *etc.*, de serpente eneo.

venerabilem, ubi dicit sic "Locus, quem elegit Dominus, apostolica sedes esse *cognoscitur.* Cum, enim, Petrus urbem fugiens exivisset, volens eum Dominus ad locum, quem elegerat, revocare, interrogatus ab eo 'Domine, quo vadis?', respondit 'Venio Romam iterum crucifigi', quod intelligens pro se dictum, ad locum pristinum est reversus." Motus, enim, Petrus lacrimis christianorum, a facie Neronis fugiens, aliam sedem eligere volebat;

sed hoc Dominus prohibuit, volens ibi *finaliter sedem Petri* permanere. Unde, non ex Petri, sed ex Christi electione *est etiam* sedes Petri; quare non potest etiam a Petro mutari. Sicut elegit Dominus Sion in templum, ut esset locus orationis, nec ex tunc licuit alibi templum facere etiam summo sacerdoti, unde peccavit Eliachim in Heliopoleos Egipti simile templum faciens illi Jerosolimorum, ut refert Josephus.

Ad hoc dicendum quod, sicut nutu Dei factus est serpens eneus quando *prefuit* in deserto; postea, vero, quando in idolatriam versus est, destructus *et* iusto <*regis iudicio*> Ezechie; ita, si nunc romani in rebellione ecclesie existerent, vel alia civitas in mundo <*apparet*> <communior> et aptior ad universalis ecclesie regimen posset papa inde *suam sedem* mutare, eadem ratione qua Petrus eam transtulit, sicut Constantinus sedem imperii a Roma Constantinopolim *transvexit.* Argumentum ad hoc 63 d., c. Quia sancta, ibi: "Sicut divina <*scriptum*>," de serpente eneo.

Sine causa autem rationabili sedem suam a Deo Rome fundatam non posset ipse papa evertere nec alibi transferre. Et si faceret, non valeret, immo etiam quantumcumque causa probabilis appareret, quia non nisi Dei contraria iussione mutandum est quod semel iussit. Sine assensu generalis concilii super hoc specialiter convocati, et Dei revelationem super hoc invocantis, non esset talis translatio facienda, quia nec propter transmigrationem, nec propter captivitatem populi Dei ad septuaginta annos, licuit locum templi quem Deus elegerat immutare. Nec est simile de mutatione Antiochie, quia illam sedem Petrus elegerat motu proprio, non speciali Domini iussione. Nec est etiam simile de serpente eneo, quem Dominus erigi fecerat, non ad perpetuitatem, sed ad temporale remedium in deserto. Nec est simile de translatione sedis imperialis, cuius auctoritas est a populo Romano, qui ius suum et potestatem in imperatorem transtulit, Inst., De iure naturali § Sed quod principi.

Although the author of the *Tractatus de potestate papae* thinks it is possible for the pope to change his residence, the author of the *De causa* appends a paragraph to the end of the discussion concluding in the negative. For Stella this fact alone is a sufficient indication that the *De causa* followed the *Tractatus* and amended it, and therefore that it could not have been written by Pierre de la Palu,[22] and Stella is undoubtedly correct. In the *Tractatus* the passage as a whole is straightforward enough. The author of the *Tractatus* wants to argue that the pope can transfer his see from Rome if he so desires. He states his basic position on lines 8-39; he raises a possible objection on lines 40-88; and he replies to the objection on lines 89-107. In the *De causa* the passage is not quite so straightforward. It is introduced as a possible objection to the doctrine that the Roman pontiff has received authority directly from God. The substance of the objection is that, if this is the case, then the pope would

[22] Stella, "A proposito," pp. 404-406; *Tractatus*, pp. 30-32.

not be able to transfer his see from Rome. The first ninety lines are given over to the statement of the objection. Surprisingly, the objection is dealt with by acknowledging the force of the argument, although it is not at all clear that this is what is happening until we get to the end (lines 108-133): because the Roman pontiff has received his authority directly from God, the pope cannot simply transfer the papacy as he wishes. Hence the section which in the text of the *Tractatus* serves as the author's reply to the objection (lines 89-107), and which in both texts is introduced by the phrase "Ad hoc dicendum quod," does not serve the same function in the *De causa*. The arguments given there are not arguments with which the author of the *De causa* agrees, and he replies to them in the final section (lines 108-133). Given that, the phrase "Ad hoc dicendum quod," although quite appropriate in the *Tractatus*, is not really appropriate at all in the *De causa*. The author of the *De causa* would have done much better, and would have clarified his argument considerably, had he written "Contra hoc obicitur quod" (or words to that effect) at the beginning of line 89, and transferred the phrase "Ad hoc dicendum quod" to the beginning of line 108. This would have had the added advantage of providing a proper introduction for his final statement on the matter, which, as the text stands, has no introduction at all. The fact that he did not do so strongly suggests that he was copying from the *Tractatus* at this point, and was not being careful enough to make the necessary adjustments.

Such adjustments have been made in our MSS B^1 and T on the one hand, and in P^2 and V^7 on the other, although not in precisely the same fashion in each pair of manuscripts. After *transtulit*, on line 29, all four manuscripts advance to line 89: *Ad hoc dicendum*. The copyists of B^1 and T then transcribe the rest of the passage, returning to line 30 to pick up the text at *Quod autem* at the end of line 133. The copyists of P^2 and V^7, however, insert the sentence: *Dicendum est quod papa non potest transferre sedem Romanam, nec alius purus homo*, at line 107 after *eneo*, and then return to pick up the text at line 30: *Quod autem*. Since of the two pairs P^2 and V^7 are marginally better at this point and avoid the problems raised above, one might be tempted to test the suggestion that P^2 and V^7 represent the original text of the *De causa* which was borrowed by the author of the *Tractatus*, although changed to suit his purpose. But this would leave the problem of having to explain how all the other manuscripts of the *De causa* could have been modified independently of the *Tractatus* to give the same reading as the *Tractatus*, a reading, again, not as suitable for the *De causa*. The only other alternative, and the one we are compelled to accept, is that the *De causa* borrows from and corrects the *Tractatus*. That being the case, two conclusions seem warranted: (1) that the *De causa* and the *Tractatus* must have different authors, and (2) that since the author of the *Tractatus* is Pierre de la Palu, the author of the *De causa* must be the only candidate other than Pierre himself, Guillaume de Pierre Godin.

These conclusions are confirmed when the *De causa* and the *Tractatus* are compared, not only with one another, but with the other works which are indisputably by Pierre de la Palu and which have some bearing on his ecclesiological views. Stella argues that Pierre de la Palu must have written the *Tractatus* between 6 January and 25 October 1317.[23] If this is correct, Pierre's commentary on the fourth book of the *Sentences* and his *Quodlibet* must both have been written before the *Tractatus*,[24] whereas his *Iudicium contra magistrum Johannem de Poliaco*, his *Conclusio contra responsionem datam per magistrum Johannem de Poly*, his *Responsiones ad ea que sibi imposuit magister Iohannes de Pollhiaco*, and his *Articuli circa materiam confessionum* must all have been written later.[25] Significantly, there is a general consistency of interpretation shared by the *Tractatus* and these other works of Pierre de la Palu on a number of important ecclesiological issues, precisely what we would expect if they

[23] Stella, "A proposito," pp. 394-395; *Tractatus*, pp. 19-21.

[24] The commentary on the fourth book of the *Sentences* (ed. Venitiis, 1493) seems to have been finished in 1313. Cf. G. Groppo, "La teologia e il suo 'Subiectum' secondo il prologo del commento alle Sentenze di Pietro da Palude O.P. (†1342)," *Salesianum*, 23 (1961): 245. The *Quodlibet* (Toulouse, Bibliothèque de la Ville, MS 744, fols. 75r-118v) seems to have been written in 1314. Cf. Koch, "Der Prozeß," pp. 401-402. Koch's dating is confirmed by *Quodlibet* 4.2, fol. 94v, where Pierre refers to the bull "Inter cunctos, que iam sunt decem anni sub bulla emanavit." *Inter cunctos* can be dated 14 February 1304.

V. Heynck argues that Pierre was still working on book four of his commentary on the *Sentences* as late as the end of 1314 or the beginning of 1315. Cf. V. Heynck, "Zur Datierung des Sentenzenkommentars des Petrus de Palude," *Franziskanische Studien*, 53 (1971): 317-327 at 325. However, the balance of the evidence seems to indicate that Pierre's commentary was substantially finished at an earlier date, even if it were subject to some revision later on. The point is not a crucial one for our present purposes, although the argument which follows would have to be recast slightly if the order of the fourth book of the commentary on the *Sentences* and the *Quodlibet* were reversed.

[25] The *Iudicium* (Vienna, Österreichische Nationalbibliothek, MS 2168, fols. 1r-12r; MS 11799, fols. 191r-215r) appears to have been written in late 1317 or early 1318. Koch points out that on two occasions Pierre maintains that the *Clementinae* were sent out *hoc anno* to the universities. (Cf. art. 10, MS Vienna 2168, fol. 9r, MS Vienna 11799, fol. 209r; and MS Vienna 2168, fol. 9v, MS Vienna 11799, fol. 210v.) Since the *Clementinae* were promulgated on 25 October 1317, the *Iudicium* must have been written between that date and the beginning of the next year, 25 March 1318. The *Conclusio* (MS Vienna 2168, fols. 17r-35r), the *Responsiones* (MS Vienna 2168, fols. 101r-111v) and the *Articuli circa materiam confessionum* (ed. J. Barbier, Paris, 1506) all appear to have been written in the period 1318-1321. Cf. Koch, "Der Prozeß," pp. 408-409, 410-412.

are indeed the work of Pierre de la Palu, and if Pierre was himself consistent in his views. What is equally as significant, however, is that on these same issues the views expressed in the *De causa* are strikingly different.[26]

One of the most significant issues separating the *De causa* and the *Tractatus* has to do with the jurisdictional power entrusted to the apostles and disciples in the early church. The author of the *De causa* makes it a fundamental point that neither the apostles nor the seventy-two disciples received any *potestas iurisdictionis* from Christ.[27] Whatever jurisdictional authority they received they received from Peter,[28] and it was Peter and his successors who divided the church into its parish and diocesan structure.[29] Although he does not devote the space to the issue that the author of the *De causa* devotes to it, the author of the *Tractatus* still makes clear that his position is fundamentally different. Although he can agree that the assignment of particular areas of jurisdiction was not undertaken by Christ himself,[30] in his view the apostles and disciples still possessed *potestas iurisdictionis* from Christ.[31] When one surveys the other works of Pierre de la Palu, it is the view expressed in the *Tractatus* which receives

26 For a different view see Koch, "Der Prozeß," p. 404 n. 50. One of the reasons why he would attribute the *De causa* to Pierre is because of "die Übereinstimmung der Ideen mit den übrigen Schriften des Paludanus gegen unsern Magister [Jean de Pouilly]."

27 For his treatment of the apostles see *De causa* **2**: 847ff.; for his treatment of the disciples see ibid. **3**: 343-471.

28 Ibid. **2**: esp. 1177-1389.

29 Ibid. **6**: 391-396. Although the view expressed by the author of the *De causa* was not a popular one, Herveus Natalis and Augustinus Triumphus would both agree with it. Cf. Herveus Natalis, *Tractatus de potestate pape* (Paris, 1647), pp. 378ff. Augustinus Triumphus has a little difficulty reconciling his views with Biblical texts which seem to indicate that Christ conferred *potestas iurisdictionis* on the apostles. Cf. *Summa de ecclesiastica potestate* (Augsburg, 1473) qu. 61.2 ad 3, qu. 88.1 ad 2 & 3. But his clear opinion seems to be that the other apostles could have received *potestas iurisdictionis* only from Peter: "totam potestatem ordinis <apostoli> immediate a Christo recipiunt. Verumtamen potestatem iurisdictionis qua possent potestatem ordinis exequi in tanta vel in tali materia non receperunt nisi a Petro post missionem Spiritus Sancti" (qu. 88.1 ad 1).

30 *Tractatus*, 1.3, p. 179.

31 Ibid. 1.3, p. 182. This was the usual view in the early fourteenth century, at least with regard to the apostles. See Alexander de S. Elpidio, *De ecclesiastica potestate* 1.5, ed. J. T. Rocaberti, *Bibliotheca maxima pontificia* 2.7 (Rome, 1698), pp. 1-40 at 6; Alvarus Pelagius, *De planctu ecclesiae*, chaps. 37 & 52, ed. Rocaberti 3, pp. 23-264 at 44 & 127; Guillelmus de Villana, *Reprobatio errorum* 4.2, ed. D. Mac Fhionnbhairr (Rome, 1977), p. 88; Herveus Natalis, *Tractatus de iurisdictione*, ed. L. Hödl (Munich, 1959), p. 28; and James of Viterbo, *De regimine christiano* 2.3, ed. H.-X. Arquillière, *Le plus ancien traité de l'Église* (Paris, 1926), p. 180. Although several of these theorists are not too clear as to when this commission of authority occurred, the text which seems to be preferred is Matthew 18:18, although Alvarus Pelagius also mentions John 20:22-23.

support, for the same view can be found in both the *Quodlibet*[32] and the *Iudicium*. In one passage in the *Iudicium* Pierre considers the doctrine of Jean de Pouilly, that priests and bishops must receive all their authority directly from Christ, because their predecessors, the apostles and disciples, received all their authority from Christ. Pierre replies by stating that, although bishops and priests receive their *potestas ordinis* from Christ just as the apostles and disciples did, it does not follow that they receive all their *potestas iurisdictionis* from Christ, even if we grant that this was true in the case of the apostles and disciples.[33] Although this does not amount to a firm statement that the apostles and disciples *did* receive *potestas iurisdictionis* from Christ, it implies as much.[34] If he really believed that this were not the case, saying so simply would have been the best way of dealing with Jean's argument. Indeed, Pierre's position in the *Iudicium* seems to be that, although the successors to the apostles and disciples in some manner or other receive their authority from the pope, and although the apostles and disciples themselves did not receive the care of specific dioceses and parishes from Christ but rather from Peter, still there were a number of occasions on which they can be shown to have received *potestas iurisdictionis* of a general nature directly from Christ himself.[35] This is the position of the *Tractatus* exactly.

In his commentary on the *Sentences* Pierre offers a view which might, at first glance at least, be thought to be irreconcilable with the *Quodlibet* and the *Iudicium*:

> Potestas que tota data est uni in suo fonte non est in aliis nisi derivata et limitata pro illius voluntate. Sed potestas iurisdictionis que est ad regendum populum tota et in suo fonte data fuit soli Petro et in eo successoribus eius quando cura ecclesie sibi soli commissa fuit, dicente Domino Joannis

[32] *Quodlibet* 4.3, fol. 96v.

[33] *Iudicium*, art. 2, MS Vienna 2168, fol. 2r-2v; MS Vienna 11799, fols. 193v-194r.

[34] At one point he states: "Unde Christus per se ordinavit primos apostolos et primos discipulos ita quod voluit quod post se et post illos Petrus loco sui alios instituerit."

[35] *Iudicium*, art. 13, MS Vienna 2168, fol. 11r-11v; MS Vienna 11799, fols. 213v-214r: "Unde quamvis posset dici quod Christus per se omnibus et singulis apostolis et discipulis quo ad personas suas quo adiuvarent, nisi Petrus per se vel per alium aliter ordinaret, subiecerit omnes gentes, secundum illud Matthei ultimo: Baptizate omnes gentes; Marci ultimo: Predicate Evangelium omni creature; Actuum 1: Eritis mihi testes in Hierusalem et Judea et Samaria et usque ad ultimum terre, quia soli Petro dixit: Pasce oves meas et agnos meos, quem etiam super totum gregem suum loco sui universalem vicarium derelinquit, probabile est quod successoribus apostolorum episcopis et successoribus discipulorum curatis per seipsum immediate nullos populos subiecit, sed vicario suo Petro et eius successoribus subiciendos dimisit. Unde auctoritate pape postmodum factum est quod iste huic diocesi tanquam episcopus, et ille huic parrochie tanquam curatus prefuit, ex quo patet quod papa, qui dioceses et parrochias instituit, potest eas dividere et unire."

> ultimo: *Pasce oves meas*. Hoc enim nulli aliorum apostolorum dictum fuit nec tunc nec ante nec post. Ergo talem potestatem plenam et perfectam habet solus successor Petri qui ob hoc papa dicitur, quia pater patrum. In aliis autem non est nisi derivata et limitata prout pape placet.[36]

Pierre states firmly that when Peter was made the first pope he received a plenitude of jurisdictional authority, which was then distributed downwards from him to the other members of the ecclesiastical hierarchy: he seems to commit himself to the view expounded in the *De causa*. However, since he also maintains that Peter was not made pope until immediately before the Ascension,[37] he may simply be describing the situation which in his view prevailed from the time of the Petrine commission on, and not necessarily be eliminating the possibility of a direct commission of authority from Christ during the preceding period. After Peter was instituted as the first of Christ's vicars here on earth, from that point on in some sense all jurisdictional authority in the church was derived from him or his successors. But while Christ was still on earth and still presiding over his church in his own person, it was up to him to distribute jurisdictional authority to his apostles and disciples, even if such jurisdictional authority did not entail responsibility in a certain area. The other alternative, of course, is to view the statement in the commentary on

[36] 4 *Sent*. 24.6.1, fol. 130r.

[37] The operative passage, as illustrated in the quotation given above, was John 21:15-17. Cf. *Tractatus* 1.2, p. 138; *Iudicium*, art. 2, MS Vienna 2168, fol. 2r-2v; MS Vienna 11799, fol. 194r. The author of the *De causa* would agree. See *De causa* **1**: 198-261. This seems to have been the usual view on the matter. The other alternative was that Christ conferred papal authority on Peter in Matthew 16:18-19. This view was favoured by Augustinus Triumphus, *Summa*, qu. 20.4 (ad 1) & 5; James of Viterbo, *De reg. christiano* 2.3, p. 180; and Guillelmus de Villana, *Reprobatio errorum* 3.2, p. 73. However, since Augustinus Triumphus also maintains that Peter did not use his papal authority until after the Ascension (*Summa*, qu. 61.2 ad 3), on one occasion at least he is inclined to regard Matthew 16 as being no more than a promise which was not fulfilled until John 21. See *De potestate collegii mortuo papa*, ed. W. Mulder in *Studia catholica*, 5 (1928-29): 46-53 at 48. Cf. Guillelmus de Villana, *Reprobatio errorum* 3.3, p. 77. This was the view favoured by Alexander de S. Elpidio, *De eccl. potestate* 2.2, p. 15; Guillelmus de Sarzano, *Tractatus de potestate summi pontificis*, chap. 5, ed. R. Del Ponte in *Studi medievali*, 3rd series, 12 (1971): 1020-1094 at 1033-1034; and Herveus Natalis, *Tractatus de potestate papae*, p. 368. Alvarus Pelagius probably deserves to be placed in this list as well. On some occasions he seems to prefer Matthew 16 (*De planctu ecclesiae*, chap. 52, p. 127; chap. 53, p. 133; chap. 55, p. 140); on others he seems to prefer John 21 (chap. 13, p. 30). Indeed, on a couple of occasions he manages to suggest that Christ bestowed papal authority on Peter in both passages (chap. 44, p. 79; chap. 58, p. 167). However, since on at least one occasion he does refer to Matthew 16 as a promise (chap. 40, p. 64), he probably feels that Peter was designated as the first of Christ's vicars in Matthew 16, but was not actually entrusted with papal authority until later.

the *Sentences* as a direct precedent for the view found in the *De causa*, but this is much less likely. If Pierre does commit himself here to a view like the one adopted in the *De causa*, he changed his mind on the matter at least twice before the *De causa* could have been written: from his first opinion on the matter to his second in the *Quodlibet* of 1314, and from his second view back to the first in the *De causa*. This does not strike one as being very probable.

The discussion of the source of jurisdictional authority in the early church leads naturally to a discussion of the source of *potestas iurisdictionis* in the contemporary church. Since the author of the *De causa* argues that it was left to Peter to distribute jurisdictional authority to the apostles and disciples in the primitive church, so he argues that it is left to the pope, the successor of Peter, to distribute jurisdictional authority to bishops and priests, the successors of the apostles and disciples, in the contemporary church.[38] In his view, all jurisdictional authority is derived, not from Christ directly, but from the pope, his vicar on earth, to whom has been entrusted a *plenitudo potestatis*.[39] However, the author of the *Tractatus* offers a substantially different view. Discussing the problem of the source of papal authority in the church, he maintains that three different opinions can be identified. The first opinion, with which no early fourteenth century theologian could agree, would make all jurisdictional authority, including papal authority, a product of human ordinance.[40] The second opinion, with which the author does not agree either, is the same

[38] For his comments on the jurisdictional authority of bishops see *De causa* **5**: 118-666; for his comments on the jurisdictional authority of priests see ibid. **6**: 25-241.

[39] Ibid. **4**: 587-951. Augustinus Triumphus would accept the argument offered by the author of the *De causa*. See *Tractatus brevis de duplici potestate prelatorum et laicorum*, ed. R. Scholz, *Die Publizistik zur Zeit Philipps des Schönen und Bonifaz VIII.* (Stuttgart, 1903), pp. 486-501 at 492; *De potestate collegii*, p. 50. Most other late medieval publicists, without necessarily accepting the argument, would accept the general point, that *potestas iurisdictionis* in the contemporary church must be derived from the pope. See Augustinus Triumphus, *Summa*, qu. 1.1; qu. 65.1; *Tractatus brevis*, p. 496; Alvarus Pelagius, *De planctu ecclesiae*, chap. 54, p. 136; Guillelmus de Sarzano, *Tractatus*, chap. 5, pp. 1033-1034; Guillelmus de Villana, *Reprobatio errorum* 4.2, p. 87; Hermannus de Scildis, *Tractatus contra haereticos negantes immunitatem et iurisdictionem sanctae Ecclesiae* 2.2, ed. A. Zumkeller (Würzburg, 1970), pp. 62-63; Herveus Natalis, *Tractatus de potestate papae*, p. 370; James of Viterbo, *De reg. christiano* 2.5, pp. 205-206. This became common doctrine among late medieval canonists as well. See R. L. Benson, *The Bishop Elect: A Study in Medieval Ecclesiastical Office* (Princeton, 1968), esp. p. 131; B. Tierney, *Foundations of the Conciliar Theory* (Cambridge, 1955), pp. 145-147; J. A. Watt, *The Theory of Papal Monarchy in the Thirteenth Century* (New York, 1965), pp. 82-83; K. Ganzer, *Papsttum und Bistumsbesetzungen in der Zeit von Gregor IX. bis Bonifaz VIII.* (Cologne, 1968), pp. 56-57.

[40] *Tractatus*, 1.3, p. 176.

as the doctrine defended in the *De causa*, although here it is attributed to Innocent III.[41] The opinion which is favoured is the third, according to which all jurisdictional authority in the church: papal, episcopal and parochial, is derived from Christ:

> Tertia opinio, que mihi videtur verior, est quod potestas pape, episcoporum et curatorum est a Christo, et preeminentia episcoporum super curatos et simplices sacerdotes, et preeminentia pape super omnes. Est, tamen, advertendum circa hec omnia quod Petrus et Apostoli et Discipuli acceperunt sic immediate potestatem a Christo, quod sine medio ministro et sacramento, quia ipse potuit rem sacramenti conferre etiam sine sacramento. Sed sequentes prelati mediante hominum electione et superioris confirmatione, quantum ad istos qui habent superiorem, adepti sunt potestatem iurisdictionis, non aliter; sed potestatem ordinis mediante sacramento et ministro sacramenti.[42]

The author of the *Tractatus* does not want to deny the papal *plenitudo potestatis* completely, of course. Hence he goes on to maintain that, since a plenitude of power has been entrusted to the pope alone, *potestas iurisdictionis* can be limited or taken away by the pope, and indeed is in some sense instituted by him.[43] It is somewhat difficult at first to appreciate how the pope could have the authority of instituting people in their *potestas iurisdictionis* when this authority comes from Christ. But as we have already seen, elsewhere in the *Tractatus* he maintains that the *potestas iurisdictionis* which Christ conferred on the apostles was of a general nature, and the division of this authority on diocesan and parochial lines was something that was done only later on the authority of Peter and his successors.[44] This would seem to imply that the jurisdictional authority

[41] Ibid. 1.3, p. 179.

[42] Ibid. 1.3, p. 182.

[43] Ibid. 2.5, pp. 261-262: "Papa non habet plenitudinem potestatis in ordine; unde in potestate ordinis alii non subduntur ei, sed equantur; presbiteri quidem, in charactere sacerdotali; episcopi, in episcopali. ... Sed papa in iurisdictione habet plenitudinem potestatis; ceteri, autem, in partem tantum sollicitudinis sunt vocati. ... Unde, in hoc alii subduntur ei, et per consequens ab eo possunt deponi. Et quando dicitur 'Quod Deus dedit, homo non potest auferre,' verum est, nisi Deo dante auctoritatem auferendi. Eo ipso, autem, quod Deus dedit pape plenam iurisdictionem, aliis partialem, volens illos huic subesse et hunc illis preesse, et ipse dedit ei potestatem instituendi et destituendi illos; sicut quamvis rex institueret immediate primo ballivos, castellanos et prepositos, si tamen ex toto submittat ballivis alios a se institutos, ex hac submissione daret eis potestatem ipsos deponendi et alios ponendi, licet potestas castellanie et preposIture non sit a ballivo, sed a rege."

[44] Ibid. 1.3, p. 181: "Ecclesia romana ceteras ecclesias et dignitates instituit, non quantum ad potestatis collationem, sed quantum ad ipsarum distinctionem et ipsarum certam situationem, quia a principio non erat per Christum facta divisio diocesium et

which Christ now confers is of an equally general nature, and it is up to the pope to make it specific by entrusting its recipient with the responsibility of a certain parish or diocese. But even if the recipient of *potestas iurisdictionis* is subject to the authority of the pope and in some sense instituted by him, this does not deny the fact that throughout the ecclesiastical hierarchy *potestas iurisdictionis* has a divine foundation.[45]

Significantly, the view which Pierre defends in the *Quodlibet* is identical with the view in the *Tractatus*, and just as in the *Tractatus*, its defence is combined with an explicit rejection of the Innocentian alternative. Rather than argue that all jurisdictional authority is derived from the pope, here Pierre argues that it comes from God. God bestows *potestas iurisdictionis* on the candidate chosen by the human law,[46] although recipients of this divine grant are still subject to the authority of their hierarchical superiors.[47] Surprisingly, the view which Pierre puts forth in the *Iudicium* is different, on a *prima facie* view much more like the position defended in the *De causa*. He does not agree with the author of the *De causa* that the apostles received all their jurisdictional authority from Peter, preferring instead to believe that they received it directly from Christ. But since Christ instituted Peter as the first of his representatives immediately

parrochiarum; sed post eius ascensionem et Spiritus Sancti missionem facta est ista distinctio per Apostolos et eorum successores, auctoritate Petri et successorum eius. Sicut in Veteri Testamento Deus dedit filiis Israel terram promissionis per se ipsum, sed Josue et Eleazarus eis ipsam distribuerunt per sortes."

[45] Significantly, although several other late medieval publicists would agree with Pierre that the apostles received *potestas iurisdictionis* directly from Christ (see n. 31), these same theorists would not agree that their successors, the bishops, also receive their *potestas iurisdictionis* directly from Christ. Pierre seems to have had a distinctive view in this regard. The other theorists all go on to explain that, after the Ascension, the apostles stood in a relationship to Peter precisely the same as the one they had had to Christ himself before. See Alexander de S. Elpidio, *De eccl. potestate* 1.5, p. 6; Alvarus Pelagius, *De planctu ecclesiae*, chap. 59 (57 according to Alvarus), p. 179; Guillelmus de Villana, *Reprobatio errorum* 4.2, p. 88; Herveus Natalis, *Tractatus de iurisdictione*, p. 28; James of Viterbo, *De reg. christiano* 2.10, p. 308. Although their statements are not identical, that of Guillelmus de Villana seems representative: "verum est, quod omnes apostoli acceperunt talem potestatem <iurisdictionis> immediate a Christo et non a Petro, quia Christus praesens <erat>, et ideo non oportebat, quod eis daret per vicarium. Modo vero Christus est absens, et ideo vult, quod omnes successores apostolorum accipiant a vicario suo. Nec in hoc sunt minoris dignitatis et virtutis, quia eandem vel aequalem habent potestatem cum apostolis, et sicut episcopi sunt Papae subiecti, ita post Christi ascensionem beato Petro fuerunt subiecti apostoli. Erat enim eorum caput et princeps, ut patet ex dictis."

[46] *Quodlibet* 4.3, fols. 96v-97r.

[47] Ibid. 4.3, fol. 97r: "Sicut enim papa, si dat alicui prebendam, non propter hoc eximit eum a potestate episcopi, quin possit eum privare si mereatur, sic etiam <Deus> dat curato potestatem ita quod in ea subsit episcopo et sic episcopo quod subsit pape."

before the Ascension, the successors to the apostles and disciples were certainly subject to the authority of Peter and his successors in jurisdictional matters. Hence, just as the apostles and disciples received their authority directly from Christ, so must their successors receive their authority from the successor of Christ, the pope.[48] Furthermore, a similar view seems to be defended in the commentary on the *Sentences*, where the pope is described as the fount of all jurisdictional authority in the church:

> Potestas que tota data est uni in suo fonte non est in aliis nisi derivata et limitata pro illius voluntate. Sed potestas iurisdictionis que est ad regendum populum tota et in suo fonte data fuit soli Petro et in eo successoribus eius quando cura ecclesie sibi soli commissa fuit, dicente Domino Joannis ultimo: Pasce oves meas. Hoc enim nulli aliorum apostolorum dictum fuit nec tunc nec ante nec post. Ergo talem potestatem plenam et perfectam habet solus successor Petri qui ob hoc papa dicitur quia pater patrum. In aliis autem non est nisi derivata et limitata prout pape placet. ... Et hoc est rationabile, quia optimum regimen unius multitudinis est quando regitur per unum suppremum a quo descendit auctoritas regendi in medios usque ad infimos. Et propter hoc regnum est optima pollicia secundum Philosophum, secundo *Polliticorum*. Sed regimen ecclesie est optime a Christo institutum. Ergo in tota ecclesia debet esse unus universalis rector a quo descendat auctoritas regendi in medios usque ad rectores infimos, et hic est papa.[49]

From this it might appear that, although Pierre differs with the author of the *De causa* on the matter of the precise nature of the New Testament precedents, for all practical purposes he has the same doctrine on the nature of the government of the church. The church has a monarchical constitution, according to which all governmental authority has been entrusted to the monarch himself, the pope, who in turn distributes it as he deems appropriate to the inferior members of the ecclesiastical hierarchy.

It is very difficult, at least at first, to see how these conflicting doctrines of Pierre can be renconciled. On the one hand we have a doctrine which stresses the fact that *potestas iurisdictionis* is derived from the pope, to whom it has been entrusted in its fullness. This view is expressed in the commentary on the *Sentences*, which was written in 1312-1313, and it is

[48] *Iudicium*, art. 2, MS Vienna 2168, fol. 2r-2v; MS Vienna 11799, fols. 193v-194r. Cf. Alexander de S. Elpidio, Alvarus Pelagius, Guillelmus de Villana, Herveus Natalis and James of Viterbo in n. 45.

[49] 4 *Sent*. 24.6.1, fol. 130r.

expressed again in the *Iudicium*, which was written in 1317-1318. On the other hand we have a doctrine which emphasizes that *potestas iurisdictionis* has a divine source. This is expressed first in the *Quodlibet* of 1314, and then later in the *Tractatus* of 1317. To suggest that Pierre changed his mind is not all that helpful, since if he did, again he changed it not once but twice: from the first doctrine to the second in the *Quodlibet* of 1314, and from the second doctrine back to the first in the *Iudicium* of 1317-1318. However, the two apparently contradictory doctrines can be reconciled along the lines which are suggested in the *Tractatus*. The author of the *Tractatus* seems to suggest that *potestas iurisdictionis* is derived from Christ in a general sense, although in any specific diocese or parish it is derived from the pope. In the *Iudicium*, which otherwise stresses the papal source of *potestas iurisdictionis*, Pierre suggests that this was the case in the primitive church, although he is not quite so clear in maintaining that the same situation still applies.[50] Following up these suggestions, one might argue that, although *potestas iurisdictionis* is derived from Christ, it makes equally good sense to maintain that it is derived from the pope as well, since it is only by the papacy that this commission of authority can be made specific. However, if this reconstruction is correct, the doctrine of Pierre de la Palu on the source of jurisdictional authority in the church is essentially the doctrine found in the *Tractatus*, and the doctrine defended in the *De causa* is significantly different.

A comparison of the doctrines of the *De causa* and the *Tractatus* on a third problem, the nature of papal government in the church, reinforces this conclusion. The author of the *De causa* maintains that in the apostolic church all governmental authority was entrusted to Peter, and that the same situation applies with regard to Peter's successor, the pope. The pope has been given a plenitude of jurisdictional authority, and it is up to him to allocate *potestas iurisdictionis* as he thinks appropriate. He concedes that the *potestas iurisdictionis* of inferior bishops and priests is "a Deo inspirante," since it is undoubtedly for the good of the church that *potestas iurisdictionis* be entrusted to them, and anything that is for the good of the church can be thought to have a divine foundation.[51] But since the *potestas iurisdictionis* of bishops and priests has no direct divine foundation, the pope's discretionary authority with regard to it is quite

[50] Cf. *Iudicium*, art. 13, MS Vienna 2168, fol. 11r-11v; MS Vienna 11799, fols. 213v-214r, quoted in n. 35.

[51] *De causa* **4**: 806-810.

extensive. The author of the *Tractatus*, however, has a view of papal authority in the church which is quite different, at least in its emphasis. Since he maintains that the apostles and disciples received *potestas iurisdictionis* from Christ, and since he maintains that even now bishops and priests receive their *potestas iurisdictionis* from Christ, he is not prepared to grant the pope the same licence in dealing with subordinate members of the ecclesiastical hierarchy, although he does recognize, of course, that the pope has been given a responsibility for the government of the entire church.

In article 5, the author of the *De causa* maintains that the pope can remove a prelate *sine culpa*. But he emphasizes that he must replace him with someone more suited for the position if he is to avoid sinful conduct.[52] With this the author of the *Tractatus* can agree; in fact, the entire passage of the *De causa* in which this point is made is copied from the *Tractatus*.[53] However, further on in the *De causa* the problem is taken up again, and on this occasion it is given a treatment which has no counterpart in the *Tractatus*. The author of the *De causa* introduces a distinction between the pope's *potentia ordinata* and his *potentia absoluta*, maintaining that, although *de potentia ordinata* the pope cannot depose a bishop or priest without reasonable cause, *de potentia absoluta* he can, and his action is valid even if he acts in complete disregard of the regular, canonically sanctioned procedures.[54] The pope can even dispense with the episcopate and parish priests entirely, at least as far as the *potestas iurisdictionis* of bishops and priests is concerned, if for some reason or other he thinks such action desirable.[55] The pope has no authority to deprive Christians of the ministers necessary for the purposes of salvation. But since the purposes of salvation could be met even if the pope chose to replace the regular bishops and priests with special legates, such action would undoubtedly be valid.[56] In all of this the author of the *De causa* admits that such papal decisions would be undesirable; even more, he

[52] Ibid. **5**: 634-647.

[53] Cf. *Tractatus* 2.5, pp. 266-267.

[54] *De causa* **6**: 1105-1123.

[55] Ibid. **6**: 1291-1335; cf. 1406-1447.

[56] Cf. Augustinus Triumphus, *Summa*, qu. 61.1 and qu. 19.5: "Potest etiam < papa > in provinciis et parrochiis eis [i.e. episcopis et presbyteris] deputatis omnia facere per seipsum vel per commissionem que ipsi episcopi vel presbyteri facere possunt, et adhuc amplius." Cf. Alexander de S. Elpidio, *De eccl. potestate* 2.2, p. 15; Alvarus Pelagius, *De planctu ecclesiae*, chap. 54, p. 137; Herveus Natalis, *Tractatus de iurisdictione*, p. 30; idem, *Tractatus de potestate papae*, pp. 376 & 384; James of Viterbo, *De reg. christiano* 2.5, p. 207.

maintains that they would be positively sinful, since the pope would be violating Christ's desires for the church.[57] But we are nonetheless left with the fact that the pope has the authority to make such decisions if he so wishes.

This kind of perspective on the nature of papal government has no parallel in the *Tractatus* or any of the other undisputed works of Pierre de la Palu. In fact, its validity is expressly denied. Although, in his controversy with Jean de Pouilly, Pierre championed the cause of the friars by exalting the papal rights of government in the church as much as possible, he never allowed himself to be led to a view of papal government like the one presented in the *De causa*: his understanding of the New Testament precedents precluded such a possibility. On his reading, the New Testament established a divine foundation for the authority of parish priests and bishops which the pope is compelled to respect.[58] Hence, because the three orders, papal, episcopal, and parochial, are all of direct divine institution, Pierre asserts expressly that "papa non potest tollere ordinem episcoporum nec curatorum ex toto, quia non habet potestatem in destructionem totius ecclesie sed in edificationem."[59] In short, on this issue, as on the others considered above, the views expressed in the works which undoubtedly were written by Pierre de la Palu, and which date from periods both before and after the writing of the *Tractatus*, are in essential harmony with the views expressed in the *Tractatus*. However, the views expressed in the *De causa* are significantly different.

One final illustration of the same point can be derived from a consideration of the different treatments which the *De causa* and the *Tractatus* accord to the papal heretic. The author of the *De causa*

[57] Cf. Augustinus Triumphus, *Summa*, qu. 19.3: "Debet enim papa in gubernando ecclesiam Dei providentiam imitari qui, quamvis possit totum orbem immediate per seipsum gubernare, non tamen facit." Cf. Herveus Natalis, *Tractatus de potestate papae*, p. 399: "quantum est de plenitudine potestatis, credo quod Papa posset facere quod nullus esset ordinarius alius ab ipso, et quod omnia quae fiunt in Ecclesia posset agere si vellet per commissarios; sed credo quod non deceret, nec etiam ut credo, expediret, quia ut credo, illa que pertinent ad regimen totius Ecclesiae non ita utiliter fierent si omnes essent commissarii, sicut ponendo quod aliqui sint ordinarii qui tam per se quam per alios possint regere populum sicut principaliter instituti in regimine populi." For a more complete discussion of the views of Augustinus Triumphus on this matter see my essay, "The Papal Sovereign in the Ecclesiology of Augustinus Triumphus," *Mediaeval Studies*, 39 (1977): 177-205.

[58] See his comments in *Quodlibet* 2.2, fols. 89v-90r. The passage is repeated in his *Articuli circa materiam confessionum*, fol. 98v.

[59] *Quodlibet* 2.2, fol. 90v; *Articuli circa materiam confessionum*, fol. 99v.

underlines the fact that no one is competent to pass judgment upon the pope. The possibility of a papal heretic has to be considered, of course, but he is careful to point out that a pope who is guilty of heresy can be considered to have deposed himself. The most that man can do is announce that such an act of self-deposition has taken place.[60] With this the author of the *Tractatus* would agree;[61] once again the entire discussion in the *De causa* is copied from the *Tractatus*. However, there is a significant difference in emphasis. Although both treatises endorse the usual canonistic solution to the problem, the author of the *Tractatus* is inclined to place more stress on papal accountability than the author of the *De causa*. Whereas the author of the *De causa* maintains that the pope *cannot* be deposed except for heresy, and that even then such a judgment is merely a *de facto* pronouncement, the author of the *Tractatus* maintains that the pope *can* indeed be deposed, but only for heresy, although the act of deposition should be regarded more as a *de facto* pronouncement than as a *de iure* judgment. Significantly, perhaps, the views expressed in the other works of Pierre de la Palu lack the nuances found in both the *Tractatus* and the *De causa*; in these works Pierre contents himself with the simple statement that an heretical pope can be deposed by a general council. As he puts it in the *Quodlibet* (1314) and repeats in the *Responsiones* (1318-1321),

> Si papa errare possit, nec in suo errore sequendus sit, sed corrigendus, sicut dicitur ad Galatas 2: *In faciem ei restiti quia reprehensibilis* etc. Tamen in

[60] *De causa* **4**: 177-229.

[61] Cf. *Tractatus* 1.3, pp. 195-196. This was a common doctrine in the early fourteenth century. See, for example, Augustinus Triumphus, *Summa*, qu. 22.1 ad 2; Aegidius Romanus, *De renunciatione papae*, chap. 9, ed. Rocaberti 2.1, pp. 1-64 at 20; Alvarus Pelagius, *De planctu ecclesiae*, chap. 6, p. 27; chap. 34, p. 37; chap. 45, p. 82; idem, *Collirium adversus hereses novas*, ed. R. Scholz, *Unbekannte kirchenpolitische Streitschriften aus der Zeit Ludwigs des Bayern (1327-1354)* 2 (Rome, 1914), pp. 491-514 at 507; Franciscus Toti de Perusio, *Tractatus contra Bavarum*, ed. Scholz, *Unbekannte kirchenpolitische Streitschriften* 2, pp. 76-88 at 81; Guillelmus de Villana, *Reprobatio errorum* 2.2, p. 64; and Hermannus de Scildis, *Tractatus* 2.4, p. 67. Indeed, there was a well established canonistic precedent for this kind of doctrine. In this regard see Tierney, *Foundations of the Conciliar Theory*, pp. 47-67; and J. M. Moynihan, *Papal Immunity and Liability in the Writings of the Medieval Canonists* (Rome, 1961), pp. 75-91. However, many fourteenth-century canonists, although for the most part firm papalists, displayed some conciliarist tendencies. See Tierney, *Foundations of the Conciliar Theory*, esp. pp. 199-219; Moynihan, *Papal Immunity and Liability*, pp. 117-124; and L. Buisson, *Potestas und Caritas: Die päpstliche Gewalt im Spätmittelalter* (Cologne, 1958), pp. 182ff. A publicist leaning in this direction was Peter Olivi. See his *Epistola ad Conradum de Offida*, ed. P. L. Oliger in *Archivum franciscanum historicum*, 11 (1918), 366-373 at 369; and his *De renunciatione papae*, ed. P. L. Oliger, ibid., 340-366 at 356.

> dubio non presumitur, nec est cuiuslibet iudicare papam errantem, sed solius concilii generalis quod propter heresim ipsum deponere potest, 40 d. *Si papa.*[62]

However, although neither the *Quodlibet* nor the *Responsiones* contain a full discussion of the problem, the treatment which they do give the issue is more easily reconcilable with the emphasis of the *Tractatus* than with the very different emphasis of the *De causa*.

Further illustrations could be given.[63] But probably enough has already been said. On a wide range of issues the views in the *Tractatus* seem to be in essential harmony with the views which Pierre de la Palu held throughout his career, whereas the same cannot be said of the *De causa*. When this is combined with the fact that the *De causa* follows the *Tractatus* and corrects it, the only conclusion to draw is that, whereas Pierre indeed is the author of the *Tractatus*, someone other than Pierre, Guillaume de Pierre Godin, must be the author of the *De causa*. The only time Pierre clearly leans in the direction of the *De causa* is in his *Conclusio*, where he offers a view of the status of the seventy-two

[62] *Quodlibet* 4.2, fol. 89v; *Responsiones*, fol. 108v.

[63] The author of the *De causa*, for example, maintains that the apostles were made priests in Luke 22: *Hoc facite in meam commemorationem* (*De causa* **2**: 163-198). This was the occasion on which they received the power of consecrating the elements of the eucharist, the principal function of priestly authority. He goes on to maintain that there is some doubt about when they received the *potestas ligandi et solvendi*, the two possibilities being John 20: *Accipite Spiritum Sanctum*; *quorum remiseritis peccata remittuntur eis* etc., and the same Luke 22 passage in which they received their *potestas celebrandi* (see the rather lengthy discussion, ibid. **2**: 200-386). Although he shows some initial favour towards the John 20 passage, largely because one can support such a choice with the authority of Aquinas, in his final statement on the problem he decides in favour of Luke 22: this he maintains is the *rationabilior opinio* (ibid. **2**: 382). Significantly, the author of the *Tractatus* opts for the other alternative (*Tractatus* 1.2, p. 126), and Pierre de la Palu does the same on the only occasion other than the *Tractatus* on which he explicitly raises the issue (4 *Sent.* 24.2.3, fol. 127r). Perhaps equally significantly, in his *Lectura Thomasina* Guillaume defends a doctrine on the ordination of priests in the contemporary church quite compatible with a parallel discussion in the *De causa* (see *De causa* **2**: 322-335), and quite compatible with the discussion of the New Testament precedents found in the *De causa*, although he says nothing about those precedents themselves. See *Lectura Thomasina* 4.24 (25 in MS 281), Vienna, Österreichische Nationalbibliothek, MS 1590, fol. 70r-70v; Klosterneuburg, Bibliothek des Augustiner-Chorherrenstiftes, MS 281, fols. 122v-123r: "In sacerdote autem imprimitur caracter in collatione calicis cum patena et materia debita, scilicet pane et vino, quia tunc datur ei potestas consecrandi corpus Christi, quod est principale officium sacerdotis. Tamen quidam dicunt quod in impositione utriusque manus, quia tunc dicitur ei: Accipe Spiritum Sanctum; quorum remiseritis peccata etc. Hoc autem ad solos sacerdotes pertinet. Tamen quia consecrare corpus Domini est principalius officium sacerdotis, magis videtur quod in collatione calicis utrumque tamen est faciendum."

disciples essentially the same as the doctrine offered in the *De causa*.[64] But rather than indicate that Pierre was responsible for the *De causa*, the isolated nature of this statement probably indicates, if it indicates anything, that Pierre read the *De causa* and was influenced by it.[65]

[64] The author of the *De causa* maintains that, with the exception of Peter, Christ did not make the apostles bishops (*De causa* **2**: esp. 388-551), nor did he make the seventy-two disciples priests (ibid. **3**: 105-341). This is quite different from the view expressed in the *Tractatus*, where the author maintains that the status of bishops was instituted in the twelve apostles and the status of priests in the seventy-two disciples (cf. *Tractatus* 1.3, p. 182; with regard to the episcopal order, see his comments in 1.2, p. 126). This latter view is the one supported in the *Iudicium* of Pierre de la Palu which followed the *Tractatus* (*Iudicium*, art. 2, MS Vienna 2168, fol. 2r-2v; MS Vienna 11799, fols. 193v-194r), and in the commentary on the *Sentences* and the *Quodlibet* which preceded it (cf. 4 *Sent.* 24.6.3, fol. 130r-130v, where he maintains that the apostles were created bishops by Christ; and *Quodlibet* 4.3, fol. 96v, where he maintains that the seventy-two disciples were made priests: "Status apostolorum et septuaginta duorum representatur et reservatur quo ad potestatem ordinis in omnibus sacerdotibus."). However, there is some indication that Pierre may have changed his mind about the disciples at least some time after 1318, for in the *Conclusio* (fol. 35r) he doubts their priestly status.

[65] This book had gone to the printer before I discovered that Anneliese Maier has argued for an earlier date for qu. 1 of Pierre de la Palu's *Tractatus de potestate papae*. On the basis of a précis which was prepared by Petrus Rogerii in 1315, Maier argues that, although one can still adhere to Stella's dating for qu. 2, qu. 1 at least must have been written in late 1314 or 1315. Cf. *Ausgehendes Mittelalter: Gesammelte Aufsätze zur Geistesgeschichte des 14. Jahrhunderts* II (Rome, 1967), pp. 308-312, and esp. 509-510. Although this complicates matters somewhat, in all likelihood the chronological order we have given to the early works of Pierre de la Palu is still the correct one. That is, Pierre most probably wrote, first the commentary on book four of the *Sentences*, then the *Quodlibet*, and then the *Tractatus*. Moreover, the precise chronological sequence of Pierre's early works is not a matter of crucial importance for the argument of this chapter, for the argument holds if they were written in some different order as well. One fact we can be certain about is that the commentary on the fourth book of the *Sentences* – indeed, the portion of it used in our analysis – was completed before qu. 1 of the *Tractatus*. As Stella has pointed out, Pierre himself refers to it explicitly at *Tractatus* 1.3, p. 182. If we test each possible chronological arrangement which might be given to Pierre's early works, eliminating only those which would have the *Tractatus* antedate the commentary on the *Sentences*, every possible arrangement leads to results similar to those discussed in this chapter. Most of Pierre's statements on the major issues parallel the doctrines of the *Tractatus*. Some of his statements, indeed, may be taken as anticipating the very different views of the *De causa*. However, whatever the order of his early works, one cannot regard any of these latter statements as evidence for Pierre's authorship of the *De causa* without also assuming that he was capable, within a relatively short period of time, of changing his mind at least twice on several central issues in his ecclesiology. The unlikelihood of such a degree of inconsistency is strong evidence against Pierre's authorship of the *De causa* and in favour of Guillaume de Pierre Godin's.

3

The Date

Since the *Tractatus de potestate papae* of Pierre de la Palu was written between 6 January and 25 October 1317, and since the *De causa* is dependent on the *Tractatus*, one might consider the early months of 1317 as a *terminus a quo* for the writing of the *De causa*. This date, however, is too early. In view of the fact that the *De causa* contains two explicit references to the *Clementinae* (**2**: 650-652; **5**: 217), the *De causa* could not have been written before 25 October 1317, the date on which the *Clementinae* were promulgated.

This date can be refined by an analysis of the relationship between the *De causa* and the *Iudicium* of Pierre de la Palu, which was written between 25 October 1317 and 25 March 1318. If the *De causa* is dependent on the *Iudicium*, the *De causa* could not have been written before November or December 1317. If the *Iudicium* is dependent on the *De causa*, the *De causa* must have been written before March 1318. Although neither alternative can be viewed with any certainty, there is more to suggest the former alternative than the latter. Clearly, if Guillaume drew from the *Iudicium* of Pierre de la Palu, he had to have a copy of it; just as Pierre had to have a copy of the *De causa* if he drew upon it for his *Iudicium*. Since there is no record of the two men having had time to meet and familiarize themselves with one another's work before the spring or summer of 1318, which was probably too late for Pierre to have used the *De causa* in his writing of the *Iudicium*, the other alternative seems more likely. Although this falls short of conclusive proof, when conclusive proof cannot be had one has to fall back on probable arguments, and in this case probable arguments suggest the *De causa*'s dependence on the *Iudicium*. Hence, given the fact that the earliest known opportunity Guillaume had for familiarizing himself with the *Iudicium* was the spring or summer of 1318, conceivably this latter date might be offered as an improvement on the *terminus a quo* suggested earlier.

A *terminus ad quem* is even more difficult to establish. Given the fact that the author of the *De causa* was certainly familiar with the case of Jean de Pouilly, and given the fact that he makes no mention of its conclusion, one might be tempted to think that it must have been written while the case was still a live issue, that is before 24 July 1321. However, although he was undoubtedly familiar with the case, Guillaume had no personal interest in it; and under those circumstances he could very well have allowed the case to be resolved without taking notice of the fact. Fortunately, however, there may be some significance in the fact that in the *Conclusio* of Pierre de la Palu we find Pierre entertaining the suggestion that the seventy-two disciples were not made priests by Christ. Since this amounts to a radical and unprecedented change of mind on his part, it is quite conceivable that he derived the idea from the *De causa*, where it is offered as one of the principal points which the work is designed to demonstrate. The suspicion that this may have been the case is heightened by the fact that Pierre offers a reason for his new-found opinion which the author of the *De causa* would also consider important: the fact that some of the seventy-two were subsequently made deacons. Moreover, like the author of the *De causa*, his doubt about the priestly status of the seventy-two does not lead him to question their power of preaching and performing miracles.[1] If Pierre was dependent on the *De causa* here, we have a *terminus ad quem* for the *De causa*, 1318, the year when the *Conclusio* likely made its appearance. At best, this amounts to an informed guess, as does the *terminus a quo* discussed earlier. But given the evidence available, the best estimate for a date for the writing of the *De causa* would be mid-to-late 1318.

[1] Cf. *Conclusio*, fol. 35r: "Quod autem dicit < Joannes de Polliaco > , Evangelia dicere septuaginta duos discipulos accepisse immediate potestatem a Christo, verum de potestate predicandi et miracula faciendi, de quo modo non queritur. Sed non est certum nec clarum de potestate ligandi et solvendi sive de potestate et ordine sacerdotali, de quibus queritur, et magis videtur oppositum, scilicet quod non fuerint per Christum ordinati in sacerdotes, quia postea de illis fuerunt septem in diacones ordinati, Actuum sexto capitulo."

4

The Manuscripts

There are thiry extant manuscripts of the *Tractatus de causa immediata ecclesiastice potestatis*. Undoubtedly several other manuscripts have been lost, such as the manuscript which appears in the fifteenth-century catalogue of the Neithart library at Ulm;[1] and unfortunately it is impossible to determine the extent of the loss because of the imprecision of many medieval catalogues. The catalogue of the library of Sixtus IV, for example, lists a number of works entitled *De potestate pape* or the equivalent, without giving further details.[2] However, the following are the extant manuscripts which I have been able to locate and use in the preparation of this edition. I have not been able to improve on the list in Kaeppeli[3] except for the addition of MS lat. 4233 of the Bibliothèque Nationale in Paris. The manuscripts are listed alphabetically by sigla. In order to conserve as much space as possible, the descriptions have been restricted to what must be regarded as the most essential information: contents, date and provenance, when known. References to complete and published descriptions have been included when such are available.

[1] Cf. P. Lehmann, *Mittelalterliche Bibliothekskataloge Deutschlands und der Schweiz*, vol. 1: *Die Bistümer Konstanz und Chur* (München, 1918), p. 340: "146. Petrus de Pallude de potestate ecclesiastica; item Erveus de potestate ecclesiastica; item Gerson de eodem; item tractatus de sacerdocio et regno; item dyalogus Okam non totaliter conpletus in papiro mixto pergameno, habet folia 402, quorum primum inc. 'circa potestatem' et fin. 'confirmatur.' Fol. 38 inc. 'non enim est' et fin. 'spiritus sancti.' Fol. 79 inc. 'que valet' et fin. 'regimen.' Fol. 130 inc. 'verum miraculum' et fin. 'procedere debui.' Fol. 162 inc. 'permanserit' et fin. 'cardinalium.' Fol. 210 inc. 'defendendi' et fin. 'dum tale.' Fol. 259 inc. 'utens iuris' et fin. 'non est unus.' Fol. 290 inc. 'quamvis videatur' et fin. 'manifestum quod.' Fol. 325 inc. '-rarium est' et fin. 'habet pro papa.' Fol. 352 inc. 'regnum' et fin. 'mortalium hoc.' Fol. 384 inc. 'nemo potest' et fin. 'sequitur capitulum 21.' Fol. 402 inc. 'Cristiane'." This corresponds to none of the extant manuscripts.

[2] Cf. E. Müntz and P. Fabre, *La Bibliothèque du Vatican au XV*^{e} *siècle* (Paris, 1887), esp. pp. 195-197.

[3] T. Kaeppeli, *Scriptores Ordinis Praedicatorum Medii Aevi* 2 (Rome, 1975), pp. 154-155.

B[1] = Barcelona, Archivo Capitular de la Catedral de Barcelona, Cod. 2 [Monastic Microfilm Project # 30273]

A fifteenth-century manuscript of uncertain provenance, although judging from the amount of conciliar material which it contains, it could have been written at Basel. The *De causa* appears without the *Epilogus*, the annotated table of contents appended to the text in most of the manuscripts. *Contents*:

1) fols. 1r-8v – Joannes de Turrecremata, "Flores sancti Thomae de potestate papae."
2) fols. 8v-11r – "Decretum domini pape Eugenii actum in concilio Florentino de reductione Armenorum."
3) fols. 11r-12v – "Decretum domini pape Eugenii depositionis et privationis Basilien."
4) fols. 12v-39r – James of Viterbo, *Tractatus de regimine christiano*.
5) fols. 39v-60v – A treatise without title and with gloss, arguing that the pope can resign his office and that he possesses temporal jurisdiction.
6) fols. 61r-68r – "Questio disputata de pape potestate super imperatorem et reges respectu temporalium. / Questio est utrum dignitas pontificalis et regalis sint due potestates distincte divise et separate. ..."
7) fol. 68r-68v – "Epistola quedam missa cum conclusionibus disputatis de pape potestate in concilio regis Francie inter oratores pape Eugenii et oratores Basiliensium."
8) fols. 69r-102v – The *De causa*. *Inc*.: "Tractus [sic] Petri de Palude de causa immediata ecclesiastice potestatis. / Incipit tractatus fratris Petri de Palude, magistri in sacra pagina et doctoris utriusque iuris, ordinis fratrum predicatorum, de causa immediata ecclesiastice potestatis, de potestate Petri, apostolorum et discipulorum Christi, ac etiam de pape potestate episcoporum et curatorum. / Circa potestatem a Christo collatam prelatis ecclesie. ..." *Expl*.: "Unde potestas que est de iure divino nullo modo subest pape ut possit eam in se tollere vel mutare, sicut patet in potestate caracteris etc. / Explicit tractatus magistri Petri de Palude ordinis predicatorum de causa immediata ecclesiastice potestatis."
9) fols. 103r-105r – "Sermo domini abbatis de Sicilia nunc archiepiscopi Panormitani factus in concilio Basiliensi per eundem in favorem sanctissimi ac beatissimi domini nostri pape Eugenii IIII[ti]."
10) fols. 105v-108r – "Decretum sanctissimi domini nostri pape Eugenii IIII[ti] missum rectori et universitati studii Senensis ad informandum eos de iusticia sua quam habet in papatu."

11) fols. 108v-111r – "Propositio facta per reverendissimum in Christo patrem dominum Julianum cardinalem Sancti Angeli, apostolice sedis legatum, in concilio Basiliensi ante recessum suum ab eodem concilio."
12) fols. 111r-117r – "Questio domini Joannis Palomar utriusque iuris doctoris: Cui parendum est, an sanctissimo domino nostro pape Eugenio IIII[to], an concilio Basiliensi tanquam superiori."
13) fols. 117v-134v – Alexander de S. Elpidio, *Tractatus de ecclesiastica potestate*.
14) fols. 134v-143v – Ptolemy of Lucca, *Determinatio compendiosa de iurisdictione imperii et auctoritate summi pontificis*.
15) fols. 144r-156v – "Questiones disputate tempore pape Benedicti de Luna de potestate pape et concilii."
16) fols. 156v-159v – "Tractatus de veritate potestatis apostolice contra decem propositiones cardinalis Cameracensis que videntur erronee."
17) fol. 160r-160v – "Quedam propositiones de concilio."
18) fol. 161r-161v – A short piece beginning with a reference to Alvarus Pelagius: "Alvarus de statu et planctu ecclesie in principio articulo quarto dicit quod nullum crimen privat papam ipso iure papatu etiam heresis si vult corrigi. ..."

B^2 = BARCELONA, Archivo Capitular de la Catedral de Barcelona, MS 16 [Monastic Microfilm Project # 30286]

A manuscript of uncertain date and provenance, although judging from the amount of conciliar material which it contains, it was probably a product of the fifteenth century, and like the other Barcelona manuscript quite possibly from Basel. It does not contain the main text of the *De causa* but only the *Epilogus*, a version of the *Epilogus* at points considerably fuller than is usually the case. *Contents*:

1) fols. 1r-14r – Franciscus Zabarella, "Tractatus scismatis editus."
2) fols. 14v-20v – "Tractatus super congregatione concilii Pisani factus per famosissimum doctorem iuris canonici dominum Dominicum de Sancto Geminiano."
3) fols. 21r-27r – "Fundamenta iuris super hiis que potest facere concilium generale Basiliense edita a reverendo patre domino abbate Sancti Honorati insule Litinensis."
4) fols. 28r-51v – "Tractatus de neutralitate vitanda. / Frequens generalium conciliorum celebratio. ..."
5) fols. 52r-128r – "Tractatus qui dicitur gubernaculum conciliorum editus per dominum Andream episcopum Magurensem."

6) fols. 129r-137r – The *Epilogus* to the *De causa*. *Inc*.: "Epilogi P. de Palude. / Epilogus tractatus de causa immediata ecclesiastice potestatis quantum ad articulos et conclusiones principales et incidentales." *Expl*.: "Deo gratias. / Expliciunt epilogi fratris Petri de Palude de ordine predicatorum patriarche Ierosolimitani."
7) fols. 138r-162r – "Tractatus de ecclesiastica potestate editus a reverendissimo in Christo patre et domino, domino Petro de Aylliaco cardinali Cameracensi."
8) fols. 163r-171v – "Collatio domini cancellarii Parisiensis, videlicet prosperum iter faciet nobis Deus, facta per dominum Joannem Jerson in concilio Constanciensi de potestate conciliorum in eodem concilio decretata."
9) fols. 172r-185r – "Tractatus reverendissimi in Christo patris domini Joannis patriarche Antiocheni ad hostendendum quod concilium generale legitime congregatum sit supra papam, et quod per papam dissolvi non possit sine consensu ipsius concilii."
10) fols. 186r-191v – "Responsio facta per oratores sacri Basiliensis concilii ad ea que in presentia prelatorum et principum regni Francie proposita fuerunt ex parte domini Eugenii pape contra supremam auctoritatem generalium conciliorum."
11) fols. 192r-193v – "Propositiones cuidam religioso ordinis Carthusiensis presentate per Nicolaum de de [sic] Cuza et suos complices in favorem pape et sedis apostolice facte."
12) fols. 193v-213v – "Sequitur declaratio circa propositiones ... superius annotatas que michi presentabantur."
13) fols. 213v-214v – "Tractatus de neutralitate principum studii Coloniensis."
14) fols. 215r-228v – "Tractatus super neutralitate principum per quendam religiosum fratrem ordinis Carthusiensis apud Coloniam, sacre theologie professorem, compilatus anno Domini 1440."
15) fols. 232r-267v – "Tractatus universitatis studii Cracoviensis de potestate concilii et pape, et que potestas sit maior."

Bl = BASEL, Universitätsbibliothek, MS B. II. 24.[4]

A fourteenth-century manuscript from the Dominican convent at Basel. See fol. 47v: "Iste liber est fratrum predicatorum domus Basiliensis, et est

[4] Cf. G. Meyer and M. Burckhardt, *Die mittelalterlichen Handschriften der Universitätsbibliothek Basel Beschriebendes Verzeichnis*. Abteilung B: *Theologische Pergamenthandschriften* 1 (Basel, 1960), pp. 193-195.

de libris reverendi magistri Theobaldi quondam provincialis Theutonie oretur pro eo." The reference here is to "Ulricus Theobaldi von Altkirch, 1390-1398 Ordensprovinzial der Teutonia, nachher Vicarius des Basler Klosters."[5] See also fol. 133v: "Iste liber est fratrum ordinis predicatorum conventus Basiliensis, et est de libris reverendi magistri Johannis de Efringen oretur pro eo." Here the reference is to "Johannes von Efringen (†1375), Basler Achtburger und Prior des Klosters 1347."[6] The manuscript was originally two separate manuscripts, the products of two different scribes. *Contents*:

1) fols. 1r-47r – The *De causa*. *Inc*.: "Tractus [sic] fratris Petri de Plaude [sic] ordinis fratrum predicatorum de causa inmediate ecclesiastice potestatis. / Circa potestatem. ..." *Expl*.: "Hec autem omnia dicta sunt nihil temere asserendo sed dando peritioribus materiam cogitandi et ut per sedem apostolicam in illis que dubia sunt veritas declaretur aut declarata alias confirmetur. / Deo gratias. Amen."
2) fols. 49(1)r-133(85)v – William of Ockham, *Opus nonaginta dierum*.

Bm[1] = BAMBERG, Staatsbibliothek, MS Patr. 152.[7]

A fifteenth-century manuscript from the Dominican convent in Bamberg.[8] *Contents*:

1) fols. 1r-13v – Thomas Aquinas, *Tractatus de divinis moribus* [*nominibus*?].
2) fols. 15r-30v – Hermannus de Scildis, *Speculum clarum nobile et preciosum sacerdotum* [cf. Hain, Repert. bibl. 14518].
3) fols. 31r-86v – Thomas Aquinas, *Sermones de sanctissimo sacramento altaris*.
4) fols. 91r-134v – Idem, *Tractatus de symbolo*.
5) fols. 135v-139v – An anonymous and incomplete "Tractatus de salutatione angelica."
6) fols. 146r-290v – The *De causa*. *Inc*.: "Incipit tractatus de potestate ecclesiastice dignitatis magistri Petri de Palude ac domini patriarche Ierosolimitani ordinis fratrum predicatorum. / Circa potestatem. ..." *Expl*. "Hec autem omnia. ... / Explicit tractatus de causa immediata ecclesiastice dignitatis et potestatis anno Domini M°CCC°XLIII [1443?] in vigilia ascensionis."

[5] Ibid., p. 195.

[6] Ibid., p. 195.

[7] Cf. F. Leitschuh, *Katalog der Handschriften der Königlichen Bibliothek zu Bamberg* 1.1 (Bamberg, 1895), pp. 534-535.

[8] Fol. 1: "predicatorum bamb. P. 18."

Bm² = BAMBERG, Staatsbibliothek, MS Theol. 227 (Q. V. 3).[9]

Another fifteenth-century manuscript from the Dominican convent in Bamberg, a bequest of "magister Johannes Hebrer."[10] In this manuscript the texts of the *De causa* and the *Epilogus* are separated by several folios. *Contents*:

1) fols. 1r-5r – Jean Gerson, *Tractatus de arte audiendi confessiones*.
2) fols. 5r-7r – Idem, *Tractatus de remediis contra recidivum in peccato*.
3) fols. 7r-33v – Joannes Nider, *Tractatus de religionibus secularium*.
4) fols. 34r-43v – Idem, *Tractatus de vera et falsa nobilitate*.
5) fols. 43v-60r – St Jerome, *Epistola de virginitate ad Paulam et Eustochium*.
6) fols. 60r-80r – "Perfectio 15 graduum Marie ex Gorra [Nic. de Gorham] super Cantica. / Uie eius pulchre. ..."
7) fols. 80v-92r – James of Viterbo, *Questiones VI*.
8) fols. 92r-129v – Alanus de Insulis, *Maxime*.
9) fols. 129v-140r – Joannes de Francofordia, *Questiones*.
10) fols. 140r-149v – "De receptione monialium et clausura. / Omne quod plurimorum se offert oculis varium consuevit habere iudicium. ..."
11) fols. 149v-156v – Jacobus Carthusianus, *Tractatus de securiori vivendi statu et modo*.
12) fols. 156v-178v – Thomas Aquinas, *Tractatus de decem preceptis decalogi*.
13) fols. 179r – 256v – The *De causa*. *Inc*.: "Incipit Petrus de Palude, de auctoritate et potestate quam prelati ecclesie militantis acceperunt a Christo. / Circa potestatem. ..." *Expl*.: "Sed certum est quod irrationabiliter ageret et peccaret etc. Et sic est finis etc. etc."
14) fols. 256v-260v – "Utrum decedentes cum solo originali puniantur aliqua pena sensus. ..."
15) fols. 261r-267v – "In nomine sancte et individue trinitatis Amen. Noverint tam presentes quam posteri sancte matris ecclesie filii. ... [According to Leitschuh, "Sex articuli quibus mag. Henricus de Oyta ab Alberto de Bohemia denunciatus fuit."]
16) fols. 268r-270r – Bernard of Clairvaux, *Formula honestae vitae*.

[9] Cf. Leitschuh, *Katalog der Handschriften* 1.1, pp. 811-814.

[10] See the top margin of fol. 1r: "Istum librum legavit magister Johannes Hebrer sacre theologie professor in suo testamento conventui Bambergensi ordinis predicatorum." Immediately beneath this we find: "R23 predicatorum Bamberge." See also fol. 2r: "Conventus Bambergensis ord. predicatorum"; and fols. 157r and 355r: "R23."

17) fols. 270v-272v – "Questio proposita coram dominis iudicibus fidei per venerandum patrem dominum episcopum Adtrabecensem die iiii mensis anno Domini M°CCCC°VII°. ... / Utrum quilibet christianus ex professione facta in baptismo. ..."
18) fols. 273r-275v – "Exemplar confessionis sacramentalis formande secundum quod quilibet se salubriter recolligere potest. / Facto signo sancte crucis. ... Edicio est cuiusdam doctoris in sacra pagina, episcopi Civitatensis, penitentiarii in Romana curia."
19) fols. 277r-290v – "Tractatus de septem viciis capitalibus. Et primo de gula incipiendo etc. / Quoniam vas celestis glorie. ..."
20) fols. 290v-300v – The *Epilogus* to the *De causa*. *Inc.*: "Primus articulus est de potestate Petri singulari. ..." *Expl.*: "Hec autem omnia. ..."
21) fols. 301r-343v – "Gloriosa dicta sunt de te civitas Dei Ps. LXXXVII. Nota quod propter sedecim causas quibus materialis civitas efficitur. ..."
22) fols. 347r-351r – "In nomine individue trinitatis, Patris et Filii et Spiritus Sancti Amen. Fratres meos quero. ..."
23) fol. 351 – "Supradictum sermonem ... in ecclesia cathedrali Magd. ad clerum pronunciavi ego frater Johannes Preen ordinis fratrum heremitarum Sancti Augustini. ..."
24) fols. 351v-355v – "Replicatio contra quartum periculum de horis canonicis. / Declarat beatus Thomas. ..."
25) fol. 356v – A postscript to fol. 136: "Sed adhuc est unum dubium de serpentibus. ... Et hec de questione que fuit in quodlibeto Heidelberge declarata per magistrum Joannem de Francfordia, sacre theologie baccalarium, anno 1405."

Bo = BURGO DE OSMA, Archivo-Biblioteca de la S. I. Catedral, MS 65.[11]

A fifteenth-century manuscript of unknown provenance. *Contents*:

1) fols. 2r-77v – The *De causa*. *Inc.*: "Circa potestatem. ..." *Expl.*: "Hec autem omnia. ... / Explicit tractatus copilatus [sic] a domino fratre Petro de Palude ordinis predicatorum, sacre pagine magistro eximio et patriarcha Ierosolimitano. / Deo gratias Amen.
2) fols. 82r-107r – "In nomine unigeniti Marie virginis incipit tractatus

[11] Cf. T. Rojo Orcajo, "Catálogo descriptivo de los códices que se conservan en la Santa Iglesia Catedral de Burgo de Osma," *Boletín de la Real Academia de la Historia*, 94 (1929): 655-792; and 95 (1929): 152-414, at 152-153.

de conceptione ejusdem inmaculate virginis editus a fratre Petro Aureoli sacre theologie magistro ordinis fratrum minorum."

3) fols. 107r-116r – "Incipit additio fratris Petri Aureoli de ordine fratrum minorum theologie magistro et archiepiscopi Auxensis. / Ad resistendum latratibus quorumdam. ..."
4) fols. 116r-116v – "Sacrosancta generalis sinodus. ..." [According to Rojo Orcajo, the pronouncement of the Council of Basel on the immaculate conception.]

Br = BERLIN, Staatsbibliothek Preussischer Kulturbesitz [formerly Preussische Staatsbibliothek], MS Elect. lat. 475 (theol. fol. 126).[12]

A fifteenth-century manuscript from the library of the cathedral chapter of Magdeburg. It was a bequest of magister Petrus Roden,[13] a canon of the cathedral, and in 1461 rector of the University of Leipzig. The manuscript was copied in Leipzig in 1460,[14] and is one of a large number of Leipzig manuscripts which Roden bequeathed to the cathedral of Magdeburg.[15]
Contents:

1) fols. 1r-311v – Augustinus Triumphus, *Summa de potestate ecclesiastica*.
2) fols. 313r-363v – The *De causa*. *Inc*.: "Petrus de Palude, de potestate collata a Christo prelatis ecclesie militantis. / Circa potestatem. ..." *Expl*.: "Hec autem omnia. ... / 1460. Lipczk."

O = OXFORD, Codrington Library, All Souls' College, MS 47.[16]

A fifteenth-century manuscript which was bequeathed to All Souls' College by Philip Polton (Archdeacon of Glouchester, †22 September 1461) in a will of 17 September 1461.[17] The College seems to have

[12] Cf. V. Rose, *Die Handschriftenverzeichnisse der Königlichen Bibliothek zu Berlin*. Dreizehnter Band: *Verzeichniß der lateinischen Handschriften* 2.1 (Berlin, 1901), p. 331.

[13] See the inside front cover: "1483. Memoria magistri Petri Roden."

[14] Fol. 311v: "Deo gratias. 1460. Lipczk"; fol. 358v: "Anno domini. 1460. Lipczk"; and fol. 363v: "1460. Lipczk."

[15] Cf. Ilse Schunke, "Die Handschrifteneinbände des Magdeburger Domgymnasiums in der Deutschen Staatsbibliothek Berlin (MSS Magdeb.)," *Zentralblatt für Bibliothekswesen*, 78 (1964): 656-678, esp. 671-674.

[16] Cf. O. Coxe, *Catalogus codicum mss. qui in collegiis aulisque Oxoniensibus hodie adservantur* 2 (Oxonii, 1852), pp. 14-15. In my description of this manuscript I am indebted to J. S. G. Simmons, Librarian of All Souls' College, who was kind enough to examine the manuscript on my behalf.

[17] N. R. Ker, *Records of All Souls' College Library, 1437-1600* (Oxford, 1971), pp. 108, 123 and 163. For details on Polton see A. B. Emden, *A Biographical Register of the University of Oxford to A.D. 1500* 3 (Oxford, 1959), pp. 1493-1494.

received the manuscript in 1462.[18] Nothing certain is known of the earlier history of the manuscript, although an Italian provenance seems likely.[19] *Contents* (following the description of Coxe):

1) fols. 1r-75r – The *De causa*. *Inc*.: "Opus magistri Petri de Palude ordinis predicatorum, patriarche Antiochensis. / Circa potestatem. ..." *Expl*.: "Hec autem omnia. ... / Amen."
2) fol. 76r – Eusebius, *Chronicon*.
3) fol. 152r – Isidore of Seville, *Chronica ab exordio mundi usque ad tempora Heraclii et Sisebuti principum*.
4) fol. 160r – Sextus Rufus, *Annumerationis Romanae historiae liber*.
5) fol. 172r – Andreas Escobar, *Sermo ad clerum die sancti Joannis apostoli et evangelistae factus coram Martino papa v et cardinalibus anno 1423*.
6) fol. 191r – Prosper of Aquitaine, *De vita contemplativa*.
7) fol. 220v – Bernard of Clairvaux, *De vita prelatorum*.
8) fol. 229r – Simonis de Salterella, *Sermones*.
9) fol. 274r – *Anonymi cujusdam de pace inter reges Franciae et Angliae* [Charles VI and Henry V].
10) fol. 279r – Joannes Hugenetti, *Collatio recitata in generali concilio Constantiensi anno 1417*.
11) fol. 287r – *Articuli concordiae inter Carolum VI regem Franciae et Henricum V Angliae regem. Dat. Trecis, 21 Mai. 1420*.

P[1] = PARIS, Bibliothèque nationale, MS lat. 1514.[20]

A fifteenth-century manuscript from the library of the "Collège de Navarre."[21] From there it passed to the collection of the abbé Drouin, and finally into the royal library.[22] *Contents*:

[18] Fol. 2r: "Liber collegii animarum omnium fidelium defunctorum in Oxon. de dono M. Philippi Polton archidiaconi Glocestr. anno Domini MºCCCCºLXIIº."

[19] The watermarks in the volume do not correspond precisely with the watermarks in Briquet. Cf. C. M. Briquet, *Les filigranes: dictionnaire historique des marques du papier dès leur apparition vers 1282 jusqu'en 1600*, 2nd edition, 4 vols. (Leipzig, 1923). But they are pretty close analogues, the watermark on fol. 20, for example, being analogous to Briquet no. 11692, and the watermark on fol. 31 being analogous to Briquet no. 11750. Such as it is, the watermark evidence throughout the volume suggests an Italian origin. But this evidence must be treated with caution, for much Italian paper was used in France and in England as well in the fifteenth century.

[20] Cf. Bibliothèque nationale, *Catalogue général des manuscrits latins* 2 (Paris, 1940), p. 49.

[21] Fol. 1r: "Pro libraria regalis collegii Navarrae"; and fol. 119v: "Pro libraria regalis collegii Campaniae, alias Navarrae, Parisiis fundati."

[22] L. Delisle, *Le cabinet des manuscrits de la Bibliothèque nationale* 2 (Paris, 1874), pp. 252-255, esp. 255.

1) fols. 1r-58v – Guillelmus de Montjoye, *Tractatus missus ad regem Carolum VII pro Eugenio IV.*
2) fols. 61r-119v – The *De causa*. *Inc*.: "Tractatus fratris Petri de Palude ordinis fratrum predicatorum de causa immediata ecclesiastice potestatis. / Circa potestatem...." *Expl*.: "Hec autem omnia.... / Finie."

P² = PARIS, Bibliothèque nationale, MS lat. 4232.

A fourteenth-century manuscript from the library of the anti-pope Benedict XIII. It was deposited in the Bibliothèque royale in 1732. Prior to that it had been the possession of Jean-Baptiste Colbert, who had acquired it in 1680 in Toulouse, where it had been part of the library of the "Collège de Foix" since the college's foundation in 1457. Earlier than that it had been in the library of Benedict XIII (Petrus de Luna) in Peniscola. But when Benedict's successor, Clement VIII, abdicated in favour of Martin V in 1429, the manuscript passed into the hands of the cardinal P. de Foix, the founder of the college in Toulouse.[23] During its period in Peniscola the manuscript did not exist in its present form, in which it contains treatises by Herveus Natalis and Hermannus de Scildis as well as the *De causa*. The catalogue which survives indicates that the *De causa* and the treatise of Herveus Natalis were bound together at that time, but along with a number of other things and not the treatise of Hermannus de Scildis.[24] There is no trace of an earlier history for the portion of the manuscript which bears the *De causa*. However, the two other portions can be identified in the catalogue of the library of Urban V at Avignon, which was prepared in May, 1369.[25] *Contents*:

[23] For this account, as well as a good description of the manuscript, see A. Zumkeller, *Hermanni de Scildis* O.S.A. *Tractatus contra haereticos negantes immunitatem et iurisdictionem sanctae ecclesiae et Tractatus de conceptione gloriosae virginis Mariae* (Würzburg, 1970), p. x. Zumkeller follows Delisle, *Le cabinet des manuscrits* 1 (Paris, 1868), pp. 486-509.

[24] Cf. M. Faucon, *La librairie des papes d'Avignon* 2 (Paris, 1887), p. 149, # 1077: "Item tractatus Petri de Pallude, patriarche Alexandrini [in the margin in a later hand: Hierosolymitani], de ecclesiastica potestate, et tractatus magistri Ervey de eadem materia; tractatus ejusdem de paupertate Christi et apostolorum; questio disputata per magistrum Raymundum Regoini de paupertate Christi et apostolorum; lectura magistri Petri Rogerii, scilicet pape Clementis VI[ti] super decretali Quia quorumdam Johannis pape; et questio disputata de paupertate per fratrem P. Johannis."

[25] Cf. Faucon, *La librairie des papes d'Avignon* 1 (Paris, 1886), pp. 93-262, esp. p. 145, # 583: "Item liber contra hereticos negantes jurisdictionem ecclesiasticam, coopertus corio viridi, qui incipit in secundo corundello primi folii *a spirituali*, et finit in penultimo folio *eterne*." Cf. also p. 175, # 955: "Item tractatus Henrici de ecclesiastica potestate, de litera curiali, coopertus postibus sine pelle, qui incipit in secundo folio *eam*, et finit in

1) fols. 1r-104v – The *De causa*. *Inc*. "Tractatus fratris Petri de Palude ordinis predicatorum de causa immediata ecclesiastice potestatis. / Circa potestatem...." *Expl*.: "Hec autem omnia.... / Explicit. Deo gratias."
2) fols. 106r-149r – Herveus Natalis, *Tractatus de potestate pape*.
3) fols. 152r-174v – Hermannus de Scildis, *Tractatus contra hereticos negantes emunitatem et iurisdictionem sancte ecclesie*.

P^3 = PARIS, Bibliothèque nationale, MS lat. 4233.[26]

A fifteenth-century manuscript of uncertain provenance. It appears in the catalogue of the royal library prepared by Nicholas Clement in 1682. Judging from Clement's description,[27] it was once in the possession of Cardinal Charles Maurice le Tellier (1642-1710), Archbishop of Reims,[28] although no trace of it can be found in the catalogue of the manuscripts of the Le Tellier library edited by Omont.[29] Nothing is known of the medieval owners of the manuscript, although an Italian provenance seems likely.[30] The scribe identifies himself on fol. 95v: "Johannes Leytan me fecit." Neither *MSS datés* nor the work of the Bénédictins de Bouveret casts any light on his identity, but both agree on a fifteenth-century date for the manuscript, the former specifying the end of the fifteenth century.[31] The *De causa* forms the entire contents of the manuscript, and occupies fols. 1r-96r.

Inc.: "Petrus de Palude de potestate ecclesiastica [this in a later hand]. / Circa potestatem...." *Expl*. (fol. 95v): "Hec autem omnia.... / Sit laus Deo patri. Johannes Leytan me fecit. (fol. 96r) Explicit tractatus conpilatus a

---

penultimo folio *obliqui*." This is the treatise of Herveus Natalis, although the cataloguer has obviously misread "Herveo" ("Tractatus editus a fratre herveo Natal....") as "Henrico."

[26] The description of this manuscript was greatly assisted by Denise Bloch of the Bibliothèque nationale, who was kind enough to examine the manuscript for me.

[27] H. Omont, *Anciens inventaires et catalogues de la Bibliothèque Nationale*, tome 3: *La Bibliothèque Royale à Paris au XVIIe siècle* (Paris, 1910), p. 387: "4267². Petrus de Palude, sive Paludanus, de potestate ecclesiastica. (Telleriano-Remensis)."

[28] Cf. Delisle, *Le cabinet des manuscrits* 1, pp. 302-319.

[29] Cf. Omont, *Anciens inventaires* 4, pp. 369-399.

[30] The watermark of the paper corresponds to no. 6453 in Briquet, and this suggests an Italian origin. But as was mentioned earlier, this evidence needs to be treated with caution due to the widespread use of Italian paper in the fifteenth century.

[31] C. Samaran and R. Marichal, *Catalogue des manuscrits en écriture latine portant des indications de date, de lieu ou de copiste [MSS datés]* 2 (Paris, 1962), p. 534; Bénédictins du Bouveret, *Colophons de manuscrits occidentaux des origines au XVIe siècle* 3 (Fribourg, 1973), p. 354.

domino fratre Petro de Palude ordinis predicatorum, sacre pagine magistro eximio, patriarcha Ierosolimitano."

P⁴ = PARIS, Bibliothèque nationale, MS lat. 12467.

A manuscript of uncertain date which entered the Bibliothèque nationale with the manuscripts from Saint-Germain-des-Prés,[32] but which was originally from the abbey of Jumièges.[33] Various estimates of its date have been offered,[34] but the portion which bears the *De causa* at least seems to date from the latter half of the fourteenth century.[35] *Contents*:

1) fols. 1r-14v – "Tractatus de ecclesiastico interdicto compositus a magistro Johanne Carderini decretorum doctore Bononiensi."
2) fols. 15r-17v – "Tractatus de absolutione ad cautelam per dominum Berengarium compositus."
3) fols. 19r-58r – Johannes de Ligniano, *Tractatus de bello*.
4) fols. 59r-118r – Idem, *Tractatus de censura ecclesiastica*.
5) fols. 119r-126v – The anonymous *Questio in utramque partem*.
6) fols. 127r-130v – The anonymous *Rex pacificus*.
7) fols. 131r-157v – John of Paris, *Tractatus de potestate regia et papali*.
8) fol. 158 – A fragment of the anonymous *Disputatio inter clericum et militem*.
9) fols. 159r-199r – The *De causa*. *Inc.*: "Tractatus de pape et prelatorum ecclesie potestate compositus per dominum Guillelmum Petri cardinalem episcopum Sabinensem. / Circa potestatem...." *Expl.*: "Hec autem omnia.... / Explicit per manus Ny. de Luccenburch nuncupatus Reffingeyrs Port. Deo gratias etc. Amen. Amen. Amen etc. / Explicit tractatus de potestate pape et prelatorum ecclesie per dominum Guillelmum Petri cardinalem episcopum Sabinensem compositus."

[32] L. Delisle, *Inventaire des manuscrits de Saint-Germain-des-Prés conservés à la Bibliothèque impériale, sous les numéros 11504-14231 du fonds latin* (Paris, 1868), p. 53.

[33] G. Nortier, *Les bibliothèques médiévales des abbayes bénédictines de Normandie* (Paris, 1971), pp. 159, 162 and 213.

[34] Delisle and Nortier attribute it to the fourteenth century. Leclercq and Bleienstein, both of whom were interested in the manuscript because it bears a copy of the *Tractatus* of John of Paris, attribute it to the fifteenth century. Vinay, who was interested in it because it contains a copy of the *Questio in utramque partem*, attributes it to the fourteenth or fifteenth century. Cf. J. Leclercq, *Jean de Paris et l'ecclésiologie du XIIIe siècle* (Paris, 1942), p. 169; F. Bleienstein, *Johannes Quidort von Paris, Über königliche und päpstliche Gewalt* (Stuttgart, 1969), p. 48; and G. Vinay, "Egidio Romano e la cosidetta 'Questio in utramque partem'," *Bollettino dell'Istituto Storico Italiano per il Medio Evo e Archivio Muratoriano*, 53 (1939): 57-58.

[35] *MSS datés* 3 (Paris, 1974), p. 733.

Pr = PRAGUE, St Vitus Cathedral MS O 50 [now in the Archives of the Prague Castle].[36]

A manuscript of the first half of the fifteenth century, a bequest of "M. Procopius de Cladrub," deacon of Prague.[37] It is devoted primarily to sermon literature, and there are too many sermons to list them all here. But, following Podlaha, the principal contents of the manuscript can be described as follows:

1) fols. 2r-10v – An alphabetical index to the sermons.
2) fols. 11r-13v – *Excerpta varia*.
3) fols. 14r-18r – Peter Damian, *Liber Gomorrianus*.
4) fols. 18v-22v – *De pluralitate beneficiorum quam periculosum sit*.
5) fols. 23r-24v – *Contra superbos miraculum de Juliano imperatore*.
6) fol. 25r – Peter of Blois, *De correctione principis epistola* X.
7) fol. 25r-25v – Idem, *Epistola* LIV *invectiva in invidum*.
8) fols. 26r-105v – *Sermones*.
9) fols. 105v-111v – *De sacerdotibus correctio* [excerpts from Joachim de Floris, *Semen scripturarum*].
10) fols. 111v-115v – *Excerpta varia*.
11) fols. 115v-116v – *Carmen: Viri fratres, servi Dei, non vos turbent verba mei....*
12) fols. 117r-125r – *Epistolae exulum catholicorum* [letters of Johannes de Inferno to Procopius de Kladrub and to Andreas de Broda, and letters of Andreas de Broda].
13) fol. 125r-125v – *Peccata prelatorum non sunt populo publicanda*.
14) fols. 125v-126v – *De Romanis edificiis*.
15) fols. 127r-132v – "Incipit conversacio Christi opposita conversacioni antichristi, ut patet ibi. Hic reprehendit Hus hereticus papam et ecclesiam...."
16) fols. 133r-137v – *Responsiones ad obiecciones et picturas Huss*.
17) fols. 137v-143v – *Tractatus responsalis ad auctoritates cuiusdam tractatuli Hussitarum de communicatione laicali sub utraque specie*.
18) fols. 144r-153v – *Sermones*.
19) fols. 155r-214v – The *De causa*. *Inc*.: "Incipit tractatus fratris Petri de Palude ordinis fratrum predicatorum de causa immediate ecclesiastice potestatis. Conclusiones quinque secuntur. / Circa potestatem...." *Expl*.: "Hec omnia dicta sunt...."

[36] Cf. Ant. Podlaha, *Soupis rukopisů knihovny metropolitní kapitoly Pražské* 2 (Prague, 1922), pp. 522-525.

[37] Fol. 1r: "Liber M. Procopii de Cladrub, sacre theologie professoris, decani ecclesie pragen."

20) fols. 214v-227v – Stephani de Páleč, *Tractatus de portis inferi*.
21) fols. 227v-229r – *Epistola baronum Bohemiae concilio Constantiensi directa*.
22) fols. 229r-242v – *Sermones*.
23) fols. 243r-244r – *Excerpta ex operibus s. Hieronymi*.
24) fols. 244v-281r – *Sermones*.
25) fols. 281v-283r – "Nota ex quo presens evangelium loquitur de consilio, quod duo principaliter sunt notanda circa consilium...."

R = REIMS, Bibliothèque municipale, MS 493.[38]

A manuscript which the authors of the catalogue entry attribute to the fourteenth century, but which might better be attributed to the late fourteenth or early fifteenth century. On the inside of the back cover, immediately below what appears to be the signature of "Guy de Roye," archbishop of Reims, there is a long inscription which states that the manuscript was once in the possession of Guy de Roye, and that it was copied by a canon of the church of Reims in 1412.[39] The description of the contents of the manuscript related in this inscription corresponds precisely to what the manuscript actually contains. But the date provided is suspect. According to Eubel, Guy de Roye died on 8 June 1409.[40] *Contents*:

1) fols. 1r-147r – "Conclusiones fratris Hymberti, ordinis Cysterciensis, abbatis de Prulliaco, super librum Sentenciarum."
2) fol. 147v- – "Hic sunt aliqui propositiones < Hymberti de Prulliaco > bene notabiles super decem libros Ethice...." [followed by "Notabilia Politicorum...," fol. 148v-; and "Notabiles proposiciones Rethorice...," fol. 149v-].
3) fols. 151r-166v – "Ad honorem Dei omnipotentis et ingenii domini mei, domini Ludovici de Melunduno, volo disputare hanc questio-

[38] Cf. *Catalogue général des manuscrits des bibliothèques publiques de France, Départements* 38.1 (Paris, 1849 –), pp. 660-662.

[39] The inscription is very faint, and is written in a hand different from that of the just completed text: "Iste liber fuit de libris bone memorie domini Guidonis de Roya, nuper archiepiscopi Remensis, qui liber continet conclusiones. ... Et sunt in isto volumine in toto folia 220, que omnia fere sunt scripta. Si quis furatus fuerit aliquid de isto libro, anathematisetur. Et fuit quotatus et folia numerata et scripta de manu domini de Asperomonte, canonici ipsius ecclesie Remensis, die XVIII^a mensis Maii, anno Domini M°CCCC°XII°. Orate Deum pro ipsis."

[40] C. Eubel, *Hierarchia catholica medii aevi* 1 (Regensberg, 1913), p. 419. Samaran and Marichal refer to this manuscript, but only to tell us that "la date de 1317 qui figure au f. 166v° est une date d'œuvre." *MSS datés* 5 (Paris, 1965), p. 655.

nem: An in uno et eodem individuo forma generis sit alia realiter et substantialiter a forma speciei.... Explicit questio de pluralitate formarum et diversitate generis et speciei, ordinata per magistrum Johannem de Leuduno et completa anno Domini 1317°, 23 die Januarii."

4) fols. 167r-220v – The *De causa*. *Inc*.: "Tractatus fratris Petri de Palude ordinis fratrum predicatorum de causa immediata ecclesiastice potestatis. / Circa potestatem...." *Expl*.: "Hec autem omnia.... / Hoc libro scripto sit laus et gloria Christo."

S = Salamanca, Universidad Literaria de Salamanca, ms 18.[41]

A fifteenth-century manuscript, a bequest of the famous conciliarist, John of Segovia,[42] at one time professor of theology at the University of Salamanca. *Contents*:

1) fols. 1r-87r – The *De causa*. *Inc*.: "... compilatus a domino fratre Petro de Palude ordinis predicatorum, magistro eximio, patriarcha Ierosolimitano, de ecclesiastica potestate. / Circa potestatem...." *Expl*.: "Hec autem omnia.... / Sit laus Deo. Explicit tractatus compilatus a domino Petro de Palude ordinis predicatorum, sacre pagine magistro eximio, patriarcha Ierosolimitano."
2) "Propositio facta in consistorio coram Benedicto papa xii pro domino Ludovico de Bavaria."
3) "Tractatus de plenitudine potestatis spiritualis et temporalis in Romano pontifice."
4) "Tractatus de questionibus armenorum."

Sr = Saint-Omer, Bibliothèque municipale, ms 382.[43]

A fifteenth-century manuscript from the Benedictine Abbey of Saint Bertin at Saint-Omer. *Contents*:

[41] Cf. Vicente de La Fuente and Juan Urbina, *Catalogo de los libros manuscritos que se conservan en la Bibliotheca de la Universidad de Salamanca* (Salamanca, 1855), p. 53. This catalogue incorrectly records the title as "De ecclesiastica pietate undecim libri." I am indebted to Teresa Santander of the Biblioteca Universitaria in my description of this manuscript. Sra Santander was not able to provide me with a microfilm of the complete manuscript. But she did send me a complete list of its contents, although, unfortunately, without folio numbers.

[42] Benigno Hernandez Montes, "En busca de manuscritos de la donación de Juan de Segovia," *Revista Española de Teología*, 34 (1974): 35-68 at 44-45 and 47.

[43] Cf. *Catalogue général des manuscrits des bibliothèques publiques de France, Départements* 3, pp. 184-185.

1) fols. 1r-70v – The *De causa*. *Inc.*: "Circa potestatem...." *Expl.*: "Hec autem omnia.... / Explicit tractatus de potestate pape editus a magistro Petro de Palude ordinis fratrum predicatorum."
2) fols. 71r-290v – Material much too copious to detail here, but which can be summed up under the title which appears on the binding: "Acta concilii Basiliensis." It begins with a letter written to the council by the patriarch of Antioch: "Compulatio [sic] domini patriarche Anthioni [sic] quomodo sacrum concilium superest supra papam. / Sacrosancte generali sinodo Basiliensi in Spiritu Sancto legitime congregate universalem ecclesiam representanti, vester devotus humilis Johannes, patriarcha Antiochenus.... / In nomine domini nostri Jesu Christi Amen. Ad ostendendum quod concilium generale legitime congregatum sit supra papam...." (fols. 71r-93v). It ends with a letter of Joannes de Ragusio and Simon Freron, canon of Orleans: "Littera magistrorum Joannis de Ragusio et Simonis Freron.... / Sacrosancte generali sinodo Basiliensi in Spiritu Sancto legitime congregate. ... Scriptum in Constantinopoli die ix[a] Februarii M°CCCC°XXXVI. Eiusdem sancte sinodi vestri humiles et devoti oratores frater Joannes de Ragusio ordinis predicatorum et Simon Freron canonicus Aurelianensis."

St = STUTTGART, Württembergische Landesbibliothek, MS theol. 4° 614.

A fifteenth-century manuscript from the Benedictine abbey in Blaubeuren.[44] The copyist of the *De causa*, David Hursler, identifies himself as a native of Urach, a community about 25 km west of Blaubeuren, and about 35 km southeast of Stuttgart, and dates his work at 1478.[45] The manuscript is prefaced by a table of contents on fol. 1v, where the *De causa* appears under two different titles: "Petrus de Palude, de ecclesiastica potestate"; and "Tractatus Petri de Palude ordinis fratrum

[44] Cf. P. Lehmann, *Mittelalterliche Bibliothekskataloge* 1, p. 15. In a list of surviving manuscripts once in the "Benediktinerkloster" in Blaubeuren, and under the rubric: "Blaubeuren, Ev.-theol. Seminar," we read the following: "... III 117 (Petrus de Palude de potestate eccl., Johannes de Turrecremata de auctoritate summi pontificis, Johannes Gerson de temptationibus, idem de laude scriptoris, psalterium B. M. V., sermones, memoriale librorum sententiarum, memoriale regulae s. Benedicti, s. XV)...." This is our manuscript precisely. See also fol. 78v: "Explicit tractatus questionum de auctoritate summi pontificis ... scriptus pro monasterio sancti Johannis baptiste in Blauburen per fratrem David Hursler Deurach."

[45] See the *explicit* of the *De causa* given below, as well as fol. 59r: "per fratrem David Deurach dyaconum. 1478."

predicatorum de causa immediata ecclesiastice potestatis." *Contents* (following the unpublished catalogue of the Württ. Landesbibliothek):

1) fols. 2r-64r – The *De causa*. *Inc*. "Circa potestatem...." *Expl*.: "Hec autem omnia.... / Explicit tractatus cum tabula de causa immediata ecclesiastice potestatis venerabilis patris ac domini fratris Petri de Palude, de ordine predicatorum, sacre theologie professoris clarissimi, ac patriarche Hierosolimitani, per fratrem David Hursler Deurach tunc diaconum. 1478."
2) fols. 65r-78v – Johannes de Turrecremata, *Tractatus de auctoritate summi pontificis*.
3) fols. 79v-81v – *Bulla indulgentiarum sanctissimi domini Pape Sixti IV data ad ecclesiam in Urach*.
4) fols. 83r-92v – *Philosophia moralis*.
5) fols. 94r-102v – Jean Gerson, *Tractatus de temptationibus nostri temptatoris* [sic].
6) fols. 103r-109v – Idem, *De laude scriptoris*.
7) fols. 110r-116r – *Compendium psalterii beate virginis Marie*.
8) fols. 126r-134r – Ludolfus Carthusiensis, *De vita Jesu*.
9) fol. 134v – *De indumentis sacerdotalibus*.
10) fols. 141r-149r – *Liber de conflictu viciorum atque virtutum*.
11) fols. 150r-165r – *Memoriale librorum sacrorum*.
12) fols. 165v-171v – *Memoriale regule Benedicti*.
13) fols. 175r-185 – *Textus algorismi*.

Sv = SEVILLE, Biblioteca Capitular Colombina, MS 7-4-11.

A fifteenth-century manuscript once the possession of the bishops of Brescia in Italy, the earliest known owner being Piero da Monte.[46] *Contents*:

1) fols. 3r-91v – The *De causa*. *Inc*.: "Incipit tractatus compilatus a domino fratre Petro de Palude ordinis predicatorum, sacre pagine

[46] Fol. 1v: "Hic liber est mei Dominici de Dominicis episcopi Brixiensis, domini pape vicarii, et fuit ex libris bone memorie dominorum Petri de Monte primo, deinde Bartolomei Malipetri, episcoporum Brixiensium, quem allatus est mihi ex (?) Brixia Romam 1465 mense Septembris." Eubel confirms the line of succession related here. See *Hierarchia catholica medii aevi* 2 (Regensberg, 1914), p. 111. Piero da Monte, *protonotarius apostolicus*, was appointed bishop of Brescia on 23 March 1442. He was succeeded by Bartholomaeus Malipiero, a canon of Padua, who was created bishop on 24 January 1457. Bartholomaeus was followed by Dominicus de Dominicis, formerly bishop of Torcello, who was created bishop of Brescia on 14 November 1464. On the library of Dominicus de Dominicis, see C. Villa, "Brixiensia. 1. La biblioteca del vescovo Domenico Domenichi. 2. Codici bresciani a Bologna: Giovanni Crisostomo Trombelli e Marco Marini," *Italia medioevale e umanistica*, 20 (1977): 243-275.

magistro eximio, patriarcha Ierosolimitano, de ecclesiastica potestate. / Circa potestatem...." *Expl.*: "Hec autem omnia.... / Sit laus Deo. Explicit tractatus compilatus a domino fratre Petro de Palude ordinis predicatorum, sacre pagine magistro eximio, patriarcha Ierosolimitano."

2) fols. 92r-94r – "Proposicio facta in consistorio coram domino Benedicto papa XII pro domino Lodovico de Bavaria a domino Johanne papa XII an< tea > excommunicato."
3) fol. 94v – "Quartus de institutione Trajani. Est autem respublica quoddam corpus...."
4) fols. 94v-97v – "Quod plenitudo potestatis spiritualis et temporalis sit in summo pontifice videtur primo sic probari posse...."

Sz = SALZBURG, Bibliothek der Erzabtei St Peter, MS b.XI.25 [Monastic Microfilm Project # 10653].

A fifteenth-century manuscript which once was a bequest of a "magister Johannes de Salina."[47] *Contents*:

1) fols. 1r-135r – Thomas Aquinas, *Questiones de malo*.
2) fols. 135r-269v – Idem, *Questiones de potentia Dei*.
3) fol. 270 – A register to the preceding works.
4) fols. 271r-314r – The *De causa*. *Inc.*: "Incipit Petrus de Palude, de potestate collata a Christo prelatis ecclesie militantis. / Circa potestatem...." *Expl.*: "Hec autem omnia.... / Et sic est finis. Deo gratias."
5) fols. 315r-326r – Nicolaus Weigl, *Tractatus de potestate ecclesie ac sacrorum conciliorum*.
6) fols. 327r-367v – Nicholas of Cusa, *Tractatus de docta ignorantia*.
7) fols. 367v-376r – Idem, *Tractatus de conjecturis*.

T = TORTOSA, La Catedral de Tortosa, MS 151.[48]

A manuscript of uncertain provenance which, according to Bayerri Bertomeu, dates from the late fourteenth or early fifteenth century. In its present form the manuscript is the product of three scribes, the first responsible for fols. 1r-12v, the second responsible for fols. 13r-56v, and

[47] On the inside cover facing fol. 1r we find a table of contents and the following inscription, written in what appears to be a fifteenth-century script: "Hunc librum testatus est Magister Johannes de Salina ibidem predicator fratribus ad S. Petrum anno etc. 76°."

[48] Cf. E. Bayerri Bertomeu, *Los Códices Medievales de la Catedral de Tortosa* (Barcelona, 1962), pp. 313-316.

the third responsible for fols. 63r-180v. Folios 51v and 57r-62v are blank. Bayerri Bertomeu argues that the two items copied by the second scribe (fols. 13r-51r and 52r-56v respectively) were written by the same anonymous author, and that the first of them was an address delivered to the Council of Constance, probably in 1416. The version of the *De causa* contained in this manuscript ends abruptly near the end of the sixth article, and does not include the *Epilogus*. *Contents*:

1) fols. 1r-9v – "Queritur de ordine seu dignitate pape temporali. Hic primo ostendo quod Christus ratione meriti plenum ius iudiciarium habet super istum mundum...."
2) fols. 9v-12v – "Ad indagandum quid iure habeat princeps Christianus in bonis Iudeorum sibi subiectorum. Est sciendum quod princeps...."
3) fols. 13r-51r – "Deus in adiutorium meum intende domine ad adiuvandum me festina. Excelsus ille propheta David de quo scriptum novimus Deum dixisse...."
4) fols. 52r-56v – "In nomine sancte et individue trinitatis, Patris et Filii et Spiritus Sancti Amen. Hiis qui pro inploratione divini auxilii sacratissimique domini nostri Jesu Christi...."
5) fols. 63r-180v – The *De causa*. *Inc*.: "Incipit tractatus fratris Petri de Palude, magistri in sacra pagina et doctoris utriusque iuris, ordinis fratrum predicatorum, de causa inmediata ecclesiastice potestatis, de potestate Petri, apostolorum et discipulorum Christi, ac etiam de pape potestate episcoporum et curatorum. / Circa potestatem...." *Expl*.: "... dicendum quod est oppositum in obiecto, ut supra dictum est, scilicet quod aliquid sit de."

U = ULM, Stadtbibliothek, MS 6740-44.[49]

A manuscript of the late fifteenth and early sixteenth centuries, probably from the Dominican convent in Ulm. The copyist of the *De causa*, who was responsible for the first 60 folios of the manuscript, was a certain Joannes Hetzler, whose signature appears at the end of the *De causa* on fol. 41r.[50] He is identified on fol. 38r as a native of Geislingen, a city 30 km north of Ulm, and within the territory of the *Reichstadt* Ulm. On fol. 38r we are also informed that the copying of the *De causa* was completed

[49] My description of this manuscript has been greatly assisted by information supplied by Dr Breitenbruch, Bibliotheksoberrat of the Stadtbibliothek Ulm, who was kind enough to examine the manuscript for me.

[50] His signature also appears on fol. 60v: "f. Joannes Hetzler 3. die Janua. 1494."

on 28 October 1514.[51] Hetzler appears to have had some connection with the Dominican convent at Worms, judging from an inscription which appears on fol. 43v, although the nature of the connection is not precisely clear.[52] Both the inscription on fol. 38r and the one on fol. 43v are written in a different hand, and the one on fol. 38r bears the signature of Paul Hug (†1537), a Dominican from the convent at Ulm.[53] On the basis of the inscriptions by Hug, it seems probable that the manuscript came to the Stadtbibliothek from the library of the Dominican convent at Ulm, which was scattered at the time of the Reformation. It is conceivable as well that Hetzler was a Dominican from the Ulm convent, and that he spent some time at the Dominican convent at Worms, although the evidence is not sufficient to allow any firm conclusions to be drawn. The manuscript is prefaced with a table of contents written in a later hand, in which the *De causa* appears under the title: "De potestate a Christo collata praelatis ecclesie." *Contents*:

1) 6740 fols. 1r-41r – The *De causa*. *Inc*.: "Circa potestatem...." *Expl*.: "Sed irrationabiliter ageret et peccaret. / Finis tabule. / F. Io. Hetzler pro singularissimo amico."
2) fols. 41r-43v – "Responsio ad quattuor questiones domini Sifridi episcopi Cyrenensis. / Querebatur primo an liceat absolutionis beneficium impendere...."
3) 6741 fols. 44r-50v – "Tractatus duarum questionum Domini Seiffridi episcopi Cyrenensis.... Explicit determinatio duarum questionum, de Iudeis scilicet et matrimonio servorum, Sifridi episcopi Cyrenensis."
4) 6742 fols. 51r-60v – "Disputatio super scismate Grecorum facta in civitate Nicea inter nuntios domini pape missos ad imperatorem et patriarcham Grecorum ex parte una, et inter eosdem imperatorem et patriarcham ex altera, anno Domini millesimo ducentesimo tricesimo tercio."
5) 6743 fols. 61r-79r – "Tractatus de usura eiusdem qui supra. / Non defecit de plateis eius usura et dolus...."

[51] Fol. 38r: "Frater Joannes Hetzelius Gyslingensis hec scripsit anno salutiferi partus quingentisimo quartadecimo supra millesimum ipso die sanctorum Symonis et Iude apostolorum." This date is confirmed by the watermark on the paper in that portion of the manuscript. This watermark, an ox head with serpent, is identical with that illustrated by Gerhard Piccard, *Die Ochsenkof-Wasserzeichen* 3 (Stuttgart, 1966), p. 784, a watermark characteristic of southwestern Germany, from Göppingen to Worms, and in use in the period 1513-1519.

[52] Fol. 43v: "F. Joannes Hetzler venerando sacre theosophiae lectori tunc heis (?) priori conventus Wormacensis scripsit."

[53] G. Geiger, *Die Reichsstadt Ulm vor der Reformation* (Ulm, 1971), p. 73.

6) 6744 fols. 83r-107r – "Queritur primo quomodo possint Christiani usuras ab eis per Iudeos extotetas [extortas?] repetere...."

V[1] = VATICAN, Biblioteca Apostolica Vaticana, MS Ottob. lat. 641.

A manuscript of uncertain provenance, probably of the fifteenth century. Nothing is known of the medieval owners of the manuscript, but in the late sixteenth or early seventeenth century it was part of the library of Giovanni Angelo, duke of Altemps.[54] The Altemps library was purchased by Pope Alexander VIII (Piero Ottoboni) in 1690, and the Ottoboni collection was in turn purchased for the Vatican Library by Benedict XIV in 1748.[55] *Contents*:

1) fols. 1r-79r – The *De causa*. *Inc*.: "Opus magistri Petri de Palude ordinis predicatorum, patriarche Antiochensis. / Petrus de Palude. / Circa potestatem...." *Expl*.: "Hec autem omnia.... / Amen."
2) fols. 80r-94v – "Tractatus domini abbatis sancti Gregorii [abbatis s. Eugendii?]. / Incipit prologus in tractatum de unitate ecclesie sub uno principatu unius summi ierarche...."
3) fols. 95r-135v – "Infra scriptum tractatum edidit reverendissimus dominus cardinalis s. Xisti natione cathelan., ordinis predicatorum, et tempore domini Eugenii pape IIII. / Quamvis ut ait beatus Jeronimus.... Explicit tractatulus de potestate pape et concilii generalis."
4) fols. 137r-154r – "Disputatio d. abbatis Sciculi de potestate pape et concilii etc."
5) fols. 155r-164v – "Disputatio domini P. Donato episcopi Paduan. quam fecit tempore concilii generalis dum presideret in eo nomine domini Martini pape quinti."
6) fols. 165r-177v – "Trium questionum de potestate pape et concilii. / An papa sit supra concilium...."
7) fols. 178r-193r – "De iurisdictione imperii et auctoritate Romani pontificis. / Quoniam apud multos...."
8) fols. 193r-194v – "Primo sciendum est quod tractare de facto scismatis...."
9) fols. 194v-198v – "Incipiunt differentie iuris canonici et civilis...."

[54] See the verso side of the initial folio, where we find a table of contents, largely illegible, and then in quite clear and modern script: "Ex codicibus Joannis Angeli / Ducis ab Altaemps / Petri de Palude varia opuscula."

[55] J. Bignami Odier, *La Bibliothèque Vaticane de Sixte IV à Pie XI* (Vatican, 1973), p. 55.

10) fols. 200r-259r – "Flores florum et multa recollata per dominum N< icolaum > abbatem de Scicilia archiepiscopum Panormitanum."
11) fols. 260r-263v – "Primo auctoritate cuius generale concilium congregetur...."
12) fols. 266r-267v – "Quod summus pontifex possit et debeat beneficia reservare. / Et primo licet ad sedem apostolicam...."
13) fol. 268r-268v – "Quod sequitur est de manu summi doctoris domini olim Dominici de S. Geminiano. / In nomine individue trinitatis amen. Quorundam curiositas...."
14) fols. 270r-296v – "Tractatus de [sic] Petri de Monte utriusque iuris doctoris de summi pontificis, generalis concilii et imperialis maiestatis origine et potestate."
15) unnumbered folio – "Tractatus domini Joannis Munionis de conciliis."
16) fols. 297r-319v – A treatise beginning "Quia frequenter audeo...."

V^2 = VATICAN, Biblioteca Apostolica Vaticana, MS Ottob. lat. 779.

Another fifteenth-century manuscript of uncertain provenance which, like MS Ottob. lat. 641, was once in the library of Giovanni Angelo, duke of Altemps.[56] On fol. 1r, a title page written in a modern hand, the *De causa* appears under the title: "Petrus de Palude de potestate Petri, apostolorum, discipulorum, summi pontificis, episcoporum et curatorum." *Contents*:

1) fols. 2r-35v – The *De causa*. *Inc.*: "Petrus de Palude.... [the rest has been cut off] / Circa potestatem...." *Expl.*: "Hec autem omnia.... /

[56] Fol. 1r: "Ex codicibus illustrissimi et excellentissimi domini Joannis Angeli Ducis ab Altaemps." The Altemps library was built from a variety of sources, including the library of the famous cardinal Sirleto (†7 October 1585). Cf. Bignami Odier, *La Bibliothèque Vaticane*, p. 55; *Premières recherches sur le fonds Ottoboni* (Vatican, 1966), p. 11. The Sirleto library, or at least most of it, was sold on 4 June 1588 to Cardinal Ascanio Colonna. When Ascanio Colonna died on 17 May 1608, he left a large part of his estate to the chapter of St John Lateran. But his will was contested by his family, and it became the occasion for a long process of litigation which was ended by the sale of the library to the Duke of Altemps on 6 August 1611. A portion of the catalogue of the Sirleto library has been published by L. Dorez, and it indicates that the Sirleto library contained at least one manuscript of the *De causa*, although it does not appear to have been either of the extant manuscripts coming from the Altemps library. The title to the *De causa* given in the catalogue entry suggests rather a manuscript related to our MSS Br and Sz. Cf. L. Dorez, "Recherches et documents sur la bibliothèque du cardinal Sirleto," *Mélanges d'archéologie et d'histoire*, 11 (1891): 457-491 at 481: "400. Petri Paludani de potestate collata praelatis Ecclesiae a Christo, et de potentia Papae respectu Ecclesiae viatorum et super terram. *In papiro et pergam.* [in-fol.]."

Explicit tractatus a venerabili patre et domino compilatus, magistro Petro de Palude, sacre theologie doctore eximio, ordinis fratrum predicatorum et patriarcha Hierosolimitano."

2) fols. 36r-57v – "Nunc considerandum est de potentia pape respectu ecclesie viatorum et supra terram. Circa quod quinque consideranda occurrunt. Primo de ipsius pape etiam residentia...."

V^3 = VATICAN, Biblioteca Apostolica Vaticana, MS Ross. 466.

A fifteenth-century manuscript[57] of probable Italian provenance. In its present form the manuscript appears to be the product of three different scribes, the copyist of the *De causa*, who writes in a fifteenth-century hand, also being responsible for fols. 58r-60r. On fol. 60r we find: "Qui scrissit scribat semper cum domino vivat / Vivat in celis Johannes nomine felix." The Bénédictins du Bouveret have been able to identify a number of manuscripts with similar colophons: Firenze Ricc. 1408, Napoli MB IV F. 36, Wien Theol. lat. 16 (53), and Quaritch n. 36.[58] All are manuscripts of the fifteenth century, and one of them at least is clearly of Italian provenance.[59] However, of the medieval owners of this manuscript nothing is known. It has only recently been acquired by the Vatican Library, since the Rossiana collection did not enter the library until 23 December 1921.[60] On the verso side of an initial folio the *De causa* is identified as "Petrus de Palude de ecclesiastica potestate." *Contents*:

1) fols. 1r-58r – The *De causa*. *Inc.*: "Circa potestatem...." *Expl.*: "Hec autem omnia.... / Sit laus Deo patri. / Explicit tractatus conpilatus a domino fratre Petro de palude, ordinis predicatorum, sacre pagine magistro eximio, patriarcha Ierosolimitano."
2) fols. 58r-60r – "Propositio facta in consistorio coram domino Benedicto papa 12° pro domino Lodovico de Bavaria a domino Johanne papa XII an< tea > excommunicato."
3) fols. 61r-130v – "De termino pontificalis potestatis, ad quid et quousque summi pontificis potestas se extendat, per concordancias teologie et iuris canonici, magistri Dominici Beneti episcopi

[57] P. O. Kristeller, *Iter italicum* 2 (London, 1967), p. 466.

[58] Bénédictins du Bouveret, *Colophons de manuscrits* 3, p. 132, Item 8491; p. 133, Item 8502; p. 134, Item 8515; p. 140, Item 8555.

[59] Cf. S. Morpurgo, *I manoscritti della R. Biblioteca Riccardiana di Firenze* 1.6 (Rome, 1896), p. 447. MS 1408 bears a colophon very similar to the colophon of our manuscript (cf. fol. 61v: "Qui scripsit scribat semper cum domino vivat. / Vivat in celis Iohannes cum domino felix."), and is described as a fifteenth-century manuscript written in Italian.

[60] Bignami Odier, *La Bibliothèque Vaticane*, p. 262.

Torcellani, ad sanctissimum patrem dominum Calistum papam tercium."

4) fols. 132r-146v – "De potestate ecclesie questio. / Circa decimam-octavam distinctionem quarti Sententiarum in qua de potestate ministrorum ecclesie tractatur. Quero utrum summi pontificis auctoritas...."
5) fols. 146v-188v – A number of short pieces, the first of which begins: "Incipit epistola Luciferi ad principes. / Lucifer princeps ecclesie tenebrarum tristia profundi...."

V^4 = VATICAN, Biblioteca Apostolica Vaticana, MS Vat. lat. 4109.[61]

A fifteenth-century manuscript written at Basel at the time of the general council.[62] Nothing is known of its medieval owners. It seems to have been acquired by the Vatican Library by the early seventeenth century at the latest, although the precise date of its acquisition is impossible to determine. The group of manuscripts to which it belongs (Vat. lat. 3553-4616) is "un mélange de nouvelles acquisitions et de manuscrits de l'ancien fonds."[63] *Contents*:

1) fols. 1r-183v – Augustinus Triumphus, *Summa de ecclesiastica potestate*.
2) fols. 196-213v – Herveus Natalis, *Tractatus de potestate pape*.
3) fols. 216r-247v – The *De causa*. *Inc.*: "Dominus P. de Palude. / Circa potestatem...." *Expl.*: "Hec autem omnia.... / Deo gratias. Amen. Explicit tractatus domini Petri de Palude ordinis fratrum predicatorum de ecclesiastica potestate scriptus Basilee in concilio generali et finitus 19[a] Marcii anno Domini M°CCCC°34°."
4) fols. 248r-259v – Herveus Natalis, *De iurisdictione et exemptione*.
5) fols. 260r-261r – "Jacobi abbatis Cist. ord. Silvaducinensis diocesis Tractatus contra impugnatores exemptionem, ab eodem editus in Vienne tempore generalis concilii."
6) fols. 261r-265v – Henricus de Bitterfeld, *Determinatio super audientiam confessionum*.

[61] For a partial description see L. Hödl, *De iurisdictione. Ein unveröffentlichter Traktat des Herveus Natalis* O.P. *(†1323) über die Kirchengewalt* (München, 1959), p. 6.

[62] See the *explicit* to the *De causa* given below, as well as fol. 178r: "Explicit summa de ecclesiastica potestate edita a fratre Augustino de Ancona ordinis fratrum eremitarum Sancti Augustini, quam scripsit frater Matheus de Valle de conventu Beluacensi, nationis Francie, ordinis fratrum predicatorum, cum esset in sacro concilio Basiliensi, et finivit in vigilia Spiritus Sancti, 30 Maii, anno Domini millesimo 433°."

[63] Bignami Odier, *La Bibliothèque Vaticane*, p. 82.

7) fols. 265v-267v – John of Paris, *Quaestio disputata de potestate pape*.
8) fol. 267v – "Item alia questio eiusdem materie. / Utrum de superioris licentia aliquis possit confiteri alteri quam proprio sacerdoti."
9) fols. 267v-270v – "Item tractatus super possessionibus et redditibus habendi."

V[5] = VATICAN, Biblioteca Apostolica Vaticana, MS Vat. lat. 4139.

A manuscript of uncertain date and provenance, although no earlier than mid-fifteenth century. Its medieval owners are unknown, but like MS Vat. lat. 4109 it had been acquired by the Vatican Library by the early seventeenth century. *Contents*:

1) fols. 1r-20r – Bernardus de Rosergio, *Tractatus de potestate legati de latere*.
2) fols. 21r-37r – A collection of excerpts from a variety of sources including Alvarus Pelagius and Augustinus Triumphus, and beginning: "Christianissimo principi domino nostro regi...."
3) fols. 37v-147r – The *De causa*. *Inc*.: "Opus magistri Petri de Palude, qui fuit magister in sacra theologia et prius decretorum doctor, et fuit postea patriarcha Antiochensis. / Circa potestatem...." *Expl*.: "Sed certum est quod irrationabiliter ageret et graviter peccaret. / Et sic est finis huius operis. Deo gratias."
4) fols. 148r-192v – Alexander de Sancto Elpidio, *Tractatus de ecclesiastica potestate*.
5) fols. 192v-207v – Idem, *Tractatus de cessione personali*.
6) fols. 208r-275v – The anonymous *Libellus de iurisdictione imperii et auctoritate summi pontificis*.
7) fols. 276r-293v – John of Paris, *Tractatus de potestate regia et papali*.

V[6] = VATICAN, Biblioteca Apostolica Vaticana, MS Vat. lat. 6586.

A seventeenth-century manuscript which was obtained by the Vatican Library before the end of the century. Volume 8 of the inventory (Vat. lat. 6449-7058) was probably prepared by the end of the seventeenth century, and describes manuscripts which entered the Vatican Library between 1640 and 1700.[64] This manuscript is in very delicate condition, is largely illegible, contains only the fourth article of the *De causa*, and is directly dependent on the 1506 edition. *Contents*:

1) fols. 1r-81v – "Tractatus de iure monarchiae fratris Guillielmi de Cremona."

[64] Ibid., p. 141.

2) fols. 87r-115v – "Tractatus de origine iurisdictionum seu de duabus potestatibus, temporali, scilicet et spirituali, a reverendissimo in Christo patre domino Petro Bertrando."
3) fols. 117r-144r – The *De causa*. *Inc*.: "Petrus de Palude, patriarcha Hierosolimitanus, ordinis fratrum predicatorum, de potestate pape. / Quartum articulum de causa immediata potestatis papalis...." *Expl*.: "... tota potestas ecclesie fuit collata Petro, nec habet ecclesia aliquam potestatem iurisdictionis nisi a Petro, quam Petro episcopus concessit."
4) fols. 145r-176v – "Defensorium ecclesiae magistri Aegidii Carlerii decani ecclesie Cameracensis."
5) fols. 181r-199v – "Durandus <de S. Porciano> de iurisdictione ecclesiastica questio 1: An potestas secularis sit a Deo."
6) fols. 203r-306r – Herveus Natalis, *Tractatus de potestate pape*.

V^7 = VATICAN, Biblioteca Apostolica Vaticana, MS Vat. lat. 7188.

A fifteenth-century manuscript of unknown provenance which once belonged to Vatican librarian Lorenzo Zaccagni (†26 January 1712).[65] The manuscript is written in at least five different hands, although the *De causa* and the *De iurisdictione* of Herveus Natalis which it also contains are written in the same hand. The *De causa* is found on fols. 31r-43v, and 126r-161v, although it is incomplete, ends rather abruptly, and the folios are not in proper sequence. Hence they need to be read in the following order: fols. 31r-43v, 138r-161v, 136r-136v, 126r-135v, 137r-137v. *Contents*:

1) fols. 1r-30r – Herveus Natalis, *De iurisdictione et exemptione*.
2) fols. 31r-43v – The first portion of the *De causa*. *Inc*.: "Circa potestatem...."
3) fol. 44r-44v – A fragment bearing the title "Moses et Belial" and beginning: "Universis Christi fidelibus atque orthodoxe sancte matris ecclesie fidei cultoribus hoc breve compendium inspectius presbiter Jacobus detheramo...."
4) fols. 45r-100v – A compendium of questions on legal matters, each followed by an appropriate reference, beginning: "ALIMENTA. An debeantur filio qui habuit patrem...."
5) fols. 103r-111v – A collection of quotations from, or paraphrases or summaries of, important papal pronouncements, organized under

[65] Ibid., p. 156, n. 103.

rubrics for popes Innocent III, Nicholas III, Boniface VIII, Clement V, Benedict XII, Gregory IX and Urban VI, and beginning: "*Cum bonus pastor*. Patriarche, archiepiscopi, episcopi, abbates, priores in curia Romana vel infra duas dictas ex[a] ecclesias eis commissas existentes...."

6) fols. 113r-118v – A collection of notes on canon law organized under appropriate rubrics, the first of which is *De summa trinitate*.
7) fol. 119r – A table of contents for the selections of papal pronouncements.
8) fol. 125v – A short note beginning: "Videas omnes constitutiones factas in concilio Constantiensi, Basiliensi...."
9) fols. 126r-161v – The remainder of the *De causa*, which needs to be rearranged in the manner described above. *Expl.* (fol. 137v): "sed verum est quod status illorum fuit...."
10) fols. 162r-173v – A fragment of an ecclesiological treatise beginning: "omnis alia potestas quantum ad correctionem abusus, quia in tota communitate Christiana...."
11) fols. 174r-200v – Another fragment entitled "Bartoli consilia" and beginning: "Ad aliud quod queritur, an per exercitium iurisdictio habita modo predicto...."

Va = VIENNA, Österreichische Nationalbibliothek, MS 2168 (Theol. 228).[66]

A manuscript of south German provenance, and of the first quarter of the fifteenth century. Nothing is known of its medieval owners, although the Hofbibliothek in Vienna had acquired it by the early seventeenth century. Folio 1r bears the catalogue number, "N° 143," of Sebastian Tengnagel, prefect of the Hofbibliothek from 1608 to 1636. Apart from the *De causa*, its contents relate exclusively to the controversy between Pierre de la Palu and Jean de Pouilly. The text of the *De causa* and the *Epilogus* are separated by several folios. *Contents*:

1) fols. 1r-12r – "Iudicium fratris Petri de Palude ordinis fratrum predicatorum, magistri in theologia, contra magistrum Johannem de Poliaco doctorem in theologia super articulis qui secuntur."
2) fols. 12v-16v – "Responsio magistri Joannis de Poly ad predicta."

[66] Cf. *Tabulae codicum manuscriptorum praeter Graecos et orientales in Biblioteca Palatina Vindobonensi asservatorum*... 2 (Vindobonae, 1868), pp. 21-22. The information contained here has been supplemented for me by Dr Eva Irblich of the Österreichische Nationalbibliothek, who was kind enough to examine the manuscript on my behalf.

3) fols. 17r-35r – "Conclusio fratris Petri de Palude contra responsionem datam per magistrum Joannem de Poly."
4) fols. 36r-101r – The text of the *De causa*. *Inc*.: "De causa immediata potestatis ecclesiastice in prelatis. / f. P. de Palude. / Circa potestatem...." *Expl*.: "... videtur esse hereticum, sicut superius est deductum."
5) fols. 101r-111v – "Responsiones fratris Petri de Palude ad ea que sibi imposuit magister Joannes de Pollhiaco dum ad obiecta sibi ab aliis idem magister Joannes in consistorio responderet, quas frater Petrus vestre sanctitati exibet iudicandas, condepnando, corrigendo vel etiam approbando sicut misericors et iusta vestra prudentia decreverit faciendum."
6) fols. 111v-118r – The *Epilogus* to the *De causa*. *Inc*.: "Epilogus tractatus de causa immediata ecclesiastice potestatis quantum ad articulos et conclusiones incidentales et principales." *Expl*.: "Hec autem omnia.... / Finito libro sit laus gloria Christo Amen."

W = WROCŁAW (Breslau), Biblioteka Uniwersytecka, MS IV F 64.[67]

A manuscript which, according to Heck, dates from the first half of the fifteenth century, and which once was in the possession of the Dominican convent at Breslau. Heck's opinion, which is based largely on the illuminations in the portion of the manuscript which bears the treatise by Jacobus de Cessulis, is that the manuscript was copied in the Dominican convent at Breslau, and that it was illuminated by a local artist named Joannes. Although Heck's argument appears quite sound, it should be pointed out that the portion of the manuscript bearing the *De causa* is written in a distinctive hand. Heck maintains that this hand is also of the fifteenth century, and Kaeppeli seems to concur with this judgment, although the sixteenth-century date which appears at the end of the *De causa* is quite clear. *Contents* (following the description of Heck):
1) fol. 1 – A fragment of a scholastic commentary on the *De generatione*.
2) fols. 2r-32r – Jacobus de Cessulis, *Liber super ludum scacorum*.
3) fols. 32v-53r – *Legenda de sancta Catherina*.
4) fols. 53v-60r – *Tractatus de demonibus*.

[67] For a complete description and extensive discussion of this manuscript see R. Heck, "Miniatury Wrocławskiego rekopisu Jakuba de Cessulis 'Liber super ludum scacorum'," *Acta Universitatis Wratislaviensis*, 23 (1964): 13-50.

5) fols. 61r-209v – Stephanus Bisuntinus, *Alphabetum narrationum*.
6) fols. 215r-248v – The *De causa*. *Inc*.: "Circa potestatem...." *Expl*.: "... Sed irrationabiliter ageret et peccaret. / 1524 / Hec omnia...."
7) fols. 249r-264r – *Liber de penitentia*, with German glosses.
8) fols. 265r-377r – Thomas Brabantinus O.P., *Liber de apibus*.
9) fols. 377r-389v – Exempla, identical to those found in MS 2107.1, fols. 135v-147r.

5

The Manuscript Filiation

The interrelationships among the manuscripts can best be described by making an initial distinction between two main groups of manuscripts, an α Group composed of OV^{1}BoV^{2}V^{5}V^{3}P^{3}SvSStU Bm^{1}PrWBlV^{4}B^{2}P^{2}V^{7}, and a β Group composed of P^{4}RP^{1}B^{1}TBm^{2}BrSzBarb.V^{6}SrVa.

The α Group

The relationships among the manuscripts of α Group can, initially at least, be represented by the following stemma, where θ represents the hyparchetype for OV^{1}BoV^{2}V^{5}V^{3}P^{3}SvS, φ the hyparchetype for StUBm^{1}PrWBlV^{4}, and ψ the hyparchetype for P^{2}V^{7}. B^{2}, which contains only the *Epilogus*, and which also belongs to α Group, is not given a place in this stemma. But further on we shall clarify its position by devoting some special attention to it.

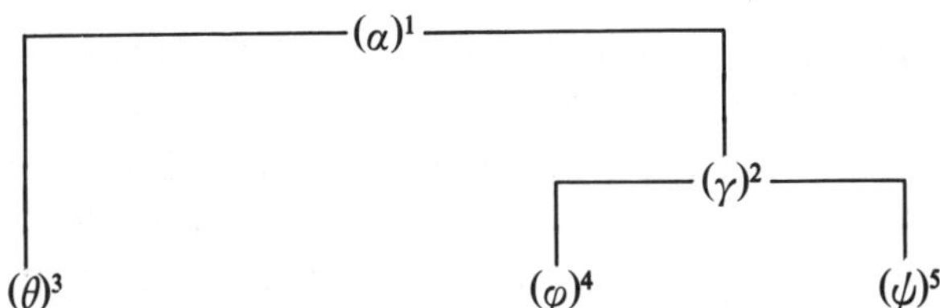

[1] Cf., for example, the reordering of the material on pp. 204-205. At line 505, immediately after "sexto," the α MSS, OV^{1}BoV^{2}V^{5}V^{3}P^{3}SvSStUBm^{1}PrWBlV^{4}P^{2}V^{7}, advance to line 510: "Secundo quia." At line 519, immediately after "corpore," these same MSS return to line 506: "Minor patet." At line 509, immediately after "ecclesie," OV^{1}Bo-V^{2}V^{5}V^{3}P^{3}SvS advance to lines 522-523: "cui obligatur." The words "eodem ... potest" (lines 509-510) are omitted, as are "dicendum ... ecclesie" (lines 520-522). At line 510, immediately after "potest," StUBm^{1}PrWBlV^{4}P^{2}V^{7} advance to line 520: "Dicendum est."

[2] Cf. n. 1 above.

[3] Cf. n. 1 above, or **2**: 481 – vel ... speciebus] sub speciebus panis et vini OV^{1}Bo V^{2}V^{5}V^{3}P^{3}SvS.

[4] Cf. **2**: 531 – quidem ... masculum] quamvis solum hominem prius [prius hominem St] masculum StUBm^{1}PrWBlV^{4}.

[5] Cf. **3**: 271 – quod^{1} ... Emmaus] de illis duobus discipulis P^{2}V^{7}.

Of the subfamilies of α Group, the one composed of P^2V^7 is perhaps the easiest to sort out. Not enough is known of the provenance of these manuscripts to trace them back to a common point of contact, although one might suggest Italian roots for each of them. However, their relationship is a fairly straight-forward one. Since P^2V^7 share conjunctive errors which also have separative force against the other manuscripts, and since each possesses errors distinctive to itself alone,[6] both must be derived independently from the hyparchetype here represented as ψ. Contamination must have entered into both P^2 and V^7, for on occasion one or the other will agree independently with $StUBm^1PrWBlV^4$, and less frequently with $OV^1BoV^2V^5V^3P^3SvS$. They also, both together and individually, have a marked affinity with manuscripts in the β Group, especially $P^4RP^1B^1T$, a phenomenon to be discussed later. This could not be explained without positing other sources for ψ in addition to γ, and other sources for P^2V^7 in addition to ψ. But, having said that, the main lines of filiation of P^2V^7 can be described by the following stemma.

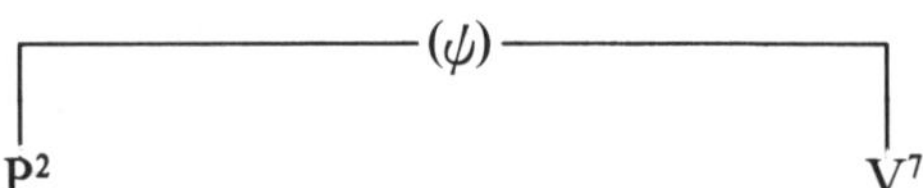

We are relatively better informed about the provenance of manuscripts $StUBm^1PrWBlV^4$, and what we know of the provenance of each suggests a German character for the group as a whole. Internal evidence bears out this conclusion: the German gloss at p. 186, line 17, for example. Unfortunately, the relationships among these manuscripts are quite complex. Again there are signs of contamination in the group, and "where contamination exists the science of stemmatics in the strict sense breaks down."[7] The chief indication of contamination is that individual members of this group of manuscripts, particularly V^4, on occasion escape the errors common to all the other members of the group. But, having said that, the following stemma could be offered as illustrative of the main lines of filiation.

[6] Cf. **1**: 169-170 – Anacletus ... ecclesia] *om.* V^7; Appendix A: 42 – qua ... simulatorie] *hom.* P^2.

[7] Paul Maas, *Textual Criticism* (Oxford, 1958), p. 48.

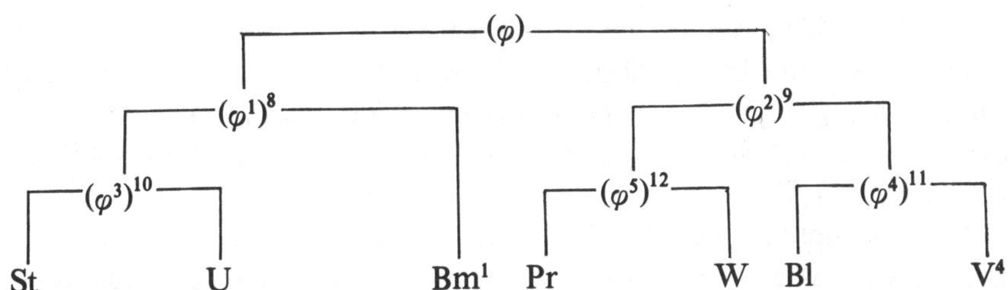

Each of StUBm^{1}PrWV^4 possesses peculiar errors distinctive to itself alone.[13] Bl does not possess its own strikingly distinctive errors, but it does share conjunctive errors with V^4 which also have separative force against StUBm^{1}PrW. Since V^4 contains most of the peculiar errors of Bl as well as distinctive errors of its own, Bl could be a direct source for V^4. But it is more likely that both are dependent on the hyparchetype φ^4. If Bl is a source for V^4, it is only one source, for there are occasions on which V^4 avoids not only the errors of Bl but of StUBm^{1}PrW as well.[14]

The stemma can be expanded to accomodate B^2 in the following manner:

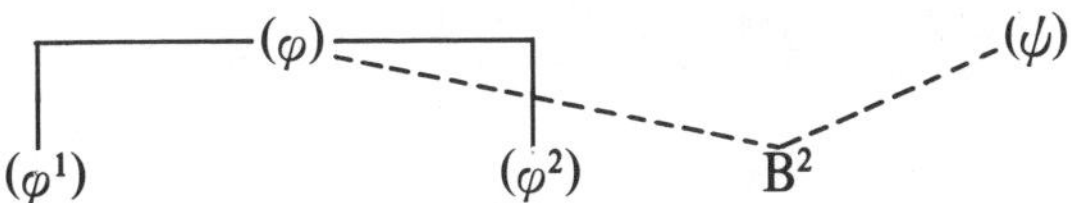

B^2 is a distinctive manuscript, possessing only the *Epilogus*, and perhaps because of that fact a much fuller version of the *Epilogus* than found in the other manuscripts. The copyist must have felt it incumbent upon him to expand upon the points made there, since the text itself was not present. However, B^2 can frequently be found sharing the conjunctive errors of

[8] The conjunctive errors of StUBm^1 or PrWBlV^4 are not particularly striking, but cf. **2**: 280 – sit] fuit PrWBlV^4, fuerit StUBm^1; and **2**: 658-659 – a Deo prepositus est] a Deo [Domino W] est prepositus PrWBlV^4, est a Deo prepositus StUBm^1.

[9] Cf. n. 8 above.

[10] Cf. **1**: 4 – preeminentia eius] primaria quod Petrus habuit potestatem a Christo StU.

[11] Cf. **6**: 1078 – futuris] *add.* episcopis potestatem iurisdictionis in utroque foro et discipulis pro se et pro omnibus futuris BlV^4.

[12] Cf. **1**: 67-68 – iudex^1 ... specialis] loci illius iudex specialis PrW.

[13] Cf. **2**: 851-852 – Sed ... iurisdictionis] *hom.* St; **2**: 568-569 – in^2 ... similibus] *om.* U; **3**: 170-191 – boni ... vobis] *om.* Bm^1; **1**: 36 – Solutio ... potestate] *om.* Pr; **1**: 142-146 – commisit ... singulariter] *hom.* W; **2**: 254-255 – iam ... legis] *hom.* V^4.

[14] Cf. Epilogus: 747-753, where StUBm^{1}PrWBl (but not V^4) reverse the order of propositions 37 and 38. To escape this error the copyist of V^4 must have had access to an additional source.

StUBm[1]PrWBlV[4] which also have separative force against the other manuscripts, and this establishes its dependence on φ.[15] It can also be found sharing with P[2] conjunctive errors which also have separative force against StUBm[1]PrWBlV[4] and the other manuscripts. (V[7] does not include the *Epilogus*.) This establishes its dependence on ψ.[16]

We are not as well informed as we would care to be about the provenance of the manuscripts in the last and largest sub-group of α Group, OV[1]BoV[2]V[5]V[3]P[3]SvS, but what we do know suggests an Italian character for this group as a whole. The relationships among these manuscripts are extraordinarily complex, and again we can suspect contamination in several members of the group. But the following stemma can be offered as an approximation illustrating the major lines of filiation.

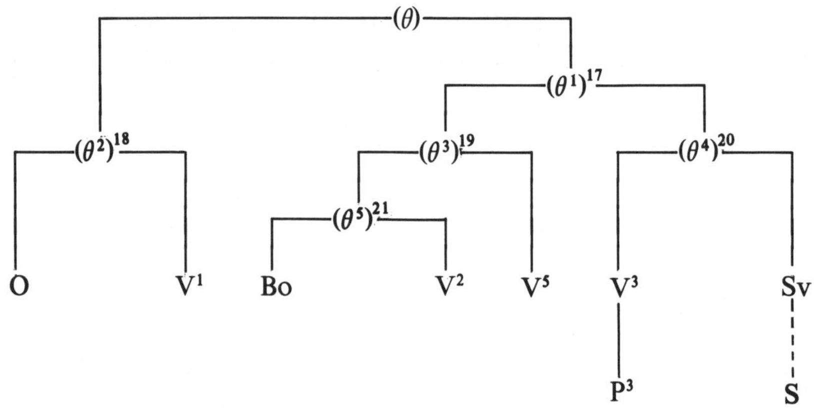

[15] Cf. Epilogus: 628 – sic ... fecerit] nam Christus non instituit immediate [immediate instituit Bm[1]] StUBm[1]PrWBlV[4]B[2].

[16] Cf. Epilogus: 768-774, where B[2]P[2] reverse the order of propositions 43 and 44.

[17] Cf. **2**: 1063 – necesse fuit ut Petrus haberet] ut Petrus OV[1], ideo prelatus devians [derivans V[5]] a fundamento Petri iurisdictionem perdit [perdidit Bo] et [*om.* Bo] sic [sicut V[3]P[3]; *add.* perdit Bo] non habens eam exercere non potest iurisdictionem, videlicet [unde licet Sv] quam [quare Bo] Petrus habuit a Christo et eam diffudit [diffundit V[3]P[3]] BoV[2]V[5]V[3]P[3]SvS.

[18] Cf. **4**: 693 – determinationi preponere sensum suum] detrahere rationibus [nominibus V[1]] OV[1].

[19] Cf. **4**: 343 – preferendo Romanam ecclesiam] preferenda Romana ecclesia BoV[2]V[5].

[20] Cf. **2**: 1027-1028 – haberet ... suum] haberet eas a Petro qui sic reciperet a Christo et sic minorasset promissum suum V[3]P[3]SvS.

[21] Cf. **4**: 68 – probabitur] *add.* scilicet infra, in [*om.* Bo] secunda conclusione principali, aliquid tangit post principium ibi [in Bo] ubi [sexto Bo]: sed quia difficile erat patriarchas etc., et ibi remittit infra. Unde vide plene in quarto [quinto Bo] articulo principali et in secunda principali conclusione, scilicet in ipsius secunde conclusionis conclusione incidenti [incidente Bo] nona et sequenti BoV[2].

Each of OBo$V^2V^5P^3$S possesses peculiar errors not found in any of the other manuscripts.[22] V^1 does not possess striking errors of this sort, although it does share conjunctive errors with O which also have separative force against Bo$V^2V^5V^3P^3$SvS. V^1 could be a source for O, but it is more likely that both are derived independently from the hyparchetype θ^2.

V^3 and Sv do not possess strikingly peculiar errors either, and the marked affinities which they bear with P^3 and S respectively suggest that P^3 could be derived from V^3 and S from Sv.[23] V^3 cannot be a copy of P^3 because of the large number of errors which are peculiar to P^3 and not repeated in V^3. There are also some errors peculiar to V^3 and not repeated in P^3, but these are not such as to rule out the dependence of P^3 on V^3. One of the weaknesses of the scribe of V^3 was his tendency to repeat individual words and phrases, and many of these repetitions are not found in P^3. But only two of the repetitions not found in P^3 are longer than two words,[24] and even these are not such as could not have been eliminated by an attentive scribe. There are also other errors in V^3 not to be found in P^3, but the following is a complete list of the errors of this sort that are to be found in the first forty pages of edited text. (This includes Appendix A, pp. 327-352, for in most of the manuscripts this material is inserted at p. 139, line 636.)

1: 34 – fuerunt] fiunt V^3 [originally *fiunt* in P^3, but corrected]
1: 43 – respondetur] respondet V^3
1: 68 – quin Petrus] quia Petrus V^3, quia Petrus non P^3 [*non* has been added above the line]
1: 83 – faciamus] faciam V^3
1: 104 – ire] in re V^3 [originally *in re* in P^3, but corrected]
1: 108 – idest] a V^3, *om.* P^3 [originally *a*, but deleted]
1: 125 – est] *om.* V^3, et P^3 [*et* has been added above the line]
1: 161 & 162 – rete] retem V^3 [originally *retem* in P^3, but corrected]
1: 180 – verisimilius] verisimilis V^3, verisimile P^3 [originally *verisimiles* in P^3, but corrected]
2: 269 – extendi] exercende V^3, exercendi P^3
2: 414 – fingere] effingitur V^3, effingere P^3

[22] Cf. **2**: 366-367 – principalem ... actum] *hom.* O; **1**: 245 – pastorem ... Ad] *om.* Bo; **4**: 709-731 – Primo ... cuius] *om.* V^2; **5**: 512-517 – universalis ... consensu] *hom.* V^5; **3**: 383 – Quia ... apostolis²] *hom.* P^3; and **3**: 331-332 – apostolorum ... et] *om.* S.

[23] Cf. **3**: 273-278 – tunc ... et] *hom.* V^3P^3; and **2**: 603-616 – ut ... sacerdotes] *hom.* SvS.

[24] Cf. **6**: 1052 – sed a Christo immediate] *rep.* V^3; Appendix A: 129-130 – eos ... Christus] *rep.* V^3.

The conclusion which this list seems to warrant is that P^3 was indeed copied from V^3. Hence, in the *apparatus criticus* readings attributed to V^3 are to be understood as also being found in P^3 unless the contrary is expressly noted. (This procedure is followed in the case of every manuscript which can be eliminated.) P^3 is a corrected manuscript, but the corrections are all such as could have been accomplished by a conscientious copyist.

The relationship between Sv and S is similar, although not exactly the same. Sv cannot have been copied from S because of the large number of errors peculiar to S not repeated in Sv. S could have been copied from Sv, although in view of the large number of errors peculiar to S, it is not likely that it is in direct unmediated descent from Sv. If it is, it is an extremely bad copy. A comparison of the two manuscripts through the first forty pages of our text (again including pp. 327-352) reveals that, except for the rubrics of Sv, S contains almost all of the errors peculiar to Sv, as well of course as many distinctive errors of its own. This naturally inclines one to suspect the ultimate dependence of S on Sv, even if they were separated by one or more lost intermediaries in which some of the errors peculiar to S were introduced. However, there are several readings in Sv not repeated in S, and these complicate the picture. If we eliminate the minor errors in Sv which could easily have been corrected by the copyist of S, we get the following.

(1) **2**: 54 – assensu] consensu $OV^1V^2V^5V^3P^3S$ (but not Sv)
(2) **2**: 98 – est²] sit Sv
(3) **2**: 328 – dantur] *add.* quod Sv
(4) **2**: 460 – Marie] *om.* $OV^1BoV^2V^3P^3Sv$ (but not S)
(5) **2**: 480 – idest] scilicet V^3P^3S (but not Sv)
(6) Appendix A: 416 – qui] quia $V^5V^3P^3S$ (but not Sv)
(7) Appendix A: 445 – quod] sed $OV^1BoV^2V^5V^3P^3S$, sic Sv
(8) **2**: 688 – solis] soli Sv
(9) **2**: 753 – auctoritatem] potestatem $OV^1BoV^2V^5S$ (but not Sv)

With numbers 2, 3, 7 and 8 we are dealing with simple errors in Sv which receive no support in any of the other manuscripts. Number 7 is doubtful, since the reading "sic" which is found in Sv was originally "si." It has been corrected to "sic," and the corrected reading could be read as "set," from which "sed" would be a logical derivation. However, in the other cases we have straightforward errors in Sv not repeated in S, and they are not manifest errors which the scribe of S, judging from the context, would be forced to correct. They could be regarded as separative errors indicating that S cannot be derived from Sv. However, in view of the fact that the total number of errors listed above is quite small, and the fact that there is no striking error, such as an omission, in Sv which is not also found in S, S could be derived from Sv, although via an intermediary in which a few corrections were supplied. Unfortunately, the source of the correcting influence is not clear. Numbers 1 and 7 suggest that the source of the corrections must have been a manuscript descended from θ. Numbers 5 and 6 are consistent with this theory, but suggest more precisely that the source of the corrections must have been a manuscript descending from θ^4. However, number 9 points away from θ^4 as the source of the correcting influence, and number 4 suggests, although not very strongly, that the source of the corrections must have been a manuscript outside of this whole group of manuscripts entirely. In the final analysis not too much is clear. The weight of the evidence seems to suggest the descent of S from Sv via an intermediary. But in the stemma given above Sv and S are joined by a broken line to signify that Sv is not an exclusive source for S.

There are several factors, however, indicating that the stemma for OV^{1}BoV^{2}V^{5}V^{3}P^{3}SvS has limitations. First of all, on many occasions V^{3}P^{3}SvS alone of these manuscripts preserve the correct reading, OV^{1}Bo V^{2}V^5 agreeing against V^{3}P^{3}SvS and the other manuscripts in significant error.[25] Errors of this sort might indicate contamination in θ^3 which could be accounted for by revising our stemma to show that θ^3 is dependent on an additional source intermediate between θ and θ^2. Secondly, the relationship of BoV^2 and V^5 is complicated by the fact that on many occasions Bo and V^2, sometimes individually and sometimes together, alone preserve the correct reading against the other manuscripts in this group. This phenomenon is particularly striking in the case of V^2,[26] and especially from the end of article 5. Readings such as these suggest contamination in the common exemplar for both of these manuscripts, and quite possibly in each of them individually, especially V^2, although the source of the contamination in V^2 cannot readily be identified.[27] Finally, there is every reason for believing that contamination and the listing of variants was present in the exemplar for the group as a whole,

[25] Cf. **4**: 603 – sedit ... finaliter] *om.* OV^{1}BoV^{2}V^5.

[26] Cf. Epilogus: 591 – nullam ... culpa] quod absolutio illorum [eorum OV^1] curatorum et episcoporum [episcoporum et curatorum Bo] sit nulla a vinculo vel [nec BoV^{3}P^{3}Sv] a culpa. Idest, non potest facere papa per excommunicationem suam in episcopos et curatos, quod non valeat absolutio eorum [illorum BoV^{3}P^{3}Sv] a vinculo vel a culpa [Idest ... culpa *om.* S], quam ipsi aliis impenderent [impenderet Bo, impedirent S] OV^{1}BoV^{5}V^{3}P^{3}SvS.

[27] V^2 shows some affinity with B^{1}T, but not enough to allow any firm conclusions. Cf. **6**: 182 – conficiendum] confitendum V^{2}B^{1}T; 183-184 – in ... equalis] *hom.* V^{2}B^{1}T.

for that is the only way one can explain the conjunctive errors of OV^1Bo-V^2,[28] $BoV^5V^3P^3SvS$,[29] and $V^5V^3P^3SvS$,[30] to give only a few examples of the combinations that can occur from time to time. If variants were present in θ, the stemma for this group of manuscripts has to be treated with caution. But the evidence for their existence is quite striking.[31]

The β Group

The relationships among the manuscripts of β Group can be represented by the following preliminary stemma, where π represents the hyparchetype for $P^4RP^1B^1T$, ρ the hyparchetype for $Bm^2BrSzBarb.V^6$, and σ the hyparchetype for SrVa. The Barbier edition is not a manuscript of course, although V^6, which is directly dependent upon it, is. But it deserves a place in the stemma in view of the fact that it appears to have been dependent on a manuscript or manuscripts closely related to Bm^2BrSz.

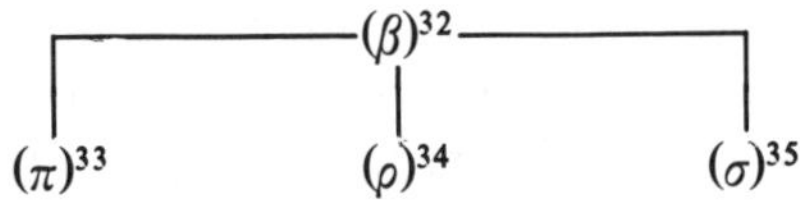

The relationship of SrVa is a straightforward one, although these two manuscripts are not very closely related. Not enough is known of the provenance of either to trace them back to a common source. Moreover, in addition to possessing peculiar errors not found in any of the others,[36] each of these manuscripts is rather idiosyncratic, Sr because it often

[28] Cf. **2**: 1266 – signavit] *add.* tanquam materiam, sicut si in aliqua [qua V^1, illa BoV^2] casa esset aurum, et claves ipsius case tradantur alicui etc. [*om.* Bo] OV^1BoV^2.

[29] Cf. **4**: 773 – Romana] *add.* nunc et semper $BoV^5V^3P^3SvS$.

[30] Cf. **5**: 377-378 – Hoc ... instituuntur] *hom.* $V^5V^3P^3SvS$.

[31] Cf. the listing of variants in the manuscripts of this group at **5**: 158 – habuerunt] habuerunt vel habuerint OV^1, habuissent vel habuerint [habuerunt Bo] $BoV^2V^5V^3P^3$, habuissent SvS.

[32] Cf. **2**: 1063 – necesse ... haberet] ut Petrus haberet $P^4RP^1B^1TBm^2BrSzSrVa$. Since this makes no sense, it is amended in Barb. to "necesse fuit ut Petrus haberet." V^6 does not follow Barb. here because it contains only article 4.

[33] Cf. **2**: 134-135 – Chrysostomus ... Joannis 4] sicut ... Joannes Chrysostomus $P^4RP^1B^1T$.

[34] Again, V^6 contains only article 4, and there is no particularly striking error of the sort we need here in that part of the treatise. But cf. **2**: 1373 – sedebitis ... duodecim^2] etc. usque ibi $Bm^2BrSzBarb$.

[35] Cf. **3**: 123-145 – Nec ... dicto] *om.* SrVa.

[36] Cf. **1**: 145-165 – Item ... meas] *om.* Sr; and **2**: 72-80 – Potest ... meos] *om.* Va.

functions as a précis, omitting large sections of the text and smoothing over the omissions with transitional sentences, Va because of the distinctive arrangement it gives to the material located in our Appendix B. Va also at times displays a marked affinity with $OV^1BoV^2V^5V^3P^3SvS$, suggesting that it might have been influenced by a manuscript descended from θ.[37] However, despite the fact that the relationship between them is a distant one, Sr and Va do share conjunctive errors that have separative force against the other manuscripts. Their relationship, therefore, can be expressed in terms of the following stemma.

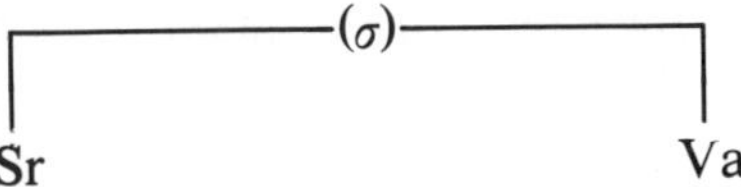

We are better informed about the provenance of the manuscripts in the second sub-family of β Group, Bm^2BrSzV^6, and the available evidence suggests a German character for the group as a whole. The provenance of V^6 is uncertain, but our lack of knowledge here is insignificant in view of the fact that V^6 is directly dependent on the Barbier edition, which also is to be grouped with these manuscripts. The relations of $Bm^2BrSzBarb.V^6$ are relatively straightforward, and can be described as follows.

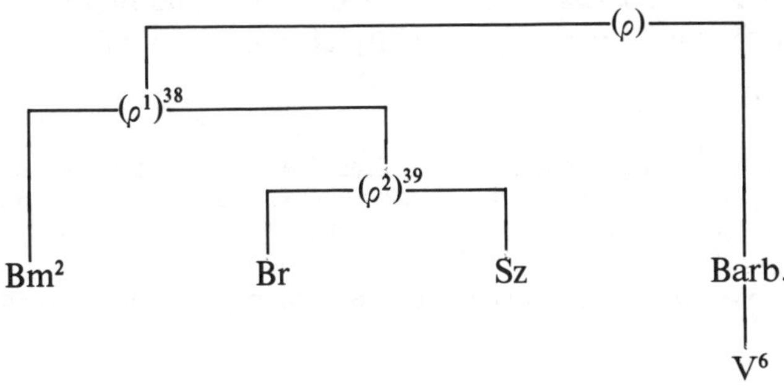

[37] Cf. **5**: 318 – partialem] particularem $OV^1BoV^2V^5Va$; Appendix A: 697 – habet] *add.* medium $OV^1BoV^2V^5V^3P^3SvSVa$. Examples could be multiplied fairly easily.

[38] Cf. the inversions on pp. 282-283. On line 956, in place of "Quorum," Bm^2BrSz give "quo tamen et cum hoc," and then advance to line 965: "de quo." On line 971, immediately after "presentem," Bm^2BrSz return to line 957: "Quod¹." On line 964, immediately after "simile," Bm^2BrSz advance to line 972: "Secunda." The words "Et ... hoc" on lines 964-965 are omitted.

[39] Cf. **2**: 392-393 – facti¹ ... sacerdotes] cum eo facti episcopi sicut facti sunt sacerdotes BrSz.

Each of Bm²BrSzBarb.V⁶ possesses peculiar errors not found in any of the other manuscripts.[40] However, V⁶, in the portion of the treatise which is contained in V⁶ (i.e. article 4), contains all the peculiar errors of the Barbier edition[41] as well as distinctive errors of its own, and this establishes its dependence on Barbier.

Unfortunately, we are not as well informed about the provenance of the members of the last remaining sub-group of β Group, P⁴RP¹B¹T. Only three allow of any firm conclusions. However, the testimony of these three is probably sufficient to warrant describing the group as a whole as French. The relationships of these manuscripts are quite complex. But the following stemma illustrates at least the main lines of dependence.

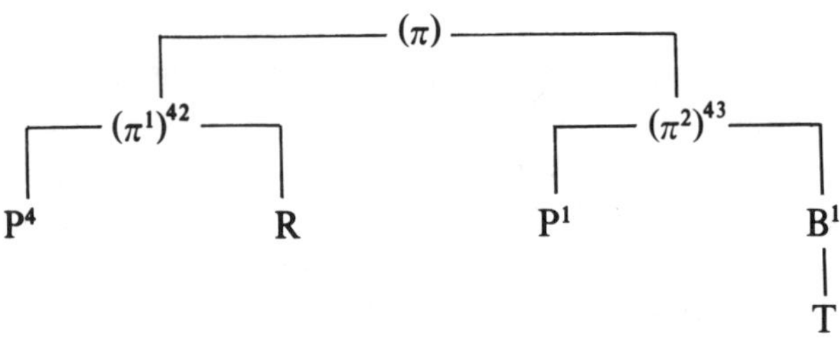

Each of P⁴RP¹T possesses peculiar errors not found in any of the other manuscripts.[44] But T possesses virtually all the errors of B¹,[45] as well as

[40] Cf. **5**: 238-239 – Sed ... potestatis] *hom.* Bm²; **3**: 81-83 – sicut ... discipulis] *hom.* Br; **2**: 504-505 – Thomas ... quod] *om.* Sz; **5**: 728-729 – ut ... divino] videlicet quod ecclesia Hierosolimitana sit fundata a Deo, vel alia particularis ecclesia Barb.; **4**: 278 – ad ... subiciendo] *om.* V⁶.

[41] Cf., for example, **4**: 321 – De iurisdictione omnium iudicum] De iure quod tamen videtur Barb.V⁶.

[42] Cf. **2**: 717-722 – quid ... apostolis] *om.* P⁴R.

[43] Cf. **2**: 530-531 – masculum ... masculum] masculum et feminam simul, et primo quidem hominem solum prius masculum P¹B¹T.

[44] Cf. **4**: 783-789 – suam ... potestatem] *hom.* P⁴; **3**: 227-230 – et² ... orare] *hom.* P¹; Appendix A: 158-160 – qui ... tunc] *om.* T. There is no striking evidence of independent error in R. But cf. **3**: 229 – pro tunc erant] erant pro tunc R; and **5**: 709 – pontificali dignitate] dignitate pontificali R.

[45] The most striking error peculiar to B¹ (and T) is the reordering of material which occurs on p. 171ff. On line 89, immediately after "dicit," B¹T advance to line 165: "fieri." On line 243, immediately after "predicandi," B¹T return to line 89: "Gregorius." On line 165, immediately after "nobiscum," B¹T advance to line 323: "dicit." On line 407, immediately after "quasi," B¹T return to line 243: "predicandi." On line 323, immediately after "duos," B¹T advance to line 408: "perfectioribus."

distinctive errors of its own, and this establishes the dependence of T on B[1]. A comparison of the two manuscripts through the first 43 pages of text (again including pp. 327-352) reveals only seven errors in B[1] which do not appear in T, and with the possible exception of the second one, all of these could quite easily have been corrected by the copyist of T:

2: 121 – synodus] sydonus B[1]
2: 222 – peccaverunt] peccaverint B[1]
2: 279 – quod] *add.* quod B[1]
2: 304 – actus] *add.* actus B[1]
2: 406 – nihil] nihi B[1]
Appendix A: 259 – meam] *om.* B[1]
2: 852 – potestatem iurisdictionis] potestatem potestatem iurisdictionem B[1]

Unfortunately, however, this is far from being the whole story. Of the five manuscripts descended from π, frequently R alone preserves the correct reading against the conjunctive error or errors of P[4]P[1]B[1]T. We have an example of this sort on p. 157, lines 1104-1105, where R and all the other manuscripts preserve what is undoubtedly the correct reading, "secundum intelligitur salvo primo, quia intelligitur dari salvo iure alterius," whereas the reading in P[4]P[1] is "secundum intelligitur dari salvo iure alterius," and the reading in B[1]T is "secundum intelligitur salvo iure alterius." Examples of this sort could easily be multiplied; conjunctive errors of P[4]P[1]B[1]T (but not R) are frequent occurrences. What they seem to indicate is that contamination has crept into R, contamination from some manuscript probably in the α Group, and more likely a manuscript descended from φ, the hyparchetype for StUBm[1]PrWBlV[4], than a manuscript descended from θ, the hyparchetype for OV[1]BoV[2]V[5]V[3]P[3]SvS.[46]

A similar point might be made about P[1], which at a few places shows a marked affinity with Va,[47] and even more about P[4]. Conjunctive errors of RP[1]B[1]T (but not P[4]) are frequent occurrences as well, for P[4] is a corrected

[46] Examples can be found suggesting each of these alternatives. Cf. **2**: 37 – predicatores] predicatione StUBm[1]PrWBlV[4], predicationes R; and **6**: 167 – recipiendi] retinendi OV[1]BoV[2]V[5]V[3]P[3]SvSR.

[47] Hence on p. 170, for example, both P[1] and Va insert several words, although not in precisely the same place. Cf. **3**: 58 – refertur] *add.* qui tamen non predicaverunt nisi de auctoritate Petri ovibus eis commissis, postquam factus est a Domino pastor eorum singulis et summus P[1]. Cf. line 68 – 8] *add.* nulli tamen discipuli immo nec apostoli predicaverunt nisi auctoritate Petri, omnibus sibi commissis, postquam factus est a Domino pastor eorum singularis et summus Va.

manuscript, and the corrections frequently obliterate the original reading. Some of these corrections were produced by scribal conjecture. On p. 160, line 1213, for example, P⁴ originally contained the reading "pro plenitudine" like RP¹B¹T, but this has been corrected to "per plenitudinem." Immediately thereafter, however, on lines 1213-1214, P⁴ has the same omission as P¹B¹T (but not R), one destructive of the sense. One would think that if the corrector of P⁴ were making systematic use of another exemplar, this error would have been corrected as well. But not all the corrections in P⁴ are to be explained in terms of the resourcefulness of the scribe. A study of the variants seems to indicate recourse to a second exemplar from the α Group, and more likely an exemplar descended from θ, the hyparchetype for OV¹BoV²V⁵V³P³SvS, than one descended from φ, the hyparchetype for StUBm¹PrWBlV⁴.[48]

Contamination in P⁴RP¹ would indicate that the stemma given above has to be treated with caution. But equally as noteworthy is the fact that, at several points throughout the treatise, questions arise about the relationship of P⁴RP¹B¹T and the Barbier edition. For example, in P⁴RB¹TBarb. the last part of article 5, that is lines 698-732 – "Minor ... caracteris," is found appended to article 6, that is at line 1447, immediately after "peccaret." In B¹TBarb. we have a case of repetition: the last part of article 5 is present in its proper location as well as at the end of article 6. In P⁴R the passage is found only at the end of article 6, although at the appropriate place in the fifth article R provides a marginal note indicating that the material in question should be inserted there. Because of missing folios, it is impossible to tell what P¹ contained or failed to contain in article 5. But unlike P⁴RB¹TBarb., P¹ ends appropriately at p. 299, line 1447, without making the mistake of repeating earlier material.

The most plausible explanation of this is provided by the following revised stemma:

[48] As in the case of R, examples can be found suggesting the latter alternative. Cf. **6**: 947 – patriarchali] parochiali StUBm¹PrWBlV⁴P⁴. However, the evidence for the former alternative is a little stronger. Cf. **5**: 235 – regis] regi OV¹BoV²V⁵V³P³SvSP⁴ [Here P⁴ has been corrected from *regis*]; **6**: 1078 – pro³] *add.* omnibus OV¹BoV²V⁵V³P³SvSP⁴; **6**: 1105 – episcopis] eis OV¹BoV²V⁵V³P³SvSP⁴; **6**: 1248 – institutus] constitutus OV¹BoV²V⁵V³P³SvSP⁴.

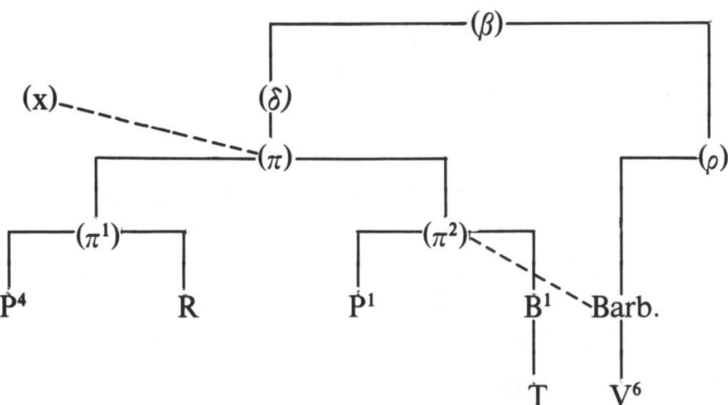

The hyparchetype for P[4]RP[1]B[1]T (π) was dependent upon an exemplar (δ) which omits the last part of article 5. This omission cannot be present in β, or the last part of article 5 would be omitted in ρ and σ as well, which is not the case. The copyist of π checked another exemplar (x), as yet unidentified, and appended the missing material to the end of the sixth article with a note that it should be inserted earlier. The copyist of π^1 repeated the note, as did the copyist of R after him, but the copyist of P[4] missed it, and so simply transferred the last part of article 5 to the end of article 6. The copyist of π^2 also properly appreciated the note which he read in π, and restored the last part of article 5 to its proper location. However, at the end of article 6 he repeated the material he had already inserted, and B[1]TBarb., all of which were dependent upon him at this point, repeated the error.

All of this is highly conjectural, but at least it provides an explanation. Moreover, the stemma on which it is based has the advantage of pointing out the contamination in the Barbier edition, which enables us to account for the frequent conjunctive errors of B[1]TBarb or P[1]B[1]TBarb.[49] It hypothesizes the existence of x which has not yet been identified. But this problem is clarified by a striking error which occurs at pp. 149-152, lines 901-984, where the words "in ... apostolis" are omitted in StUBm[1]Pr WBlV[4]P[2]V[7] as well as in P[4]RP[1]B[1]T. An error of this magnitude can only be explained in terms of their joint dependence on a common source, and that common source would be γ, the hyparchetype already discovered for StUBm[1]PrWBlV[4]P[2]V[7]. Having discovered γ, one might wonder about the need for hypothesizing the existence of δ. However, the example discussed in the preceding paragraph indicated that π must have been dependent on

[49] Cf. **5**: 99 – confirmare] *add.* quia papa non potest mutare naturam sacramentorum a Christo institutam [institutorum B[1]T] sicut [*om.* Barb.] patet exemplo apostolorum [*add.* c. confirmare B[1]T] B[1]TBarb. One can also find examples of conjunctive errors of P[1]B[1]TBarb., P[4]P[1]B[1]TBarb. and P[4]RP[1]B[1]TBarb.

two different exemplars, one of which omitted the last part of article 5, and one of which did not. γ cannot have made such an omission because it is not made in φ or ψ. β cannot have made it because it is not made in ρ or σ. δ is inserted between β and π because of the usual affinities of π with ρ and σ. β, therefore, or another source derived from β, would have been the source on which π was normally dependent.

There is one additional striking error which we must consider before this discussion can be brought to a close. On p. 149, line 901, immediately after "invenitur," $P^2V^7P^1B^1T$ attempt to solve the problem of the omission discussed in the last paragraph by inserting five lines. Examples of conjunctive errors in $P^2V^7P^1B^1T$ or $P^2V^7B^1T$ could easily be multiplied. A good example of the latter kind of error is the reordering of the material which, with their differences, $P^2V^7B^1T$ share on pp. 202-204. On line 446, immediately after "transtulit," $P^2V^7B^1T$ advance to line 477: "Ad hoc." On line 486, immediately after "eneo," P^2V^7 insert the words "dicendum est quod papa non potest transferre sedem Romanam nec alius purus homo," and then return to line 446: "Quod autem." B^1T postpone this move several lines. But then on line 500, immediately after "naturali," B^1T return to line 446: "Quod autem," omitting the words "Sed ... principi." The reordering is complete when on line 476, immediately after "Josephus," P^2V^7 advance to line 487: "Sine," while B^1T advance to line 501: "Secundo." Errors of this sort indicate that, in addition to the contamination in π discussed above, there is also contamination in ψ, requiring the following revisions to our stemma. In this stemma, as before, θ represents the hyparchetype for $OV^1BoV^2V^5V^3P^3SvS$, φ the hyparchetype for $StUBm^1PrWBlV^4$, ψ the hyparchetype for P^2V^7, π the hyparchetype for $P^4RP^1B^1T$, π^2 the hyparchetype for P^1B^1T, ρ the hyparchetype for $Bm^2BrSzBarb.V^6$, and σ the hyparchetype for SrVa. When it is expanded in accordance with the stemmata given earlier, the result is a final stemma outlining the major lines of filiation of the manuscripts.

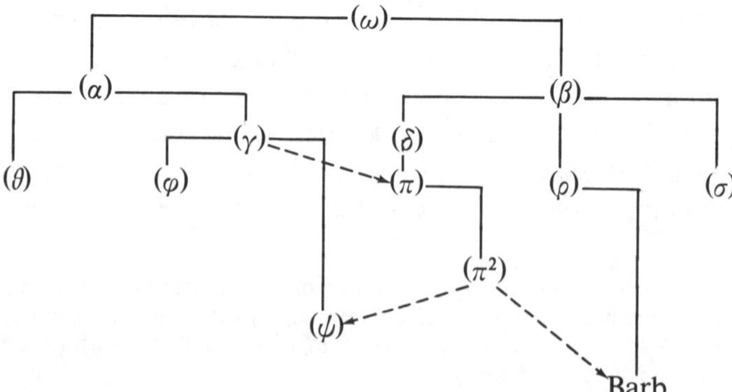

6

Principles Governing the Edition of the Text

The situation with which the stemma confronts us is a difficult one. We have already noted contamination in individual manuscripts, as well as the presence of variants in the hyparchetype θ. To complicate matters even further, variants were probably present in ω, and then again in α and β, for only the presence of variants quite early in the manuscript tradition could explain the mixing that sometimes occurs, the agreement, for example, of θ (OV^{1}BoV^{2}V^{5}V^{3}P^{3}SvS) with π (P^{4}RP^{1}B^{1}T) in some significant error against γ (StUBm^{1}PrWBlV^{4}P^{2}V^{7}), ρ (Bm^{2}BrSzBarb.V^{6}) and σ (SrVa).[1] But, despite the difficulties, the situation is not hopeless. In most cases it is still possible to reconstruct α and β, and where α and β agree we can be certain of the reading in the archetype. The most serious problems are encountered where α and β differ, and where there are no good reasons for preferring one reading to the other. The criterion I have used in such situations is that β should be followed because it contains fewer recognizable errors than does α, and although this criterion may be thought to need no justification, it can be put to a test. Indeed, the test, which is described below, functions as a check to everything done so far in two important ways. In addition to confirming our impression of the general preferability of β, it provides assurance that there is no "best" manuscript, or "best" group of manuscripts, which should have been followed consistently.

As was already noted, at several points in the *De causa* Guillaume copies extensively from the *Tractatus* of Pierre de la Palu, and, on one occasion at least, from *Quodlibet* v of Jean de Pouilly. Given the fact that Guillaume was copying, the text which we have produced following the method described above should be closer to the texts on which Guillaume was dependent than any text we could produce by adopting any other

[1] Cf., for example, **2**: 645 – Apostolis omnibus $\gamma\rho$Va] *inv.* $\theta\pi$; **2**: 1125 – agnati θ(-Bo) π (-B^{1})Va] cognati BoγB$^{1}\rho$; and **3**: 233 – dicitur $\varphi\rho$] *om.* $\theta\psi\pi$. For the key to the interpretation of these references see the discussion on the *apparatus criticus*, pp. 93-96.

procedure. Hence all the significant common passages were carefully compared. The premises behind this comparison were the following. First, it was assumed that these common passages could not be expected to be mirror images of one another. Allowances had to be made for the fact that we have no critical edition of the *Quodlibet*, and that the critical edition of the *Tractatus* which we do have is based upon the one extant manuscript. Hence the texts of the *Quodlibet* and the *Tractatus* used as our standards in this comparative exercise could be somewhat different in detail from the texts which Guillaume had available to him. Allowances also had to be made for the fact that at points Guillaume may have chosen to depart from the text before him; even though he was copying it, there undoubtedly were places where he chose to adopt his own phraseology rather than simply copy wholesale the text in front of him. However, if the procedure adopted for establishing the text of the *De causa* was the correct one, any reading which is present in the text which Guillaume was copying but which is not found in the *De causa* should receive either no support whatever from the manuscripts of the *De causa*, or only support which is scattered among various manuscripts.

To expand this a little further, if the readings in the *Tractatus* or *Quodlibet* not adopted in the *De causa* received no support in any of the manuscripts of the *De causa*, two explanations would be possible for each variation: (1) that the reading in the *Tractatus* or *Quodlibet* is peculiar to the particular manuscript of it in question, and hence was not the reading which Guillaume encountered; or (2) that Guillaume deliberately chose to depart from the text he was copying. Clearly, such cases would not cast doubt on the procedures used to establish the text of the *De causa* in the first place. Similarly, if the variations received support scattered among the various manuscripts of the *De causa*, again there would be two possible explanations for each variation: (1) that the reading in the *Tractatus* or *Quodlibet* is peculiar to the particular manuscript in question, but that individual copyists of the *De causa*, through the process of emendation or error, happened upon the same reading; or (2) that the reading in the *Tractatus* or *Quodlibet* is the one which Guillaume encountered, but that he modified the text he had before him, although subsequent copyists restored the original through their errors or emendations. As long as the support for the readings in the *Tractatus* or *Quodlibet* did not consistently come from any particular manuscript or manuscripts, there would be no reason for doubting the editorial procedure. If, however, the variations were to receive consistent support from some particular manuscript or manuscripts, this manuscript or group of manuscripts would be closer to what Guillaume was copying, and hence perhaps should have been followed for the purposes of establishing the text of the *De causa*.

Because of the limitations of space, not all of these common passages can be reproduced here: a few representative examples will have to suffice. In each case, however, the analysis supported the same conclusion. One of the common passages has already been supplied above (pp. 15-18). When the manuscripts of the *De causa* are consulted to see if any of them support the readings found in the *Tractatus* and not repeated in our edition of the *De causa*, one can produce the following short list:

> 9-10 sedem suam mutare $\psi\pi(\text{-P}^{1)}\sigma$ | 15 sedem specialem Bo | episcopalem] *om.* Bo | 42 illud $\alpha(\text{-P}^{2)}\rho^{2}$Sr | 50 illam $\varphi(\text{-}\varphi^{5})\rho^{1}$ | 58 etc. Sz | 62 sunt BoSvφ^{3}PrψB$^{1}\rho^{2}\sigma$ | 91 prefuit V^{7} | 96-97 apparet BoP^{2}BrVa | 99-100 suam sedem $\psi\pi(\text{-B}^{1})$Barb.Sr, suam suam Va | 106 etc.] *om.* $\theta^{2}\rho^{1}$.

Most of the readings peculiar to the *Tractatus* and not repeated in our edition of the *De causa* receive no support in the manuscripts of the *De causa* whatever. What support there is is scattered among a variety of manuscripts. The support for the reading "illud" on line 42 might suggest that we would have been wise to follow α at that point. This is a situation in which α and β provide equally possible readings, and we have chosen to follow β for the edition of the *De causa*, although the reading in α is closer to the text which Guillaume was copying. However, if we had followed α in such cases with the same consistency with which we have followed β, we would have produced a text much further removed from the text which Guillaume was copying. The following list makes this clear:

> 41 tollere legem domini sui] legem domini sui [*inv.* V^{2}] tollere α | 47 successor alius] *inv.* $\varphi\theta^{2}\theta^{3}$Va | 56 Dominus] *om.* α | 81 non potest etiam] etiam [*add.* a Petro θ^{4}] non potest [potuit θ^{4}] $\theta\varphi$ | 90 quando] *add.* populus $\theta\varphi$ | 91 profuit] fuit $\theta^{1}\varphi$.

Much the same conclusion emerges from a comparison of the *De causa* and the *Quodlibet* of Jean de Pouilly at the one point in the *De causa* where it is certain Guillaume is copying the *Quodlibet*.

De causa immediata ecclesiastice potestatis **6**: 292-380.	Jean de Pouilly, *Quodlibet V*, Biblioteca Apostolica Vaticana, MS Vat. lat. 1017, fols. 214r-215r.
Contra hoc autem arguunt alii sic dicentes. Scriptura sacra statum curatorum dicit esse institutum et ipsos a Christo. Quia accipio tanquam manifestum quod status *in quo est* potestas	*Sed sacra Scriptura* statum curatorum dicit esse institutum et ipsos a Christo. Quia accipio tanquam manifestum quod status *aut* potestas

et iurisdictio *continuatur* in diversis temporibus ab illo a quo fuit institutus a principio *cum institutus fuit*, et conservatur in omnibus temporibus sequentibus, et quod successor alicuius in aliqua dignitate, officio aut statu ab illo eodem instituitur in illo a quo antecessor institutus est, cum in eodem statu *succedat* quasi eadem persona cum illo, ut patet per inductionem in omnibus baillivis, prepositis, prioribus, magistris ordinum, et sic *de* aliis, alias successor nullomodo censeretur quasi eadem persona cum antecessore. Sed status et potestas *et iurisdictio* discipulorum septuaginta duorum *continuatur* in sacerdotibus *curatis*, sicut status apostolorum et potestas et iurisdictio in episcopis, et succedunt sacerdotes curati septuaginta duobus discipulis sicut episcopi succedunt apostolis. *Ergo* sequitur quod ab illo eodem a quo status discipulorum fuit *institutus* a principio modo est institutus *status curatorum*, et a quo fuerunt instituti *discipuli* sunt instituti curati, habentes auctoritatem et iurisdictionem ab illo eodem a quo et discipuli septuaginta duo.

Sed status *discipulorum* a Christo est institutus, et ipsi ab eo instituti et missi, potestatem ab ipso Christo immediate accipientes, non ab aliquo apostolorum, sicut nec alii apostoli a Petro. ... *Item* Matthei ultimo in fine, dicit Dominus in monte Galilee, parum ante ascensionem: "Euntes *ergo*, docete omnes gentes" – ecce eis dat officium predicandi – "baptizantes eos in nomine Patris, et Filii, et Spiritus Sancti" – ecce potestatem *baptizandi* dat eis. Marci ultimo: "Euntes in mundum universum, predicate Evangelium omni creature." Et sequitur post: "Illi *autem profecti predicaverunt*

et iurisdictio, *continuatus* in diversis temporibus, ab illo a quo fuit institutus a principio *est institutus* et conservatur *et continuatur* in omnibus temporibus sequentibus, et quod successor alicuius in aliqua dignitate, officio aut statu ab illo eodem instituitur in illo a quo *eius* antecessor institutus est, cum in eodem statu *succedit* quasi eadem persona cum illo, ut patet per inductionem in omnibus baillivis *et* prepositis, prioribus, magistris ordinum, et sic *in* aliis, alias successor nullomodo censeretur quasi eadem persona cum antecessore.

Sed status et potestas discipulorum septuaginta duorum *continuatus est* in sacerdotibus *creaturis, et* sicut status apostolorum et potestas et iurisdictio in episcopis, et succedunt sacerdotes curati septuaginta duobus discipulis sicut episcopi succedunt apostolis. ... *Igitur* sequitur quod ab illo eodem a quo status discipulorum fuit a principio modo est institutus, et a quo fuerunt instituti sunt instituti curati, habentes auctoritatem, *potestatem* et iurisdictionem ab illo eodem a quo et discipuli septuaginta duo.

Sed status *septuaginta duorum* a Christo est institutus, et ipsi ab eo instituti et missi, potestatem ab ipso Christo immediate accipientes, non ab aliquo apostolorum, sicut nec alii apostoli a Petro. ... *Et* Matthei ultimo in fine, dicit Dominus in monte Galilee, parum ante ascensionem: "Euntes *igitur*, docete omnes gentes" – ecce eis dat officium predicandi – "baptizantes eos in nomine Patris, et Filii, et Spiritus Sancti" – ecce *dat eis* potestatem. Dat eis Marci ultimo *dicentes*: "Euntes in mundum universum, predicate Evangelium omni creature." Et sequitur post: "Illi *perfecti autem predicarunt* ubique, Domino cooperante et sermonem confirmante sequentibus signis."

Dices quod ibi non fuerunt septuaginta duo *quando* hoc dixit apostolis. Immo fuerunt, et hoc negare videtur maxime hereticum et contra Scripturam que *alias salvari non potest*. Quia Actuum 2, quando reversi sunt de monte Oliveti unde *Christus ascendit*, dixit Petrus: "Oportet ex his viris qui nobiscum sunt congregati omni tempore quo intravit et exivit Dominus Jesus inter nos, incipiens a baptismate Joannis usque in diem qua assumptus est a nobis, testem resurrectionis eius nobiscum fieri unum ex istis." Et statuerunt duos, Joseph et *Mathiam, qui* fuerunt de *septuaginta duobus* discipulis. *Ergo* ipsi et alii discipuli fuerunt in ascensione Christi cum Christus iterato misit eos ad predicandum et baptizandum. Immo si debeat *illa* Scriptura verificari, oportet eos, scilicet septuaginta duos, fuisse semper cum Christo *sicut* et duodecim. *Ergo et apostoli* et discipuli omnes immediate *sunt a Christo* instituti, et ab *illo* acceperunt sine medio potestatem. Unde et Paulus, *2* ad Corinthios 10, dicit: "Nam et si amplius *aliquid gloriatus fuero* de potestate nostra quam dedit *nobis* Dominus," non alius. *Ergo nec Petrus. Item* Actuum 9: "Vas electionis" etc.

Et Actuum 13: "Segregate mihi *Paulum* et Barnabam ad opus ad quod assumpsi eos," et ad Galatas, in principio: "Paulus apostolus, non ab *homine* electus, neque per hominem, sed per Jesum Christum et Deum Patrem." Et pari ratione vel maiori alii apostoli quos immediate vocavit, ut Matthei 4: Petrum et Andream, Ja-

ubique, Domino cooperante et sermonem confirmante sequentibus signis."

Dices quod ibi non fuerunt septuaginta duo *quare* hoc dixit apostolis. Immo fuerunt, et hoc negare videtur maxime hereticum et contra *sacram* Scripturam que *aliter non potest salvari*. Quia Actuum 2, quando reversi sunt de monte Oliveti unde *ascendit Christus*, dixit Petrus: "Oportet ex his viris qui nobiscum sunt congregati omni tempore quo intravit et exivit Dominus Jesus *Christus* inter nos, incipiens a baptismate Joannis usque in diem qua assumptus est a nobis, testem resurrectionis eius nobiscum fieri unum ex istis." Et statuerunt duos, Joseph et *Mariam, et* fuerunt de discipulis. *Igitur* ipsi et alii discipuli fuerunt in ascensione Christi cum Christus iterato misit eos ad predicandum et *ad* baptizandum. Immo si debeat *ista* Scriptura verificari, oportet eos, scilicet septuaginta duos, fuisse semper cum Christo et duodecim. *Igitur* et discipuli omnes immediate *a Christo sunt* instituti, et ab *ipso* acceperunt sine medio potestatem. Unde et Paulus, *12* ad Corinthios 10, dicit: "Nam et si amplius *gloriatus fuero aliquid* de potestate nostra quam dedit Dominus," non alius. *In edificatione dedit*, Actuum 9: "Vas electionis etc., *mihi iste ut portet nomen meum*" etc.

Actuum 13: "Segregate mihi *Saulum* et Barnabam ad opus ad quod assumpsi eos," et ad Galatas, in principio: "Paulus apostolus, non ab *hominibus* electus, neque per hominem, sed per Jesum Christum et Deum Patrem." Et pari ratione vel maiori alii apostoli quos immediate vocavit, ut Matthei 4: Petrum et Andream, Jacobum et Joannem, filios Zebedei, et Matthei 9 et *Marci* 2: Mattheum. Et ad Galatas 2, super illo verbo: "Cum venisset Petrus Antiochiam, in *facie* restiti ei," Glossa: "Tanquam par, hoc enim non auderet nisi sciret *se non* imparem fore." Non *ergo* ab ipso *potestatem* habuit. *Ergo* a Christo.

Sequitur *ergo* quod status curatorum et ipsi sint a Deo immediate instituti, et ab ipso habent immediate potestatem. Status enim *istorum* et illorum non est alius et alius, sicut status isti non sunt alii quam *erant* ante centum annos. Sed est unus *status* continuatus *a Christo semper*, et potestas a *Christo* data illis continuata in istis. Quare enim potestas a Christo collata Petro continuata est in *summo* pontifice, et potestas collata aliis apostolis non est continuata in aliis episcopis, et potestas collata discipulis non est continuata in *curatis*, non potes dicere. Et ideo curati sunt *vere* ordinarii, habentes iurisdictionem ordinariam, non iure humano sibi *datam*, sed a Christo immediate, in prima institutione ecclesie, in qua hos duos ordines et solum instituit. Et non sunt vicarii episcoporum, sed Jesu Christi, ab ipso instituti, inferiores tamen et minores episcopis, nec ab *ipsis* possunt destitui nisi rationabili causa, sicut nec episcopi a papa, cum non sint eorum vicarii sed Christi. Item episcopi habent *inferiorem* potestatem a Deo immediate *sub papa*, *sed* non a papa.

Quia tunc, sede papali *vacante*, potestas in prelatis inferioribus periret, sicut sensus, absciso capite, deficiunt in ceteris membris. Et si ita esset, adhuc manifestius constat quod episcopus

cobum et Joannem, filios Zebedei, et Matthei 9 et *Matthei* 2: Mattheum. Et ad Galatas 2, super illo verbo: "Cum venisset Petrus Antiochiam, in *faciem* restiti ei," Glossa: "Tanquam par, hoc enim non auderet *facere* nisi sciret *non se* imparem fore." Non *igitur* ab ipso *in potestate* habuit. *Igitur* a Christo.

Sequitur *igitur* quod *status episcoporum et ipsi et* status curatorum et ipsi sint a Deo immediate instituti, et ab ipso habent immediate potestatem. Status enim *illorum* et illorum non est alius et alius, sicut status isti non sunt alii quam *essent* ante centum annos. Sed est unus *annus non* continuatus *in diversis personis*, et potestas a *toto* data illis continuata *est* in istis. Quare enim potestas a Christo collata Petro continuata est in *Romano* pontifice, et potestas collata aliis apostolis non est continuata in aliis episcopis, et potestas collata discipulis non est continuata in *creaturis*, non potes dicere. Et ideo curati sunt *veri* ordinarii, habentes iurisdictionem ordinariam, non *in* iure humano sibi *dandam*, sed a Christo immediate, in prima institutione ecclesie, in qua hos duos ordines et solum instituit. Et non sunt vicarii episcoporum, sed Jesu Christi, ab ipso instituti, inferiores tamen et minores episcopis, nec ab *episcopis* possunt destitui nisi rationabili causa, sicut nec episcopi a papa, cum non sint eorum vicarii sed Christi. Item episcopi habent *inferiores* potestatem a Deo immediate, *aut a propria persona*, non a papa.

Quia tunc, sede papali *beata*, potestas in prelatis inferioribus periret, sicut sensus, absciso capite, deficiunt in ceteris membris. Et si ita esset, adhuc manifestius constat quod episcopus ordinatus, tempore vacationis illius, et consecratus, nullam penitus haberet potestatem. Et cum illa vacatio possit durare multis annis, sequeretur quod potestas ecclesie totaliter periret, *quod* nepharium est dicere.

Consimiliter potest argui quod curati suam potestatem non habent nec a papa nec ab episcopis. *Ergo* etc. Ex quo patet quod nec papa a prelatis potest potestatem datam a Christo eis auferre et aliis non prelatis dare, nec statum ecclesie a Christo institutum destruere et immutare, cum sit ei data potestas in edificationem et non *in* destructionem, sicut et apostolo, 2 ad Corinthios 10. Et hoc pulchre dicit Urbanus papa, 25 q. 1 Sunt *quidam*:

"Inde novas leges condere *potest* unde evangeliste aliquid nequaquam dixerunt. Ubi vero *Dominus* vel eius apostoli et eos sequentes sancti patres *finaliter* aliquid diffinierunt, ibi nec novam legem Romanus pontifex dare *potest*, sed potius quod predicatum est usque ad animam et sanguinem confirmare debet. Si enim quod docuerunt apostoli et prophete, quod absit, destruere *niteretur*, non sententiam dare sed magis errare *convinceretur*."

ordinatus, tempore vacationis illius, et consecratus, nullam penitus haberet potestatem. Et cum illa vacatio possit durare multis annis, sequeretur quod potestas ecclesie totaliter periret, *quia* nepharium est dicere.

Consimiliter potest argui quod curati suam potestatem non habent nec a papa nec ab episcopis. *Igitur* etc. Ex quo patet quod nec papa a prelatis potest potestatem datam a Christo eis auferre et aliis non prelatis dare, nec statum ecclesie a Christo institutum destruere et immutare, cum sit ei data potestas in edificationem et non destructionem, sicut et apostolo, 2 ad Corinthios 10. Et hoc pulchre dicit Urbanus papa, 25 q. 1 *c.* Sunt *quidem, ubi sic dicit*: "*Sciendum vero sine operatione est quod*

inde novas leges condere *potuit* unde evangeliste aliquid nequaquam dixerunt. Ubi vero *dicunt* vel eius apostoli et eos sequentes sancti patres *sententialiter* aliquid diffinierunt, ibi nec novam legem Romanus pontifex dare *potuit*, sed potius quod predicatum est usque ad animam et sanguinem confirmare debet. Si enim quod docuerunt apostoli et prophete, quod absit, destruere *mitterentur*, non sententiam dare sed magis errare *convincerentur*."

Again, most of the readings peculiar to the *Quodlibet* and not repeated in the *De causa* receive no support in any of the manuscripts of the *De causa*, and such support as is provided is scattered among a variety of manuscripts:

4 sacra Scriptura StW | 16 succedit Sr | 18 et B^1Bm^1 | 31 institutus] *om.* Bo | 32 status] *om.* θ^2 | 33 discipuli] *om.* V^5 | 34 auctoritatem] potestatem $V^2\rho^2$ | 52 profecti] perfecti BoV^2V^3Va | 59 non potest salvari Bm^1 | 65 Christus P^3 | 70 Mariam Br | 74 ad U | 75 ista Va | 79-80 a Christo sunt instituti $Bo\rho^2$ | 83-84 gloriatus [glorificatus Bo] fuero aliquid $BoBm^1$ | 86-87 electionis] *add.* est iste mihi Bm^1, mihi iste [*om.* V^5] est [*inv.* Bo] θ | 99 Matthei UBm^1W | 102 faciem $\theta\varphi$(-V^4)B^1Barb. | 117 est θ(-V^2) |

122 creaturis φ^5 | 123 veri $\varphi(-\varphi^5)$ | 131 episcopis OW | 159 quidem OV^{2}StWV^{4}P^{4}B$^1\rho$(-Bm^2)Va | 166 sententialiter O

The support for "faciem" on line 102 might suggest that α should have been followed. Furthermore, there is one point in this common passage where we have preserved the agreement of the two texts only by deliberately choosing the α reading over the β reading. This occurs on line 99, where "et^2" is omitted in π(-P^1)ρ. However, in this situation α has been followed because it offers clearly the superior reading. If we had chosen to follow α where α and β offer readings equally plausible, the text of the *De causa* would have differed from the text of the *Quodlibet* in five additional places.

42-43 in fine dicit] dicit [*om.* V$^2\varphi^5$; dixit θ^2BoV^5, dicitur Sψ] in fine α | 95-96 alii apostoli] apostoli alii [aliqui V^2] α | 99 Mattheum] *om.* α | 156 et] *om.* α(-Bm^1)B^1 | 163 aliquid nequaquam] nequaquam aliquid [aliud S, aliqui V^2] α(-V^7).

There is one additional common passage which should be considered because of the rather peculiar results it yields.

De causa immediata ecclesiastice potestatis **4**: 177-229.

Ad secundum dicendum quod papa in nullo casu quamdiu est papa, propter quodcumque crimen, potest nec a concilio, nec a tota ecclesia, nec a toto mundo deponi, non solum quia est superior; sed quia est a Deo, qui sibi Romani presulis, quamdiu presul est, iudicium reservavit, 9 q. 3 Aliorum. Sed quando labitur in heresim, tunc eo ipso precisus est ab ecclesia et desinit esse caput, et tunc deponitur de facto, *non* de iure, quia "qui non credit iam iudicatus est," de iure scilicet. Hoc est autem iudicium, quia eo ipso quod hereticus est, ab ecclesia precisus est. Non potest autem caput a corpore precisum, quamdiu est *precisum*, caput *esse* illius corporis *a quo est precisum.* Unde papa per hoc desinit esse caput corporis *ecclesie*, quod ab illo prescinditur per heresim, *ipso facto, secundum*

Pierre de la Palu, *Tractatus de potestate papae* 1.3, pp. 195-196.

Est, autem, advertendum quod secundum communem opinionem papa non iudicatur, nec condemnatur aut deponitur, nisi pro heresi, 40 d., Si papa.

Et tunc *magis* deponitur de facto, *quam* de iure, quia "qui non credit iam iudicatus est," de iure, scilicet. Hoc est autem iudicium, quia eo ipso quod hereticus est ab ecclesia precisus est. Non potest, autem, *esse* caput a corpore precisum quamdiu est caput illius corporis; unde papa per hoc desinit esse caput *illius* corporis, quod ab illo prescinditur per heresim.

illud Deuteronomii 17: "Non poteris alterius gentis hominem super te facere regem." Unde hereticus non potest esse nec manere papa, quia extra ecclesiam non possunt haberi claves ecclesie. Per alia autem peccata est caput languidum, *quod* non propter hoc desinit esse caput, *nec potest a membris per consequens iudicari.* Quod ergo Marcellinus papa, qui idolatraverat, non *fuit* iudicatus *de facto*, sed dictum est ei: "Tu ipse iudica causam tuam," 21 d. Nunc autem, hoc est quia non erat hereticus, *quia* a fide nunquam deviaverat animo, sed metu tormentorum sacrificaverat idolis. *Item* falsa est glossa *in* predicto capitulo, Si papa, dicens quod de quocumque alio crimine notorio *papa*, si est *incorrigibilis*, potest accusari et amoveri, quia contumacia est heresis, et contumax dicitur infidelis. Quia hoc est *non proprie sed* solum metaphorice, sicut et simonia dicitur heresis. Et ideo quidquid agat papa quamdiu est papa, nunquam iudicari potest nec condemnari, *non propter hoc tantum*, quia nullus inferior potest iudicare superiorem quamdiu superior est, *de lege communi, ut arguitur De maioritate et obedientia c. Cum inferior, sed potissime propter hoc, quod papatus, qui non est ab homine, non potest ab homine iudicari.* Unde propter quodcumque crimen quo papa non desinit esse *papa, sicut est omne aliud preter heresim proprie dictam, papa ab homine* iudicari non potest. Sed reprehendi potest, sicut Paulus in *faciem* restitit Petro, quia reprehensibilis erat, ita quod in malis non est ei obediendum, sed resistendum. Unde si cogeret gentes judaizare, non vere quia

Per alia, autem, peccata est caput languidum, *quia* non propter hoc desinit esse caput.

Quod, ergo, Marcellinus papa, qui idolatraverat, non *sit* iudicatus, sed dictum est ei "Tu ipse iudica causam tuam," 21 d., Nunc autem, hoc est quia non erat hereticus, *cum non esset pertinax, immo penitebat et* a fide nunquam deviaverat animo, sed metu tormentorum sacrificaverat idolis. *Unde* falsa est glossa predicto capitulo Si papa, dicens quod de quocumque alio crimine notorio, si est <*incorruptibilis*>, potest accusari et amoveri, quia contumacia est heresis et contumax dicitur infidelis, quia hoc est solum metaphorice, sicut et simonia dicitur heresis. Et ideo, quidquid agat papa quamdiu est papa, nunquam iudicari potest, nec condemnari, quia nullus inferior potest iudicare superiorem, quamdiu superior est. *Nunquam, enim, inferior iudicat superiorem, sed e converso, De maioritate et obedientia, c. Cum inferior.*

Unde propter quodcumque crimen, quo papa non desinit esse, iudicari non potest; sed reprehendi potest, sicut Paulus in *facie* restitit Petro, quia reprehensibilis erat; ita quod in malis non est ei obediendum, sed *est* resistendum. Unde, si cogeret gentes iudaizare, non vere, quia tunc esset hereticus, sed simulatorie, *sicut Petrus faciebat ad Galatas 2*, resistendum esset.

Quid ergo fiet si *papa* sit ita malus moribus quod destruat ecclesiam Dei? *Respondeo*: duplex est remedium. Unum, quod dictum est, exemplo Pauli, quia in facie *est ei* resistendum, sicut etiam monachi, licet non possint abbatem suum deponere, non tamen tenentur ei in malis obedire, sed ei resistere quousque per superiorem remedium apponatur. Unde si papa vellet totum thesaurum ecclesie dare parentibus suis, aut ecclesiam sancti Petri destruere et facere palatium parentibus *suis, aut* eis dare patrimonium Petri, quod non licet, vel aliquid huiusmodi, non esset permittendum, sed esset ei resistendum *et* non obediendum, *sine tamen ipsius depositione*. Secundum remedium est exemplo beati Hylarii, qui contra Leonem papam prevaluit orando, quia orandum esset pro ipso a tota ecclesia, quod Deus ipsum corrigeret, vel *de medio* amoveret; nec unquam *Deus sic* ecclesiam suam despiceret quin eam exaudiret. Et esset contra eum concilium convocandum per cardinales, si ipse nollet *convocare*, ut per illud *moneretur*, vel Deus imploraretur, et remedium apponeretur in resistendo malis que vellet facere, ne ecclesia periclitaretur. Aliud est exemplum de hoc remedio, nam Anastasius papa periit scelere proprio et iustorum orationibus percussus, 19 d. Anastasius.

tunc esset hereticus, sed simulatorie, resistendum esset.

Quid, ergo, fiet si sit ita malus moribus quod destruat ecclesiam Dei. *Responsio*: Duplex est remedium. Unum, quod dictum est, exemplo Pauli, quia in facie *ei est* resistendum. Sicut etiam monachi, licet non possint abbatem suum deponere, non tamen tenentur ei in malis obedire, sed ei resistere quousque per superiorem remedium apponatur. Unde, si papa vellet totum thesaurum ecclesie dare parentibus suis, aut ecclesiam sancti Petri destruere et facere palatium parentibus, *et* eis dare patrimonium Petri, quod non licet, vel aliquid huiusmodi, non esset permittendum; sed esset ei resistendum, non obediendum.

Secundum remedium est exemplo beati Hylarii, qui contra Leonem papam prevaluit orando, quia orandum esset pro ipso a tota ecclesia quod Deus ipsum corrigeret vel amoveret, nec unquam *sic Deus* ecclesiam suam despiceret quin eam exaudiret. Et esset contra eum concilium convocandum per cardinales, si ipse nollet *se corrigere*, ut per illud <*moveretur*>, vel Deus imploraretur, et *quod* remedium apponeretur in resistendo malis, que vellet facere, ne ecclesia periclitaretur. – Aliud est exemplum de hoc remedio, nam Anastasius papa periit scelere proprio et iustorum orationibus percussus, 19 d., Anastasius.

Once again most of the readings peculiar to the *Tractatus* and not repeated in the *De causa* receive no support in the manuscripts of the *De causa*. But there is a difference in this case, for what is quite striking is the amount of support which is found in Va:

19 precisum^1] *add.* esse θ(-V^2) | precisum^2] *om.* θ | 20 esse] *om.* θ | 21 a quo est precisum] *om.* π^1Va | 24 ipso facto] *om.* Va | 32-33 nec ... iudicari] *om.* Va | 35 de facto] *om.* Va | 38-39 cum non esset pertinax immo penitebat immo Va | 42 Unde Va | 61-63 sicut ... homine] *om.* Va | 65 facie $\theta\psi\rho$ | 69 sicut ... ad Galatas 2] *om.* Va | 71 papa] *om.* Va | 75 ei est Bm^1 | 84 suis] *om.* Bm^{1}W | 87-88 sine ... depositione] *om.* $\varphi^3\rho^1$ | 93 de medio] *om.* Va | 94 sic Deus B^1 | 98 moveretur V^{5}V^{3}SBlρ^1.

This might suggest that Va is the most reliable of our manuscripts, the one to be followed whenever possible. However, although one can point to a number of occasions on which Va alone contains the precise reading to be found in the *Tractatus*, there are also many occasions on which Va departs from both the *Tractatus* and our edition of the *De causa*. In this same common passage we can produce the following list:

15 est^2] *om.* Va | 20 caput esse illius corporis] illius corporis esse caput Va | 23 quod] quia $\psi\sigma$ | 40-41 deviaverat] *add.* a fide Va | 46 et] ac Va | 48 est non proprie] proprie non est Va | 50 Et^2] *om.* Va | 51 agat] agit ρ^2Va | papa^1] *om.* Va | 64-65 in faciem restitit] restiti in faciem Va | 85 aliquid] aliud ρ^1Va | 86 permittendum] permittendus π(-P^1)Barb.Va | 91 ipso] eo Va.

Hence any attempt to rely on Va consistently would end in serious difficulties. The same might be said of the θ manuscripts (OV^{1}Bo V^{2}V^{5}V^{3}P^{3}SvS), which on occasion seem prominent in their agreement with the *Tractatus*, and of every other manuscript or sub-group of manuscripts. Clearly, there is no "best" manuscript or manuscripts on which we could have relied to reconstruct the text of the *De causa*. We could have chosen to follow α, but doing so with the same consistency with which we have followed β, that is, when there are no good grounds for preferring one to the other, would have produced in this passage as in the others considered above a number of additional differences between the *De causa* and the text we know the author of the *De causa* was copying:

17 hereticus est] *inv.* α | precisus est] *inv.* α(-St) | 30 alia] *om.* $\theta\varphi$ | autem peccata] peccata autem φ, peccatum autem θ | 52 iudicari potest] potest [*add.* amoveri V^3] iudicari α | 76-77 non possint abbatem suum] abbatem suum [*om.* φ] non possint [possunt θ^2BoV^{5}Sv, possent S] $\theta\varphi$.

Although this test seems to verify our editorial procedure, the case of Va discussed above does indicate the need for a certain amount of caution. One might be tempted to explain the curious parallelism between Va and the *Tractatus* noted above by suggesting that Va represents an early recension of the *De causa*, a version of the text in which Guillaume, at certain points at least, followed the *Tractatus* more closely than in his final version. On this assumption, the readings peculiar to Va are certainly quite significant. Alternatively, one might suggest that the copyist of Va had a copy of the *Tractatus* at his disposal, was aware of Guillaume's dependence on it, and so made some revisions in his copy of the *De causa* to bring it more into line with the *Tractatus*. This certainly is not probable, but it is at least possible. We do know that the copyist of Va was familiar with the work of Pierre de la Palu, since Va contains a number of Pierre's minor treatises in addition to the *De causa*. Hence among the other things which we know he had, the copyist of Va may very well have had a copy of the *Tractatus*. Furthermore, we know from the colophon that the copyist of Va thought that the *De causa* was written by Pierre. Hence the similarity of their subject matter could have led him to compare the two treatises, find at least some of the common passages, and make revisions in his copy of the *De causa*. If we could be certain that this was the case, the readings distinctive to Va would deserve no special consideration. But since this explanation is a simple hypothesis and no more, and not at all as probable as the first one considered above, we have to be prepared to admit the possibility at least that at various points (unfortunately impossible to determine) Va may be alone in preserving for us Guillaume's original text.

Our apparatus would be grossly overloaded if we were to record all the variants of Va. But there is one point at least where Va deserves serious consideration. At **2**: 635, immediately after "conclusionibus incidentalibus," most of our manuscripts continue with a long section beginning with the words: "Item confirmant aliqui istam opinionem quibusdam auctoritatibus dicentes sic...." Significantly, however, this section is missing in Bm²BrSzBarb.Sr, and although the copyist of Va does include it, he does so only with two important changes: a change in its position in relation to the rest of the text, and a significant change in the ordering of its parts. One might question whether this section should be considered an authentic part of the text of the *De causa* in the first place. If π has been governed by γ, then the only β-based manuscript we have attesting to its authenticity is Va. However, the authority of Va is probably sufficient to warrant the conclusion that this passage is indeed authentic; and this view is reinforced by the fact that the points which it raises are perfectly consistent with the general position adopted in the *De causa*, and in many respects a legitimate development of it. However, it is somewhat more difficult to decide (1) whether the passage should be included as part of the text at p. **2**: 636, or whether it should be transferred to the end and treated as an appendix as Va seems to suggest, and (2) whether the passage should be given the arrangement found in the majority of our manuscripts, or whether our choice should fall on the arrangement given in Va.

On the assumption that Va represents an early recension of the *De causa*, both these questions might be answered in Va's favour. Moreover, this could be done without doing violence to our stemma. If π has been governed by γ, and an error of omission has occurred in ρ, only σ is left to attest to what was present in β. The fact that Sr commits the same error of omission as ρ might seem surprising, but not if one supposes that the passage in question was originally an appendix. For Sr frequently functions as a précis, omitting large sections of the original text, and for the author of a précis an appendix would be a reasonable candidate for omission. Hence Va deserves serious consideration, for it is quite conceivable that Va alone reflects what was present in β.

A consideration of internal evidence is of some help here. With regard to the first of the problems mentioned above, the position of the passage, on a *prima facie* view at least not even the evidence of Va itself is unambiguous. At the end of **2**: 635 there is a sign in the text of Va which is repeated in the margin along with the following: "Require infra versus finem ad tale signum ... alias rationes." If we refer ahead to the end of the text as directed, at fol. 92r we find the section in question, although a significantly different version of the same, along with the sign used before and the following marginal comments: "Quere supra articulo secundo, de potestate apostolorum, conclusione vii, de potestate episcopali, ante obiectiones, ad tale signum folio xlvi ... circa principium." Given the fact that these marginal comments are not really clear and could be taken to mean that the material is to be inserted at **2**: 636, the agreement of all the other manuscripts containing this section might incline us to incorporate it into the text itself. However, at the end of **4**: 708 the same sign as encountered above is repeated in both the text and the margin with directions substantially the same. This would seem to indicate that, as far as Va is concerned, the additional material is to be treated as an appendix and not an integral part of the text. The nature of the additional material itself reinforces the testimony of Va: it has all the characteristics of an afterthought, which could appropriately enough be read in connection with the material in article 2, but which digresses too far from the second article, particularly in its handling of papal authority vis-à-vis the bishops, to be a part of it. Further, the evidence of the *Epilogus*, the annotated table of contents included in all of our manuscripts with the exception of $V^5V^7B^1TV^6$, is also significant at this juncture. Although the *Epilogus* lists all the principal points raised in the treatise, the points made in this section are not included in the list. For these reasons, therefore, I have decided to follow what appears to be the suggestion of Va, and regard this section as an appendix to the text (Appendix A) rather than an integral part of the text itself.

With regard to the second matter, there is once again a strong temptation to follow Va, although the lack of corroborating evidence would preclude a firm decision in Va's favour. Basically the purpose of the appendix is to list further arguments which could be given in support of the author's case, and to deal with objections which could be raised against it. The arrangement which is found in all the other manuscripts containing the appendix has the advantage of having the author deal immediately with objections after they are raised. The disadvantage is that there are some awkward transitions at those points where the author has finished his handling of some particular objection and wants to return to the task of listing arguments in his favour. This is particularly noticeable at Appendix A: 170, 263, 576, and 672. For the most part, the arrangement given in Va avoids these problems. In the Va arrangement the objections are allowed to accumulate while the principal arguments are being given, and then all are dealt with at once at the end. This leads to smoother reading, but at the expense of having the objections and the replies separated by several pages in many cases. Since the overwhelming number of manuscripts give the first form, and since there is no additional evidence to corroborate the testimony of Va on the matter, the first form should be given preference (Appendix A). But since Va alone is correct in not incorporating the appendix in the text, and since the arrangement in Va is not inferior but rather in some respects superior, Va has been given as well for comparative purposes (Appendix B).

7

The Two Apparatus

There are two kinds of apparatus for each page of text, an *apparatus fontium* which is self-explanatory and needs no further comment here, and an *apparatus criticus*. Given the number of manuscripts which have been used in the preparation of the present edition, a complete *apparatus criticus* would be out of the question. It would also be of doubtful utility, for the vast majority of the readings would be simple *lectiones singulares* which, by sheer force of numbers, would obscure the more important matters which the *apparatus* should draw to the reader's attention. Basically, the apparatus has been designed to serve two purposes: to illustrate the lines of filiation of the manuscripts, and to provide the reader with an alternative or alternatives when there is genuine doubt about the reading which should be adopted. Both of these purposes can be fulfilled, and the size of the *apparatus* kept within reasonable bounds, by suppressing (except for extensive omissions) variants peculiar to individual manuscripts, or variants scattered among unrelated manuscripts. Hence for the most part the *apparatus* notes only significant variants which were present in θ, φ, π, ρ, or σ, the readings of ψ being recorded only when there is dissent in one of the major manuscript families. More specifically, the *apparatus* records the agreement of all the manuscripts of any of the major groups when they agree in some significant error. It also records the dissent of any individual member of the group where it does not share the reading common to the others, unless the dissent is due to an omission of a few words or lines not otherwise worth recording. It does not record the fact that a manuscript unrelated to the group shares the same significant reading if it could easily have come to share the same reading by coincidental scribal error. However, if its agreement could not easily be explained as a simple coincidence, then it is recorded as a possible sign of contamination. The meaning of "significant" in this context will be clarified shortly; in what follows I shall describe in detail how the different manuscript families have been treated.

To describe first the major families descended from α, the *apparatus* records the variants of StUBm^{1}PrWBlV^4 where these manuscripts agree in significant readings against the other manuscripts. It also records the variants common to all but one or two of these manuscripts: Bm^{1}PrWBlV^{4} or StUBm^{1}PrW, for example. But a reading found only in StUBm^{1} is not recorded unless at least PrW (or BlV^{4}) possess a distinctive reading different from that found in StUBm^{1} on the one hand and BlV^{4} (or PrW) and the remaining manuscripts on the other. In that case the reading in PrW is recorded as well. Similarly a reading found in only PrWBlV^{4} is not recorded unless at least Bm^{1} (or StU) possesses a distinctive reading different from that found in PrWBlV^{4} on the one hand and StU (or Bm^{1}) and the remaining manuscripts on the other. The second major family of manuscripts descended from α has been handled in much the same way. The *apparatus* records the variants of OV^{1}BoV^{2}V^{5}V^{3}P^{3}SvS where these manuscripts agree in significant readings against the other manuscripts. It also records the variants common to all but one or two of these manuscripts: OV^{1}BoV^{2}V^{5}V^{3}P^{3} or OV^{1}BoV^{2}V^{5}SvS, for example. But readings found only in OV^{1}BoV^{2}V^{5} are not recorded unless at least V^{3}P^{3} (or SvS) possess a distinctive reading different from that found in OV^{1}BoV^{2}V^{5} on the one hand and SvS (or V^{3}P^{3}) and the remaining manuscripts on the other. Similarly a reading found only in BoV^{2}V^{5}V^{3}P^{3}SvS is not recorded unless at least O (or V^{1}) possesses a distinctive reading different from that found in BoV^{2}V^{5}V^{3}P^{3}SvS on the one hand and V^{1} (or O) and the remaining manuscripts on the other.

With regard to the manuscripts descended from β, I have noted significant variants common to SrVa, Bm^{2}BrSzBarb. or Bm^{2}BrSz. In the first case the agreement of both manuscripts has been necessary; in the last case I have noted instances of the agreement of two of the three manuscripts when the third has a reading different from all the other manuscripts. I have also noted the agreement of P^{4}RP^{1}B^{1}T as well as P^{4}RP^{1}. Since T is derived from B^{1}, the agreement of P^{4}RP^{1} represents the testimony of three of the four independent manuscripts of the family. Because of the dependence of T on B^{1}, the agreement of P^{1}B^{1}T, although it is a frequent occurrence, is not noted unless at least P^{4} (or R) possesses a distinctive reading different from that found in P^{1}B^{1}T on the one hand and R (or P^{4}) and the remaining manuscripts on the other. Although it represents a slight departure from the principle of dealing only with the major families, I have also noted the agreement of P^{2}V^{7}P^{1}B^{1}TBarb., P^{2}V^{7}B^{1}TBarb., P^{2}B^{1}TBarb., V^{7}B^{1}TBarb. or P^{1}B^{1}TBarb. because of the frequency of such combinations, and because of the light they cast on P^{2}, V^{7} and Barb. But the agreement of B^{1}TBarb., P^{2}B^{1}T, V^{7}B^{1}T and P^{2}V^{7}B^{1}T has been noted only in the most striking cases.

To include all the variant readings which meet these criteria would still leave an *apparatus* much too large to be useful. A second principle for reducing the *apparatus* needed to be established, and the principle chosen was that it should be restricted to what could reasonably be regarded as significant variations. Hence the *apparatus* does not record variations in the rubrics, the majority of which could be eliminated on grounds already discussed in any case, for the individual copyists seem to have taken considerable liberty in this regard. The rubrics adopted in the text (Primus Articulus, Prima Conclusio etc.) are simplified and standardized forms provided by the editor. Further, unless there is genuine doubt about the reading in the archetype, readings are not preserved if they fall into the following categories. The first category is that of simple errors in references: *Matthei* for *Marci*, for example. The second category is that of simple alternatives between (or among) which it is often difficult to distinguish in the manuscripts themselves: *ergo/igitur, dicit/dixit* (in quotations), *econtrario/econverso, huius/huiusmodi, responsio/respondeo* and *dicens/dicat/diceret* (when preceded by "quasi"). The third category is that of minor matters largely of a scribal nature: variations in the use of *etc.* at the end of quotations, variations in the use of *ad* in readings such as *ad Galatas* or *ad Titum*, minor variations in word order such as simple inversions, or minor variations in quotations of familiar passages, such as *Quorum remiseritis peccata/Quorum remiseritis*, where the words are used as a formula. The key phrase here is "unless there is genuine doubt about the reading found in the archetype." Hence, a simple inversion, such as *ecclesia Romana/Romana ecclesia*, is not noted even if shared by all the members of one of the major families. It is, however, if it is found in all the manuscripts descended from α.

The mechanics of the *apparatus criticus* are fairly straight-forward. Variants are recorded by line. Individual entries on the same line are separated by a single stroke (|). With the exception of fol. (fols.) for folio (folios), the abbreviations used are those recommended by Dondaine,[1] and they are given above at pp. xx-xxii. A lemma is provided unless there could be no possible confusion about the word or words on which the variant reading occurs, and it is set apart from the list of variants by a single squared bracket (]). A squared bracket has been preferred to a colon because of its greater visibility. The choice between a positive and a

[1] A. Dondaine, "Abréviations latines et signes recommandés pour l'apparat critique des éditions de textes médiévaux," *Société internationale pour l'étude de la philosophie médiévale*, 2 (1960): 142-149.

negative rendering of the variants has been determined by the exigencies of each case. If the reading adopted in the text is thought to have sufficient authority to place it beyond doubt, the manuscripts attesting to it are left to be understood, and the entry takes the following form: Romana] Rome φ. This should not be taken to mean, however, that every other manuscript apart from StUBm^{1}PrWBlV^4 agrees in the reading "Romana," for there may be scattered *lectiones singulares* not worth preservation. If the reading adopted in the text is uncertain, the manuscripts attesting to the reading are specified in the following manner: Romana π] *om.* θρσ; Rome φ. Enclosed square brackets contain information about the dissent of individual manuscripts, and the point of reference is always the immediately preceding word unless the entry itself clearly specifies otherwise. For example:

> 22 ecclesia apostolica Romana] Rome ecclesia [*inv.* U] apostolica [*om.* St] φ(-Bm^1).

This means that at line 22, where the text reads "ecclesia apostolica Romana," the reading "Rome ecclesia apostolica" is found in PrWBlV^4, the reading "ecclesia Rome apostolica" is found in U, and the reading "Rome ecclesia" is found in St. Bm^1 dissents from the other members of the group in giving the same reading as adopted in the text. The entry "*inv.* U" clearly refers to the two preceding words; the entry "*om.* St" refers only to "apostolica," the word immediately preceding. If St omitted the entire phrase, the entry would take the form: ecclesia apostolica Romana] *om.* St; Rome ecclesia [*inv.* U] apostolica φ(-StBm^1).

The most complex kind of entry found in the *apparatus criticus* takes the following form:

> 22 ecclesia apostolica Romana] *om.* θ; Rome ecclesia [*inv.* U] apostolica [*om.* St] φ(-Bm^1); *add.* Petri ψ, Petri apostoli π.

This means that at line 22, where the text reads "ecclesia apostolica Romana," the φ manuscripts (StUBm^{1}PrWBlV^4) give the same readings as in the preceding example; the θ manuscripts (OV^{1}BoV^{2}V^{5}V^{3}P^{3}SvS) omit the entire phrase; the ψ manuscripts (P^{2}V^7) add the word "Petri," to give the reading: "ecclesia apostolica Romana Petri"; and the π manuscripts (P^{4}RP^{1}B^{1}T) add the words "Petri apostoli," to give the reading: "ecclesia apostolica Romana Petri apostoli."

8

Orthography, Capitalization and Punctuation in the Present Edition

To a large extent, questions concerning orthography, capitalization and punctuation have been answered in terms of the personal decision of the editor. The spelling of proper names has been regularized. Hence *Hieronymus* is preferred to *Ieronimus, Chrysostomus* to *Crisostomus, Cyrillus* to *Cirillus* and *Jesus* to *Ihesus*. With regard to spelling in general, the manuscripts display a considerable variety. Hence, to provide some consistency, the spelling found in the classical Latin dictionary of Lewis and Short has been adopted, unless there is a clear consensus in the manuscripts for an alternative form. Because such consensus is frequently present, many of the most prominent features of typical medieval orthography have been retained: *pre-* rather than *prae-* in words such as *preferre*, for example, and *e* rather than *ae* in words such as *hec*. *Im-* has been retained in words such as *immediate* even though many manuscripts prefer *in-*, for in most of the manuscripts the initial *im-* or *in-* is abbreviated in such a way as would allow it to be expanded in either fashion. Because the sense demands it, I have also retained the distinction between *concilium* and *consilium*, equivalent to the distinction in English between "council" and "counsel," even though the manuscripts show no consistency in this regard.

The system of capitalization has been decided in terms of the editor's preference as well. Proper names and the books of the Bible are capitalized, but most other words are rendered in lower case letters. The only exceptions, which require no explanation, are *Evangelium, Scriptura, Deus,* and other words referring to the Deity (such as, depending on the context, *Filius* and *Dominus*). In titles to Latin works only the first word and proper nouns are capitalized, unless the title also contains the title of another work, in which case its first word is also capitalized. The punctuation has been determined by the exigencies of the text itself. Some of the longer, more convoluted sentences have been separated into two or more sentences, or broken down by means of parentheses or dashes, to enhance readability.

9

The Edition of 1506 and the Present Edition

Hitherto the only edition of the *De causa* available to scholars has been the relatively rare edition of Jean Barbier, published in Paris in 1506.[1] Fournier mentions a second edition of 1647,[2] and Laurent mentions an edition which was published in Salamanca in 1552,[3] but I have not been able to verify either of these references.[4] The volume in which the Barbier edition appears begins with the words "In hoc volumine continentur," and then provides a list of contents. In addition to the *De causa* it contains Durandus de S. Porciano, *De iurisdictione ecclesiastica*; a *Tractatus de legibus* attributed to Durandus de S. Porciano but which is not his; Pierre de la Palu, *Circa materiam confessionum*; John of Paris, *Tractatus de potestate regia et papali*; Herveus Natalis, *Tractatus de potestate pape*; and the anonymous *Rex pacificus*. The *De causa* appears on fols. 25r-81r, although the folios are unnumbered throughout the volume.

[1] See the description in B. Moreau, *Inventaire chronologique des éditions parisiennes du* XVI*e siècle* 1 (Paris, 1972), p. 191, no. 57; and in P. Renouard, *Imprimeurs et libraires parisiens du xvi*e *siècle* 3 (Paris, 1979), pp. 76-77, no. 93. Moreau lists the following locations: Amiens, Bibliothèque municipale; Cambrai, Bibliothèque municipale; Cambridge, University Library; Cologne, Universitäts- und Stadtbibliothek; Deventer, Stadsen Athenaeumbibliothek; Durham, University Cosin's Library; Evora, Biblioteca publica (incomplete); León, Real Colegiata San Isidoro; London, British Library (2 copies, 1 incomplete); Oxford, Bodleian Library; Paris, Bibliothèque nationale (2 copies), Bibliothèque de l'Arsenal, Bibliothèque Sainte-Geneviève (incomplete), Bibliothèque de la Faculté des lettres et de la Faculté des sciences (Sorbonne) (incomplete); Poitiers, Bibliothèque municipale; Seville, Biblioteca Colombina. To this list should be added the Biblioteca Apostolica Vaticana.

[2] P. Fournier, "Pierre de la Palu, théologien et canoniste," *Histoire littéraire de la France*, 37 (1938): 65 n. 1.

[3] M.-H. Laurent, "Le testament et la succession du cardinal dominicain Guillaume de Pierre Godin (1260-1336)," *Archivum Fratrum Praedicatorum*, 2 (1932): 228 n. 90.

[4] Sr Justo García Morales, of the Centro Nacional del Tesoro Documental y Bibliográfico in Madrid, informs me that he and his colleagues have no knowledge of a Salamanca edition of the *De causa*. There was, however, a Salamanca edition of Pierre de la Palu's commentary on the fourth book of the *Sentences*, and this edition was published in 1552. Laurent's reference to a Salamanca edition of the *De causa* appearing in the same year may have been the product of multiple confusion which arose originally because of the attribution of the *De causa* to Pierre.

Inc.: "Tractatus fratris Petri de Palude ordinis predicatorum de causa immediata ecclesiastice potestatis. / Circa potestatem...." *Expl.*: "Hec autem omnia.... / Finit tractatus reverendi domini fratris Petri de Palude, patriarche Ierosolimitani, ordinis fratrum predicatorum, de causa immediata ecclesiastice potestatis. Impressus Parisius per Iohannem Barbier impressorem pro Iohanne Petit librario commorante in vico sancti Iacobi sub intersignio Leonis Argenti. Anno nostre salutis M.CCCCC.VI."[5]

As was noted earlier, the Barbier edition shows marked affinities with Bm²BrSz on the one hand and P⁴RP¹B¹T, especially P¹B¹T, on the other. Both of these groups of manuscripts are descended from β, and since it is the β tradition which has been followed in the present edition, the differences between the Barbier edition and the present edition are not as marked as they otherwise might have been. However, the differences are still quite considerable, for unlike the Barbier edition, the present edition has been based on a collation and analysis of all the extant manuscripts.

To anyone who has worked with the Barbier edition its defects are obvious, for there are places where, because of *lacunae* or corruptions of various sorts, it is barely readable. Its single most serious defect is its omission of the material which in the present edition is located in Appendix A. In what follows I have listed only the differences between the Barbier edition and the present edition which appear in article one. Since there are 119 such differences, an average of over ten per page, it is believed that the present edition is significantly different and, I would hope, a marked improvement as well.

1: 2 – apostoli] *om.* Barb. | sunt] *add.* vidende Barb.
1: 3 – prelatione] potestate Barb.
1: 15-20 – Ego ... illud] *om.* Barb.
1: 23-24 – intelligendum est] intelligitur Barb.
1: 29 – exprobrat] exprobat Barb.
1: 33 – donatus] dotatus Barb.
1: 34 – quod] quia Barb. | novo] *add.* testamento Barb.
1: 37 – recipit] recepit Barb. | nec] et Barb.
1: 40 – inter] super Barb.

[5] On Jean Barbier and Jean Petit see P. Renouard, *Répertoire des imprimeurs parisiens* (Paris, 1965), pp. 19-20, 339-341; and *Imprimeurs et libraires parisiens* 3, pp. 55-59. Although as a matter of convenience I have consistently referred to the Barbier edition, and have even referred to Barbier as editor in the Bibliography and in the List of Abbreviations and Symbols, whether Barbier's role was that of an editor in any precise sense of the term is another question. As the colophon quoted above indicates, Barbier was the printer acting on behalf of the book-seller, Jean Petit. Renouard and Moreau both seem to regard Philippe Grivel as the editor of the entire volume, although the evidence for this is unclear.

1: 41 – Verum] unde Barb.
1: 44 – dicens] diceretur Barb.
1: 47 – non imparem] non nuperem Barb.
1: 58 – eius] *om.* Barb.
1: 59 – Sed] solutio Barb.
1: 60 – sibi] *om.* Barb.
1: 64 – et] *om.* Barb.
1: 66 – inquietari] inquietate Barb.
1: 68 – quia] *om.* Barb.
1: 70 – curiam] curam Barb.
1: 76 – dissidentibus] dissidenentibus Barb. | uni] *om.* Barb.
1: 82 – Quod] quia Barb.
1: 83 – 7] 9 Barb.
1: 84 – te] est Barb.
1: 85 – constituit] *om.* Barb.
1: 87 – eius] suis Barb. | beatissimus] *add.* Petrus Barb.
1: 88 – accepit] acceperit Barb.
1: 91 – dicit sic] *inv.* Barb.
1: 92 – Jesu Domino] *inv.* Barb.
1: 93 – 22] *add.* et Barb.
1: 94 – Theophylus] Crisostomus Barb.
1: 98 – econtrario] econverso Barb.
1: 102 – movent] movet Barb. | illuc] illud Barb.
1: 104 – pro ... ire] illud ire pro salute populi Barb.
1: 105 – primatum] *om.* Barb.
1: 106 – ecclesiam] *add.* primatum Barb. | habuit] habuerit Barb.
1: 107 – 21 d.] *inv.* Barb. | novo] nono Barb.
1: 110 – acceptante] acceperunt Barb.
1: 113 – Petro tamen] *inv.* Barb.
1: 114 – iidem] idem Barb.
1: 115 – quod est] idest Barb.
1: 118 – habuit] haburit Barb.
1: 120 – thesaurarios] thesauros Barb.
1: 125 – thesaurarium] thesaurarimum Barb.
1: 130 – dominus] *om.* Barb.
1: 132 – autem] *om.* Barb.
1: 134 – Bulgarorum] Burgarorum Barb. | pertractans] practicans Barb.
1: 135 – Ter te] certe Barb.
1: 136 – timidus] tremidus Barb.
1: 138 – tunc] nunc Barb.
1: 140 – confirmo] *add.* idest do Barb.
1: 141 – invicem] *om.* Barb. | dissidendo] dividendo Barb.
1: 144 – alii] alteri Barb.
1: 146 – singulariter] *om.* Barb. | collata] *add.* singulariter Barb.
1: 147-148 – Quemadmodum] quomodo Barb.

1: 151 – reservantur] *add.* extra Barb.
1: 152 – accepit] acceperit Barb.
1: 153 – iurisdictione] *add.* dicit Barb.
1: 157 – immo] ideo Barb.
1: 159 – rete] rethete Barb.
1: 164 – trahenda] trahanda Barb.
1: 167 – principalis] de potestate episcopali et Barb.
1: 168 – episcopalem] *add.* et Barb. | factus et] est Barb.
1: 172 – prevalebunt] prevalebant Barb.
1: 175 – propagatio naturaliter] *inv.* Barb.
1: 178 – poterat] poterant Barb. | ecclesiastica sacramenta] *inv.* Barb.
1: 181 – Luce 24] Joannis 20 Barb.
1: 182 – et qui] unde Barb.
1: 183 – cathalogo] *add.* sanctorum Barb.
1: 185 – esse] *om.* Barb.
1: 188 – illud] ipsum Barb. | commissum] ipsum Barb.
1: 189 – explicari] expleri Barb. | iurisdictione omnium iudicum] Iure. do. Barb.
1: 191 – sacramentum] sacramenta Barb. | sed] *om.* Barb.
1: 192 – alias] alios Barb.
1: 193 – officium] effectum Barb.
1: 201 – sed] *om.* Barb.
1: 203 – absentant] obsentant Barb.
1: 206 – Que] hec Barb.
1: 207-208 – fieri aliorum principem] principem fieri Barb.
1: 209 – ipse] *om.* Barb.
1: 210 – querente] attestante Barb.
1: 211 – Consideremus] Considerandum nobis est Barb. | Deus] *add.* omnipotens Barb.
1: 212 – se] seipsum Barb.
1: 213 – respondente] respondet Barb.
1: 217 – Tradite] credite Barb.
1: 223 – potestas] potentia Barb.
1: 224 – sacramentum eucharistie] *inv.* Barb.
1: 226 – que] quo Barb.
1: 231 – idest] *om.* Barb.
1: 233 – 21 d.] *om.* Barb. | Ipsi] Christi Barb. | datus] *add.* Petro Barb.
1: 235 – dari] *om.* Barb.
1: 235-236 – et bene] *om.* Barb.
1: 238 – temporis] operis Barb.
1: 238-239 – tu ... dicens] *hom.* Barb.
1: 242 – Mirentur] *add.* in hac causa Barb. | Dominum] *add.* nostrum Barb.
1: 243 – posuit] apposuit Barb.
1: 246 – factus est] *inv.* Barb.
1: 249 – firmamentum] fundamentum Barb.
1: 260 – summus] *om.* Barb. | suus] avi Barb.

Tractatus de causa immediata ecclesiastice potestatis

Circa potestatem a Christo collatam prelatis ecclesie sex per ordinem sunt videnda. Primo de potestate Petri. Secundo de potestate apostolorum. Tertio de potestate discipulorum. Quarto de potestate pape. Quinto de potestate episcoporum. Sexto de potestate curatorum.

Primus Articulus

Quantum ad primum, circa potestatem Petri apostoli singularem, sunt quinque conclusiones principales. Prima de prelatione Petri super alios apostolos. Secunda de preeminentia eius super totam ecclesiam. Tertia de plenitudine potestatis Petri. Quarta de dignitate episcopali ipsius. Quinta de tempore collationis istorum.

Prima Conclusio

Prima conclusio est quod Petrus a Christo habuit potestatem super omnes apostolos tanquam princeps et prelatus eorum, quod patet sic. Quia sicut paterfamilias aliis filiis aliquem unum quasi primogenitum preponit, quem facit heredem universalem, alios vero heredes particulares sub illo, sicut Genesis 27, Jacob, cui dedit primogenita, dixit Isaac: *Esto dominus fratrum tuorum*, sic Christus, qui dixit apostolis: *Omnes vos fratres estis*, Matthei 23, unum de apostolis, scilicet Petrum, quasi primogenitum aliis preponere voluit. Unde dicit Cyrillus super illud Luce 22: "Ego rogavi pro te, ut non deficiat fides tua": *Omissis ceteris, venit ad Petrum ceteris prelatum*. Item Augustinus, *De verbis Domini*, tractans illud Matthei 14: "Petrus ambulabat super aquas": *Primo apostolo, idest Petro, in ordine apostolorum firmo et precipuo, in quo figurabatur ecclesia* etc. Item Cyrillus, super illud: "Et tu aliquando conversus confirma fratres tuos":

desunt B^2V^6

2 de potestate $\theta\psi\pi^2$ | apostoli] *om.* ρSr | singulari $\theta\psi\pi^2$ | 4 preeminentia eius $\psi\pi^2$Barb.Va] primaria eius [prima via eius O] prelatione θ, primaria quod Petrus habuit potestatem a Christo φ^3, primaria eius potestate Bm^1, primaria potestate eius Pr, primaria eius W, primatia eius $\varphi^4\pi^1$, potestate eius Bm^2, primatu eius Sr | 5 ipsius] *om.* θ(-O)ψ; eius φ | 8 conclusio est] *om.* γ(-V^4) | habuit a Christo potestatem φ, habuit [habet O] potestatem θ, a Christo positus est ψ | 12 dedit] *add.* Deus $\psi\pi^2$ | 15 super illud] *om.* ρ^1 | 15-20 Ego ... illud] *om.* ρVa | 15-16 Ego ... te] Petre [*add.* ego P^3] pro te rogavi θ | 17 14] *add.* quod φ | 18 aquas] *add.* dicit [dixit P^1] π(-P^4)

12-13 Gen. 27:29 | 13-14 Matt. 23:8 | 15-17 *Cat. aur. in Luc.* 22.9, 2:289B (2:316A) | 15-16 Luc. 22:32 | 17-19 *Cat. aur. in Matt.* 14.5, 1:235A (1:255A) | 17-18 Matt. 14:29 | 20-25 *Cat. aur. in Luc.* 22.9 (Theophylactus), 2:289B (2:316A) | 20 Luc. 22:32

Quasi dicens: postquam me negato ploraveris et sic penitueris, corrobora ceteros, cum te principem apostolorum deputaverim. Hoc enim decet te qui mecum robur es et petra ecclesie. Unde sequitur: *Hoc autem intelligendum est non solum de apostolis qui tunc erant, ut roborarentur a Petro, sed de omnibus qui usque ad finem mundi futuri sunt fidelibus.* Item super illud Joannis 21: *Pasce agnos meos*, dicit Chrysostomus: *Eximius enim apostolorum erat Petrus, et os discipulorum, et vertex collegii. Unde et negatione deleta, committit ei prelationem fratrum. Et negationem quidem ei non exprobrat, sed dicit: Si diligis me, preside fratribus.* Item Petrus pre ceteris a Christo accepit claves. Unde super illud Matthei 16: *Tibi dabo claves regni celorum*, dicit Rabanus: *Qui enim regem celorum maiori pre ceteris devotione confessus est, merito pre ceteris collatis clavibus regni celestis donatus est.*

Contra tripliciter, primo quod omnes fuerunt pares. Unde 21 d. *In novo* dicitur: *Ceteri apostoli cum eodem*, scilicet Petro, *pari consortio honorem et potestatem acceperunt.* Solutio: verum est de potestate ordinis, sacerdotalis primo et episcopalis tandem, que non recipit magis nec minus. Sed non est verum de potestate iurisdictionis.

Secundo, quod saltem Petrus et Paulus fuerunt equales, Ambrosius, 2 q. 7: *Beati Petrus et Paulus eminent inter apostolos universos, et peculiari quadam prerogativa precellunt. Verum inter eos quis cui preponatur incertum est. Puto enim illos equales esse meritis qui equales sunt in passione* etc. Sed ad hoc respondetur per hoc quod dicit "meritis," quasi dicens prelatione impares. Sed sicut etiam dicit Gregorius in fine primi *Dialogi*: *meritis specialiter martirii pares.* Unde eadem questione *Paulus* dicit Hieronymus: *Paulus Petrum reprehendit, quod non auderet nisi se non imparem sciret*, ubi subiungit Gratianus: *Hoc non de officio*

desunt B²V⁶

22 te²] *om.* α | 23 Unde] ubi φ | 25 qui] *om.* φ | ad] in φ | illud] *om.* θ(-Bo) | 30 a Christo] *om.* α | a ... claves ρσ] accepit a Christo claves π | 31-32 maiori pre ceteris] manifesta ρ¹ | 32 devotione] *add.* ceteris ρ¹ | merito] *add.* illis Bm², illi BrSz | 33 dotatus φV⁷Barb. | 34 primo] *add.* videtur θ | quia ρ | novo] *add.* testamento π²Barb.Sr | 37 nec] et V⁷π²ρ | 39-40 fuerunt ... Paulus] *hom.* ρ¹ | 40 Beatus θ(-Bo) | inter] super ρ | peculiari] speciali ψπ² | 41 preexcellunt [excellunt OS] θ(-Bo) | Verum] unde ρ | 42 meritis [meriti S] esse α | 44 Sed sicut] et [*om.* Bo] sic θ | Isidorus θψπ | 45 eadem questione] 2 q. 7 π(-R)

25-62 Item ... Sacrosancta: cf. Pierre de la Palu, *Tractatus de potestate papae* 1.3, pp. 185-186 | 25-29 *Cat. aur. in Joan.* 21.3, 2:590A (2:646B) | 25-26 Joan. 21:15-16 | 30-33 *Cat. aur. in Matt.* 16.3, 1:252B (1:273B) | 30-31 Matt. 16:19 | 34-36 Gratian, D.21 c.2 | 39-43 Gratian, C.2 q.7 c.37 | 44-45 Cf. Gregory the Great, *Dialogorum libri quattuor* 1.12 (PL 77:213-216), ed. U. Moricca (Rome, 1924), p. 70 | 45-49 Gratian, C.2 q.7 c.33

ecclesiastice dignitatis, sed de puritate vite et sanctitate conversationis intelligitur. Solus enim Petrus inter apostolos primatum gerebat. Unde Augustinus, eadem questione c. *Puto, quod sine ulla sui contumelia Cyprianus episcopus Petro apostolo comparatur quantum attinet ad martyrii coronam. Ceterum magis vereri debeo, ne in Petrum contumeliosus existam. Quis enim nesciat ipsum apostolatus principatum cuilibet episcopatui preferendum ? Sed etsi distat cathedrarum gratia, una tamen est martyrum gloria.*

Sed contra hoc est stilus curie Romane in indulgentiis, in quibus ostenditur illorum paritas per hec et similia verba: De beatorum Petri et Pauli apostolorum eius auctoritate confisi, centum dies de iniunctis penitentiis relaxamus. Sed dicendum quod solus Petrus fuit superior, et omnes alii sibi subditi, etiam Paulus. Sed ideo in gestis papalibus Paulus Petro coniungitur quia urbem suo martyrio consecrarunt, et in passione socii fuerunt, 22 d. *Sacrosancta.*

Tertio videtur de Jacobo quod fuerit maior Petro, quia ille qui iudicat inter omnes videtur maior et prelatus. Sed Jacobus tulit sententiam in questione legalium, Actuum 15, Petro et Paulo allegantibus, dicens: *Ego iudico non inquietari eos qui ex gentibus convertuntur.* Solutio: Jacobus iudicavit, non tanquam iudex omnium, sed tanquam iudex illius loci specialis, non quin Petrus potuisset iudicare si voluisset, sed quia voluit illi deferre in loco suo. Sicut papa, quando est in civitate alia, non aufert propter hoc officialem nec curiam episcopo illius civitatis, sed de his que ibi emergunt ei iudicium dimittit.

desunt B^2V^6

50 eadem questione] q. 2 [ibidem 2 q. 7 Bo, q. 21 V^5] θ| sui] *om.* $V^1Bo\psi\pi^2$Barb.; sua θ(-V^1Bo)φ | 51 attinet B^1Barb.σ] *om.* P^4P^1; obtinet [optet O, legitur P^3] αR, pertinet ρ^1 | 52 Ceteris $\psi\pi$(-P^4), In ceteris θ(-Bo)| 53 ipsum] Romani [*om.* φ^5; illum Romani U] α; *add.* Romani π^2 | 55 est] *om.* ρ^1 | martyrii $\psi\pi^2\sigma$ | 57 et[1]] etiam φ(-Pr) | 58 eius] *om.* πBarb. | iniunctis] *om.* α(-Bo)π | 59 penitentiis] indulgentiis θ(-Bo) | 60 Sed] et $\theta\psi\rho^1$ | papalibus] specialibus [spiritualibus Bo] α(-θ^4)R | 61 consecravit ρ^1 | 64 prelatus] *add.* aliorum θ | 68 quin Petrus] quia [quando V^7] Petrus non [*om.* V^3S] α | 69 aliqua $\psi B^1\rho^1$ | 70 his] eis π | 71 ei] *om.* $\psi\pi$ | dimittit] *add.* eis π

50-55 Gratian, C.2 q.7 c.35 | 62 Gratian, D.22 c.2 | 65-66 Act. 15:19

Secunda Conclusio

Secunda conclusio principalis est quod Petrus a Christo habuit prelationem super totam ecclesiam universalem. Quia in uno corpore non debent esse plura capita, sed unum tantum, alias esset monstrum, et illis dissidentibus membra non possent bene regi. Unde uni corpori suo mistico Christus Petrum sicut caput unum prefecit. Propter quod, super illud: *Tibi dabo claves regni celorum*, dicit Glossa: *Specialiter eam Petro concessit ut ad unitatem nos invitaret. Ideo enim eum principem apostolorum constituit, ut ecclesia unum principalem Christi haberet vicarium ad quem diversa membra ecclesie recurrerent, si forte inter se dissentirent. Quod si diversa capita essent in ecclesia, unitatis vincula rumperentur*. Item super illud Luce 7: *Ait Petrus ad Jesum* etc.: *Faciamus hic tria tabernacula*, Damascenus: *Non te Dominus tabernaculorum, sed universalis ecclesie constructorem constituit: verba tua tui discipuli, oves tue mandaverunt effectum, Christo tabernaculum construentes, nec non et servis eius*. Item Leo papa, 24 q. 1: *Cum beatissimus apostolus a Domino accepit principatum*. Item Chrysostomus, *Super Actus Apostolorum*: *Petrus a Filio super omnes que Filii est potestatem accepit, non ut Moyses in gente una, sed in universo orbe*. Item Cyrillus Alexandrinus in *Libro thesaurorum* dicit sic: *Cui,* scilicet Petro, *omnes iure divino caput inclinant, et primates mundi tanquam Jesu Domino obediunt*. Item super illud Luce 22: *Tu aliquando conversus confirma fratres tuos*, dicit Theophylus: *Petrus obtinuit ut esset antistes mundi*.

Sed contra illud est, et videtur quod ecclesia sit maior Petro, quia nullus mittitur ab inferiore. Sed in primitiva ecclesia Petrus legitur missus ab apostolis et senioribus, sicut dicitur Actuum 8: *Miserunt Petrum et*

desunt B²V⁶

75 illis] *add.* se $\psi\pi^2$ | 76 dissentientibus ρ^1 | 80 constituerat ρ^1 | 82 Quia ρ | 84 te] et ρ^1 | 85 constituit] *om.* ρ; *add.* hec φ | 86 constituentes [constituens W] $\gamma\pi^2$, constituentes vel [et V⁵] construentes [constituens vel construens Bo] θ | 87 eius] suis ρ | 89 omne [*om.* Bm¹] φ | que] quod φ, qui θV⁷$\pi^2\rho^1$ | est] sunt θ(-V¹)$\psi\pi^2$ | accepit potestatem $\theta\pi$ | 90 universo] toto θ | 92 primates] potestates ρ^1 | 93 22] *add.* et ρ | 94 Theophylus [Hieronymus P¹] $\gamma\pi$] Chrysostomus $\theta\rho$Sr

78 Matt. 16:19 | 78-83 *Cat. aur. in Matt.* 16.3, 1:252B (1:274A) | 83-87 *Cat. aur. in Luc.* 9.7, 2:133A (2:145B) | 83-84 The reference should be Luc. 9:33 | 87-88 Gratian, C.24 q.1 c.16 | 88-92 Item ... obediunt: Cf. Pierre de la Palu, *Tractatus de potestate papae* 1.3, p. 193 | 88-90 *Contra er. Gr.*, p. 323 | 90-92 *Contra er. Gr.*, p. 324 | 93-94 *Cat. aur. in Luc.* 22.9 (Theophylactus), 2:289B (2:316B) | 93 Luc. 22:32 | 97-98 Act. 8:14

Joannem etc. Ergo Petrus non fuit maior nec superior illis, sed econtrario. Solutio: missio per auctoritatem est a superiore et maiore, sicut papa mittit legatum et rex baillivum. Sed missio per consilium potest esse ab inferiore, et sic concilium dicitur mittere regem quando vadit alicubi de consilio etiam subditorum, qui per consilium suum movent eum ad illuc proficiscendum. Et sic apostoli et seniores miserunt Petrum per consilium suum, suadentes ei pro salute populi illuc ire.

Secundo, videtur quod Petrus primatum super alios apostolos et super ecclesiam non habuit a Christo, sed solum a voluntate aliorum apostolorum et ecclesie. Quia dicitur 21 d. *In novo*: *Ipsumque principem eorum esse voluerunt*, idest apostoli voluerunt Petrum esse principem suum et per consequens totius ecclesie, cuius ipsi fuerunt prelati. Solutio: apostoli alii voluerunt voluntate consequente et acceptante Dei ordinationem super hoc, non autem voluntate antecedente et causante. Unde Anacletus papa, 22 d. *Sacrosancta*: *Inter beatissimos apostolos quedam fuit discretio, et licet omnes apostoli essent, Petro tamen a Domino concessum est*, supple: primo et principaliter; *et ipsi iidem inter se idipsum voluerunt, ut reliquis omnibus preesset apostolis, et Cephas, quod est caput, et principium teneret apostolatus*.

Tertia Conclusio

Tertia conclusio principalis est quod Petrus a Christo habuit plenitudinem potestatis. Quia sicut rex, preter particulares thesaurarios, vult habere unum de quo magis confidit super omnes thesaurarios suos, per cuius manum omnia transeant — sicut Actuum 8, eunuchus Candacis, regine Ethiopum, *erat super omnes gazas eius*, et sicut rex pharao Joseph constituit dominum domus sue et principem omnis possessionis sue — sic Christus super omnes thesauros regni celorum, quod est ecclesia iustorum, voluit esse unum universalem thesaurarium

desunt B^2V^6

102 suum] *om.* $\psi\rho^1$ | ad] *om.* ρ^1 | 105 alios $\theta\rho$Va] *om.* $Bm^1Pr\varphi^4\psi\pi Sr$; omnes φ^3W | super] *om.* φ | 107 Quia] *om.* γ; nam $\theta(-V^1)Sr$, unde Va | principem] *om.* θ | 108 eorum] *om.* $\theta\psi$ | 110 acceperunt ρ | 113 distinctio ρ^1 | 114 iidem $UPr\varphi^4R\sigma$] idem [id P^1, quidem O] $\alpha(-UPr\varphi^4)\pi^2\rho$ | 115 quod est $\psi\pi^2Sr$] quod $\pi^1\rho^1$Va, et $\theta\varphi$, idest Barb. | 116 principatum θ | 120 de quo] cui θ | suos] *add.* et $\theta(-O)$ | 121 manus θ | 124 sic] *add.* et $V^1\theta^3\varphi\psi\pi^2Sr$ | 125 est] *add.* in $\psi\pi(-R)$ | iustorum] sanctorum α | unum] *add.* principem et θ

107-108 Gratian, D.21 c.2 | 112-116 Gratian, D.22 c.2 | 118-131 Tertia ... eum: cf. Pierre de la Palu, *Tractatus de potestate papae* 1.3, p. 191 | 121-122 Act. 8:27 | 122-124 Cf. Gen. 41:37-44

qui haberet plenam dispensationem totius thesauri. Sed quia infidelitatem Jude fuerat expertus, voluit ponere fidelem Petrum super hoc opus. Unde Petrus, Luce 12: *Domine, ad nos dicis hanc parabolam, an ad omnes?* Et Dominus tunc dixit Petro singulariter: *Quis, putas, est fidelis dispensator et prudens quem constituit dominus?* etc. *Amen dico vobis super omnia bona sua constituet eum.*

Confirmatur autem hoc auctoritate Grecorum dupliciter. Primo, quod Petro Christus dedit plenitudinem potestatis, Chrysostomus, *Ad consulta Bulgarorum*, pertractans illud Joannis ultimo: *Dicit ei tertio*: "*Amas me?*" ex persona Christi loquens: *Ter te interrogo an me diligas, quia ter trepidus ac timidus me negasti. Nunc autem reductus, ne credant te fratres gratiam et clavium auctoritatem* – supple: promissam prius, nondum tamen datam, sed tunc dandam – *amisisse* – idest amittere debere, idest iuxta promissum non recepturum esse – *quia amas me, coram ipsis iam tibi confirmo quod meum est plenum.* Et ne si essent plures insolidum universales thesaurarii < qui > thesaurum diriperent invicem dissidendo, soli Petro inter apostolos Christus singulariter commisit plenitudinem potestatis. Quod autem hec plenitudo potestatis soli Petro collata fuerit, dicit Cyrillus, patriarcha Alexandrinus, in *Libro thesaurorum*: *Nulli alii quam Petro Christus quod suum est plenum, sed ipsi soli dedit.* Item quod soli Petro singulariter hec preeminentia sit collata a Christo patet per Ambrosium, 24 q. 1: *Non turbatur navis que Petrum habet* etc. *Quemadmodum enim turbari poterat cui preerat Petrus, qui ecclesie fundamentum est. Denique etsi aliis imperatur ut laxent retia, soli tamen Petro dicitur: "Duc in altum," hoc est in profundum disputationum*, quia

desunt B^2V^6

126 plenariam ρ^1 | fidelitatem α | 127 Jude] *om.* γ; Petri θ | fuit π | 128 Domine] Dominus $\theta\psi$ | dicit $O\theta^4\psi$, dixit $V^1\theta^3$ | 128-129 Et Dominus] *om.* $\alpha\rho^2$ | 129 tunc] tamen $OBo\theta^4$, cum $V^1V^2V^5\psi\pi^1$ | 130 dominus] *om.* ρ | 132 quia θ | 135 te] *om.* $\psi\pi^2$ | diligis θ | 136 ac] et α | 137 supple] supra ρ^1 | 138 tunc] nunc φ | amisisse] *add.* et φ | 138-139 idest^1 ... esse] *om.* αVa | 140 tibi] ter [te θ^3] θ | confirmo] *add.* idest do ρ; idest amittere te non debere, idest [*om.* U] iuxta promissum [promissam U] nunc te recepturum esse φ; idest [et ψ] amittere debere [admiti debet Bo], idest iuxta promissum [proximum non ψ; *add.* te OSv, non V^1Bo] recepturum [receptum OBo] esse $\theta(-V^3)\psi$; idest iuxta promissum te recepturum esse V^3 | 141 invicem] *om.* ρ | 142 Christus] *om.* θ | 143 soli] *om.* θ | 145-165 Item ... meas] *om.* Sr | 146 hec] *om.* ρ^1 | 148 turbari] *add.* non θ(-Bo) | 149 imperat π

128-131 Luc. 12:41-44 | 132-145 Confirmatur ... dedit: cf. Pierre de la Palu, *Tractatus de potestate papae* 1.3, p. 185 | 133-140 *Contra er. Gr.*, p. 324 | 134 Joan. 21:17 | 144-145 *Contra er. Gr.*, p. 323 | 145-165 Item ... meas: cf. Pierre de la Palu, *Tractatus de potestate papae* 1.3, pp. 193-194 | 147-150 Gratian, C.24 q.1 c.7

scilicet sibi cause maiores fidei reservantur, *De baptismo* c. *Maiores*. Sed quod cum hoc Petrus a Christo accepit preeminentiam singularem in iurisdictione, Ambrosius, 24 q. 1: *Est aliud piscandi genus et apostolicum, quo genere solum Petrum piscari Dominus iubet, dicens: "Mitte hamum, et eum piscem qui prius ascenderit, tolle,"* ubi dicit Glossa quod *per hamum intelligitur iurisdictio, quia hamo, idest ferro, carnes putride resecantur.* Unde quia Petrus habet potestatem ligandi et solvendi pre aliis, immo solus in hoc habet plenitudinem potestatis, ideo sibi soli dictum est: *Mitte hamum*. Sed per rete intelligitur inquisitio veritatis. Unde super illud Joannis ultimo: *Dixit eis Jesus: "Afferte de piscibus quos prendidistis nunc." Ascendit ergo Simon Petrus, et traxit rete,* dicit Gregorius in homilia quod ideo dicitur singulariter ascendere et rete cum piscibus trahere, quia ipsi a Domino ecclesia specialiter est commissa, scilicet ad portum salutis, et ad Christum cum fidelibus trahenda, et ipsi specialiter est dictum: *Pasce oves meas*.

Quarta Conclusio

Quarta conclusio principalis est quod Petrus a Christo immediate habuit potestatem et dignitatem episcopalem, ab ipso factus et consecratus episcopus. Unde Anacletus papa, 21 d. *In novo*, dicit: *Ipsi,* scilicet Petro, *primo pontificatus in ecclesia Christi datus est, dicente Domino ad eum: "Tu es Petrus, et super hanc petram edificabo ecclesiam meam, et porte inferi non prevalebunt adversus eam; et tibi dabo claves regni celorum." Hic igitur ligandi atque solvendi potestatem primus accepit a Domino.* Et ratio huius est quia Dei perfecta sunt opera. Unde sicut Deus in creatione

desunt B^2V^6

151 sibi] *om.* α | reservantur] *add.* sibi θ(-V^1V^3), eidem extra φ, ut dicit ψ | Sed] Patet ergo $\psi\pi^2$ | 152 cum hoc] *om.* $\varphi^3\psi\pi^2$Va; tantum φ(-φ^3) | acceperit $\theta^3\varphi\pi^1$Barb. | 153 iurisdictione] *add.* dicit $\varphi\rho$ | 155 qui] quem ρ^1 | ascenderit] apprehenderis ρ | dicit] *add.* sic θ | 160 Dicit $\psi\pi^2$ | ei $\psi\pi$ | 167 principalis] de potestate episcopali et ρ | 168 episcopalem] *add.* et ρ | ipso] *add.* Christo $\psi\pi^2$, est ρ | factus et] *om.* ρ | 169 dicit] *add.* sic φ | scilicet] sancto φ | 170 Christi] *om.* θ | ad eum] *om.* $\theta\varphi^1$ | 173 Hic igitur ligandi] *om.* α | primus $\pi^1\rho$(-Br)Va] prius π^2Br, primo α | Domino] Christo ρ^1 | 174 Deus] Dominus θ | creatione] *add.* mundi θ

151 X. 3.42.3 | 153-155 Gratian, C.24 q.1 c.8 | 155-156 *Decretum Gratiani, seu verius decretorum canonicorum collectanea, ab ipso Gratiano Concordantia discordantium canonum inscripta, ... commentariis Hugonis ac Joannis Teuthonici aliorumque iuris utriusque peritorum illustrata ...* (Paris, 1550), C.24 q.1 c.8, Glossa: *Hamum*, fol. 471v | 159-165 Gregory the Great, *Quadraginta homiliarum in Evangelia libri duo* 2.24.4 (PL 76:1185) | 160-161 Joan. 21:10-11 | 169-173 Gratian, D.21 c.2

homines perfectos fecit, ex quibus propagatio naturaliter procedere potuit, sic Deus apostolos, quos principia ecclesie in recreatione fecit, sic perficere debuit ut per eos ecclesia propagari posset. Sed sine episcopo ecclesia non poterat proficere, a quo solo omnia ecclesiastica sacramenta possunt ministrari. Ergo oportuit quod Christus, pontifex, recedens, aliquem loco sui episcopum relinqueret. Sed si aliquem fecit, verisimilius est de Petro, qui ceteris dignior fuit – ut dicit Chrysostomus super illud Luce 24: "Apparuit Simoni": *Primo digniori et fideliori omnibus apparuit* –, et qui in catalogo apostolorum semper et ubique primus ponitur, Matthei 10, Luce 6, Actuum 3. Unde Augustinus, super illud Joannis 13: "Venit ergo ad Simonem Petrum": *Quis enim nesciat primum apostolorum esse beatissimum Petrum ?* Unde beatum Petrum episcopum fecit, quod patet auctoritate Scripture, Joannis 21, ubi dicit: *Pasce oves meas, pasce agnos meos.* Cui enim aliquid committitur, et illud sine quo commissum explicari non potest, *Ff. De iurisdictione omnium iudicum* 1.2. Sed pascere gregem dominicum perfecte non potest nisi episcopus. Quia agni, per sacramentum confirmationis pasti, fiunt arietes pro fide, sed certantes oves per sacramentum ordinis fiunt matres spirituales alias gignentes. Ergo imponendo sibi pastum gregis, imposuit sibi officium pastoris et episcopi. Siquidem ipse sine sacramento rem sacramenti dare potuit per potestatem excellentie quam in sacramentis habuit, unde solo illo verbo Petrum episcopum fecit.

desunt B^{2}V^6

176 principes $\theta\psi\pi^2$ | creatione $\theta\pi^1$ | 180 episcopum] *om.* φ | 181 qui] *add.* pre θ | ut] unde φ | 182 Primo] *add.* ut $\psi\pi^2$ | et^2] unde ρ | qui] *om.* $\psi\pi^2\rho$ | 183 apostolorum] sanctorum ρ^1 | 185 nesciat] *add.* ipsum Petrum Oθ^4, ipsum V$^1\theta^3$ | esse] *om.* ρSr | 186 beatissimum Petrum] *om.* Oθ^4; beatum [*om.* B^1] Petrum π | 187 dicitur γ(-W)π^2 | 188 enim] *add.* committitur φ | illud] ipsum ρ | commissum] ipsum ρ | 189 potest] *add.* De officio delegati [*add.* c. θ^3] Preterea [*om.* Bo] θ(-V^1) | 191 confirmationis] eucharistie φ | pasti] *add.* per sacramentum confirmationis φ | arietes] constantes φ | pro fide] per [pro R] fidem $\theta\psi\pi$; *add.* certantes Oθ^4 | sed] *om.* $\varphi^3\rho\sigma$; scilicet φ(-φ^3) | 192 matres] *om.* $\theta\psi\pi^2$; fecunde vel [et St] fertiles [steriles Bm^1] φ | spirituales] *add.* vel [et P^4] π | alias] actus φ, alios ρ; *add.* oves θ(-V^1) | gignentes $\rho\sigma$] exequentes [per exequentes V^5] $\alpha\pi$ | 194 ipse] Christus θ(-V^1) | 195 potentiam ρ^1 | potestatis excellentiam θ^3, potestatis excellentiam et excellentie potestatem Oθ^4 | sacramento θ(-V^1)

181-182 *Cat. aur. in Luc.* 24.3, 2:315A (2:345B) | Luc. 24:34 | 183 Matt. 10:2 | 184 Luc. 6:14 | The reference should be Act. 1:13 | 184-186 *Cat. aur. in Joan.* 13.2, 2:505A (2:553A) | 184-185 Joan. 13:6 | 187-188 Joan. 21:15-17 | 188-189 *Dig.* 2.1.2

QUINTA CONCLUSIO

Quinta conclusio principalis est quod Christus predictam eminentiam potestatis et dignitatis episcopalis Petro ante resurrectionem suam non contulit. Quia quamdiu ipse corporaliter inter homines vivens per seipsum ecclesiam rexit, nulla necessitas [sed] nec decentia nec utilitas fuit quod ipse alium loco sui poneret. Sed solum quando per ascensionem se absentare debuit, sicut prelati tunc demum, quando se absentant ad magnum tempus, loco sui constituunt vicarium generalem. Unde super illud Luce 22: *Facta est autem contentio inter eos quis eorum esset maior*, dicit Gregorius: *Que contentio videtur habuisse motivum, quod cum Dominus ab hominibus transmigraret, oportebat aliquem eorum fieri aliorum principem, quasi Domini vicem gerentem*, quasi dicens: antequam ipse transmigraret non erat necesse. Unde Petrus non est factus pastor ecclesie ante resurrectionem, querente Gregorio in *Homilia resurrectionis*, et habetur 50 d.: *Consideremus cur Deus eum, quem cuncte ecclesie preficere disposuerat, ancille vocem pertimescere et se negare permisit*; et respondente: *Ut is, qui futurus erat pastor ecclesie* etc., quasi dicens: nondum erat.

Item Chrysostomus, super illud Luce 22: "Facta est contentio inter eos": *Credenda erat Petro populorum innumera multitudo.* Quod autem ibidem dicit Chrysostomus: *Tradite erant Petro claves regni celorum*, intelligendum est promissione non datione, quia dictum est sibi: *Tibi dabo*. Promissionis enim verbum est hoc, sicut dicit apostolus in simili, ad Hebreos 11, quia nullus habet claves ligandi nec solvendi nisi sacerdos, *De penitentia* d. 1 § *Ex his*. Nullus autem debuit esse sacerdos ad

desunt B^2V^6

201 sed] *om.* ρ | 204 Unde] ut ρ^1 | 206 Que] hec ρ | videtur] dicitur θ | 207 migraret φ | oportebat] decebat φ | 208 aliorum] *om.* ρ | 209 ipse] *om.* ρVa | 210 querente [*add.* domino W] Gregorio $\varphi\pi^1$Va] querit [queret S] Gregorius θ, querendum [*add.* est B^1] ergo ut $\psi\pi^2$, attestante Gregorio ρ | 211 Consideremus] confundere videtur ρ^1 | cur] *om.* ρ^1 | 213 respondente $\psi\pi^1P^1$Va] respondet $\theta\varphi B^1$Barb., responderent ρ^1 | is qui] his quibus θ | 216 innumera] summa $\theta\psi$ | multitudo] *om.* θ | 217 ibi [illi V^1] θ | Tradite] credite φ(-W)π^1Barb. | 221 Nullus] *add.* fuit $\psi\pi^2$ | autem] aut π^2, nec ψ | debet θ(-Bo)

205-208 *Cat. aur. in Luc.* 22.7 (Graecus), 2:288A (2:314B) | 205 Luc. 22:24 | 210-214 Gratian, D.50 c.53 | 215-217 Cf. John Chrysostom, *In Petrum apostolum et in Heliam prophetam* (PG 50:727). In the general context of Luke 22 (Peter's denial) he says: "Petro committendae erant claves ecclesiae, imo potius committebantur ei claves celorum, eidemque concredenda erat multitudo populi." | 215-216 Luc. 22:24 | 218 Matt. 16:19 | 219-220 Heb. 11? | 220-221 Gratian, *De poen.* D.1 c.60

conficiendum sacramentum altaris antequam ipsum sacramentum esset institutum, quia frustra esset potestas que non posset reduci ad actum. Unde ante cenam, in qua fuit institutum sacramentum eucharistie, nullus fuit factus sacerdos, nec per consequens habuit potestatem ligandi nec solvendi in foro conscientie, quia potestas clavium in illo foro que respicit corpus Christi misticum fundatur super potestate que habetur super corpus Christi verum; unde eam presupponit. Item non obstat quod dicit idem Chrysostomus super illud Matthei 16: "Super hanc petram edificabo ecclesiam meam": *Erigit eius sensum, et pastorem facit ipsum*, quia exponendum est: idest promittit se facturum. Quia antequam essent oves per passionem redempte, non oportebat eis pastorem preficere. Similiter ad auctoritatem Anacleti, 21 d.: Ipsi pontificatus datus est dicente Domino: *Tu es Petrus*, et quod ligandi et solvendi potestatem accepit. Exponendum est: datus, idest dari promissus, et accepit in spe. Unde dicit Glossa ibi, et bene, quod Petrus non est factus episcopus nec pastor ecclesie nisi quando dictum est sibi: *Pasce oves meas, pasce agnos meos*, quod non est promissio futuri temporis – quasi dicens: tu pasces – sed collatio presens, quasi dicens: pasce, idest ex nunc potestatem pascendi accipe, scilicet per administrationem omnium sacramentorum quibus ecclesia pascitur. Et hoc est quod habetur *De electione* c. *Significasti*, ubi dicitur: *Mirentur Dominum Jesum Christum, qui, cum ovium suarum Petro curam committeret, conditionem posuit, dicens: "Si diligis me, pasce oves meas,"* quasi dicens: tunc committebat, non ante commiserat. Unde tunc primo eum pastorem et episcopum animarum fecit. Ad idem est auctoritas Ambrosii, 50 d. c. *Fidelior*, ubi dicit Ambrosius quod *fidelior factus est Petrus postquam fidem se perdidisse deflevit, atque ideo maiorem gratiam reperit quam amisit. Tanquam enim bonus pastor tuendum gregem accepit, ut qui ante infirmus fuerat, omnibus fieret firmamentum*, quasi

desunt B^2V^6

223 potentia $\psi\rho$ | 226 que] *om.* ψ; qui π^2, quo [in quo ρ^2] $\theta\rho$ | 228-261 unde ... infectus] *om.* Sr | 229 super illud] *om.* α | 230 eius sensum] ei consensum θ | quia] quod α | 231 idest] *om.* $\alpha\rho$ | 235 dari] *om.* ρ | ibidem ρ^1 | 235-236 et bene] *om.* ρ | 236 ecclesie] *om.* α | 238 temporis] operis ρ | 238-239 tu ... dicens] *hom.* ρ | 241 dicitur] *add.* quod ρ^1 | 242 mirantur θ, miremur φ | Christum] *om.* α(-W) | 243 apposuit ρ | dicens] *om.* θ | 244 committebat] *add.* et θ | 249 fundamentum $V^1\theta^3\rho$, firmamentum vel fundamentum θ^4, fundamentum vel firmamentum O

229-230 *Cat. aur. in Matt.* 16.3, 1:251B (1:273A) | Matt. 16:18 | 233 Gratian, D.21 c.2 | 235-236 *Decretum Gratiani* ..., D.21 c.2, fol. 31v | 237 Joan. 21:15-17 | 241-243 X. 1.6.4 | 246-249 Gratian, D.50 c.54

dicens: non est factus pastor gregis antequam fleret peccatum, quod fuit in passione, nec per consequens ante resurrectionem. Quia nec decuit Christum dare alicui plenitudinem potestatis quousque innotuisset quod data esset sibi omnis potestas, nec decebat esse simul nisi unum summum pontificem. Unde Christo ascensuro debuit Petrus fieri episcopus summus et pastor ovium redemptarum, et non antequam summus pontifex Christus per proprium sanguinem introivit semel in sancta. Unde contra legem fuit quod Anna et Cayphas simul in vita sua, licet alternis annis, erant summi pontifices. Unde super illud Joannis 18: *qui erat pontifex anni illius*, dicit Beda: *Sonat contrarium legi, in qua preceptum erat ut unus esset summus pontifex, quo mortuo succederet ei filius suus. Sed iam pontificatus ambitione erat infectus.*

desunt B²V⁶

252 alicui] aliter [alteri U] φ(-φ⁵) | 255-261 et² ... infectus] *om.* Va | 256 intraverit [intravit BoSv] θ| 259 legis θφ| 260 esset] erat ρ¹| summus] *om.* ρ| ei] sibi [*om.* W] α| suus] *om.* ψρ¹ | Sed] sic ρ¹ | 261 infectus] *add.* tempore Christi θ(-V¹)

258-261 *Cat. aur. in Joan.* 18.4, 2:559B (2:613B)| 258-259 Joan. 18:13

Secundus Articulus

Quantum ad secundum articulum principalem, de potestate a Christo collata immediate aliis apostolis, sunt octo conclusiones. Prima de potestate miracula faciendi. Secunda de potestate predicandi. Tertia de potestate metendi temporalia. Quarta de potestate baptizandi. Quinta de potestate sacerdotali. Sexta de potestate clavium ordinis. Septima de potestate episcopali. Octava de potestate iurisdictionis.

Prima Conclusio

Prima conclusio principalis, de potestate miracula faciendi, est quod eam habuerunt omnes apostoli immediate a Christo, non a Petro. Immo nec quicumque alius miracula unquam faciendi potestatem a puro homine habuit, nec habere potuit, sed a solo Deo. Matthei 10 dedit illis potestatem spirituum immundorum. Matthei 3 dedit illis potestatem curandi infirmitates et eiciendi demonia. Luce 9 dedit eis potestatem super omnia demonia. Tamen, licet potestatem faciendi miracula non habuerint a Petro, habuerunt tamen eam sub Petro et minorem Petro. Unde in illius usu omnes deferebant Petro, sicut et Joannes, qui fuit maior post Petrum, fecit. Unde primum miraculum factum per apostolos post Spiritus Sancti missionem factum est per Petrum, Actuum 3, dicentem claudo erigendo: *Quod autem habeo, hoc tibi do. In nomine Jesu Nazareni, surge, et ambula.*

desunt B^2V^6

3 octo] *add.* principales φ | 7 potestate iurisdictionis ρSr] clavibus iurisdictionis θ(-S)ψR, potestate clavium iurisdictionis φS, potestate et clavibus [aliquibus T] iurisdictionis π(-R) | 9 Prima] *add.* ergo θ | 11 quisquam ρ | faciendi] fecit qui [licet Va] hanc ρVa | 12 sed] nisi φ | 13 immundorum] *add.* et $\psi\pi^2$ | 13-14 infirmitatem α(-OBo) | 14-15 Luce ... demonia] *hom.* $\theta\varphi^3V^4V^7$ | 15 habuerint $V^2V^3Bm^1\varphi^4P^2$RBarb.] habuerunt $V^1BoV^5Sv\varphi^3\varphi^5V^7\rho^1\pi$(-R)$\sigma$, fuerunt O | 16 illius] illo $\psi\pi^2$ | 17 sicut] sic [sed φ^3] α | 19 dicendo $\theta\pi^2$ | 20 hoc] *om.* ρ^1 | nomine] *add.* Domini θ(-V^3)

12 Matt. 10:1 | 13 The reference should be Matt. 10:8 | 14 Luc. 9:1 | 19-21 Act. 3:6-7

Et apprehensa manu eius dextra, levavit eum; et in gestis apostolorum Petri et Pauli, in deiectione Simonis Magi quem demones per aerem portabant, Paulus Petro legitur detulisse. Quod autem minorem Petro patet, quia per umbram Petri sanabantur infirmi, Actuum 5, quod de aliis apostolis non invenitur.

Secunda Conclusio

Secunda conclusio principalis est de potestate predicandi, quod apostoli acceperunt eam immediate a Christo ante passionem ad predicandum Judeis, Matthei 10: *In viam gentium ne abieritis* etc. *Euntes autem predicate, dicentes: Quia appropinquavit regnum celorum*, Matthei 3, Luce 9. Post resurrectionem autem iterum a Christo missi sunt ad predicandum toti mundo, Matthei ultimo: *Euntes docete omnes gentes*; Marci ultimo: *Predicate Evangelium omni creature*; et postea: *Illi autem profecti predicaverunt ubique, Domino cooperante*. Quamvis autem, Christo adhuc eos per se regente, ante passionem non subessent regimini Petri, nec in predicando nec in aliis, tamen postquam ab ipso est factus pastor ecclesie, ut si etiam predicatores inter se dissiderent – sicut facta est dissentio inter Paulum et Barnabam, ita ut ab invicem discederent, Actuum 15 – esset superior qui eos reuniret, in hoc et in aliis subfuerunt Petro. Unde ubicumque presens erat in predicando, sibi omnes alii deferebant. Unde in Pentecostem primum sermonem ipse fecit, Actuum 2; et de Petro dicitur, 21 d. *In novo*: *Primus ad fidem populum virtute sue predicationis adduxit, verboque instituit*.

Item nullus sapiens princeps mittit exercitum contra hostes, quin det eis unum principalem ducem et capitaneum ad cuius oris imperium omnes

desunt B^2V^6

21 dextra] *om.* θ | levavit] sanavit π(-R) | 22 in] de [*om.* W] α(-Bo) | eiectione [erectione Bo] θ | 23 Petro^2] *add.* habuerunt [habuerint θ^4] θ | 30 predicate] *add.* Evangelium π | appropinquavit ψπσ] appropinquabit θφρ | 31 9] *add.* et πVa | 33 ultimo] *add.* euntes ρ | autem] *om.* ρ^1 | 34 ubique] *om.* θ(-O) | 37 si] *add.* forte φ | etiam] *om.* ρ^1 | predicatione φ, predicantes $\psi\pi^2$ | dissentirent ρ^1 | 38 ab] ad ρVa | dissentirent ρ^1 | 39 eos] omnes ρ | reuniret] *add.* et π | subfuerunt] *add.* sibi [*om.* V^3] scilicet θ | 41 ipse] *om.* ρ^1 | 42 populum] *om.* α | virtutem φ(-U) | 43 instituit] instruxit ρ

21-23 Cf. F. M. Fiorentini ed., *Vetustius occidentalis ecclesiae martyrologium* (Lucca, 1668), pp. 109-110 | 24 Act. 5:15 | 29-30 Matt. 10:5-7 | 30 Matt. 3:2 | 31 Luc. 9:2 | 32 Matt. 28:19 | 33 Marc. 16:15 | 33-34 Marc. 16:20 | 39 Act. 15:36-41 | 41-42 Act 2:14-40 | 42-43 Gratian, D.21 c.2

alii debent obedire. Sicut Genesis 26, Abimelech, rex Gerare, habuit ducem militum Phicol; Genesis 39, pharao, rex Egipti, Putiphar principem exercitus; et sic de aliis. Unde quia ecclesia est *terribilis ut castrorum acies ordinata*, et apostoli fuerunt celestis aule milites, belli triumphales duces habentes arma spiritualia, et specialiter gladium spiritus, quod est verbum Dei, debuerunt habere unum capitaneum, scilicet Petrum, qui propter hoc dictus est Cephas, quasi caput aliorum, a quo in acie ordinarentur. Unde ab ipso facta est divisio et ordinatio predicatorum et predicationum, licet de consilio et assensu aliorum, sicut etiam papa agit de consilio cardinalium. Quia ad rectorem communitatis pertinet instituere subrectores, quasi vicarios suos, non ad subditos, qui ex quo alicui subsunt, vel propria voluntate vel superioris ordinatione, ex tunc sine illius assensu non possunt super se alterum ponere. Inde est quod ex quo cura totius ecclesie fuit Petro soli a Christo commissa, qui etiam dixit: *Fiat unum ovile, et unus pastor,* et illum unum designans dixit Petro: *Pasce oves meas*, ex tunc nullus nisi auctoritate Petri habuit oves pascere nec regere ubicumque. Unde et ipsius fuit ordinare alios pastores, vocando in partem sollicitudinis. Unde ipsius erat ordinare de successore Jude in apostolatum, sed dedit electionem aliis. Similiter de diaconis, officialibus et predicatoribus ipsius fuit ordinare et eos sub se ponere, sed voluit electionem aliis committere, dicens Actuum 6: *Considerate ex vobis viros boni testimonii* etc., *et elegerunt Stephanum* etc., sicut etiam Moyses constituit sub se principes. Quamvis per se posset eligere, dedit tamen electionem populo dicens, Deuteronomii 1: *Date ex vobis viros sapientes* etc. Unde omnis electio vel institutio ad aliquam rectoriam in tota ecclesia Dei oportet quod fuerit a Petro vel eius successore collata, et divisio provinciarum et diocesum ab eo facta, 80 d. *In illis*. Potest etiam probabiliter dici quod post Pentecostem potestatem seu auctoritatem predicandi habuerunt alii apostoli omnes a Petro, et non immediate a Christo, propter servandam in omnibus uniformiter ecclesie unitatem. Dicitur autem Christus post resurrectionem eos misisse ad docendum et

desunt B^2V^6

47 militem θ(-O)$\psi\pi$(-R) | 53 divisio] *om.* α | 54 assensu] consensu θ(-BoSv)ρ^1 | 55 consilio] consensu π | 56 non ad] super $\psi\pi^2$ | 58 consensu θ | 61 auctoritate] per auctoritatem αVa | 63 erat] fuit $\alpha\pi^2$ | 67 sic $\theta\pi^1$ | 68 constituit BoSt$\psi\pi^2$BrBarb.Sr] constituturus θ(-OBoV^5)$Bm^1Pr\varphi^4\pi^1$Va, constituens OBm^2Sz, constitutus V^5U, constitutos W | 75 propter] ad φ | uniformiter] *om.* ρ | 76 Christum $\psi\pi^2$

46 Gen. 26:26 | 47 Gen. 39:1 | 48-49 Cant. 6:3 | 60 Joan. 10:16 | 61 Joan. 21:17 | 66-67 Act. 6:3-5 | 69-70 Deut. 1:13 | 72 Gratian, D.80 c.2

predicandum, dando eis os et sapientiam, et sermonem confirmando sequentibus signis que sibi retinuit, non dando eis per se auctoritatem sed per Petrum, cui totum pabulum ovium per verbum Dei commisit, dicens: *Pasce oves meas, pasce agnos meos.*

Tertia Conclusio

Tertia conclusio principalis est quo ad potestatem metendi temporalia ab illis quibus spiritualia seminarent, quia et hanc Christus apostolis omnibus dedit per seipsum immediate a principio, dicens, Matthei 10: *Dignus est enim operarius cibo suo.* Unde 1 ad Corinthios 9: *Si nos vobis spiritualia seminamus, non magnum est si nos carnalia vestra metamus?* quasi dicens: non. Et postea subdit: *Dominus ordinavit his qui Evangelium annuntiant de Evangelio vivere.* Sed hanc potestatem servientem potestati predicandi et baptizandi, sicut et illas, post Pentecostem acceperunt alii a Petro, ne quis mitteret falcem suam in messem alienam spiritualiter vel temporaliter. Unde eius fuit metropoles et dioceses dividere, suam cuique assignando. Sicut Josue divisit terram in funiculo distributionis, quam Dominus non ipse dedit, ita etiam in ecclesia, quam non Petrus sed Christus suo sanguine acquisivit, Petrus loco Christi apostolis divisit et distribuit partes suas. Unde ad Galatas 2: *Jacobus, Cephas, et Joannes, qui videbantur columne esse, dextras dederunt michi et Barnabe societatis, ut nos in gentes, ipsi autem in circumcisionem*, ubi apparet quod illa prima divisio predicationum facta est per Petrum. Si dicatur quod facta est eque per alios duos – immo et Jacobus ibi preponitur Petro, et ideo videtur principalius facta ab eo – dicendum est quod immo, quantum ad auctoritatem facta est a solo Petro, cui omnium ovium, non solum que perierant ex Israel, sed etiam aliarum totius mundi soli cura erat commissa, secundum illud: *Alias oves habeo, et illas oportet me adducere, et fiat unum ovile et unus pastor,* Joannis 10. Illi autem duo ibi

desunt B^2V^6

77 et^2] *om.* ρ | sermonem] *add.* eorum φ | 83 apostolis] *om.* θ | 85 enim] *om.* $θρ^2$ | 86 non] *om.* θUBarb., ne φ(-U) | nos] *om.* θ | 87 his] ei [et P^1, eum P^4] π | 88 nuntiant θ(-S), annuntiavit [annuntiat B^1] π | 91 dividere] *om.* ρ; dimittere π(-P^4) | suam cuique] suamque $V^1V^2V^5$, suumque $Oθ^4$, unicuique ρ | 92 assignando Va] assignare *cet. mss.* | 93 non^1] *om.* $ψπ^2$Va | 94 Petrus] *om.* θ(-Bo) | 96 Barnabe] *add.* ut $ρ^1$ | 97 illa] ista θ | 99 videtur] *add.* esse θ(-Sv)$π^1$ | 102 ex Israel π(-P^1)Barb.Va] *om.* $θ^2V^5γP^1ρ^1$; in Israel Bo$V^2θ^4$ | 104 et^1] ut θ

80 Joan. 21:15-17 | 84-85 Matt. 10:10 | 85-86 1 Cor. 9:11 | 87-88 1 Cor. 9:14 | 92-93 Cf. Num. 34:16ff | 95-97 Gal. 2:9 | 103-104 Joan. 10:16

nominantur tanquam principales consiliarii et coadiutores Petri. Quod autem ibi Jacobus preponitur non est ratione maioritatis simpliciter, sed quia in Hierusalem, ubi facta est illa ordinatio, preerat specialiter.

Simili modo etiam dicendum est ad epistolam super cessatione legalium, scriptam non nomine solius Petri, sed apostolorum et seniorum, Actuum 15: *Apostoli et seniores fratres* etc., quasi nec Petrus nec alius solus preesset omnibus, sed apostoli et seniores et episcopi et presbyteri quasi equaliter. Et in fine capituli dicitur quod Paulus *ambulabat* etc., *precipiens custodiri precepta apostolorum et seniorum*. Non dicit Petri, quia sicut antiquitus omnia concilia fiebant auctoritate pape, sic et nunc, 27 d. per totum, *De electione* c. *Significasti*, in fine. Et tamen ordinationes conciliorum non ex nomine solius pape recitabantur nec scribebantur, sed nomine omnium patrum qui in concilio interfuerunt. Quia illud attribuebatur Spiritui Sancto non homini, quia *ubi sunt duo vel tres congregati in nomine meo, ibi sum in medio eorum*, Matthei 18. Unde in actis conciliorum solet dici: "placuit omnibus," vel "statuit sancta synodus," vel aliquid huiusmodi. Ideo tunc in illo primo concilio, quod auctoritate Petri fuit congregatum et definitum, Petrus non sibi sed Spiritui Sancto et toti congregationi, cuius meritis illud revelatum fuit, similiter attribuebat id quod ibi factum fuit. Unde ibi dicunt in principio epistole: *Visum est Spiritui Sancto et nobis*. Et consimiliter potest responderi ad multas instantias similes que occurrunt.

Quarta Conclusio

Quarta conclusio principalis est de potestate baptizandi, scilicet quod omnes apostoli habuerunt a Christo immediate potestatem baptizandi ante passionem. Quia baptizabant, ut dicitur Joannis 4, *quamvis Jesus non baptizaret, sed discipuli eius*, qui non presumpsissent baptizare nisi a

desunt B^2V^6

106 autem] *om.* σ | 107 quia] *om.* φ | 108-126 Simili ... occurrunt] *om.* Sr | 108 etiam] *om.* π(-R) | 110 quasi] *add.* diceret Br, dicat V^1BoV^5, dicens S, d. OV^2V^3SvSz | nec^1] *add.* solus ρ | 111 et^2] *om.* φV^7 | 113 precipiens] precipiat ρ^1 | 114 sic φ(-φ^3)π(-R)SzBarb.] *om.* $V^1\theta^3$; sicut O$\theta^4\varphi^3\psi$RBm^2BrVa | 115 in fine] *om.* ρ | 117 patrum ρ^1Va] *om.* απ; patrium Barb. | 118 attribuebant [attribuebat Pr] α | 120 conciliorum] aliorum ρ^1 | 123 similiter] humiliter θ, simpliciter φ | 124 id θ(-BoV^5)P^2Rρ(-Sz)] *om.* π(-R); illud BoV^5φSz | ibi^1] sibi ρ^1 | factum ibi [ibi *om.* W] α | fuit] fuerat θ | dicitur $\psi\pi^2$, dicuntur π^1 | 126 similes] *om.* α

110 Act. 15:23 | 112-113 Act. 15:41 | 115 Gratian, D.17 | X. 1.6.4 | 118-119 Matt. 18:20 | 125 Act. 15:28 | 130-131 Joan. 4:2

Christo auctoritatem habuissent. Unde Joannis 1 dixerunt pharisei Joanni: *Quid ergo baptizas, si tu non es Christus, neque Elias, neque propheta?* quasi dicentes: non debes. Sed sciendum est quod Chrysostomus dicit in loco preallegato, Joannis 4, quod discipuli non baptizabant baptismo Christi in Spiritu Sancto, quia nondum erat Spiritus datus, quia nondum erat Jesus glorificatus. Unde sicut Joannes non sacerdos baptizabat suo baptismo, ita et apostoli, licet nondum sacerdotes, poterant sine offensa baptizare eodem baptismo vel simili baptismate. Sed Augustinus et Alcuinus dicunt quod immo apostoli baptizabant baptismo Christi, in quo dabatur Spiritus Sanctus, non tamen visibiliter sicut post Spiritus Sancti missionem. Et hoc etiam poterant facere apostoli licenter, licet nondum essent sacerdotes, quia nec ipsi nec alii erant futuri ante cenam, et tamen, ut ibi dicit Augustinus, ipsi erant a Christo baptizati. Unde hec sunt verba Augustini: *Neque enim ministerio baptizandi defuit, ut haberet baptizatos servos per quos ceteros baptizaret*, et idem habetur *De consecratione* d. 4 *Quando ab Hierosolimis*, et capitulo sequenti. Apostoli enim non debuerunt aliquid predicare quod non prius ipsi facerent, sicut dicebat Paulus ad Romanos 15: *Nichil audeo loqui eorum que per me non efficit Christus*. Unde nec debuerunt predicare nec dare baptismum Christi nisi prius baptizati eodem baptismo. Sed in defectum omnis sacerdotis nove legis poterant baptizare, sicut nunc licet etiam layco baptizare quando non potest haberi copia sacerdotis, ut dicit Isidorus, et habetur *De consecratione* d. 4 *Constat*. Item post resurrectionem data est eis a Christo potestas et auctoritas baptizandi omnes ubique, Matthei ultimo: *Docete omnes gentes, baptizantes eos*, quod dictum est non solum Petro sed undecim discipulis qui abierant in Galileam. Ut tamen unitas ecclesie servaretur, et a capite Petro omnis actus hierarchicus originaretur, noluit

desunt B^2V^6

134 est] *om.* γ | Chrysostomus] Augustinus θ, sicut π | 135 Joannis 4] Joannes Chrysostomus π | 136 Spiritus] *add.* Sanctus θ | nondum] non θ | 139 Sed] sicut dicit α | 141 datur φ | 142 etiam] enim φ | licenter] licite ρ | nondum] non ψσ | 143 quia] quod φ(-Pr) | et tamen] tunc [*add.* alias tamen Bo] θ | 144 dicit Augustinus] dicitur θ | ipsi] *om.* θψ | 145 defuit] *add.* scilicet Christus [Christo U] φ | 146 et] *om.* θψ | 147 capitulo] *om.* α(-$θ^4$) | 148 dixit $ρ^1$Sr | 149 effecit θ(-BoV^2V^3)ψRVa | 150 nec[1]] non π(-P^1) | 151 defectu γ$π^2$Sr | 152 legis] *add.* etiam $ρ^1$ | baptizare[2]] baptizato θ(-BoP^3Sv)φ(-W)P^2R$ρ^2$Va | 158 actus] *om.* $ρ^1$

132-133 Joan. 1:25 | 134-146 For Augustine, as well as the comments of Chrysostom and Alcuin, see *Cat. aur. in Joan.* 4.1, 2:381AB (2:418AB) | 146-147 Gratian, *De cons.* D.4 c.147-148 | 149-150 Rom. 15:18 | 153-154 Gratian, *De cons.* D.4 c.19 | 155-156 Matt. 28:19

Christus eos baptizare nisi ex Petri commissione et ordinatione. Sed ideo eis immediate mandat baptizare, ut ab eo, non a Petro, credatur baptismum habere virtutem, et ut eos doceret veram formam baptizandi.

Quinta Conclusio

Quinta conclusio principalis est de potestate sacerdotali conficiendi corpus et sanguinem Christi, scilicet quod istam habuerunt a Christo immediate omnes apostoli, et eam receperunt in die cene et non ante. Quod autem ante cenam nullus debuerit fieri sacerdos evangelicus patet per rationem supra tactam, quia scilicet obiectum precedit potentiam et non econtrario, sicut dicitur secundo *De anima* quod obiecta sunt priora potentiis. Unde cum obiectum potentie sacerdotalis principale sit sacramentum eucharistie, prius debuit illud sacramentum institui quam respectu illius hec potentia dari. Secunda ratio est quia lex et sacerdotium debent se concomitari, sicut dicitur ad Hebreos 7: *Translato sacerdotio, necesse est ut legis translatio fiat.* Quod exponens Augustinus ibidem, et habetur *De constitutionibus* c. *Translato*, dicit sic: *Quia enim simul et ab eodem et sub eadem sponsione utraque data sunt, quod de uno dicitur necesse est ut de altero intelligatur.* Unde quia lex nova non est confirmata nisi in passione, sicut dicitur ad Hebreos 9: *Ubi testamentum est, mors necesse est ut intercedat testatoris*, ideo, instante passione in cena, consummata est institutio omnium sacramentorum nove legis, et ideo tunc etiam sunt instituti dispensatores sacramentorum. Sunt autem facti per illa verba: *Hoc facite in meam commemorationem*, Luce 22; dicta sunt in traditione calicis, sicut etiam in traditione calicis cum verbis equipollentibus fit sacerdos. Nam dicere *hoc facite*, idest potestatem accipite hoc faciendi, equipollet ei quod dicitur: *accipe potestatem celebrandi*. Quia enim Christo subest cum voluerit posse, dicendo *hoc*

desunt B^2V^6

161 veram formam] *inv.* α(-θ^2BoBm^1) | 167 tactam] dictam π(-R) | 170 primo θ | 171 ratio] *om.* θ(-O) | 172 dicitur] ostenditur [*om.* φ^5] φ | 173 ut] et Bm$^1\varphi^4\pi$(-B^1); *add.* et $\varphi^3\varphi^5$ | ibidem] *om.* ρ | 175 et sub] ab ρ^1 | 177 passione] *add.* Christi θ(-Bo) | testamentum] *add.* mortis [mors Bo, monstratis V^5] θ(-θ^4) | est] *om.* θ | mors] *om.* $\theta\rho$ | 178 intercedat] *add.* mors θ(-Bo)ρ | 178-179 instante ... consummata] *om.* θ | 179 institutio] constitutio φ | 180 facti] *add.* sacerdotes φ | 181 22] *add.* que $\theta^1\varphi$ | 182 etiam] *add.* nunc P$^2\pi^2$ | 183 dicere] dicit ρ | 184 dicitur] est dicere φ | accipe] accipite φ | 185 Christus [*om.* φ^5] V^{1}V$^2\varphi$, Christus vel Christo θ^4 | posse] vasse θ(-Bo)

168 Aristotle, *De anima* 2.4 (415a14-22) | 172-173 Heb. 7:12 | 173-176 X. 1.2.3 | 177-178 Heb. 9:16 | 181 Luc. 22:19

facite, idest corpus et sanguinem meum conficite, quod non potest conficere nisi verus sacerdos, ut dicitur *De summa trinitate* c. 1 § *Una vero*, et 95 d. *Ecce*, ideo tunc fecit eos sacerdotes, ut sit sensus: *hoc facite*, idest faciendi potestatem accipite. Unde est magis verbum potestatem conferentis quam precipientis, quia statim potestatem faciendi acceperunt; non tamen statim fecerunt, quia non celebraverunt ante Pentecostem. Et quia omnes duodecim apostoli ibi fuerunt et communicaverunt secundum omnes sanctos preter Hylarium – qui dicit Judam non communicasse, quia illud verbum Lucas refert dictum inter sumptionem corporis et calicis – ideo omnes equaliter facti sunt sacerdotes, quibus omnibus equaliter illud dictum est: *Hoc facite in meam commemorationem*, etiam Judas. Quia fictio recipientis sacramentum non impedit receptionem caracteris, licet impediat effectum gratie secundum Augustinum.

Sexta Conclusio

Sexta conclusio principalis, de potestate ligandi et solvendi in foro conscientie, est quod eam omnes apostoli receperunt eque immediate a Christo et simul et semel et equaliter. Sed quando hoc fuerit dubium esse potest. Unde circa hoc notanda sunt duo certa et tertium dubium.

Primo, certum est quod non fuit eis data hec potestas ante cenam, quia ante cenam, ut dictum est, non fuerunt ipsi facti sacerdotes. Non sacerdos autem non potest habere claves ordinis, nec potentiam ligandi nec solvendi in foro conscientie, quia *solis sacerdotibus ligandi solvendique potestas a Deo tradita est*, *De penitentia* d. 1 c. *Si cui* § *Ex his*, sicut olim sacerdotes soli iudicabant inter lepram et non lepram. Unde Matthei 8: *Vade, ostende te sacerdoti*, et Luce 17: *Ite, ostendite vos sacerdotibus*.

desunt B^{2}V^6

188 et 95 d. Ecce] *om.* θ; Extra d. Ecclesie γ | 189 verbum] *om.* θ | 196 illud] *om.* φ^{1}ρ | 197 recipientis] accipientis θ | sacramentum] *om.* α | 198 gratie] *om.* θ | 200 principalis] *add.* est θ | 201 est] *om.* θ | 202 et^3] *om.* ρ^1 | fuit αB^{1}Barb.Sr | 203 Unde] *om.* θ; et ideo ρ | hoc] *add.* tria φ | tertium] unum ρ | 204 Primum V^{5}θ^{4}ρ | 205-206 Non^2 ... non] Nullus autem nisi sacerdos θ | 207 solvendique] atque solvendi in foro conscientie [in ... conscientie *om.* Barb.] ρ | 209-210 Matthei ... et] *om.* θ | 210 Ite] *om.* θ(-S); vade S | sacerdotibus] *add.* et Matthei 8: Vade [*om.* P^3] et [*om.* V^1] ostende te sacerdoti θ

187-188 X. 1.1.1 | 188 Gratian, D.95 c.6 | 193-194 Cf. *Cat. aur. in Matt.* 26.7 & 8 (Matt. 26:26 & 29), 1:385A & 386B (1:421A & 423A) | 196 Luc. 22:19 | 197-198 The reference has not been identified. | 207-208 "Si cui" should be "Voluissent": Gratian, *De poen.* D.1 c.60 | 208-209 Cf. Deut. 17:8-9 | 209-210 Matt. 8:4 | 210 Luc. 17:14

Unde ante cenam, in qua primo facti sunt apostoli sacerdotes, non acceperunt ipsi potestatem ligandi nec solvendi in foro conscientie. Quod ergo dictum est eis omnibus duodecim simul Matthei 18: *Quecumque alligaveritis super terram erunt ligata et in celo, et quecumque solveritis super terram erunt soluta et in celo*, est verbum promissionis de futuro, non collationis in presenti, propter causam predictam, sicut etiam simile verbum dictum Petro Matthei 16: *Quodcumque ligaveris* etc., fuit promissionis verbum, ut supra dictum est.

Secundo, certum est quod ista potestas fuit data apostolis ante Pentecostem, quia post passionem Christi confessio de mortali commisso post baptismum fuit de necessitate salutis, sicut et baptismum. Unde cum omnes apostoli peccaverunt mortaliter Christum derelinquendo, et Petrus specialiter ter negando, alii fere omnes, excepta beata virgine, desperando vel discredendo, omnes per consequens indigebant absolutione sacramentali. Unde Christus eis defecisset in necessariis si non alicui dedisset potestatem absolvendi eos. Et quia Petrus indigebat confiteri sicut et alii, ideo preter ipsum debuit hec potestas dari alicui alii apostolo, et pari ratione omnibus, ut non usque ad Pentecostem necesse haberent omnes confessiones differre. Qui enim predicaturi erant: *Confitemini alterutrum peccata vestra*, ut dicitur Jacobi 5, prius ipsi confessi sunt propria, que, scilicet, post baptismum commiserant. Et quia ante cenam baptisati fuerant, ut dictum est, et post cenam peccaverunt, ut dictum est, et a Christo sibi subtracto sacramentaliter absoluti non sunt, Christo mortuo obligati ad confitendum, et penitentes, saltem in die resurrectionis, et confiteri volentes ut supponitur, utpote habentes intellectum Scripturarum, saltem ex tunc debuerunt habere ministrum qui posset eos solvere et ligare. Et si posset videri Petrum a Domino absolutum quando respexit Dominus Petrum et egressus flevit amare, non tamen sic legitur de aliis.

desunt B^{2}V^6

214 ligaveritis θ| 215 est] fuit [ubi θ^2] θ| 216 in] de π| 217 dictum] *add.* est $\varphi\rho\sigma$| etc.] *add.* et φ| 218 supra dictum est π(-B^1)BrVa] dictum est supra θ(-P^{3}Sv)φ(-StBm^1)ψB^1, est supra dictum Bm^2, supra dictum SzBarb., dictum supra P^{3}Bm^1, supra St, dictum est Sv| 219 Secundum ρ| illa ρ^1| 223 ter] *om.* θ| 224 discredendo] discedendo ρ^1| 226 eos] *om.* $\alpha\sigma$| 228 omnes] *om.* ρ| 229 confessionem γ| 230 ut dicitur] *om.* θ; ut salvemini φ| Jacobi 5] *om.* φ| prius] *om.* φ; primo [*add.* enim (ante Bo) $\theta^2\theta^3$] θ| 231 commiserunt θ(-V^{2}Sv)ρ^1| 232 post ... et] *hom.* θ| 234 obligati] *add.* fuerunt $\varphi\rho^2$, erant ρ(-ρ^2), sunt σ| confitendum et penitentes] penitendum et confitendum ρ| et^2] *om.* ρ| 236 absolvere α| 238 egressus] *add.* foras B$^1\rho$| legimus ρ

213-215 Matt. 18:18| 217 Matt. 16:19| 229-230 Jac. 5:16| 237-238 Cf. Luc. 22:61-62, Matt. 26:75, Marc. 14:72

Nec forte illa absolutio fuit talis que liberaret a debito confitendi, quia etiam ille respectus fuit tantum spiritualis secundum Augustinum.

Dubium autem est tertium, scilicet utrum potestatem ligandi et solvendi acceperint in cena, quando facti sunt sacerdotes, an in die resurrectionis, quando dictum est eis Joannis 20: *Accipite Spiritum Sanctum: quorum remiseritis peccata, remittuntur eis; et quorum retinueritis, retenta sunt.* Et videtur quod in cena per illa verba: *Hoc facite*. Primo quidem, propter id quod communiter dicitur, quod unus et idem est caracter sacerdotalis, qui est potestas conficiendi et absolvendi. Ideo non potest una potestas dari sine alia, quia, ut dicitur 4 *Metaphisice*, quecumque sunt unum et idem simul generantur. Unde cum illis tunc sit data potestas conficiendi, per consequens et potestas absolvendi. Secundo, quia si Deus a principio mundi statim quando fuit peccatum adhibuit remedium per sacramentum penitentie congruum illi tempori, multo magis in nova lege, que perfectior est, hoc facere debuit. Unde cum apostoli, baptisati et communicati sacramentis nove legis, iam pertinerent ad eam, peccantes, eadem nocte statim debuerunt habere remedium sacramenti penitentie nove legis, quod est per confessionem et absolutionem, quod tamen non habuissent nisi tunc data fuisset potestas ligandi et solvendi. Tertio, quia dato quod potestas conficiendi et <potestas> ligandi et solvendi essent distincte, sicut aliqui dicunt, quia potentie distinguntur per obiecta, et iste potentie habent diversa obiecta, sicut corpus Christi verum et corpus Christi misticum seu peccata, nihilominus quia una fundatur super aliam sicut accessorium super principale, eo ipso quod Christus dedit primam et principalem potestatem, scilicet conficiendi, simul videtur dedisse potestatem accessoriam absolvendi. Secundum hoc autem diceretur quod

desunt B^{2}V^{6}

239 ista [ipsa V^{5}, ita St, alta U] $\theta\varphi$ | liberaret] *add.* eum θ^{1}, data [datur P^{2}] potestas $\theta^{2}\psi$ | 240 iste θ | 241 autem est θ(-Bo)φ^{3}V$^{4}\rho$] est autem [tamen φ^{5}] BoBm$^{1}\varphi^{5}$Bl$\psi\pi$Va | tertium] *om.* B$^{1}\rho^{1}$ | 243 Joannis 20] *om.* θ | 245-246 propter id quod $\varphi^{4}\pi$(-B^{1})Barb.Va] propter illud quod φ(-φ^{4})P^{2}B$^{1}\rho^{1}$Sr, propter hec O, propter quod V^{1}V^{7}, quia θ^{1} | 247 Ideo] cum [tamen θ^{2}, et Bo] θ, tunc ψ | 248 dicitur] habetur π(-R) | Metaphisicorum [Mach' W] θ(-Bo)$\varphi\pi$ | 250 per consequens] *om.* α | 257 tunc] *om.* φ | esset γ | 258 conficiendi et [*om.* Sr] ligandi et solvendi P^{4}Sr] ligandi et [atque Sv] solvendi et [*add.* potestas θ^{4}] conficiendi $\theta^{4}\psi\pi^{2}$, ligandi et solvendi θ(-θ^{4})Rρ(-Sz)Va, solvendi et ligandi Sz, conficiendi [confitendi φ^{1}] et solvendi φ | 262 quod] quo ρ | 263 simul] similiter ρ^{1} | 263-264 potestatem] *om.* π | 264 accessoriam] *add.* scilicet π

240 Cf. *Cat. aur. in Luc.* 22.14, 2:296B (2:325A) | 243-244 Joan. 20:22-23 | 245 Luc. 22:19 | 248 Aristotle, *Metaphysica* Γ.2 (1003b22-30)

Christus in verbis illis: *Accipite Spiritum Sanctum*, dedit eis Spiritum Sanctum insufflando, non aliquam potestatem. Per hoc etiam quod sequitur: *Quorum remiseritis* etc., non dedit eis potestatem ligandi et solvendi quam iam habebant, sed declaravit usum potestatis in cena eis date extendi ad alium actum quam fuisset declaratum. Unde non dixit remittite, et remittetur, sicut ibi dixit *Hoc facite*, sed dixit *Quorum remiseritis*, scilicet per potestatem quam habetis. Sed quia perdiderant Spiritum Sanctum quem in baptismo receperant, dat eis de novo Spiritum Sanctum ut digne absolvant. Confirmatur opinio, quia si prius non dedisset eis potestatem ligandi et solvendi, sed tantummodo tunc eis dedisset insufflando et dicendo *Accipite* etc., quod factum et dictum fuit presentibus et non absentibss, Thomas, unus ex duodecim qui absens erat, non accepisset a Christo potestatem ligandi et solvendi, quod est inconveniens.

Alia vero opinio potest imaginari, quod in illis verbis: *Quorum remiseritis* etc., sit eis de novo data potestas ligandi et solvendi quam prius non habebant, et hoc tripliciter. Uno modo supposito quod potestas conficiendi et absolvendi sit una res simplex et indivisibilis. Et tunc per illa verba: *Hoc facite*, nulla potestas eis fuisset data consecrandi, nec fuissent facti sacerdotes, sed solum fuisset eis factum preceptum vel monitio, quod quandocumque ex tunc communicarent vel celebrarent, quandocumque eis data potestate, essent memores passionis Christi. Et hoc videtur innui 1 ad Corinthios 11, ubi apostolus, repetens illa verba: *Hoc facite in meam commemorationem*, et quasi exponens, dicit in secunda vice ad consecrationem sanguinis: *Hoc facite quotienscumque bibetis in meam commemorationem*, quasi dicens: commedite et bibite in memoriam mortis mee. Unde secundum hoc non est verbum ad conficientes sed ad communicantes, sicut glosse innuunt utrobique. Unde consequenter

desunt B^2V^6

265 eis] *om.* θ | 267 non] nec θ | 269 extendi] *om.* π^1Va; exercendi [exercende θ^4(-P^3)] $\theta\varphi^3\varphi^4$ | 271 perdiderunt $\theta\varphi$ | 274 tunc] *add.* eam φ | 279 Alia vero] secunda ρ | opinio] *add.* dicit quod ρ | 280 sit] fuit φ^2, fuerit φ^1 | 281 tripliciter] casu π | 282 sint [sicut U, fuit V^1P^3W] θ(-Bo)φ(-Bm^1), sunt ψ | simpliciter φ(-φ^4) | 283 eis fuisset [fuisse B^1] π] eis fuit Sr, fuit eis ρVa, fuit V^5, fuisset α(-V^5) | 285 quandocumque²] quacumque $\psi\pi^2$ | 286 innui] *om.* φ; verum θ(-Bo)ψ, unde alias innui Bo | 287 illa verba] illud φ | 288-290 et ... commemorationem] *hom.* θ(-V^3) | 288 dicit] *om.* ρ^1; dixit φ | ad] ante π(-R) | 291 secundum] *om.* φ | 292 glossa innuit θ(-V^2)Bm^1Pr$P^2\rho^1$

265 Joan. 20:22 | 267 Joan. 20:23 | 270 Luc. 22:19 | 270-271 Joan. 20:23 | 275 Joan. 20:22 | 279-280 Joan. 20:23 | 283 Luc. 22:19 | 286-290 1 Cor. 11:25 | 292 Cf. *Liber vite. Biblia cum glosis ordinariis et interlinearibus* (Venice, 1495), 1 Cor. 11:25, 4:1226v

subiungit ad communicantes non conficientes: *Quotienscumque enim manducabitis panem hunc, et calicem bibetis, mortem Domini annunciabitis*, per quod videtur illud non esse potestatis collatio, sed admonitio debite perceptionis sacramenti. Et hoc supposito, diceretur quod in istis verbis: *Quorum remiseritis* etc., facti sunt de novo sacerdotes, et collata est eis utraque potestas, que est una res per expressionem unius actus. Quia cum potestas ligandi et solvendi non possit esse sine potestate consecrandi si sint una res, per consequens ista data et illa datur. Unde sicut ex forma sanguinis, quamvis sit minus principalis, conficitur sanguis per se, sed est ibi corpus per naturalem concomitantiam, dato quod consecrans prius non confecisset per se corpus Christi hostiam consecrando, ita etiam, licet absolvere sit actus minus principalis caracteris sacerdotalis quam conficere, nihilominus tamen Christus dicendo *Quorum remiseritis*, et sic exprimendo actum minus principalem, dedit potestatem absolvendi ex vi verborum, sed potestatem conficiendi ex naturali concomitantia, vel magis ex naturali identitate.

Secundo modo, secundum opinionem aliam qua potest imaginari alia potestas realiter consecrandi et alia absolvendi, potest dici quod in cena facti sunt sacerdotes, recipientes per illa verba: *Hoc facite*, potestatem consecrandi, et in resurrectione per illa: *Quorum remiseritis*, potestatem absolvendi.

Tertio modo, si dicatur quod est unus caracter ampliatus, sicut dicunt quidam de ordine sacerdotali et episcopali, quod quando sacerdos consecratur in episcopum, non additur novus caracter, sed ampliatur preexistens ad duos novos effectus, scilicet confirmare et ordinare, ad quos non se prius extendebat, ita etiam potest dici quod caracter sacerdotalis, impressus a Christo apostolis in cena per illa verba: *Hoc facite*, ad effectum consecrandi, ampliatus est postmodum a Christo in resurrectione per illa verba: *Quorum remiseritis*, ad effectum absolvendi.

desunt B^2V^6

295 esse] est ρ^1 | 298 Quia cum] quamvis φ | 299 absolvendi θ(-BoSv) | 300 sint] fuit φ | res] *add.* et θ | ista] illa ρ^1 | 301 efficitur ρ^1 | 303 per se] *om.* π | 306-307 ex ... potestatem] *om.* θ | 308 naturali] *om.* ρ^1 | 309 qua] *om.* π^2; que π^1Sr, secundum quam ρ^1 | imaginari] *add.* quod sit φ | 310 et] *om.* $\gamma\pi$(-B^1)σ | 311 recipientes] *add.* tunc α | 312 illa] *add.* verba θ | 315 quod] *add.* sicut φ | 316 additur] *add.* sibi [nisi Bo] θ | 318 quos] quod ρ | non se prius πBm²Barb.] non prius se φ, se prius non $\theta^4\rho^2$, prius se non $\theta^2\theta^3$, prius non se ψ, se non prius Sr, prius non Va | 320 & 321 effectum] officium $\psi\pi^2$

293-295 1 Cor. 11:26 | 297 & 305 Joan. 20:23 | 311 Luc. 22:19 | 312 Joan. 20:23 | 319 Luc. 22:19 | 321 Joan. 20:23

Et iste opiniones locum habent in consecratione sacerdotum que fit cotidie, quia in diversis horis et seorsum dicitur sibi in traditione calicis cum patena: *Accipe potestatem celebrandi missas* etc., per quod sibi datur caracter sacerdotalis ad consecrandum. Cum hoc etiam seorsum per manus impositionem datur sibi Spiritus Sanctus per illa verba: *Accipite Spiritum Sanctum, quorum remiseritis peccata, remittuntur* etc. In quibus verbis, si sunt diverse potestates, potest dici quod seorsum dantur. Si autem est una et eadem, tunc magis videtur dari tota potestas in verbis que exprimunt actum principalem, et in aliis verbis non datur aliqua potestas nova, sed exprimitur et declaratur usus potestatis ad novum actum qui non fuerat expressus. Si vero est unus caracter non indivisibilis sed ampliabilis et extensibilis, tunc per illa verba: *Accipe potestatem*, dicendo illi qui ordinatur cum traditione calicis, datur caracter ad consecrandum. Et per illa: *Quorum remiseritis*, ampliatur idem caracter ad absolvendum.

Inter has autem opiniones videtur improbabilior illa opinio que dicit apostolos non factos sacerdotes in cena per illa verba: *Hoc facite*, sed in resurrectione per illa: *Quorum remiseritis*, propter rationes dictas, maxime propter hoc: quod Thomas non fuisset factus sacerdos qui presens non erat, licet absens Spiritum Sanctum recipere potuisset si alias dispositus fuisset. Sicut Numeri 11, de illis septuaginta viris quibus erat dandus Spiritus Sanctus, *remanserunt in castris duo viri* etc., *super quos requievit Spiritus; nam et ipsi descripti fuerant, et non exierunt ad tabernaculum*. Sed licet Christus absentem corpore potuisset consecrare, non tamen est credibile quod ipsum consecrasset. Immo nec quod tunc Spiritum Sanctum receperit, nam reversus dixit: *Nisi videro in manibus eius fixuram clavorum* etc., *non credam*. Unde cum pertinacia et obstinatione infidelitatis non videbatur habere Spiritum Sanctum. Unde nec presens

desunt B^2V^6

322 ille ρ^1 | 324 Accipite ρ^1Va | 325 etiam] *om.* θ | seorsum] *om.* ρ | 328 sint θ | 329-330 verbis ... verbis] verbis [*om.* St] primis [premissis Bm^1; verbis primis *inv.* U] ita quod in verbis secundis [secundis verbis St] φ | 333 ista φ | Accipite φ(-St)ρ^1 | 335 illa] ista φ; *add.* verba $\theta\varphi^3$W | 336 videtur] *om.* α | improbabilior] *om.* $\theta\psi$; probabilior [*add.* est φ] $\varphi\pi$(-R) | opinio] *om.* ρ | 337 non] *om.* $\varphi V^7\pi$(-R) | sed] non [et non B^1] $\varphi\pi$(-R) | 338 predictas π | 341 Sicut] sic φ | 342 etc.] ecclesiastici [*om.* Bo] $\theta\psi$, ecclesiastici idest custodes tabernaculi [tabernaculi custodes W] φ | 343 Spiritus] *add.* Sanctus θ(-V^3) | et[1]] *om.* φ | fuerunt π(-R) | exierant ρ | 344 absente [absens P^1] $V^7\pi$(-R)Va, absentes ρ | posset ρ | 346 nam] *add.* ipse θ | 348 videtur habuisse φ | nec] licet φ | presens] prius ρ^1

337 Luc. 22:19 | 338 Joan. 20:23 | 341-343 Num. 11:26 | 346-347 Joan. 20:25

cum illa obduratione recepisset. Sed potestatem consecrandi et absolvendi equaliter bonus et malus accipere potest, sed absens corpore a consecrante non solet.

Quod autem per illa verba: *Hoc facite*, potius quam per ista: *Quorum remiseritis*, facti fuerunt sacerdotes innuit Innocentius III, *De penitentia* d. 6 c. 1 § *Laboret*, ubi dicitur: *Ideoque non petat sacerdotes ab unitate ecclesie divisos*. Cum enim prius dixisset: *Qui confitetur sacerdoti meliori quam potest confiteatur*, infert quod sacerdoti malo, specialiter scismatico, non confiteatur. Unde redarguit Judam qui penitens ivit ad phariseos relinquens apostolos, quasi dicens: reliquit bonos sacerdotes, ivit ad malos, ubi videtur supponere tunc fuisse apostolos sacerdotes, quod fuit inter cenam et resurrectionem, quo tempore Judas peccavit et laqueo se suspendit, Matthei 27. Tunc igitur facti sunt sacerdotes per illa verba: *Hoc facite*, et non post resurrectionem per illa verba: *Quorum remiseritis*, per quecumque verba sit eis data potestas ligandi et solvendi. Et confirmatur, quia licet Christus per utraque verba, immo etiam sine verbis, eos potuerit ordinare, rationabilius tamen debuerunt ordinari per verba exprimentia actum principalem ordinis, sicut illa: *Hoc facite*, ratione consecrationis quam refert li hoc, quam per verba exprimentia actum secundarium, qualia sunt illa: *Quorum remiseritis*. Nec obstat quod inducitur 1 ad Corinthios 11, quia illa verba, licet dicantur communicantibus et non conficientibus, nihilominus dicta sunt etiam celebrantibus, et per illa data est potestas celebrandi presentibus. Sic igitur apostoli facti sunt sacerdotes in cena, accipientes potestatem consecrandi, que est principalis.

Sed in resurrectione per illa verba: *Quorum remiseritis*, acceperunt potestatem quo ad actum secundarium. Et hec est opinio Thome, 4 *Sententiarum* 24 d., et hec est magis consona dictis sanctorum. Et tunc

desunt B^{2}V^6

349 ista θ | Sed] *om.* φπ(-R); et ψ | absolvendi] *add.* quam quidem potestatem φ, quam B^1 | 350 recipere θ | consecrante] consecratione ρVa; *add.* consecrari φ | 352 illa] ista θ | ista] illa πρ^1 | 354 Laboret] 1 [*om.* Bm^1; et V^5] α | ubi] ibi πSr | dicitur ρ] *om. cet. mss.* | 356 quam] *add.* cito θ(-Bo) | 358 ivit] et ivit [ivitque V^3] θφ^1 | 359 ubi] *om.* θψ | videtur] *add.* Innocentius φ | 361 illa] hec π | 362 verba] *om.* π(-B^1)ρ | 363 quecumque] *add.* etiam φ(-Bm^1) | absolvendi θ(-V^3)π(-T)Barb. | 364 potuisset [posset et potuisset Bm^1] α, potuit σ | 366 sicut illa] *om.* α | 367 refert ... quam] *hom.* θ | secundarium [secundum Bm^1, secundum alium U] actum α(-θ^{2}BoS) | 368 ista θ(-V^2) | 369 ista φ(-St) | 370 illa] *add.* verba θ | 371 est] *om.* V^{1}V^{2}V^{5}ψπ(-P^4)Sr | 374 opinio] *add.* beati θ, sancti ψ

352 Luc. 22:19 | 352-353 Joan. 20:23 | 353-356 Gratian, *De poen.* D.6 c.1 | 361 Matt. 27: 3-5 | 361-362 Luc. 22:19 | 362 Joan. 20:23 | 366 Luc. 22:19 | 368 Joan. 20:23 | 368-369 1 Cor. 11:25-26 | 373 Joan. 20:23 | 374-375 Thomas Aquinas, 4 *Sent.* 24.2.3 ad 2

dicendum est quod Christus, etiam Thome absenti corpore, dedit eandem potestatem. Vel potest dici quod in cena dedit utramque potestatem, sed tunc innotuit altera. Et sic dictum Thome salvatur, quia res dicitur fieri quando innotescit. Unde sicut Christus dixit de se post resurrectionem: *Data est mihi omnis potestas*, non quod tunc esset sibi data de novo, sed quod tunc erat manifestata, ita dicitur tunc *Quorum remiseritis*, non novam potestatem dando, sed declarando datam. Et hec est rationabilior opinio. Quod ergo dicit ibi Gregorius in homilia: *Principatum superni iudicii sortiuntur, ut vice Dei quibusdam peccata retineant, quibusdam relaxent*, exponendum est: *sortiuntur*, idest sortiti esse monstrantur, et eodem modo ad alias quam plures auctoritates similes.

Septima Conclusio

Septima conclusio est de potestate pontificali, scilicet quod alii apostoli non acceperunt a Christo potestatem episcopalem immediate, nec facti sunt ab eo episcopi sicut Petrus, sed magis a Petro mediate vel immediate, solo vel cum alio aut cum aliis. Et primo quidem patet quod non omnes alii apostoli sunt simul facti cum Petro episcopi, sicut simul cum eo facti sunt sacerdotes, quia dicitur 66 d. § *Porro*, quod *Hierosolimorum primus archiepiscopus, beatus Jacobus, a Petro et Jacobo et Joanne apostolis est ordinatus*. Ex quo arguitur, quia sicut semel baptizatus non rebaptizatur, ita nec semel in episcopum consecratus iterum ordinatur, 68 d. c. *Sicut semel*. Sed Jacobus tunc fuit per apostolos ordinatus; ergo non erat prius a Domino in episcopum consecratus. Et ita non omnes apostoli saltem fuerunt a Christo immediate facti episcopi.

Sed ad hoc dicunt quidam quod illud capitulum loquitur de unctione visibili tantum qua illi eum consecraverunt. Sed prius erat invisibiliter unctus a Domino, sicut sanctificatus in utero vel baptizatus baptismo

desunt B^2V^6

376 est] *om.* σ | etiam] *om.* ρ^1 | eandem] *om.* ψ; utramque [*add.* alias hanc et secundariam Bo] $\theta(-\theta^4)$, hanc secundariam θ^4, consecrandi φ | 377 potestatem¹] *add.* aliter hanc secundariam potestatem V^2 | 379 dicit π(-R) | 380 tunc] *om.* θ | sibi] *om.* σ | 381 quod $\pi(-B^1)\rho^1$] *om.* φV^3; quia $\theta(-V^3)\psi B^1$Barb.σ | manifesta ρVa | tunc²] *om.* $\gamma(-P^2)$ | 386 consimiles [*om.* B^1] πVa | 391 aut] vel γ | 394 et¹] *om.* θ | 395 quia] quod $\theta\psi\pi^2$ | sicut] *om.* ρ^1 | rebaptizatur] baptizatur θ | 396 consecratus] ordinatus φ | iterum] *add.* non ρ^1 | 402 vel] *add.* etiam ρSr

380 Matt. 28:18 | 381 Joan. 20:23 | 383-385 *Cat. aur. in Joan.* 20.3, 2:583A (2:639B) | 393-395 Gratian, D.66 c.2 | 396-397 Gratian, D.68 c.1

flaminis nihilominus baptizatur. Sed secundum hoc habetur propositum, quia sanctificatus in utero vel baptizatus baptismo flaminis non est sacramentaliter baptizatus. Unde adhuc habet recipere verum sacramentum baptismi in actu, ac si nihil eorum habuisset. Ita etiam secundum hoc, licet beatus Jacobus et alii recepissent Spiritum Sanctum, et de terra Christo insufflante, et de celo Christo mittente in die Pentecostes, non tamen propter hoc fuerunt sacramentaliter in episcopos consecrati. Unde erant similiter ex integro consecrandi.

Alii dicunt quod non ordinaverunt eum, sed tantum formam ordinandi aliis ostenderunt. Sed istud est contra decretalem *De celebratione missarum* c. *De homine*, ubi dicitur: *Abicienda sunt falsa remedia, que veris sunt periculis graviora.* Unde fingere falsam consecrationem ad ostendendum quomodo debet fieri vera consecratio nullomodo est licitum, cum solo verbo sine alio exemplo facti potuit clare dici quod episcopus non consecraretur nisi a tribus, sive alias fuisset sic factum, sive non, quia oportuit quod primus a tribus vere consecratus consecraretur sine exemplo vero. Nec in cultu Christiane religionis debuit adhiberi exemplum falsum nec fictum secundum Augustinum, quia *ecclesia in suis actionibus fraudem aliquam non debet adhibere, De donationibus* c. *Per tuas*.

Tertii dicunt quod non in episcopum sed in archiepiscopum eum ordinaverunt, sicut textus sonat cum dicit: *Primus archiepiscopus*. Sed nec istud valet, quia aut loquuntur de vera consecratione et ordinatione pontificali de qua querimus, et tunc episcopus, quando fit archiepiscopus, nullomodo ordinatur nec consecratur aliqua alia ordinatione nec consecratione, etiam si fieret patriarcha vel papa, aut loquuntur de promotione simplici episcopi in archiepiscopum, que est per electionem

desunt B^2V^6; 410 *post verbum* consecrandi *deest* Sr

405 habet] potest θ | 406 actuali ρ^1 | eorum] istorum θ(-V^5), ipsorum V^5, illorum $\varphi^2\psi$Va, horum φ^3Sr | etiam] et $\theta\varphi$(-U) | 407 terra] gratia $\theta P^2\pi^2$ | Christo] Christi θ | 409 sacramentaliter] statim ρ^1 | 410 similiter π^1Barb.Va] *om.* θ(-θ^4); iterum θ^4, simpliciter $\gamma\pi^2$, sibi ρ^1, simul Sr | 411-452 Alii ... Petrus] *om.* Sr | 412 illud φ(-Bl)π^2 | 414 veris] ceteris $\psi\pi^2$ | confingere [confingetur V^5] $\theta^2\theta^3$, effingere θ^4, effigiare ρVa | 415 quomodo] quod [*add.* alias quomodo V^1 Bo] $\theta\psi$, qualiter φ | deberet [debeat B^1] γ(-St)π | 416 alio] aliquo $\varphi\rho^1$ | 418 quia] et [*om.* Bo] sic θ^1, quod ρ^1 | oportuerit ρ^1 | primus] *add.* consecrandus [ex tunc V^5] θ^1 | consecratus] *om.* θ^1; consecratis φ | consecraretur] *om.* ρ^1 | 419 sine] sicut φ | exhiberi θ | 420 nec] vel α | 425 ista [ita St] $\theta\varphi$ | valent φ | loquitur [loquimur Bo] θ(-V^3)π(-R) | vera] una ρ^1 | et] in φ(-V^4) | 427 nec²] vel $\psi\pi^2$

412-414 X. 3.41.7 | 420-422 X. 3.24.5 | 424 Gratian, D.66 c.2

inferiorum, vel per provisionem superioris vel pallii concessionem, et ista non oportet quod fiat a tribus episcopis. Immo electio vel postulatio fit a canonicis, et quando fiebat electio metropolitani a suffraganeis, sicut tempore beati Nicholai, fiebat non a tribus sed ab omnibus. Provisio vero, que fit per superiorem, fit ab ipso solo. Item exemplum illud non esset ad propositum, ubi queritur de vera episcopi consecratione, a quot et a quibus debet fieri. Hoc etiam est contra Remigium, qui agens de ista ordinatione non utitur verbo archiepiscopi sed episcopi. Unde super illud Matthei 10, ubi ponuntur nomina apostolorum, Jacobus Alphei etc., dicit Remigius de isto Jacobo: *Cuius meriti fuerit, testes sunt apostoli qui eum episcopum Hierosolimitane ecclesie ordinaverunt.*

Quarti dicunt quod ordinaverunt, idest intronizaverunt eum ad administrationem certi loci. Prius enim erat episcopus, sed sine titulo. Nec ista expositio valet ad propositum, quia cum intronizatio differat ab ordinatione, ea que fiunt in uno non dant formam nec exemplum in alio, alias cum intronizatio possit fieri per archidiaconum sine episcopo, pari ratione ordinatio, quod est hereticum. Dato ergo quod Petrus cum Jacobo et Joanne intronizare potuerunt Jacobum sic eum honorando tali solemnitate, non tamen hoc faciendo dedissent formam ordinandi que ibi ponitur, ut minus quam a tribus episcopis nullatenus episcopus ordinetur. Et sic adhuc stat argumentum, scilicet quod beatus Jacobus non fuit a Christo factus episcopus, cum fuerit postea ab aliis factus. Et sic non omnes apostoli fuerunt a Christo facti episcopi sicut Petrus.

Secundo dico quod nullus apostolus preter Petrum factus est a Christo episcopus, quod patet tripliciter. Primo, quia nihil est asserendum de divinis nisi quod ex Scripturarum testimoniis vel ratione probari potest. Primum probatur per Dionysium et Hieronymum in homilia: *Ecce ego mitto ad vos*, ubi loquens de opinione quadam de Zacharia, filio Barachie,

desunt B^2V^6; 452 *usque ad verbum* Petrus *deest* Sr

430 per] *om.* $\psi\pi^2$ | ista] ita φ, illa ρ^1 | 431 fit] *om.* $P^2\pi(-B^1)\rho$ | 432 et] verum φ | aliquando φ | metropolitanorum $\psi\pi^2$ | 433 fiebat] *om.* α | tribus] *add.* fiebat θ^2 | omnibus] *add.* fiebat θ^1 | 434 ab ipso] a papa φ | 436 deberet [debeat Bm^1] $\alpha(-\theta^4 St)$ | illa ρ^1 | 439 illo ρ^1 | meriti] *om.* ρ^1 | 442 archiepiscopus θ | 443 illa ρ^1 | 445 cum] sicut ρ^1 | 449 episcopus] *om.* θ | ordinaretur $\varphi^1 W$ | 450 scilicet] *om.* ρ^1 | 454 quod] et hoc θVa, et γ | 455 ratione] *add.* efficaci θ | 456 Ecce] *add.* quod ρ^1 | ego] *om.* θ | 457 quadam] *add.* et θ

432-433 Cf. Jacobus a Voragine, *Legenda aurea*, chap. 3, ed. Th. Graesse (Dresdae & Lipsiae, 1896), p. 23 | 437-440 *Cat. aur. in Matt.* 10.1, 1:163B (1:174B) | 438 Matt. 10:2-4 | 456-459 Cf. Thomas de Hibernia, *Manipulus florum*, British Library Add. MS 24, 129, fol. 139r. The quotation is attributed to Jerome, *Ad metuadem virginem*.

dicit sic: *Quod dictum, quia ex Scripturis non habet testimonium, eadem facilitate contempnitur qua probatur*. Secundum de ratione per Augustinum, in sermone *De assumptione beate Marie virginis*, ubi dicit: *Fiat ergo ipsa ratio auctoritas, sine qua nec valet auctoritas*. Alios autem apostolos a Petro nulla ratione convincitur factos esse a Christo episcopos, nec auctoritate. Ergo etc.

De auctoritate quidem patet, quia in Canone non inveniuntur verba ad hoc sufficientia. Nihil enim eis dictum est in communi ad potestatem sacerdotalem pertinens nisi illa tria que inducta sunt. Primo quidem illud Matthei 18: *Quecumque alligaveritis*. Sed per illud non sunt ipsi facti episcopi propter tria. Primo, quia Petrus per similia verba et etiam maiora, Matthei 16: *Quodcumque ligaveris*, non fuit factus episcopus. Secundo, quia ipsi nondum erant sacerdotes, nec per consequens poterant fieri episcopi. Tertio, quia illud fuit promissio, non alicuius potestatis nec episcopalis nec sacerdotalis collatio, ut dictum est. Ergo etc.

Secundo, illud Luce 22: *Hoc facite in meam commemorationem*. Sed nec per hoc facti sunt episcopi, quia per verba consecrationis non efficitur plus quam per illa significetur, nisi propter naturalem concomitantiam et inseparabilem ad principale significatum vel accessoriam. Sed potestas pontificalis non est accessoria nec necessario consequens ad sacerdotalem, et illa verba non indicant nisi nudum actum sacerdotalem quem potest facere quilibet simplex sacerdos, scilicet consecrare corpus et sanguinem Christi, quod importat cum dicit: *Hoc facite*, scilicet quod feci, idest eucharistiam, vel corpus et sanguinem esse sub speciebus. Ergo per illa verba non fecit eos nisi simplices sacerdotes.

Tertio, illud quod dicitur Joannis 20: *Quorum remiseritis* etc. Sed nec per istud sunt ordinati episcopi, quia cum ordinatio episcopi sit distincta

desunt $B^{2}V^{6}$

458 Quod] *om.* θ | quia] quod θ | 459-460 per Augustinum] Augustinus [Augustini φ^{3}] φV^{7} | 460 beate] *om.* γ | Marie] *om.* θ(-V^{5}S) | dicit] *add.* sic ρ | 461 non $\psi\pi^{2}$ | valet] patet ρ^{1} | 462 esse] *om.* [etiam R] π | 464 in Canone] *om.* θ | verba] *om.* α | 464-465 ad hoc] *om.* θ | 465 enim] *om.* θ | 466 illa] ista $\theta\psi$ | 467 ligaveritis [ligaveris $V^{5}\theta^{4}\psi$] α(-Pr)ρ(-Bm^{2}) | 470 erant] *add.* facti θ | 471 promissum θ | non] nec ρ^{1}Va | 473 Secundum θ(-Bo) | 475 et] *om.* ρ^{1} | 476 principalem [*om.* V^{4}] significationem φ | accessoriam [accessionem W] $\varphi P^{4}B^{1}$Barb.] accessorium $\theta\sigma$, accessoria [accessionum V^{7}] $\psi RP^{1}\rho^{1}$ | 477 necessario] *om.* φ | consequens] concomitans φ | 478 ista θ | 481 vel ... esse] *om.* θ | speciebus] *add.* panis et vini θ | 484 illud γ(-φ^{4}) | distincta est ρ^{1}

459-461 Augustine, *De assumptione Beatae Mariae Virginis*, chap. 2 (PL 40:1144) | 467 Matt. 18:18 | 469 Matt. 16:19 | 473 & 480 Luc. 22:19 | 483 Joan. 20:23

ab ordinatione simplicis sacerdotis, non est verisimile quod illud per quod proprie et precise facta est ordinatio primorum episcoporum dicatur communiter omni illi qui ordinatur in simplicem sacerdotem. Unde cum in omni ordinatione simplicis sacerdotis dicatur ab episcopo cuilibet ordinando: *Accipe Spiritum Sanctum, quorum remiseris* etc., non est verisimile quod illa verba fuerint propria et precisa ordinatio primorum episcoporum qui fuerunt summi sacerdotes, quia etiam in lege alia erat ordinatio simplicium sacerdotum, alia summi.

Et confirmatur, quia verba sacramentalia prolata a ministro sunt eiusdem virtutis in effectu sacramentali sicut prolata a Christo, sicut patet in forma sacramenti eucharistie, in qua verba illa: *Hoc est corpus meum*, illud idem efficiunt quod effecerunt in Christo ea dicente. Si ergo Christus, dicendo illa verba: *Accipite Spiritum Sanctum* etc., fecisset apostolos episcopos, qui iam erant facti sacerdotes in cena quo ad caracterem sacerdotalem per illa verba: *Hoc facite* etc., sibi dicta in traditione panis et calicis, pari ratione episcopus, dicens illa verba, scilicet *Accipite Spiritum Sanctum, quorum remiseritis* etc., illi qui iam factus est sacerdos per verba sibi dicta in traditione calicis cum pane et vino: *Accipe potestatem celebrandi missas* etc., faceret eum episcopum, quod est absurdum. Item Thomas, qui presens non erat illis verbis, non fuisset factus episcopus. Item quod per neutra verba, scilicet *Hoc facite* et *Quorum remiseritis*, sint facti episcopi patet, quia sicut dicit Anacletus, 21 d. *In novo*: *Petro primo pontificatus in ecclesia Christi datus est.* Sed illa verba dicta sunt simul et semel apostolis, et per consequens habuerunt suum effectum unum et indivisibilem, et sine ordine prioris et posterioris. Ergo tunc non est datus pontificatus alicui primo. Sic ergo nulla auctoritas Canonis cogit dicere alios apostolos a Petro factos esse episcopos a Christo.

Item nec ratio cogit, immo magis oppositum, propter tria. Primo, quia sicut in creatione humani generis, ut esset maior unitas Deus fecit ex uno

desunt B^{2}V^6

487 omni illi] cum illis [illo Bo] θ | ordinantur θ | simplices sacerdotes [sacerdote V^3] θ | 489 ordinando] *om.* ρ | Accipite γ(-P^2) | remiseritis θ(-O)φπ(-R)σ | 490 quod] *add.* per φ | fuerint] *om.* φ; fuerunt $\pi^1\rho^1$, sint π^2 | precisa] *add.* facta fuerit φ | 492 sacerdotum] *add.* et ρ | 493-510 Et ... primo] *om.* Va | 493 sacerdotalia ρ^1 | 496 in] *om.* [a φ^5] φ | 499 sibi θψSr] *om.* π; eis φ, supra ρ^1, sic Barb. | 500 scilicet α(-StBm^{1}W)π(-P^4)] *om.* StBm^{1}WP^{4}ρSr | 501 ille [item ille θ^2] $\theta\rho^2$B^1 | per] *add.* illa π(-R) | 502 sibi] supra π | Accipite γ(-StP^2) | 503 celebrandi missas] *om.* α | 506 primo] *om.* ρ | 510 alicui pontificatus α | 511 factos esse] *om.* α(-θ^4); *inv.* θ^4 | Christo] *add.* esse [*om.* φ^5] factos [ordinatos St] α(-θ^4)

497 Joan. 20:22 | 499 Luc. 22:19 | 505 Luc. 22:19 | Joan. 20:23 | 506-507 Gratian, D.21 c.2

esse hominum genus, ut dicit Paulus, Actuum 17, quia primo fecit masculum, et ex illo fecit feminam, ex quibus duobus omnes processerunt, sic ad servandam ecclesie unitatem non fecit Deus duos aut tres episcopos a quibus alii fierent, ut essent plura capita et principia, sed debuit facere unum episcopum tantum, a quo ceteri fierent. Immo si ita esset impossibile quod unus episcopus faceret alium nisi essent duo aut tres, sicut quod unus homo faciat alium, sicut ad servandam unitatem Deus fecit unicum primum hominem, et de illo fecit feminam quam ille non poterat facere, qui duo ex tunc ceteros generarent, ita Christus fecisset unum episcopum, et ex illo secundum, et ex illis tertium, si non unus episcopus posset consecrare alium episcopum. Nunc autem, quia sola prohibitio ecclesie obstat ut non consecretur episcopus nisi a tribus, quam Petrus ipsemet fecit, cui ipse non subfuit, fecit Christus solum Petrum episcopum, a quo postmodum alii omnes sunt facti.

Secundo patet idem, quia sicut in prima rerum creatione Deus solum fecit seminaria sine quibus res esse non possunt – unde in speciebus que non generantur nisi a mare et femina fecit duo supposita, masculum et feminam, simul quidem in ceteris, sed in homine prius masculum ratione iam dicta; non autem fecit supposita reptilium que per putrefactionem generantur, nec in aliis plus quam duo supposita, quia illa sufficiunt ad generandum – ita in ecclesia, quia unus episcopus sufficit ad alium consecrandum, nec est nisi propter solemnitatem ab ecclesia inventum quod tres concurrant – sicut unus sacerdos sufficit ad consecrandum corpus Christi, sed tamen in quibusdam ecclesiis in ordinibus sacerdotum vel ordinationibus episcoporum ordinati concelebrant ordinatori propter reverentiam et maiorem solemnitatem – ideo Christus non debuit per se

desunt B^{2}V^6

514 esse] omne [homine V^7] γP^4 | dicit] *om.* θ(-Bo) | 515 fecit] *om.* πSr | 518 ita] *add.* non $\psi\pi^2$ | 519 impossibile] *add.* esset [erunt Bo] $\theta^2\psi\pi^2\rho$, fuisset Sr | aut] vel θ | 520 homo] *om.* $\psi\pi^2$ | alium] *add.* tunc φ, sed $\psi\pi^2$ | conservandam [servandum W] φ(-Pr) | unitatem] *add.* generis humani [*inv.* Bm^1] φ | 521 Deus $\varphi\pi^2\rho^1$] *om.* $\theta\pi^1$Barb.σ | fecit^1] *om.* θ | unum π | ille] *add.* solus θ(-θ^4) | 522 poterat] *add.* solus θ^4 | generarent] *add.* fecit Deus a principio θ(-Bo) | Christus] *add.* non [*exp.* V^7] $\psi\pi^2$ | fecisset] *add.* nisi π^2 | 523 episcopum] *om.* θ | illo] isto φ | 524 Nunc autem quia] sed quoniam [quin V^1; *add.* quia Bo] θ | 526 cui] *add.* scilicet prohibitioni [prohibitione St, prohibitionem Bl] φ | 527 postmodum] *om.* θ | 531 simul [similiter Br] ... homine [hominem π^1] prius masculum $\pi^1\rho\sigma$] simul [semel U] quamvis solum hominem prius [prius hominem St] masculum φ, simul et primo quidem [quod V^7] hominem solum prius masculum $\psi\pi^2$, simul quidem solum hominem prius masculum θ(-θ^4), simul quidem preter hominem quem prius solum fecit θ^4 | 533 ista θV^7 | 535 ab ecclesia] ecclesie $\theta\pi^2$ | 536 concurrant] consecrant [consecrent U] φ | 538 ordinationibus] *om.* θ^4; ordinibus θ^2V$^5\rho^1$ | ordinatori] *om.* θ^4; ordinationem [ordinati Bo, ordinatione V^5] θ(-θ^4) | 539 ideo] unde ρ^1

514 Act. 17:26

facere nisi unum episcopum a quo ceteri fierent, ex quo unus sufficit. Ille autem unus non debuit esse alius quam Petrus, de quo dicit glossa Actuum 1 in catalogo apostolorum ubi primus nominatur: *Petrus primus ponitur, quasi pastor et princeps.*

Tertia ratio est quia in ecclesia non debet esse minor unitas nec minus bonus ordo quam fuit in synagoga. Sed in illa, ad bonam ordinationem et unitatem ipsius, pertinuit quod Moyses, legis lator, non faceret simul per se plures episcopos, sed unum tantum, scilicet Aaron, a quo omnes alii immediate vel mediate postmodum processerunt. Ergo Christus, nove legis lator, ecclesie ordinator, non debuit facere plures episcopos, sed unum tantum, scilicet Petrum, a quo omnes alii immediate vel mediate postmodum fierent.

Videtur ergo rationabiliter iste fuisse processus in ordinatione episcopali apostolorum, scilicet quod Petrus factus fuit solus episcopus a Christo ante ascensionem. Post Spiritus Sancti autem missionem, sive ipsa prima die dominica sive alia, Petrus solus episcopus fecit Joannem episcopum. Deinde Petrus cum consecrato Joanne fecit Jacobum Zebedei, quibus tribus factis, tunc ordinavit Petrus quod deinceps non ordinaretur episcopus nisi a tribus episcopis. Et ad ostendendam formam huius, ipse cum duobus predictis ordinavit Jacobum, ut dicitur 66 d. § *Porro*, licet propter raritatem episcoporum, quando apostoli fuerunt divisi, non potuerit hec forma semper servari. Ideo Paulus forte solus Timotheum et Titum ordinavit episcopos, qui separatus a Barnaba non habebat in societate sua episcopos nisi quos postea fecit, nam Lucas, Demas, Silas et huiusmodi non erant episcopi. Sed quando potuerunt habere duos, tunc cum eis ordinabant, non soli.

desunt B^{2}V^{6}

544 est] *om.* σ | nec] et θ | 546 unitatem] bonitatem ρ^{1} | simul] *om.* σ | 546-547 per se] *om.* α | simul per se π] per se simul ρ | 548 vel mediate] *om.* φ | mediate vel immediate θ | 549 lator] *om.* π(-R); *add.* et φσ | ecclesie] *om.* π(-R) | 550 vel mediate] *om.* P^{2}π(-R) | 552 Videtur] *om.* ρ | rationabiliter] *om.* ψσ; rationabile φ; *add.* quod α | ille ρ^{1} | fuisse πσ] *om.* ψ; fuit [fuerit UBm^{1}] θφρ | 553 fuit OπSr] fuerit [fuerat Sz] α(-O)ρVa | 554 autem] *om.* ρ^{1}σ | sive] cum [in V^{3}, et in Sv] θ(-Bo) | 556 cum] *om.* θπ(-R) | consecrante V^{3}φRBarb.Va | 558 episcopis] *om.* ρ | ostendendam] videndam [evidentiam V^{7}] γ, videndum θ | 560 raritatem] paucitatem φ, unitatem ψθ^{4}, raritatem alias unitatem O, unitatem alias raritatem V^{1}, unionem vel raritatem Bo | apostoli] *om.* θ^{1}(-Bo) | divisi] *om.* θ^{2}φ; dispersi ψ; *add.* ab invicem θ^{1} | 561 potuit θ(-V^{1}BoV^{2})WP^{1}σ | 563 Lucas] *add.* et ρ | Silas] *om.* ρ | 564 huiusmodi] hii φ, quidam alii θρ | poterant ψ, poterat π | 565 ordinaverunt φ, ordinabat π | solus π

541-543 *Liber vite. Biblia cum glosis ordinariis et interlinearibus*, Act. 1:13, 4:1314r | 559 Gratian, D.66 c.2 | 561-562 Cf. Eusebius, *Historia ecclesiastica* 3.4 (PG 20:219)

Ratio autem quare filii Zebedei creduntur prius a Petro in episcopos ordinati est: quia illi post Petrum fuerunt maiores et honorabiliores, et hos cum Petro Christus ceteris preferebat, ut patuit in transfiguratione, in suscitatione filie archisynagogi, in oratione in orto et similibus, in quibus hos solos, quasi familiares secretarios, secum assumpsit, Matthei 9, 17, 26. Unde super illud Luce 7: *Non permisit intrare secum quemquam nisi Petrum et Joannem et Jacobum*, dicit Theophylus: *Solum hos intromisit tanquam discipulorum vertices*. Item Matthei 17, super illud: *Assumpsit Jesus Petrum, Jacobum et Joannem*, dicit Chrysostomus: *Ideo hos assumpsit, quia aliis potiores erant*. Item super illud quod ibi sequitur: *Quare nos non potuimus eicere illum*, dicit Chrysostomus: *Columne ille non aderant, Petrus, Jacobus et Joannes*. Quod autem alter Jacobus diceretur columna cum Petro et Joanne, ad Galatas 2, est quia Jacobus Zebedei iam erat martyrio coronatus. Quod autem Joannes fuerit maior licet iunior fratre, ideo sibi prelatus, patet super illud Matthei 10: *Et Andreas frater eius*, ubi dicit Chrysostomus: *Marcus autem post duos vertices, Petrum et Joannem, Andream numerat*, ubi innuit Petrum et Joannem inter apostolos fuisse sublimiores. Item super illud ibidem: *Jacobus Zebedei et Joannes frater eius*, dicit Chrysostomus: *Vide autem quia non secundum dignitatem ordinat. Mihi enim videtur Joannes non aliis solum, sed etiam fratre maior esse*.

Ex predictis apparet falsa glossa super illud capitulum 66 d. *Porro*, que dicit quod a principio in primitiva ecclesia *omnes apostoli erant simplices sacerdotes, et tamen poterant consecrare episcopos. Nam Moyses simplex sacerdos erat, et tamen consecravit Aaron in pontificem. Nec tunc erat*

desunt B^2V^6

566 credantur α(-V^7) | 567 ordinati] consecrati [consecrari O] θ | maiores] *add.* fuerunt φ(-W) | 568 ceteris] *om.* θ(-θ^4); pre [cum St] ceteris $\theta^4\gamma$(-W) | transfiguratione] *add.* et θB^1 | 569 filii θ(-Boθ^4)$Bm^1W\varphi^4V^7P^4$Barb. | archisynagogi] *add.* et θ | et similibus] *om.* σ | 570 solos] *om.* ρ^1 | familiariores $\theta^4\varphi^2\psi\pi$(-B^1)Barb. | 571 illud] *om.* φ(-U) | 572 Petrum et [*om.* $W\psi\rho^1$] Joannem et Jacobum $\varphi^2\psi\pi\rho$] Petrum Jacobum et Joannem $\theta\varphi^1$, Jacobum Petrum et Joannem Va | Solum] *om.* ρ | 573 tanquam] quasi ρ^1 | 574 Jesus] *om.* θ | 579 maior] minor ρ^1 | 580 iunior] minor [*om.* P^4] $\psi\pi$ | fratre] *add.* et φ | 581 Marcus] martyr [Matt. V^3, martyr alius Marcus Bo] θ | 583 illo π(-P^4) | 585 quod θ | enim] autem α | 586 etiam] *om.* $\theta\psi$ | fratre etiam φ(-St) | 590 erat^1] fuit [*om.* W] φ | pontificem] episcopum π

570 Matt. 9:18-26; 17:1-13; 26:36-46 | 571-573 *Cat. aur. in Luc.* 8.8 (Theophylactus), 2:121A (2:132B) | 571-572 The reference should be Luc. 8:51 | 573-575 *Cat. aur. in Matt.* 17.1, 1:259A (1:280A) | 573-574 Matt. 17:1 | 575-577 *Cat. aur. in Matt.* 17.5, 1:263B (1:285B) | 576 Matt. 17:18 | 578 Gal. 2:9 | 580-582 *Cat. aur. in Matt.* 10:1, 1:162B-163A (1:174A) | 580-581 Matt. 10:2 | 583-586 *Cat. aur. in Matt.* 10:1, 1:163A (1:174A) | 584 Matt. 10:3 | 587-591 *Decretum Gratiani* ..., D.66 c.2, fol. 116v

differentia inter episcopum et simplicem sacerdotem, 95 d. Olim. Quia sicut Augustinus dicit, in prima rerum creatione non queritur quid Deus facere potuerit, sed quid decuerit, et quid ratio et natura rerum requireret. Cum autem dicat apostolus: *Quod minus est, sine ulla contradictione a meliore benedicitur*, ad Hebreos 8, et philosophi asserunt quod nihil agit ultra suam speciem, licet Christus per simplicem sacerdotem de potentia absoluta possit facere episcopum, non tamen decet, nec congruit officiis quod minor faciat maiorem, dans alteri quod non habet. Nec per consequens est verisimile quod Christus voluerit per simplices sacerdotes, qui sunt inferiores, summos sacerdotes, qui sunt episcopi, consecrare. Unde considerandum est quod Moyses, licet non esset sacerdos et pontifex unctus visibiliter cum Aaron, quem fecit pontificem, et cum filiis eius, quos fecit simplices sacerdotes, ut habetur Levitici 7, et recitatur 21 d. c. 1, erat tamen dignior illis et virtute maior illis in omnibus. Quia in illis ordinibus non erat caracter, nec illi sacerdotes habebant claves, sed tantum offerebant pro populo, et erant mediatores orando, quod multo melius faciebat Moyses. Secundum veritatem autem in ecclesia nulla est maior dignitas quam sacerdotalis, excepta pontificali. Unde omnis non episcopus est inferior eo, et per consequens non decuit quod non episcopus episcopum consecraret, nec est possibile apud homines, etiam de potentia absoluta.

Sed Christus, verus *sacerdos in eternum secundum ordinem Melchisedech*, et *pontifex futurorum bonorum*, licet equivoce sacerdos et episcopus ad alios, in quo non fuit caracter nec consecratio visibilis, tamen fuit

desunt B^2V^6

593 requirerent π(-R) | 595 asserant α(-BoUBm^1)P^4P^1 | 602 unxit π | cum^1 φBarb.Va] *om.* $\pi\rho^1$; tamen $\theta\psi$Sr | 603 simplices] *om.* π | 603-616 ut ... sacerdotes] *hom.* Sv | 604 virtute] *add.* et π | 606 orando] *om.* $\theta^2\gamma$; ad Deum [eum P^3] θ^1 | 607 Moyses] *add.* et illa erant in synagoga in umbra. Unde et Moyses Christum figurabat [signabat V^2] θ^1 | nulla] non ρ | 608 quam ... pontificali φ] sacerdotali [sacerdotalis RP^1] nec in ea pontificali $\theta^2\psi\beta$, pontificali et post eam sacerdotali V^3, pontificali et postea [et postea *om.* Bo] sacerdotali nec in ea pontificali θ^3 | 612 Sed] Vel dicas quod non est recurrendum [occurendum Bo] ad potentiam absolutam Dei ad considerandum actus quos exercuit inter homines [omnes V^2V^5]. Potius debemus episcopum [ipsum θ^3] allegare legitime processisse [processit V^2] ea lege que [*om.* V^3] sibi apparet placuisse [placuisset P^3]. Dicas igitur [ergo V^5] quod θ^1

591-593 Cf. Augustine, *De diversis quaestionibus octoginta tribus* 46.2 (PL 40:30; CCL 44A:72) | 594-595 The reference should be Heb. 7:7. | 603 The reference should be Lev. 8. | Gratian, D.21 1ª Pars | 612-613 Heb. 5:6, 7:17; cf. 5:10, 6:20 | 613 Heb. 9:11

dignior ceteris. Sicut ergo Moyses consecravit Aaron in pontificem, et filios eius in simplices sacerdotes, a quo Aaron derivatus est pontificatus ad omnes alios, sicut ad filium suum Eleazarum, indutum vestibus eius, Numeri 20, postmodum ad Phinees, et sic de aliis, sic Christus per se immediate fecit Petrum episcopum, a quo postmodum in omnes pontificatus derivatus est, et per se fecit alios apostolos simplices sacerdotes. Unde 21 d. *In novo* dicit Anacletus: *In novo testamento post Christum a Petro sacerdotalis cepit ordo, quia ipsi primo pontificatus in ecclesia Christi datus est.* Ex exponitur: *sacerdotalis*, idest pontificalis, sicut sacerdos ponitur pro episcopo, *De consecratione* d. 1 *Solemnitates*. Quia cum alii fuerint eque cito facti sacerdotes sicut ipse et non ab ipso, non potest dici ab ipso incepisse simplex sacerdotalis ordo. Similiter, si ipse fuisset a Christo factus episcopus, licet prius tempore, et alii a Christo, non ab ipso, non propter hoc ab ipso proprie cepisset pontificalis ordo. Sed propter hoc quod ab ipso sunt facti omnes alii episcopi mediate vel immediate, et ipse a Christo, ideo vere dicitur quod ab ipso post Christum cepit pontificalis ordo, quod requirit unitas ecclesie habere, scilicet unum caput a quo dona fluant. Unde 19 d. *Ita Dominus* dicitur sic de Petro: *Ut ab ipso quasi a quodam capite dona sua velut in corpus omne diffunderet.* De hoc articulo iterum dicetur infra, sexto articulo, tertia conclusione principali, 9, 10, 11 conclusionibus incidentalibus.

. . . .

Contra hoc autem arguitur multipliciter. Primo quod omnes apostoli facti fuerunt episcopi a Christo, quia sicut simul ab ipso facti sunt omnes sacerdotes, ita simul debuerunt ab eo fieri episcopi. Solutio: non est simile, quia Petrus inquantum sacerdos non fuit maior aliis, quia omnes sacer-

desunt B^2V^6; 635 *post verbum* incidentalibus *deest* Sr

616 quo] *add.* quidem φ | 617 ad²] *om.* ρ^1 | 618 20] *add.* et α | post [postea St] α | sic²] *add.* et φ | 620 per se] *om.* $\theta\psi$ | 621 Unde] ut α(-W); *add.* in ρ^1 | 623 Christi] Dei θ | 624 pro episcopo] pro Christo [*add.* alias episcopo Bo] $\theta\pi^1$, 20 [*add.* d. Bm^1] φ | Solemnitas π(-R) | 625 fuerint $\theta^4\varphi$(-W)Bm^2Barb.Va] fuerunt $\theta^2\theta^3\psi W\pi\rho^2$ | eque] tam φ | ipse] *add.* Petrus φ | ab] sub γ | 626 incepisse $\theta\rho$Sr] cepisse $\gamma\pi$Va | simplex] simpliciter $\psi\pi^2\rho^1$ | 627 et] etiam φ | alii] *add.* tunc φ | 628 non² ... ipso] *hom.* αB^1 | 630 verum est dicere π(-R) | 633 quodam] *om.* $\psi\pi^2$ | 635 principali] *add.* item etiam [in φ^5] φ, cum $\psi\pi^2$ | 9 ... incidentalibus] *om.* ρ | incidentibus θ | 637-845 Contra ... incidentibus] *om.* Sr | 638 ipso] eo $\psi\pi$ | omnes] *om.* ρVa | 639 debuerunt] *add.* omnes Bm^1 | eo] *add.* omnes $\theta^2\theta^3\varphi^2$ | fieri] *add.* omnes $\theta^4\varphi^3$ | Solutio] *om.* π(-R)

615-616 Cf. Ex. 29:1ff | 618 Num. 20:22-29 | Cf. Eccli. 45:28-31 | 621-623 Gratian, D.21 c.2 | 624 Gratian, *De cons.* D.1 c.16 | 632-633 Gratian, D.19 c.7

dotes sunt pares simpliciter. Unde ad illam paritatem sacerdotalem inter illos ostendendam, Christus simul et semel fecit eos sacerdotes in cena, et dedit simul, vel datam declaravit, parem potestatem ligandi et solvendi in foro conscientie in resurrectione, quando dixit: *Quorum remiseritis* etc. – Cyprianus, 24 q. 1 *Loquitur*: *Apostolis omnibus post resurrectionem suam parem potestatem tribuit* – quia sacerdoti ut sic non debetur potestas iurisdictionis, sicut sunt multi sacerdotes sine cura animarum et subditis. Sed episcopo, qui dicitur super intendens, preter potestatem ordinis debetur potestas iurisdictionis et populus subditus. Unde rationabiliter statutum est in concilio Viennensi quod *nullus de pastore provideat ecclesie cathedrali, sibi qualitercumque subiecte, que clero careat et subditis Christianis, De electione* c. *In plerisque*, quia episcopus sine subditis est quodammodo in opprobrium dignitatis. Licet ergo omnes episcopi sint pares quo ad potestatem ordinis, non tamen simpliciter, quia non quo ad potestatem iurisdictionis, que per se debetur episcopo de congruitate, secundum quam archiepiscopi sunt supra episcopos, et patriarche supra illos, que preeminentia est a Petro, qui divisit provincias et dioceses, ut dicit Clemens, 80 d. *In illis*. Sed super hos omnes Petrus a Deo prepositus est. Unde ad significandum quod in episcopatu erat maior aliis, non debuit simul fieri episcopus cum aliis, sed ipse a Christo solus, et alii postea ab eo, ut dictum est. Petrus enim non fuit maior sacerdos aliis, quia non habuit aliam nec maiorem potestatem sacerdotalem. Sed fuit maior episcopus, non quia habuit aliam aut maiorem potestatem sacramenta ministrandi, sed quia habuit maiorem potestatem iudicandi, super intendens toti mundo.

Secundo, contra hoc est Augustinus, qui dicit, in libro *De questionibus Veteris et Novi Testamenti*, quod Christus omnes apostolos fecit episcopos. Respondetur dupliciter: uno modo quod fecit omnes episcopos, sed

desunt B^2V^6Sr

645 Cyprianus] Unde dicit Cyprianus [Cyprianus dicit ρ^2] ρ | Apostolis omnibus $\gamma\rho$Va] *inv.* $\theta\pi$ | 646 potestatem] *add.* eis ρ | sacerdotio [sacerdos φ^5] α | 647 sicut sunt] cum sint φ | animarum] *om.* ρ^1 | 650 institutum ρ | 654 sint] fuerint π(-R) | 656 secundum quam] quamquam φ | sint [sicut W] φ | 657 ipsos [episcopos St, archiepiscopos U] φ | 660 debuit] *om.* φ(-St); poterat St, debet θ^4 | 661 postea] *om.* π(-R) | 663 aut] vel ρ | 668 Respondetur $\varphi\pi^2$Barb.] respondeo $\theta\psi$, responsio π^1Bm^{2}Va, solutio ρ^2 | dupliciter] dicitur ρ^1 | omnes] *om.* ρ^1

644 Joan. 20:23 | 645-646 Gratian, C.24 q.1 c.18 | 650-652 *Clem.* 1.3.5 | 658 Gratian, D.80 c.2 | 666-667 Cf. Pseudo-Augustine, *Quaestiones Veteris et Novi Testamenti* 1.93 (PL 35:2287; cf. CSEL 50:163-165)

differenter, quia Petrum per se, alios per Petrum, sicut dicit propheta, et in Joanne repetit Christus: *Erunt omnes docibiles Dei*, scilicet quidam immediate, alii mediate. Secundo potest dici omnes fecisse episcopos, idest sacerdotes. Sepe enim episcopus ponitur pro simplici sacerdote, sicut probat Hieronymus per illud Actuum 20: "Posuit vos Spiritus Sanctus episcopos": *idest presbyteros*, quod ibi probat Beda per hoc quod loquitur ad seniores unius civitatis Ephesi, in qua non erat nisi unus episcopus. Quia sicut dixit Clemens, 80 d. c. *In illis*, Petrus *in singulis civitatibus singulos et non plures constitui precepit episcopos*. Secundo probat Hieronymus per episcopos intelligi presbyteros, 93 d. *Legimus*, per hoc quod apostolus dicit ad Titum 1: *Reliqui te Crete, ut constituas per civitates presbyteros*, quorum conditionibus descriptis, subiungit dicens: *Oportet enim episcopos sine crimine esse*, quod non esset ad propositum nisi per episcopos intelligeret presbyteros.

Tertio contra, *De summa Trinitate* c. 1 § *Una*, ubi dicitur quod sacramentum eucharistie *nemo potest conficere nisi sacerdos qui rite fuerit ordinatus secundum claves quas ipse concessit apostolis Jesus Christus*. Sed constat quod sacerdos non ordinatur a clave sacerdotali, sed solum ab episcopali. Ergo videtur quod Christus apostolis tradidit claves pontificales a quibus solis presbyteri ordinantur, et non solum sacerdotales; et per consequens quod Christus non solum Petrum sed etiam alios apostolos fecit episcopos, et non solum simplices sacerdotes. Solutio sicut prius, quia Christus omnibus concessit claves pontificales, sed Petro per se, aliis per Petrum, non autem aliis per seipsum. Quia enim Christus dedit apostolis omnibus per seipsum claves sacerdotales, ideo omnibus ipse dixit: *Quorum remiseritis* etc., sive illud fuerit collatio sive collationis facte declaratio. Idem etiam illis simul omnibus prius illas se daturum promisit, Matthei 18: *Quecumque alligaveritis* etc., iuxta morem suum quo facta ardua pronuntiabat priusquam faceret ea. Si ergo similiter per seipsum

desunt B^2V^6Sr

669 se] *add.* et θ | 670 scilicet] *om.* π | 671 alii] *add.* autem θ(-BoV^2) | 672 episcopus] *om.* ρ^1 | 674 ibi] sic φ | 679 ut] *add.* ea que desunt [sunt V^5] corrigas et θ | 681 episcopum [*om.* π^1] π | 683 § Una] *om.* π(-R) | 685 claves] *add.* ecclesie θ | 688 solis] soli $\varphi\pi^2$ | 692 aliis] alios fecit θ^1 | seipsum] seipsos $\theta^2\gamma$(-U); *add.* episcopos θ^1 | enim] *om.* α | 695 Item φV^7

670 Joan. 6:45 | 673-674 Jerome, *Ep.* 146, *Ad Evangelum presbyterum* (PL 22:1193; CSEL 56:308-309) | Act. 20:28 | 674-675 Bede, *Expositio Actuum apostolorum* 20.28 (PL 92:986), ed. M. L. W. Laistner (Cambridge, Mass., 1939), p. 76 | 676-677 Gratian, D.80 c.2 | 678 Gratian, D.93 c.24 | 679-680 Tit. 1:5 | 681 Tit. 1:7 | 683-685 X. 1.1.1 | 694 Joan. 20:23 | 696 Matt. 18:18

esset eis daturus claves episcopales sicut et Petro, ita promisisset eis prius sicut et Petro. Non fecit autem, sed soli Petro, cui dixit singulariter: *Tibi dabo claves regni celorum, et quodcumque ligaveris* etc. Ubi etiam notat Origenes plus promissum Petro per illud quam apostolis per aliud. Unde cum dixerit Petro: *Quodcumque ligaveris ligatum erit, et quodcumque solveris solutum erit in celis*, Matthei 18 apostolis dixit: *Quecumque ligaveritis erunt ligata, et quecumque solveritis erunt soluta in celo*. Origenes: *Non dixit in celis sicut Petro, sed in celo uno. Unde non sunt tante perfectionis sicut Petrus.* Petro enim, dando episcopatum et summum, dedit claves in celo visibili et invisibili, et sic in celis. Ceteris autem dedit claves in foro conscientie quasi in celo invisibili, non autem in foro exteriori, quod est celum visibile, et sic in uno celo tantum. Vel dicendum quod illa auctoritas de clavibus concessis apostolis probat propositum, quia ibi dicitur sic: quod illas claves *concessit apostolis eorumque successoribus Jesus Christus*. Loquitur autem de clavibus pontificalibus, que differunt a sacerdotalibus, quia claves dici possunt non solum scientia discernendi et potentia ligandi et solvendi, per quas homo introducitur vel eicitur de ecclesia, sed potestas dispensandi thesaurum ecclesie, idest sacramenta, sicut dispensator sub clave custodit ea que debet dispensare, et discernit et iudicat quid, quale, quantum, cui dispenset. Unde claves episcopales, prout differunt a sacerdotalibus, sunt potestas confirmandi et ordinandi. Has igitur Christus tradidit apostolis aliis sicut et eorum successoribus. Sed constat quod successoribus non tradidit eas per se, sed per episcopum consecrantem. Ergo non per se sed per Petrum consecrantem tradidit illas claves aliis apostolis.

desunt B^2V^6Sr

698 et St$\psi\pi$Va] *om.* ρ; etiam [esset Sv] $\theta\varphi$(-St) | promisisset] pronuntiasset φ | eis] *om.* ρ^1 | prius] *om.* ρVa | 699 autem] *add.* hoc φ | 700 Ubi] ibi φ | etiam α(-V^5V^3)Va] *om.* $V^5\rho^2$; et $V^3\pi Bm^2$Barb. | 702 dixerit $\psi\pi$Va] dixit [dicit V^4] $\theta\varphi\rho$ | erit] est π(-R) | 703 erit] *add.* et [etiam $V^1\theta^3$] α(-SvUW) | 704 alligaveritis θ(-Bo) | soluta] *add.* et α(-θ^4) | 705 dicit π(-R)Barb. | sicut] nisi φ | uno] *om.* φ | 706 et] *om.* θ | 707-708 et² ... invisibili] *hom.* θ^2 | 707 et² ... celis] *om.* θ | Ceteris] aliis θ^1 | autem] *add.* non θ^1(-V^2) | 708 claves ... autem] *om.* θ^1 | 709-722 Vel ... apostolis] *om.* Va | 710 apostolis] *om.* α | 712 Christus] *add.* non φ | 713 quia] que φ | claves] *add.* idest [scilicet St] sacerdotales φ | 714-715 et¹ ... ecclesia] *om.* ρ | 714 introducitur] intromittitur φ, intrat θP^2 | 717-722 quid ... apostolis] *om.* π^1 | 717 quid quale quantum] qualiter et $\psi\pi^2$ | 718 sacerdotalibus] *add.* sicut $\psi\pi^2$ | 719 igitur] similiter [simul W] φ | 720 quod $\theta\varphi^2\psi$] *add.* eorum $\varphi^1\rho$ | 722 apostolis] episcopis $\psi\pi^2$

699-700 Matt. 16:19 | 700-701 Cf. *Cat. aur. in Matt.* 18.5 (Matt. 18:18), 1:274A (1:297B) | 702-703 Matt. 16:19 | 703-704 Matt. 18:18 | 711-712 X. 1.1.1

Quarto, sic arguit glossa, 66 d. § *Porro*, per illud quod habetur 21 d. *In novo*, ubi dicitur: *Ipsi*, scilicet Petro, *primo pontificatus in ecclesia Christi datus est*. Et post pauca: *Ceteri vero apostoli cum eodem pari consortio honorem et potestatem acceperunt*. Sed non habuissent honorem et potestatem pari consortio nisi fuissent pontifices sicut Petrus, et ab eodem simul, licet post, sicut in eadem missa plures episcopi, unus post alium, consecrantur. Ergo videtur quod Dominus omnes fecit episcopos simul et semel, licet Petrum prius, sicut simul lavit pedes discipulorum, licet prius Petri, sicut dicit Augustinus. Dicendum quod illa paritas non est intelligenda quo ad omnia, sed quantum ad hoc, quod ipsi fuerunt episcopi sicut ipse, sed non cum ipso, nec a Christo, sed postea facti ab ipso Petro. Et tunc facti episcopi fuerunt pares quo ad potestatem consecrationis, non obstante quod fuerunt ab eo facti, sicut episcopus consecratus est par consecranti in potestate ordinis.

Quinto arguit glossa ubi supra sic: *Episcopi successerunt in locum apostolorum, 68 d. Quorum. Ergo et apostoli fuerunt episcopi*. Solutio: apostoli fuerunt episcopi, sed non per hoc, nec statim cum hoc, quod fuerunt apostoli, quod sic patet. Quia principalius facti sunt apostoli ad hoc, ut essent predicatores, quam ad hoc, ut essent episcopi. Unde Luce 9, ubi Christus misit apostolos predicare, dicit Cyrillus: *Oportebat discipulos eum ubique terrarum predicare. Hoc enim erat opus electorum ab eo ad apostolatus officium*. Sed ipsi non statim quod ex discipulis sunt electi et

desunt B^2V^6Sr

724 dicitur] arguitur π | scilicet] *om.* π(-R) | 728 post[1]] *add.* eum $\psi\pi^2$ | missa] villa [ecclesia φ^5] γ | plures] *add.* quid [quam P^4P^1], quale, quantum, cui dispenset. Unde claves episcopales, prout differunt a sacerdotalibus, sunt potestates confirmandi et ordinandi. Has igitur [ergo P^1] Christus tradidit apostolis aliis sicut et eorum [*om.* R] successoribus [successoribus eorum P^4]. Sed constat quod successoribus non tradidit eas per se, sed per episcopum consecrantem. Ergo non per se sed per Petrum consecrantem tradidit illas claves aliis a Petro [a Petro: apostolis R] et π(-B^1) | episcopi ... alium] *om.* B^1 | 729 fecerit ρVa | 730 licet[1]] sed θ | discipulorum] apostolorum θ | prius[2]] primo ρ^1 | 731 Dicendum] *add.* est φ | 732 quantum] quo α | 733 facti] et φ | 734 episcopi] *om.* π(-R) | 734-735 consecrationis] consecrandi ρ^1 | 735 fuerunt] *add.* episcopi π | est] *add.* per consecrationem π(-R) | 736 par consecranti] *om.* P^4P^1; consecratori par B^1 | 737 successerant φ(-St) | loco π(-R)ρ^1 | 738 et] *om.* ρ^1 | 740 ut] quod $\theta\psi$Va | 741 ut] quod $\theta\rho^2$Va | 742 discipulos] *add.* sequi φ | 743 predicare] *om.* φ

723 Cf. *Decretum Gratiani* ..., D.66 c.2, fol. 116v | 723-726 Gratian, D.21 c.2 | 731 Cf. *Cat. aur. in Joan.* 13.2 (Joan. 13:6), 2:505A (2:553A) | 737-738 *Decretum Gratiani* ..., D.66 c.2, fol. 116v | 741 Luc. 9:2 | 742-744 Cf. Cyril of Alexandria, *Explanatio in Lucae evangelium*, chap. 9 (PG 72:642). These are not the words of Cyril, but the thought is not alien to him. In his commentary he concentrates on the miraculous powers granted to the apostles. But he emphasizes that these powers were designed to serve the apostles' primary purpose of preaching.

assumpti in apostolos predicaverunt, sed postea. Unde cum Lucas, sexto capitulo sui Evangelii, dixisset: *Vocavit discipulos suos, et elegit duodecim ex ipsis, quos et apostolos nominavit*, postea, octavo capitulo, narrat quod *ipse iter faciebat per civitates et castra, predicans et evangelizans regnum Dei, et duodecim cum illo*, super quo verbo dicit Theophylus: *Non docentes aut predicantes, sed instruendi ab eo.* Sed postea, nono capitulo, dedit eis auctoritatem predicandi primo quando, convocatis duodecim apostolis, postea misit illos predicare regnum Dei. Quomodo enim predicabunt nisi mittantur? Ergo illa missio dedit eis auctoritatem predicandi et non status apostolatus, et multo minus apostolatus dedit eis dignitatem episcopatus, nisi in spe. Quia non fuerunt episcopi antequam essent sacerdotes, quod non fuerunt ante cenam, cum tamen diu ante fuerint apostoli.

Preterea Petrus fuit ante alios episcopus, 21 d. *In novo.* Sed ipse non fuit episcopus factus ante resurrectionem, ut dictum est in quinta conclusione primi articuli. Ergo multo minus alii. Si dicatur Aaron simul factus est sacerdos et episcopus; ergo et Petrus. Respondeo: non est simile, quia iam erat populus Israel collectus, cui Aaron erat preficiendus. Unde statim debuit fieri episcopus, ne oves in deserto errarent sine pastore. Sed ovibus ante passionem non redemptis, non convenienter pastor novus fuisset datus. Item nec Aaron vivente, qui erat summus pontifex, debuit alius collega fieri, sed solum eo mortuo successit Eleazarus. A sanctis etiam patribus in conciliis rationabiliter est statutum quod, vivente episcopo, alter non substituatur eidem. Unde cum Christus esset pontifex et summus, et in utroque vellet sibi Petrum substituere, non decuit quod hoc faceret ante mortem, nec per consequens apostoli alii fuerunt episcopi pro

desunt B^2V^6Sr

747 narratur ρ^1 | 748 castella θ | 748-751 predicans ... apostolis] *om.* V^3 | 748-750 predicans ... eo] *om.* $\theta\varphi$ | predicans ... instruendi] *om.* ψ | 749 Theophylus ρVa] Thomas π | 750 eis] *om.* ρ^1 | 751 auctoritatem] potestatem θStBm^1 | vocatis $B^1\rho$ | apostolis] *add.* dedit eis [*om.* W; illis St] potestatem etc. φ | 753 Ergo ... missio] In ipsa enim missione φ | statum [statim UBm^1] φ | 754 multo minus] nihilominus ρ^1; *add.* per statum φ, status ψB^1 | dignitatem] potestatem ρ^1 | 756 fuerint θ(-OBo)$P^2\pi^1$Barb.Va] fuerunt OBo$\varphi V^7\pi^2\rho^1$ | 757 episcopos φ (-φ^3)RP^1 | 761 statim] Aaron φ | 764-765 debuit ... fieri] poni [*om.* θ^2] debuit [debet Sv] alius [alter Bo] collega θ, debuit esse collega φ, debuit dari alius collega [*om.* V^7] ψ | 766 in conciliis] in concilio ρ^1, in concusse et $\theta^2\theta^3$, in concusse [incusse V^3] et a Romana ecclesia θ^4 | institutum ρ | 766-767 quod ... eidem] idem φ | 768-769 hoc faceret] *om.* α | 769 mortem] *add.* Christi φ(-U)

745-747 Luc. 6:13 | 747-749 Luc. 8:1 | 749-750 *Cat. aur. in Luc.* 8.1 (Theophylactus), 2:109B (2:119A) | 750 Luc. 9:2 | 757 Gratian, D.21 c.2 | 764-765 Cf. Num. 20:22-29

tunc. Et quantum ad hoc eis succedunt episcopi, quantum ad episcopatum quem habuerunt finaliter, et administrationem spiritualium et temporalium aliqualem. Sed videtur quod apostoli sint facti episcopi quando dictum est eis Joannis 20: *Quorum remiseritis* etc., per illud quod ibi dicit Gregorius in homilia: *Ecce non solum de semetipsis securi fuerunt*, scilicet per illud: "Accipite Spiritum Sanctum," *sed etiam principatum fraterni iudicii sortiuntur, ut vice Dei quibusdam peccata retineant, quibusdam relaxent. Quorum nunc in ecclesia episcopi locum tenent, solvendi atque ligandi auctoritatem suscipiunt qui gradum regiminis sortiuntur*. Solutio: sicut probatum est, per illud quod est commune simplicibus sacerdotibus apostoli non sunt facti episcopi. Sed verum est quod illi qui tunc acceperunt vel accepisse monstrati sunt potestatem sacerdotalem postea acceperunt episcopalem, que plenius potest solvere et ligare, quia in foro exteriori et interiori, cum prima solum in interiori (quia excommunicatio est proprius actus episcopi). Et ad hoc se refert Gregorius quando dicit episcopos tenere locum eorum.

Sexto, arguit sic predicta glossa. Quia dicitur de Juda, et scriptum est in Psalmo et Actuum 1: *Episcopatum eius accipiat alter*. Si autem Judas fuit episcopus, multo magis alii, et per consequens ante resurrectionem, antequam ipse laqueo se suspendit. Et constat quod non ab alio quam a Christo. Ergo omnes apostoli ante passionem a Christo facti sunt episcopi. Solutio: Judas non fuit episcopus secundum veritatem, sed solum fuit apostolus et sacerdos. Et quando dicitur: *Episcopatum eius accipiat alter*, exponendum est, idest presbyteratum sive sacerdotium, sicut supra dictum est. Quia in Scriptura unum pro alio frequenter accipitur propter hoc, quod est unus et idem ordo sive caracter, licet ampliatus, et quia in primitiva ecclesia quandoque simul ordinabantur aliqui sacerdotes et epis-

desunt B^{2}V^{6}Sr

772 apostoli] *om.* ρ | 774 securi BoγBarb.Va | 775-776 principatum fraterni iudicii πVa] principatum sanctum [secundum Bo, superni V^7, sanctum vel secum θ^4] iudicii θψ, principatum divini iudicii [iudicii divini St] φ, superni iudicii principatum ρ | 777 Quorum] *om.* ρ^1 | episcopi] equum θφ | 779 commune] *add.* omnibus ρ | 781 vel ... sunt] *om.* φ | vel accepisse] *om.* $\theta^2\theta^3\psi$; vel accipere V^3 | 782 quia] *om.* φ | 783 prima] *add.* sacerdotalis possit θ^1 | solum] *add.* possit φ(-U), etiam π(-R) | 784 actus θφ] *om.* Va; mucro $\psi\pi^1$, mutatio P^1, operatio B^1, murus Bm^2, usus ρ^2, nuncio Barb. | 786 sic] sicut γ(-Uφ^5) | predicta] prius dicta φ(-W) | 787 1] et ρ^1 | 787-788 Judas ... resurrectionem] *om.* ρ^1 | 789 suspendit] *add.* fuit episcopus ρ^1 | a] *add.* primo ρ^1 | 790 omnes] *add.* alii θ | 792 dicitur] *add.* et ρ^1 | 793 sive] vel ρ^1

773 Joan. 20:23 | 773-778 *Cat. aur. in Joan.* 20.3, 2:583A (2:639B) | 787 Ps. 108:8; Act. 1:20

copi, sicut etiam cum diaconi ordinabantur, simul recipiebant inferiores ordines. In exteriori etiam conversatione episcopi humiliter cum presbyteris conversabantur, nec se efferebant. Unde vulgus nesciebat differentiam inter illos, que tamen semper fuit, etiam de iure divino, ex quo episcopus potest confirmare et ordinare, quod non potest simplex sacerdos. Unde pro confirmatione in Samariam miserunt ad eos Petrum et Joannem, pro eo quod nondum erant alii apostoli facti episcopi. Alias potius misissent minores quam maiores, cum isti duo essent vertices aliorum, ut supra dictum est. Ex quo etiam confirmatur illud quod supradictum est, scilicet Petrum fecisse primo episcopum Joannem quam aliquem aliorum.

Quod autem super illud Luce 9: *Assumpsit Jesus Petrum et Jacobum*, dicit Ambrosius: *Jacobus ascendit qui prius solium sacerdotale conscendit*, illud exponitur quasi mistice, prout martyr dicitur sacerdos, seipsum Deo offerens hostiam vivam, pro qua evolat ad celum, per proprium sanguinem introiens in tabernaculum non manufactum. Unde Jacobus Zebedei dicitur primus ascendisse solium sacerdotale quia, inter apostolos primus martyrio laureatus, per sacrificium martyrii solium celi conscendit. Vel quia Ambrosius et Augustinus fuerunt illius opinionis, quod Jacobus, primus Hierosolimorum episcopus, interfuit transfigurationi, ut dicit Augustinus super epistolam ad Galatas et Ambrosius ibidem. Secundum hoc, Jacobus primus solium sacerdotale conscendit, non quia prius fuerit ordinatus in sacerdotem quam alii, cum omnes simul fuerint facti ut dictum est, nec quod prius fuerit ordinatus in episcopum a Christo, cum hoc fuerit solus Petrus, nec primus a Petro, sed potius Joannes, sed quia prior habuit sedem distinctam sibi assignatam, quam sedem importat solium, et non ipsum ordinem episcopalem. Prima enim sedes episcopalis specialis apostolorum fuit Hierosolimitana Jacobi, secunda Antiochena Petri.

desunt $B^{2}V^{6}$Sr

800 tamen] *add.* differentia φ | semper] *om.* ρ^{1} | de] *om.* θ | 802 in Samariam] Samarie [*om.* U] φ | 805 aliorum] apostolorum θ | 805-806 Ex ... est] *hom.* $P^{4}\rho$ | 811 pro qua] per [pro P^{4}] quam π(-R)Va | 814 primo θ, prius ρ^{1} | 816 transmigrationi ρ | 818 Secundum hoc] sed φ | 819 prius] primus $\pi^{2}\rho^{1}$ | fuerint $V^{1}BoV^{2}V^{3}\varphi(-\varphi^{5})P^{2}$] fuerunt $OV^{5}Sv\varphi^{5}V^{7}\beta$ | 821 primus] prius ρ^{1} | 822 prior] prius $\theta\varphi^{5}$, primam φ^{1} | distinctam] destinatam ρ^{1} | sedem²] *om.* φ | 824 specialis] *om.* π(-R)

802-803 Cf. Act. 18:14 | 808-809 *Cat. aur. in Luc.* 9.6, 2:131B (2:143B) | 808 Luc. 9:28 | 817 The reference has not been identified.

Vel exponendum est: *Episcopatum eius accipiat alter*, idest apostolatum, sicut ibi postea dicitur: *Accipe locum ministerii huius et apostolatus, de quo prevaricatus est Judas*. Apostolatus autem non habet annexum episcopatum, sicut dictum est. Et patet in Paulo, qui dicit de seipso ad Galatas 1: *Paulus apostolus, non ab hominibus, neque per hominem, sed per Jesum Christum*. Quamvis autem Paulus non fuerit inferior aliis apostolis, non tamen fuit simul a Christo episcopus factus, sed ab apostolis ordinatus cum Barnaba, quando Actuum 13, ad iussum Spiritus Sancti, *imponentes illis manus, dimiserunt eos*, et recitatur 75 d. *Quod die*. Similiter Mathias, Domini sorte electus, *annumeratus est cum undecim apostolis*, Actuum 1, qui tamen non potuit a Christo cum aliis in episcopum consecrari, nec propter hoc minus fuit verus apostolus. Sic igitur Mathias, Paulus, Barnabas, veri apostoli sicut et ceteri, qui tamen non fuerunt facti episcopi a Christo sed ab homine puro, ostendunt quod status apostolatus in aliis non requirebat quod fierent episcopi a Christo. Sed hoc fuit privilegium Petri, quem Christus loco sui summum pontificem consecravit. Sic Moyses Josue, imponens ei manum, generalem sui vicarium derelinquit, Numeri 27. De hoc iterum dicetur infra in ultimo articulo, ultima conclusione principali, 9, 10, 11 conclusionibus incidentibus.

Octava Conclusio

Octava conclusio est de potestate iurisdictionis: quod eam alii apostoli a Christo non habuerunt immediate, sed quamcumque habuerunt a Petro habuerunt. Primum patet tripliciter, primo sic. Ab illo a quo aliquis non habet aliquem subditum, ab illo non habet aliquam potestatem iurisdictionis. Sed alii apostoli a Christo non habuerunt populum subditum. Ergo nec a Christo habuerunt potestatem iurisdictionis. Maior patet, quia cum nullus possit solvere nec ligare nisi subditum, *cum a non suo iudice*

desunt B^2V^6; 844-845 *usque ad verbum* incidentibus *deest* Sr

827 Accipere φ(-W)ρ | huius] eius ρ | 828 autem] etiam ρ^1 | 832 episcopus] *om.* α(-U) | 833 quando πVa] *om.* $\alpha\rho$ | a iussu ρ^1 | 834 eos] illos ρ | Quod tue [tunc V^5] θ, q. [*om.* St] φ | 835 annumeratus] et numeratus ρ^1 | 836 tamen] *om.* θ | 838 et] *om.* αB^1 | 842 Sic] sicut $\theta U\varphi^5$Va, sicuti γ(-Uφ^5) | 843 dereliquit $BoV^2\theta^4\varphi(-\varphi^4)B^1\rho(-Bm^2)$ | hoc] *add.* tamen $\theta(-V^3)$ | 844 conclusionibus] *om.* ρ | 844-845 incidentibus $\theta(-V^1BoV^2)\pi(-R)$] *om.* ρ; incidentalibus $V^1BoV^2\gamma R$ | 847 conclusio] *add.* principalis θ | alii] *om.* $\theta\pi^2$Va | 849 illo] isto φ | 852 quia] *om.* φ | 853 nec] vel $\theta\sigma$

826 Act. 1:20 | 827-828 Act. 1:25 | 829-831 Gal. 1:1 | 833-834 Act. 13:2-3 | 834 Gratian, D.75 c.5 | 835-836 Act. 1:26 | 843 Num. 27:18-23 | 853-855 X. 5.38.4

ligari nullus valeat vel absolvi, De penitentiis et remissionibus, Quod autem, potestas iurisdictionis qua aliquis potest solvere et ligare dicitur relative ad subditum. Relativa autem posita se ponunt, et perempta se perimunt. Unde sicut si non est servus non est dominus, propter quod, secundum Augustinum, *Deus non fuit Dominus quousque habuit creaturam servam*, ita si non est subditus non est prelatus nec iudex qui possit eum iudicare, ad Romanos 14: *Tu quis es qui iudicas alienum servum ? Suo domino stat, aut cadit*. Si autem habenti subditos quo ad certos casus amplietur iurisdictio super illos, adhuc dantur sibi de novo subditi quo ad illud ad quod non erant. Et sic cui non dantur subditi, illi non datur potestas iudiciaria, que fuit maior. Minor patet, quia si Christus dedisset aliis a Petro subditos, aut omnes, aut aliquos. Non est dicendum quod dederit eis aliquos et aliquos non, quia Christus populos apostolis non divisit, sed dixit omnibus et singulis, Matthei ultimo: *Docete omnes gentes*, et Marci ultimo: *Predicate Evangelium omni creature*. Nec est fingere quos quibus subiecerit. Nec est similiter dicendum quod subiecerit omnes omnibus, quia pluralitas principatuum non est bona, ut dicitur 12 *Metaphisice*, et ideo concluditur ibidem: unus ergo princeps. Unde Christus non bene ordinasset populum Christianum si dedisset omnibus et singulis duodecim principes aut quattuordecim, et quemlibet in solidum. Non ergo omnes subiecit omnibus, sed uni solum, alias ovilis Christi non fuisset unus pastor sed plures, contra illud Joannis 10: *Fiet unum ovile, et unus pastor*.

Secundo sic, quia si Christus dedisset apostolis potestatem iurisdictionis, aut plenam et omnimodam sicut Petro, aut particularem, limitatam et

desunt B^2V^6

854 vel] nec α | 854-855 Quod autem] nam φ | 855 potestas] *add.* enim ρ^1 | posset [possit P^4] π(-R) | et] vel ρ^1 | 860 posset $\theta^2\theta^3\rho$ | quis $Bo\theta^4\varphi$(-W)$B^1Br\sigma$] *om.* $\theta^2V^2V^5$; qui $SW\psi\pi(-B^1)\rho$(-Br) | 862 illos] illo φ | 863 illud] *add.* quo π | 865 omnes] *add.* dedisset φ(-W) | aliquos] *add.* dedisset W | 866 dedit π | eis] *om.* θ | populos] ipsis ρ^1 | 867 dicit π(-R) | 868 ultimo] *om.* [iterum St, item U] $\gamma(-Bm^1)\pi Sr$ | 869 quos] quod ρ^1 | Nec ... subiecerit] *hom.* π | 872 Christus] Dominus ρ^1 | 874 solum] totum θ, soli ρ^1 | 874-875 alias ... plures] alias unius ovilis Christi unus non esset [*add.* si non unus omnium V^2] pastor si [sed θ^3] plures essent θ^1; alias ovile Christi si non unus omnium pastor sed plures esset θ^2; alias [*add.* enim St] ovile Christi [ubi U] non esset [non esset *om.* Bm^1; non erat U] unum nec unus omnium [*om.* V^4] ovium [*om.* φ^3] pastor sed plures φ | 878 particulariter φ

858-859 Cf. Thomas Aquinas, *Summa theologica* 1.13.7 esp. ad 6 (Turin, 1922) 1:86A-88B esp. 88B; cf. Augustine, *De trinitate* 5.16 (PL 42:922; CCL 50:224-225) | 860-861 Rom. 14:4 | 867-868 Matt. 28:19 | 868 Marc. 16:15 | 870-871 Aristotle, *Metaphysica* Λ.10 (1076a4) | 875-876 Joan. 10:16

coartatam. Sed neutram eis dedit. Ergo nullam. Maior patet per sufficientem divisionem. Minor patet quo ad primam partem, scilicet quod non dedit aliis apostolis plenam et omnimodam, quia quod per superhabundantiam dicitur uni soli convenit. Unde summa potestas uni soli dari debuit. Et cum per plenitudinem potestatis intelligamus illam qua non est alia maior, si alii apostoli habuissent plenitudinem potestatis, Petrus non fuisset maior eis, nec superior, nec princeps eorum, cuius contrarium probatum est in primo articulo, ubi etiam probatum est quod soli Petro data est plenitudo potestatis. Non igitur aliis apostolis data est potestas plena, que fuit prima pars minoris. Item nec potestas iurisdictionis coartata et limitata, quia non est fingere certitudinem illius limitationis. Nec ex Evangeliis haberi potest quin potius, ubicumque potestatem iudiciariam Christus videtur apostolis dare vel promittere, non addit limitationem, nec quantum ad subditos, de quibus est prima ratio, nec quantum ad gradus vel casus iurisdictionis in se, de quibus est ista secunda ratio. Sicut quando promisit, Matthei 18: *Quecumque alligaveritis super terram, et quecumque solveritis*, non dicit que vel aliqua, sed *quecumque*, nec dicit in hac vel in illa terra, sed *super terram*. Et similiter quando dedit vel datam potestatem eis innotuit, Joannis 20: *Quorum remiseritis, et quorum retinueritis*, non dicit horum vel illorum, sed indeterminate *quorum*, nec dicit hec peccata vel illa, sed indefinite *peccata*. Ergo etc.

Tertio, quia quidquid collatum est a Christo apostolis invenitur in Novo Testamento. Sed ibi non invenitur quod Christus aliis apostolis a Petro contulerit aliquam potestatem iurisdictionis. Ergo Christus nullam illis contulit. Maior patet, quia Novum Testamentum sufficienter describit

desunt B^2V^6; 901 *post verbum* invenitur *desunt* $\gamma\pi$

881 omnimodam] *add.* iurisdictionis potestatem θ | 883 soli] *om.* θ(-V^3)φ(-W) | 884 alia] *om.* φ | plenam potestatem ρ^1 | 887 Non] nec ρ^1 | apostolis [*om.* φ^5] aliis α(-SBm^1) | 891 viderit $\psi\pi^2$, videretur θ^2, visus fuerit θ^1 | vel] aut ρ^1 | 892 de quibus] circa quos φ | prima ratio] limitatio φ | 893 illa ρ^1 | 894 secunda ratio] limitatio φ | 896 nec] non ρ^1 | 897 vel] *add.* quando θ | innotuit eis [*om.* φ^5] α | 899 dicit $V^4V^7\pi$(-R)BrBarb.] *om.* V^3; dixit α(-$V^3V^4V^7$)$RBm^2Sz\sigma$ | 900 peccata] illa γ | Ergo etc.] *om.* σ | 901 est] *om.* φ | invenitur] innuitur ρ^1; *add.* in Sacra Scriptura. Sed nihil invenitur in ea per quod probetur quod [*om.* P^1] apostoli alii a Petro potestatem iurisdictionis habuerunt [habuerint ψ] immediate a Christo, ut deducetur [deduceret V^7] statim [statim deducetur B^1] . Ergo etc. Maior [minor V^7] patet de se. Minor probatur [*inv.* ψ], ad cuius evidentiam sciendum est quod $\psi\pi^2$ | 901-984 in ... apostolis] *om.* $\gamma\pi$ | 902 invenitur] innuitur ρ^1 | 903-904 aliquam ... contulit] *hom.* ρ^1

894-895 Matt. 18:18 | 897-898 Joan. 20:23

gesta Christi et potestatem ab eo ecclesie collatam. Unde Actuum 1: *Primum quidem sermonem* etc., usque ibi: *docere*. Si enim Vetus Testamentum describit sufficienter potestatem datam ministris eius, sicut summo sacerdoti, minoribus sacerdotibus et levitis, sicut decimas, primitias, armum pectus et huiusmodi eorum iura, Levitici 8, Numeri 18, multo magis Novum Testamentum debet describere potestatem a Christo datam ministris eius qui preferuntur illis, sicut probat apostolus, 2 ad Corinthios 3. Minor patet discurrendo per potestates a Christo apostolis collatas, que supra dicte sunt.

Primo enim patet de potestate miracula faciendi, quia per illam non est eis data potestas iurisdictionis aliqua, quia miracula possunt fieri non subditis sicut subditis. Immo signa sunt data infidelibus, 1 ad Corinthios 14, de quibus dicit: *Quid ad nos de his qui foris sunt iudicare*, 1 ad Corinthios 2.

Secundo, nec per potestatem predicandi data est eis potestas iurisdictionis, quia predicatio potest fieri non subditis. Nec oportet quod auditores sermonis, qui se subiciunt aut subiciuntur alicui ad audiendum, propter hoc subiciant se vel subiciantur illi ad iudicandum. Sicut fratribus predicatoribus et minoribus datur auctoritas predicandi confluentibus ad loca eorum vel alibi. Non tamen propter hoc datur eis potestas aliqua iudicandi.

Tertio, nec per potestatem baptizandi data est eis potestas iudicandi, quia etiam non subditi baptizantur. Immo cum baptismus sit ianua sacramentorum, et per consequens ecclesie que non iudicat illos qui foris sunt, potestas baptizandi non importat potestatem iudicandi, quamvis per ecclesiam sit postea prohibitum quod nullus baptizet extra necessitatem alienum, quia sacramenta a suis prelatis sunt recipienda, 18 q. 2 *Abbatibus*. Sed hec prohibitio a principio non fuit.

Quarto, nec per potestatem temporalia metendi. Si enim Deus ordinavit his qui Evangelium annuntiant de Evangelio vivere, non propter hoc dedit

desunt $\gamma\pi$V^6

907 describit sufficienter V$^1\theta^3$SvBm^{2}Barb.Va] *inv.* OV^{3}Sρ^2Sr | 908 decimas] *add.* et θ | 909 armum] *add.* et θ | 911 datam] *add.* apostolis θ | eius ministris θ | 914 enim] *om.* σ | 915 eis] *om.* σ | 924 eorum loca θ | 930-931 baptizet [baptizaret ρ] extra [contra Br] necessitatem alienum ρSr] extra [*om.* V^3] necessitatem baptizet alienum θ, extra necessitatem alienum baptizet Va | 933 Deus ρSr] Dominus θVa | 934 annuntiant Bm^{2}Barb.σ] nuntiant $\theta\rho^2$

905-906 Act. 1:1 | 909 Lev. 8:7-9, 13 | Num. 18:8ff | 911-912 2 Cor. 3:7-11 | 916-917 1 Cor. 14:22 | 917-918 The reference should be 1 Cor. 5:12. | 931-932 Gratian, C.18 q.2 c.18

potestatem evangelistis excommunicandi predicatos nisi talia ministrent. Sic enim Dominus ordinavit Levitici 19: *Non morabitur apud te opus mercenarii usque mane*. Non tamen propter hoc mercenarius fit iudex eius cui operatus est, sed per iudicem faciet eum compelli. Unde si Christus dixit: *Edentes et bibentes que apud illos sunt*, non propter hoc dixit quod, si non dederint, excommunicate eos. Immo magis videtur dixisse oppositum quando dixit, Matthei 10: *Quicumque non receperit vos, nec audierit sermones vestros, exeuntes foras* etc., *excutite pulverem de pedibus vestris*. Et Luce 10 additur: *in testimonium super illos*, quod non est dicere tradite eum Sathane excommunicando.

Quinto, nec per potestatem sacerdotalem conficiendi, quam acceperunt in cena, quia illam habet etiam degradatus, scismaticus et hereticus, qui omnes vere conficiunt corpus Christi, apud quos tamen nulla est potestas iurisdictionis. Quia non possunt solvere nec ligare, ut dicitur 24 q. 1 *Audivimus*, ibi: *Qui extra ecclesiam sunt, nec ligare possunt nec solvere*, qui tamen possunt vera sacramenta conficere, sicut dicit Augustinus *Contra Faustum*, et habetur 24 q. 4 *Quid faciat*.

Sexto, nec per potestatem ligandi et solvendi in foro conscientie, quia et illam potest quis habere qui nullam habet iurisdictionem nec subditum. Sicut sacerdos monachus non prelatus ita habet caracterem sacerdotalem et claves ordinis, que sunt scientia discernendi et potentia ligandi et solvendi, sicut papa, qui tamen penitus nullam habet potestatem iurisdictionis nec aliquem subditum, nec in foro conscientie nec in foro exteriori, nec aliquem potest solvere nec ligare, nisi detur de novo sibi ab aliquo potestas iurisdictionis ordinaria vel delegata. Ergo per nullam istarum sex potestatum a Christo apostolis collatarum est eis potestas iurisdictionis collata, qua quemcumque in foro conscientie possent solvere nec ligare.

desunt $\gamma\pi$V[6]

935 excommunicare σ | predicatos θ] predicaturos Bm[2], predicatores ρ^2, predicantes Va, aliquos Sr, illos quibus predicant Barb. | 945 conficiendi] *add.* corpus [*add.* Christi V[5]] sive [seu Sv, suum Bo] eucharistiam θ^1 | 948 ut Bm[2]Barb.Va] sicut θ | 955 et[1]] ac θ(-Bo) | 956-957 iurisdictionis potestatem θ | 958 nec[2]] vel θ(-V[3]) | 960 illarum ρ^1 | 961 quecumque θ(-BoSv)Va | nec V[1]V[2]V[3]SvBarb.Va] vel BoV[5]Bm[2], et OSρ^2

936-937 Lev. 19:13 | 939 Luc. 10:7 | 941-943 Matt. 10:14 | 943 The reference should be Marc. 6:11. | 948-949 Gratian, C.24 q.1 c.4 | 950-951 The reference should be 23 q. 4: Gratian, C.23 q.4 c.25

Septimo, nec per illud quod dictum est eis Matthei 18: *Quecumque alligaveritis super terram* etc., usque ibi: *erunt soluta et in celo*. Primo quidem quia per illud nihil penitus eis datum est, sed solum promissum, sicut supra dictum est. Sed quia Deus verax est in promissis, si illud fuit promissio Christi, oportet quod quandoque sit facta solutio, *quia quecumque promisit potens est facere*, ad Hebreos 11, et non solum potens sed etiam volens et complens, sicut dicit apostolus ad Titum 1: *Promisit qui non mentitur Deus*. Ergo in omnibus apostolis quandoque completum fuit illud: *Quecumque alligaveritis* etc., sicut in Petro illud: *Quodcumque solveris super terram*, sive hoc fuerit per illa verba: *Quorum remiseritis peccata*, sive per alia, sive tunc, sive alias. Et quia *non tardat Dominus promissionem suam*, ut dicitur 2 Petri 3, sicut Christus ante ascensionem suam implevit in Petro illud: *Quodcumque solveris*, ita implevit illud in apostolis: *Quecumque alligaveritis*.

Sed secundum sanctos plus est promissum Petro per illa verba: *Tibi dabo claves* etc., et per consequens plus datum, quam apostolis per illa verba: *Quecumque alligaveritis*, vel *Quorum remiseritis*, vel quecumque alia. Unde Origenes, ut supra dictum est, super illud: *Quecumque alligaveritis*, dicit: *Non dicit in celis sicut Petro, sed in celo, quia non fuerunt tante perfectionis ut Petrus*. Loquitur autem non de perfectione virtutis personalis, sed de perfectione potestatis respectu aliorum, sicut verba sonant. Cum ergo in apostolis fuerit tandem duplex potestas, scilicet ordinis et iurisdictionis, quam distinctionem iura faciunt, dicendo quod confirmatus in episcopum potest ea que sunt iurisdictionis (sicut iudicare, corrigere, excommunicare, absolvere et huiusmodi), non autem ea que sunt ordinis episcopalis (sicut consecrare res aut personas), *De electione* c. *Transmissam*, et similiter episcopus non episcopo potest committere ea que sunt iurisdictionis, non autem ea que sunt ordinis, *De consecratione*

desunt B^2V^6; 984 *usque ad verbum* apostolis *desunt* $\gamma\pi$

963 Septimo] unde ρ^1 | 967 facta sit θ | 975 illud²] *om.* θ | 980 illud] his ρ^1 | 982 ut] sicut θ | 984 fuit φ, est $\psi\pi^2$ | tandem] *om.* $\psi\pi^2$; tantum φBarb. | 986 iudicare] *om.* ρ^1 | 987 ea] *om.* $\theta^4\gamma$ | 988 res aut personas] *om.* P^1; regit [regere Bo] autem personas $\theta\psi$, ecclesias [*add.* confirmare St] aut [et ordinare St] personas φ, aut personas confirmare π^2(-P^1)

963-964 Matt. 18:18 | 967-968 The reference should be Rom. 4:21. | 969-970 Tit. 1:2 | 971 Matt. 18:18 | 971-972 Matt. 16:19 | 972-973 Joan. 20:23 | 973-974 2 Pet. 3:9 | 975 Matt. 16:19 | 976 Matt. 18:18 | 977-978 Matt. 16:19 | 979 Matt. 18:18 | Joan. 20:23 | 980-982 *Cat. aur. in Matt.* 18.5, 1:274A (1:297B) | 980-981 Matt. 18:18 | 988-989 X. 1.6.15 | 990-991 X. 3.40.9

ecclesie vel altaris c. *Aqua*, igitur Christus per illa verba: *Tibi dabo claves* etc., promisit utrasque claves, scilicet tam ordinis quam iurisdictionis. Quia quando dixit: *claves regni celorum*, non distinguens has aut illas, de omnibus intellexit: argumentum *De privilegiis* c. *Quia circa*. Ergo omnes claves regni celorum, per quas scilicet ecclesia militans intrat in triumphantem, et per quas homo de ecclesia eicitur et in eam introducitur, sive sint claves ordinis, per quas hoc fit directe et immediate, sive claves iurisdictionis, que primis clavibus deserviunt preparando et exequendo, omnes istas claves sive ambas Christus promisit Petro dare et dedit. Et quia non promisit sibi mittere per alium, sed dixit: *Tibi dabo*, ideo etiam dedit per seipsum. Et quia dixit: *Super hanc petram edificabo ecclesiam meam*, quod non solum de Christo principaliter sed etiam de Petro post Christum sancti exponunt, cum quidquid est in toto edificio solidetur in fundamento, ideo omnis potestas ecclesie primo collata est Petro. Immo non est data ecclesie nisi in Petro, licet non sit data Petro propter se sed propter ecclesiam.

Est autem sciendum quod potestas ordinis per sui multiplicationem in nullo diminuitur. Unde per hoc quod sunt multi sacerdotes vel multi episcopi non minuitur caracter, quin ita possit sacerdos conficere et absolvere in foro conscientie, si habet subditum, sicut si esset solus, et similiter episcopus ordinare et confirmare. Per hoc autem quod potestas iurisdictionis alii datur non a iudice, minuitur potestas iudicis, quia non possunt esse plures domini eiusdem rei insolidum, nec possessores, nec per consequens duo iudices vel prelati eiusdem populi subditi insolidum, nisi unus habeat ab alio, et tunc non minuitur potestas conferentis. Sicut si rex dat totam potestatem suam baillivo vel preposito in certo loco, in nullo per hoc eius potestas diminuitur. Sed tunc committens est insolidum, non autem

desunt B^{2}V^6

991 Aqua] *add.* considerandum autem quod [*om.* U] potestas miraculorum, predicandi [*om.* U], temporalia metendi, conficiendi [confitendi φ^5], absolvendi in foro conscientie nullam penitus iurisdictionem important [importat UBm^1] de se [de se *om.* St; in se W], ubi etiam notandum quod φ | igitur] *om.* $\varphi\pi$Sr | igitur Christus ρVa] Christus igitur [ergo V^{5}Sv] θ | 992 promisit] *add.* Petro $\psi\pi^2$ | 993 dicit π(-R) | aut γ(-Pr)πBm$^2\sigma$] vel θPrρ(-Bm^2) | 995 scilicet] *om.* ρ | 997 et immediate] *om.* α | 999 illas ρ^1Sr | 999-1000 Petro ... promisit] *hom.* π(-R) | 1000 sibi] *om.* α(-θ^4); sicut θ^4 | per alium] per filium $\theta^2\theta^3$(-Bo), de Paraclito θ^4 | 1001 seipsum] se θ^2, se ante ascensionem θ^1 | 1004 ideo] a [*om.* RP^1] Deo π | 1004-1005 primo ... ecclesie] non fuit [est θ^2] θ | 1008 multi^2] *om.* θ | 1010 si^2] *add.* etiam $\theta^2\theta^3$, habet vel [*om.* Sv] θ^4 | 1012 alicui φ | non^1] *om.* $\theta^2\theta^3$; ut [et φ^5] φ | 1017 minuitur $\theta\varphi^1$W | Sed] et θ

991 Matt. 16:19 | 994 X. 5.33.22 | 1000 Matt. 16:19 | 1001-1002 Matt. 16:18

commissarius proprie loquendo. Sed dicitur insolidum quantum ad hoc, quod potest totum et totaliter iudicare sicut alius. Vel sic quod ambo habeant a tertio, et tunc iurisdictio unius diminuit iurisdictionem alterius, sive eius virtutem, quantum ad effectum saltem, sicut plus potest unus dominus vel prepositus quando est solus in una villa quam quando sunt duo. Ergo si Christus promisit Petro dare omnes claves ecclesie, scilicet tam claves ordinis quam iurisdictionis, dando per se claves ordinis alii in nullo minoravit promissum. Quia per hoc quod cum Petro fuerunt multi sacerdotes, ipse non potuit minus conficere quam ante. Sed dando alii claves iurisdictionis per seipsum sic quod non haberet a Petro, minorasset promissum suum. Sicut si rex promitteret alicui quod daret ei totam senescalliam regendam et iudicandam, et postea medietatem vel partem eius traderet alii iudicandam et regendam, qui potestatem suam iudiciariam et regendam non haberet nec recognosceret ab illo senescallo, sed a rege solo, et reliquam potestatem daret senescallo primo, certum est quod non integraret promissum. Sed si daret sibi aliquas personas aptas ad regimen et iudicium, quas ipse senescallus assignaret sub se in sui adiutorium, dando eis limitando et auferendo potestatem suam sicut vellet et expediens subditis iudicaret, per hoc in nullo potestatem eius diminueret nec lederet, sed iuvaret, et promissum perficeret et compleret.

Quia igitur Christus Petro commisit claves iurisdictionis ecclesie, idest totam potestatem iudicandi in ecclesia, si aliquam iurisdictionem per se alii contulisset qui non eam a Petro haberet nec recognosceret, minorasset nec integrasset promissionem suam. Et ideo nulli alii per se eam dedit, nec per consequens dare promisit, quia facit quod promittit. Sed per hoc quod apostolos sacerdotes fecit, et habiles ad recipiendum iurisdictionem in foro conscientie, prout Petrus eis vellet dare et auferre et limitare, prout sibi videretur ad edificationem ecclesie, non ad destructionem, in nullo promissum suum falsificavit nec minoravit. Si etiam Christus fecisset apostolos episcopos, non dando eis populum subditum, per hoc non

desunt B²V⁶

1019 et] vel θ | 1020 tunc] sic αVa | 1021 effectum] *add.* eius θ | 1024 quam] *add.* claves [etiam St] γ | 1026 conficere] facere ρ¹ | 1029 et¹] vel θ | 1030 que π(-B¹), quod ρ¹ | 1030-1031 potestatem ... regendam] eam θ | 1031 regendam] rectoriam [rectoria W] φ | non] *om.* φ | illo] ipso θ | 1032 et ... senescallo] *om.* ρ | potestatem] partem φ | 1034 assignaret] assumeret ψσ | 1036 subditis [subditus φ⁵P²] expediens α | per] quod ρ | 1037 nec] vel ρ | 1038 igitur] similiter [enim φ⁴] φ | Christus] *om.* ρ¹ | commisit] *om.* θ; promisit φ | idest] et φV⁷ | 1039 ecclesia] *add.* promisit θ¹, dedit θ² | 1040 cognosceret θ²BoV⁵P²π | 1042 consequens] *add.* eam StBm¹φ⁵ | dare] *add.* eam Uφ⁴ | 1043 recipiendum] habendum ρ¹ | 1044 vellet [voluit S] eis θφ(-φ⁴) | 1045 ecclesie] *om.* π(-R)

fuisset diminuta potestas Petri ad consecrationem, quia non minus posset confirmare et ordinare quam ante. Sed non ita decet facere episcopum sine populo subdito et iurisdictione, sicut simplicem sacerdotem. Unde modo decente dignitatem episcopalem, non potuit Christus facere alium episcopum a Petro quin abstulisset Petro quod dederat, vel non implevisset quod promiserat.

Igitur per promissionem quam fecit Petro dicens: *Super hanc petram edificabo ecclesiam meam*, quia a fundamento procedit omnis et tota soliditas edificii in superioribus partibus, a quo si divertunt parietes corruunt, et tanto gravius quanto sunt altius, promisit ei quod ab ipso derivaretur et originaretur omnis altitudo prelationis et iurisdictionis ecclesie. Unde quicumque prelatus et iudex ecclesiasticus, eo ipso quod divertit a fundamento Petri, corruit a prelatione et iurisdictione, quia iurisdictionem datam ecclesie non potest quis ei auferre nec extra ecclesiam portare, quod esset sponsam Christi dote sua spoliare. Et quia nemo dat alteri quod non habet, <necesse fuit ut Petrus haberet> unde ab ipso proflueret. Sequitur: *Tibi dabo claves regni celorum*, idest ecclesie militantis, quia secundum Gregorium, regnum celorum est ecclesia iustorum. Cum autem paterfamilias dat dispensatori omnes claves domus sue, per consequens dat sibi custodiam et gubernationem omnium que sub clavibus continentur ad regimen familie, et omnes qui sibi subduntur subicit ei in domo illa, non sicut domino, sed sicut dispensatori. Nec de rebus sub clavibus contentis aliquis habet ius accipiendi quidquam nisi secundum eius ordinationem. Unde per illud Dominus promisit dare Petro custodiam omnium ovium suarum, et dispensationem omnium

desunt B^2V^6

1048 ad] et φ | consecratio $\varphi(-\varphi^4)$ | 1049 quam ante] *om.* θ | 1051 decente] dante $\psi\pi^2$ | 1052 substulisset θ | 1055 et tota] *om.* ρ^1 | 1056 divertant π(-R) | 1057 et] etiam θ(-Bo) | ei] *om.* π | 1058 originaretur $\psi\pi$Va] ordinaretur $\theta\varphi\rho$ | 1063 necesse ... haberet Barb.] ut Petrus haberet β(-Barb.); ut Petrus $\theta^2\psi$; ideo prelatus devians [derivans V^5] a fundamento Petri iurisdictionem perdit [perdidit Bo], et [*om.* Bo] sic [sicut V^3; *add.* perdit Bo] non habens eam exercere non potest iurisdictionem, videlicet [unde licet Sv] quam [quare Bo] Petrus habuit a Christo et eam diffudit [diffundit V^3] θ^1; ideo nullus citra Deum ulli [illi St] unquam dare [dari UW] potuit ut sit super [*om.* W; supra Bm^1Pr] corpus Christi misticum tante potestatis ut Petrus φ | unde] *add.* quod θ^1 | 1064 proflueret] profluit de quo [quod St] φ | 1072 omnium ovium suarum ρ^1] omnium suarum ovium π^2Barb., ovium suarum omnium π^1Sr, omnium suarum V^7, omnium suorum Va, ovium suarum $\alpha(-V^5V^4V^7)$, suarum ovium V^5V^4

1054-1055 Matt. 16:18 | 1064 Matt. 16:19 | 1065-1066 Cf. Gregory the Great, *Quadraginta homiliarum in Evangelia libri duo* 1.12.1 (PL 76:1119), 2.38.2 (PL 76:1282)

sacramentorum et sacramentalium, et omnem iurisdictionem per quam oves introducuntur et excluduntur, et per consequens omnem clavem ordinis et iurisdictionis, non solum quo ad habitum, immo etiam quo ad actum nullatenus impeditum. Unde sequitur: *Et quodcumque ligaveris super terram* etc., idest quidquid in quocumque foro et per quamcumque clavem solveris vel ligaveris ratum erit in celis, idest in celo empireo, vel occulto Dei iudicio.

Per hoc autem quod apostolis postea promisit: *Quecumque alligaveritis super terram* etc., non promittit ipse eis claves iurisdictionis per seipsum, quia tunc diminueret promissionem factam Petro, ut ostensum est. Nec etiam promisit eas dare per alium, scilicet per Petrum, quia tunc habuissent ipsi, saltem a Petro, eas per totum mundum, quia non dicit super hanc terram vel illam, sed *super terram* indefinite, quod nec de facto fuit, sed Thomas Indiam, Mattheus Ethiopiam, Andreas Achaiam, Joannes Asiam, et sic de aliis iudicarunt. Nec etiam decuit quod toti mundo preesset nisi unus solus, nec quod ceteri vocarentur nisi in partem sollicitudinis. Unde per illud non promittit eis nisi claves ordinis sacerdotalis, per quas quilibet sacerdos potest solvere et ligare in foro conscientie omnes sibi alias subditos. Unde sensus est: *Quecumque alligaveritis super terram* etc., idest: dabo vobis potestatem per quam poteritis absolvere ab omni peccato, et ligare omnem hominem, quem et prout vobis subiecerit ille cui omnium hominum prelationem promisi, et cuius est vobis subditos ministrare. Unde istud non intelligitur de potestate iurisdictionis – alias contradiceret promissioni facte Petro, ut ostensum est – sed solum de potestate ordinis, et sic non contradicit.

Si queratur quare illa verba dicta Petro: *Quodcumque solveris et ligaveris* etc., intelliguntur in utroque foro et de utraque potestate – ista autem verba similia: *Quecumque alligaveritis et solveritis*, que etiam

desunt B^2V^6

1074 introducuntur] intromittuntur φ | 1077 et] idest ρ^1 | 1080 postea promisit [*inv.* P^2] apostolis $\theta\psi$, postea [*om.* W] apostolis dicit [*inv.* W] φ | 1081 ipse eis $V^3\varphi^4\pi$(-B^1)Va] *inv.* [ipse *om.* Bo] $\theta^2\theta^3\varphi^1\rho^1$ | 1083 eas] eis [*om.* Barb.] $\theta P^1\rho$ | 1084 ipsi] *om.* ρ | 1085 terram[1]] petram [portam V^5] θ(-Bo) | quia θ | 1088 solus] *om.* π | 1091 alias] *om.* $\theta\varphi^1\psi P^4B^1$ | 1095 subditis ρ^1Va | illud θ | 1097 contradicit] *add.* sed π(-R) | 1098 ista φ | 1099 intelligantur [intelligatur Bo] $\theta\rho$(-Sz) | ista] illa $\pi\rho$

1076-1077 Matt. 16:19 | 1080-1081 Matt. 18:18 | 1086-1087 Cf. Isidore, *De ortu et obitu patrum*, chap. 81 (PL 83: 154) | 1091-1092 Matt. 18:18 | 1098-1099 Matt. 16:19 | 1100 Matt. 18:18

dicuntur in plurali, *quecumque*, et illa in singulari, *quodcumque*, non intelliguntur nisi in foro conscientie et de potestate tantum ordinis et non iurisdictionis – dicendum quod hoc est quia, quando princeps dat duo privilegia, unum prius alterum posterius, secundum intelligitur salvo primo, quia intelligitur dari salvo iure alterius, *C. De emancipationibus liberorum* 1. *Nec avus*. Quia ergo promissio facta apostolis in communi secuta est promissionem factam Petro, gratia posterius promissa apostolis intelligitur salva gratia primitus Petro data vel promissa. Et quia non potest intelligi de clavibus iurisdictionis sine detrimento Petri, sed de clavibus ordinis sicut dictum est, ideo promissio facta apostolis intelligitur de clavibus ordinis tantum. Promissio vero facta Petro per illa verba: *Quodcumque solveris* etc., intelligitur secundum principium promissionis, ubi promiserat sibi, non has aut illas claves determinate, sed claves absolute, et per consequens ambas et omnes claves ecclesie, quia super ipsum promiserat se fundaturum ecclesiam. Ideo illa verba dicta Petro intelliguntur de utrisque clavibus et in utroque foro. Non ergo per illa verba: *Quecumque alligaveritis et solveritis*, fuit data apostolis aliqua potestas iurisdictionis.

Octavo, nec per illud Joannis 20: *Quorum remiseritis peccata, remittuntur eis; et quorum retinueritis, retenta sunt*, propter tria. Primo quia, secundum unam opinionem, per illa verba nihil est eis datum de novo, sed solum declaratum illud quod erat eis collatum in cena quando facti fuerunt sacerdotes, quod non pertinebat nisi ad claves ordinis quas solas includit caracter sacerdotalis, et non aliquam potestatem iurisdictionis.

Secundo, patet de potestate iurisdictionis in foro exteriori, per quam homo ligatur excommunicando et solvitur absolvendo, quia per illam non dimittuntur nec retinentur peccata proprie et directe, sed solum per

desunt B^2V^6

1102 et^2] *om.* $P^4\rho\sigma$ | 1104-1105 salvo ... intelligitur] *hom.* P^4P^1 | 1105 primo ... salvo] *hom.* B^1 | 1107 est] *add.* post θ | 1111 vero] autem θ | 1112 principium] privilegium φ | 1115 ipsum] *add.* secundum quod θ | 1119 Octavo] simili modo [similiter V^4] φ, iterum ψ | 1121 quia] enim θ | verba] *om.* θ | nihil] non θ | datum] *add.* aliquid [aliud O] θ | 1122 illud] *om.* ρ | collatum] datum ρ^1Sr | 1123 fuerunt] sunt $\theta\varphi^3$W | 1124-1125 et ... iurisdictionis] *om.* θ | 1127 homo] *om.* φ | absolvitur θ | 1128 dimittuntur $\psi\pi\sigma$] dimidiantur $\theta^2\theta^3$, adminuuntur V^3, diminuuntur Sv, remittuntur $\varphi\rho$ | retinentur] remittuntur $\theta\psi$ | directe] *add.* nec retinentur θ^4

1105-1106 *Cod.* 8.48.4 | 1112 Matt. 16:19 | 1117 Matt. 18:18 | 1119-1120 Joan. 20:23

absolutionem et retentionem que fit in foro conscientie. Unde cum dicitur: *Quorum remiseritis peccata* etc., manifestum est quod non loquitur de absolutione a sententia excommunicationis maioris vel minoris que fit in foro contentioso, nec per consequens de retentione que fit per excommunicationem, sed de absolutione a peccatis que fit in foro conscientie, per quam directe peccata remittuntur, et de retentione ei opposita in eodem foro, per quam scilicet sacerdos negat absolutionem indigno.

Tertio, quod per illa verba Christus eis nullam potestatem iurisdictionis dedit etiam in foro conscientie patet, quia ubi eadem ratio, ibi idem ius; et ubi eadem causa, ibi idem effectus. Sed constat quod eadem verba dicuntur cuilibet ordinato in sacerdotem, et ab illo qui potest dare utramque potestatem, puta ab episcopo diocesano, et tamen per illa verba nulla potestas iurisdictionis datur sacerdoti. Verbi gratia. Episcopus ordinat in sacerdotem aliquem non curatum secularem vel regularem dicendo ei inter alia: *Accipe Spiritum Sanctum, quorum remiseris peccata remittuntur eis, et quorum retinueris retenta sunt*. Constat autem quod sacerdos sic ordinatus ab episcopo non per hoc habet quod possit subditos episcopi ordinantis excommunicare nec absolvere in foro exteriori, nisi cum hoc faciat eum officialem suum, vel alias ei committat audientiam alicuius cause. Item per hoc non habet ipse quod illos de diocesi quoscumque possit absolvere nec ligare in foro conscientie, nisi cum hoc fiat ipse penitentiarius, vel episcopus det ei aliquam curam, vel specialiter sibi committat audientiam confessionum. Sicut ergo per ista verba eadem que dicit episcopus illis quos ordinat in sacerdotes non datur aliqua potestas iurisdictionis in aliquo foro, nec aliqua prelatio, sed solum datur potestas ordinis sacerdotalis, per quam ordinatus tantum potest solvere et ligare in foro conscientie quantum papa, si haberet tantum de subditis sicut papa, sicut etiam per potestatem conficiendi tantum potest conficere

desunt B^2V^6

1129 cum] *om.* θ | 1131 a] de $θ^2θ^3φ$ | maioris vel minoris] *om.* σ | 1134 dimittuntur θφ | de] *om.* φ | 1137 eis] eidem φ | 1138 dederit $V^1θ^3φ(-φ^3)ρ$(-Sz)Va | etiam] nec etiam φ | ibi] *om.* [et Bm^1] α(-W)π($-B^1$) | 1138-1139 et ... ibi] *om.* θ | 1139 eadem[2]] *add.* causa ubi [ibi P^4P^1] π(-R) | 1141 puto φ(-StPr)$ρ^1$ | episcopo] ipso π | et] *om.* π(-R) | illa] ista φ($-φ^5$) | 1145 autem] *om.* θσ | 1150 quacumque π | solvere πSr | nec] vel α | hoc] *om.* π(-R) | 1151 curam] causam θ | 1152 illa $θ^2θ^3ρ^1$ | 1155 absolvere $ρ^1$ | 1157 conficere] *add.* pauper φ

1130 Joan. 20:23

quantum papa, si tantum haberet de vino et de pane — unde quando sacerdos fit papa, non augetur in eo potestas ordinis, sed augetur eius obiectum seu materia per additionem potestatis iurisdictionis — ita similiter per ista verba: *Quorum remiseritis* etc. dicta apostolis, sive fuerint collativa sive collationis declarativa, non est eis data nec declarata aliqua potestas iurisdictionis in aliquo foro, nec aliqua prelatio, nec aliorum subiectio, nec facta eis submissio. Sed solum data vel declarata potestas ligandi et solvendi prout se tenet ex parte caracteris, sine qua nullus cuiuscumque commissione in foro conscientie potest quemcumque solvere nec ligare, cum qua et per quam quilibet habens eam potest absolvere quemlibet a quolibet sibi subditum et inquantum subditum. Unde sensus est: *Quorum remiseritis* etc., idest: habete vel habetis potestatem ligandi et solvendi a quibuscumque peccatis quoscumque a Petro vobis subiciendos prout subiecerit, non aliter, quia intelligitur salvo iure Petri, ut dictum est. Apparet igitur per ea de quibus magis videtur in Novo Testamento, quod alii apostoli a Christo nullam potestatem iurisdictionis receperunt. Et per consequens relinquitur quod omnis potestas iurisdictionis quam habuerunt apostoli et qua usi fuerunt, specialiter post Christi ascensionem, fuit a Petro eis collata.

Et hoc patet tripliciter, primo sic ex precedentibus. Omnis potestas particularium iudicum in regno aut est immediate a rege aut eius vicario generali. Sed potestas iurisdictionis in apostolis non fuit a Christo rege, et solus Petrus in toto regno celorum fuit eius vicarius generalis. Ergo omnis potestas iurisdictionis in apostolis fuit a Petro. Maior patet, quia cum omne imperfectum a perfecto sumat originem, ut dicit Boethius, oportet quod omnis particularis iurisdictio, et per consequens imperfecta, derivetur a plena et perfecta, sive illa plenitudo et perfectio in illo in quo est sit ab alio, sive a seipso, hoc est a nullo alio. Sicut videmus quod aut rex ponit per seipsum prepositos et castellanos in senescalliis et baillivis,

desunt B^{2}V^6; 1176 *post verbum* collata *deest* Sr

1158 papa] dives φ | si] *add.* tamen φ(-W) | 1159 eius] *om.* π(-R) | 1161 illa θψρ^1Va | 1162 collativa] conferentia [cum felicia V^7] α | 1163 nec^1] vel π(-B^1) | 1164 facta] *add.* est π(-R)Barb.Va | vel] et π(-R) | 1171 subiciendos] *add.* et ρ^1 | quia] quoniam $\theta^2\theta^3$(-Bo), quam θ^4U, quod φ(-U) | 1172 videretur RρVa | 1177-1370 Et ... Solutio] *om.* Sr | 1177 sic] sicut [ergo φ^3] φ | ex] in φ | 1179 et] sed θV^{4}ρ | 1184 in illo] *om.* ρ^1; illa [in illa R] π | qua ρ^1 | 1185 sit] fit π(-B^1)Barb. | alio^1] aliis π | 1186 castellarios φ(-W)RP^1 | et^2] *add.* in θ(-Bo)

1161 & 1169 Joan. 20:23 | 1181-1182 Cf. Boethius, *De consolatione philosophiae* 3 prosa 10 (PL 63:764-765; CCL 94:52-53; CSEL 67:64-65)

aut ipsi senescalli et baillivi, qui sunt eius vicarii generales in provinciis sibi decretis, ponunt ipsos immediate vel per alios mediate. Et hec fuit maior. Minor patet quo ad primam partem, scilicet quod apostoli non habuerunt immediate a Christo aliquam iurisdictionem, per illud quod modo dictum est. Et confirmatur declarando, quia per nulla verba alia magis videtur apostolis dedisse potestatem iudiciariam quam per illa, Matthei 18: *Quecumque alligaveritis* etc., que videntur respicere forum contentiosum, et per illa, Joannis 20: *Quorum remiseritis peccata* etc., que videntur respicere forum conscientie. Sed per neutra illa verba concessit eis potestatem iurisdictionis in aliquo foro, ut visum est. Ergo etc.

Et confirmatur iterum istud, quia per illa verba que fuerunt equaliter dicta aliis apostolis et Petro omnibus fuit equaliter attributa potestas vel declarata, sicut dicit Cyprianus, et habetur 24 q. 1 *Loquitur*: *Quamvis apostolis omnibus post resurrectionem suam parem potestatem tribuat, et dicat: "Accipite Spiritum Sanctum,"* etc. Si ergo illud intelligeretur de potestate iurisdictionis, tunc alii accepissent equalem potestatem iurisdictionis cum Petro. Aut ergo Petrus, nec post nec ante, aliam potestatem a Christo accepit, et tunc a Christo nullam maiorem ceteris habuisset, aut Petrus ante vel post maiorem accepit, et tunc Christus vel Petro vel illis quod prius dederat abstulit, quod est absurdum, quia beneficium principis decet esse mansurum. Quod autem illud sequatur patet, quia si prius dederat Petro plenam potestatem, et postea dedit aliis non per ipsum, minorata fuit iurisdictio Petri quando coniudices accepit ab alio, et non a se, qui prius solus per se potuit iudicare. Si autem posterius dedit Petro, tunc multum minoravit id quod apostolis dederat liberum, a solo Deo habitum et subiectum, quando illud postea Petro subiecit. Nam Christus per plenitudinem potestatis quam Petro commisit sibi omnem aliam iurisdictionem submisit. Et sic quod dederat vel dare promiserat apostolis liberum dedit vel fecit servum, quod est inconveniens, sicut si ille qui promisisset dare edes liberas, vel sicut sunt quando erant libere, postea eis

desunt B^2V^6Sr

1188-1189 Et ... maior] *om.* φ | 1189 quo] quantum ρ | 1195 ista φ | 1197 iterum] dictum φ | istud] illud φ^3Wπ(-R) | 1198 omnibus] *om.* ρ | equalis θφ(-φ^5) | 1201 intelligitur V^7π(-R)Va | 1202 recepissent θ | 1207 istud θ(-V^2) | 1208 Petro dederat α(-V^2St) | dedit] *om.* θ | non] tunc φ | 1209 Petri] *om.* $\theta^2\theta^3\psi$; sua θ^4 | quando] qui ρ^1 | non] *om.* φ | 1210 dedit] dederit ψπVa | 1211 multo θφ | illud [*om.* St] $\varphi\rho^1$ | 1212 istud θ | 1213 pro plenitudine $\theta^2\theta^3\psi\pi$(-P^4) | 1213-1214 sibi ... submisit] *hom.* π(-R) | 1215 si] *om.* ρVa | 1216 promiserat $\theta^2\theta^3\varphi V^7$, promisit θ^4P^2

1193 Matt. 18:18 | 1194 Joan. 20:23 | 1199-1201 Gratian, C.24 q.1 c.18

imponeret servitutem. Sic igitur a Christo non habuerunt apostoli potestatem iurisdictionis.

Quod autem Petrus fuerit Christi vicarius generalis supra probatum est in primo articulo. Et confirmatur 1 Esdre 7, ubi Artaxerses, rex regum, Esdre, quasi suo vicario generali, dat potestatem constituendi omnes iudices in provincia sue vicarie, dicens: *Tu autem Esdra* etc., *constitue iudices et presides, ut iudicent omni populo.*

Secundo, patet idem sic. Quia omnis unitas cognationis et generis ab uno principio procedit, sicut illi dicuntur esse agnati et unum genere paterno qui habuerunt unum patrem a quo primitus processerunt, et illi dicuntur esse cognati sive unum genere materno qui processerunt ab una matre. Unde gradus consanguinitatis accipiuntur per comparationem ad primum stipitem, in quo omnes fuerunt unum, ut dicitur *Ff. De gradibus* 1. *Iurisconsultus.* Unde etiam, ut esset perfecta unitas et cognatio in genere humano, de qua dicit Iurisconsultus, *Ff. De iustitia et iure* 1. 2: *Cum inter nos natura cognationem quamdam constituerit, constat hominem homini insidiari nephas esse*, Deus, ut supra dictum est, ex uno fecit hominum genus, Actuum 17, Genesis 2. Ergo cum congregatio ecclesie sit una, que etiam est quedam cognatio, de qua Christus dicit: *Omnes vos fratres estis* – immo per caritatem omnes fideles fratres sunt – ideo oportet quod ista cognatio ab uno originetur. Et quia diceretur quod istud unum principium est Christus, de cuius plenitudine omnes accepimus, ipse Christus voluit Petrum facere suum vicarium, ut etiam ab ipso post se spiritualis gratia et potestas derivaretur. Unde hoc negare est rumpere ecclesie unitatem, sicut dicit Cyprianus, 24 q. 1 *Loquitur*, ubi dicit de Christo: *Ut unitatem*

desunt B^2V^6Sr

1217 Sic] *om.* π(-R) | 1219 fuerit] fuit φ(-Bm^1) | 1221 quasi] *om.* θ; ut ψ | dedit ρ | 1223 presides] presbyteros π | presides et iudices θ(-BoV^5)φ | 1224 Secundo] et φ | 1225 isti φ | esse] *om.* ψρ | agnati θ(-Bo)π(-B^1)Va] cognati BoγB^1ρ | 1226 primitus] *om.* φ | 1227 esse] *om.* ρ | 1231-1232 inter ... quamdam] cognatio unionem quamdam φ | inter nos natura P^4Va] *om.* ψ; unitas vera alias humana natura [vera O] $θ^2$, humana natura alias unitas natura Bo, humana natura V^2, unitas natura V^5, unitas vera $θ^4$Barb., intuat vera R, natura P^1, nam cum B^1, unitas una [unam $ρ^2$] $ρ^1$ | 1233 Deus] unde θρ | fecit] *add.* Deus $θ^4$ | 1234 Cum ergo α | 1235 Omnes] *add.* autem ψπ(-B^1)Va | 1236 illa $ρ^1$ | 1237 congregatio ρ | originetur] *add.* principio θ | 1238 accipimus γ(-Bm^1Pr) | 1239 suum] summum φ | 1239-1240 et potestas] *om.* φ

1220-1223 1 Esdr. 7:25 | 1229-1230 *Dig.* 38.10.10 | 1231-1233 The reference should be to 1.3: *Dig.* 1.1.3 | 1234 Act. 17:26 | Gen. 2:7ff | 1235 Matt. 23:8 | 1241-1247 Gratian, C.24 q.1 c.18

manifestaret, unitatis eiusdem originem ab uno incipientem sua auctoritate disposuit. Hoc erant utique ceteri apostoli, quod Petrus fuit, pari consortio prediti et honore et potestate, scilicet apostolatus et sacerdotali a Christo, et tandem pontificali a Petro. *Sed ab unitate exordium proficiscitur*, idest a solo Petro post Christum potestas et prelatio derivatur, *ut ecclesia Christi una esse monstraretur*. Ad idem est quod dicit Leo papa, 19 d. *Ita Dominus*: *Huius muneris sacramentum ita Dominus ad omnium apostolorum officium pertinere voluit, ut in beatissimo Petro, summo apostolorum omnium, principaliter collocaret, ut ab ipso quasi quodam capite dona sua velut in corpus omne diffunderet, ut exortem ministerii se intelligeret esse divini, qui ausus fuisset recedere a soliditate Petri*. Unitas ergo ecclesie et prelatorum fraternitas requirit quod potestas prelationis in ecclesia a Petro originetur et procedat.

Tertio sic. Illud quod fuit totum et totaliter datum Petro, in quibuscumque inveniatur, processit a Petro. Sed tota potestas iurisdictionis quam habuerunt apostoli fuit data Petro. Ergo eam habuerunt ab illo. Maior patet, quia *id quod nostrum est sine facto nostro ad alios transferri non potest*, ut dicit regula iuris, *Ff. De regulis iuris* 1. *Id quod nostrum*. Unde res que semel facta est mea, a quocumque postea iuste habeatur, oportet quod hoc sit per meam concessionem. Minor patet, quia potestas apostolorum fuit potestas ecclesie, cum ipsi essent membra ecclesie. Tota autem potestas ecclesie fuit collata Petro, immo non est collata ecclesie nisi in persona Petri. Unde Augustinus dicit, et habetur 24 q. 1 *Quecumque*: *Quando Petrus claves accepit, ecclesiam sanctam signavit*, quasi dicens: ecclesia in Petro et Petrus pro ecclesia a Christo claves accepit, per quod patet quod omnes claves ecclesie Petro fuerunt collate. Unde quicumque eas habet a Petro postea eas accepit, loquendo de

desunt B^2V^6Sr

1243 Petrus] *om.* φ | 1244 et[1]] *om.* $\theta\psi B^1$ | honore $P^2B^1\rho$] honoris α(-P^2)Va, honor π(-B^1) | potestate $P^2B^1\rho^1$] potestatis α(-P^2)RBarb.Va, potestas P^4P^1 | sacerdotalis [*add.* potestas V^2V^5, potestatis Bo] θ | 1245 pontificalis θ^4 | 1246 derivetur [derivaretur θ^2] $\theta\psi$ | 1247 esse] *om.* π | Ad] Quod ρ^1 | 1248 Huius] *add.* inquit φ | Dominus[2]] *om.* $\theta^2\theta^3\rho$Va | 1249 beato α | 1250 principaliter] principe [*om.* S; principem V^1] θ | collocaretur φ | 1252 esse] *om.* φ | esse intelligeret θ | divini] *om.* φ | 1253 prelatorum] *add.* et $\pi^1\rho$ | fraternitas] superioritas [supernitas P^1] π(-R) | 1258 id $\psi\pi$(-P^4)Barb.Va] illud $\theta\varphi P^4\rho^1$ | 1259 Id] *om.* $\theta\psi$ | 1261 hoc $\theta V^7\pi$(-B^1)Va] *om.* γ(-V^7)$B^1\rho$ | 1265 Quecumque] *add.* quod [et Bo] α(-St) | sanctam] suam ρ^1 | 1266 significavit [sanctificavit W, significat V^7] $\theta^4\gamma$ | in ... ecclesia] *hom.* π(-R) | 1268 habet [habeat ψ] eas [*add.* habet St] α

1247-1252 Gratian, D.19 c.7 | 1258-1260 *Dig.* 50.17.11 | 1264-1266 The reference should be *Quodcumque*: Gratian, C.24 q.1 c.6

clavibus iurisdictionis, in quibus Christus plenitudinem et primatum sibi dedit. Quia de clavibus ordinis nihil plus habuit ipse quam minimus sacerdos vel episcopus, nisi quod prius tempore et a digniori factus est episcopus.

Contra hoc autem opponitur multipliciter. Primo auctoritate Pauli, qui dicit 1 ad Corinthios 5: *Iudicavi tradere huiusmodi hominem Sathane in interitum carnis*, ex quo habetur quod apostolus Paulus illum excommunicavit, et per consequens habuit potestatem excommunicandi. Sed hanc potestatem ipse habuit a Domino, secundum illud 2 ad Corinthios ultimo: *Ut non durius agam secundum potestatem quam Dominus dedit mihi*. Ergo Paulus apostolus potestatem iurisdictionis habuit a Deo.

Solutio sicut dicitur ad Romanos 13: *Non est potestas nisi a Deo*, scilicet mediate vel immediate. Unde apostolus habuit potestatem a Deo mediante Petro. Vel ideo ipse et alii in primitiva ecclesia dicebantur habere potestatem iurisdictionis specialiter a Deo, licet non haberent nisi mediante Petro, quia habebant virtutem executivam a Deo, sicut ordinarius mandat executioni sententiam delegati quando ille per se non sufficit. Unde quia in primitiva ecclesia excommunicati statim a diabolo arripiebantur, ideo dicebantur excommunicantes habere virtutem a Deo, quia excommunicando consequenter tradebant Sathane in interitum carnis, quod non erat nisi virtute divina. Quod enim Petrus Ananiam et Saphiram mentitos Spiritui Sancto morte damnavit, Actuum 5, non fuit virtute clavium, sed speciali operatione virtutum, de qua 1 ad Corinthios 12: *Alii operatio virtutum*, idest miraculorum.

Secundo opponitur, quia sancti in diversis locis per illud Matthei 18: *Quecumque alligaveritis*, et Joannis 20: *Quorum remiseritis* etc., dicunt apostolis collatam fuisse potestatem ligandi et solvendi in foro exteriori, per excommunicationem et censuram ecclesiasticam. Unde super illud: *Quecumque alligaveritis*, dicit Hieronymus: *Potestatem tribuit apostolis, ut sciant,* [*quod*] *qui a talibus condemnantur, humanam sententiam divina*

desunt B²V⁶Sr

1273 multipliciter] *om.* ρ^1 | 1275 habetur] patet ρ^1 | 1276 et ... excommunicandi] *hom.* θ | 1277 ultimo] *add.* Hec [Hoc θ^4] absens scribo θ | 1278 non] *add.* presens θ | Dominus] Deus ρ | 1279 a Deo] *om.* π(-R) | 1282 Vel] *om.* φ | 1288 interitu ρ^1 | 1298 quod] *om.* θ^4P⁴; ut φ^3, et ψ | damnantur [dominantur Sv(-S)] θ

1274-1275 1 Cor. 5:3-5 | 1277-1278 2 Cor. 13:10 | 1280 Rom. 13:1 | 1290 Act. 5:1-11 | 1291-1292 1 Cor. 12:10 | 1293-1294 Matt. 18:18 | 1294 Joan. 20:23 | 1297 Matt. 18:18 | 1297-1299 *Cat. aur. in Matt.* 18.5, 1:274A (1:297B)

sententia corroborari. Item Hylarius ibidem per hoc: *Ad terrorem maximi metus, quo ad presens omnes continentur, immobile severitatis apostolice iudicium omnibus demonstravit*. Item super illud Joannis 20: *Quorum remiseritis* etc., dicit Gregorius in homilia: *Principatum superni iudicii sortiuntur*, ubi etiam dicit Gregorius quod *sententia pastoris sive iusta sive iniusta timenda est*, loquens de sententia excommunicationis. Ergo videtur per illa verba data esse a Christo apostolis potestas iurisdictionis.

Solutio: sicut supra dictum est, ille auctoritates quantum ad sensum litteralem non possunt intelligi de potestate ligandi et solvendi in foro exteriori. Sed solum in foro conscientie quo ad caracterem, non autem quo ad executionem ligandi et solvendi in illo, que requirit concursum iurisdictionis in illo foro, que differt a iurisdictione in foro exteriori sicut patet, quia possunt esse sine invicem. Sicut officialis habet iurisdictionem in subditos episcopi contentiosam in foro exteriori, et nullam in foro interiori. Penitentiarius autem episcopi, inquantum huiusmodi, non habet iurisdictionem in subditos eius in foro exteriori, sed solum in foro conscientie. Quia officialis, qui potest excommunicare et absolvere ab illa sententia quam tulit, a nullo peccato potest absolvere. Econtrario penitentiarius, inquantum huiusmodi, potest absolvere a peccatis, non autem ab aliqua sententia excommunicationis, nisi sibi specialiter committatur, quia fori sunt distincti et per consequens habent iurisdictiones distinctas. Hoc autem est commune omni iurisdictioni et omni foro, quod in nullo foro potest quis nisi subditum solvere nec ligare. Sed hoc habent proprium isti fori, quod aliquis est subditus alicui quo ad unum forum qui non est subditus quo ad alium, sicut exemplificatum est. Unde per illa verba non est data iurisdictio apostolis nec prelatio in aliquo foro litteraliter, ut dictum est.

desunt B²V⁶Sr

1299 terrorem] timorem θ| 1300 qua γ| 1301 Item] unde ρ¹| 1302 superni] summi ρ¹ | 1303 etiam dicit φ¹P²ρ(-Sz)] *inv.* θ²θ³φ²Va; tunc dicit π(-B¹), dicit θ⁴B¹Sz | 1306 iste θ| auctoritates] *add.* non possunt intelligi α | 1307 non possunt intelligi] *om.* α | 1309-1310 illo ... in²] *hom.* φ| 1309 que] quod θ(-Sv)| 1310 que ... foro] *hom.* θ| 1311 quia] quando θ| potest π(-R) | sine] et si non [*add.* in P⁴] π(-P¹) | invicem] iurisdictione θ| 1321 absolvere θφ¹ρ¹| nec ligare πVa] *om.* α; vel ligare ρ| 1323 forum] *om.* θ| 1324 ista φ

1299-1301 *Cat. aur. in Matt.* 18.5, 1:274A (1:297B)| 1301-1304 *Cat. aur. in Joan.* 20.3, 2:583A (2:639B)| 1301-1302 Joan. 20:23| 1303-1304 Cf. Gregory the Great, *Quadraginta homiliarum in Evangelia libri duo* 2.26.6 (PL 76:1201)

Ad primam auctoritatem dicendum quod ibi non est facta collatio, sed promissio, etiam de potestate in foro conscientie, quam ante cenam non debuerunt habere. Sed quia promissio Dei non fallit, ideo Hieronymus ita loquitur de potestate promissa ac si esset data, dicens *potestatem tribuit* etc., idest tribuere promittit. Similiter, quod dicit Hylarius: *Immobile severitatis apostolice iudicium demonstravit*, exponendum est: *severitatis apostolice*, idest potestatis non tunc date, sed tunc promisse. Quod autem illa promissio non respiciat forum contentiosum sed conscientie, patet per Hylarium consequenter post verba predicta: *severitatis apostolice iudicium demonstravit*, ubi exponens illud iudicium subdit: *Ut quos in terris ligaverint, idest peccatorum vinculis innexos reliquerint, et quos solverint, concessione scilicet venie acceperint in salutem, hi in celis ligati sunt et soluti*. Ad illud Gregorii dicendum quod illud sic exponitur in sensu mistico, non historico. Per potestatem enim eis a Christo datam ligandi et solvendi in foro conscientie signabatur potestas prelationis eis danda a Petro in foro utroque, sine qua non poterant exequi potestatem primam, nisi scilicet Petrus eos fecisset prelatos et iudices, dando eis subditos, primo et principaliter in foro conscientie quantum ad peccantes voluntarios ad penitentiam, et deinde in foro exteriori ad cohercendum per censuram ecclesiasticam illos qui aliter non possunt corrigi, 11 q. 3 c. *Nemo*. In quo quidem foro exteriori idem est dare potestatem iurisdictionis et dare subditos, quia ad iudicandum in foro exteriori una tantum potestas, scilicet iurisdictionis, requiritur, que non est aliud quam relatio talis superioritatis ad subditos. Unde talis potestas non est sine subditis sicut nec prelatio sine subiectione. Sed ad iudicandum in foro interiori

desunt B^{2}V^{6}Sr

1327 non] *om.* ρ^1 | 1328 debuit [*add.* ullus (nullus V^4) φ(-φ^5)] α(-θ^4) | 1328-1329 ita loquitur] ista φ | 1330 promisit θ | 1333 ista θ | 1336 ligaverint BoStψ] ligaverunt θ^2V^{2}V^5φ(-St)Va, ligaverit θ^4, ligaveris π(-R), ligaveritis Rρ | reliquerint [relinquerint V^7] $\psi\pi$(-P^4)] reliquerunt $\theta\varphi$Va, relinquerit P^4, reliqueritis ρ | solverint BoSt$\psi\pi$(-P^4)] solverunt θ(-Bo)φ(-St), solvit P^4, solveritis ρ, subderunt Va | 1337 scilicet] idest θ | acceperint $\psi\pi$Barb.] acceperunt $\theta\varphi$Va, acceperit ρ^1 | 1338 illud^1 $\theta\pi$Barb.] aliud $\gamma\rho^1$Va | dicendum] *om.* φ | 1339 historico] *add.* quod θ | 1340 signabatur] significabatur $\theta^4\psi$Barb., figurabatur φ, significatur Va | data θ | 1341 potestatem] *add.* suam ρ^1 | 1342 et ... subditos] *om.* ρ^1 | eis] eos φ(-StW) | subditos] iudices [*om.* U] φ | 1345 per ... ecclesiasticam] *om.* ρ | 1350 interiori] exteriori θ^2V^{2}V^{5}StBm^1φ^5, conscientie θ^4

1329 *Cat. aur. in Matt.* 18.5, 1:274A (1:297B) | 1330-1332 *Cat. aur. in Matt.* 18.5, 1:274A (1:297B) | 1335-1338 *Cat. aur. in Matt.* 18.5, 1:274A (1:297B) | 1345-1346 Gratian, C.11 q.3 c.41

requiritur duplex potestas, quarum una est qualitas et res absoluta caracteris, scilicet sacerdotalis indelebilis; alia est res relata, scilicet potestas iurisdictionis. Unde quod dicit Gregorius per illa verba: *principatum superni iudicii sortiuntur*, exponendum est: idest sortituri esse prefigurantur. Et quod dicit: *sententia pastoris timenda est*, intelligens de excommunicatione, verum est, et habetur per illa verba in simili et in sensu mistico, non historico.

Tertio opponitur de multis auctoritatibus que dicunt apostolos a Christo factos iudices et principes mundi, et sic intelliguntur a sanctis et a tota ecclesia, sicut est illud: *Constitues eos principes super omnem terram*. Et Luce 11: *Ipsi iudices vestri erunt*, dixit Christus Judeis de apostolis. D.21 *In novo* < dicitur > quod in locum apostolorum episcopi surrexerunt. Et 68 d. *Quorum* ponitur verbum Augustini super Psalmo: *Pro patribus tuis nati sunt tibi filii. Constitues eos principes super omnem terram*, qui dicit quod episcopi sunt successores apostolorum, et per hoc sunt principes populorum. Nemo autem potest plus iuris in alium transferre quam ipse habeat. Si ergo episcopi propter hoc a Deo constituuntur principes, quod succedunt apostolis, ergo multo magis ipsi apostoli fuerunt a Deo constituti principes.

Solutio: apostoli sunt immediate a Christo constituti principes et iudices totius mundi ad iudicandum cum Christo, sicut assessores assistendo, in die iudicii, secundum illud Matthei 19: *Cum sederit Filius hominis in sede maiestatis sue, sedebitis et vos super sedes duodecim, iudicantes duodecim tribus Israel*. Hanc autem potestatem iudiciariam non habent alii apostoli a Petro, sed omnes a Christo cum Petro, sicut patet in auctoritate inducta. Et de ista possunt intelligi due prime auctoritates. Sed apostoli sunt constituti principes et iudices ecclesie a Petro, determinatis sibi ab eo diversis terris et subditis, 80 d. *In illis*, et idem est de episcopis suo modo,

desunt B²V⁶; 1370-1378 *usque ad verbum* Solutio *et post verbum* illis *deest* Sr

1352 caracter γ(-U)ρ | 1353 Gregorius] *add.* quod ψπρ¹ | 1354 sortituri πVa] sortiti αρ | 1355 presignantur [prenoscitantur scilicet presignantur W] φ(-UBm¹)V⁷ | intelligendum est [*add.* alias esse Bo] θ | 1359 a²] *om.* θ²θ³ρ | 1361 dixit] dicit π(-R) | 1362 dicitur Barb.] *om. mss.* | loco ρ¹ | 1363 exponitur ρ¹ | 1365 et] *om.* ρ | 1367 principes] iudices φ | quia α | 1370 constituti] *om.* φ | 1371 assessores] *add.* et ρ | 1375 cum Petro] *om.* θ | 1377 determinate φ | 1378 divisis θ(-Bo)φ(-U) | 1378-1389 et² ... illis] *hom.* Sr

1353-1354 *Cat. aur. in Joan.* 20.3 (Joan. 20:23), 2:583A (2:639B) | 1355 Cf. Gregory the Great, *Quadraginta homiliarum in Evangelia libri duo* 2.26.6 (PL 76:1201) | 1360 Ps. 44:17 | 1361 Luc. 11:19 | 1361-1362 Gratian, D.21 c.2 | 1363 Gratian, D.68 c.6 | 1363-1364 Ps. 44:17 | 1372-1374 Matt. 19:28 | 1378 Gratian, D.80 c.2

ut postea dicetur. Quod autem dicitur: *Constitues eos principes*, intelligendum est non per te sed per tuum vicarium. Et licet ille sit sensus misticus et verus quem ponit Augustinus, ut patres dicantur apostoli et filii episcopi, tamen sensus litteralis videtur esse de patriarchis et apostolis. Quia sicut duodecim patriarche fuerunt capita duodecim tribuum Israel in synagoga, et de qualibet tribu fuit unus princeps, ita apostoli duodecim facti sunt principes ecclesie. Sed sicut sub Moyse dati sunt ab eo iudices toti populo, Exodi 18, Deuteronomii 1, et sub Josue etiam duodecim tribubus et earum principibus ipse divisit terram, sic et apostolis Petrus, Christi vicarius, potestatem iudiciariam tribuit et territoria divisit, sicut dicit Clemens predicto capitulo, 80 d. *In illis*.

desunt B^2V^6Sr

1379 dicitur] *add.* Deo [de Deo V^5, de eo StVa] $\theta\varphi$Va | 1380 iste θ | 1384 et] *om.* $\theta\rho^1$ | quibus tribubus $\theta^2\theta^3P^4B^1$ | 1384-1385 ita ... principes] *hom.* φ | 1384 duodecim apostoli θ | 1385 Sed] *om.* φ | 1386 18] *add.* et $\theta^4\psi B^1\rho$ | etiam] et θ | 1387 ipse] idem ρ^1; *add.* scilicet Moyses φ | sic] sicut $\pi(-P^4)$ | et^2] etiam ρVa | Petrus] *om.* ρ; *add.* et π(-R) | 1389 predictus $\theta\varphi$ | capitulo] eadem [*om.* S] θ

1379 Ps. 44:17 | 1386 Ex. 18:25-26 | Deut. 1:15-17 | 1389 Gratian, D.80 c.2

Tertius Articulus

Quantum ad tertium articulum principalem, de potestate a Christo data discipulis, sunt tres conclusiones principales. Prima, quod discipuli ante cenam acceperunt a Christo potestatem apostolis in multis similem, non equalem. Secunda, quod a Christo non acceperunt potestatem ordinis quamcumque. Tertia, quod nec potestatem iurisdictionis in foro aliquo.

Prima Conclusio

Prima conclusio, quod discipuli acceperunt a Christo ante cenam similem potestatem apostolis, non equalem, patet intelligendo primo totum articulum istum, non de quibuscumque discipulis Christi, sed tantum de septuaginta duobus. Siquidem discipuli Christi accipiuntur tripliciter. Uno modo ipsimet apostoli qui ex discipulis in apostolos sunt electi, semper tamen perseverantes in disciplina et doctrina Christi. Unde Joannes quasi semper vocat eos discipulos, et Matthei ultimo: *Undecim discipuli abierunt in Galileam*, et Marci ultimo: *Recumbentibus undecim discipulis* etc. Secundo modo accipiuntur discipuli quicumque auditores eius, et maxime qui eum sequebantur, non ut sanarentur, sed ut audirent eum et imbuerentur doctrina eius, etiam qui non perseveraverunt, sicut dicitur Joannis 6: *Multi discipulorum eius abierunt retro.* Et has duas acceptiones discipulorum Christi tangit Augustinus super illud Joannis: *Et post hoc descendit Jesus Capharnaum, ipse et mater eius et fratres eius et discipuli eius*, ubi dicit Augustinus: *Scriptura evangelica et apostolica non solum illos duodenos appellat discipulos eius, sed omnes qui in eum credentes magisterio eius ad regnum celorum erudiebantur.* Et neutro

desunt B^2V^6

3 principales] *om.* θ| discipuli] *add.* Domini ρ^1| 4 in multis] multis $\theta^2V^2V^5$, multum θ^4, multis alias multum Bo| similem] *add.* sed θ| 5 Christo] *add.* ante [*exp.* P^1] cenam π(-R)| 9-10 totum primum ρ^1| 10 illum ρ^1| 11 Christi] *om.* θ| 17 sanarentur] ei adhererent et [ut φ^5] ipsum sequerentur φ| 21 Jesus] *add.* in $\theta^4\varphi^1\rho$Va| ipse] *om.* ρ^1| 22 ubi] ut θ| 23 eius] *om.* θ

14-15 Matt. 28:16| 15-16 Marc. 16:14| 19 Joan. 6:67| 20-24 *Cat. aur. in Joan.* 2.3, 2: 361A (2: 396B)| 20-22 Joan. 2:12

istorum modorum agitur hic de discipulis. Tertio modo accipiuntur discipuli Christi illi septuaginta duo quos elegit ex tota turba discipulorum – postquam ex illis duodecim apostolos elegerat – quos misit *in omnem civitatem et locum quo erat ipse venturus*, sicut dicitur Luce 10. Et de istis solis discipulis nunc est nobis sermo.

Istis septuaginta duobus discipulis Christus ante cenam, dum iret predicando, dedit, et si non parem aut equalem, consimilem tamen potestatem illi quam prius dederat apostolis quantum ad tria. Primo quidem et principaliter dedit eis potestatem predicandi sicut apostolis fecerat, et quasi per eadem verba. Sicut enim dixit apostolis Matthei 10: *Euntes predicate, dicentes quod appropinquavit regnum celorum*, ita dixit discipulis Luce 10: *Dicite illis, quia appropinquavit in vos regnum Dei*. Et quod per illam missionem habuerunt ipsi potestatem predicandi innuit Cyrillus super illud Luce 10: *Etiam demonia subiciuntur nobis in nomine tuo*, ubi dicit: *Videbantur gaudere magis quod facti sunt miraculorum actores, quam quod facti sunt predicationis ministri*. Tamen non videntur habuisse tam generalem auctoritatem predicandi sicut apostoli, quia discipuli, sicut quidam nuncii et precursores, missi sunt solum illuc quo Christus ibat, Luce 10: *Et misit illos binos ante faciem suam, in omnem civitatem et locum quo erat ipse venturus*. Sed apostoli egressi circuibant per *castella, evangelizantes et curantes ubique*, Luce 9. Similiter nec post resurrectionem invenitur sic dedisse auctoritatem predicandi discipulis sicut apostolis, quia in Galilea dixit undecim discipulis: *Euntes, docete omnes gentes*, Matthei ultimo, et in die resurrectionis dixit, recumbentibus undecim discipulis: *Euntes in mundum universum, predicate Evangelium omni creature*. Non sic autem legitur de septuaginta duobus discipulis. Si autem dicatur quod illud Actuum 1: *Eritis mihi testes in Hierusalem, et in omni Judea et Samaria, et usque ad ultimum terre*, dictum est discipulis et non solum apostolis, quia omnibus qui convenerant, qui interrogabant

desunt B^2V^6

25 illorum ρ^1 | 27 duodecim] *om.* α | 28 ipse] *om.* ρ^1 | 29 solum ρ^1 | sermo] *add.* ergo ρ^1Va, igitur SrBarb. | 30 Christi ρ^1 | 31 dedit] *add.* potestatem φ | 31-32 potestatem] *add.* predicandi dedit ρ^1 | 33 fecerat] *om.* φ | 34 eadem] ea φ | enim dixit $\pi^2\sigma$] enim dicit $\pi^1\rho$, eam [iam Bm^1] dedit [*inv.* φ^5] θ(-S)φ, dederat S | 35 dicentes] *om.* φ; docentes ρ^1 | quod] quia φ | dixit $P^1\rho^2\sigma$] dicit π(-P^1)Bm^2Barb., dedit α | 43 Et^1] *om.* ρ^1 | illos] eos θ | 46 predicandi] *om.* φ | 46-47 sicut ... Euntes] *om.* ρ^1 | 47 docentes ρ^1 | 48 resurrectionis] ascensionis $\psi\pi^2$Va | 49 discipulis] *om.* α(-θ^4)π(-B^1) | 50 creature] *add.* Marci ultimo [*om.* V^3] θ | 52 omni] *om.* φ | 53 solis $\psi\pi$(-P^1)

27-28 Luc. 10:1 | 34-35 Matt. 10:7 | 35-36 Luc. 10:9 | 37-40 *Cat. aur. in Luc.* 10.5, 2: 146B (2: 160B) | 38 Luc. 10:17 | 43-44 Luc. 10:1 | 44-45 Luc. 9:6 | 47-48 Matt. 28:19 | 49-50 Marc. 16:15 | 51-52 Act. 1:8

eum dicentes: *Domine, si in tempore hoc* etc., dicendum quod per illud non dedit potestatem predicandi discipulis sive essent presentes sive non, quia non erant apti ad predicandum resurrectionem quousque essent saltem diaconi, ut dicetur in fine huius tractatus. Unde illud solum ad apostolos refertur. Item nunquam in predicando habuerunt discipuli tantam potestatem quantam apostoli. In cuius signum dixit Petrus Actuum 1: *Oportet ex his qui nobiscum sunt congregati*, quod specialiter dicitur de septuaginta duobus, *testem resurrectionis eius nobiscum fieri*, quasi dicens: nos apostoli sumus principales testes et predicatores ipsius. Unde illis principaliter predicatio appropriatur, Actuum 4: *Virtute magna reddebant apostoli testimonium resurrectionis Jesu Christi, Domini nostri.* Immo nullus discipulorum in Actibus legitur predicasse nisi postquam fuerunt in diaconos ab apostolis ordinati. Tunc enim primo beatus Stephanus usque ad martyrium predicavit, Actuum 6 et 7, deinde Philippus, Actuum 8.

Secundo autem, ad confirmationem predicationis, ut dictis mirabilibus fidem preberent facta mirabiliora, sicut Christus dedit apostolis predicando potestatem miracula faciendi, sic et septuaginta duobus discipulis. Unde sicut apostolis dixit Matthei 10: *Infirmos curate*, ita dixit discipulis Luce 10: *Curate infirmos*, ubi dicit Theophylus: *Ut operantes miracula homines ad suam predicationem attraherent.* Non tamen creduntur tantam virtutem et potestatem miracula faciendi habuisse a Christo sicut apostoli. Unde apostolis dictum est Matthei 10: *Infirmos curate, mortuos suscitate, leprosos mundate, demones eicite*, cum septuaginta duobus discipulis tantummodo dictum sit Luce 10: *Curate infirmos qui in illa sunt*, et postea: *Dedi vobis potestatem calcandi super serpentes* etc., sicut Paulus viperam in ignem excussit, Actuum 28.

Tertio, quia prohibuit discipulis sicut et apostolis portare pecuniam predicando. Sicut enim dixerat apostolis: *Nihil tuleritis in via, neque virgam, neque peram* etc., sic prohibuit discipulis Luce 10: *Nolite portare*

desunt B^2V^6

54 etc.] *add.* ad hoc [hec Barb.] ρ, adhuc Va | 55 predicandi] *om.* θ | 59 1] *om.* $B^1\rho^1$Va | 61 testes $B^1\rho$ | 62 ipsius] *om.* θ | 67 et] *om.* $\varphi(-\varphi^3)\pi\sigma$ | 69 autem] *om.* φ | 72 sicut] *add.* de $\theta\psi\pi\rho$ | 72-73 ita ... infirmos] *hom.* ρ | 73 Theophylus] Hieronymus θ | 78 tantum ρVa | 79 vobis] *om.* ρ^1 | sicut] sic enim φ | 80 in ignem] *om.* α | percussit θ | 81 et] *om.* $\theta^4\gamma$Va | 81-82 portare ... apostolis] *hom.* ρ^1

54 Act. 1:6 | 59-61 Act. 1:21-22 | 63-64 Act. 4:33 | 67-68 Act. 6:9-15, 7:1-60, 8:5-6 et passim | 72 Matt. 10:8 | 73 Luc. 10:9 | 73-74 *Cat. aur. in Luc.* 10.3 (Theophylactus), 2: 145A (2: 159A) | 76-77 Matt. 10:8 | 78 Luc. 10:9 | 79 Luc. 10:19 | 80 Act. 28:3-5 | 82-83 Luc. 9:3 | 83-84 Luc. 10:4

sacculum neque peram etc. Ideo dedit discipulis potestatem metendi temporalia sicut et apostolis. Unde sicut dixerat apostolis Matthei 10: *Dignus est operarius cibo suo. In quamcumque civitatem aut castellum intraveritis, ibi manete* etc., sic dixit discipulis Luce 10: *In eadem domo manete, edentes et bibentes que apud illos sunt; dignus est enim operarius mercede sua.* Ubi dicit Gregorius in homilia: *Ecce qui peram et sacculum portare prohibuit, sumptus et alimenta ex eadem predicatione concessit.*

De potestate autem baptizandi, quam apostoli habuerunt ante resurrectionem, quamvis dicatur Joannis 4: *Quamvis Jesus non baptizaret, sed discipuli eius*, ubi non specificantur apostoli, tamen non creditur quod alii discipuli ab apostolis eam acceperint, nec ea usi fuerint. Nec post resurrectionem est data septuaginta duobus discipulis, sicut undecim discipulis qui abierunt in Galileam, quando dictum est illis solis Matthei ultimo: *Docete omnes gentes, baptizantes eos in nomine Patris, et Filii, et Spiritus Sancti.* Unde nec in Actibus, quando passim apostoli baptizabant, leguntur discipuli baptizasse quousque ab apostolis acceperunt potestatem in diaconos ordinati, sicut Philippus diaconus baptizavit eunuchum et plures alios in Samaria, Actuum 8. Quia tunc licebat diaconis baptizare, quod hodie non licet nisi in necessitate, 93 d. *Diaconos, De consecratione* d. 4 *Constat.*

Secunda Conclusio

Secunda conclusio principalis est de potestate ordinis, quod eam non habuerunt discipuli a Christo. Nam quod non habuerunt ordinem episcopalem a Christo, nec fuerunt facti ab eo episcopi, certum est. Quia septuaginta duo discipuli, licet a tempore sue designationis fuerint maiores aliis communibus discipulis, semper tamen fuerunt minores duodecim apostolis, quia illa erat caterva regalis. Quod etiam patet, quia electio est a

desunt B^2V^6

84 peram] pecuniam φ | etc.] *add.* et α | discipulis] eis [*om.* V^2] θ | 85 et] *om.* φ^1WVa | 86 castellum] locum ρ | 87 dixit] *add.* septuaginta duobus θ | 88 enim] *om.* ρVa | 89 *Post verbum* dicit *praeterit verba interiacentia* (i.e. Gregorius ... nobiscum) *et procedit ad verbum* fieri (lineam 165) B^1 | 90 portare] *om.* ρ^1 | alimenta] illicita ρ^1 | 91 autem] *om.* $\alpha(-\varphi^1)$ | 94 ea] *om.* ρ^1 | fuerunt $\theta^2\theta^3\rho^1$, sint θ^4 | 95-96 discipulis[2]] apostolis [*om.* Bo] θ | 96 solum ρ^1 | 97 baptizate [baptizare V^2] $\theta(-V^3)$ | 107 fuerint θ(-BoS) | 108 sue] *om.* φ | fuerunt $P^4\rho\sigma$ | 109 communibus] quibusdam ρ^1

85-87 Matt. 10:10-11 | 87-89 Luc. 10:7 | 89-90 *Cat. aur. in Luc.* 10.3, 2: 144B (2: 158B) | 92-93 Joan. 4:2 | 97-98 Matt. 28:19 | 101 Act. 8:12-13, 38 | 102 Gratian, D.93 c.13 | 102-103 Gratian, *De cons.* D.4 c.19

minori statu ad maiorem. Unde cum ex discipulatu Mathias sit electus ad apostolatum, certum est quod apostoli semper fuerunt maiores discipulis. Sed apostoli non sunt facti episcopi a Christo nisi solus Petrus, ut probatum est in secundo articulo. Ergo multo minus discipuli. Item Barnabas fuit de septuaginta duobus, ut dicitur in *Ecclesiastica historia*, secundo libro primo capitulo, qui tamen a Christo non fuit factus episcopus, sed ab apostolis cum Paulo, Actuum 13.

Quod etiam non habuerunt a Christo ordinem sacerdotalem, idest quod non fuerunt facti a Christo sacerdotes, apparet, quia Christus non fecit sacerdotes nisi in cena, quando dixit: *Hoc facite in meam commemorationem*. Sed tunc non erant ibi nisi duodecim apostoli, de quibus solum faciunt mentionem Matthei 26, Marci 14, Luce 22. Ergo discipuli alii non fuerunt ab eo facti sacerdotes. Nec obstat quod apostoli inungebant oleo infirmos, quod est proprium sacerdotum, Jacobi 5, Marci 6: *Ungebant oleo multos egrotos et sanabantur*, quia illa unctio erat medicinalis, licet miraculose, non sacramentalis. Nec obstat Chrysostomus, qui ibi dicit quod *Jacobus in epistola sua canonica simile dicit* – loquitur de sacramento extreme unctionis, quinto capitulo, ubi dicit: *Ungant eum oleo* – quia utraque unctio est similis, non eadem. Nec obstat quod ibi Beda dicit: *Unde patet ab ipsis apostolis hunc sancte ecclesie morem esse traditum, ut energumini, vel alii quilibet egroti, ungantur oleo pontificali benedictione consecrato*, quia unctio energumini non est sacramentum. Et sicut baptismus Joannis erat principium baptismi Christi, sic ista unctio

desunt B^{2}V^6

114-117 Item ... 13] *om.* ρVa | 115 dicitur in] dicit π | 116 secundo libro primo [*om.* φ^5] capitulo φ^2] libro secundo capitulo primo St, tertio libro primo capitulo Bm^1, quinto libro primo capitulo U, primo et secundo capitulis θ, secundo vel primo [in V^7] capitulo ψ, primo vel secundo capitulo P^4, primo vel tertio capitulo R, primo libro tertio capitulo π^2, primo libro nono capitulo Sr | tamen] cum θ(-Bo) | 117 Actuum 13] *om.* α | 119 a Christo facti $\theta^2\theta^3\varphi$(-Bm^1) | quia] quod ρ^1 | 122 14] *add.* et θB$^1\rho^1$ | alii] *om.* γ | 123-145 Nec ... dicto] *om.* σ | 123 ungebant πBarb. | 124 sacerdotis ρ^1 | 125 ista θ(-V^2) | 126 miraculosa ρ | 127 epistola] *om.* $\theta\rho$ | sua] *om.* φ | canonica sua $\theta\rho$ | simile dicit] *om.* ρ; *add.* et θW, ubi φ^1, idest Pr$\varphi^4\psi$ | 128 Ungatur [Ungantur V^2] θ, Ungens [Ungentes B^1] π, Ungat Barb. | eum] cum θ | 129 ibi] ibidem ρ | 130 hunc] huic ρ^1 | sancte] eundem θ, communem φ | 131 traditum] cum [ut Sv, tamen V^7] dicunt [dicit V^{2}V^7] $\theta\psi$, inductum [eductum Bm^1] φ | 133 illa ρ^1

115-116 Eusebius, *Historia ecclesiastica* 2.1 (PG 20: 135); cf. 1.12 (PG 20:118) | 117 Act. 13:2-3 | 120-121 Luc. 22:19 | 122 Matt. 26:20 | Marc. 14:17 | Luc. 22:14 | 124 Jac. 5:14 | 124-125 Marc. 6:13 | 126-127 *Cat. aur. in Marc.* 6.2, 1: 475A (1: 516B) | 129-132 *Cat. aur. in Marc.* 6.2, 1: 475A (1: 516B)

non sacramentum fuit, sed preambula ad verum sacramentum et eruditio ad ipsum. Vel si fuit verum sacramentum, Christus solus non sacerdoti potuit illud committere quando non erant sacerdotes nove legis, nec ante eucharistiam institutam esse debebant.

Dato etiam quod apostoli tunc fuissent facti sacerdotes, non sequitur quod septuaginta duo discipuli, de quibus hoc non legimus, sicut legitur de apostolis, ante electionem discipulorum et post electionem apostolorum. Item non obstat quod dicit Hieronymus, quod *Jesus Christus, filius Dei, discipulos suos sacramentis divinis imbuens, ut universis gentibus conversionem ad Deum nuntient, imperat,* quia ibi accipitur sacramentum sacrum secretum pro revelatione sapientie divine, non pro sacramento ordinis proprie dicto. Preterea ex sacerdotibus non fiunt diaconi, quia tunc, vel ordo iteraretur, si prius fuissent diaconi et sacerdotes, vel ordo perverteretur, si prius fierent sacerdotes quam diaconi, quorum utrumque est inconveniens, *De sacramentis non iterandis*, et *De clerico per saltum promoto*, per totum. Sed ex septuaginta duobus discipulis Christi septem facti sunt diaconi, Actuum 6. Ergo non fuerunt facti sacerdotes a Christo.

Si dicatur quod septem diaconi non fuerunt de septuaginta duobus, contra dupliciter. Primo quia illi diaconi, quasi archidiaconi, sunt electi ad predicandum Evangelium, licet sub apostolis, sicut patet in predicatione beati Stephani, et Philippi, qui etiam propter hoc dictus est evangelista, non quia Evangelium scripserit, sed quia predicaverit, secundum illud 2 ad Timotheum 4: *Opus fac evangeliste.* De hoc enim Philippo dicit Lucas Actuum 21: *Intrantes domum Philippi evangeliste, qui erat unus de septem, mansimus apud eum.* Ad predicandum autem Evangelium apostoli preeligebant discipulos qui secum cum Domino fuerant, et eius facta viderant et verba audierant, propter quod erant testes credibiliores.

desunt B^2V^6; 151 *post verbum* Christo *deest* Sr

134-135 et ... sacramentum] *hom.* ρ^1 | 137 institutum φ, instituta ψP^4B^1 | debebat γ | 139 hoc] hic [*om.* V^5; alias hic hoc Bo] $\theta^2\theta^3B^1\rho^1$ | legimus] legitur α | legitur] legimus ρ | 141 Item non] nec ρ | quod[1]] quia π | Hieronymus] *add.* in sua canonica [cronica π(-B^1) Barb.] $\pi\rho$ | 142 divinis] *om.* ρ | gentibus] *add.* ad φ | 148 clericis φ | 149 promotis φ | 150 fuerunt] *add.* ante φ(-UW) | facti] *om.* φ(-Bm^1) | 152-246 Si ... discipuli] *om.* Sr | 153 dupliciter] dicitur ρ^1 | quia] quod ρ^1 | 154 sub] ab θ | 155 beati] sancti φ(-St) | 156 scripsit [scripserat Bo] θ(-V^1V^5)$\psi\pi$ | predicavit $\theta^1\psi B^1$Va | 157 enim] *om.* φ^1; etiam $\theta\varphi^2$ | 159 autem] *om.* φ | 161 quod] hoc π(-R)

141-143 The quotation has not been identified. | 148-149 X. 1.16; X. 5.29 | 150 Act. 6:2-7 | 156-157 2 Tim. 4:5 | 157-159 Act. 21:8

Unde in electione beati Mathie dixit beatus Petrus Actuum 1: *Oportet ex his viris, qui nobiscum sunt congregati in omni tempore quo intravit et exivit inter nos Dominus Jesus, incipiens a baptismate Joannis usque in diem qua assumptus est a nobis, testem resurrectionis eius nobiscum fieri unum ex istis.* Inter omnes autem discipulos post apostolos certum est quod illi septuaginta duo inseparabilius adherebant Christo et familiarius. Unde ex illis assumptus est Mathias in apostolum et septem in diaconos.

Secundo probatur istud sic, quia in electione septem diaconorum dixerunt duodecim multitudini: *Considerate ex vobis viros boni testimonii septem, plenos Spiritu Sancto et sapientia, quos constituamus super hoc opus.* Constat autem quod inter centum viginti super quos Spiritus Sanctus ceciderat in die Pentecostes, et recenter postea conversos, melioris testimonii et magis probati erant post apostolos ipsi septuaginta duo, quos post illos Christus elegerat et diutius cum eo et propinquius fuerant conversati. Unde ex septuaginta duobus discipulis, non quibuscumque aliis, et Mathias electus est in apostolum et Stephanus et alii in diaconos.

Tertio, quia aut fuerunt de noviter post Pentecostem conversis, aut de antiquis Christi discipulis. Non de noviter conversis, quia apostolus prohibet neophitum ordinari. Si de antiquis, magis verisimile est quod de septuaginta duobus quam de aliis, quia debuerunt se conformare Christo in preeligendo et preferendo quos ipse preelegerat et post apostolos aliis pretulerat, et ad predicandum miserat immediate post apostolos. Unde cum diaconi primi et immediate legantur predicasse ante omnes alios, etiam ante Barnabam, qui postea in apostolum est electus – unde Actuum 6, statim diaconis ordinatis, dicitur: *Verbum Dei crescebat*, scilicet crescente numero predicatorum – prius beatus Stephanus predicasse legitur, et postea Philippus Actuum 8.

desunt B^2V^6Sr; 177 *post verbum* diaconos *deest* Va

162 beatus] *om.* $\theta\psi$ | Actuum 1] *om.* θ | 163 omni] *om.* π; eo ρVa | 165 nobiscum] *om.* α | *Post verbum* nobiscum *praeterit verba interiacentia* (i.e. fieri ... duos) *et procedit ad verbum* dicit (lineam 323) B^1 | 166 istis] ipsis π(-P^1) | 167 et] quia [qui V^3] θ | 169 illud θ(-BoV^5V^3)$\varphi^3P^4B^1$ | 170-191 boni ... vobis] *om.* Bm^1 | 171 septem] *om.* φ | 172 autem] *om.* π | centum viginti] septuaginta duos [*om.* Sv$P^2\rho^1$] $\theta P^2\rho^1$ | 173 et] *add.* ita φ | postea] *add.* ad π(-R) | 174 post apostolos] *om.* ρ | 176 conversati] *add.* et ab eo edocti ρ | 177 apostolum] episcopum ρ | 178-245 Tertio ... historie] *om.* Va | 180 ordinari] *add.* sed φ | 181 debuerunt] *om.* φ | 182 eligendo ρ | 183 Unde] *om.* ρ | 184 primo φ | et] *om.* $\theta^4\gamma$ | 185 etiam] *om.* [et Bo] θ | 187 predicatorum] *add.* unde ρ | 188 predicasse legitur θ^1] *om.* ρ; predicasse $\theta^2\psi\pi$, predicasse connititur [convincitur φ^3] φ | et] *om.* ρ | post π(-B^1) | Philippus] *add.* leguntur predicasse ρ

162-166 Act. 1:21-22 | 170-172 Act. 6:3 | 179-180 Cf. 1 Tim. 3:6 | 186 Act. 6:7 | 187-188 Cf. Act. 6:9ff., 7:1ff., 8:5-6 et passim

Si dicatur quod fuerunt de antiquis discipulis, sed non de septuaginta duobus, quia illi iam erant sacerdotes – unde convocantes duodecim multitudinem, dixerunt: *Considerate ex vobis* etc., quasi dicentes: de turbis discipulorum, non de illis segregatis, sunt electi – non valet, quia tunc in electione diaconorum nullam vocem habuissent illi septuaginta duo, quod est absurdum. Unde in illis verbis apostolorum, appellatione multitudinis dubitante, contra duodecim intelliguntur septuaginta duo, sicut patet Actuum 4: *multitudinis credentium* etc. Et postea: *Joseph, qui cognominatus est Barnabas* etc., *posuit ante pedes discipulorum*, qui tamen erat unus de septuaginta duobus. Sed respectu apostolorum dicitur esse de multitudine.

Sed contra, quia Mathias fuit unus de septuaginta duobus, ut dicit Isidorus, *De ortu et obitu patrum*, in cuius electione Petrus, alloquens turbam, dixit: *Oportet ex his qui nobiscum sunt congregati*. Non dicit ex vobis, per hoc innuens quod de gremio septuaginta duorum, non de aliis, erat eligendus. Cum autem de electione diaconorum fit sermo, Actuum 12, dicitur multitudini: *Considerate ex vobis*. Non dicit ex his qui nobiscum sunt, sicut prius, ut excludat septuaginta duos quasi iam sacerdotes. Sed cum sacerdotes sint preferendi diaconis, si septuaginta duo omnes fuerunt sacerdotes, tunc ipsi debuerunt ante diaconos predicare, cuius contrarium innuit textus Actuum. Unde quidam dicunt probabiliter quod non omnes septem fuerunt de septuaginta duobus, sed quidam sic et quidam non. Quia enim nescit tarda molimina Spiritus Sancti gratia, sicut Paulus a Deo vocatus subito nihil minus habuit a ceteris apostolis, sic et aliquis de illis qui, licet recenter Spiritum Sanctum acceperant, potuit equari vel preferri illis septuaginta duobus. Unde alloquentes duodecim multitudinem discipulorum antiquorum et novorum Christi et suorum,

desunt B^{2}V$^{6}\sigma$

189 sed] et θP^{4}P^{1} | 190 quia] et ρ^{1} | 192 segregatis] *add.* qui ρ | 193 illi septuaginta duo] septuaginta duo discipuli θ | 194 multitudinis] *add.* credentium φ | 195 dubitante] *om.* $\varphi\rho^{1}$ | contra duodecim] *om.* φ | 195-196 sicut ... etc.] nam φ | 196 Joseph] *add.* autem ρ | 196-197 cognominabatur ρ | 197 Barnabas] *om.* ρ | discipulorum] apostolorum ρ | 200 quia] *om.* θ | ut] sic [sicut B^{1}] π, ubi ρ^{1} | 201 obitu] *add.* sanctorum ρ | electionem ρ^{1} | 202 turbam] *om.* ρ | 203 duorum] *om.* $\pi^{1}\rho^{1}$ | 204 diaconorum] *add.* etiam ρ^{1} | 205 dicit] dicitur θ | 206 duos] *om.* Pr$\varphi^{4}\psi\pi$(-P^{1})ρ^{1} | 207 duo] *om.* Pr$\varphi^{4}\psi\pi\rho^{1}$ | 210 omnes] *om.* φ | duobus] *om.* ρ^{1} | sic] *om.* φ | 212 sic] sicut $\alpha\pi$ | et φ] *om.* $\theta\psi\pi$Barb.; vel Bm^{2}, quod ρ^{2} | 213 decenter π | receperant θ^{2}, receperat θ^{1} | 214 duobus] *om.* Prφ^{4}V$^{7}\pi$(-B^{1})ρ^{1} | 215 multitudini θ | suorum] servorum π(-P^{4})

191 Act. 6:3 | 196 Act. 4:32 | 196-197 Act. 4:36-37 | 201 Isidore, *De ortu et obitu patrum*, chap. 79 (PL 83: 153) | 202 Act. 1:21 | 204-205 The reference should be Act. 6:3.

dixerunt: *Considerate ex vobis*, idest sive de septuaginta duobus sive de aliis, et non se restrinxerunt ad septuaginta duos sicut fecerant in electione Mathie, ante adventum Spiritus Sancti, quando supponendum erat preelectos a Christo esse meliores. Sed electi a Christo non erant preferendi a Spirito Sancto sed coequandi, qui, dividens singulis prout vult, fecit Stephanum precellere, quem aliqui dicunt non fuisse de septuaginta duobus.

Sed ex quo aliqui de septuaginta duobus facti sunt diaconi, patet quod non erant prius sacerdotes, et hoc innuunt duodecim, dicentes: *Non est equum nos ministrare mensis*, et postea: *Nos autem orationi et verbo instantes erimus*. Siquidem episcopi et sacerdotes debent solis spiritualibus vacare, sicut predicare et pro populo orare et sacrificia offerre, sed diaconorum est etiam in temporalibus ministrare, unde cum dicunt: *Nos autem orationi et verbo*, innuunt quod ipsi soli pro tunc erant sacerdotes, qui habebant pro populo orare. Et cum hoc omnes episcopi erant, vel saltem plures, quia in plurali dicitur: *Imposuerunt eis manus*. Postea vero de discipulis facti sunt sacerdotes, qui ex tunc fuerunt maiores diaconis. Unde Actuum 15 dicitur ad apostolos et presbyteros: *Et convenerunt apostoli et seniores*, idest presbyteri. Postea dicit de Juda et Sila: *Viros primos in fratribus*, qui non essent primi supra diaconos nisi essent sacerdotes, nec antea diaconi predicassent ante ipsos si iam fuissent sacerdotes, maxime si a Christo habebant auctoritatem predicandi. Quia presbyter semper prefertur diacono, 93 d. *Legimus*, c. ultimo, maxime in predicando secundum illos qui sunt contrarie opinionis, et dicunt curatum in predicando debere preferri illi qui habet a papa vel episcopo officium predicandi, pro eo quod curatus habet a Christo secundum eos. Unde si septuaginta duo a Christo fuissent facti sacerdotes, et a Christo habuissent

desunt $B^2V^6\sigma$

216 idest] scilicet ρ | sive^1] *om.* ρ | duobus] *om.* $\varphi^2\psi\pi$(-B^1)ρ^1 | sive^2] vel ρ | 217 duos] *om.* $\varphi^2\psi RP^1\rho^1$ | fecerunt ρ^1 | 219-220 preelectos ... preferendi] *om.* ρ | 220 sed] hoc ρ | 222 duobus] *om.* $\varphi^2\psi\pi^1\rho^1$ | 223 duobus] *om.* $\varphi^2\psi R\rho^1$ | 224 et hoc] etsi π(-R) | 226 eramus [vaccabimus B^1] π | solum $\theta\varphi^1\rho^1$ | 227 vacare] intendere $\theta\psi$, instare [insistere U] φ | sicut] verbum ρ | 229 et verbo] instabimus φ, etc. θ | pro tunc] *om.* α | 229-230 sacerdotes ... erant] *hom.* α | 230 erant] *om.* ρ | 231 plures] *add.* ex eis episcopi φ | 233 dicitur $\varphi\rho$] *om.* $\theta\psi\pi$; *add.* quantum [quod Bm^1, quando Pr] φ(-W) | 234 idest] *om.* ρ | presbyteri] *add.* et φ | de Juda] et Judam φ | Silam φ | 235 super φ | 236 antea] etiam θ, alii π(-R) | ipsos] eos ρ | 238 Legimus] *om.* ρ | 240 in] *om.* ρ | 242 a Christo^2] *om.* θ

216 Act. 6:3 | 224-225 Act. 6:2 | 225-226 Act. 6:4 | 231 Act. 6:6 | 233-234 Act. 15:6 | 234-235 Act. 15:22 | 238 Gratian, D.93 c.24 & c.26

immediate auctoritatem predicandi, pro illo tempore debuissent preferri in predicando diaconis ab apostolis ad predicandum ordinatis, cuius contrarium innuit ordo historie.

Tertio patet quod septuaginta duo discipuli non acceperunt a Christo potestatem ligandi et solvendi in foro conscientie, sive claves ordinis quod idem est. Quia illa potestas datur simul cum potestate consecrandi, sive sit una et eadem res cum illa, ampliata vel indivisibilis, sive sit alia; vel saltem non datur nisi habenti illam, quia *solis sacerdotibus ligandi solvendique potestas a Deo tradita est*, ut dicitur *De penitentia* d. 1 § *Ex his*, supple: in foro conscientie. Unde cum septuaginta duo non fuerint facti sacerdotes a Christo, nec ab alio ante Pentecostem, ut probatum est, manifestum est quod nec a Christo acceperunt potestatem ligandi nec solvendi in foro conscientie.

Sed contra hoc videtur quod septuaginta duo discipuli erant presentes quando Christus dixit apostolis Joannis 20: *Quorum remiseritis peccata, remittuntur eis; et quorum retinueritis, retenta sunt*. Sed tunc apostoli receperunt potestatem ligandi et solvendi, vel declarationem de iam recepta, et eadem ratio erat de discipulis. Ergo et discipuli eandem et eodem modo receperunt a Christo potestatem ligandi et solvendi, scilicet in foro conscientie.

Maior patet per auctoritatem Petri inductam Actuum 1, ubi dicit, specialiter de septuaginta duobus: *Oportet ex his viris, qui nobiscum sunt congregati in omni tempore quo intravit et exivit inter nos Dominus Jesus, incipiens a baptismate Joannis usque in diem qua assumptus est a nobis, testem resurrectionis* etc. Sed constat quod illa verba fuerunt dicta apostolis medio tempore quod fluxit inter baptisma Joannis et ascensionem Christi. Ergo discipuli erant congregati cum apostolis illo tempore

desunt B²V⁶; 245 *usque ad verbum* historie *deest* Va; 246 & 258 *usque ad verbum* discipuli *et post verbum* tunc *deest* Sr

243 *Post verbum* predicandi *redit ad verbum* Gregorius (lineam 89) B¹ | illo] quo π(-R) | 246 Christo] *add.* immediate ρ | 248 consecrandi] *add.* idest conficiendi corpus Christi φ | 250 solum ρ¹ | 251 a Deo] *om.* ρ¹ | d. 1] *om.* ρ¹ | 252 duo] *add.* discipuli P¹ρVa | fuerint V²Sv(-S)StBm¹φ⁴P²B¹Barb.Va] fuerunt θ(-V²Sv)Uφ⁵V⁷π(-B¹)ρ¹ | 253 alio] eo θ², eo [ea Sv] in cena nec ab eo θ¹ | 254 Christo] *add.* nec ab alio π(-R) | nec²] atque π | 256 quod θ(-Bo)ψP⁴ρ¹Va] quia Boφπ(-P⁴)Barb. | 258-314 apostoli ... tunc] *om.* Sr | 259-261 vel ... scilicet] *om.* ρ¹ | 260 et²] *om.* θ | 263 introductam θ | 263-264 specialiter loquitur φ | 264 Oportet] *om.* φ | 267 verba] *om.* π | 268 apostolis] *om.* ρ¹ | 269 apostolis] *add.* in π(-R)

250-251 Gratian, *De poen.* D.1 c.60 | 257-258 Joan. 20:23 | 263-267 Act. 1:21-22

quando illa verba a Christo dicta fuerunt eis. Preterea hoc patet per illud quod habetur Luce 24, ubi dicitur quod illi qui inerant in Emmaus, qui erant de septuaginta duobus, revertentes in Hierusalem, invenerunt congregatos undecim, et tunc Christus ostendit eis manus, pedes et latus, sicut dicunt Lucas et Joannes. Et tunc addit Joannes quod insufflavit et dixit: *Accipite Spiritum Sanctum, quorum remiseritis* etc., ex quo patet quod illi duo fuerunt presentes, qui tamen exiverant villam. Ergo multo magis alii septuaginta. Preterea ibi expresse dicitur quod invenerunt congregatos undecim, et eos qui cum ipsis erant, qui maxime videntur fuisse septuaginta. Ergo illi erant presentes. Preterea si undecim apostoli erant ibi congregati propter metum Judeorum, pari ratione erant ibi alii discipuli, qui ita vocabantur discipuli Jesu sicut apostoli. Unde si apostoli timebant, discipuli habebant eque timere et se abscondere et includere sicut illi, sicut etiam Joseph ab Arimathia erat discipulus Jesu *occultus propter metum Judeorum*, ut dicitur Joannis 19. Immo quia apostoli erant audaciores ceteris, sicut patuit Actuum 8, in prima persecutione magna, que facta est in ecclesia que erat Hierosolimis post mortem beati Stephani, propter cuius metum omnes dispersi sunt per regiones Judee et Samarie, sed apostoli propter metum erant congregati in cenaculo clauso, ad quod Jesus, ianuis clausis, intravit, multo magis alii discipuli erant ibi.

Minor patet quantum ad hoc, quod tunc apostoli illam potestatem aut receperunt aut eius declarationem, per supradicta secundum omnem opinionem. Alia vero pars minoris, scilicet quod erat eadem ratio de discipulis, patet, quia ex quo erant equaliter presentes, equaliter ad eos dicta sunt illa verba, et equaliter audita; ergo et equaliter operata. Sicut etiam verba consecrationis super multas hostias equaliter consecrant omnes hostias presentes, quamvis alie sint maiores alie minores, alie magis alie minus albe, vel rotunde, vel aliquid huiusmodi, ex quo omnes

desunt B^2V^6Sr; 278 *post verbum* erant *deest* P^1

270 Preterea] *om.* ρ^1 | illud $P^1\rho$Va] hoc $\alpha\pi$(-P^1) | 271 ubi dicitur Uρ] *om.* π^2; ubi dicit $\theta\varphi$(-U)π^1Va | inerunt π(-P^1) | 271-272 qui erant] *om.* ρ^1 | 273 manus] *add.* et $\theta\psi$ | 276 fuerunt] erant φ^1W | 278 - 4: 497 qui² ... remedium] *om.* P^1 | 279 illi] *add.* qui ρ^1 | decim ρ^1 | 281 Jesu] *add.* Christi θ | 283 occultus] *add.* tamen αRBarb. | 285 ceteris] aliis θ | ut θ | 287 omnes] *add.* discipuli φ | Samarie] *add.* preter apostolos ρVa | 288 sed] si ρVa | quod] quos $\theta\pi$(-R) | 290 aut] *om.* πVa | 291 eius] *om.* $\gamma\pi$ | 294 sunt] *om.* φ | equaliter¹] *om.* α | et²] *om.* ρ^1 | Sicut] *om.* θ(-Bo) | 295-296 equaliter ... hostias] *hom.* $\psi\pi$(-R) | 296 sunt $\pi^1\rho^1$ | alie²] *add.* sint B^1, sunt π^1 | 297 magis] *add.* albe θ

271 Luc. 24:33-40 | 274 Cf. Joan. 20:19-20 | 274-275 Joan. 20:22-23 | 283-284 Joan. 19:38 | 285 Act. 8:1

sunt panis de tritico, quia secus si alique essent non de frumento que non sunt consecrabiles. Unde quamvis mulieres, et precipue beata Virgo, essent presentes in cenaculo cum apostolis et discipulis, sicut dicitur Actuum 1: *Hi omnes*, scilicet undecim apostoli, *erant perseverantes unanimiter in oratione, cum mulieribus, et Maria matre Jesu, et fratribus eius*, idest discipulis, secundum illud Matthei 12: *Extendens manus in discipulos suos, dixit: "Ecce mater mea et fratres mei,"* quia tamen mulieres non sunt capaces potestatis solvendi et ligandi, quam nec beate Virgini Christus conferre voluit, *De penitentiis et remissionibus* c. *Nova*, ideo mulieres presentes per illa verba nihil receperunt. Sed discipuli erant capaces sicut apostoli, ex quibus multi postea facti sunt etiam episcopi, sicut beatus Martialis, Maximinus, et alii, et Mathias apostolus. Ergo cum essent eque presentes sicut apostoli, eadem ratio fuit in eis sicut in apostolis de recipiendo illam potestatem vel eius promissionem aut signum.

Solutio: dato quod discipuli presentes fuerint, tamen per illa verba non receperunt potestatem illam nec recepte declarationem. Quia pro tunc non erant capaces, non quidem propter impedimentum sexus perpetuum sicut mulieres, sed quia non erant sacerdotes ante Spiritus Sancti missionem, ut supra probatum est, nec per consequens erant capaces clavium ordinis, ligandi scilicet et solvendi, in foro conscientie, que solis sacerdotibus sunt concesse, ut sepe dictum est. Et ideo non erat eadem ratio de ipsis, qui sacerdotes non erant, et de apostolis, qui in cena facti fuerant sacerdotes.

Secundo videtur quod septuaginta duo discipuli a Christo facti fuerunt sacerdotes, quia super illud Luce 10: *Designavit Dominus et alios septuaginta duos*, dicit Beda: *Sicut duodecim apostolos formam episcoporum premonstrare nemo est qui dubitet, sic et hos septuaginta duos figuram presbyterorum, idest secundi ordinis sacerdotum, gessisse*

desunt $B^2P^1V^6$; 314 *usque ad verbum* tunc *deest* Sr

298 panes θ | secus] *add.* esset ρ | non^1] *om.* φ | 302 orationibus ρ^1 | 303 idest] et ρ^1 | manum γ(-Bm^1)ρ | 308 etiam] *om.* $\theta\varphi^3$ | 309 Martialis] *add.* et $\theta^1\varphi$ | et alii] *om.* θ; et Silas φ | et^2] *om.* π | cum] *add.* omnes φ(-φ^5) | 310 in^1] de φ | in^2] de φ | 318 scilicet] *om.* $\theta^2\theta^3\varphi^3WV^4$ | solum $\theta^2\theta^3\rho^1$ | 320 de] *om.* φ | fuerant $\varphi^2P^2\pi$(-P^4)Va] fuerunt P^4Bm^2Barb., sunt [*add.* vel fuerant V^7] $\theta\varphi^1V^7\rho^2$ | 323 *Post verbum* duos *praeterit verba interiacentia* (i.e. dicit ... quasi) *et procedit ad verbum* perfectioribus (lineam 408) B^1 | Sicut] *add.* formam φ | apostolos] apostolorum φ | formam] typum φ | 324 nemo ... hos] *om.* π(-R) | 325 figuram] formam θ | sacerdotum] sacerdotes [*om.* Bo] θ, sacerdotium ρ^1

301-303 Act. 1:14 | 303-304 Matt. 12:49 | 306 X. 5.38.10 | 307-309 Cf. Act. 1:21-26 | 322-323 Luc. 10:1 | 323-326 Bede, *In Lucae evangelium expositio* 3.10.1 (PL 92: 461; CCL 120: 213-214) *sciendum est*. Sed secundi ordinis presbyteri vel sacerdotes sunt ita vere sacerdotes sicut sunt episcopi et etiam sicut papa. Ergo discipuli fuerunt sacerdotes.

Solutio: nulla consequentia est: septuaginta duo discipuli figuram gesserunt sacerdotum; ergo fuerunt sacerdotes. Sicut etiam, Exodi 15, duodecim fontes Elim gesserunt figuram apostolorum, nec fuerunt apostoli, et septuaginta palme discipulorum, nec propter hoc fuerunt discipuli. Et baptismum Joannis fuit figura baptismi Christi, non tamen fuit in Spiritu nec in remissionem peccatorum sicut baptismum Christi, sed tantum in aqua. Sicut etiam pontifex et sacerdos legales gerebant figuram episcopi et sacerdotis evangelici habentium claves; non tamen ipsi habebant claves. Et Christus, sacerdos secundum ordinem Melchisedech, non tamen fuit Melchisedech. Et dato quod septuaginta duo fuissent sacerdotes, sicut multi ex eis fuerunt facti post Pentecostem, non tamen sequitur quod fuissent facti a Christo, sed ab apostolis vel aliis episcopis, sicut et sacerdotes nostri temporis.

Tertia Conclusio

Tertia conclusio principalis est de potestate iurisdictionis in septuaginta duobus discipulis Christi, quod scilicet ipsi a Christo immediate non habuerunt aliquam potestatem iurisdictionis in aliquo foro, quod patet tripliciter. Primo per omnes rationes quibus hoc probatum est in apostolis, arguendo sic. Potestas que non est collata a Christo maioribus in dignitate, potestate et prelatione non est ab eo collata minoribus. Sed apostoli fuerunt maiores illis discipulis, nec eis Christus contulit potestatem iurisdictionis. Ergo multo minus discipulis.

Maior patet, quia in potestatibus debite ordinatis nihil potest inferior quod non possit superior. Alias, si inferior haberet potestatem iuris-

desunt $B^2P^1V^6$

326 est] esse ρ^1 | 329 consequentia nulla est [*om.* θ^4] θ, nulla est consequentia φVa | 331 duodecim] *om.* θ^1(-BoV^2)ρ^1; et θ^2 | apostolorum] *add.* duodecim ρ^1 | nec] non autem ρ^1 | fuerunt] *add.* propter hoc θ | 332 septuaginta] *add.* duo $\theta\pi$(-P^4)Sr | palme] *add.* gesserunt figuram septuaginta duorum θ | 333 fuit figura] figuram φ | 334 nec] et φ | in²] *om.* φ(-U) | 335-337 Sicut ... Melchisedech] *om.* σ | 335 Sicut] sic α(-V^4) | legales $\psi\pi$] legalis $\theta\varphi$, regales ρ | 337 Et] *om.* π(-R); vel φ | 338 non ... Melchisedech] *hom.* ρ | fuit] *om.* $\gamma\pi^1$ | duo] *add.* discipuli θ | 339 ex eis] eorum θ | 343-344 in ... discipulis] septuaginta duorum [*add.* Christi φ(-W)] discipulorum αB^1 | 344 Christi] *om.* $\theta\varphi$ | 346 in] de $\varphi\rho$ | 347 sic] *add.* quod $\theta\psi$, quia φ | 352 Alias] quia θ

330 Ex. 15:27 | 337 Cf. Heb. 5:6, 7:17; cf. also 5:10, 6:20

dictionis quam non habet superior, inferior posset iudicare superiorem, quod est contra rationem, cum agens sit prestantius patiente secundum Augustinum, et contra iura, *De maioritate et obedientia, Cum inferior*.

Minor patet quantum ad primam partem, scilicet quod apostoli alii a Petro non receperunt a Christo immediate potestatem iurisdictionis, per ea que dicta sunt in secundo articulo, conclusione ultima. Item quo ad aliam partem, quod discipuli fuerunt minores apostolis, quia sic se habuerunt ad apostolos sicut sacerdotes simplices se habent nunc ad episcopos, 21 d. *In novo*. Sed constat quod episcopi sunt maiores in omni potestate, dignitate et prelatione simplicibus sacerdotibus. Ergo et apostoli discipulis. Item Actuum 1 ex septuaginta duobus discipulis electus est Mathias in apostolum, ut supra dictum est. Electio autem est ad aliquid maius, semper enim de minori statu eligitur quis ad maiorem. Ergo maior fuit status apostolorum quam discipulorum. Item ex septuaginta duobus electi sunt septem diaconi, ut supra dictum est. Quia non est verisimile quod de noviter conversis fuerunt assumpti, cum apostolus prohibeat neophitum ordinari, 1 ad Timotheum 3, 48 d. c. 1. Ergo de antiquis Christi discipulis, et de magis probatis et melioribus, sicut lex dicit: de potioribus ad munera nominandis facta est electio. Huiusmodi autem erant septuaginta duo. Ideo de illis sunt electi diaconi. Et quia electio est ad altiorem statum, ideo etiam diaconi facti, fuerunt altiores et maiores discipulis. Sed tamen etiam tunc suberant apostolis, utpote ab ipsis, quasi eorum vicarii, constituti ad opus ministerii, ut dicitur Actuum 6. Unde dicit Cyprianus, et habetur 93 d. *Dominus*: *Diaconos autem post ascensionem Domini in celum apostoli sibi constituerunt episcopatus sui et ecclesie ministros*. Si ergo discipuli, etiam facti diaconi, fuerunt minores apostolis, multo magis ante. Ergo etc.

desunt $B^{2}P^{1}V^{6}$; 362 *post verbum* discipulis *deest* Sr

353 habet $\theta\psi\pi^{1}$Barb.Va] haberet φB^{1}Sr | inferior] *om.* α(-Sv)Va | 354 contra] *add.* omnem [communem Br] ρ | 360 nunc] *om.* $\theta\rho$Sr | 361 potestate] *add.* et σ | 362 et^{1}] *om.* φ(-UBm^{1}) π | Ergo ... discipulis] *om.* α | et^{2}] *om.* ρ^{1} | 362-471 Item ... principalis] *om.* Sr | 369 3] *add.* in ρ^{1} | 370 et^{2}] idest ρ^{1}; *add.* de θ | de potioribus] *om.* ρ^{1}Va | 371 erant] *om.* $\theta^{2}\theta^{3}$(-Bo); sunt θ^{4} | duo] *om.* $\pi^{1}\rho^{1}$Va | 374 utpote ab ipsis] *om.* ρ^{1}; utpote sub [*om.* ψ] episcopis $\theta\psi$ | 376 Dominus] *add.* dicitur ibi [ubi S] θ, ubi dicitur P^{2} | ascensionem $V^{2}\varphi^{1}PrP^{2}\rho$Va] assumptionem θ(-V^{2})W$\varphi^{4}\pi$ | 378 apostolis] *add.* ergo θ | ante] alii α | Ergo etc.] *om.* θ

354-355 Cf. Aquinas, *Summa theologica* 1.79.2 (1: 510B); cf. also Augustine, *De Genesi ad litteram* 12.16 (PL 34: 467; CSEL 28: 402) | 355 X. 1.33.16 | 360-361 Gratian, D.21 c.2 | 363 Act. 1:21-26 | 366-367 Cf. Act. 6:1-8 | 369 1 Tim. 3:6 | Gratian, D.48 c.1 | 370-371 The reference has not been identified. | 375 Act. 6:2-4 | 375-377 Gratian, D.93 c.25

Secundo patet istud sic, quia si discipuli accepissent potestatem iurisdictionis a Christo, aut accepissent eam simul cum apostolis, aut per se seorsum. Sed neutro modo acceperunt. Ergo etc.

Maior patet per sufficientem divisionem. Minor patet quo ad omnes partes, primo quod non cum apostolis. Quia si cum apostolis, hoc fuisset maxime per illa verba, Matthei 18: *Quecumque alligaveritis*, vel per illa: *Quorum remiseritis*, quia per illa verba sancti communiter dicunt potestatem collatam apostolis, vel promissam aut declaratam. Sed per illa discipuli non receperunt potestatem iurisdictionis cum apostolis, non quia non essent capaces, sicut fuit dictum de potestate ligandi et solvendi in foro conscientie, sed propter alia duo. Primum, quia illa verba non sunt dicta nisi apostolis, sive discipuli presentes essent, sive non. Nam quod prima verba, scilicet illa: *Quecumque alligaveritis*, non sint dicta discipulis sed tantum apostolis, dicit ibi Hieronymus per hec verba: *Potestatem tribuit apostolis, ut qui a talibus* etc. Licet autem nomen discipuli sit commune apostolis et septuaginta duobus, non tamen econtrario. Unde si esset dictum utrisque, Hieronymus non uteretur nomine proprio sed communi. Item Hylarius ibidem: *Immobile severitatis apostolice iudicium demonstravit*. Item quod illa verba: *Quorum remiseritis* etc., non sint dicta discipulis sed tantummodo apostolis, innuit Gregorius, qui dicit ibidem: *Horum*, scilicet quibus dictum est: "Quorum remiseritis et retinueritis," *horum*, inquit, *nunc in ecclesia episcopi locum tenent, qui ligandi atque solvendi auctoritatem suscipiunt, cum locum regiminis sortiuntur*. Sed episcopi non tenent locum discipulorum, sed solum apostolorum, 68 d. *Quorum*. Ergo solis apostolis illud dictum est, et non discipulis. Item super illud Luce 24: *Sedete in civitate quousque induamini virtute ex alto*, dicit sic Ambrosius: *Consideremus quomodo secundum Joannem acceperunt Spiritum Sanctum. Hic autem in civitate iubentur sedere quousque*

desunt $B^2P^1V^6$Sr

379 Secundo] sed [*add.* alias secundo Bo] θ | 383 hoc] licet φ | 384 illa²] *add.* Joannis 20 θ | 388 sicut] *add.* supra θ^1, superius ψ | 389 Primo θ | 390 presentes essent [fuissent φ^1] $\theta^4\gamma$(-WV^4)Rρ] *inv.* $\theta^2\theta^3WV^4B^1$Va | 391 sunt [*om.* St] γ(-P^2) | 403 solis] solum $\varphi^1\rho^1$ | 404 illud] *om.* φ(-V^4) | quousque] donec θ(-S) | 405 sic] similiter ρ^1 | quomodo] quantum φ; *add.* ubi [et ubi Barb.] ρ | 406 iubentur] roborentur θ, roboretur π^1, roboranti B^1 | quousque] donec θ

384 Matt. 18:18 | 385 Joan. 20:23 | 391 Matt. 18:18 | 392-393 *Cat. aur. in Matt.* 18.5, 1: 274A (1: 297B) | 396-397 *Cat. aur. in Matt.* 18.5, 1: 274A (1: 297B) | 397 Joan. 20:23 | 398-401 *Cat. aur. in Joan.* 20.3, 2: 583A (2: 639B) | 402-403 Gratian, D.68 c.6 | 403-412 *Cat. aur. in Luc.* 24.6, 2: 318B-319A (2: 350B) | 404 Luc. 24:49

induantur virtute ex alto. Sed Spiritum Sanctum vel illis undecim quasi perfectioribus insufflavit, et reliquis postea tribuendum promittit, et secundum hoc illa verba, sicut et insufflatio, ad solos apostolos referuntur, *vel eisdem ibi insufflavit, hic promittit. Nec videtur esse contrarium, cum divisiones sint gratiarum. Ergo aliam insufflavit ibi operationem, hic aliam pollicetur.* Videtur autem ex contextu verborum quod li. "eisdem" refertur ad apostolos, ut illis et sit facta insufflatio et sit facta promissio, licet non soli illi sed centum viginti fuerunt participes illius promissionis.

Secundo apparet quod illa verba non sunt dicta discipulis sicut apostolis, intelligendo ea de potestate iurisdictionis. Quia per illa verba eadem non potuerunt illi quibus fiebant difformem nec inequalem sed parem per omnia recipere potestatem, cum eadem causa, agens in materia simili, eundem pariat effectum, qui non variatur nisi aut propter diversitatem agentis aut materie, 8 *Metaphysice.* Unde si illa verba dicta sunt discipulis sicut apostolis, sic quod receperunt discipuli cum illis similem potestatem, ergo receperunt et equalem, sicut etiam per illa verba apostoli receperunt parem potestatem, aut par signum, ut dicitur 24 q. 1 *Loquitur.* Hoc autem est inconveniens, quia non fuerunt eis pares tunc in potestate, sicut nec postea quando illi facti sunt episcopi et isti diaconi. Immo etiam tunc subfuerunt eis sicut archidiaconi episcopis, qui sunt post eos et eorum vicarii et clerici et ministri, *De officio archidiaconi* c. 1 et c. *Ad hec.*

Tertio, dato quod illa verba essent dicta discipulis sicut apostolis, adhuc illa verba non intelliguntur, nec in istis nec in illis, de potestate iurisdictionis, sed solum de potestate ordinis, que maxima est et finis alterius, et principaliter apostolis promissa et exhibita, fundata super dignissimam potestatem, que est conficere corpus Christi, et ei annexa, sicut supra dictum est.

desunt $B^2P^1V^6$Sr

407 *Post verbum* quasi *redit ad verbum* predicandi (lineam 243) B^1 | 408 promisit $\theta^2\theta^3$, promittitur [permittendum W] φ | 409 et] etiam θφ(-W) | 411 ibi [*om.* Bo] insufflavit θφ | 412 li.] licet π | 413 insufflatio ... facta] *hom.* θ | sufflatio π(-R) | 414 licet] sed π(-R) | illi] *om.* φ | sed] *add.* et [etiam Pr] φ(-W) | fuerint θ(-Sv)Prφ^4 | 416 verba] *om.* φ($-V^4$) | 417 fiebant $\theta^4\gamma$] fiebat $\theta^2\theta^3\beta$ | nec] et θ | 418 eadem causa] *om.* φ; eadem cum $\theta^2\theta^3$, eadem per causa [eam S] θ^4, idem ψ | 420 materie] *add.* per philosophum ρ^1 | 421 sunt] *om.* θ | sicut] *add.* et π | 423 apostoli] *add.* inter se φ | 425 illi] isti φ | et] *om.* φ | isti] illi φ | 427 et^4] *om.* πρ | 429 sicut] *add.* et φ(-St) | 432-433 dignissima [dignam Bo, dignissimam V^3] potestate [potestatem Bo] α | 433-434 sicut ... est] *om.* θ

420 Aristotle, *Metaphysica* H.4 (1044a25-32) | 423-424 Gratian, C.24 q.1 c.18 | 427-428 X. 1.23.1 & 7

Alia pars minoris patet, scilicet quod discipuli non acceperunt seorsum ab apostolis per se a Christo potestatem iurisdictionis, quia hoc nunquam legitur, nec per consequens est fingendum. Nam in nulla potestate seorsum eis data, sicut est potestas predicandi, miracula faciendi, temporalia metendi, quas tres per se eis Christus contulit, Luce 10, includitur potestas iurisdictionis, etiam quando ille potestates amplius apostolis sunt concesse, sicut ostensum est in secundo articulo, ultima conclusione.

Tertio apparet principalis conclusio, quia aut esset eis data potestas iurisdictionis pertinens ad synagogam, sive legem veterem, aut ad ecclesiam, sive legem novam. Sed neutro modo. Ergo etc.

Maior patet per sufficientem divisionem. Minor patet quo ad primam partem, quia ibi non habebant potestatem nisi pontifices, sacerdotes aut levite secundum ritum illum consecrati, qui ex ipsa sua consecratione consequebantur ius sibi debitum et potestatem, sicut summus pontifex in arduis et difficilibus iudicandi, Deuteronomii 17, sacerdotes iudicandi inter lepram et non lepram, levite decimas percipiendi. Sed septuaginta duo discipuli nihil horum fuerunt, aut si ante fuerant, tamen a Christo secundum hunc ritum non fuerunt consecrati. Ergo a Christo non receperunt aliquam potestatem pertinentem ad legem veterem, quam Christus venerat non dare sed evacuare. Nec etiam ista est ad propositum, quia querimus de potestate clavium regni celorum, que non erant in veteri lege, etiam apud sacerdotes, quia non erat aperta ianua regni celorum.

Secundo, patet minor quo ad secundam partem, scilicet quod discipuli non acceperunt a Christo illam potestatem iurisdictionis que pertinet ad legem novam, et dicitur potestas ecclesiastica. Quia illa ex officio sive statu ordinarie non competit nisi episcopo aut sacerdoti, sicut abbati, vel curato, aut diacono, sicut archidiacono, qui omnes possunt excommunicare subditos, vel simpliciter vel in casu, de consuetudine vel de iure. Nam

desunt $B^2P^1V^6$Sr

438 faciendi] *add.* et ρ | 439 eis [*om.* V^5Sv] Christus contulit θStπBarb.] Christus eis contulit γ(-St)ρ^1, Deus contulit eis Va | 440 etiam quando] immo etiam φ | 441-442 ultima conclusione $Bm^1\pi^1$Barb.Va] *inv.* α(-Bm^1); ultime conclusionis $B^1\rho^1$ | 443 eis] *om.* φ | 447 pontifices] *add.* et θ(-S), vel φ(-W), aut SW | 448 illum] *om.* φ | 452 fuerunt] *add.* consecrati ρ^1 | fuerant θ(-Bo)ψRBm^2Va] fuerunt Bo$\varphi B^1\rho$(-Bm^2) | 453 hunc] *add.* Judaicum φ | fuerunt] fuerant $\theta^2\theta^3\varphi$(-Bm^1W)π^1 | 456 erat φ | 459 illam] *om.* φ | 461 ordinario φ

439 Luc. 10:1-20 | 449-451 Deut. 17:8-9; cf. Num. 18:21-31 | 453-455 Cf. Matt. 5:17

archidiaconi et simplices curati magis hoc habent de consuetudine quam de iure, *De excessu prelatorum* c. *Ad hoc, De officio ordinis* c. 2. Sed septuaginta duo discipuli ante Spiritus Sancti missionem non erant episcopi, nec sacerdotes, nec diaconi nec archidiaconi. Quinimmo ex eis postea septem sunt diaconi per apostolos ordinati, ut dictum est. Ergo eorum statui non competebat quod a Christo reciperent potestatem iudiciariam pertinentem ad ecclesiam et legem novam, in qua eis debuerunt curati succedere, quia de illa est intentio principalis.

desunt $B^2P^1V^6$Sr

464 archidiaconus $Bm^1Pr\varphi^4\psi B^1$ | et] vel [*om.* W] φ | 465 excessibus $\gamma(-P^2)$ | hoc] *add.* et $\gamma(-V^7)$ | 470 et] sive [*add.* ad θ^2] θ | 471 ista θ, illis φ^1

465 X. 5.31.2 | Perhaps the reference should be *De officio iudicis ordinarii*: cf. X. 1.31.2. This, however, is not at all to the point. | 467-468 Cf. Act. 6:1-8

Quartus Articulus

Quantum ad quartum articulum, de causa immediata potestatis papalis, sunt tres conclusiones principales. Prima quod potestas papalis non est ab ecclesia. Secunda quod est a solo Christo immediate. Tertia quod ab ipso est omnis iurisdictio ecclesiastica et spiritualis in tota ecclesia et in toto mundo.

Prima Conclusio

Prima conclusio principalis, quod potestas pape propria, qua preeminet toti ecclesie, habens in ea plenitudinem potestatis, non sit ab ecclesia, patet triplici ratione, quarum prima talis est. Si preeminentia pape quam habet super alios episcopos et totam ecclesiam esset ex statuto ecclesie, ecclesia posset illam mutare et transferre et papam a papatu deponere. Sed non potest. Ergo non est ab ea.

Maior patet, quia omnem statum et preeminentiam quam ecclesia per se statuit et non Christus ecclesia potest destituere, quia statuendo non potest sibi legem imponere a qua non liceat ei recedere, sicut dicit lex de testatore, *Ff. De lege* 1. 1 *Si quando*. Unde quia coepiscopi non successerant apostolis sicut episcopi, nec discipulis sicut presbyteri et curati, et per consequens non erant a Christo sed ab ecclesia instituti, ideo potuerunt ab ecclesia de iure destitui, et fuerunt de facto amoti. Similiter Templarii, per ecclesiam confirmati, de novo sunt per eam infirmati, et omnes ordines mendicantes post Lateranense concilium instituti, preter aliquos certos, *De religiosis domibus* c. 1 *Libro sexto*. Similiter etiam

desunt B^2P^1

4 ipsa π, papa $\theta^2\theta^3$ | 8 Prima] *add.* ergo [igitur Bm^1] α(-SvV^7) | pape] *om.* $\theta^4\psi$; papalis $\theta^2\theta^3$ | propria] *om.* $\alpha(-\theta^4)$ | eminet φ | 12 Sed] *add.* hoc $\theta\psi$ | 15 destruere θ(-V^{2}V^3)ψ | 17 quia] sicut [*om.* U] φ | coepiscopi] discipuli θ, episcopi σ; *add.* idest chorbischoff φ | 18 successerunt α | apostolis] *add.* nec ρ^1 | sicut[1]] sic [si Sz] ρVa | 19 constituti θ | 20 amoti] *add.* et φ | 21 eam] ecclesiam $\theta^2\theta^3\psi$ | et] ut ρ^1 | 22 constituti θ | 23 certos] *om.* ρ

8-37 Prima ... edificationem: cf. Pierre de la Palu, *Tractatus de potestate papae* 1.3, pp. 182-183 | 17 *Dig.* 32.1.22 | 23 *Sext.* 3.17.1

preeminentia patriarchatus, que alii ex statuto ecclesie debebatur, ad Constantinopolim translata est, et facta est secunda sedes post Romam, que prius non erat, 22 d. *Renovantes*; et ipsi patriarche a patriarchatu sepe per ecclesiam depositi esse leguntur. Et sic patet tota maior quo ad tres partes suas.

Minor patet, primo quo ad primam partem de amotione totali dignitatis papalis, quia ecclesia non potest facere illud per quod unitas ecclesie destrueretur, quia hoc esset contra statutum Christi, qui voluit ecclesiam esse unum ovile, Joannis 10. Hoc autem non esset nisi haberet unum caput, sicut ipsemet dixit: *Fiat unum ovile et unus pastor*, quasi dicens: alias non esset unum ovile nisi esset unus pastor. Non ergo potest ecclesia facere quod non sit papa, idest quod in ea nullus sit omnibus superior, sed sint equales omnes patriarche aut omnes episcopi, quia dicit apostolus: *Non est mihi data potestas in destructionem, sed in edificationem.*

Secundo patet minor quo ad translationem sedis papalis, idest quod tota ecclesia sine papa, puta sede vacante vel alias, non potest transferre sedem pape nec alibi constituere, nec aliis quam cardinalibus electionem conferre. Quia illud quod Petrus vel alius papa quilibet rationabiliter et divino nutu statuit ecclesia destruere non potest, nec ad se retrahere illud quod legitime in alios transtulit, vel transferenti consensit. Sed Petrus sedem suam Rome rationabiliter et Dei nutu statuit. Papa etiam, quicumque ille fuerit, rationabiliter cardinalibus ius eligendi papam dedit, universali ecclesia in concilio generali ius suum eligendi in illos transferente, vel pape transferenti ante vel post consentiente. Ergo ecclesia sine papa istud destruere non potest.

Maior patet quo ad primum, quia cum papa sit maior ecclesia, et inferior non possit tollere statutum superioris, ecclesia non potest tollere constitutionem papalem. Et si in particulari per consuetudinem particularem preiudicetur constitutioni pape, hoc est quia sic papa vult. Vel si

desunt B^{2}P^{1}

24 debebatur] *add.* a Constantino φ | ad] *om.* φ(-φ^{4}) | 26 ipsi] episcopi π | 31 destruatur [destruetur V^{3}] θ(-Sv) | esset] est σ | 33 Fiet B^{1}ρ^{1}Sr | 34-35 potest ... facere] potest facere ecclesia θ^{2}θ^{3}Va, ecclesia potest facere Sφ(-W) | 38 papalis] *om.* θ | idest quod] scilicet quod θ^{2}θ^{3}, idest quo Sv, in quo V^{3}, idest ρ^{1} | 41 et] *om.* γ | 42 destituere φ | 43 legitime] libere ρ^{1} | transferri [transferre BoSvUW, transferrit V^{4}] α | 44 Rome] *om.* θφρ | 47 transferenti] transferendi [transferende W] φ | 50 statum [*om.* St] φ | 51-52 particularem] *om.* θ

26 Gratian, D.22 c.6 | 32-33 Joan. 10:16 | 37 2 Cor. 13:10 | 38-72 Secundo ... firmate: cf. Pierre de la Palu, *Tractatus de potestate papae* 1.3, pp. 187-188

dicatur quod generalis ecclesie consuetudo preiudicat ubique statuto pape, hoc est etiam ex statuto pape, qui vult statuta sua per contrariam consuetudinem abrogari, 4 d. *In istis* et c. sequentibus. Item patet maior quo ad aliam partem, quia donatio inter vivos facta simpliciter non potest revocari nisi ex ingratitudine donatarii.

Minor patet, de sede scilicet, quod Petrus eam Rome statuit rationabiliter, per illud Ambrosii, 2 q. 7 *Beati*, ubi dicit quod apostoli martyrium pertulerunt *in urbe Roma, que principatum et caput obtinet nationum, ut ubi erat caput superstitionis, illic caput quiesceret sanctitatis, ut ubi gentilium principes habitabant, illic etiam ecclesiarum principes morarentur*. Quantum vero ad ius eligendi papam cardinalibus tributum, sciendum quod primus qui ministros pape cardinales vocavit videtur fuisse beatus Silvester. Sed quod a solis cardinalibus sit papa eligendus, et quod alias non apostolicus sed apostaticus habeatur, probatur 23 d. *In nomine Domini*, 79 d. c. 1 c. 2. Quod vero de consensu universalis ecclesie illud ius sit cardinalibus attributum infra probabitur. Quod autem divino nutu Romanus episcopus sit Petri successor patet 19 d.: *Sic omnes sanctiones apostolice sedis*, intelligens de Romana, cui presidebat Agathon papa qui loquitur, *accipiende sunt tanquam ipsius divina voce Petri firmate*.

Tertio patet minor quantum ad depositionem pape personalem. Quod autem papa a nullo possit deponi patet 9 q. 3: *Nemo iudicabit primam sedem. Neque enim ab augusto, neque a clero, neque a regibus, neque a populo iudex iudicabitur*, ita quod nec aliquis de clero, nec totus clerus, nec aliquis de populo, nec totus mundus potest papam iudicare nec deponere.

Sed videtur quod ista ratio non valeat propter duo, primo quia diceretur quod hec impossibilitas sedem aut personam papalem deponendi vel

desunt B^2P^1

55 In istis] *om.* ρ^1 | 56 datio φ | 60 Roma θ(-BoV^5Sv)$Bm^1\varphi^4\psi\pi^1$Sr] Romana BoV^5Sv$\varphi^3\varphi^5B^1\rho$Va | principalium π | 61 ut] et θ(-Sv, *non* S) | illuc ρ | 62 ut] et $\theta\psi$ | principes¹] idola [idolum W] φ | 63 vero] *om.* θ | papam] *om.* ρ | 67 1] *add.* et α(-BoBm^1) | 68 ius] *om.* φ | tributum α | probatur $B^1\rho^1$ | 70 intelligendum ρ^1 | 71 divine φ | 73 personalem] *om.* $\theta^2\theta^3$; et papalem θ^4 | 74 a nullo possit] non possit ab aliquo θ | 75 regalibus φ | 76 totus] aliquis ρ^1 | 77 nec³] vel ρ^1 | 79 illa ρ^1 | dicetur $\psi\rho$

55 Gratian, D.4 c.3-6 [Stella corrects the reference to *In istis temporibus* and cites D.4 c.4.] | 59-63 Gratian, C.2 q.7 c.37 | 66-67 Gratian, D.23 c.1 | 67 Gratian, D.79 c.1 c.2 (?) [Stella: D.79 c.1 c.3] | 69-72 Gratian, D.19 c.2 | 73-78 Tertio ... deponere: cf. Pierre de la Palu, *Tractatus de potestate papae* 1.3, p. 194 | 74-76 Gratian, C.9 q.3 c.13

mutandi non est quia papatus sit a Deo, sed quia papatus est superior status in ecclesia et in mundo, dato quod sit ab ecclesia vel a mundo. Et ideo quia inferior non potest iudicare superiorem, *De maioritate et obedientia* c. *Cum inferior*, ecclesia vel mundus, quamvis super se papam posuerint et non Christus, non possunt eum deponere, nec eius sedem transferre vel destruere, 40 d. *Si papa*. Sicut monachi super se faciunt abbatem, qui tamen eum non possunt deponere nisi habeant hoc ex privilegio superioris; sicut etiam populus super se facit regem, quem tamen non deponit, etiam quando meruit deponi. Secundo quia papa potest propter heresim deponi et penitus amoveri, 40 d. *Si papa*. Si autem papatus non esset ab homine sed a Deo, propter nullam heresim posset ab homine papa deponi, quin semper remaneret verus papa, sicut propter heresim non potest deponi ab ordine episcopali vel sacerdotali, quin semper remaneat verus episcopus et verus sacerdos, propter hoc quod ille caracter est a Deo.

Dicendum ergo ad primum, quod quantumcumque donatio inter vivos sit de natura sua irrevocabilis, potest tamen propter ingratitudinem revocari, habens tacitam conditionem gratitudinis annexam, si donatarius ingratitudinem committat. Sed donator non debet eam auctoritate propria revocare quamdiu habet copiam superioris. Sed supposito quod donatarius non habeat superiorem, vel sit talis quod ad ipsum non possit haberi recursus per viam iustitie, potest donator sibi ius dicere, sicut in aliis casibus in quibus licet se sine iudice vindicare, et debitorem capere fugientem. Eodemmodo, quamvis voluntate propria aliquis se alterius subiciat servituti, si tamen ille abutatur dominio, licet servo clamare in libertatem. Et in casu ubi non posset haberi superioris copia, posset servus auctoritate propria iugum excutere servitutis.

Unde populus qui super se regem voluntarie constituit, dans ei super se dominationem utique propter bonum regimen non tyrannidem, siquidem

desunt B^2P^1

82 dato ... mundo] *hom.* ρ | 83 quia] *om.* θVa | 85 posuerint] posuerunt $\pi\rho^1$ | 89 deponit] deponunt φ | 90 removeri ρ^1 | 92 sicut] nam $\theta^2\theta^3$, sed θ^4 | 93 potest] *add.* aliquis θ^4(-P^3) | deponi] *add.* aliquis [quis V^2] $\theta^2\theta^3P^3$ | 96 primum $\theta^2\theta^3$Barb.Va] primam $\theta^4\gamma\pi$Sr, propositum ρ^1 | 97 tamen potest α(-V^7) | 99 ingratitudinem] *add.* non $\theta\beta$ | debet] valet θ | 101 vel] et θP^2; *add.* si [sit St] habet ille φ | 104 Eomodo ρ^1 | 105 reclamare ψ, proclamare $\pi\sigma$ | 106 posset[1]] possit θ(-V^5) | posset[2]] potest autem ρ^1 | 107 iugum] *om.* θ | servitutem [servitute S] θ | 108 qui] cum π(-R)

83-84 X. 1.33.16 | 86 & 90 Gratian, D.40 c.6

illius confirmatio pertineat ad superiorem, tunc non habet electus ab eis prelationem, sed a confirmante. Unde non possunt ipsi auferre illud quod ei non dederunt, licet ad dationem disposuerint, sed qui confirmat dat. Unde, ut inde procedat cure privatio unde datio processit, coram illo superiore habent ipsum accusare deponendum. Et hec est ratio quare canonici vel monachi suum superiorem non deponunt, sed ad superiorem referunt, quia ipsi non dant ei illam dignitatem eligendo, sed superior confirmando. Et idem esset si ex privilegio superioris electus haberetur pro confirmato, quia per hoc haberet electus ius a sic privilegiante, nisi ille committeret eis depositionem.

Quando autem superior ex solo consensu populi habet regimen, sine confirmatione superioris et sine privilegio, quo regimine abutitur, in illo casu et non in alio possunt ipsi revocare donationem suam. Sed adhuc non debent sibi ius dicere in causa sua si ille habet alias superiorem ratione delicti, et si non ratione regiminis. Immo coram illo habent proponere causas, et ille deponere. Et isto modo, licet papa non habeat confirmare omnem regem qui consensu populi a principio regimen sumpsit, nihilominus tamen potest deponere omnem talem, non solum propter heresim aut scisma aut aliud crimen intollerabile in populo, sed etiam propter insufficientiam. Utpote, si quis idiota sensu vel impotens viribus in regno preesset, propter cuius insufficientiam regnum fidelium periclitaretur, talis certum est quod mereretur deponi, quia bonum commune preferendum est privato. Debet autem deponi per superiorem, et quia illi de regno, sive sint proceres sive alii, sunt inferiores eo, et inferior non potest iudicare superiorem, ideo non potest ab eis deponi. Sed

desunt B^2P^1

110-111 ab eis prelationem $P^2\rho$] ab eis prelationem ab ipsis $V^7\pi\sigma$, prelationem ab ipsis φ, confirmationem ab ipsis θ^2, iurisdictionis [iurisdictionem Boθ^4(-S)] sive cure dationem ab ipsis eligentibus θ^1 | 111 ipsi] illi ρ^1, sibi ψ | illud] *om.* θ | 112 ei] *om.* θ | disposuerant [disposuerat P^3] θ^1(-Bo), disposuerunt Boγ(-Bm^1PrP^2)$\pi\rho^2$ | dat] *add.* vim [verum sacramentum φ^3] φ | 113 Unde¹] attamen [*om.* φ^3; activam Pr] φ | ut ... unde] *hom.* π(-R) | 114 ipsum] illum θ | Et] *om.* φ(-Bm^1) | 116 ei] illi θ | dignitatem] *add.* ipsum θ | 117 superioris] *add.* esset quod [quia V^2] θ^1, esset $\theta^2\rho$ | electus] *add.* quia $\theta^2\rho^1$, qui ψ, quod π^1, et Barb. | 118 electus ius] ius [illius Bm^2] electionis ρ, electionis ius Sr | sic] suo α | privilegiato ρ^1 | 118-119 nisi ... depositionem πSr] *om.* ρVa; ubi [nisi Sv, ibi V^7] donum [dominium θ^4, demum P^2, dictum V^7] iste [ille ψ] tenet [teneret $\theta^4\psi$] illius dispositione [depositione V^7] $\theta\psi$, quia iam totum donum ille [*om.* Bm^1] teneret [tolleret Pr] illius φ | 121 quo] qui ψB^1 | regimine] *add.* si φ | abutatur θ | 122 adhuc] ad hoc ρ^1 | 123 debent] *om.* φ; debet ρ^1 | iste θ | habeat ρ^1 | 125 isto] illo ρ^1 | 126 populi] proprio ρ^1 | 131 meretur θ(-V^2V^3)ψB^1Va | 132 est] *add.* bono θ

125-155 Et ... facienda: cf. Pierre de la Palu, *Tractatus de potestate papae* 2.5, p. 266

quia papa est superior eo in spiritualibus, et per consequens in temporalibus quantum necesse est pro bono spirituali ipsius et aliorum, et adminus ratione delicti, et ille sana conscientia non potest retinere regnum ad quod est insufficiens et indignus, per consequens papa potest eum monere ut regno cedat, quod sine peccato non potest retinere. Quod, si nolit facere, excommunicetur, quia ad officium pape spectat *de quocumque mortali peccato corripere quemlibet Christianum, et si correctionem contempserit, per districtionem ecclesiasticam cohercere, De iudiciis* c. *Novit*. Quod, si in excommunicatione perseveret, potest ipsum, ut dictum est, deponere, et subditos ab eius subiectione absolvere, sicut scismaticum propter contumaciam et inobedientiam pertinacem, et quia excommunicatus legitimis actibus et officiis publicis non debet fungi, et scismatici dignitate et cingulo militie sunt nudandi, 24 q. 1 *Qui circa*, 15 q. 6 c. penultimo. Sed si subditi non meruerunt perdere ius eligendi, non potest papa sine eis alium substituere. Quod ergo dicitur 15 q. 6 *Alius*, quod Zacharias papa Ludovicum regem Francorum deposuit, et Pipino, patri Karoli, regnum tradidit – ibi dicit glossa: proceribus *deponentibus consensit* – quia tante potestatis erat inutilis, quod intelligendum est quo ad institutionem, que per proceres fieri debuit. Sed depositio auctoritate pape non procerum facta fuit, que a solo superiore fieri potuit. Sed electio erat ab inferioribus facienda.

Sed si princeps, qui totum ius suum habet a consensu populi, non haberet in terris quocumque modo aliquem superiorem, et mereretur deponi, tunc subditi vel maiores, qui omnes subditos representant, possent eum deponere auctoritate iuris naturalis et divini, quod dat repetitionem iuris sui in defectum superioris. Et isto modo Romani licite malos principes deposuerunt, qui superiorem nesciebant. Immo etiam regimen

desunt B^2P^1

135 eo] eius [eis Sz] ρ^1 | 136 temporalibus] *add.* in φ | spirituali] *add.* conservando φ | et^2] *om.* σ | 137 iste [ista θ^2S] θ | salva $\psi\rho^1$ | regimen ρ^1 | 138 indignus] *add.* et θ | 140 nollet ρ^1 | excommunicet γBm^{2}Barb. | 142 cohercetur θ^2V$^5\rho^1$, coherceatur [excerceatur S] θ^4 | 145 et^2] *add.* ex [*om.* St] hoc etiam φ | 146 excommunicatus] *add.* et φ(-Bm^1) | 147 denudandi ρ | citra ρ | 148 penultimo] *add.* et [*om.* π^1Va] ultimo $\pi\sigma$ | subditi] proceres sive electores predicti φ | 151 regimen θ(-V^5)φ(-W) | ibi] idest [*om.* Sr] P$^2\pi\sigma$ | 152 potestati γ | inutilis] *om.* θ(-Bo) | 154 fieri] *add.* debuit et θ | 158 tunc] *om.* φ | 159 quod dat] per φ | 160 illo ρ^1 | malos] alios θ | 161 qui] quia θ

140-143 X. 2.1.13 | 147 The reference should be *Qui contra*: Gratian, C.24, q.1 c.32 | 147-148 Gratian, C.15 q.6 c.4 | 149 Gratian, C.15 q.6 c.3 | 151-152 *Decretum Gratiani* ..., C.15 q.6 c.3, fol. 367r

regum abiecerunt quod super se erexerant, *Ff. De origine iuris* 1. 2 § *Exactis deinde regibus*. Si autem ille superior non ab eis sed a Deo superioritatem haberet, quamvis malus esset et indignus, nihilominus tamen ab inferioribus deponi non posset, qui ei prelationem non dederunt, nec per consequens auferre possunt, sicut patuit in Saule, rege Israel. Qui quamvis iam factus esset indignus regno propter iniquitates suas, non tamen licuit populo abicere iugum eius, propter quod David in Christum Domini noluit mittere manum suam, superioris sui, Dei scilicet, ipsum iudicio derelinquens, 1 Regum 24, 26. Unde si papatus est a Deo, nulla ratione potest ab homine dissolvi, Actuum 5: *Si ex Deo est, non poteritis dissolvere*. Sed si esset ab ecclesia, posset deponi per eam ex quo superiorem non habet, quamvis alias ecclesia sit inferior, quia hoc fit auctoritate Dei concedentis in defectum iudicis donationem propter ingratitudinem auctoritate propria revocare, sicut licuit Hebreis iugum excutere pharaonis; et huiusmodi modus licendi inferius apparebit.

Ad secundum dicendum quod papa in nullo casu quamdiu est papa, propter quodcumque crimen, potest nec a concilio, nec a tota ecclesia, nec a toto mundo deponi, non solum quia est superior; sed quia est a Deo, qui sibi Romani presulis, quamdiu presul est, iudicium reservavit, 9 q. 3 *Aliorum*. Sed quando labitur in heresim, tunc eo ipso precisus est ab ecclesia et desinit esse caput, et tunc deponitur de facto, non de iure, quia *qui non credit iam iudicatus est*, de iure scilicet. Hoc est autem iudicium, quia eo ipso quod hereticus est, ab ecclesia precisus est. Non potest autem caput a corpore precisum, quamdiu est precisum, caput esse illius corporis

desunt B^{2}P^{1}

163 iste θ | superior] *om.* φ | 164 malus] in aliis θ | et] *om.* θ | 165 qui] quia θ | 166 consequens] *add.* eam St, ei U | auferre] *add.* eam sibi [ei V^{4}] $\varphi(-\varphi^{3})$ | possent [posset W] φ(-V^{4}) | Qui] quia θ | 167 factus esset iam [iam esset factus UW] α | 168 David] dicendum πBm^{2}Barb. | 170 24] *om.* ρ^{1}; *add.* et $\theta\psi$ | 171 Si] sed ρ^{1} | est] *om.* ρ^{1} | poteritis] potestis $\theta^{2}\theta^{3}$Bm^{1}Prφ^{4}, potestatis V^{3}, potuistis Sv, potest φ^{3}W | 172 esset] est φ | 173 quamvis alias] cum [*om.* W] etiam [et φ^{5}] tota φ, quam non alias ρ^{1} | inferior] *add.* eo. Secus est autem [*inv.* φ^{3}] de principe qui, exigente [exigenta φ^{3}] culpa sua, deponi meretur [mereretur W], qui, quia totum ius suum habet a consensu populi, si abutatur potestate a populo sibi concessa, tunc [tamen φ^{3}] subditi, non habentes aliquem ad quem [*add.* subditi φ^{5}] possint [possent W] recursum habere [recurrere φ^{3}], cum [tamen W, eum Bl] auctoritate iuris naturalis [*inv.* W] deponere possunt. Nec mirum φ | fit] *om.* φ | 174 defectum θP$^{2}\pi$Sr] defectu $\varphi\rho$Va | 176 et $\gamma\pi$Sr] *om.* $\theta\rho$ | huiusmodi] alius ρ | modus] *om.* $\psi\pi$(-R); ius $\theta^{2}\theta^{3}$ | 177 Ad] *om.* φ | 183 de ... iudicium] *om.* π(-R) | scilicet] *om.* θ(-V^{3}) | 184 est hereticus α | est precisus α(-St) | 185 precisum^{1}] *add.* esse [est V^{2}] θ | est] esse Bm^{1}Wφ^{4} | precisum^{2}] *om.* θ | esse] *om.* θ

162-163 *Dig.* 1.2.2 § 3 | 170 1 Reg. 24: esp. 7; 26: esp. 9-11 | 171-172 Act. 5:39 | 177-229 Ad ... Anastasius: cf. Pierre de la Palu, *Tractatus de potestate papae* 1.3, pp. 195-196 | 180-181 Gratian, C.9 q.3 c.14 | 183 Joan. 3:18

a quo est precisum. Unde papa per hoc desinit esse caput corporis ecclesie, quod ab illo prescinditur per heresim, ipso facto, secundum illud Deuteronomii 17: *Non poteris alterius gentis hominem super te facere regem*. Unde hereticus non potest esse nec manere papa, quia extra ecclesiam non possunt haberi claves ecclesie. Per alia autem peccata est caput languidum, quod non propter hoc desinit esse caput, nec potest a membris per consequens iudicari. Quod ergo Marcellinus papa, qui idolatraverat, non fuit iudicatus de facto, sed dictum est ei: "Tu ipse iudica causam tuam," 21 d. *Nunc autem*, hoc est quia non erat hereticus, quia a fide nunquam deviaverat animo, sed metu tormentorum sacrificaverat idolis. Item falsa est glossa in predicto capitulo, *Si papa*, dicens quod de quocumque alio crimine notorio papa, si est incorrigibilis, potest accusari et amoveri, quia contumacia est heresis, et contumax dicitur infidelis. Quia hoc est non proprie sed solum metaphorice, sicut et simonia dicitur heresis. Et ideo quidquid agat papa quamdiu est papa, nunquam iudicari potest nec condemnari, non propter hoc tantum, quia nullus inferior potest iudicare superiorem quamdiu superior est, de lege communi, ut arguitur *De maioritate et obedientia* c. *Cum inferior*, sed potissime propter hoc, quod papatus, qui non est ab homine, non potest ab homine iudicari. Unde propter quodcumque crimen quo papa non desinit esse papa, sicut est omne aliud preter heresim proprie dictam, papa ab homine iudicari non potest. Sed reprehendi potest, sicut Paulus in faciem restitit Petro, quia reprehensibilis erat, ita quod in malis non est ei obediendum, sed resistendum. Unde si cogeret gentes judaizare, non vere quia tunc esset hereticus, sed simulatorie, sicut Petrus faciebat ad Galatas 2, resistendum esset.

Quid ergo fiet si papa sit ita malus moribus quod destruat ecclesiam Dei? Respondeo: duplex est remedium. Unum, quod dictum est, exemplo

desunt B²P¹

187 quia ψσ | 188 hominem] *om.* θ | super te] *om.* α; super se ρ¹ | 190 habere [manere U] φ(-StPr) | alia] *om.* θφ | peccata autem φ, peccatum autem θ | 191 quod] et φ | 193 sed] *add.* tantum ρ | iudica] iudicas ρ¹ | 195 sacrificavit θ | 196 papa] *add.* 40 d. θ | 198 et²] aut ρ¹ | 199 Quia hoc] quod φ | non est [*om.* Bo] α(-θ²) | 200-201 potest [*add.* amoveri V³] iudicari α | 202 possit φ(-W) | 204 non²] nec π | 206 omne] *add.* illud θ | 207 facie θψρ | 209 vere] *add.* quidem φ | 210 resistendum] *add.* ei θ⁴ | 211 esset] *add.* ei [sibi V⁵] θ²θ³ | 212 fieret ρ¹ | esset [*om.* U] φ | malus] *add.* in θ²θ³π | moribus] omnibus π

188-189 Deut. 17:15 | 193-194 Gratian, D.21 c.7 | 196 *Decretum Gratiani* ..., D.40 c.6, fol. 65v | 203 X. 1.33.16 | 210 Gal. 2:11

Pauli, quia in facie est ei resistendum, sicut etiam monachi, licet non possint abbatem suum deponere, non tamen tenentur ei in malis obedire, sed ei resistere quousque per superiorem remedium apponatur. Unde si papa vellet totum thesaurum ecclesie dare parentibus suis, aut ecclesiam sancti Petri destruere et facere palatium parentibus suis, aut eis dare patrimonium Petri, quod non licet, vel aliquid huiusmodi, non esset permittendum, sed esset ei resistendum et non obediendum, sine tamen ipsius depositione. Secundum remedium est exemplo beati Hylarii, qui contra Leonem papam prevaluit orando. Quia orandum esset pro ipso a tota ecclesia, quod Deus ipsum corrigeret, vel de medio amoveret; nec unquam Deus sic ecclesiam suam despiceret quin eam exaudiret. Et esset contra eum concilium convocandum per cardinales, si ipse nollet convocare, ut per illud moneretur, vel Deus imploraretur, et remedium apponeretur in resistendo malis que vellet facere, ne ecclesia periclitaretur. Aliud est exemplum de hoc remedio, nam Anastasius papa periit scelere proprio et iustorum orationibus percussus, 19 d. *Anastasius*.

Vel potest responderi secundo, quod licet inferior inquantum huiusmodi non possit deponere superiorem, tamen electus qui confirmatione non indiget, aut hoc ipsum habet ex privilegio superioris (et tunc ab illo habet ius suum, non ab electoribus, et per consequens ab illo est, non ab electoribus, deponendus, nisi ipsam etiam depositionem ille superior electoribus committat), aut hoc ipsum habet ille electus ex hoc, quod illud ad quod eligitur de se nulli alteri est subiectum. Et tunc illa dignitas, que non habetur ab alio homine quam ab ipsis electoribus, nisi sit in se speciale et immediatum donum Dei, habetur totaliter ab illis electoribus. Et ideo in casu in quo ille presidens non haberet superiorem, etiam ratione delicti, vel haberet, sed ad illum non posset commode recursus haberi, si ipse mereretur deponi, illi subditi, a quibus habet totum ius suum, possent

desunt B^{2}P^1

214 faciem φ(-Bm^1) | 214-215 abbatem suum [*om.* φ] non possint [possunt θ^{2}BoV^{5}SvW, possent S] θφ | 219 patrimonium] *add.* beati [sancti Sv] θ | aliud ρ^{1}Va | 220 permittendus πBarb.Va | esset] *om.* θ | et non obediendum] *om.* θ | obediendum] obeditur ρ^1 | 220-221 sine ... depositione] *om.* ρ^1 | 221 exemplo] *om.* ρ^1 | 223 vel] aut B^{1}ρ | de] a ρ^1 | 226 moveretur ρ^1 | 227 in] etiam ρ^1 | 228 exemplum] *om.* θ | papa] *om.* φ | 229 percussus] *add.* est θ | 232 aut] *om.* ψ; et φ | habet] potest ρ^1 | 233 illo^2] isto φ | 234 etiam] *om.* B^{1}ρ | 235 habeat φ | 237 in se] *om.* ψπ(-R) | 238 ipsis θVa | 239 iste θ | etiam] et ρ | 240 vel] *add.* si ψB^{1}Barb. | haberet] haberetur Rρ^1 | sed] *om.* ψB^{1}Barb.; si ρ^1 | 241 mereretur [merentur Sv] θBm^{1}Wπ(-P^4)SzBarb.Sr] meretur γ(-Bm^{1}W)P^{4}Bm^{2}BrVa

221-222 Cf. Jacobus a Voragine, *Legenda aurea*, chap. 17, Graesse 99 | 229 Gratian, D.19 c.9

ipsum deponere, donationem revocando, duplici auctoritate. Uno modo auctoritate Dei, ut dictum est, propter defectum iudicis; alio modo auctoritate propria, tanquam superiores eo in casu isto. Nam in se sibi submittendo, expresserunt vel intenderunt non eum sibi superponere in casu ubi superioritate abuteretur. Quando illud contingit, ipse desinit esse superior in effectu, et fit sicut prius communitati subiectus. Et sic, sicut inferior a superiore, potest ab ea iudicari et deponi, vel depositus declarari. Sed ille qui habet superioritatem a Deo, non a subditis, nisi per heresim a communitatis corpore dividatur, semper manet communitate superior. Unde non potest ab ea aliquatenus iudicari. Et ideo semper solius Dei, qui solus superior eius est, iudicio reservatur.

Secunda ratio talis est. Potestas que excedit potestatem ecclesie non est ab ecclesia, quia nemo dat alteri quod non habet. Sed potestas pape solius excedit potestatem totius residue ecclesie, quia in omnibus aliis ecclesiis a Romana est pars potestatis; in sola Romana, idest in solo papa, est plenitudo potestatis, 11 d. *Consequens*, ut dictum est. Ergo potestas pape non potest esse ab ecclesia.

Sed videtur quod illa ratio non valeat, quia in omni electione regis vel principis rex electus habet maiorem potestatem quam aliquis de populo, immo quam tota communitas, quia ipse iudicat totam communitatem, et tamen ipse habet quidquid habet a populo, quasi potestas regia sit in populo virtute, licet non sit in eo formaliter. Ita etiam posset dici de potestate papali, quod licet non sit in ecclesia formaliter, extra ipsum est tamen in ecclesia virtute, idest in electoribus qui in hoc totam ecclesiam representant. Si dicatur quod papa preest toti mundo; nunquam autem totus mundus convenit, nec per se nec per procuratores ad hoc constitutos, ad constituendum super se caput unum; ergo non potest dici a

desunt B^2P^1

242 duplici] *add.* ratione sive θ | 244 isto] illo ρ^1 | in^2] *om.* $\theta^4\psi\rho$Va | 245 superponere ψB^1Bm^2Br] supraponere φ(-StW), supponere [supponet P^4] θ^4StWπ^1SzBarb.σ, preponere [proponere V^5] $\theta^2\theta^3$ | 246 abuteretur] *add.* et φ, unde ρ^1 | ipse] *om.* $B^1\rho$ | 247 in effectu] de facto α | fit] sit π | sic] *om.* $\varphi(-\varphi^5)$Sr | sicut^2] *om.* $\theta\psi$Va | 248 superior ab inferiore α | ab ea] *om.* $\theta\psi$ | et ... declarari] *om.* π(-R) | 249 iste $\theta\varphi$ | subditis] subiectis φ | per] propter θ | 250 superior] *add.* ut dicitur θ | 251 Unde] *om.* $\theta\pi$; ergo ψ | semper] *om.* ρ | 258 potest esse] est θ | 259 ista θBarb.σ | 261 quam] *add.* totus populus seu ρ^1 | 262 tamen] *om.* φ | regis θ | 263 licet] sed ρ^1 | potest θ | 264 quia π(-R)Barb.Sr | extra ipsum] *om.* φ | 265 electoribus] *add.* et ρ^1 | 267 convenit] *om.* B^1Barb.; congregatur ρ^1 | procuratores] *add.* suos [sed P^4] $\theta\pi$(-R) | 267-268 hoc ... ad] *hom.* θ | 268 dici] *om.* $\theta\varphi$ | a] *om.* φ(-W)

253-258 Potestas ... ecclesia: cf. Pierre de la Palu, *Tractatus de potestate papae* 1.3, p. 183 | 257 Gratian, D.11 c.2 [The reference should be C.2 q.6 c.11-12.]

subditorum consensu habere hanc preeminentiam. Dicendum quod infideles, subtrahentes se ab obedientia ecclesie Romane, non debent habere vocem in electione superioris, sed solum ei obedientes de facto, quorum consensus, per eorum voluntatem, translatus est in illos qui eligunt. Unde de voluntate totius mundi potest dici prepositus.

Dicendum ergo ad hoc quod quilibet in eo in quo non est alicui subiectus potest se alteri submittere, *Qui filii sunt legitimi* c. *Per venerabilem*. Et ideo populus nulli subiectus potest sibi rectorem preficere, cui se submittat iudicandum in humanis et civilibus. Et sicut liber homo, vendens se ad pretium participandum se emptori subiciendo, facit eum dominum suum, sic populus, se subiciendo voluntarie alicui ut principi vel rectori, facit eum principem suum, dans ei super se potestatem in civilibus et humanis; et ista potestas erat in illo virtute, inquantum erat potens se subicere. Sed potestatem spiritualem non potest populus conferre. Unde nullo consensu populus potest sibi aliquem preficere in curatum, nec se alicui subicere ut curato, sic quod det ei potestatem se absolvendi in foro conscientie, cum illa potestas non sit nisi a Deo. Ideo nulla consuetudine sola potest quis sibi eligere confessorem, *De penitentiis* c. 2 *Libro sexto*, nec similiter potest sibi aliquem preficere in episcopum, sic quod ab eis habeat potestatem confirmandi et ordinandi, quod non est nisi a Deo. Ita similiter, cum papa in eo quod papa habeat plenitudinem potestatis, ex qua potest aliqua, que totus mundus non habet formaliter nec virtute, sicut quod potest dare indulgentiam plenissimam, quod potest restringere materiam sacramenti matrimonii, multiplicare ministerium confirmationis et ordinis, et huiusmodi, ista potestas, que non respicit humanum iudicium nec civile, non est in virtute populi eligentis. Unde adhuc stat argumentum.

Tertia ratio talis est. Quia si potestas vel preeminentia pape esset ab ecclesia, hoc esset per aliquod concilium generale. Sed per nullum concilium hoc potuit fieri. Ergo non est ab ecclesia. Maior patet, quia tota ecclesia non congregatur nisi in conciliis generalibus, in quibus ipsa est

desunt B²P¹

275-276 se ... potest] *hom.* ρ | 275 sint θ(-Bo) | 277 iudicandum] *om.* φ | homo] *om.* φ | 279 suum] *add.* dans ei super se potestatem θ | 280 ei] *om.* φ | 281 ista] illa θ(-Sv)ρ^1 | 283 populus] *om.* π(-R) | 287 Libro sexto] l. di. [*add.* alias li. 6 Bo] $\alpha\rho$ | potest sibi] possunt aliqui $\theta^2\theta^3$, potest quis θ^4 | 288 eis] eo θ^4 | 289 in ... papa] *hom.* θVa | habet ρ^1Sr | 293 ista] *om.* [ita V³] θ(-Sv); illa ρ^1 | que] *om.* ρ^1

275-276 X. 4.17.13 | 286-287 *Sext.* 5.10.2 | 296-309 Tertia ... Significasti: cf. Pierre de la Palu, *Tractatus de potestate papae* 1.3, p. 183

tota in virtute per hoc, quod ibi quilibet episcopus representat totam diocesim suam, vel solus, vel cum procuratoribus collegiorum. Unde proprie dicitur tota ecclesia facere quod ibi fit, non quod aliter nec alias, sicut canonici omnes dicuntur facere quod faciunt in capitulo ad hoc congregato, non quod quilibet per se facit ut sunt singulares persone. Probatio minoris, quia illud quod habet auctoritatem et robur ab aliquo non dat illi auctoritatem nec potestatem, quia causa inquantum causa nihil accipit ab effectu. Sed papa dat auctoritatem et robur omnibus conciliis generalibus. Ergo ab ipsis non accipit ipse potestatem, *De electione* c. *Licet* et c. *Significasti*.

Sed contra hoc est, et videtur quod ecclesia Romana habeat primatum ab ordinatione universalis ecclesie sive conciliorum tripliciter. Primo per simile de imperatore, quia sicut papa preest in spiritualibus, que sunt propria clero, sic imperator in temporalibus, que sunt propria populo. Unde isti duo sunt quasi duo magna luminaria in mundo. Sed imperator preest populo in temporalibus ab electione populi. Ergo papa in spiritualibus ab electione cleri. Argumentum, 93 d. *Legimus*, in medio, ubi dicit Hieronymus quod exercitus facit imperatorem.

Responsio: non est simile, quia imperator non habet potestatem nisi temporalem, terrenam et mundanam, quam populus se ei subiciendo potest ei dare. Licet enim *privatorum consensus iudicem non faciat eum qui nulli iurisdictioni preest, C. De iurisdictione omnium iudicum* 1. *Privatorum*, tamen populi consensus potest facere iudicem in temporalibus. Sed in spiritualibus nullorum hominum consensus facit iudicem illum qui non est per quamcumque submissionem. Unde nulla submissione potest se quis subicere excommunicandum illi qui alias excommunicare non potest. Unde quia papa, ut papa, habet spiritualem potestatem qualis non est in tota reliqua ecclesia, ut dictum est, ideo illam per nullam electionem solam acquirere potest.

Secundo arguitur per illud quod dicitur 3 q. 6 *Dudum*, ubi dicitur quod sancti apostoli successoresque eorum *sanctam Romanam ecclesiam*

desunt B²P¹

300 tota] totaliter ρ¹ | 302 quod²] autem [aut W] φ | 304 quelibet θ | per se] persone θ²V²V⁵, persona θ⁴, persona per se Bo | facit] *om.* α; faciat π(-R)Barb. | 305 quia] quod φ | 307 recipit [recepit S] θ¹, recipiat θ² | 308 Licet] Lites φ | 309 et] *om.* πVa | 310 hoc] *om.* φ | primatum] papatum ρ¹ | 314 in] *add.* toto ρ | 320 consensus] *add.* possit facere θ | 324 est] preest [*add.* sibi θ⁴] θ | 328 solum θ⁴φ, aliquis θ²θ³ | 329 dicitur¹] habetur θP²

308 X. 1.6.6 | 309 X. 1.6.4 | 316 Gratian, D.93 c.24 | 320-322 *Cod.* 3.13.3 | 329-331 Gratian, C.3 q.6 c.9

primatem omnium ecclesiarum esse voluerunt. Ex quo videtur, cum apostoli et eorum successores fuerint puri homines, quod a puris hominibus ecclesia Romana habuit principatum.

Solutio: sicut supra dictum fuit de Petro, ita et hic de sua ecclesia dicendum est quod a solo Deo, primo et principaliter, habuit principatum de iure. Sed a conciliis et patribus volentibus voluntati Domini obedire, sicut debebant, de facto obtinuit principatum.

Sed tertio obicitur contra hoc, et videtur quod immo econtrario principaliter a conciliis, consequenter autem a Domino approbante. Quia dicitur 17 d.: *Huic etiam sedi*, scilicet Romane, *primum apostoli Petri meritum, deinde secuta iussione Domini conciliorum reverendorum auctoritas singularem in ecclesiis tradidit potestatem.*

Et dicendum quod, licet in preferendo Romanam ecclesiam aliis meritum Petri precesserit Domini iussionem quantum ad hoc, quod Dominus in persona Petri ecclesiam fundavit, et ibi voluit esse primatum ubi Petrus finaliter resideret, tamen Petrus fuit causa meritoria tantum, sed Christus effectiva, concilia vero sequentia causa executoria de facto tantum.

Secunda Conclusio

Secunda conclusio principalis, scilicet quod papa preeminentiam et plenitudinem quam habet in ecclesia non habet ab homine sed a Deo, probatur multipliciter. Primo sic: successor Petri habet in tota ecclesia, non ab homine sed a Deo, preeminentiam super omnes et plenitudinem potestatis. Papa sive pontifex Romanus est huiusmodi. Ergo etc.

Maior patet, quia illa plenitudo et preeminentia potestatis que fuit in Petro transiit ex dono Christi ad Petri legitimos successores. Sicut enim

desunt B^2P^1

331 primatem] potestatem ρ^1 | videtur] *add.* quod $B^1\rho$Va | 332 fuerint θ^4(-S)UPr$\varphi^4\pi$Bm^2] fuerunt $\theta^2\theta^3$SStBm^{1}W$\psi\rho$(-Bm^2)σ | 333 habuerit $\pi\sigma$ | 334 fuit] est θ | hic] hoc ρ^1 | 335 habuit] *add.* potestatem et $\theta^2\theta^4$ | principatum] *add.* et potestatem θ^3 | 339-340 Quia dicitur] *om.* α | 340 Petri] *om.* ρ^1 | 344 precessit ρ^1Va | 345 ecclesiam] *om.* θ | primatum] papatum ρ^1 | 346 tamen] *om.* ρ | 347 vero] *om.* π(-R) | executoria] executiva exequendo [*om.* Bo; executorio θ^4] θ | 348 tantum] *om.* π(-R)Va | 350 principalis] *add.* est [est quod V^3] θ | 351 sed] *add.* habet θ(-V^2) | 353 super] inter ρ^1 | 356 transit $\theta^2\theta^3\varphi$

340-342 Gratian, D.17 c.6 | 355-413 Maior ... datas: cf. Pierre de la Palu, *Tractatus de potestate papae* 1.3, pp. 186-187

Adam quedam dona a Deo habuit personalia, sicut omnem scientiam, quedam vero pro sua posteritate in statu innocentie, sicut originalem iustitiam, sic et Petrus quedam dona a Christo habuit pro sua persona, sicut miracula, ut quod ad eius umbram sanarentur infirmi, quedam vero pro successoribus suis in ecclesia. Et hec sunt illa sine quibus ecclesia non staret, sicut claves ligandi et solvendi, aliter porte inferi prevalerent adversus eam. Unde hanc plenitudinem potestatis per quam ecclesia resistit mundo et diabolo Christus contulit Petro pro se et pro suis successoribus. Unde Cyrillus, ubi supra: *Sicut Christus accepit a patre dux et sceptrum ecclesie gentium ex Israel egrediens super omnem principatum et potestatem, et super omne quodcumque est, ut ei genua cuncta curventur,* <*plenissimam potestatem*> *sic et Petro et eius successoribus plenissime commisit.* Item *De renuntiatione* c. *Quanto* dicit Innocentius: *Potestatem transferendi pontifices ita sibi retinuit Dominus et Magister, quod eam soli beato Petro vicario suo, et per ipsum successoribus suis prebuit et concessit.*

Minor patet, quia successor Petri in plenitudine et preeminentia potestatis sive papatu est solus episcopus Romanus. Ubi est advertendum quod sedes episcopi dicitur non prima in qua sedit, sed ultima in qua finaliter resedit legitime translatus. Petrus igitur, qui super universalem ecclesiam sedit, a principio nullam determinatam sedem sibi appropriavit, sed sedem Hierosolimitanam Jacobo, fratri Domini, dimisit. Postea vero Antiochie primo sedit, sed et illam sedem reliquit Ignatio martyri, disciplo sancti Joannis evangeliste. Postea vero Romam venit, et illuc sedem suam transtulit et immobiliter illic resedit. Unde non Antiochia prima sed Romana ultima debet dici sedes Petri. Unde qui in sede

desunt B^2P^1

357 a Deo] *om.* Boφ | a Deo quedam dona θ(-Bo) | 360 sicut] scilicet θ(-S) | miracula] *add.* faciendi θ | 364 pro^2] *om.* θ | 365 Cyrillus] sensus $\theta^4\varphi$, alias Cyrillus sensus O, sensus alias Cyrillus V^1, Cyrillus et sensus Bo | 367 et^2] *om.* θ | omne] *om.* φ | est] *om.* θ | genua $B^1\rho$Va] genu $\alpha\pi^1$Sr | 368 cuncta] *om.* $\theta\varphi$ | curventur $\psi B^1\rho$] curvetur $\theta\varphi$RSr, curentur P^4, curverentur Va | plenissimam potestatem] *om.* φBarb.; plenissima potestate B^1, plebs [lex Bo, proles P^4] nostra potestatem [potestate π^1] *cet. mss.* | et^1] *om.* π(-R)Barb. | 369 commisit] *add.* universe plebis potestatem Barb. | Quando φ | 371 beato] *om.* $\theta\varphi^3$Wψ | 372 suis] *om.* ρ^1 | 375 episcopi] Petri $V^2\gamma B^1$, Christi [*om.* V^5; *add.* alias Petri θ^2Bo] θ(-V^2) | 376 resedit] residet ρ^1 | legitime translatus] *om.* ρ^1 | igitur] *om.* φ | super V^2Sv$\varphi\rho$Va] supra θ^2Bo$V^5V^3\psi\pi$Sr | 377 sibi] *add.* determinavit vel [sive O] θ | 379 martyri] *om.* ρ | 380 evangeliste] *add.* et π | illuc] *om.* π(-R); illic [ibi Sv] θ(-V^3)

359-360 Cf. Act. 5:15 | 362-363 Cf. Matt. 16:18-19 | 365-369 *Contra er. Gr.*, p. 323 | 369-372 The reference should be *De translatione*: X. 1.7.3.

Romana legitime constituitur successor Petri efficitur, et per consequens plenus et perfectus vicarius Christi.

Aliud autem est de electione episcopi, aliud de electione archiepiscopi. Quia electio episcopi debet pertinere ad clericos omnes sue diocesis, vel ad maiores clericos, sicut ad ecclesiam cathedralem, quia preficitur solum diocesi. Sed archiepiscopus preficitur sue diocesi specialiter et toti provincie communiter. *Quod autem omnes tangit ab omnibus debet approbari.* Unde quantum est de primitivo iure eligendi, non ad solam ecclesiam cathedralem, cuius specialiter interest, sed ad suffraganeos, quibus preficitur, spectat electio archiepiscopi. Et ita olim servabatur, propter quod in electione beati Nicholai in metropolitanum Mirreorum, in ecclesiam convenerunt episcopi suffraganei tanquam principales, ad quos solos electio pertineret si archiepiscopus nullam sedem determinatam haberet. Sed quia difficile est semper suffraganeos convocare, constitutum est de consensu omnium ad quos spectat, quod ad solam ecclesiam cathedralem spectat electio archiepiscopi sicut et episcopi. Sic igitur, si Petrus mortuus fuisset antequam Rome sedem elegisset, ad primitivam totam ecclesiam, vel de eius consensu ad solos apostolos, quasi suffraganeos, pertinuisset electio successoris Petri. Sed postquam Rome resedit, de iure communi et ad patriarchas, ratione universalis ecclesie, et ad clerum Romanum, ratione appropriationis, spectabat electio, ut videtur. Sed quia difficile erat patriarchas convocare, nec erat tutum simplicibus canonicis tantum negotium committere, papa loco patriarcharum et canonicorum Romanorum cardinales instituit qui papam eligerent, concurrente tamen in hoc consensu ecclesie generalis, sicut infra plenius ostendetur. Unde qui sic in Romanum pontificem eligitur est verus Petri

desunt B^2P^1

385 episcopi] *add.* et $\theta B^1\rho^1$ | de electione²] *om.* φ | 387 clericos] *om.* σ | solum] sue π(-R) | 393 in²] *om.* φ (*in marg.* V^4) | in³ Va] ad P^4; *om.* Barb. *et cet. mss.* | 394 ecclesiam [ecclesiarum Sv] $\theta\psi\pi$Va] ecclesie φ, ecclesia ρSr | episcopi] *om.* θ(-Bo) | 395 solum ρ^1 | si] sic ρ^1 | 397 spectabat [spectet Sz] ρ | 398 cathedralem] *om.* φ | 400-401 vel ... suffraganeos] *om.* θ | 400 de] *om.* φV^7 | eius] *om.* ρ^1 | 402 resedit] fuit [fuerit S] θ^1, elegit sedem θ^2 | et¹] *om.* $\theta(-V^3)\pi$(-R) | 403 approbationis V^5, approbationis [appropriationis V^3] et etiam [*add.* ratione S] appropriationis $\theta(-V^5)$ | spectat φBarb.Va | 405 tantum ... committere] tantum $\theta^2\theta^3$, tantum [tamen V^3] istud relinquere θ^4 | negotium] regimen σ | 405-406 papa ... patriarcharum] *om.* θ | 406 instituerunt θ | 407 in] ad φ | 408 vere θ(-Bo)

389-390 *Cod.* 5.59.5.2 | 392-394 Cf. Jacobus a Voragine, *Legenda aurea* 3.2, Graesse

successor et Christi plenus vicarius. Unde dicit canon concilii Chalcedonensis: *Si quis episcopus predicatur infamis, liberam habeat licentiam appellandi ad beatissimum antique Rome quem habemus Petrum, petram refugii, et ipsi soli libera potestate, loco Dei, sit ius discernendi episcopi criminati infamiam, secundum claves a Domino sibi datas.*

Item probatur ista conclusio, scilicet quod potestas pape sit a Deo, auctoritate Cyrilli in *Libro thesaurorum*, qui tractat illud Matthei 16: *Tu es Petrus, et super hanc petram edificabo ecclesiam meam, et porte inferi non prevalebunt adversus eam.* Dicit sic: *Secundum autem hanc Domini promissionem, ecclesia apostolica Petri ab omni seductione et heretica circumventione immaculata manet, super omnes prepositos et episcopos, et super omnes primates ecclesiarum et populorum in suis pontificibus, in fide plenissima et auctoritate Petri.* Item 21 d. *Quamvis*: *Sancta Romana ecclesia catholica et apostolica nullis synodochicis constitutis ceteris ecclesiis prelata est, sed evangelica voce Domini et Salvatoris nostri Jesu Christi primatum obtinuit.* Item 22 d. *Omnes*: *Non ergo quelibet terrena sententia, sed illud verbum quo constructum est celum et terra, per quod denique omnia condita sunt elementa, Romanam fundavit ecclesiam.* Item sequenti capitulo: *Sacrosancta Romana ecclesia et apostolica non ab apostolis, sed ab ipso Domino et Salvatore nostro primatum obtinuit.* Item ibidem: *Prima ergo sedes celesti beneficio Romana ecclesia.* Item ibidem: *Hec vero apostolica sedes caput et cardo, ut prefatum est, a Domino, et non ab alio constituta est.* Item septima auctoritas ad idem, *De consecratione* d. 1 *Basilicas*, ubi dicitur sic in fine de ecclesia Romana: *Ubi Dominus ecclesie totius posuit principatum.*

desunt B^{2}P^1

409 dicit] ait θ | 410 episcopus] *om.* α | 412 et] cum φ | 413 criminalis φ | 414 probatur] *om.* α | illa ρ^1 | scilicet] *om.* θ | Deo] *add.* videtur [*add.* probari V^3, approbari Sv] θ, probatur γ | 415 tractans ρVa | illud] *add.* verbum ρ | 417 Dicit] *om.* θψ; dicens φ | sic] *om.* α | 418 et] *om.* φ | 420 primates] potestates ρ^1 | pontificibus] *add.* et ρ^1 | 423 Salvatoris] *add.* Domini θ | 424 primatum] papatum ρ^1 | Item] *om.* πSr | d.] *add.* super θ | ergo] enim [*om.* BoSv] θ(-V^3) | 425 constitutum α | 427 ab] *add.* ipsis θ | 428 ab ipso] a θ | 429 Prima ... ibidem] *hom.* θ^{2}V^3 | ecclesia] *add.* primatum obtinuit θ^{3}Sv | 430 apostolica sedes] ecclesia apostolica θ; *add.* et ρ | 431 ab] *om.* ρ^1 | Item ... auctoritas] *om.* α | septima] videtur ρ^1 | consecratione] constitutionibus γ(-U) | 433 principatum] fundamentum θ

409-413 *Contra er. Gr.*, p. 324 | 415-421 *Cat. aur. in Matt.* 16.3, 1: 252A (1: 273B) | 415-417 Matt. 16:18 | 421-424 Gratian, D.21 c.3 | 424-426 Gratian, D.22 c.1 | 427-431 Gratian, D.22 c.2 | 431-433 Gratian, *De cons.* D.1 c.6

Contra hoc autem arguitur dupliciter. Primo quia, secundum hoc, papa non posset sedem suam a Roma mutare et alibi transferre. Hoc autem est inconveniens. Ergo et primum. Quod autem hoc sit inconveniens, et quod papa ex causa rationabili possit mutare sedem suam, dupliciter patet. Primo quod ponat Rome alium episcopum, et ipse presideat omnibus ecclesiis universaliter et nulli specialiter. Secundo quod ipse sedem suam transferat ad aliam specialem sedem episcopalem, novam vel veterem. Primum patet, quia in his que sunt iurisdictionis non minus potest papa quam Petrus in eo quod papa. Sed Petrus usquequo venit Antiochiam fuit sine sede speciali, et ab illo tempore quo Antiochie Ignatium constituit quousque Rome sedit. Ergo et papa sic potest esse sine speciali sede. Per idem patet secundum, quia et Petrus sedem suam de Antiochia Romam transtulit. Quod autem illud sequatur patet, quia homo non potest destruere fundamentum Dei, dicente apostolo 2 ad Timotheum 2: *Firmum fundamentum Dei stat*. Si ergo ecclesia Romana a Christo est fundata, ergo papa non potest sedem apostolicam alibi transferre nec aliquo modo mutare, quod esset Dei fundamentum destruere. Et confirmatur quod nec ipse Petrus potuisset mutare si vixisset, quia servus non potest tollere legem domini sui. Unde id quod Petrus fecit proprio capite papa successor potest tollere. Sed illud quod Petrus fecit divina iussione videtur quod nec ipsemet Petrus, et multo minus quicumque successor alius, possit revocare.

Sedes autem Petri electa est Rome de speciali Domini iussione. Ergo nullus purus homo potest istam sedem alibi transferre nec aliter mutare. Maior probata est. Minor patet per illud quod scribit Marcellus papa universis episcopis per Antiochiam constitutis, 24 q. 1 *Rogamus*: *Ipse est caput totius ecclesie cui ait Dominus: "Tu es Petrus, et super hanc petram*

desunt B^{2}P^1

434 Primo] *add.* quidem φ | papa] *om.* φ | 435 mutare et] *om.* θ | 437 commutare φ | sedem suam mutare ψπσ | dupliciter] *om.* φ | patet dupliciter θσ | 440 sedem] *add.* scilicet ρ^1 | 441 iurisdictionis] *add.* eiusdem θ | 443-444 quo ... sedit] Antiochie resedit quousque Romam venit, et tunc ibi [ibidem Bo] Ignatium [*add.* in Antiochia V^3, in Antiochiam Sv] constituit et Rome sedit [resedit θ^4] θ^1 | 443 quo] *om.* φ | 445 quia] quod θ | 446 *Post verbum* transtulit *praetereunt verba interiacentia* (i.e. Quod ... Josephus) *et procedunt ad verbum* Ad (lineam 477) ψB^1 | homo non] nemo ψB^1 | 447 Dei] *om.* φ | 450 quod^2] quia θφ^1PrψB^1 | 451-452 legem domini sui [*inv.* V^2] tollere α | 452 id] illud α(-P^2) | 454 et] vel [*om.* Pr] φ | alius successor $\theta^2\theta^3\varphi$Va | 455 mutare θ | 457 illam [suam φ^5] $\varphi\rho^1$ | alibi] *om.* φ | aliter] alibi ρ | 459 per] in ρ^1 | 460 Dominus] *om.* α

434-486 Contra ... eneo: cf. Pierre de la Palu, *Tractatus de potestate papae* 1.3, pp. 188-190 | 447-448 2 Tim. 2:19 | 459-462 Gratian, C.24 q.1 c.15

edificabo ecclesiam meam." Eius enim sedes primitus fuit apud vos, que postea iubente Domino Romam translata est. Hunc autem iussum Domini exponit Innocentius, *Qui filii sint legitimi* c. *Per venerabilem*, ubi dicit sic: *Locus quem elegit Dominus apostolica sedes esse dinoscitur. Cum enim Petrus urbem fugiens exivisset, volens eum Dominus ad locum quem elegerat revocare, interrogatus ab eo: "Domine quo vadis?" respondit: "Venio Romam iterum crucifigi," quod intelligens pro se dictum, ad locum pristinum est reversus.* Motus enim Petrus lacrimis Christianorum, a facie Neronis fugiens aliam sedem forte eligere volebat, secundum illud Matthei 10: *Cum autem persequentur vos in civitate ista, fugite in aliam.* Sed hoc Dominus prohibuit, volens ibi sedem Petri finaliter permanere. Unde non ex Petri sed ex Christi electione facta est sedes Petri; quare non potest etiam a Petro mutari. Sicut elegit Dominus Sion in templum, ut esset locus orationis, nec ex tunc licuit alibi templum facere, etiam summo sacerdoti. Unde peccavit Eliachim in Eliopoleos Egipti simile templum faciens illi Hierosolimorum, ut refert Josephus.

Ad hoc dicendum quod, sicut nutu Dei factus est serpens eneus quando profuit in deserto, Numeri 21; postea vero, quando in idolatriam versus est, destructus est iusto iudicio regis Ezechie, 4 Regum 18; ita si nunc Romani in rebellione ecclesie existerent, vel alia civitas in mundo appareret communior et aptior ad universalis ecclesie regimen, posset papa, forte de voluntate Dei interpretativa, inde sedem suam mutare eadem ratione qua Petrus eam Romam transtulit, sicut Constantinus sedem imperii a Roma Constantinopolim transtulit, ei Romana privilegia

desunt B^2P^1

462 Domini] *om.* φ | 463 sic] *om.* π(-R) | 470 ista] una θ, illa ρ^1 | 472 ex^2] *om.* θ(-BoV^{5}S) | Christi electione] ipsa electione Domini φ | 472-473 non ... Petro] etiam non potest a Petro $\theta^2\theta^3\varphi$, etiam a Petro non potuit θ^4 | 473 mutare $\varphi(-\varphi^3)$ | 475 Egipti] *om.* φ | 476 ut ... Josephus] *om.* ρ^1 | *Post verbum* Josephus *praeterit verba interiacentia* (i.e. Ad ... principi) *et procedit ad verbum* Secundo (lineam 501) B^1; *praeterit verba interiacentia* (i.e. Ad ... eneo) *et procedit ad verbum* Sine (lineam 487) ψ | 477 quando] *add.* populus $\theta\varphi$ | 478 fuit $\theta^1\varphi$ | 479 iusto] *add.* Dei θ | Sedechie [*add.* tempore θ^4] θ | 480 Roma φ | ecclesie] *om.* φ | existeret φ | 481 communior] melior φ | 482 inde suam sedem $\psi\pi$Barb.Sr, inde suam suam Va, sedem suam inde ρ^1 | transmutare θ | 483 eam] sedem suam θ | Rome θ | 484 sedem] *add.* suam θ | Romana] bona θ

463-468 X. 4.17.13 | 470 Matt. 10:23 | 473-474 Cf. Ps. 131:13 | 475-476 The reference should be to Onias: cf. Flavius Josephus, *Antiquitates Judaicae* (Venice, 1480) xxx.4 | 478 Num. 21:89 | 479 4 Reg. 18:4

concedendo. Argumentum ad hoc, 63 d. c. *Quia sancta*, ibi: *Sicut divina Scriptura* etc., de serpente eneo.

Sine causa autem rationabili sedem suam a Deo Rome fundatam non posset ipse papa evertere nec alibi transferre. Et si faceret, non valeret, immo etiam quantumcumque causa probabilis appareret, quia non nisi Dei contraria iussione mutandum est quod semel iussit. Sine assensu generalis concilii super hoc specialiter convocati, et Dei revelationem super hoc invocantis, non esset talis translatio facienda, quia nec propter transmigrationem, nec propter captivitatem populi Dei ad septuaginta annos, licuit locum templi quem Deus elegerat immutare. Nec est simile de mutatione Antiochie, quia illam sedem Petrus elegerat motu proprio, non speciali Domini iussione. Nec est etiam simile de serpente eneo, quem Dominus erigi fecerat, non ad perpetuitatem, sed ad temporale remedium in deserto. Nec est simile de translatione sedis imperialis, cuius auctoritas est a populo Romano, qui ius suum et potestatem in imperatorem transtulit, *Inst.*, *De iure naturali* § *Sed quod principi*.

Secundo arguitur sic, quia papa potest papatui cedere et resignare. Sed non posset si potestas sua esset a Deo. Ergo non est a Deo. Maior patet per multa exempla summorum pontificum qui renuntiaverunt, et specialiter sancti Petri de Murrone, qui post hoc in sanctum canonizatus est, qui etiam hoc ipsum declaravit, ut patet *De renuntiatione* c. 1 *Libro sexto*. Minor patet dupliciter. Primo, quia matrimonium, in quo est vinculum divinum, etiam non consummatum, nulla renuntiatione potest tolli. Ergo nec vinculum inter papam et ecclesiam, quod est vinculum divinum. Si papatus est de iure divino et ipse sit sponsus ecclesie, eodem iure nulla

deest B^2; 497 *usque ad verbum* remedium *deest* P^1

486 etc.] et queritur ρ^1 | *Post verbum* eneo *add. verba* dicendum est quod papa non potest transferre sedem Romanam nec alius purus homo, *et tunc redit ad verbum* Quod (lineam 446) ψ | 487 fundatam] situatam ρ | 488 ipse] *om.* $\theta\pi$ | alibi] alio [alias W] $\varphi(-\varphi^3)\pi^1$Va, in alio [aliquo V^7] ψ | 490 Dei [*om.* Bm^1] contraria [*om.* U] $\theta\varphi$(-W)$\pi\rho^2$] contraria [causa W] Dei W$\psi\rho(-\rho^2)\sigma$ | iussit] *add.* nec φ | consensu ρ^1 | 491 Dei] *om.* φ | 492 est φ | 494 Deus] Dominus π(-R) | 495 elegit α | 496 etiam] *om.* π(-R) | 500 Inst. ... naturali] *om.* ρ^1 | Inst.] illud fuit ψ, illud patet B^1 | *Post verbum* naturali *om. verba* Sed ... principi *et tunc redit ad verbum* Quod (lineam 446) B^1 | principi] *add.* placuit [placuerit θ^2V^2] α | 501 Sed] *add.* hoc θ | 505 *Post verbum* sexto *praeterit verba interiacentia* (i.e. Minor ... potest) *et procedit ad verbum* Secundo (lineam 510) α | 506 dupliciter] *om.* α | Primo] *om.* α | 509 *Post verbum* ecclesie *om. verba* eodem ... potest (lineas 509-510), *et tunc, praeteriens verba interiacentia* (i.e. Secundo ... corpore, lineas 510-519), *et omittens verba* Dicendum ... ecclesie (lineas 520-522), *procedit ad verbum* cui (lineam 522) θ

485-486 Gratian, D.63 c.28 (Gratian) | 500 *Inst.* 1.2.6 | 505 *Sext.* 1.7.1

renuntiatione nec resignatione tolli potest. Secundo, quia si potestas papalis est a Deo, sicut potestas caracteris sacerdotalis et episcopalis, sicut sacerdos et episcopus nulla renuntiatione possunt perdere claves ordinis, quin semper remaneant ille verus sacerdos et ille verus episcopus, quantumcumque perdant curam et regimen suarum ecclesiarum, ita papa nulla renuntiatione perdere poterit ius papatus nec potestatem papalem quam habet a Deo, nec claves ecclesie commissas Petro, nec per consequens quin semper remaneat verus papa. Nec per consequens poterit esse alius verus papa eo vivente, ne sint duo capita in eodem corpore.

Dicendum est quod papa potest papatui cedere, et cedendo desinere esse papa, si cardinales acceptent, alias non. Sunt enim in acceptatione papatus duo: unum est ius suum quod ei acquiritur; aliud est ius ecclesie cui obligatur. Cuilibet autem licet renuntiare iure suo in omni eo in quo non est alteri subditus nec obligatus, *C. De episcopis et clericis*, et *C. De pactis, Si quis in conscribendo*. Sed qui se semel obligavit non potest se ad libitum liberare. Igitur papa papatui ex parte quidem sua renuntiare potest. Sed quia semel se obligavit ecclesie, ex illa parte renuntiare non potest nisi de assensu cardinalium, qui in omnibus que ad papam spectant vicem ecclesie representant. Est enim papa obligatus ex quo acceptavit ecclesiam regere. Unde nisi ecclesia quittet ipsum et consentiat, non videtur quod renuntiare possit. Sed consentientibus illis potest. Secundum hanc distinctionem debet intelligi declaratio predicta, *De renuntiatione* c. 1, ubi dicit: *Romanum pontificem posse libere resignare*, scilicet iuri suo. Sed non se posse excutere a iugo nisi sponsa sua consentiente.

Ad primam probationem in contrarium dicendum quod non est simile de clavibus ordinis, que adherent ossibus persone inseparabiliter et ipsam

deest B^2

510 *Post verbum* potest *praeterit verba interiacentia* (i.e. Secundo ... corpore) *et procedit ad verbum* Dicendum (lineam 520) γ| 512 ordinis] *om.* θ| 513 remaneat $P^4\rho^1$Va| et] *om.* φ| ille^2] iste θπ(-B^1)| 516 Petro] *om.* θ| nec^2] *om.* [et U] φ| 517 per consequens^2] *om.* φ| 518 eo] ipso [Christo V^2] θ| 519 *Post verbum* corpore *redit ad verbum* Minor (lineam 506) α| 520-522 Dicendum ... ecclesie] *om.* θ| 520 cedendo] cedens φ| 521 enim] *om.* ρ^1| 523 omni eo in] *om.* θ| 524 nec] non σ| obligatur π(-P^1)σ| 525 Sed] et ρVa| potest] *om.* φ(-Bm^1) | 526 liberaret [liberarius W] φ(-Bm^1) | 530 quittet] *add.* quitdare est verbum gallicum et est idem quod deobligare [obligare Bm^1W] φ| 531 potest] *add.* et [papa et S] θ| 533 posse libere] possibile $\varphi\pi^2$ | 534 se] *om.* ρ^1 | 536 que] *add.* illo Bm^2, illi ρ^2 | 536-537 ossibus ... sequuntur] *om.* ρ^1 | 536 persone inseparabiliter] *om.* φ| persone] tempore V^3, pape V^5Svψ, pape alias [vel V^2] episcopo et sacerdoti θ^2V^2, vel episcopo et sacerdotis et pape Bo| ipsum [ipsa θ^4(-S)] θ

520-534 Dicendum ... consentiente: cf. Pierre de la Palu, *Tractatus de potestate papae* 1.3, p. 200| 524-525 *Cod.* 1.3.50, 2.3.29| 532-533 *Sext.* 1.7.1

sequuntur. Unde caracter ordinis sacerdotalis et episcopalis sicut et baptismalis sunt indelebiles in anima. Unde si resurgeret episcopus vel sacerdos, verus episcopus et sacerdos esset, potens conficere, confirmare et ordinare sicut prius. Unde illa potestas non debetur sedi nec statui, sed persone. Cum enim moritur curatus vel episcopus, successor non succedit ei in ordine, sed habet necesse ordinari. Sed potestas papalis debetur statui, non persone. Unde non acquiritur per personalem consecrationem, sed eo ipso quod aliquis est in sede, acquirit et habet illam potestatem. Eo ipso quod sedem perdit, potestatem perdit, que semper remanet in ipsa sede que non moritur, *De rescriptis* c. *Si gratiose, Libro sexto*. Esse autem in sede est humanum et liberum, dependens ex voluntate eligentium et acceptantis. Et quia nihil tam naturale est quam unumquodque dissolvi eo genere quo ligatum est, propter quod omnes obligationes que solo consensu mutuo contrahuntur consensu contrario distrahuntur et etiam dissolvuntur, inde est quod vinculum obligationis inter papam et ecclesiam solo consensu contractum contrario consensu dissolvitur, et renuntiando in manibus cardinalium acceptantium desinit esse in sede, et perdit per consequens potestatem que remanet in sede, et acquiritur succedenti in sede ex ipsamet successione. Quod non potest dici de clavibus ordinis, quia ille semper sequuntur personam, et nulli statui debentur.

Per idem respondetur ad aliud de matrimonio carnali, quia in eo consensum mutuum per verba de presenti, que sunt verum sacramentum, sequitur vinculum divinum, quod est subiective non in anima, sed in toto composito. Unde tamdiu durat quamdiu utrumque suppositum, sicut tamdiu manet corpus et sanguis Christi sub speciebus quamdiu manent species. Unde illud vinculum, quod est quid divinum et res sacramenti, sequens non nudum consensum, sed sacramentum integratum ex consensu et verbis in personis habilibus, non potest ab homine dissolvi

deest B^2; 565 *post verbum* personis *deest* P^1

539 et] vel θ(-S) | 540 ista θ | nec] vel θ | 542 statui] papatui [*om.* φ^5] φ | 544 potestatem] *add.* et ρSr | 546 c.] *add.* et ρ^1 | 548 est] *om.* θ | 550 etiam] *om.* σ | 551 dissolvuntur] *add.* re [et V^2; *add.* non B^1] existente integra [integre V^1V^2] $\alpha\pi^2$ | obligationis] *om.* θ | 552 solo ... consensu²] *om.* θ | 555 succedenti] sedenti θ | in sede] *om.* $\theta^2\theta^3$; in ea θ^4 | 556 iste θ | 558 Per] ad θ, quod ρ^1 | eo] *add.* per α(-θ^4P^2)P^1 | 561 quamdiu] quam ρ; *add.* durat φ | 563 vinculum] divinum ρ^1 | quid divinum] quoddam vinculum ρ^1 | 564 ex] in φ | 565 verbis] *add.* et φ | 565 - 6: 684 habilibus ... discipulos] *om.* P^1 | 565 personis habilibus] personalibus ρ^1

546 *Sext.* 1.3.5

secundum illud: *Quod Deus coniunxit homo non separet.* Sed consensus cardinalium eligentium representantium consensum sponse ex una parte, et consensus electi quasi sponsi ex alia, per quecumque verba expressus, non est sacramentum, nec etiam sacramentale. Unde ex opere operato nullum habet effectum divinum quo ad vinculum. Sed remanet illud vinculum pure humanum, solo consensu hominum contractum. Unde consensu contrario potest tolli, eadem ratione qua et sponsalia de futuro, que non sunt sacramentum. Unde non consequitur ea aliquod vinculum divinum, propter quod consensu contrario dissolvuntur, saltem auctoritate ecclesie, que tamen non posset hoc facere si inde nasceretur divinum vinculum, sicut est in matrimonio per verba de presenti. Unde obligatio que est inter prelatum quemcumque et suam ecclesiam magis assimilatur sponsalibus quam matrimonio, quantum ad illud quod dictum est. Unde potestas papalis, prout est in sede Romana, habet fundamentum divinum non humanum, et ideo nunquam destruitur. Sed prout est in persona que est in sede solum per consensum humanum, habet fundamentum humanum duplex, scilicet ipsum hominem et illum consensum, que sunt destructibilia. Unde quolibet illorum destructo, destruitur potestas, non in se, sed in illa persona in qua erat per accidens, per hoc scilicet quod erat in sede.

Tertia Conclusio

Tertia conclusio principalis, quod omnis potestas iurisdictionis ecclesiastice et prelatio in ecclesia procedit, derivatur et originatur a papa vel a sede papali, idest ab ecclesia Romana, probatur tripliciter. Primo ex precedentibus cum auctoritatibus Grecorum sic. Sicut se habuit Petrus postquam fuit papa ad apostolos et ad discipulos et primitivam ecclesiam, sic se habet papa Romanus ad omnes alios prelatos ecclesie, et ad omnes

desunt B^{2}P^1

566 Quos $\theta\psi\rho$(-Bm^2) | 571 pure] per $\theta^2\theta^3$, vere θ^4 | solum [*om.* Bo] consensum $\theta^2\theta^3$ | 573 ea] *om.* $\theta\psi$; in sponsalibus φ | 582 humanum] *om.* φ | illum] ipsum θ | 583 eorum [illorum aut eorum S] $\theta\pi$(-R) | 587 principalis] *add.* est θ | 588 procedit] *add.* et φ | originaliter [originatur Sv] et [*om.* V^3] derivatur θ(-Bo), generaliter a papa et etiam derivatur Bo | 589 papali] apostolica θ | idest ... Romana] *om.* θ; *add.* quod ρ | 590 precedentibus ... Grecorum] auctoritatibus Grecorum precedentibus ρ | Grecorum] *om.* φ | 591 ad^2] *om.* [*in marg.* V^1] $\theta^2\theta^3\psi\pi$(-R)Va | et^2] *add.* ad $\theta\rho^1$ | 592 Romanus] *om.* φ | alios] *om.* φ

566 Matt. 19:6; Marc. 10:9

alias ecclesias. Sed Petrus sic se habuit ad illos quod a Petro habuerunt omnem potestatem iurisdictionis, non a Christo immediate. Ergo papa sic se habet ad istos quod ab ipso habent omnem potestatem iurisdictionis.

Maior patet, quia papa Romanus in omni preeminentia, plenitudine et dignitate iurisdictionis succedit plene et perfecte Petro, ut probatum est in probatione minoris precedentis rationis. Et iterum probatur tripliciter auctoritatibus Grecorum. Prima synodi Nicene, que magne auctoritatis semper fuit apud eos et totam ecclesiam Dei, in qua inter cetera legitur sic: *Ecclesia Romana semper primatum habuit semperque habere debet*. Quod autem dicit *semper habuit* intelligendum est ex quo ecclesia fuit, et ex quo primus in ea Petrus sedit, et in ipsa finaliter resedit. Secundo patet istud per auctoritatem concilii alterius apud eos, ubi dicitur sic: *Veneramur secundum Scripturas et canonum definitionem sanctissimum antique Rome episcopum primum esse et maximum omnium episcoporum*. Dicit autem *antique Rome* ad differentiam Constantinopolis, quam Constantinus, illuc sedem suam transferens, et privilegiis urbis Romane extollens, novam Romam voluit appellari. Tertio patet istud auctoritate concilii Chalcedonensis, ubi inter cetera legitur quod tota synodus acclamavit Leoni pape: *Leo sanctissimus apostolicus et ecumenicus*, idest universalis patriarcha, *per multos annos vivat*. Quod autem episcopi successerunt loco apostolorum, et curati et omnes inferiores prelati loco discipulorum, probatur 21 d. *In novo*, 68 d. *Quorum*.

Secundo probatur sic. Omnis iurisdictio et prelatio, sive potestas cuiuslibet persone ecclesiastice, procedit et derivatur originaliter et principaliter ab institutore et fundatore ecclesie cui presidet, et dignitatis seu potestatis vel etiam prelationis qua fungitur et in qua residet. Sed omnes alie ecclesie et dignitates earum sunt institute et fundate ab ecclesia

desunt B^2P^1

596 plenitudine] *add.* et [*om.* ρ^2] potestate ρσ | 603 primus] *om.* θ | istud] idem [*om.* Bo] θV^7, illud ρ^1 | 604 eos] ipsos ρVa | 605 definitionem] sanctificationem [sanctionem U] φ | 606 esse] etiam ρ^1 | 608 Rome θφ(-Pr) | 609 istud] *om.* $\theta^2\theta^3$; idem θ^4, illud π(-R)ρ^2 | 612 successerint $\theta^2V^2V^5\gamma$(-StW)B^1 | 615 sive] *add.* auctoritas sive ρ^1 | 616 derivatur] *add.* et θ | originaliter] originatur α(-V^4P^2) | et^2] *om.* θ | 617 principaliter] principiatur [principatur φ^3] φ(-V^4) | presidet] *add.* insuper principium et origo totius [*inv.* W] φ | et^2] *om.* φ | 618 etiam] *om.* π(-R) | 619 et fundate] *om.* α(-Sv)

598-612 Et ... vivat: cf. Pierre de la Palu, *Tractatus de potestate papae* 1.2, p. 136 | 599-601 c.6 – see Mansi 2: 679. Cf. Conc. Chalced., act. 16, Mansi 7: 443. | 604-606 *Contra er. Gr.*, p. 322 | 609-612 *Contra er. Gr.*, p. 323 | 614 Gratian, D.21 c.2 | Gratian, D.68 c.6

Romana, ipsa vero a solo Christo. Ergo potestas et dignitas ecclesie Romane est a solo Christo. Omnis vero alia potestas iurisdictionis et prelationis in omnibus aliis rectoribus et prelatis procedit ab ecclesia Romana vel a papa, quod idem est. Quia non intelligitur quod a papa ratione persone, sed ratione status et dignitatis in qua est.

Maior patet, quia cum solum fundamentum sit principium et origo totius edificii, omnes autem alie partes sint principiate et originate, impossibile est quod fundamentum principietur sive originetur ab aliis partibus, sed necessarium est econtrario. Unde illa ecclesia que fundata est a solo Christo, fundans omnes alias, originatur et derivatur a solo Christo, non ab aliis. Alie vero ab ipsa. Et cum persona ab ecclesia trahat dignitatem et potestatem, non econtrario, oportet quod omnis persona ecclesiastica accipiat dignitatem et potestatem a fundatore ecclesie et dignitatis cui preest et in qua presidet.

Minor autem patet auctoritate Nicholai pape, 22 d. *Omnes*, ubi dicitur sic: *Omnes sive primatie cuiuslibet apicem, sive metropoleon primatus, aut episcopatuum cathedras, vel ecclesiarum sive cuiuslibet ordinis dignitatem instituit Romana ecclesia. Ipsam vero solus ipse fundavit qui beato Petro, vite eterne clavigero, terreni simul et celestis imperii iura commisit.* Si dicatur ad minorem quod Romana ecclesia non instituit dignitatem nec potestatem ecclesiarum nec cathedrarum, sed Christus, sed ipsa instituit personas in eis, sicut glossa videtur dicere, non valet. Quia quando locus aliquis non habet episcopum actu nec aptitudine, idest non habet ius habendi, per consequens non est civitas nec ecclesia cathedralis. Unde idem est dare ecclesie cathedram episcopalem et dare episcopum. Cum autem Christus non distinxerit ecclesias nec dioceses, eius vicarius Petrus et eius successor, assignando novas sedes episcopales, per consequens in omnibus illis novas cathedras erexerunt et fundamentum iecerunt. Unde ecclesia Romana non solum instituit et fundavit personas in prelationibus

desunt B^2P^1

621 Christo] *add.* et ρ | 623 a^1] *om.* φ | quod a] *om.* φ | 626 sunt θ(-BoV^3) | 627 sive] et θ | 629 fundans ... Christo] *hom.* ρ^1Sr | 632 accipiat] habeat ρ | 633 in qua] cui θ | 634 autem] *om.* $\theta\psi$ | Nicholai ρ^1] *om.* φBarb.; Anacleti θ, Alexandri [*add.* undecimi B^1] π, A. [si V^7] $\psi\sigma$ | pape] *om.* φ | 635 Omnes] Deus ρ^1 | primatie Boθ^4(-S)σ] *om.* ρ^1; primitie $\theta^2V^2V^5$S, primatias [primitias W] φ, primarie ψ, primative π, patriarche Barb. | cuiuslibet] *om.* θ; quaslibet φ | apicem] *om.* φ | 636 vel] aut θ(-V^3) | 645 distinxit [destruxerit Bo, destruxit Sv] θ | Petrus] *om.* φ | 646 sui successores φ | episcopales] *add.* et ρ^1 | 647 novas] *om.* θ

634-638 Gratian, D.22 c.1 | 641 Cf. *Decretum Gratiani* ..., D.22 c.1, fol. 33r

ecclesiasticis, de ipsis providendo aut eas in sedibus instituendo, sive modum institutionis ordinando. Immo etiam ipsas ecclesias cathedrales erexit et sedes et dignitates fundavit, sicut dicitur in preallegato capitulo, 80 d. *In illis*, ubi dicit Clemens sic: *In illis vero civitatibus quibus olim apud ethnicos primi flamines atque primi legis doctores erant, episcoporum primates vel patriarchas beatus Petrus poni precepit, qui reliquorum causas et maiora negotia in fide agitarent. In illis autem in quibus dudum apud predictos ethnicos erant eorum archiflamines, quos tamen minores esse tenebant quam predictos flamines, archiepiscopos per se precepit. In singulis vero reliquis civitatibus singulos non plures episcopos constitui precepit, qui episcoporum tantum vocabula sortirentur; quoniam nec inter ipsos apostolos par fuit institutio, sed unus prefuit omnibus.*

Tertio patet idem per alias duas auctoritates. Primo auctoritate Gregorii, 2 q. 6 *Decreto*, ubi dicitur sic: Sancta Romana ecclesia *ita vices suas aliis impartivit ecclesiis, ut in partem sint vocate sollicitudinis, non in plenitudinem potestatis*. Secundo auctoritate Julii pape in capitulo sequenti, dicentis sic: *Ipsa namque ecclesia que prima est ita vices suas reliquis ecclesiis credidit largiendas, ut in partem* etc. Ista enim impartitio sive largitio vicum suarum non potest intelligi de particulari, speciali et accidentali commissione quam papa fecit quibusdam ecclesiis quo ad primatiam et dignitatem legationis, nec de cotidianis commissionibus quas fecit ecclesiasticis personis, tum quia istud non convenit nisi certis et paucis ac determinatis ecclesiis et personis – auctoritates autem loquuntur de omnibus aliis ecclesiis in communi – tum quia ista commissio est accidentalis. Illa autem que sunt per accidens non cadunt

desunt B^2P^1

651 erigendo [exigendo V^3] θ | fundando θ | 652-660 ubi ... omnibus] *om.* Sr | 653 episcopos φ, apostolorum ρ^1 | 654 patriarchas Bo$\theta^4\varphi$Barb.] patriarche $\theta^2V^2V^5\psi\pi\rho^1$, patriarcha Va | 656 maiores φ(-U) | 657 per se] *om.* $\theta^2\theta^3$; preesse θ^4, poni [constitui U] φ, institui Barb. | In] et φ(-U) | 658 singulos] *add.* et θ^4B^1Barb. | plures] *add.* et $\psi\pi$Va | 659-660 quoniam ... omnibus] *om.* $\pi^1\rho$ | 660 instituens $\theta^4\psi B^1$ | *Post verbum* omnibus *praeterit verba interiacentia* (i.e. Tertio ... potestatis) *et procedit ad verbum* Secundo (lineam 664) Sr | 662 aliis] *om.* $\varphi\pi$(-R)Va | 663 ecclesiis ... vocate] *om.* π(-R) | 664 plenitudine $V^7\pi$(-R) | *Post verbum* potestatis *praeterit verba interiacentia* (i.e. Secundo ... etc.) *et procedit ad verbum* Ista (lineam 666) Sr | Secundo UBm^1PrρSr] secunda α(-UBm^1Pr)πVa | auctoritate B$m^1\varphi^5\rho$Sr] auctoritas [auctoritates Bl; *add.* est V^4] α(-B$m^1\varphi^5$)πVa | 666 credidit] tradidit [*add.* alias credit Bo] $\theta\rho^1$ | partem] *add.* sollicitudinis θVa | *Post verbum* etc. *redit ad verbum* Tertio (lineam 661) Sr | 667 et] *om.* φ | 670 fecit $\theta^2\theta^3\varphi^1W\pi$(-R)$\sigma$] facit Pr$\varphi^4\psi$R$\rho$, facit et fecit θ^4 | 671 ac] et [*om.* O] θ, sic $\psi\pi$(-R) | 672 ista] illa ρ^1

652-660 Gratian, D.80 c.2 | 661-664 Gratian, C.2 q.6 c.11 | 664-666 Gratian, C.2 q.6 c.12

sub arte, 2 *Metaphysice*. Unde auctoritates sunt intelligende de potestate quam habent ecclesie communiter, et non accidentaliter, quod scilicet omnis talis procedat ab ecclesia Romana.

Inter has autem auctoritates, licet videantur prima facie credibiliores ille Grecorum, quasi testimonium et confessio inimicorum contra se ipsos, quam auctoritates Romanorum pontificum, que sunt quasi testimonium in causa propria, ut dicatur cuilibet eorum: *Tu de teipso testimonium perhibes; testimonium tuum non est verum*; tamen secundum veritatem auctoritates Romanorum pontificum sunt efficaciores in hoc et in sequentibus, si attendamus illud verbum Christi ad Petrum pro se et pro sede sua, Luce 22: *Ego rogavi pro te Petre ut non deficiat fides tua*. Ex quo habetur quod Romana ecclesia in fide errare non potest, nec de eius fide dubitare licet, sed in omnibus est sequenda. *Unde ipse sanctus Ambrosius se in omnibus sequi magistram sanctam Romanam ecclesiam profitetur*, 22 d. *Omnes*, in fine. Unde cum per predictas auctoritates constet Romanam ecclesiam et Christi vicarios tanto tempore tenuisse, docuisse et per Sacram Scripturam confirmasse ipsam Romanam ecclesiam a Christo factam fundamentum aliarum, et alias instituisse et in partem sollicitudinis vocasse et alias eius vices gerere, temerarium est tantorum patrum determinationi preponere sensum suum, et minime mutanda sunt que longam interpretationem habuerunt. Nec est credendum ecclesiam Romanam a fide errasse, nec Scripturam Sacram pervertisse, quod est etiam hereticum, propter appetitum glorie et honoris. Et potest ipsa econtrario dicere cum Christo: *Ego testimonium perhibeo de meipso; testimonium meum verum est, quia testimonium perhibet de me pater*, idest Christus, qui eam fundavit et hoc privilegium sibi dedit. Immo dicere oppositum videtur hereticum et erroneum, quia hoc est ecclesie Romane auferre privilegium a Christo sibi datum, secundum illud 22 d. *Omnes*, ubi dicitur sic: *Non dubium est, quia quisquis cuilibet ecclesie ius suum detrahit, iniusticiam facit. Qui autem Romane ecclesie privilegium ab ipso*

desunt B^2P^1

676 omnes tales [*om.* ψ] procedant $\psi\rho$ | 678 inimicorum] *om.* φ | 680 Tu] *om.* θ(-Bo) | 683 si] sed ρ^1 | 684 Luce 22] *om.* ρ | Petre] *om.* θ | 687 se] *om.* α | sanctam] *om.* ρ^1 | 689 docuisse] *om.* $\psi\pi$(-R) | 692 est] *om.* ρ^1 | 693 determinationi] decretis ψB^1 | 694 longinquam ρ^1 | 695 Sacram] *om.* α | 696 potest] *add.* enim π | 697 cum] *om.* $\pi\sigma$ | meipso] *add.* et θ | 699 qui] *add.* eque π(-R) | 702 quia] quod θ | 703 trahit $\theta^2V^2V^5\psi\rho^1$, subtrahit $\theta^4\varphi$

674 Aristotle, *Metaphysica* A.1 (981a15-16); cf. B.6 (1003a14) | 680-681 Joan. 8:13 | 684 Luc. 22:32 | 686-688 Gratian, D.22 c.1 | 697-698 Joan. 8:14-18 | 701-706 Gratian, D.22 c.1

summo omnium ecclesiarum capite traditum auferre conatur, hic proculdubio in heresim labitur; et cum ille vocetur iniustus, hic est dicendus hereticus. Cum enim iste auctoritates dicant esse privilegium ecclesie Romane quod eam solam Christus fundavit, dicere quod alias sicut istam Christus fundavit est eius privilegium impugnare.

Contra hoc autem arguitur septem mediis. Primo sic: ecclesia que fundavit et instituit certas alias in determinatis partibus mundi tantum non fundavit nec instituit ecclesias omnes per universum mundum. Sed ecclesia Romana, sive sedes Petri, est huiusmodi. Ergo etc. Maior patet, quia illud est ius singulare, cuius contrarium est ius commune. Unde qui fundavit aliquas ecclesias singulariter non fundavit omnes universaliter et communiter. Minor patet 11 d. *Quis nesciat*, ubi dicit sic Innocentius: *Manifestum est in omnem Italiam, Galliam, Hispaniam et Africam atque Siciliam insulasque interiacentes nullum instituisse ecclesias nisi eos quos venerabilis apostolus Petrus aut successores eius constituerunt sacerdotes ibidem.* Iste autem sunt modica pars mundi et universalis ecclesie, et frustra dicerentur institute a Romanis pontificibus singulariter si alie omnes essent ab eis institute equaliter. Ergo iste sole sunt ab ea instistute.

Responsio: omnes ecclesie et dignitates et cure ecclesiastice sunt institute a Romanis pontificibus mediate vel immediate. Sed ille que ibi nominantur immediate, quia beatus Petrus immediate misit discipulos suos ad fundandum diversas ecclesias, sicut beatum Marcum Alexandriam, Potentianum Favinianum in Franciam Senonas; et similiter beatus Clemens sanctum Dionysium Parisius, et sic de aliis. Ceteri vero ab apostolis missi ad fundandum alias ecclesias missi sunt ad hoc ipsum mediate a Petro, inquantum et apostoli, non auctoritate sua sed Petri generalis vicarii Christi, eos miserunt, cuius etiam Petri auctoritate ipsimet apostoli exercuerunt omnem iurisdictionem qua functi sunt. Unde

desunt B^2P^1

706 dicunt π(-R) | 707 solam γ(-Stφ^5)Rρ(-ρ^2)Va] solus θSt$\varphi^5\pi$(-R)Sr, solum ρ^2 | 707-708 dicere ... fundavit] *hom.* $\theta\rho^1$ | 708 sicut] *add.* et φ | impugnare πBarb.] auferre contrarium asserere θ^1, auferre $\theta^2\gamma$, enervare $\rho^1\sigma$ | 709-731 Primo ... cuius] *om.* V^2 | 709 Primo sic] *om.* ρ^1 | 710-711 certas ... instituit] *hom.* ρ^1 | 710 alias] ecclesias [*om.* V^5W] $\theta\varphi$ | 711 nec] vel π(-R) | omnes] *om.* φ | omnes ecclesias θVa | 714 ecclesias] *om.* π(-R)Barb. | 716 atque] ac [et P^4] πBarb. | 721 essent] fuissent ρ^1 | iste] ille ρ^1 | 723 et^1] *om.* π(-R)Barb. | ecclesiastice] ecclesie ρ^1 | 725 nominavit [nominat Sz] ρ^1 | 726 suos] *om.* $B^1\rho$ | 729 missi^1] missis π(-R); *add.* sunt θ | fundandum] faciendum θ | alias] *om.* θ | 730 mediante Petro αB^1 | et] etiam φ | 732 omnem] *om.* φ

715-719 Gratian, D.11 c.11

Actuum 13 dixit Spiritus Sanctus: *Segregate mihi Saulum et Barnabam in ministerium ad quod assumpsi eos*, quasi dicat: licet eos elegerim et assumpserim ad officium regiminis, volo tamen quod per vos ad illud promoveantur, ab aliis segregati. Quod dictum ecclesie in communi intelligitur dictum principaliter Petro, eius singulari et summo rectori.

Secundo arguitur sic: ecclesia Romana non potest instituisse nec fundasse nec auctorizasse nec dotasse illas ecclesias, cathedras et dignitates que ipsam precesserunt. Sed multe ecclesie cathedrales et dignitates ecclesiastice ipsam precesserunt. Ergo impossibile est quod illas fundaverit, instituerit seu dotaverit, et per consequens non omnes ipsa fundavit nec auctorizavit. Maior patet, quia semper causa precedit effectum suum. Minor patet, quia antequam Romana ecclesia fundata esset, ecclesia Hierosolimitana erat fundata, facta sedes metropolitana, habens archiepiscopum Jacobum fratrem Domini, 66 d. § *Porro*. Item Antiochena a Petro, in qua primum discipuli appellati sunt Christiani, fundata erat, et sic de multis aliis.

Solutio: Romana ecclesia omnes alias fundavit et instituit, tam priores tempore quam posteriores, sed differenter. Nam cum ipsa non sit fundamentum aliarum nisi per hoc, quod ipsa est sedes Petri cui dictum est: *Tu es Petrus, et super hanc petram edificabo ecclesiam meam*, posteriores se tempore ipsa fundavit directe, per suos sponsos qui tunc erant, mediate vel immediate earum fundamenta faciendo et cathedras erigendo. Priores vero se tempore ipsa fundavit tripliciter. Unomodo earum fundamenta iaciendo non per se tunc, sed per hoc quod fuit sponsa eius finaliter qui eas fundavit primordialiter. Quia enim dicitur Genesis 2 de viro et uxore quod *erunt duo in carne una*, et per consequens quod de uno dicitur attribuitur alteri, maxime de pertinentibus ad dotem, et inter prelatum et ecclesiam est quoddam matrimonium spirituale, ideo factum prelati dicitur factum sue ecclesie, non solum pro tempore post contractum matrimonium, sed etiam ante. Unde sicut dicimus quod homo Christus fundavit terram super aquas, quia eam fundavit idem ipse qui est

desunt B²P¹

734 licet] cum π(-R)Barb. | 736 dictum] *add.* est θ | 737 principaliter] singulariter φ | 739 cathedrales θφB¹ | 740 ecclesie ... et] *om.* φ | 741 illas] ipsas ρ¹Va | 745 esset] est φ | fundata] *add.* et θ⁴φB¹ | 748 aliis multis α | 750 tempore] *om.* θ | 754 earum] eorum θπBarb. | faciendo] iaciendo φρ¹ | 759 et] *om.* φ | 761 ecclesie sue αρ¹ | 762 etiam] *om.* π(-R)Barb.

733-734 Act. 13:2 | 746 Gratian, D.66 c.2 | 752 Matt. 16:18 | 757-758 Gen. 2:24

filius Dei, licet antequam esset homo, ita ecclesia Romana, sponsa tandem Petri, dicitur fundasse illa que ipse fundavit etiam antequam esset sponsus eius. Vel dicitur secundo: illas fundasse, idest in suis fundamentis sustinuisse, retinuisse et solidasse. Nam nisi se tenerent in fide et doctrina et obedientia Romane ecclesie, a suo fundamento recederent et corruerent, 19 d. *Ita Dominus*, ubi dicitur: *Ut exhortem ministerii se intelligeret esse divini, qui ausus fuisset discedere a soliditate Petri.* Vel tertio, quando dicitur ecclesia Romana esse fundamentum aliarum, exponitur, idest ecclesia vel sedes Petri. Et tunc verificatur de ecclesia Petri semper, sed de Romana pro tempore quo cepit esse ecclesia Petri, et pro tempore precedente de Antiochena, quando ibi residebat, et pro tempore primevo de ecclesia primitiva cui Petrus presidebat, inde mittens alios huc et illuc.

Tertio idem patet per Bernardum, libro tertio *De consideratione ad Eugenium papam*, ubi dicit: *Erras si ut summam ita et solam institutam a Deo vestram apostolicam dignitatem existimas. Si hoc sentis, dissentis ab ipso qui ait: "Non est potestas nisi a Deo," ad Romanos 13: "Omnis anima sublimioribus potestatibus subdita sit." Non ait sublimiori, tanquam in uno, sed sublimioribus, tanquam in multis. Non ergo tua sola potestas a Domino; sunt et mediocres, sunt et inferiores.*

Dicendum quod si papa existimaret dignitatem et potestatem suam esse solam a Deo constitutam, excludendo dignitatem et potestatem ordinis sacerdotalis et pontificalis, dicendo illas non esse eque immediate a Deo sicut suam, ipse erraret. Quia potestas et dignitas ordinis in omnibus ordinatis equaliter est a Deo, ut patet quinto articulo, prima conclusione, et sexto articulo, prima conclusione. Item si papa existimaret dignitatem et potestatem sue iurisdictionis sic esse solam a Deo quod nulla alia esset a Deo, nec mediate nec immediate, erraret et dissentiret ab apostolo dicente:

desunt B^{2}P^1

765 Petri] Christi $\theta^2\theta^3\gamma$(-P^2) | 767 retinuisse] *om.* ρ^1 | nisi] ubi non ρ^1 | doctrina et [*add.* in φ^3] fide α | 769 Domino φ(-U) | intelligerent [intelligerunt P^4] V$^7\pi\rho^1$ | 770 tertio] *om.* π(-R)Barb. | 771 esse] est [in O] θ, esset ρ^1 | 772 sed] si θ^2Barb., videlicet θ^3V^3, scilicet Sv | 773 Romana] *add.* nunc et semper θ^1(-V^2) | tempore^1] *add.* sequenti de θ^2 | quo ... tempore] *hom.* θBarb. | 774 sedebat φ | pro] de φ(-φ^5) | 775 et] vel ρ^1 | 776 idem patet] patet illud θ^2, obicitur [arguitur V^5] θ^1 | De consideratione] *om.* θ | 777 papam] *om.* θ; *add.* secundum ρ^1 | ut] sicut ρ^1 | 778 vestram $\psi\sigma$] *om.* $\theta\rho^1$; tuam φ, nostram πBarb. | 782 sunt^2] *om.* α | 785 et θ^1(-Bo)$\varphi^1\psi\rho^1$Va] *om.* θ^2Bo$\varphi^2\pi$Barb.Sr | pontificalis] *add.* aliorum φ | illam θ | 787 ordinatis] *om.* α | quinto] primo ρ^1 | 788 et^1 αP^4] *om.* RρVa | sexto] secundo ρ^1

769-770 Gratian, D.19 c.7 | 776-782 St. Bernard, *De consideratione* 3.4.17 (PL 182: 768), ed. J. Leclercq and H. M. Rochais in *S. Bernardi Opera* 3 (Rome, 1963), pp. 379-493 at p. 444

Non est potestas nisi a Deo, scilicet mediate vel immediate. Sed si existimat suam potestatem iurisdictionis solam esse immediate a Deo, omnem autem aliam potestatem iurisdictionis ecclesiastice non esse a Deo immediate sed mediante sua, non errat, nec dissentit ab apostolo dicente: *Non est potestas nisi a Deo*. Quia non intelligit immediate, alias tolleretur omnis potestas delegata et prepositorum et baillivorum, que non sunt a Deo nisi mediantibus superioribus, qui istis vices suas committunt.

Ad illud quod sequitur: *Non ait sublimiori, tanquam in uno, sed sublimioribus, tanquam in multis,* non vult ipse dicere quin papa sit inter omnes sublimissimus et solus altissimus in omni terra, sed quod cum eo sunt sublimes ut curati, sublimiores ut episcopi. Et quod concludit: *Non ergo tua sola potestas a Domino; sunt et mediocres, sunt et inferiores,* concedendum est, modo predicto, scilicet quod sunt omnes a Domino. Sed illa pape immediate, episcoporum mediocris, curatorum inferior mediate, referendo ad potestatem iurisdictionis. Nam referendo ad potestatem ordinis omnes sunt eque immediate, ut sepe dictum est. Vel potest dici quod status et potestas etiam iurisdictionis ordinarie in episcopis et curatis est a Deo inspirante. Nam cum bonum sit eos esse in ecclesia, et omne bonum regimen ecclesie, que Spiritu Sancto regitur, a Deo inspiretur, non est dubium istos status esse a Deo inspirante. Sed propter hoc non sequitur quod sint a Deo eos per se immediate instituente, et eis potestatem conferente. Immo mediante vicario Christi in terris. Sicut Spiritu Sancto inspirante sanctus Benedictus et alii sancti religiones fundaverunt. Tamen non propter hoc Deo immediate, sed ecclesia Romana approbante, et confirmante et instituente ipsos ordines, et privilegia largiente.

Quarto patet idem per Rabanum super illud Matthei 16: *Tibi dabo claves* etc. *Hec*, inquit, *solvendi atque ligandi potestas, quamvis soli Petro*

desunt B^2P^1

791-795 scilicet ... Deo] *hom.* ρ^1 | 791 existimaret [estimaret V^3S] θ | 792 potestatem sue P^2B^1Barb. | 792-793 omnem autem $\varphi(-\varphi^3)R\sigma$] omnemque $\theta St\psi B^1$Barb., et aliorum U | 800 omnem terram π(-R)Barb. | 802 et[1]] *om.* ρ^1 | 804 illa] sola et summa φ | 807 etiam] *om.* π(-R)Barb. | 809 inspiratur [inspirantur S] $\theta(-V^5)$, inspirante V^5Barb. | 810 illos ρ^1 | 812 conferente] *add.* immediate φ | Immo ... vicario] unde nec [non φ^3] sunt immediati [immediate St] vicarii φ | 813 sancti] *add.* religiosi θ^2Bo | religiones] religiosi θ^1(-Bo) | 814 Deo immediate $\pi^1\sigma$] a Deo immediate [immediate a Deo V^3] αBarb., sunt a Deo immediate $B^1\rho^1$ | 816 patet ... illud] obicitur illud Bo, obicitur per illud quod dicit glossa V^2, obicitur per illud quod dicitur in Evangelio V^5, obicitur per illud [*add.* Matthei 16 V^3] glosse super illud θ^4 | Rabanum] Urbanum ρ^1, id quod est θ^2

791 Rom. 13:1 | 798-799, 801-802 St. Bernard, *De consideratione* 3.4.17 (PL 182: 768), Leclercq and Rochais 444 | 816-819 *Cat. aur. in Matt.* 16.3, 1: 252B (1: 274A) | 816-817 Matt. 16:19

data videatur a Domino, tamen et ceteris apostolis datur, nec non etiam nunc in episcopis et presbyteris omni ecclesie.

Respondeo: potestas data Petro datur ceteris apostolis, episcopis, presbyteris, a Domino et a Petro. A Domino quidem immediate quo ad potestatem ordinis, mediate quo ad potestatem iurisdictionis. A Petro autem datur similiter utraque, sed illa ordinis ministerialiter sive instrumentaliter, illa vero iurisdictionis principaliter. Quia videretur Petro auferri illud quod primo fuit sibi datum vel promissum si sine eo et non per eum alteri daretur potestas iurisdictionis, ut dictum est.

Quinto patet idem per Leonem papam in quodam sermone de apostolis, ubi tractans illud Matthei 16: *Tibi dabo claves regni celorum*, dicit: *Transivit in alios apostolos ius istius potestatis, et ad omnes ecclesie principes decreti huius constitutio commeavit. Petro enim hoc ideo singulariter creditur, quia cunctis ecclesie rectoribus Petri forma preponitur.*

Solutio: ius potestatis huius transivit et commeavit a Petro in apostolos et principes ecclesie, vel a Deo per Petrum, et hoc innuit verbum transitus et commeationis que important motum, in quo non est transitus de extremo ad extremum nisi per medium. Unde cum ista potestas primo transivit a Deo ad Petrum, et post Petrum ultimo ad alios, consequens est quod transiverit ad ultimos per Petrum quasi per medium. Et hoc etiam sonat finis auctoritatis, quando dicit Petro hoc singulariter creditur tanquam ab eo aliis dispensandum, secundum illud 1 ad Corinthios 9: *Dispensatio mihi credita est*, quia Petrus est *dispensator fidelis et prudens, quem constituit Dominus super familiam suam*, Luce 12.

Sexto idem patet per Dionysium, *De ecclesiastica hierarchia*, ubi prius, ubi dicitur sic: *Divinus pontificum ordo primus est divinarum ordinatio-*

desunt B^2P^1

818 ceteris] *om.* π(-R)Barb. | 823 datur] *om.* α | ministraliter θV^7 | 824 ista φ | 825 auferre $\theta\varphi^3\varphi^5$ | primo] *om.* θ^4 | fuit primo sibi $\theta^2\theta^3 StBm^1\varphi^4$, sibi fuit primo U, primo fuit W, sibi primo sibi fuit Barb. | 827 idem] illud [*om.* Bm^1] $\theta^1\gamma(-UP^2)$ | 830 huius] *om.* θ | 834-838 et² ... Petrum] *hom.* φ^3 | 835 et ... transitus] *hom.* $\varphi(-\varphi^3)$ | 836 ad] in $\theta^4\varphi$ | primo] *om.* θ | 837 transiverit $\theta(-Sv)B^1Va$ | ultimo] ulterius ρ^1 | 838 transivit $\theta^2\theta^3\varphi B^1$ | 840 secundum] sic ρ^1 | 841 Dispensatio ... est¹] *om.* α | credita $B^1(-T)\rho^1$] tradita $\pi(-B^1)$Barb.Va, data Sr | Petrus] potestatis ρ^1 | est²] *om.* θ; fuit φ, sit ψ | et prudens] *om.* α | 842 suam] *add.* ut det [dicit P^4] illis etc. πVa | 12] *add.* Dispensatio mihi [*om.* φ^3] credita est 1 [2 Bo] ad Corinthios 9 [1 ... 9 *om.* γ] α | 844 ubi] *om.* ρ^1 | divinarum φ] in Deo [ideo V^3] θ, de numero ψ, de iudicio β | 844-845 ordinationum] ordinationis π(-R)Sr

827-832 Leo the Great, *Sermo* 4.3 (PL 54: 151; CCL 138: 19) | 828 Matt. 16:19 | 840-841 1 Cor. 9:17 | 841-842 Luc. 12:42 | 843-853 Ps.-Dionysius, *De ecclesiastica hierarchia*, chap. 5, ed. P. Chevallier in *Dionysiaca* (Paris, 1937), 2: 1333-1334

num, vel secundum aliam translationem: *Ordinum secundum Deum inspicientium sublimissimus et novissimus idem*, ubi habet alia translatio: *Summus et ultimus idem*. Et sequitur: *Etenim in ipsum perficitur et impletur omnis hierarchie dispositio. Etenim omnem hierarchiam videmus in Jesum consummatam, sic unamquamque in proprium divinum summum sacerdotem*, ubi alia translatio habet: *Etenim in ipso terminatur et impletur omnis nostre hierarchie ornatus. Sicut enim universam hierarchiam videmus in Jesum terminatam, ita unamquamque in proprio divino hierarcha*. Ex quo habetur quod omnis hierarchia ecclesiastica, de qua loquitur ibi Dionysius, immediate reducitur ad Christum, quod non esset nisi omnis potestas in hierarchia ecclesiastica esset immediate a Christo. Unde commentator ibidem: *Ordo episcopalis pre ceteris ordinibus ecclesiasticis proximus est Deo et ultimus, idest consummativus aliorum, quia in ordine episcopali consummatur et impletur omnis ornatus ecclesiastice hierarchie. Sicut enim universa hierarchia in Domino Jesu consummatur, ita et quelibet specialis hierarchia terminatur in proprio hierarchico*. Ecce quod omnis hierarchia terminatur et reducitur in Christum. Unde et in eodem commento Maximi habetur: *Sicut universa hierarchia, angelica et humana, in Domino Jesu consummatur, sic et quelibet hierarchia in proprio hierarcha*. Sed constat quod hierarchia angelica reducitur absque medio in Christum, quia est caput hominum et angelorum secundum apostolum. Constat etiam quod quelibet hierarchia in proprium hierarcham sine medio reducitur. Quare tota hierarchia

desunt B^{2}P^{1}

845 translationem] ordinationem B^{1}Barb. | Ordinum] oportet [*add.* est U] divinum φ | 846 item π(-R)Barb.Sr | ubi] *om.* ρ^{1} | 847 item ρ^{1} | proficiscitur [perspicitur V^{3}, proficitur W] θφρ^{1} | 851 universam] omnem ρ^{1} | 852 Jesum] Deum θ^{4}γ, Deo θ^{2}θ^{3} | in^{2}] non πBarb.Va; *add.* unoquoque ρ^{1} | 853 hierarcha] hierarchiam [hierarcham V^{2}] θ, hierarchico Sr, hierarchia Barb. *et cet. mss.* | 853-855 de ... ecclesiastica] *hom.* ψ | 853-854 de ... Dionysius] *om.* φ | 854 qua] *add.* hierarchia ecclesiastica [*inv.* Va] πVa | 854-856 quod ... Christo] *hom.* ρ^{1} | 860 hierarchia] *om.* θ | 861 hierarchico RBarb.Va] hierarcha V^{1}V^{2}Uφ^{4}, hierarchia θ(-V^{1}V^{2})StBm^{1}φ^{5}Tρ^{1}Sr, hierarchio B^{1}(-T)P^{4}, hierarch. ψ | 864 hierarcha V^{1}BoUBm^{1}PrV^{4}Bm^{2}BrSr] hierarchia [*add.* hierarcha V^{3}(-P^{3})] θ(-V^{1}Bo)StWBlB^{1}Sz, hierarchico ψBarb., hierarchica π^{1}Va | 865 absque medio] immediate ρ^{1} | in] ad ρ^{1} | 867 proprium α(-BoSBm^{1}W)] propriam [propria R] SBm^{1}WπBarb.Va, proprio ρ^{1}, propriis Bo | hierarcham θ(-BoV^{5}Sv)φ(-Bm^{1}W)] hierarchiam BoV^{5}SvBm^{1}WπBarb.Va, hierarchic. ψ, patriarcha ρ^{1} | Quare] ergo et φ

856-864 Petrus Hispanus, *Expositio in librum De ecclesiastica hierarchia*, chap. 5, ed. P. M. Alonso in *Pedro Hispano. Exposicao sobre os livros do Beato Dionisio Areopagita* (Lisbon, 1957), pp. 123-242 at p. 201

ecclesiastica, per immediatam receptionem potestatis a Christo, immediate reducitur in Christum.

Solutio: ordo pontificum est divinus, non quia potestas iurisdictionis pontificalis sit a Deo immediate, sed quia ipse ordo est a solo Deo principaliter ipsum ordinem in animam imprimente. Item ordo pontificum est sublimissimus et novissimus, summus et ultimus, in quo perficitur omnis hierarchie dispositio, secundum potestatem caracteris, in qua omnes episcopi sunt equales, nec papa excellit. Et loquendo de reductione in Deum, que est per potestatem ordinis, ita immediate reducimur in Deum per quemlibet pontificem sicut per papam, cum papa non possit ministrare plura sacramenta quam minimus episcopus. Et de ista potestate conceditur quod in omnibus sit equaliter a Deo. Non autem loquitur de potestate iurisdictionis, in qua dicere quemlibet episcopum esse summum et sublimissimum est hereticum. Quia licet quilibet episcopus sit summus sacerdos, tamen unus solus est summus pontifex.

Quod dicunt, quod ex illis verbis Dionysii habetur quod omnis ecclesiastica hierarchia reducitur immediate ad Christum, verum est sicut in perficientem et consummantem principaliter in omni sacramenti datione, et sicut in finem ultimum, non in papam nec in alium purum hominem isto modo. Quod ulterius dicunt, quod hoc non esset nisi omnis potestas in ecclesiastica hierarchia esset immediate a Christo, non a Petro, dicendum quod non est verum nisi de potestate ordinis, nec sequitur aliquomodo de alia potestate. Nam quando dicit Dionysius quod omnis hierarchia consummatur et terminatur in Jesu, intelligendum est sicut in fine suo proprio, et sicut in primo et supremo hierarcha, a quo sunt omnes principatus hierarchie immediate vel mediate. Sed non oportet quod omnes immediate pro tempore post ascensionem, pro quo posuit hierarcham alium loco sui.

Quod dicit commentator, quod ordo episcopalis pre ceteris est proximus Deo et ultimus, omnia hec manifeste sonant potestatem ordinis, quam omnes concedunt esse immediate a Deo, et pontificalem esse digniorem

desunt B^2P^1

869 in $\theta^2\theta^3\psi\pi^1\sigma$] ad $\theta^4\varphi B^1\rho$ | 870 pontificatus ρ^1 | quod πBarb. | 871 est] *add.* scilicet θ | 873 est] *om.* πBarb. | et novissimus] *om.* ρ^1 | 879 illa ρ^1 | Non] nos φ | 880 loquimur φ | 881 esse] *om.* ρ^1 | 883 Quod^1] *add.* autem θ(-V^3) | 884 ad] in θ(-O) | 886 et] *om.* [non V^3] θ | in finem] *om.* φ | nec in] *om.* ρ^1 | 887 hominem] *add.* nisi ρ^1 | illo ρ^1 | 890 dicit] *add.* ibi ρ^1 | 892 hierarcha θ(-V^5P^3S)StPrV^4Br] hierarchia $V^5P^3S\varphi$(-StPrV^4)π^1Bm^2SzSr, hierarchico ψBarb., hierarchio B^1, hierarchica Va | 895 hierarcham θ(-V^5Sv)φ^3V^4Bm^2BrSr] hierarchiam V^5SvB$m^1\varphi^5$BlSz, hierarchicum ψBarb., hierar^{am} π^1, hierarchium B^1, hierarchicam Va

sacerdotali, et per consequens omni alia. Dico autem digniorem sacerdotali inquantum ipsam includit, et aliquid superaddit, sicut omne totum est dignius sua parte. Sed si ad invicem distinguerentur ut diverse partes, ordo sacerdotalis, qui est potestas conficiendi corpus et sanguinem Christi, et pontificalis, qui est potestas confirmandi et ordinandi, multo dignior esset ordo sacerdotalis per se quam pontificalis per se.

Quod dicunt postea, quod angelica hierarchia reducitur in Christum absque medio, non videtur esse verum. Quia infima hierarchia reducitur in Deum mediante media, et illa mediante suprema, et in qualibet hierarchia inferior ordo per superiorem, que reductio intelligitur, non quo ad divine essentie visionem, quam omnes angeli habent sine medio, sed quantum ad revelationem misteriorum gratie. Unde cum revelationes angeli non accipiant a Deo nisi mediante anima Christi – sicut dicitur in prologo super Apocalypsim: *Revelavit tota trinitas Christo secundum humanitatem. Christus vero Joanni per angelum*, et per consequens Christus angelo secundum illud in quem desiderant angeli prospicere utique ab eo illuminandi de misteriis Dei – si igitur omnes angeli reducerentur in Christum sine medio ab ipso purgandi, illuminandi et perficiendi, tunc angeli omnes reducerentur in Deum sine medio angelico, licet per medium Christum, quod est contra doctrinam Dionysii in *De angelica hierarchia*, ubi exponens illud Isaiae: *Quis est iste qui venit de Edom* etc., dicit quod est vox inferiorum angelorum ad superiores ab eis illuminandorum, qui et ipsi illuminantur a Christo dicente: *Ego qui loquor iustitiam* etc., Isaiae 63. Non ergo verum est quod angelica hierarchia reducatur in Christum sine medio.

Ad probationem: Christus caput est hominum et angelorum, dicendum quod hoc est ad oppositum. Quia in hominibus non quilibet reducitur immediate per seipsum in Christum, sed per sacerdotes et episcopos

desunt B²P¹

899-900 et ... sacerdotali] *hom.* θP²π(-R) | 899 consequens] *add.* dignitati [dignitate Bm¹W] φ | omnia ρ¹ | 901 distinguantur φ | 903 et ordinandi] *om.* φ | 904 est θ | ordo] *om.* α | 905 postea] *om.* α | quod²] *om.* θ | hierarchia [*add.* angelorum seu V⁴] angelica γρ¹, hierarchiam angelicam θ | reduci θ | 906 absque] *add.* omni ρ¹ | Quia] nam φ | 907 media ... mediante] *hom.* π(-R)Barb. | 910 quantum] *om.* φ | ministeriorum θ(-V¹BoV³)ρ¹Va | 914 Christus] *om.* φ | perspicere Bm¹Wφ⁴ | 916 purgandi] *add.* et θψ | 918 in] *om.* θ(-V³)φ | 919 exponendo ρ¹ | Isaiae] *add.* 63 ρ¹ | 925 oppositum] propositum nostrum [probationem nostram W] φ

912-913 *Liber vite. Biblia cum glosis ordinariis et interlinearibus*, Prefatio Gilberti Pictaviensis in Apocalypsim Joannis, 4: 1371 | 918-919 Cf. Ps.-Dionysius, *De caelesti hierarchia*, chap. 7 (*Dionysiaca* 2: 853-855) | 919-920, 921-922 Is. 63:1 | 926-927 Cf. Ps.-Dionysius, *De ecclesiastica hierarchia*, chap. 5 (*Dionysiaca* 2: 1330ff.)

reducuntur inferiores, secundum Dionysium. Quod ulterius dicunt quod tota hierarchia ecclesiastica reducitur in Christum immediate per immediatam receptionem potestatis a Christo, de potestate ordinis verum est, non de alia. Ad probationem quod quelibet hierarchia reducitur in proprium hierarcham sine medio, dicendum quod verum est de hierarcha infimo, non de summo, ad quem fit reductio per medium, que etiam mediatio potest esse per collationem potestatis, sicut papa dat potestatem legato suo vel delegato, et ille subdelegato. Et isto modo papa dat episcopo, et ille curato.

Septimo idem patet per Hieronymum, *Contra Jovinianum*, qui dicit: *Supra Petrum fundatur ecclesia, licet idipsum super ceteros apostolos fiat.*

Solutio: ecclesia fundata est super Petrum dupliciter. Unomodo quia super fidem Petri, qua pre omnibus et pro omnibus respondit: *Tu es Christus, filius Dei vivi*, et super hanc petram fidei fundata est ecclesia. Sed quia omnes apostoli sicut Petrus predicaverunt fidem, ideo etiam ipsi cum Petro sunt ecclesie fundamenta, secundum illud Apocalypsis 21: *Murus civitatis habens fundamenta duodecim, et in ipsis nomina duodecim apostolorum.* Sed non eque solida, quia sola ecclesia Petri non potest errare a fide. Secundo modo fundata est ecclesia super Petrum quia super potestatem Petri, idest potestas ecclesie super potestatem Petri, quia totum fundamentum potestatis ecclesie est super hoc quod Petro est promissum et datum pro ecclesia, 24 q. 1 *Quecumque.* Et sic non est fundata super alios apostolos, quia tota potestas ecclesie fuit Petro collata, nec habet ecclesia aliquam potestatem iurisdictionis nisi quam Christus Petro concessit.

desunt B^{2}P^1

931 hierarcham θ^1(-V^{5}S)φ(-Bm^{1}W)Bm^{2}BrSr] hierarchiam SBm^{1}WSz, hierarchum θ^2, hierarchicum ψP^{4}Barb., hierarchicam RVa, hierarchium B^1, hierarch. V^5 | hierarcha θ(-OV^{5}S)φ(-W)Bm^{2}BrSr] hierarchia OV^{5}SWπ(-P^4)Sz, hierarchico ψBarb., hierarchica P^{4}Va | 932 quem] *add.* quidem supremum φ | 934 vel] et ille B^{1}Barb. | isto] illo ρ^1 | 935 ille] *om.* φ | 937 Supra] super ρ^1 | petram $\theta^4\varphi$(-St) | 939 qua] quia π(-R)Barb. | 940 fidei] *om.* φ | fundata] edificata φ(-φ^5) | 943 duodecim^2] *om.* θ | 945 super^{1+2}] supra π(-R)Barb. | 948 per ecclesiam πBarb.

936-937 Jerome, *Adversus Jovinianum* 1.26 (PL 23: 258) | 939-940 Matt. 16:16 | 942-944 Apoc. 21:14 | 948 The reference should be *Quodcumque*: Gratian, C.24 q.1 c.6.

Quintus Articulus

Quintus articulus principalis est de potestate episcoporum, habens tres conclusiones principales, quarum prima est de potestate ordinis episcopalis, secunda de potestate iurisdictionis quantum ad personas ipsorum episcoporum, tertia de potestate ecclesiarum cathedralium quibus presunt.

Prima Conclusio

Prima ergo conclusio, de causa immediata potestatis ordinis episcopalis, est quod omnes episcopi habent potestatem ordinis eque immediate et eque perfectam in sua essentia, et eque virtuosam in suo effectu, a Christo sicut habet papa.

Primum autem dictum, scilicet de equalitate immediationis, sic patet. Quia sicut omnes alii episcopi habent istam potestatem a Christo non nisi mediante sua consecratione et episcopo consecrante uno vel pluribus, sic nec papa, qui ad hoc quod sit verus episcopus ita indiget consecrari sicut minimus episcopus. Quia ipse papa non est super sacramenta, sed sub eis, et subiacet Christo sicut et alii Christiani, et legibus et ordinationibus Christi. Unde sicut si non fuisset confirmatus indigeret sacramento vero confirmationis sicut alii, ita si non erat prius in episcopum consecratus indiget consecrari sicut alii. Nec potest ipse dispensare in substantia consecrationis, licet possit dispensare in ritu et sollemnitate circa se, sicut nec circa alium, quia consecratio episcopalis non est quid sacramentale tantum ab ecclesia institutum, sicut est consecratio abbatis, ecclesie vel altaris, sed est verum sacramentum, idest pars et complementum ordinis sacerdotalis, qui est pars principalis et finalis ordinis. In hac autem immediatione cause plus habuit Petrus ceteris episcopis et successoribus

desunt $B^2P^1V^6$

2 principalis] *om.* $B^1\rho^1\sigma$ | 3 principales quarum] *om.* π(-R)Barb. | 4 personam ρ^1 | 5 quibus] *add.* ipsi [*add.* episcopi Bo] θ | 7-8 episcopalis ... ordinis] *hom.* π(-R)Barb. | 8 immediatam [immediata Bl] $\theta\varphi$ | et] *om.* θ | 9 a Christo] *om.* ρ^1 | 12 illam ρ^1 | 14 nec] et [etiam V^4] φ | qui] quo φ | 15 papa] *om.* φ | supra θ | 16 Christiani] *om.* π(-R) | 17 vero ρSr] *om.* θB^1Va; vere $\gamma\pi^1$ | 18 ita] sic $\theta\psi$; *add.* et ρ^1 | 19 sicut] *add.* et π(-R) | Nec] non ρ^1 | 24 qui $\varphi P^2 R\sigma$] que $\theta V^7\pi$(-R)ρ | 25 cause] aliquid φ, cure ρ^1 | episcopis] apostolis φ | et] etiam θ

suis, quia ipse fuit a Christo factus episcopus verus sine alio ministro, et sine exteriori unctione, per hec verba: *Pasce oves meas, pasce agnos meos.* Idest accipe potestatem perfectiores ordinandi ad generandum filios ecclesie, et imperfectiores confirmandi ad pugnam visibilem et invisibilem – quia pastus animali ministrat materiam generationis et fortificat ipsum –, que duplex potestas integrat essentialiter potestatem episcopalem quantum ad id quod est sibi proprium, et quod addit ad potestatem sacerdotalem. Item accipe potestatem custodiendi, regendi et disponendi ovile meum quantum ad omnia necessaria et utilia ad salutem, directe et indirecte, principaliter et secundario, que est proprie potestas papalis. Unde Christus per illa verba fecit eum simul et semel verum episcopum et verum papam. Item in hoc plus habuit Petrus quam omnes alii episcopi, etiam successores sui, quod ab ipso processerunt omnes alii episcopi, etiam quo ad potestatem ordinis, inquantum ab ipso Petro, primo et solo episcopo a Christo facto, omnes alii mediate vel immediate sunt postea ordinati, quod non potest dici de aliquo successore ipsius, quia omnes sunt a puro homine ordinati, nec ab illis sunt omnes alii ordinati.

Secundo dico quod omnes episcopi habent istam potestatem ordinis a Christo eque plenam, magnam, integram et perfectam quantum ad suam essentiam sicut papa, quia ordo episcopalis in sua essentia non recipit magis nec minus. Unde a quocumque habetur, totus et totaliter habetur. Unde plenitudo potestatis, quam habet papa super alios, non pertinet ad potestatem ordinis in qua non precellit alios sed equatur eis, sed ad potestatem iurisdictionis in qua preeminet universis. Unde sicut alii episcopi, qui habent potestatem limitatam et coartatam, possunt ea que sunt iurisdictionis ante suam consecrationem equaliter sicut post, *De electione* c. *Transmissam*, sic papa potest omnia que pertinent ad plenitudinem potestatis sive talem statum. Inde est quod papa est verus papa ante consecrationem, quamvis electus et confirmatus in episcopum

desunt $B^2P^1V^6$

26 verus episcopus α | ministerio π(-R)Barb. | 30 animali ρ^1] *om.* α; animalis σ, alia B^1, al. π^1, aliis Barb. | 31 ipsum] *add.* fetum φ | potestatem essentialiter α | 32 id] illud $B^1\rho^1$ | et] *add.* quantum ad id θ | 33 regendi [*add.* et θ] custodiendi α | 34 salutem] sacramentum θ | et²] vel θ | 35 propria ρ^1 | 38 etiam] et θ | ipso] eo θ | processerant ρ^1 | 40 sunt] fuerunt φ(-W) | 42 nec ... ordinati] *hom.* ρ^1 | illo φ | 43 habent] *om.* $\theta\varphi$ | ordinis] *add.* habent φ | 45 essentiam] *add.* receperunt θ | recipit] *add.* nec $\varphi(-\varphi^5)$ | 46 nec] et ρ^1 | 48 excellit [excedit Bo] θ | sed²] *add.* quantum θ, pertinet φ | 50 coartatam] ecclesiasticam φ | 51 equaliter] *om.* ρ^1 | 53 sive] *add.* ad θ | 54 quamvis] quamquam non ρ^1

27 Joan. 21:15-17 | 51-52 X. 1.6.15

non sit verus episcopus ante consecrationem, quia episcopus principaliter est nomen ordinis. Unde sicut non est sacerdos ante ordinationem sacerdotalem, sic nec episcopus ante episcopalem. Sed papatus est nomen dignitatis, sicut cura, decanatus, archidiaconatus et huiusmodi. Unde sicut aliquis est verus curatus, decanus, archidiaconus etiam antequam habeat ordinem debitum illi dignitati, ita est papa verus et essentialiter ex quo rite electus assensit, antequam consecretur in episcopum, potens omnia que potest papa ut papa, idest que sunt iurisdictionis. Unde potest facere personas habiles et inhabiles ad matrimonium, statuere et destituere consecrationes que non sunt sacramenta, non episcopo committere, quod non potest simplex episcopus nec ante nec post consecrationem suam, *De consecratione ecclesie* c. *Aqua*. Item indulgentias dare, gratias facere et omnia que ad solam iurisdictionem pertinent.

Tertio dico quod omnes episcopi habent a Christo potestatem ordinis eque virtuosam in suo proprio effectu sicut papa, quia *idem manens idem semper est natum facere idem*, 2 *De generatione*. Unde cum sit idem caracter specie, non maior nec minor in ceteris sicut in papa, quidquid potest papa per solum ordinem episcopalem hoc potest etiam quilibet episcopus. Dico autem in suo proprio effectu ad differentiam eius quod potest ex adiuncto. Verbi gratia: confirmare et ordinare sunt propria episcoporum de iure divino. Unde in his non minus potest minimus episcopus quam papa. Sed facere talia per alium includit potestatem ordinis et iurisdictionis. Unde, ratione inclusi, hic plus potest papa quam simplex episcopus, quia consecratus potest committere simplici sacerdoti confirmationem, 95 d. *Pervenit*, quod non potest simplex episcopus, *De consuetudine* c. *Quanto*.

desunt B^{2}P^{1}V^{6}

57 episcopalem] *add.* consecrationem ψB^{1}Barb. | nomen] *add.* domini [dominii Sz] et [*om.* Bm^{2}] ρ^{1} | 58 cura] curatus ψB^{1}Barb.Sr; *add.* seu pastoratus [pastoria Bm^{1}] φ | 59 curatus] *om.* ρ^{1}; *add.* seu pastor φ | decanus] *add.* vel $\theta^{2}\theta^{3}$, et θ^{4}V^{7} | 61 potens] potest φ | 62 Unde potest θBarb.] *om.* Sr; unde $\psi\beta$(-SrBarb.), ut [unde Bl] est φ | 63 inhabiles] non habiles θ | et^{2} θ(-S)Uψ] *om.* Sφ(-U)β | 65 consecrationem [confirmationem O] suam θ] *om.* Barb. *et cet. mss.* | 66 ecclesie] *add.* vel altaris α | A quo γ | et] *om.* π(-R)Barb. | 70 est] *add.* aptum ψB^{1}Barb. | natum] *om.* θ(-Bo) | natum est facere [*inv.* Bm^{1}] φ | generatione] *add.* et corruptione θ | 72 solum] solam [solum S] ordinationem vel θ | 75 minimus] *om.* π(-R)Barb. | 77 ordinis et] *om.* θ | hoc ρ^{1} | 79 95 d. Pervenit] quod est contra predicta θ | non] etiam nunquam [*inv.* Sv] θ | 79-84 De ... predicta] *om.* θ

65-66 X. 3.40.9 | 69-70 Aristotle, *De generatione et corruptione* 2.10 (336a27-28). Cf. *Les Auctoritates Aristotelis: Un florilège médiéval*, ed. J. Hamesse (Louvain and Paris, 1974), p. 170. | 79 Gratian, D.95 c.11 | 79-80 X. 1.4.4

Sed contra hoc arguitur, quia illa commissio aut pertinet ad potestatem ordinis aut iurisdictionis. Si ordinis, cum sit equalis in omnibus episcopis, omnis episcopus poterit committere non episcopo confirmationem, quod est contra predicta. Si autem pertinet ad potestatem iurisdictionis, tunc posset committere papa antequam esset consecratus sicut et alia iurisdictionis. Hoc autem est inconveniens, quia si posset per alium, posset etiam per seipsum. Consequens est falsum; ergo et antecedens.

Probatio consequentie, quia virtus non est maior in effectu quam in causa. Si ergo simplex sacerdos alius a papa, virtute sibi commissa, et per consequens a virtute papali causata, potest confirmare, multo magis papa existens simplex sacerdos, virtute papali existente in eo formaliter, potest hoc facere. Si dicatur contra hoc: *quia inter dantem et accipientem debet esse distinctio personalis*, *De institutionibus* c. ultimo. Unde cum simplex sacerdos non possit ista nisi ex dono pape, et papa non possit sibiipsi aliquid dare, per consequens nec potest ipse hoc facere. Dicendum quod papa nihil potest sibi dare, sed eo quod habet a Deo potest uti non minus per se quam per alium. Unde si per simplicem sacerdotem papa non episcopus posset confirmare, multo magis ipse, idest simplex sacerdos, per se posset confirmare. Probatio antecedentis, scilicet quod papa simplex sacerdos non episcopus non possit per se confirmare, quia papa non potest mutare naturam sacramentorum a Christo institutam. Sed natura confirmationis a Christo instituta, sicut patet exemplo apostolorum, est quod confirmatio non fiat nisi a potestate episcopali, *De consecratione* d. 5 *Manus*. Ergo nisi sit episcopus confirmans aut mandans, impossibile est quod sit confirmatio.

Dicendum quod illa commissio non pertinet ad alteram potestatem, sed ad utramque simul iunctam. Unde nisi committens sit verus papa et verus episcopus, non potest committere non episcopo confirmationem, que

desunt B²P¹V⁶

81 hoc] *om.* φ(-Bm¹) | 82 equalis] episcopalis π, equaliter ρ¹ | 83 potest ρ¹ | 85 alia] *add.* consecrationis et θ²Bo, consecrationis θ⁴, consecratione V⁵ | 86 est] esset θ | si] *add.* papa θ | 89 sacerdos] *om.* ρ¹ | papa] *add.* in φ | 90 a virtute] auctoritate φ | causata] *om.* θ | 90-91 causata ... papali] sibi in ρ¹ | 91 eodem θ | 92 facere] *add.* sed θ | hoc²] *om.* σ | quod α | 93 ultimo] finali θ | 94 illa ρ¹ | pape] proprie [pape Bm¹] loquendo [locando W] φ | sibi [*om.* Bm¹] φ | 95 donare θ | non θVa | ipse] *om.* θB¹Barb.Va | 98 idest P²π¹ρ¹] scilicet [si O; *add.* et φ³] θφ, etiam B¹, idem σ, et Barb. | simplex] papa φ | 99 scilicet] *om.* ρ¹ | 101 immutare θ | 104 confirmans] consecrans [consecratus WV⁴] φ | 106 Dicendum] *add.* est ergo θ | potestatem] partem ρ¹; *add.* tantum θB¹ | 107 nisi] si θ | 108 non¹] *om.* θ(-S)

92-93 X. 3.7.7 | 103-104 Gratian, *De cons.* D.5 c.4

semper fit virtute episcopali, vel sola, quando fit ab episcopo, vel episcopali et papali, quandocumque fit a non episcopo. Unde tunc plus potest simplex sacerdos non papa quam simplex sacerdos papa. Quia simplex sacerdos non papa potest confirmare ex commissione alicuius, puta pape episcopi. Simplex autem sacerdos papa non potest confirmare, nec iure suo, cum non sit episcopus, nec ex commissione alterius, quia non est alius papa, nec ex commissione sua sibi facta, non solum quia non potest sibi dare, sed quia non posset dare alteri, ut visum est.

Secunda Conclusio

Secunda conclusio principalis huius articuli de potestate iurisdictionis episcopalis, quantum ad personas ipsorum episcoporum, est quod omnis potestas quam habent episcopi communiter ligandi et solvendi, et quecumque alia superaddita ordini episcopali, quam scilicet habet in utroque foro episcopus habens populum sibi subditum super episcopum qui nullos habet subditos, est a papa et non solum subest pape. Et ista patet sex rationibus, primo ex his que dicta sunt duobus modis.

Uno modo, quia papa se habet ad episcopos sicut Petrus se habuit ad apostolos. Sed apostoli omnem potestatem iurisdictionis habuerunt a Petro. Ergo episcopi omnem huiusmodi potestatem habent a papa. Maior patet, quia sicut episcopi tenent locum apostolorum quem finaliter habuerunt, 68 d. *Quorum*, sic papa tenet locum Petri in plenitudine potestatis, ut dictum est in secunda conclusione precedentis articuli. Et probatur iterum, quia Cyrillus Hierosolimitanus patriarcha, ex persona Christi loquens Petro, dixit sic: *Tu cum fine, ego sine fine. Cum omnibus quos loco tui ponam, pleno et perfecto sacramento et auctoritate, cum eis ero sicut sum et tecum*. Minor patet per ea que dicta sunt in secunda parte

desunt B^{2}P^{1}V^6

109 ab episcopo] episcopo etiam a [*om.* BoV^2] non [domino O] episcopo θ, a solo episcopo [Christo Bm^2] ρ^1 | 110 episcopali] *add.* simul φ | et] vel ρ^1 | quando θ | a non episcopo] ab episcopo papa non episcopo scilicet simplici sacerdoti θ | 111 papa^1] *add.* in hoc θ | 114 nec^1] *om.* θ | 115 ex] *om.* φ | 116 sed] hoc ρ^1 | nec $\psi\rho^1$Va | posset] *add.* etiam θ | dare] *om.* ρ^1 | 119 quantum ... episcoporum] *om.* ρ^1 | ipsorum] eorum scilicet θ | 123 nullum θ | subditum θ | et ... pape] *hom.* θ | non solum] simpliciter φ | illa ρ^1 | 124 prima π(-R)Barb. | 125 quod π(-P^4)Barb. | 127 habuerunt π(-R) | 129 Quorum] per totum θ | 132 Tu ... ego] sicut tecum [*add.* est W] sic ero φ | ego] *add.* sum ψB^{1}Barb. | 134 sum] *om.* θ

129 Gratian, D.68 c.6 | 130-134 Et ... tecum: cf. Pierre de la Palu, *Tractatus de potestate papae* 1.3, p. 190 | 131-134 *Contra er. Gr.*, p. 324

octave conclusionis <secundi> articuli, ubi probatum est quod omnes apostoli post Christi ascensionem receperunt a Petro omnem potestatem iurisdictionis quam habuerunt.

Secundo probatur sic eadem conclusio ex predictis. Omnis potestas iurisdictionis ecclesiastice procedit a papa. Sed omnis potestas iurisdictionis in episcopis ut sic est potestas ecclesiastica. Ergo omnis talis est a papa. Maior patet per illud quod probatum est in tertia conclusione precedentis articuli. Minor patet, quia episcopus est sponsus sue ecclesie. Unde et anulum portat.

Tertio patet idem sic. Ab illo habet aliquis potestatem iurisdictionis a quo habet principaliter et perfecte statum cui debetur illa potestas, a quocumque illa potestas illi statui sit annexa. Sed omnis episcopus et curatus habet a papa principaliter et perfecte statum cui debetur potestas iurisdictionis. Ergo omnes episcopi et curati habent a papa potestatem iurisdictionis quam habent inquantum sunt episcopi et curati.

Maior patet, quia quidquid est causa cause est causa causati, ut probatur 2 *Metaphysice*. Unde si alicui castro debetur alta iustitia, undecumque sit illi acquisita, et rex det illud castrum alicui cum suis pertinentiis, ad quem regem de iure quocumque pertinet dare illud castrum pleno iure, licet rex non dederit illam iurisdictionem illi castro, sed forte fuerit sibi acquisita antequam veniret ad manum regis, nihilominus tamen ille cui rex dat castrum tenet et habet utrumque a rege, scilicet castrum et pertinentias, et per consequens iustitiam ei annexam, dato quod non omnes predecessores habuerunt illud a rege. Dico autem principaliter et perfecte, quia secus si accidentaliter et adminiculative, sicut presentatus ad aliquod beneficium non habet ius illius a presentante, sed ab instituente qui confert. Nec episcopus habet perfecte iura episcopatus a canonicis eligentibus, quia indiget confirmatione, a quo magis habet quam ab electoribus.

Minor patet, quia omnis episcopatus cum suis iuribus integre et perfecte, a quocumque habeatur, aut habetur a papa immediate providente, aut habetur secundum ordinationem factam a papa, et que

desunt $B^2P^1V^6$

135 octave ψB^1Barb.] ante θ^2, prime Bo, secunde P^4, quinte *cet. mss.* | secundi] primi Barb. *et mss.* | 141 illud] id ψRBarb.σ | 146-147 et curatus] *om.* α | 147-148 principaliter ... papa] *hom.* ρ^1 | 151 castro] *om.* ρ^1 | debetur] *add.* aliqua [alia W] $\theta\varphi$ | alta] *om.* φ | 152 illi] illa θ | 153 quocumque] *add.* modo ρ^1 | 154 fuit $\theta^2\theta^3$St$Bm^1W\rho^1$Sr | 155 manus θ | 156 castrum[1]] *om.* φ | et pertinentia ρ^1, cum pertinentiis suis θ | 158 habuerunt vel habuerint θ^2, habuissent vel habuerint [habuerunt Bo] θ^3V^3, habuissent Sv, habuerint $\varphi(-\varphi^5)$Barb.Va | 161 episcopatus] *om.* θ | 162 confirmatore $\varphi(-Bm^1)$

151 Aristotle, *Metaphysica* a.2 (994a10-15)

habet vigorem a papa. Et per consequens quicumque habet episcopatum habet ipsum a papa, immediate vel mediante lege sua, et integre et perfecte, et hec fuit minor.

Unde sequitur conclusio, quod dato quod status episcopatus in se non sit a papa sed a Christo, dato etiam quod illi statui non a papa sed a Christo sit annexa potestas iurisdictionis, quia tamen papa dat huic persone illum statum integre et perfecte et principaliter, vel per se immediate vel mediantibus electoribus et confirmante, qui a papa habent ius hoc faciendi et modum, et per consequens iste qui sic habet habet a papa. Dato quod ille status non habeat illam potestatem a papa, et dato etiam quod essent aliqui alii apostoli vel alii qui alio modo habuissent et non a papa, sed a Christo vel aliter, tamen omnes qui secundum formam iuris papalis dignitates ecclesiasticas assequuntur non possunt dici non eas habere a papa, nisi dicendo quod non habent eas iuste, nec secundum iura canonica, et quod non habent canonicam institutionem. Quia nullum ius divinum ordinat modum nec formam dignitates ecclesiasticas obtinendi, sed relinquit hec particularia iuri positivo. Unde ab auctore huius iuris habentur ista a quocumque canonice possidentur. In quo apparet per oppositum quod non solum papatus non est ab homine, sed a Deo, immo etiam quod nec habetur ex dono hominis, sed ex dono Dei solum. Unde omnis alia dignitas ecclesiastica habetur perfecte ex dono hominis, sed ista ex solo dono Dei, quod sic patet.

Constat enim quod papa, si haberet papatum ab aliquo homine, quod haberet illum a cardinalibus, quia ipsi habent maius ius in conferendo papatum vel cooperando ad illum habendum quam tota reliqua ecclesia Dei, undecumque illud habeant. Nam si aliquis eligeretur in papam a duabus partibus cardinalium, et tota ecclesia Dei alia et totus mundus eligeret alium, electus a cardinalibus esset verus papa. Sed papa non habet

desunt $B^2P^1V^6$

166 quicumque] qui θ | 167 papa] *add.* mediate vel θ | vel] ut [*om.* θ^4] videlicet θ | 168 hoc π(-R) | 169 status] *om.* θ | 171 huic] illi θ | 173 qui] quia θ(-BoV^5V^3), scilicet ρ^1 | habent θRσ] habuit φ, habet $\psi\pi$(-R)ρ | 174 iste] *om.* θ; ille ρ^1 | habet[2]] *om.* Sv$\varphi\pi$(-R)Bm^2 | habet a papa $V^3\psi$R$\rho^2\sigma$] a papa habet $\theta^2\theta^3$Barb. | 174-175 Dato ... papa] *hom.* ρ^1 | 175 ille] iste θ | habet πBarb. | 176 alii[1]] *om.* φ | apostoli] *om.* θB^1 | vel alii] *om.* $\theta B^1\rho^1$ | 178 dici non] *om.* θ | habere] *add.* nisi θ | 179 nisi] nec ρ^1 | eas] *om.* α | 180 Quia] nam [non S] θ | 181 nec] vel π(-R)Barb. | 182 sed] quia θ | hec] secundum ρ^1 | Unde] nam θ | actore π(-P^4)ρVa | 183 habent θ, licet videtur ρ^1 | illa ρ^1 | quacumque ρ^1, quo θ | 184 a] ex θ(-OS) | 185 non γB^1Va | sed] *add.* ista π(-R)Barb. | solo π(-R)Barb. | 186 alia] *om.* φ | 187 sola ex φ | 188 enim] *om.* θ | 190 vel] *add.* in θ | 191 habuerunt θ^2BoV^5, habuerint V^2, habetur πBarb. | 192 alia ... mundus] *om.* θ | 193 papa[2]] *om.* θ

a cardinalibus qui se elegerunt ius papatus integre et perfecte. Ergo a nullo homine illud habet.

Maior patet per illud quod dictum est, et per illud quod post electionem cardinalium, ad hoc quod electus sit papa verus non requiritur confirmatio humana, nec per consequens alia collatio ab homine. Requiritur tamen consensus electi. Constat autem quod consensus suus nihil dat sibi, tum quia nemo potest dare quod non habet, nec sibi nec alteri, tum etiam quia *inter dantem et accipientem debet esse distinctio personalis, De institutionibus* c. ultimo. Unde consensus electi bene est causa sine qua non sibi acquiritur ius, sed nunquam est causa principalis per quam sibi acquiritur. Restat ergo quod, si habet ab homine papatum, habet a cardinalibus, que fuit maior.

Probatio minoris, quia quanto aliquis habet minus ius in re, tanto minus potest eam dare, quantum est de se et de lege communi. Nam quod creditor potest alienare pignus cuius non est dominus, maritus autem alienare non potest fundum dotalem cuius est dominus, hoc est ex speciali legis ordinatione, certis de causis concedentis primum unde fit legis auctoritate, et prohibentis secundum. Sed canonici habent maius ius in episcopatu, sede vacante, quam cardinales in papatu. Quia apud capitulum, sede vacante, residet tota potestas et iurisdictio episcopi de iure communi, nisi in paucis casibus, *De maioritate et obedientia, His que* in fine, c. *Cum olim, De hereticis* c. *Ad abolendam* in principio. Econtrario autem potestas et iurisdictio pape, sede vacante, non devolvitur ad cardinales nisi in paucis casibus, ut in *Clem. De electione* c. *Ne Romani*. Sed canonici eligentes episcopum non dant sibi ius episcopatus integre et perfecte, sed indiget confirmatione superioris. Ergo nec cardinales eligendo dant ius pape, sed indiget superiore confirmante et dante. Et quia *quod minus est a meliore benedicitur*, ad Hebreos 8, et papatu seu papa

desunt $B^2P^1V^6$

194 se] eum θV^7B^1, ipsum P^4 | 195 habet illud $\theta\varphi^1$W | 196 et ... quod] *om.* π(-R)Barb. | 197 quod] *add.* papa θ | verus papa $\theta\varphi$ | requireretur π(-R) | 198 alia] aliqua φ(-W) | collatio] approbatio φ | 200 quod non habet] *om.* ρ^1 | 201 recipientem $\theta^2V^2V^5\rho^1$ | 206 quia] *om.* φ | habet aliquis α | ius] *om.* αVa | 208 non] *om.* ρ^1 | autem θ] vero ψ; *om.* Barb. *et cet. mss.* | 210 certis] cunctis ρ^1 | 210-211 unde ... auctoritate] *om.* θ^2V^5; ut sit θ^1(-V^5) | 212 episcopatum φ | papatum φ | 215 olim] Cayn φ | 216 sede vacante] *om.* θ | 220 eligendo] *add.* papam ei [*om.* Sv] θ | ius ... dante] *hom.* φ | superiore ... dante] confirmatione vel datione superioris et dante [ante $\theta^2\theta^3$] istam [illum Sv] confirmationem [infirmationem P^3] etc. θ | Et^2] *om.* ρ^1; sed θ | 221 benedicitur] unde dicitur φ

201-202 X. 3.7.7 | 214-215 X. 1.33.11 | 215 X. 1.33.14 | X. 5.7.9 | 217 *Clem.* 1.3.2 | 221 The reference should be Heb. 7:7.

nullus homo purus nec aliquis status ecclesie est maior nec superior, sed solus Deus, ideo impossibile est quod papa ab homine puro vel ab aliquo statu hominum confirmetur, sive quod ille status alicui detur et confirmetur nisi a solo Deo. Unde ceteri prelati ab homine ponuntur in suo statu. Sed Deus per se ponit hominem in statu papali, sicut innuit auctoritas Cyrilli inducta, quando dicit ex persona Christi Petro: *Cum omnibus quos loco tui ponam.*

Quarta ratio talis est. Omnis potestas iurisdictionis in aliqua communitate, in quacumque persona sit particulariter et coartate, est totaliter et perfecte ab illo qui preest illi communitati cum plenitudine potestatis. Sed papa preest toti ecclesie cum plenitudine potestatis in spiritualibus. Ergo omnis potestas iurisdictionis spiritualis in omnibus personis ecclesiasticis tenetur et habetur a papa.

Maior patet, quia omnes de regno subditi regis illud in quo ei subduntur tenent a rege, et recognoscunt se ab eo tenere. Sed non totaliter et simpliciter habent ab eo, quia non habet in eos plenitudinem potestatis. Sed in baillivos, prepositos et alios quos ipse ad libitum instituit et destituit, dicitur ipse habere plenitudinem potestatis, et isti simpliciter et totaliter habent officia sua ab eo. Moyses etiam presidens synagoge cum plenitudine potestatis illi tempori debita ponebat omnes officiales, et ab eo habebant omnes iudiciariam potestatem, Exodi 18. Romani etiam, quando perfecte dominabantur mundo, in omnibus provinciis ponebant presides, prefectos, rectores, proconsules et legatos, quorum institutio ab eis totaliter dependebat, non sinentes quemquam regnare iure suo, estimantes se aliter non habere plenitudinem regiminis perfectam. Unde et Judei dicebant, confitentes monarchiam Romanorum: Non habemus regem nisi Cesarem, Joannis 19. Legitur etiam Judith 3 quod Nabuchodonosor preceperat principi militie sue Holoferni, *ut omnes deos terre exterminaret, videlicet ut ipse solus deus diceretur ab his nationibus que possent*

desunt $B^2P^1V^6$

223 puro vel] ponitur ut ρ^1 | 224 sive] et θ | 224-225 alicui ... Deo] *om.* ρ^1 | 226 per se] *om.* θ | 227 quando dicit] *om.* ρ^1 | 229-230 universitate φ | 230-231 est ... illo] est [et S] sub illo θ, ab illo est φ, tenetur et habetur ab illo ψ | 230 totaliter] *om.* π(-R)Barb. | 235 regis] regi θ | ei] *om.* φ | 237 in eos] *om.* ρ^1 | 239 et^1] idest ρ^1 | 241 debita γSr] *om.* B^1Barb.; debite θVa, debitam $\pi^1\rho^1$ | 242 omnes] *om.* ρ^1 | quando] *om.* θ | 243 dominabantur] *add.* toti θB^1 | mundo] *add.* et θ | ponebant in [*om.* St] omnibus provinciis α | 245 existimantes $\theta\pi$(-R)Barb. | 246 et] *om.* θ | 247 confitentes] *om.* φ; propter $\theta\psi$ | monarchiam] *add.* esse φ | 250 videlicet] *om.* θ | his] omnibus θ

227-228 *Contra er. Gr.*, p. 324 | 242 Ex. 18:25-26 | 248 Joan. 19:15 | 248-251 Judith 3:13

Holofernis potentia subiugari, quasi non reputaret se plene et perfecte preesse si cum eo alius preesset qui ab eo suam prelationem non haberet nec recognosceret, sicut Dei est non habere superiorem. Unde ex communi animi conceptione omnium qui intelligunt quid est quod dicitur per nomen plenitudinis potestatis, habetur quod ille solus habet plenitudinem potestatis et iurisdictionis in aliqua communitate qui sic toti preest quod ab ipso procedit omnis iurisdictio et potestas ad alios qui sub ipso presunt in illa communitate, et hec fuit maior.

Minor patet, et quantum ad preeminentiam pape super totam ecclesiam, et quantum ad plenitudinem potestatis in spiritualibus, per ea que dicta sunt de Petro in primo articulo, secunda et tertia conclusione, et per ea que dicta sunt de papa in quarto articulo, prima et secunda conclusione. Sed hec preeminentia et plenitudo non est quantum ad potestatem ordinis in qua est equalis aliis, ut dictum est, sed tantum quantum ad potestatem iurisdictionis. Unde sequitur conclusio, quod licet potestas ordinis in aliis non sit ab eo simpliciter, tamen omnis potestas iurisdictionis in quibuscumque personis ecclesiasticis, et per consequens episcopis, est totaliter et simpliciter a papa. Et qui negant se tenere ab eo suam potestatem, simpliciter dicentes se habere a solo Deo, quamvis recognoscant eum superiorem aliis verbis, tamen hoc ipso negant se ei subditos, sicut patet in simili. Quia illi de regno non recognoscunt regem superiorem suum, nec se subditos regi in aliquo, nisi in eo quod tenent ab eo. Unde in Franco allodio, quod dicunt se a nullo tenere nisi a Deo, dicunt se non subdi nisi Deo, nec in illo recognoscunt superiorem nisi Deum. Illi ergo prelati qui dicunt se non tenere a papa potestatem et auctoritatem suam, sed a solo Deo, eo ipso negant se subesse pape in illa, et sic negant papam primatem in ecclesia, qui est error Grecorum. Ulterius autem principes et barones, qui in suis terris recognoscunt regem superiorem, sed dicunt se non habere suas iurisdictiones et dominia ex sola regis commissione, sicut prepositi et baillivi, sed dicunt in eis se habere ius proprium a parentibus vel aliunde acquisitum, eo ipso negant

desunt $B^2P^1V^6$

257 iurisdictio] auctoritas φ | 258 hec] illa φ, hoc π(-R) | 261-262 et² ... conclusione] *hom.* ρ^1 | 264 equaliter ρ^1 | 265-266 Unde ... iurisdictionis] *hom.* ρ^1 | 265 in aliis] quantum ad alios φ | 268 tenere] habere φ | ab eo] *om.* φ | 271 cognoscunt φ(-W) | 273 Unde] ut φ | 274 dicunt ... Deo] *hom.* φ | non] nulli θ | recognoscere θ, recognoscant ψ | 276 Deo] *add.* ipsi ρ^1 | 276-277 se ... negant] *hom.* Wψ | 276 pape in illa] *om.* φ | 277 papam] illum $\theta^2\theta^3$, illum ipsum V^3, ipsum Sv | 280 sicut] *add.* habent φ | in eis] *om.* θ | 280-281 in eis [ea Sr] se habere Rσ] se in eis habere γ(-Bm^1W)B^1Barb., se habere in eis $Bm^1W\rho^2$

regi, non quidem superioritatem simpliciter, sed plenitudinem potestatis in illis, dicentes quod tantum in certis casibus habet se intromittere de illis que ad se immediate pertinent. Et ideo episcopi et prelati, qui recognoscunt quidem se subesse pape in sua potestate et auctoritate, sed cum hoc dicunt quod eam non habent simpliciter ex commissione et largitione ecclesie Romane vel sedis apostolice sed a Deo, negant pape plenitudinem potestatis.

Quinto sic, quia si potestas iurisdictionis est immediate a Christo in episcopis et curatis et non a papa, sicut et potestas ordinis sive caracteris, tunc sicut papa non potest dare solo verbo nec auferre potestatem ordinis episcopo vel curato per quamcumque depositionem seu degradationem quin semper remaneat caracter, quia non potest auferre illud quod non dedit – sicut propter hoc non potest tollere vinculum matrimonii, quia scriptum est Matthei 19: *Quod Deus coniunxit homo non separet* – ita non posset papa solo verbo dare nec auferre potestatem iurisdictionis episcopo vel curato, nec ipsos deponere nec degradare, quod est negare pape plenitudinem potestatis. Argumentum ad hoc, *Auth. De defensoribus civitatum* § *Iusiurandum*, coll. 3, ubi dicitur sic: *Non habente licentiam clarissimo provincie iudice removendi eum, sed si quid videtur agere non recte, nunciare ad gloriosissimos prefectos, ut inde ei fiat cure privatio unde datur*.

Ad hanc autem rationem videtur sic posse responderi, quia papa non habet plenitudinem potestatis in ordine. Unde in potestate ordinis alii non subduntur ei sed equantur, presbyteri quidem in caractere sacerdotali, episcopi in episcopali, licet in quibusdam accidentalibus circa potestatem ordinis habeat aliquam preeminentiam, ut dictum est alibi. Unde a potestate ordinis non potest eos papa deponere nec destituere quantum ad

desunt $B^2P^1V^6$

282 potestatis] superioritatis [potestatis sive superioritatis V^2] θ | 283 illis[1]] *add.* vel potestatis θ(-V^2) | ceteris $\theta^4\pi$Barb.Va | intromittere] *add.* in illis et [*om.* Bo] θ | 285 sed] *add.* tamen ψ | 286 cum] tamen [tantum U] φ(-W) | 289 Christo] Deo α | 290 et[3]] est θ | sive] et φ, seu ρ^1 | 292 seu] vel θ | 294 sic φ(-U) | potest] *add.* ipsi R$Bm^2Br\sigma$, ipse B^1Sz | 295 Quos $\theta Bm^1\varphi^2P^2$Barb. | 297 nec[2]] vel φ | degradare] *add.* de se tantum quia ρ^1 | 297-299 quod ... civitatum] *om.* ρ^1 | 298 hoc] *add.* in θ | 301 recte] perfecte ρ^1 | 304 Unde] nam θ, nec γ | alii] *om.* θ | 305 sacerdotali] *add.* et $\theta\varphi$

289-298 Quinto ... potestatis: cf. Pierre de la Palu, *Iudicium*, art. 1, MS Vienna 2168, fol. 1v; MS Vienna 11799, fol. 192r | 295 Matt. 19:6; cf. Marc. 10:9 | 298-302 *Auth.* 3.2.1 § 1 = *Nov.* 15.1 § 1 | 303-323 Ad ... rege: cf. Pierre de la Palu, *Tractatus de potestate papae* 2.5, pp. 261-262

essentiam caracteris, non ideo quia habent eam a Deo, sed quia non est in ea illis superior, immo par, et par in parem non habet imperium, sed tantummodo superior in inferiorem, *De maioritate et obedientia* c. *Cum inferior, Ff. De arbitris* 1. *Nam et magistratus*. Sed papa in iurisdictione habet plenitudinem potestatis. Ceteri autem in partem tantum sollicitudinis sunt vocati, 2 q. 6 *Decreto* et c. sequenti. Unde in hoc alii subduntur ei, et per consequens ab eo possunt deponi. Et quando dicitur: quod Deus dedit homo non potest auferre, verum est nisi Deo dante auctoritatem auferendi. Eo ipso autem quod Deus dedit pape plenam iurisdictionem, aliis autem partialem, volens illos huic subesse et hunc illis preesse, eo ipso dedit pape potestatem instituendi et destituendi illos. Sicut quamvis rex statuerit per se immediate primos baillivos, castellanos et prepositos, si tamen ex toto submitteret baillivis illos a se institutos, ex hac submissione daret eis potestatem ipsos deponendi et alios ponendi, licet potestas castellanie et prepositure non sit a baillivo sed a rege.

Et dicendum quod ista solutio confirmat propositum. Quia si ex plenitudine potestatis papalis est quod ipse omnem episcopum et curatum possit destituere et alium instituere, sequitur quod omnis episcopatus et cura, et omne beneficium ecclesiasticum, tenetur et habetur ab eo simpliciter. Quia aliquis dicitur habere aliquid ab alio, non solum quando illud sibi dat inter vivos, sed etiam quando illud sibi relinquit in testamento, non solum pure et simpliciter, sed etiam sub conditione vel modo, dum tamen non oporteat ipsum propter hoc aliquid magnum dare aut facere. Quia tunc, impleto modo vel conditione, non totaliter haberet

desunt $B^2P^1V^6$

312 et] *om.* φ | 313-314 in ... sollicitudinis π(-P^4)] tantum in partem sollicitudinis γ(-φ^3)Sr, in partem sollicitudinis tantum ρ^1 | 313 tantum] *om.* $\theta\varphi^3P^4$Va | 317 dedit] *add.* auctoritatem θ(-Bo) | pape] *add.* et [auctoritatem et Bo] θ | 320 instituerit [instituit Bo, institueret θ^4(-S)] θ, statueret γ(-V^4)Rρ^1 | per se immediate] *om.* θ | baillivos] *add.* et θP^2, deinde statueret [constitueret W] φ | castellarios $\theta\varphi$(-St)B^1 | et] atque φ | 320-321 si ... toto] ex toto et in totum si tamen [tantum V^3] demum istis [illis O] θ, et eosdem castellarios atque prepositos a se institutos $Bm^1\varphi^5$Bl, a se institutos φ^3V^4 | 321 baillivis φB^1Barb.Va] *om.* θ; baillivos $\psi\rho^1$, baillivo P^4Sr, baillivus R | illos ... institutos] *om.* φ; alios θ | hac] *om.* θ | 322 ponendi] instituendi ρ^1 | licet] sed ρ^1 | 323 castellature [castellarie Bm^1, castellare Bl] $\theta\varphi$, castellae Bm^2, castellani ρ^2 | 326 episcopus [*om.* Sz] ρ^1 | et²] *add.* omnis θ | 327 curatus ρ^1 | 328 alio] aliquo θ | 329 sibi¹ ... vivos] sibi inter vivos dat [datur θ] α(-W), inter vivos sibi dat W | etiam] *om.* ρ^1 | sibi²] *om.* π(-R)Barb. | relinquitur θ | 330 vel] et φ | 332 aut facere] *om.* π(-R)Barb.

311-312 X. 1.33.16 | 312 The reference should be *De receptis*: *Dig*. 4.8.4. | 314 Gratian, C.2 q.6 c.11-12

illud a testatore. Vel sic immo etiam ille qui succedit ab intestato de iure, eo ipso quod testator potuit alteri dare et sibi auferre, dicitur habere a testatore. Omnis autem potestas et dignitas ecclesie, sive beneficium quodcumque legitime habitum, aut habetur immediate ex gratia pape conferentis vel providentis – et tunc talis est bene ingratus si non recognoscit se habere a papa illud. Et sive recognoscat illud beneficium in se esse a papa sive non, tamen se habere illud a papa et ex dono eius vere negare non potest. Unde tales in episcopos sic promoti solent dicere Dei et apostolice sedis gratia se electos vel episcopos. Quia sicut donatarius, quidquid habet ratione donationis, totum habet a donante, ita et isti, qui nihil iuris habent in suis beneficiis nisi ex collatione pape, totum ius suum habent a papa immediate, sed mediate a Deo, a quo bona cuncta procedunt – aut potestas vel dignitas ecclesiastica habetur aliter quam per immediatam collationem pape. Et tunc oportet quod ille qui habet eam, si sit in ea canonice institutus, quod hec institutio sit in testamento pape. Quia in iure canonico, quod est testamentum papale, idest testatio mentis et scriptura indicans voluntates et ordinationes summorum pontificum de patrimonio Christi in quo disponendi habent plenariam potestatem, cavetur modus quo debent beneficia et dignitates ecclesiastice obtineri, sic tamen quod promovendus nihil ad hoc det aut agat quod faciat simoniam. Et tunc, concurrente institutione canonica, sub forma scilicet et modo a papa quasi a testatore appositis, iste obtinet potestatem vel dignitatem ecclesiasticam, et per consequens censetur a papa institutus sub illis forma et modo. Et sic habet a papa potestatem et dignitatem illam, sicut heres, institutus sub conditione vel modo, illis existentibus, habet nihilominus hereditatem a testatore. Item quia papa potest quemlibet deponere et cui vult dare, et tenet et valet utrumque, eo ipso quod non aufert videtur dare. Unde isto modo, quasi ab intestato, habet quilibet ab eo, etiam aliter quam per eius gratiam promotus. Et sic semper sequitur quod omnis potestas et

desunt $B^2P^1V^6$

333 illud] *om.* θ | Vel] ut φ(-W) | ille] libere θ | successit φ | 334 poterit B^1, poterat P^4Barb. | diceretur θ | 335 ecclesie $P^4\rho^1\sigma$] ecclesiastica αB^1, ecclesia R, etiam Barb. | 338 recognoscit] recognoscat $\theta\psi$ | Et] sed [*om.* Bm^1] φ | 338-339 in se] *om.* γ | esse a papa in se θ | 341 vel episcopos] *om.* φ | sic θ(-Bo) | 342 ita] sic θ | 345 habetur] *om.* θ | aliter habetur $\varphi(-\varphi^3)$ | 346 collationem] concessionem vel provisionem [promissi O, promissionem V^1BoV^2Sv] θ | pape] *add.* habetur θ | 347 institutio] *add.* sua θ | in^2] *om.* ρ^1; ex θ | testamento] testimonio ρ^1; *add.* vel in testamento V^5 | pape] *add.* vel in testamento [testimonio BoV^2] pape $\theta(-V^5)$ | 350 potestatem] *add.* et γ | 352 quod^1] *add.* qui π(-R)Barb. | promovendus] *add.* est π(-R)Barb. | aut] vel γ | 354 ille ρ^1 | vel] et $\varphi\rho^1$ | 355 illis] tali φ, illo ρ^1 | 355-356 modo et forma ρ^1 | 360 isto] illo ρ^1

dignitas ecclesiastica que legitime et canonice habetur a papa vel a sede papali habetur. Quando autem dicitur contra modum arguendi, quod licet utraque potestas, ordinis scilicet et iurisdictionis, sit immediate a Deo non a papa, papa tamen potest dare et auferre ad libitum unam non aliam, quia super unam habet plenitudinem potestatis, non super aliam, est oppositio in adiecto, quia papa non est super ius divinum sed sub. Unde super potestatem que est de iure divino, quecumque sit illa, non potest ipse habere plenitudinem potestatis. Immo nec aliquid potestatis. Unde adhuc stat argumentum, scilicet quod si potestas iurisdictionis esset a Deo sicut potestas ordinis, non posset dare nec auferre unam plus quam aliam.

Sexto sic, quia si potestas episcoporum et curatorum est eque immediate a Christo sicut potestas pape, tunc episcopi electi canonice non indigerent ab homine confirmari, nec curati ad curam per patronos legitime presentari. Nec indigerent ab episcopo institui, nec oporteret quod ab alio eis cura committeretur, sicut nec papa indiget, qui electus canonice a solo Christo confirmatur et instituitur. Hoc autem dicere est ecclesiasticum ordinem perturbare, quia curati ab episcopis instituuntur, qui ecclesias eis committunt et curam animarum. Unde mirum est dicere quod ille cui ab aliquo cura animarum committitur non habeat illam curam immediate ab illo. Episcopus etiam ab archiepiscopo, et ille a papa confirmatur, et qui confirmat dat. Unde confirmatus a confirmante habet illam potestatem quam acquirit per ipsam confirmationem. Et sic patet quod, cum archiepiscopus sive patriarcha recipiat a papa immediate suam potestatem, et ab illo episcopus, a quo curatus, quod omnis alia potestas ecclesiastica derivatur a papali, mediate vel immediate. Immo quia nemo dat alteri quod non habet, nisi in virtute eius qui habet, archiepiscopus, confirmando episcopum, dat ei immediatam iurisdictionem in subditos

desunt B^{2}P^{1}V^6

362-363 a papa vel a sede papali [apostolica θ] habetur [habeatur θ] $\theta\rho$Sr] habetur [tenetur ψ] a papa vel a sede papali [*inv.* U] $\gamma\pi^1$, a papa habetur vel a sede papali B^1 | 364 scilicet] videlicet θ | 366 oppositum θ(-V^5)$\psi\rho^1$ | 367 obiecto π(-R)Sr | super^1] supra θ(-Bo) | 368 potestate θ^1(-Bo)γ(-W)Va | ipse] *om.* ρ^1 | 369 ad hoc ρ^1 | 370 stat] *om.* ρ^1 | scilicet] *om.* θ | 371 nec] vel [aut V^3] θ | 373 a] *add.* Deo vel a θ | 374 curati $\theta\varphi$] *om. cet. mss.* | 375 legitime] *om.* ρ^1 | presentati α(-BoP^2) | Nec^1 ρ^2Sr] non W; *om.* Barb. *et cet. mss.* | episcopo] ipso πBarb.Sr | oportet θ(-V^{2}Sv)V^7 | 376 alio] aliis θ | 377-378 Hoc ... instituuntur] *hom.* V$^5\theta^4$ | 378 instituuntur] instituti videantur [videntur V^1] θ^2 | 379 curas θ | 382 confirmat] *add.* vim φ | dat] *add.* potestatem ψB^{1}Barb. | Unde] et φ | 383 Et] *om.* θ | 384 recipiet π(-R) | 387 eius qui habet] unde quilibet πBarb.

372-395 Sexto ... supra: cf. Pierre de la Palu, *Iudicium*, art. 1, MS Vienna 2168, fol. 1v; MS Vienna 11799, fols. 192r-193r

non in virtute propria, quia ipse non habet eam in subditos suffraganeorum nisi in certis casibus. Ergo dat eam in virtute pape. Et sic episcopus habet a papa suam iurisdictionem immediate, loquendo de immediatione virtutis, quamvis mediante archiepiscopo, loquendo de mediatione suppositi. Et cum episcopus quidquid habet habeat a papa, qui episcopus instituit curatum, patet quod et potestas curati est a papa immediate et mediate, distinguendo ut supra.

Sed ad hoc videtur sic posse responderi. Diceretur enim quod omnis potestas, papalis, episcopalis et parochialis, habetur a Deo dupliciter, unomodo in primis episcopis et curatis, qui habuerunt a Deo sine quocumque medio, aliomodo in eorum successoribus, in quibus etiam habetur a Deo dante, non tamen nisi illi qui fuerit ab hominibus legitime electus. Unde sicut quando laicus patronus presentat episcopo ad beneficium aliquem, et episcopus acceptans ei confert illud beneficium, iste non habet vocem in capitulo nec alia iura spiritualia a laico presentante sed ab episcopo instituente, non minus quam ille cui episcopus totum confert, ita dicerent illi qui sunt contrarie opinionis quod primis episcopis et curatis, puta apostolis et discipulis, Christus totaliter et ex toto potestates et dignitates per se solum contulit, eas instituendo et confirmando. Sed de successoribus eorum ecclesie sponse sue dedit quasi presentationem, retinens sibi institutionem. Unde omni illi qui rite per ecclesiam promovetur ad statum a Deo institutum, sicut est status pape, episcoporum et curatorum, Deus confert potestatem illi statui debitam. Et isto modo curatis debentur decime de iure divino et confessio de iure divino, quia Deus dat ipsam curam animarum cui ipse annexuit et dedit ista iura in personis discipulorum.

Sed in hoc est differentia inter potestates et dignitates ecclesiasticas, quod ille que habent superiorem in ecclesia, ad hoc quod dentur a Deo alicui persone, oportet quod instituantur vel confirmentur canonice a superiore. Et sic presentati ad curam non recipiunt eam, nec habent in ea ius divinum, sed tantum humanum, quousque sint ab episcopo instituti. Et tunc quando episcopus confert eis curam animarum, committens eis

desunt $B^2P^1V^6$

389 subditis θ | 392 mediatione] immediatione σ | 394 et^1] *om.* ρ^1; etiam φB^1Sr | et^2] vel θUBm^1W | 397 habetur $\varphi^5\pi$] habentur Barb. *et cet. mss.* | 399 eorum] suis θ | 400 dante] *om.* θ | ille $\theta(-V^3)$ | fuerunt π(-R)Barb. | 401 electi π(-R)Barb. | 403 iste] ille ρ^1 | alia] aliqua θ | 404 episcopo] ipso π | 407 solum] ipsum θ | 409 omni] omnis [omnes Sv] $\theta(-V^3)$, enim π^1, eum B^1, cum Barb.σ | 412 isto] illo ρ^1 | 412-413 et ... divino] *hom.* ρ^1 | 414 illa ρ^1 | 416 illi $\theta\varphi^3WV^4$ | que] qui $\theta\varphi^2$ | 417 instituentur ρ^1 | vel] et ρ^1 | canonice] *om.* θ | 418 recipient [recipiant U, recipiens Pr, recipientes W] φ | 419 sint] *om.* π^1Barb.; sunt V^7B^1

parochiam in spiritualibus, intelligendum est quod confert ministerialiter non principaliter, eo modo quo sacerdos absolvens dicit: *Ego absolvo te a peccatis tuis*, qui tamen non absolvit nec remittit peccata sua principaliter, sed solus Deus principaliter. Ille autem sacerdos solum ministerialiter, vel declarat a Deo remitti. Ita enim possent imaginari illi qui probabilius vellent istam opinionem defendere, quod sicut dicit Dionysius quod ordo sacerdotalis procedit ab episcopo ordinante, qui dicit: *Accipe potestatem celebrandi missas* etc., per quod non intelligitur ipse episcopus principaliter caracterem imprimere, sed Deo imprimenti solum ministerium prebere secundum illud: *Dei adiutores sumus*, propter quod potestas caracteris non dicitur esse simpliciter ab episcopo ordinante, sed a Deo imprimente, ita posset imaginari in potestatibus et statibus de quibus agitur, que isti dicunt esse de iure divino sicut potestatem et statum papalem, quod quando episcopus confert curam animarum, intelligitur eam conferre ministerialiter, sed Deus principaliter. Et similiter quando episcopus confirmatur ab archiepiscopo, vel ille a papa, et datur ei cura pastoralis, sive instituitur in ea, quod Deus, qui eam instituit principaliter, eam tribuit. Sed confirmatio superioris est sicut causa sine qua non, vel ministerialis et instrumentalis, sicut in potestate caracteris. Quando autem dignitas a Deo instituta est talis quod nulla alia est maior ea in ecclesia, nec aliquis prelatus maior illo, tunc non requiritur ad hoc quod illa conferatur a Deo superioris confirmatio, quia non habet. Sed requiritur et sufficit consensus illorum ad quos spectat electio. Unde sicut papa habet a Deo potestatem suam sicut Petrus, quia succedit Petro in dignitate a Deo instituta, non obstante quod ipse ad hanc dignitatem perveniat mediante electione humana, quam Petrus habuit sola electione divina, ita episcopi et

desunt $B^2P^1V^6$

421 parochias θ | in spiritualibus] spiritualiter [in spiritualiter R] π^1Barb., specialem B^1 | ministraliter θ | 423 sua] *om.* φ | 424 ministraliter θ | vel] *om.* πBarb. | 426 istam] illam ρ^1 | 428 per] *om.* $\pi\rho$ | ille θ | 429 solum] *om.* φ | 430 propter] et sicut patet φ | 431 episcopo] *om.* θ^2BoV^2; eo $V^5\theta^4$ | 434 intelligitur [intelligere S] $\theta^4B^1\rho$Va] intelligatur $\alpha(-\theta^4)\pi^1$Sr | 435 ministraliter θ | similiter] *add.* dicendum φ | 436 vel] et θ | 438 superioris] *om.* θ | est] sit θ^1, fit θ^2 | sicut] *om.* θ | 439 ministraliter θ | instrumentaliter [mistraliter O] θ | in potestate caracteris] imponens caracterem B^1Barb. | 440-441 ea ... prelatus] illa et [*om.* Bo] sic [sicut BoP^3] in illa nullus est θ | 441 illo] isto φ; *add.* sic instituendo θ | 442 quia] *add.* superiorem φ | 443 Unde] *om.* $\theta\psi\rho^1$ | Unde sicut] sicut [si Bm^1] igitur φ | 444 sicut] *add.* et φ | 446 Petrus habuit] assecutus est Petrus φ

426-428 Cf. Ps.-Dionysius, *De ecclesiastica hierarchia*, chap. 5 (*Dionysiaca* 2: 1337) | 430 1 Cor. 3:9

curati habent suam potestatem et auctoritatem immediate a Christo, sicut et apostoli et discipuli, quibus in eadem dignitate a Christo instituta succedunt, non obstante quod illi acceperunt a Christo sine medio confirmante, isti autem mediante confirmatione vel institutione. Et pari ratione isti habent eque immediate a Deo sicut papa, non obstante quod habeant mediante electione et confirmatione quo ad episcopos, vel mediante presentatione et institutione quo ad curatos. Ipse autem papa ex sola electione sine hominis confirmatione.

Dicendum ergo ad ista quod de illa successione apostolorum et discipulorum, utrum in episcopis et curatis suam potestatem faciat esse immediate a Deo sicut potestatem pape, infra dicetur. Sed quantum tangit articulum principalem, dicendum quod papa potest dici habere immediate potestatem a Deo, non obstante quod eam habet mediante electione cardinalium, sicut etiam discipuli potestatem faciendi miracula, immo etiam potestatem predicandi et metendi temporalia, quod tunc acceperunt immediate a Christo, non obstante quod fuerunt electi ab apostolis et non immediate a Christo sicut ipsi apostoli quibus dicit: *Ego elegi vos*. De discipulis autem ceteris, quia erat turba discipulorum eius copiosa, ut dicitur Luce 6, elegerunt de mandato Domini apostoli illos septuaginta duos, sicut dicit Anacletus papa, 21 d. *In novo*, loquens de apostolis: *Ab eis electi sunt septuaginta duo discipuli*. Sed Dominus per se eos misit et eis potestatem dedit, non apostoli eligentes. Et eodemmodo cardinales eligentes non dant pape potestatem et auctoritatem papalem, sed ipse Deus. Et hoc bene confitentur illi qui sunt contrarie opinionis, addentes quod est idem de episcopis et curatis, quod falsum est.

Ad illam ergo probationem que inducta est, dicendum quod non est simile de potestate caracteris et de potestate iurisdictionis. Quia si Deus ita daret episcopo et curato curam pastoralem et parochialem quando

desunt $B^2P^1V^6$

447 auctoritatem et potestatem $\theta\varphi^3$W | a] *add.* Deo vel a θ(-V^5) | Christo] *add.* vel a Deo V^5 | 448 et[1]] *om.* $\theta\psi$Va | 449 succeditur ρ^1 | illi] *om.* φ | receperunt OBoV^5Sv, receperint $V^1V^2V^3$ | 450 isti ... confirmatione] *hom.* $\psi\rho^1$ | institutione $\theta^2\theta^3$UWπ(-R)] institutore $\theta^4\gamma$(-UW)RBarb.σ, instituente ρ^1 | 451 sicut] *add.* a φ(-U) | 452 et] *add.* mediante φ | 453 et] sive θ, seu [scilicet W] γ | 455 ista] illa ρ^1 | 457 a Deo] *om.* φ | 458 potest dici] dicitur φ | 459 habeat θ(-V^5Sv)ψB^1Va | 461 temporalia] *om.* θ | quod] quam θ(-V^3)ψ, pro φBarb.Sr | 463 ipsi apostoli R$\rho^1\sigma$] apostoli Christi [*om.* Bo] θ, Christi apostoli $\psi\pi$(-R)Barb., duodecim [septem W] apostoli [apostolis St] φ | 464 ceteris] *add.* dicitur θ | 466 papa] *om.* θ | eis] *add.* inquit $\theta\varphi$ | 467 eis] *om.* φ | 470 Et] ex [ex *sed corr. ad* et P^4] π | 473 caracteris ... potestate] *hom.* π(-R)Barb. | de[2]] *om.* φ(-φ^5)

463 Joan. 15:16 & 19 | 465 Luc. 6:17 | 466-467 Gratian, D.21 c.2

confirmantur et instituuntur canonice sicut dat eis caracterem sacerdotalem et episcopalem, ut ita liceat loqui quando ordinantur, tunc sicut de iure divino est aliquis certus et determinatus modus quo ad substantiam forme et materie, quem papa mutare non potest, per quem datur potestas caracteris, quamvis accidentalia que pertinent ad ritum et solemnitatem mutare possit, ita etiam de iure divino esset certus aliquis modus quo dignitas episcopalis et cura pastoralis darentur quem papa mutare non posset. Unde sicut papa non potest dare cuicumque vult quocumque modo vult potestatem caracteris nisi modo a Deo instituto, ita etiam non posset dare ad libitum et placitum episcopatus et curas quibuscumque vellet. Quia valde ridiculum esset dicere quod dona divina non Dei voluntate sed humana, etiam irrationabili, dispensarentur ad libitum, contra illud quod de uno donorum Dei dicitur secunda Canonica Petri: *Non enim voluntate humana allata est aliquando prophetia, sed Spiritu Sancto inspirati, locuti sunt sancti Dei homines.* Constat autem quod papa ad libitum et placitum, per se, per alium, verbo, scripto, sicut sibi placet, ponit et deponit episcopum et curatum. Et quamvis circa hoc possit peccare, ut infra dicetur, nihilominus tamen valet et tenet institutio et destitutio.

Non sic autem est de papatu, qui est donum Dei. Non enim potest ipse dare papatum ad libitum, nec in morte, nec in vita. Nec potest ad libitum mutare modum constituendi papam, sed est in constitutione pape aliquid de iure divino, quod ipse mutare non potest. De iure enim divino est quod successor Petri sit per electionem et per consensum ecclesie. Et hoc est consonum iure naturali, quia nullus iuste preest alicui multitudini nisi de eius consensu, aut de superioris ordinatione vel provisione. De primo, dicit Leo papa quod *nulla ratio sinit ut illi inter episcopos habeantur qui*

desunt $B^2P^1V^6$

477 certus] *om.* $\theta\psi$; specialis φ | 478 materie] *om.* ρ^1 | quem[1] [quod St] φ(-W)ρ(-Bm^2)Sr] quam θW$\psi\pi$$Bm^2$Va | quem[2]] quam $\psi\pi$(-R)Barb.Va | 479 accidentalia] etiam [ad P^4] omnia [illa P^4, det B^1] alia π(-R)Barb. | 480 esset certus] tunc esset φ | 481 quem] quam $\psi\pi$(-R) | 483 vult] *om.* θB^1Barb. | 485 vellet] *add.* et φ | Quia] quod ψB^1Barb. | ridiculosum $\theta^2\theta^3\varphi$Sr | est θ | 486 etiam] et π(-R)Barb. | 489 sancti] aliquando θ | autem] *om.* φP^2; enim θ | 490 se] *add.* et θ | verbo] *add.* et θ | 491 et[1]] *om.* $\psi\pi^1$Barb.σ | 492 tenet et [*om.* W] valet $\theta\varphi$ | 494 est[1]] *om.* θ | ipse] *add.* papa θ(-V^3) | 495 potest ad libitum] *om.* φ | 497 enim] *om.* $\theta\varphi$ | 498 sit] fit π | per[2]] *om.* $\theta B^1\rho$ | 500 de[1]] *om.* ρ^1; *add.* eius π(-R)Barb. | promissione ρ^1Va, permissione B^1Barb. | 501 ut] quod ρ^1

487-489 2 Pet. 1:21 | 501-502 Gratian, D.23 c.1; cf. D.62 c.1

nec a clericis sunt electi nec a plebibus expetiti, 23 d. *In nomine Domini*. De secundo patet, quia ex quo aliquis ordinarie presidet alicui multitudini iure suo, potest ponere super eam quem vult in adiutorium sui et vice et loco sui quamdiu preest. Deus autem ecclesie sue immediate non providit nisi de Petro. Unde per consequens, quia non providit de persona nominatim successore Petri, ecclesie electionem dimisit. Unde de iure naturali et divino est quod papa non faciat sibi successorem, nec post mortem, nec post resignationem, quando non preest, licet quamdiu vivit papa loco sui possit ponere legatos et vicarios ubi vult et sicut vult. Sed est de iure naturali et divino quod ex electione universalis ecclesie, vel illorum ad quos de consensu universalis ecclesie translatum est ius eligendi, sicut sunt hodie cardinales, 23 d. *In nomine Domini*, 79 d. c. 1, fiat papa.

Quod autem ius eligendi papam de consensu universalis ecclesie, vel illorum in quos universalis ecclesia quantum ad hoc ius suum transtulit, vel qui eam representant – hoc est de consensu concilii generalis precedentis vel sequentis, qui est consensus universalis ecclesie, quia ad tractandum de hoc quod tangit universalem ecclesiam habent potestatem – sit translatum in cardinales, sicut ius eligendi imperatorem de consensu populi fuit translatum in senatores, patet. Quia dato quod a principio hoc non fuisset, quia illi canones prius inducti non faciunt de hoc expressam mentionem, tamen certum est quod postea fuerunt multa concilia generalia in quibus est virtus universalis ecclesie ad ordinandum de pertinentibus ad eam, que concilia, non solum dissimulando scienter, sed etiam expresse approbaverunt, quod vice totius ecclesie ad cardinales pape electio pertineret, quedam alia superaddendo. Sicut in concilio cui prefuit Alexander tertius fuit ordinatum quod fieret a duabus partibus cardinalium, *De electione* c. *Licet*. Postmodum sub Gregorio decimo in concilio Lugdunensi multa sunt addita, *De electione* c. *Ubi maius*, et postmodum a Clemente. Et quamvis Romanus pontifex circa accidentalia posset aliqua variare, circa substantialia tamen non. Unde sine assensu

desunt $B^2P^1V^6$

503 patet] *add.* idem ρ^1 | quia] *om.* π(-R)Barb. | ordinatione ρ^1 | 510 Sed] sic [sicut St] α | 511 quod] *add.* papa fiat [fiet V^5] $\theta(-V^2)$ | de electione $V^5\theta^4$, per electionem θ^2Bo | 514 fiat papa] *om.* $\theta(-V^2)$Barb. | 516 in] ad θ | 525 eam] eadem [eandem φ^5] φ, ea ρ^1 | que] *add.* quidem φ | 528 fieret] *add.* electio $\theta(-V^2)$ | 530 superaddita θ | maius] prius φ | 531 Clemente] *add.* quinto eodem titulo Ne Romani $\theta(-V^2)$ | circa] erga φ | 532 possit $\theta(-V^2)$

513 Gratian, D.23 c.1 | Gratian, D.79 c.1 | 529 X. 1.6.6 | 530 *Sext.* 1.6.3 | 531 Cf. *Clem.* 1.3.2

ecclesie universalis, idest concilii generalis, non posset ipse statui cardinalium ius eligendi auferre et aliis dare in quos nunquam consensit ecclesia universalis, quia tunc ille electus non esset electus de consensu universalis ecclesie. Sed tunc electus a cardinalibus, nisi essent a cardinalatu depositi, esset verus papa, quidquid predecessor statuisset, quia quamdiu manent cardinales, in eis residet consensus ecclesie ad eligendum.

Similiter non posset papa statuere quod electus a minore parte cardinalium esset papa, quia nec ille haberet consensum ecclesie. Quia nunquam videtur facere communitas illud quod facit minor pars, sed illud quod maior, et maxime illud quod faciunt due partes, *Ff. Ad municipales* l. *Quod maior, De his que fiunt a maiori parte capituli* c. 1, c. *Ex ore*, c. ultimo, 65 d. c. 1, 2, 3, *C. De decur.* ... l. 2, l. 11. Utrum autem posset statuere quod possit eligi a maiori parte sola, aut quod cardinales non includantur, contra ordinationem concilii, potest dubitari, non quin papa possit statuere contra statutum concilii, sed quia non potest statuere contra statutum Dei, quod est quod papa non eligatur nisi de consensu ecclesie, vel illorum in quos ad hoc ipsum ecclesia consentit, quasi per modum compromissi perpetui. Unde cum ecclesia consenserit quod solum due partes cardinalium possint facere, non pauciores, et quod tali vel tali modo procedatur, non aliter, videtur contrario modo electus non esse electus de consensu ecclesie, nec per consequens secundum ius divinum. Unde non valet electio nec statutum pape de hoc quod est contra ius divinum, ut posset alicui videri. Verius tamen videtur quod papa posset hoc immutare, quia hoc solum habet ecclesia a Deo, quod sine eius vero consensu non fiat papa. Cum autem verus consensus communitatis sit consensus maioris partis explicitus vel implicitus, idest consensus maioris partis illorum cui tota communitas hoc commisit, hoc solum habet ecclesia a iure divino. Quidquid autem circa hunc consensum superaddit positivum

desunt $B^2P^1V^6$

535 iste θ | 537 quidquid] *add.* etiam φ | 542 illud²] id θ(-OBoV^2)V^7 | 544 1] *add.* et α | 545 ultimo] finali θ | 2¹] *add.* et α(-St)Sr | 546 possit $\varphi(-\varphi^3)\pi\sigma$] posset $\theta\varphi^3\psi\rho$ | non] *om.* π(-R)Barb. | 550 ipsa πBarb. | consentit] consensit [confessit W] αVa | 551 consenserit] consensit $\theta\psi$ | 552 possunt πBarb.Sr | quod] *om.* πBarb. | 553 videtur] *om.* π(-R)Barb. | esset [est Barb.] π(-R)ρ | 555 de hoc] *om.* φ | 555-556 quod ... immutare] *om.* θ | 556 Verius] *om.* π(-P^4) | posset²] possit ρ^1 | 557 quia] quod φ(-St) | 559 explicitus ... partis] *om.* ρ^1 | vel] non π(-P^4)Barb. | partis²] *add.* illius communitatis [*om.* $V^2\theta^4$] vel θ

543-544 The reference has not been identified. | 544 X. 3.11.1 | X. 3.11.3 | 544-545 X. 3.11.4 | 545 Gratian, D.65 c.1-3 | The reference has not been identified.

et humanum est, nec habet robur nisi ab auctoritate pape, qui est super concilia. Unde potest, si vult, talia revocare.

Supponatur ergo quod de iure divino est aliquis certus modus creandi papam, scilicet electio ecclesie vel illorum in quos ius suum transtulit, quem papa nec auferre nec revocare potest, licet circa illud possit multa statuere, illo substantiali modo semper in suo robore perdurante, cum non sit dare aliquem talem substantialem modum de iure divino attingendi ad curam parochialem vel episcopalem contra quem papa non possit pro libito ad illam aliter promovere, patet quod illa non sunt donum Dei sicut potestas caracteris, aut sicut papatus, sed donum hominis, scilicet pape, secundum cuius instituta talia proferuntur. Unde adhuc stat argumentum, quod scilicet ipsa institutio seu confirmatio superioris, que est quedam datio et vera collatio cure parochialis et episcopalis, indicant quod sunt ab homine, non a Deo sicut papatus, qui a Deo non ab homine confirmatur. Nec est simile de potestate ordinis cum suo effectu sacramentali qui, cum fiat realiter in anima in qua solus Deus agit principaliter, non potest principaliter esse ab homine. Sed potestas iurisdictionis non est nisi quedam relatio superioritatis ad subditos ordinata ad actus exteriores. Unde potest principaliter ex dono hominis provenire.

Contra istam autem conclusionem arguitur tripliciter. Primo de hoc quod dicitur Actuum 20: *Attendite vobis, et universo gregi in quo vos Spiritus Sanctus posuit episcopos regere ecclesiam Dei.* Ex quo videtur, sive loquatur ad episcopos proprie dictos, sive ad presbyteros large dictos episcopos, sive ad utrosque, quod illi de quibus loquitur ponuntur in regimine a Spiritu Sancto, sicut successores Petri in loco eius ponuntur a Christo, et per consequens habent potestatem sui regiminis non ab homine sed a Deo, sicut ipsemet papa.

desunt $B^2P^1V^6$

562 ab] ex θ | que πBarb. | 564 Supponitur ρ^1 | 566 quem] quod $V^7\pi$(-R)Barb.Sr | possit] *om.* πBarb. | 567 cum] *add.* autem θ(-V^2Sv)P^4, ergo ψ | 569 contra] *om.* θ | quod θ(-V^2) | posset π(-R) | 570 sunt] sit [sint V^2] α | 571 aut] ac φ(-φ^5)π(-R) | sed] hoc ρ^1 | 572 statuta $\theta\rho^1$ | conferuntur θ(-V^2)φ | ad hoc ρ^1 | 573 quod] quia φ(-U) | institutio] constitutio φ | 575 qui a Deo] quia [qui V^5Sv] θ | ab] *om.* θ(-BoV^5Sv)R | 576-577 cum fiat] confertur solum [*om.* P^4] π(-R) | 577 qua θB^1Sr] quam γ(-UBm^1)RBm^2Va, quantum Uρ^2, que Bm^1Barb. | principaliter] *om.* $\theta\varphi$ | 577-578 non [nec Va] potest principaliter [*add.* etiam W] esse [*inv.* $P^4\rho^1$] ab homine [ab homine esse W] $\varphi\pi^1\rho^1\sigma$] principaliter ab homine esse non potest [poterit Sv] θ(-V^2), specialiter esse ab homine V^2, est a Deo sed ministerialiter potest esse ab homine ψBarb., est a Deo sed ministerialiter et non principaliter ab homine B^1 | 579 superioris θ | 580 pervenire $Bm^1W\varphi^4$ | 581 illam ρ^1 | conclusionem] *om.* πBarb. | 583 videtur] habetur θ | 584 dictos[1]] *om.* α | 585 ponantur φ | 587 sui] *om.* θ

582-583 Act. 20:28

Responsio: utrique ponuntur a Christo in sedibus suis quandocumque legitime et canonice ascendunt. Sed differenter, quia papa, qui nullo homine sibi confirmante nec dante papatum ibi ponitur, a solo Deo immediate illic constituitur. Hanc enim immediationem non tollit electio que non dat sibi papatum. Sed episcopi et curati non solum ab hominibus presentantur vel eliguntur, sed etiam ab homine habente in virtute illud quod ipsi habent in potentia eis ius conferente instituuntur, et ab homine recipiunt illud quod accipiunt. Sicut differenter sunt electi ab hominibus discipuli ad predicandum et discipuli ad ministrandum viduis et similiter predicandum. Quia primi sunt ab apostolis electi, sed non ab apostolis missi nec constituti in officio predicationis, sed ab ipsomet Domino. Unde ab ipso solo habuerunt potestatem qua ante passionem usi sunt. Sed post Pentecostem, *convocantes duodecim multitudinem discipulorum, dixerunt: "Considerate ex vobis viros* etc. *quos constituamus super hoc opus;" et elegerunt Stephanum* etc. Hos statuerunt ante conspectum apostolorum, et orantes imposuerunt eis manus, et ordinaverunt diaconos, et fecerunt archidiaconos ad visitandum et predicandum. Unde isti electi a discipulis, quia tamen constituti non immediate a Christo sed ab apostolis, potestatem acceperunt ab eis, non sicut habuerunt primi a Christo, nullo alio medio dante. Item episcopi et curati digne et rite promoti dicuntur positi a Spiritu Sancto, non potestatem immediate conferente, sed collationem inspirante.

Secundo arguitur sic. Si episcopi et curati potestatem et auctoritatem suam non haberent immediate a Christo sed totaliter a papa, quasi eius baillivi et prepositi, tunc ipsi possent ad libitum deponi sine culpa sua et sine causa. Sed ipsi non possunt licite sine culpa amoveri etiam a papa. Ergo etc. Maior patet, quia rex potest amovere baillivum et prepositum ad libitum sine peccato, et papa revocare legatum suum et delegatum sine culpa. Minor patet, quia dicit apostolus 2 ad Corinthios ultimo: *Potestatem*

desunt $B^2P^1V^6$

590 qui] *om.* π(-R) | 591 homine] *om.* φ | sibi] *om.* ψ; se [*om.* V^2Sv] θφ | 592 immediate] *add.* ibi θ(-V^2) | electio] *add.* cardinalium φ | 595 ipsi] episcopi θBarb. | 597 similiter] insuper etiam cum hoc [*om.* U] ad φ | 598 predicandum] *om.* π(-R)Barb. | 599 Unde] nam φ | 600 qua] quia ρ^1 | 601 cum vocantes [vaccantes B^1] πBarb. | discipulorum] *om.* φ | 602-603 et elegerunt] *om.* πBarb. | 603 constituerunt $\theta\varphi^5$ | 606 instituti ρ^1 | non] *add.* fuerunt φ | 607 receperunt θ(-V^2) | 608 alio] *om.* θ; autem ρ^1 | digne BoγB^1Sr] digni θ(-Bo)$\pi^1\rho$Va | 614 etiam] *om.* $\varphi\rho^1$ | a papa] *om.* $\varphi^5\rho^1$ | 615 prepositum] *add.* suum θ(-V^2) | 615-616 ad libitum] *om.* θV^7 | 616 subdelegatum ρ^1 | 617 culpa] *add.* sua θ(-V^2)

601-603 Act. 6:3-5 | 617-618 2 Cor. 13:10

quam Dominus dedit mihi in edificationem, non in destructionem. Qui autem utitur potestate ad oppositum eius ad quod est sibi data abutitur ea, et per consequens peccat. Ergo qui sine causa destituit bonum prelatum peccat.

Responsio: argumentum non probat quin ille dignitates sive potestates sint a papa, quia dato quod essent ab eo, adhuc posset peccare quod dedit legitime indebite revocando. Unde dicendum quod huiusmodi officia sunt a papa. Sed episcopi et curati sunt procuratores et non domini. Nam si essent facti veri domini per suam ordinationem, sicut donatarius per donationem inter vivos, sine eorum culpa et ingratitudine non posset donatio revocari. Unde sciendum quod cum papa possit deponere principem laicum et prelatum ecclesiasticum, non tamen equaliter. Quia principem laicum, vassallum suum vel extraneum, non potest deponere sine iusta et rationabili causa, tali scilicet quod ille sit indignus illo principatu, et meruerit illud perdere et eo privari. Et si sine tali causa privet ipsum, non solum peccat conando, sed etiam nihil agit privando, sicut non valet sententia a non suo iudice lata. Sed in prelatis ecclesie secus est, quia non sunt domini sed procuratores. Unde sicut administrator superior qui habet plenam potestatem potest instituere et destituere inferiores administratores, et tenet quidquid facit, etiam quando minus bonum instituit et meliorem destituit, licet in hoc ipse peccet, ita etiam papa, ponendo et deponendo personas ecclesiasticas, licet peccet nisi pro meliori ecclesie hoc faciat, tamen tenet quod facit. In tantum autem procedit ratio que dicit eos esse procuratores non dominos, quod sine omni peccato suo et alieno potest papa deponere minus bonum et ponere meliorem. Quia in officiis rei publice queritur utilitas publica, non privata. Unde si prelatum non delinquentem et bonum amoveat ut meliorem ponat, non peccat, nec ille conqueri potest, sicut nec procurator quando a domino revocatur, quia ab onere relevatur, et non aliquod ius sibi

desunt B^{2}P^{1}V^{6}

619 eius] *om.* γ(-U) | sibi] *om.* θ | 622 iste πBarb.Va | 627 vivos] *add.* tunc φSr | eorum] eius θ(-V^{2})ψ | posset] *add.* eorum ρ^{1} | 629-630 et ... laicum] *hom.* ρ^{1} | 630 vel extraneum] *om.* ρ^{1} | 631 tali] *om.* α | illo] isto φ | 632 illud] *om.* απBarb. | illud perdere ρ^{1}Va] *inv.* Sr | eo] *om.* πBarb. | Et^{3}] *om.* ρ^{1} | 633 privat [privatur W] φ | conando] donando ψB^{1}Barb. | 635 est] *om.* πσ | sicut] sciendum quod [*om.* Bm^{2}] ρ^{1} | 636 plenitudinem potestatis πBarb. | et destituere] *om.* ψπBarb. | 638 et θ(-V^{2})ψB^{1}Sr] *om.* V^{2}π^{1}ρVa | et ... destituit] *om.* φ | 638-639 in ... licet] *hom.* π(-R)Barb. | 644-645 ponat meliorem α | 645 non peccat] *om.* V^{2}πBarb. | iste [isti P^{3}] θ

628-650 Unde ... sua: cf. Pierre de la Palu, *Tractatus de potestate papae* 2.5, pp. 266-267

aufertur. Sed secus in principibus laicis, qui sunt veri domini eius quod habent. Res autem sua non est alicui auferenda sine culpa sua. Unde nec feudum a vassallo, et multo minus quod aliquis habet a nullo alio potest sibi auferri sine culpa sua.

Adhuc tamen est advertendum, quod licet rex possit amovere baillivum suum ad libitum, tamen sine culpa eius non debet eum confundere, nec diffamare sine causa. Unde si sine culpa eius et utilitate populi eum amoveat, peccat, ledens famam proximi sine causa, ledens etiam subiectos, propter quod dicunt iura quod procurator post litem contestatam non debet amoveri sine causa, et tutor qui amotus est ab administratione ex dolo vel lata culpa est infamis. In istis ergo amotionibus <officialium civilium> est considerandum quod, quando sunt simpliciter instituti, <tunc rex vel imperator> non potest eos amovere sine eorum culpa quin peccet, quia facit contra prohibitionem iurium quibus tenetur obedire. Unde et licet ab eius sententia appellare, sicut cotidie appellant ab episcopo abbates et curati sine sua culpa depositi. Sed papa legibus humanis solutus est. Unde sine peccato suo potest amovere prelatum a sua prelatione quamvis ille non peccaverit, et quamvis etiam bonus sit, dum tamen meliorem ponat. Sed bene merito debet honeste secundum statum suum necessaria providere.

TERTIA CONCLUSIO

Tertia conclusio principalis est de potestate iurisdictionis episcopalis quo ad ipsas sedes episcopales et ecclesias cathedrales, quod etiam ipse ecclesie et sedes episcopales in se potestatem et dignitatem quam habent non habent immediate a Christo, sed a papa et ab ecclesia Romana habent omnem potestatem et auctoritatem quas habent, quod patet tripliciter. Primo sic: quia in omni genere illud quod est maxime tale est causa omnium aliorum, non solum ut habeantur ab alio, sed etiam ut sint illa in seipsis et in sua natura. Sed potestas papalis inter omnes ecclesias est

desunt $B^2P^1V^6$

647 secus] *add.* est $\theta\rho^1$ | 648-650 Unde ... sua] *hom.* ρ^1 | 652 libitum] *add.* non [unde θ^2] α | non] *om.* α | 653 et] *add.* sine θ(-V^2) | 654 proximi] *add.* sui θ(-V^2) | 655 subiectos γ(-V^4)RρVa] subditos $\theta V^4\pi$(-R)Sr | 658 officialium civilium Barb.] prelatorum *mss.* | 659 tunc ... imperator Barb.] papa Br, iure papa Sz, papa non papa Bm^2Sr, minor papa [pape U] *cet. mss.* | 660 quin] *add.* immo θ(-V^2) | 661 et] *om.* θ(-V^2)$Bm^1\psi$; etiam φ(-Bm^1) | 663 Unde] *om.* ρ^1 | 664 a sua prelatione] *om.* θ | 666 suum] *add.* sibi θ(-V^2) | 671 non ... habent[2]] immediate a sede apostolica et a papa et ecclesia Romana [*om.* O] habent et ab ipsa debent recognoscere θ(-V^2) | a[1] ... sed] nisi φ | 672 quas] quam $\varphi\pi$(-R)Barb. | 674 ut[1]] *add.* alia [ipsa alia Bo] θ(-V^2V^3) | alio] illo θ(-V^2)$\psi\pi$(-P^4)Barb. | illa] ita [*om.* W; ista St] φ | 675 sua] sui $\theta\varphi$(-UBm^1) | papalis] pape φ | omnes] *add.* potestates φSr | ecclesiasticas αSr

maxima. Ergo ipsa est causa omnibus aliis potestatibus ecclesiasticis, non solum personis que in illis instituuntur, sed etiam ut sint in se et in sua natura. Maior patet per Aristotelem, 2 *Metaphysice*, ubi probat quod sicut ignis, quia est calidissimus, est causa omnium calidorum et etiam calorum omnium imperfectorum, sic quod est maxime ens et verum est causa entitatis et veritatis in his que sunt magis et minus talia, etiam ipsius entitatis et veritatis diminute in se. Minor patet, scilicet quod papa in ecclesia habet summam et maximam potestatem, et omnes alii coartatam et limitatam. Ergo sequitur conclusio, scilicet quod omnes ecclesie habent ab eo suam potestatem limitatam, et illa earum potestas limitata ab ipsa eius potestate plena procedit.

Secundo probatur idem sic, quia omnis ecclesia cathedralis habet potestatem episcopalem ab illo cuius auctoritate fundatur. Sed omnis ecclesia cathedralis fundata est auctoritate pape. Ergo omnis ecclesia cathedralis habet omnem potestatem, dignitatem et auctoritatem episcopalem a papa, sive ecclesia Romana quod idem est. Maior patet, quia sicut se habet fundator materialis ecclesie ad eius dotem corporalem, sic spiritualis ad spiritualem. Sed ille est causa dotis ecclesie corporalis quam habet ex sua fundatione. Ergo et ille spiritualis. Sed dos spiritualis ecclesie cathedralis, ex hoc ipso quod cathedralis est, est habere insignia episcopalia, potestatem, dignitatem, auctoritatem et iurisdictionem. Ergo hec omnia habet ipsa ab illo cuius auctoritate fundatur et erigitur in cathedralem. Minor patet, quia nullus potest sedem episcopalem construere de novo nisi papa aut eius auctoritate.

desunt $B^2P^1V^6$; 698 *post verbum* cathedralem *deest* P^4

677 in[1]] *om.* φ(-U) | ut sint] *om.* B^1Barb.; ut sicut π^1Va | sui $\theta\varphi^3\varphi^5$ | 678 Aristotelem] *add.* in ρ^1 | 679 quia] qui $\theta\pi$(-R)Barb. | etiam] *om.* φ | 680 est[2]] *add.* maxime [maxima Br] ρ^1 | 681 etiam] et πBarb. | ipsius] *om.* ρ^1 | 682 diminute] *om.* φ | in se] *om.* θ | scilicet quod] quia φBarb. | 684 Ergo ... conclusio] *om.* $V^2\gamma$; sequitur ergo [*om.* Bo] $\theta(-V^2)$ | scilicet] *om.* $\theta(-V^2)B^1Bm^2$Barb.; eo φ | 685 et] *add.* quod $\theta(-V^2)$ | 686 eius ... plena] plena potestate pape [*om.* Bo; *inv.* Sv] $\theta(-V^2)$ | 687 probatur] patet θ | 689-690 fundata ... cathedralis] *hom.* $\pi^1\rho^1$Sr | 689 est] *om.* $\theta(-V^2)$ | pape] *add.* existit $\theta(-V^2)$ | 691 sive] *add.* ab θ | 692 spiritualis] spiritualiter [*add.* edificator Barb.] π(-R)Barb. | 694 iste [ipse O] $\theta(-V^2)$Va | 695 est[2]] *om.* [dicitur U] $\varphi\pi$Barb.Va | 696 episcopalia] temporalia θ(-Bo), spiritualia φ | et $\theta(-V^2)W\rho$] *om.* $V^2\varphi(-W)\pi\sigma$ | 696-697 Ergo ... auctoritate] *om.* π(-R)Barb. | 697 habet] sunt $\theta(-V^2)$ | ipsa] *om.* θ | 698 cathedralem] *add.* et ab illo habet $\theta(-V^2)$ | 698-732 Minor ... caracteris] *om.* P^4 | 698 episcopalem] cathedralem φ | 699 constituere ψB^1Barb.Va

678 Aristotle, *Metaphysica* a.1 (993b24-27)

Tertio patet idem sic. Quia si sedes et potestas et dignitas episcopalis, ubicumque sunt, essent a Deo et non a papa, papa non posset eas auferre nec transferre nec dividere nec unire. Sed consequens est falsum. Ergo et antecedens. Probatio consequentie, quia papa non potest tollere nec mutare nec minuere ius divinum, quia servus non potest tollere legem domini sui, 25 q. 1 *Sunt quidam*. Si ergo ubicumque est constitutio ecclesie cathedralis illa dicatur fundata a Deo et non ab homine, et de iure divino non humano, papa non potest illam destruere nec mutare. Minor patet, scilicet falsitas consequentis, quia papa multas civitates privavit pontificali dignitate. Est etiam statutum generale quod civitas culpabilis in hostili persecutione cardinalis eoipso est dignitate pontificali privata, preter Romam, *De penis* c. *Felicis, Libro sexto*. Papa etiam potest episcopatus transferre, et non solum personas sed etiam sedes, sicut de facto frequenter apparet et de iure, *De translatione episcoporum*, per totum. Ipse etiam dividit et unit episcopatus, sicut in eodem titulo habetur.

Et confirmatur per apostolum, qui dicit: *Firmum fundamentum Dei stat*, 2 ad Timotheum 2. Unde si alie ecclesie sunt a Deo fundate sicut ecclesia Romana, tunc sunt ita immobiles sicut ipsa Romana ecclesia, quam nec papa potest destruere nec dividere nec unire. Et dato quod papa ex causa rationabili posset sedem suam mutare localiter, forte cum concilio generali, tamen sedem papalem non potest ipse destruere, nec dividere, nec diminuere in aliquo sedis apostolice potestatem etiam cum consensu concilii generalis. Si ergo dicamus, gratia exempli, quod sedes Hierosolimitana, que fuit sedes Jacobi apostoli, sit eque fundata a Deo sicut sedes Petri, tunc non poterit papa ecclesiam Hierosolimitanam privare episcopo, nec alibi transferre, nec dividere, nec diminuere eius

desunt B^{2}P^{4}P^{1}V^6

701 papa^2] *om.* φ | 702-703 nec^3 ... nec] *om.* B^{1}Barb. | 702 unire] mutare ρ^1 | Sed] *om.* θSr | 703 consequentis θ(-V^{2}V^3) | 705 sui] *om.* αB^{1}Barb. | Sunt] sicut [*om.* V^2] αB^{1}Barb. | 705-706 constitutio ecclesie θRσ] institutio ecclesie φρ^2, constituta ecclesia ψB^{1}Bm^{2}Barb. | 706 dicitur θ(-V^{2}V^3) | et^1] *om.* φ | 707 Minor] *om.* ψB^{1}Barb. | 708 scilicet] *om.* B^{1}Barb.; autem ψ | consequentie θ | 709 civitas] *add.* que est θ(-V^2) | culpabilis] in [*om.* V^2] culpa θψB^{1}Barb. | 711 Romanam [ecclesiam Romanam Bm^1] φB^1 | 713 apparuit θ(-V^2) | 714 habetur] dicitur V^2, dicitur et De excessis prelatorum Sicut unire θ(-V^2) | 715 fundamentum] firmamentum ψB^{1}Barb. | 717 ecclesia^1] et φ | tunc sunt] essent ψB^{1}Barb. | ipsa] *om.* θ | 718 unire] minuere ψB^{1}Barb., mutare ρ^1 | Et] *om.* θ | 719-720 cum ... generali] de consensu concilii generalis [*om.* Bm^1] φ | 721 minuere ψB^{1}Barb. | apostolice] *add.* dignitatem vel [aut B^1] θB^1 | 725 minuere γB^{1}Barb.

705 Gratian, C.25 q.1 c.6 | 711 *Sext.* 5.9.5 | 713-714 X. 1.7 | 715-716 2 Tim. 2:19

potestatem, quod est absurdum. Si dicatur: non est simile de aliis ecclesiis super quas est papa, et de Romana in qua ipse est, sed super ipsam non est, dicendum quod est oppositum in adiecto, ut supra dictum est, dicere scilicet quod aliquid sit de iure divino et tamen sit subditum pape, quia papa non est supra ius divinum sed sub ipso. Unde potestas que est de iure divino nullomodo subest pape ut possit eam in se tollere vel mutare, sicut patet in potestate caracteris.

desunt $B^2P^4P^1V^6$

726 dicatur] *add.* quod $B^1\rho$ | 727 papa] ipse θ(-V^2) | sed] et θ | 728 dicendum] *add.* est $\theta^2Bo\theta^4\psi$ | obiecto θ | 730 super φP^2 | 731 in] sub ρ^1 | vel] et ρ^1

Sextus Articulus

Quantum ad sextum articulum principalem, de potestate curatorum, sunt tres conclusiones principales conformiter ad articulum precedentem. Prima de potestate ordinis sacerdotalis. Secunda de potestate iurisdictionis in utroque foro quo ad personas curatorum. Tertia quo ad ipsas curas et ecclesias sive rectorias parochiales in se ipsis.

Prima Conclusio

Prima igitur conclusio, de potestate ordinis sacerdotalis, est quod curati et omnes sacerdotes, quantumcumque infimi, habent potestatem ordinis sacerdotalis, qui est caracter sacerdotalis, potestas scilicet conficiendi et ligandi et solvendi in foro conscientie omnem suum subditum, eque immediate et eque perfectam in se et eque virtuosam in suo effectu proprio a Christo sicut papa et episcopi, sicut dictum est de potestate episcopalis ordinis, et propter idem. Quia caracter ab omni a quo habetur a Deo habetur, sed mediante sacramento et ministro episcopo, et non suscipit magis nec minus in se, nec potest plus in uno quam in alio, quantum est de se. Nam quod episcopus possit solvere et ligare plus quam curatus, et papa plus quam alii omnes, non est ex augmento caracteris sacerdotalis, sed ex adiuncta potestate iurisdictionis, que plures sibi subdit. In hoc autem fuit privilegium apostolorum, qui omnes in cena a Christo, non mediante alio ministro, nec exteriori ritu, facti sunt sacerdotes, accipientes claves ordinis a Christo immediate, vel tunc, vel in die resurrectionis, ut dictum est in secundo articulo principali.

desunt B^{2}P^{1}V^6

3 conformiter] *add.* respondentes θ(-V^2) | 4 Prima] *add.* est θ(-V^2)ψB^1 | 5 ipsas] *om.* φ | 6 sive] seu ρ^1 | 8 conclusio] principalis est [*om.* RBarb.] πBarb. | sacerdotalis] *add.* qui [que V^7] est caracter ψB^1 | 10 qui ... sacerdotalis] *hom.* ρ^1 | potestatem ρ^1 | conficiendi] *om.* ρ^1 | et γ(-Bm^{1}φ^5)π^{1}σ] *om.* θBm^{1}φ^{5}B^{1}ρ | 11 absolvendi θ | sui [*om.* W; sibi St] φ(-U) | 12 immediatam θ | et^1] *om.* θ | 13 sicut^2] ut θ | 14 episcopali θBm^{1}φ^2 | ordinis] *om.* θ | propter idem] pape item ψB^{1}Barb. | 17 Nam quod] non est quod θ(-V^2), quod V^2, non quod P^2, non quin V^7, quod vero φ | potest φ | 18 et] nec θ(-V^2) | non] *om.* θ(-V^{2}V^3); nec V^{2}V^{3}ψB^1 | est] *om.* θ | 19 sed] *add.* hoc est P^{2}B^{1}Barb., hec V^7 | ex] de [*om.* V^2] θ | 20 qui] quod [quia V^2] θV^7

Secunda Conclusio

Secunda conclusio principalis, de potestate iurisdictionis in foro conscientie quo ad curatos, est quod curati potestatem iurisdictionis, qua habent subditum sibi populum ad ligandum et solvendum in foro conscientie de iure, et in foro exteriori secundum quid de consuetudine, quam non habent presbyteri non curati, habent eam non a Deo immediate sed mediante papa. Nec solum sic quod habeant a papa hanc potestatem ministerialiter, aut sicut a causa sine qua non, eo modo quo habent ab episcopo potestatem caracteris, sed sic quod habent a papa principaliter et simpliciter, licet sub Deo. Et hoc patet per omnes rationes per quas probatum est de episcopo, cum sit eadem ratio per omnia de curato, preter quas sunt alie quinque rationes communes etiam episcopis et curatis, quarum prima talis est. Si potestas iurisdictionis episcoporum et curatorum, qua possunt solvere et ligare in utroque foro, non esset a papa sed a Deo, papa non posset ad se trahere illa que ad ipsorum iurisdictionem pertinent, per se vel per alium iudicando, sed deberet ad eos remittere omnia de quibus ipsi habent potestatem iudicandi. Sed consequens est falsum. Ergo et antecedens.

Probatio consequentie per rationem et per exemplum. Per rationem quidem, quia nulli facit iniuriam qui iure suo utitur. Sed ius alienum non potest homo sine iniuria usurpare. Unde cum is qui mandata iurisdictione utitur nihil proprium habeat, si is qui iurisdictionem dedit eam ad se retrahat in solidum vel in parte, iure suo utitur et ideo nemini iniuriatur. Propter quod, si episcopi et curati omnem potestatem et iurisdictionem quam habent in utroque foro habent ab ecclesia Romana, que vices suas aliis ecclesiis impartitur, tunc Romanus pontifex causas ad illos pertinentes ex sua commissione in utroque foro potest ad se trahere, per se vel per alium iudicando, sine hoc quod ad inferiores remittat. Et sicut in

desunt $B^2P^1V^6$

25-26 foro conscientie] foro utroque [*inv.* θ^2] θ | 26 qua] quam γB^1Barb.Sr | 27 habent] *add.* super φB^1, ad Sr, in Barb. | 28 conscientie] ecclesie π(-R)Barb. | secundum quid $V^2\gamma$(-W)R] secundum [sed Barb.] quod $\theta(-V^2)W\pi$(-R)Barb.Sr, hoc quidem ρ^1 | consuetudine] *add.* habent $\theta(-V^2)$ | 30 habent πBarb. | 31 ministraliter $\theta(-BoV^2)$ | eo] *add.* videlicet $\theta(-V^2)$ | 33 Et hoc] hoc etiam θ | 34 cum] quasi $\theta^2\theta^3$, quod θ^4 | preter] propter ρ^1 | 35 et curatis] *om.* ρ^1 | 38 attrahere π(-R)Barb. | 39 debet π | 40 omnia] talia ρ^1 | 44 iniuria] *add.* sibi $\theta(-V^3)$ | mandata] *add.* idest commissa φ | 45 dedit eam [*add.* scilicet θ] iurisdictionem αB^1 | 46 partem α(-Sv) | 47 et iurisdictionem] iurisdictionis ρ^1Va | 49 illos] illas [alios V^2] $\theta(-V^3)\rho^1$ | 50 in utroque foro] *om.* ρ^1 | retrahere $\theta(-V^2V^3)\rho^1$ | 51 iudicando] *add.* non preiudicando $\theta(-V^2)$ | sine] super θ | quod] quo $\theta(-V^2)$ | remittat] *om.* θ; remittatur φ

43 Cf. Gratian, D.50 c.17

foro exteriori causam ad episcopum pertinentem potest ei subtrahere, per se vel per alium iudicanao, nec habet ad eum remittere litigantes, sic etiam in foro conscientie parochianos curati vel episcopi, etiam de casibus ad illos pertinentibus, potest per se vel per alium audire et solvere et ligare sine hoc quod ad eos habeat remittere iterum confessuros vel etiam absolvendos. Sed sicut causas feudales eorum qui non sunt vassalli ecclesie non debet papa vel non potest ad se trahere, per se vel per alium cognoscendo, sed debet ad dominum feudi remittere litigantes, alias iuri alieno detraheret et peccaret, et forte etiam non valeret, nisi propter illius domini defectum, *De foro competenti* c. *Ex tenore*, c. *Ex transmissa*, c. *Licet*, *De iudiciis* c. *Novit*, *Qui filii sint legitimi* c. *Per venerabilem*, ita si potestas curatorum vel episcoporum in subditos in foro conscientie non est a papa sed habent eam a Deo, non potest papa, vel saltem non debet, per se nec per alium eorum subditos sic absolvere quin ad eos remittat absolvendos, nec similiter episcopus subditos curatorum. Et idem est in foro exteriori. Falsitas consequentis apparet, quia papa omnibus de mundo iudices petentibus solet dare, etiam in causis ad episcopos pertinentibus. Ipse etiam et summus penitentiarius dant sicut quando et quibus volunt parochianis licentiam eligendi sibi idoneum confessorem, qui possit eos absolvere, non de casibus papalibus, de quibus inferiores non possent conqueri, immo de casibus episcoporum et curatorum, de quibus non est sedes apostolica requirenda, in quo videtur magis episcopis et curatis preiudicium afferri. Et sic absolventes non remittunt ad eos sibi confessos iterum confessuros, nec ab eis iterum absolvendos. Ergo etc.

Si dicatur quod consequentia non est ad propositum, quia prima pars loquitur de delegatis (episcopi autem et curati sunt ordinarii; unde non est simile), et secunda pars loquitur de illis iudicibus laicis super quos papa non habet plenitudinem potestatis sicut habet in spiritualibus, dicendum

desunt $B^2P^1V^6$

52 potest] *add.* papa φ | 53 etiam] et φ | 54 vel] et $\theta(-V^2)$ | etiam] *om.* ρ | 55 pertinentes $V^2\pi$Barb.σ | alios θ | et^1] *om.* $\theta V^7\rho^1$ | et ligare] *om.* πBarb. | 56 iterum] *om.* θ | vel etiam] ut $\theta(-V^2)$ | 57 absolvant [absolvat Sv] $\theta(-V^2)$ | 58 retrahere [*add.* vel ρ^1] $\psi\rho^1$ | 60 etiam] ideo θ | 61 c. Ex tenore] *om.* B^1Barb.; *add.* et $\theta(-V^2)\pi^1$ | transmissa] *add.* et $\theta(-V^2V^3)\pi$ | 62 sunt $\varphi\pi$Barb.σ | 64 vel] *om.* $\varphi\pi(-R)$Barb. | 65 remittat] *add.* prius $\theta(-V^2)$ | 66 Et] *om.* φ | est] *om.* φ | 68-69 solet ... pertinentibus] *hom.* $\theta(-V^2)\varphi$ | dare ... pertinentibus] *om.* V^2 | 68 episcopos] ipsos ρ^1 | 69 Ipse etiam et] ipse et etiam φ, sicut etiam $\theta^1(-V^5)$, sic etiam θ^2V^5, etiam ψ | dant] *om.* $\pi(-R)$ | sic $\theta^2\theta^3\varphi$Sr | 70 parochianis] *add.* aliorum $\theta(-V^2)$ | 71 papalibus] *add.* tantum $\theta(-V^2)$ | 72 casibus] *om.* ρ^1 | 73 apostolica] *add.* consulenda vel $\theta(-V^2)$ | magis] *om.* θ | 75 confessuros ... iterum^2] *om.* θ | Ergo etc.] *om.* θ | 78 et] sed ρ^1 | 79 potestatis] *om.* $\varphi(-V^4)$

61 X. 2.2.11 | X. 2.2.6 | 61-62 X. 2.2.10 | 62 X. 2.1.13 | X. 4.17.13

quod non obstat primum, quia papa potest dare iurisdictionem ordinariam, que non minus est ab eo quam delegata, et ab eo revocabilis sicut illa. Unde legatus pape a latere, qui est ordinarius, non minus habet a papa iurisdictionem suam quam simplex delegatus, nec minus ei subiacet revocando. Unde per hoc quod episcopi et curati sunt ordinarii, non sequitur quod non habeant a papa iurisdictionem revocabilem. Quia papa potest dare iurisdictionem ordinariam non solum persone ad vitam aut ad aliud tempus, sed etiam officio vel statui aut dignitati in perpetuum, sicut aliqui archiepiscopi sunt legati pape ex dignitate, sicut est Cantuariensis archiepiscopus, *De officio legati* c. 1. Similiter nec secundum valet, quia eoipso quod potestas divina est, soli Deo subiacet. Nec papa habet plenitudinem potestatis super potestatem divinam, immo nihil potestatis super eam, sicut nec super ius divinum. Ex quo oportet quod potestas iurisdictionis, in qua et super quam papa habet plenitudinem potestatis, sit ab homine, non immediate a Deo.

Secundo patet idem per apostolum ad Titum 1: *Reliqui te Crete, ut constituas per civitates presbyteros*, ubi loquitur non solum de constitutione que est per ordinationem, que non concernit certum locum, sed de constitutione per collationem cure animarum, que habet populum subiectum et est potestas iurisdictionis. Unde videtur quod curati ipsam potestatem pastoralem habent ab episcopo. Eodemmodo inducitur illud Innocentii, 21 d. c. 1, circa finem, ubi dicitur quod *apostoli in singulis civitatibus episcopos et presbyteros ordinaverunt*, idest ordinatos in suis sedibus posuerunt, et sic idem quod prius.

Tertio patet idem sic. Quia si potestas curatorum et episcoporum, qui habent populum subditum in utroque foro, est a Deo immediate non a papa, cum potestas divina non possit a suo effectu impediri ab homine sicut nec potestas nature, sicut papa non potest facere quin ignis comburat stuppam si eam habet, ita non poterit facere per quamcumque

desunt $B^2P^1V^6$

81 delegatio φ^1V^4 | et] *add.* est φ | 82 a[1]] de θ(-V^2) | 83 subiacet [subiaceret φ^5V^4] ei [*add.* in θ(-V^2)] αVa | 84 revocandus $\rho^1\sigma$ | 87 vel] aut ρ^1 | 88 episcopi θ(-V^2) | est] *om.* φ | 89 archiepiscopus] *add.* totius Anglie primas πBarb. | 91 potestatem] *add.* Dei φ(-U) | potestatis[2]] *add.* habet φ | 92 eam] *add.* habet θ(-V^2) | sicut] *om.* φ | 93 iurisdictionis] *om.* πBarb. | in] etiam ρ^1 | 98 constitutione] *add.* que est [*om.* θ^4] θ | cure] *om.* ρ^1 | animarum] *om.* $\varphi\rho^1$ | 100 pastoralem] parochialem [episcopalem V^2] θ | habeant φ | Eodemmodo inducitur] per [secundum St] α | 102 et] *add.* etiam π(-R) | 105 populum] *om.* ρ^1

89 X. 1.30.1 | 95-96 Tit. 1:5 | 101-102 "Innocentii" should be "Gratiani": Gratian, D.21 1[a] pars.

excommunicationem quin episcopus possit excommunicare et curatus a peccatis absolvere. Consequens est falsum. Ergo et antecedens. Maior probata est uno modo. Probatur alio modo. Quia si potestas iurisdictionis in episcopis et curatis ita est a Deo in eis sicut potestas caracteris sacerdotalis et episcopalis, sicut non potest papa, episcopum et curatum excommunicando vel deponendo aut etiam degradando, impedire quin sacerdos vere conficiat, episcopus vere ordinet et confirmet, sic nec quin uterque vere absolvat et liget in utroque foro. Falsitas consequentis apparet, quia excommunicatus non habet usum clavium, nec etiam executionem in aliquo foro. Unde sententia ab eo lata non tenet ipso iure, *De sententia et re iudicata* c. *Ad probandum*.

Si dicatur quod papa potest excommunicato populum subtrahere, et ideo non valet sententia lata in non subditum, licet iurisdictio sit de iure divino, sicut potest de facto subtrahere materiam eucharistie sacerdoti, et tunc non poterit celebrare, non est simile. Quia cum potestas iurisdictionis et prelationis non sit aliud quam relatio ad subditos, et relativa posita se ponunt, et perempta se perimunt, et si est pater de iure divino, habet et filium de iure divino, si episcopi et prelati habent potestatem prelationis et curam animarum de iure divino, per consequens habent subditos de iure divino. Et per consequens subditi non possunt eis subtrahi iure humano nisi de facto, sicut panis potest subtrahi sacerdoti volenti conficere, et tunc non poterit conficere, non quia panis desinat esse materia consecrationis, sed quia desinit esse materia presens, et consecratio requirit materiam debitam et presentem. Sed non potest facere quin panis de iure sit materia

desunt $B^2P^1V^6$

109 excommunicationem] *add.* vel suspensionem [supplicationem Sv] θ(-V^2) | curatus] curam ρ^1 | 110 peccatis] predictis ρ^1 | 111 modo²] *om.* α(-V^2V^4) | 112 caracteris] *om.* ρ^1 | 115 sacerdos] *add.* iste [ille V^2, ipse V^5] θ | 116 vere] *om.* φ | foro] *add.* poterit [poterat Sv] quandocumque [quomodocumque V^1V^5, quocumque V^3, quemcumque Sv] efficere θ(-V^2) | 118 tenet] *add.* in aliquo foro θ | ipso] *add.* de φ | 119 sententia et] *om.* θ(-V^2) | re] *om.* φ | 120 Si] *add.* autem θ | excommunicare V^7π(-R), excommunicari Barb., excommunicando ρ^1Va | 122 sicut] *add.* papa θ | de facto] *om.* θ | subtrahere de facto ψπ^1Barb.σ | et] *om.* φ | 125 et²] ut [unde Sv] θφSr | pater] *add.* est filius [*inv.* φ^5] et si est pater φ | de] *om.* φ | 125-126 habet ... divino] *hom.* ρ^1 | 125 et³] *om.* B^1; etiam θσ | 127 divino] *add.* et θψ | consequens] *add.* et [etiam θ^4] θ | 128-129 Et ... facto] et sic [per consequens Bo] nec [non Bo] possunt [*add.* eis Bo] subtrahi nisi de iure divino nisi de facto θ(-V^2), nisi eis subtrahatur [subtrahantur St] de facto [defectio Bm^1] φ | 128 subditi] *om.* ρ^1 | 129 potest subtrahi] *om.* πBarb. | 131 presens] presentis consecrationis [*om.* P^4] π(-R) | 132 Sed] *add.* papa BoV^5, subtrahens φ | facere] *add.* papa $\theta^2\theta^4$ | de iure] *om.* ρ^1

119 X. 2.27.24

sacramenti, et quin presens de facto [non] possit confici. Ita absolutioni sacramentali, que requirit materiam presentem, potest materia de facto subtrahi, et sic absolutio impediri. Sed si de facto non subtrahatur, non potest de iure subtrahi si subiectio est de iure divino, et per consequens non poterit papa impedire episcopum vel curatum quin vere absolvat sibi penitentialiter confitentem, sicut nec quin vere conficiat panem presentem. Sed excommunicatio et absolutio contraria non requirunt materiam presentem in prospectu, sed solum in districtu, quia extra territorium ius dicenti impune non paretur. Unde si episcopus et curatus habent populum subditum in foro exteriori de iure divino, nisi de facto expellantur de parochia et diocesi, per nullam excommunicationem desinunt esse materia sua quin possint ab eis absolvi et ligari, quia ius divinum per hominem non potest solvi. Si dicatur quod absolutio penitentialis facta ab excommunicato non valet, quia scienter ei confitendo penitens novum peccatum committit, ideo non est capax, non valet. Quia possibile est quod confitens nescit curatum excommunicatum, et sic non ponit obicem. Item in foro exteriori cessat instantia in quo indistincte non tenet absolutio nec excommunicatio facta ab excommunicato.

Quarto sic, quia si potestas iurisdictionis in episcopo et curato per quam sunt proprii sacerdotes ita est de iure divino sicut potestas caracteris per quam sunt sacerdotes, tunc cum homo teneatur de iure divino confiteri proprio sacerdoti omnia peccata sua mortalia, quero quis est ille sacerdos cui debet fieri illa confessio. Si dicant quod est episcopus vel sacerdos, aut intelligunt quod isti soli sunt proprii sacerdotes et non papa. Tunc papa non poterit audire confessiones sine licentia ipsorum, sicut nec alienus sacerdos sine licentia proprii sacerdotis, *De penitentiis* c. *Omnis utriusque sexus*. Si autem intelligant quod papa sit proprius sacerdos de casibus

desunt B^{2}P^{1}V^{6}

133 non θ(-V^{2})β] *om.* V^{2}γ | Ita] *add.* in V^{7}B^{1}Barb. | absolutioni [absolutionem V^{5}] α(-UV^{7})Sr] absolutione UV^{7}B^{1}Barb., absolutio [*add.* in π^{1}Va] π^{1}ρ^{1}Va | 134 sacramentali] sacramentalis ρ^{1}; *add.* subditi θ(-V^{2}) | materiam] *om.* φ | materia] mihi ρ^{1} | 137 vel] et φ(-St) | vere] *om.* ρ^{1} | 138 quin] *om.* π(-R)Barb. | vere] *om.* αρ^{1} | conficiat] consecret [consecrat W] α(-Bo) | 140 in prospectu] in conspectu π^{1}, inspectu B^{1}Barb. | 141 impune] *om.* ρ^{1} | 142 nisi] si φ | 144 solvi α(-φ^{5}V^{4}) | 145 potest] *add.* tolli vel θ(-V^{2}) | 147 committit] *add.* et θ(-V^{2}) | est^{1}] *add.* absolutionis φ | 148 potuit obicere θ | 153 cum] si θ | 154 ille] *add.* proprius θ | 155 debet] dicitur ρ^{1} | ista θ | dicant π(-P^{4})Barb.σ] dicatur [datur S, dicitur Sz] αP^{4}ρ^{1} | 156 sacerdotes proprii [proprie St] α | papa^{1}] *add.* et ρ^{1} | 157 ipsorum] eorum αVa | 158 penitentiis] *add.* et remissionibus θBarb.Sr | 159 autem] dicatur quod φ | intelligunt θπ(-R)Barb.

158-159 X. 5.38.12

papalibus, episcopus de episcopalibus, curatus de parochialibus, tunc nec papa nec episcopus poterunt absolvere de casibus curatorum nisi de licentia ipsorum, nec papa de casibus episcoporum nisi de licentia eorum, propter idem. Si autem intelligant quod papa est proprius sacerdos ubique, episcopus de omnibus preter quam de papalibus in sua diocesi, curatus de suis in sua parochia, sequuntur tria inconvenientia.

Primum est quia uni potentie passive respondent plures active, quia uni potentie recipiendi sacramentum penitentie, que est peccator penitens, respondet triplex activa, scilicet papalis, episcopalis et parochialis, quod est absurdum. Quia tantum unum uni opponitur secundum speciem per se primo, quamvis per accidens plura secundum numerum possint opponi eidem. Unde cum potentia activa et passiva referantur ad invicem et sint opposita relative, cuilibet potentie active proprie respondet sua passiva propria, quod non est si potentia pape, episcopi et curati sint independentes ab invicem, et quelibet per se equaliter a Deo. Secundum inconveniens est quia potestas divina poterit frustrari etiam de iure divino. Quia qui habet plures proprios sacerdotes de eodem iure, cum non teneatur confiteri cuilibet sed cui vult, poterit semper ire ad unum vel duos et nunquam ad alium vel alios. Et sicut hoc potest unus penitens, ita et omnes. Et sic vel in papa, vel in episcopo, vel in curato frustrabitur potestas divina ab eo ad quod per se et principaliter ordinatur, quod est inconveniens ut videtur. Tertium inconveniens est quia sicut potestas divina sacerdotalis est una et equalis in omni sacerdote ad conficiendum, et potestas episcopalis una et equalis in omnibus episcopis ad confirmandum et ordinandum, ita debet esse una et equalis per se potestas divina ad iudicandum subditum in foro conscientie, et una ad iudicandum in foro exteriori. Hoc autem non est si potestas iurisdictionis a Deo sit in papa, episcopo et curato, quia constat quod iste non sunt equales de natura sua, sed pape est plena, ceterorum coartata.

desunt $B^2P^1V^6$

162-163 nec ... idem] *om.* ρ^1 | 162 nec ... eorum] *om.* θSr | eorum] ipsorum φ | 163 intelligunt π(-R)ρ(-Bm^2) | 165 sequentur σ | tria] talia ρ^1 | 166 quia[1]] quod $\theta\varphi^3\varphi^5$ | potentie] persone π(-R)Barb. | uni[2]] *om.* θ | 167 potentie] potestati $\theta\sigma$, persone B^1Barb.; *add.* passive ψ | recipiendi $\rho^1\sigma$] retinendi θR, receptive φ, reconciliandi P^4Barb., conferendi B^1, que [qui P^2] est penitens [*om.* P^2] recipiens ψ | que ... penitens] *om.* ψ | 168 triplex activa] et [*om.* BoV^5V^3; sibi V^2] activa tripliciter θ | 171 eisdem θ(-Bo) | 172 relatione π(-R)Sr | 173 potentia] potentie φ(-UBm^1) | 174 ab] ad $\psi\rho^1$Va | quilibet $V^7\pi$Barb. | 175 quia] *add.* secundum [*om.* Pr] hoc φ | 177 vel] aut α(-θ^3U) | 178 potest] habet θ | 179 in[3]] *om.* φ(-U) | 180 divina] sua φ | 181 est] *om.* $\theta\varphi$(-Bm^1); ut videtur ψ | 182 sacerdotalis] sacramentalis α | 183 episcopalis] *om.* φ | 187 ille [illi Barb.] $B^1\rho$

Sed si potestas iurisdictionis in solo papa est a Deo, in ceteris autem ex commissione pape, cessant omnia ista inconvenientia. Primo quidem, uni potentie passive respondet una activa, quia potentie ligabili et solubili passive, que est unius rationis in uno foro, respondet una sola activa in papa. Verbi gratia, respectu fori conscientie ad retinendum requiritur penitens subditus. Respectu igitur penitentie, que est fundamentaliter potentia receptiva sacramenti, respondet pro potentia activa caracter sacerdotalis, qui est unius rationis in omnibus sacerdotibus, et sic una potentia passiva habet unam per se activam. Item subiectioni, que est dispositio potentie passive sine qua non est receptiva absolutionis, respondet per se potestas iurisdictionis in solo papa, qui solus est proprius sacerdos de iure divino, potens solvere et ligare, et solus de iure divino tenetur audire confessiones, et cui omnes tenentur confiteri. Per accidens autem fiunt proprii sacerdotes quibus et sicut ille commiserit confiteri possumus. Similiter in foro exteriori una est potentia passiva ligabilis et solubilis, sicut et sententia excommunicationis est unius rationis. Nam excommunicatio maior et minor suspensio et interdictum non differunt nisi secundum magis et minus in eadem specie, vel saltem in eodem genere. Et per consequens potestas ligandi et solvendi in illo foro, idest potestas excommunicandi, per se primo debet esse unius rationis. Si enim calor est unius rationis, per consequens et potentia calefaciendi, que habet speciem ab obiecto. Unde potestas iurisdictionis in utroque foro per se de iure divino est in solo papa, cui soli in Petro dictum est: *Tibi dabo claves regni celorum*, quod nulli apostolorum dictum est nisi Petro. Unde cum Deus Petro tradiderit omnes claves et nulli apostolorum, loquendo de clavibus iurisdictionis, nullus aliorum habuit has claves nisi quantum Petrus tradidit, qui eas solus habuit pro omnibus. Unde dicit Innocentius, 21 d. c. 1, quod Christus Petro *pro omnibus et pre omnibus claves regni celorum tribuit*. Unde a solo Petro sunt petende iste claves ab omnibus, qui eas

desunt $B^2P^1V^6$

190 illa φP^2 | 192 activa] *om.* φ | 193 retinendum $\theta\pi$Barb.] recipiendum $\psi\rho^1\sigma$; penitendum φ | 195 caracteris π(-R)Barb. | 196 potentia] *om.* πBarb. | 199 solus] *om.* θ^2BoV^5 | est] *om.* Bm$^1\varphi^2$ | est solus θ^1(-BoV^5)$\varphi^3\rho^1$ | 200 potest φ | 201 fiunt] *add.* alii φ | 202 proprii] Christi [alii Bo] $\theta\psi$ | confiteri possumus θ(-V^2)] *om.* Barb. *et cet. mss.* | 203 passiva] *om.* ρ^1 | 204 rationis] *om.* ρ^1 | 207 consequens] *add.* omnis $\theta\psi$ | potestas^1] actus φ | 208 primo] *add.* et [*om.* θ^2V^5] principaliter θ(-V^2) | 209 calefactiva θ | 210 Unde] cum θ | 213 tradidisset θ, tradidit ψ | omnes claves] *om.* θ | 214 nisi] *add.* in $\theta\rho$ | Petro φ(-St) | 215 tradiderit πBarb. | pro] pre φ | 217 tribuit] tradidit φ | iste] ille ρ^1

211-212 Matt. 16:19 | 215-217 "Innocentius" should be "Gratianus": Gratian, D.21 1ª pars.

accepit pro omnibus. Item per hoc cessat secundum inconveniens, quia potestas ligandi et solvendi non potest frustrari in papa, nec propter defectum materie sicut in aliis, qui possunt perdere omnes subditos. Non autem papa, quia ecclesia tota non potest deficere. Item non potest frustrari per hoc quod eatur ad alium eo contempto, quia itur ad eum quando itur ad eius vicarium ordinarium vel delegatum. Tertium etiam inconveniens cessat, quia potestas iurisdictionis in papa est una a qua cetere derivantur. Quia in hoc differt potestas iurisdictionis a potestate caracteris, quia illa de sui natura potest committi, quia in iurisdictione inest etiam iudicis dandi licentia. Non sic autem potestas ordinis, cuius usus non potest committi non habenti eam, *De consecratione ecclesie vel altaris* c. *Aqua*.

Quinto patet idem sic. Quia si curati non haberent ab episcopo et papa potestatem iurisdictionis, nec episcopi a papa, papa non posset iudices dare nec legatos mittere ad dioceses episcoporum nisi propter eorum negligentiam vel defectum, nec episcopi confessores et predicatores per dioceses. Consequens est falsum. Ergo et antecedens. Consequentia patet per simile, quia papa non mittit inquisitores per terras regum et principum ad puniendum et corrigendum, quia non habent ab eo suas iurisdictiones et iustitias. Ergo similiter si episcopi non habent suam iurisdictionem ab eo, non debet eis mittere legatos, et pari ratione nec episcopus predicatores et confessores per parochias. Falsitas autem consequentis apparet, *De officio legati*, per totum, *De officio < iudicis > ordinarii* c. *Inter cetera*, ubi episcopi mittunt per dioceses predicatores et confessores.

Tertia Conclusio

Tertia conclusio principalis, de potestate curatorum per comparationem ad statum et ad ecclesias ipsorum, est quod omnes ecclesie parochiales et

desunt $B^2P^1V^6$

218 Item] et α | 222 eatur] eant φ | 223 ordinarium] *om.* φ | 226 illa] *add.* que iurisdictionis sunt φ | sua π(-R)Barb.Va | possunt φ | 226-227 quia² ... licentia] etiam ei qui in iurisdictione non est alias $\theta(-V^2)$ | 226 quia²] *add.* et π(-R) | 227 iudicis] subditus usus φ | danda πBarb. | licentiam φ | potestas] de potestate θ | 229 Equa π(-R)Barb.Va | 230 et] *add.* a $\theta(-BoP^3)V^7$ | 231 papa²] *om.* φπ(-R)Barb. | 232 nisi] etiam φ | 233 vel] et [*om.* S] θφ | 238 legatos] *add.* vel [*om.* Sv] delegatos [delegatus P^3] $\theta(-V^2)$ | et ... nec $\theta(-V^2)$] nec pari ratione [per rationem W] ipse nec [*om.* U] Barb. *et cet. mss.* | 239 et] *om.* ρ^1; nec γ | autem] *om.* $\theta(-V^2)$ | 240 legati] *add.* et delegati $\theta(-V^2)$ | totum] *add.* et $\theta(-V^2)$ | 243 comparationem] *add.* et $\theta(-BoV^2)$ | 244 ecclesias] ecclesiam [ecclesiarum S] θψ | ipsorum] eorum ρ^1 | omnes] eorum B^1Barb.

228-229 X. 3.40.9 | 239-240 X. 1.30 | 240 X. 1.31.15

cure simplices, quidquid habent potestatis spiritualis in quantum huiusmodi, totum habent a papa sive ecclesia Romana, quod patet ex predictis in quarto articulo de papa, in ultima conclusione, ubi probatum est a papa procedere omnem potestatem iurisdictionis in ecclesia. Item in precedenti articulo, ultima conclusione, ubi probatum est omnes ecclesias et cathedras a Romana ecclesia erectas et fundatas. Iterum probatur tripliciter, primo quia dictum est Petro: *Super hanc petram edificabo ecclesiam meam*, ex quo patet quod tota ecclesia Dei fundata est super soliditate Petri. Ergo aut ecclesie parochiales et cathedrales non sunt de ecclesia Dei, aut sunt fundate auctoritate Petri. Unde Cyprianus, et habetur 24 q. 1 *Loquitur*, probans unitatem ecclesie ex unitate fundamenti, quod est Petrus post Christum, dicit quod in ecclesia servatur unitas in origine ab uno capite, sicut multi radii ab uno sole, multi rami ab una radice, multi rivi ab uno fonte procedunt, intelligens illud unum principium esse Petrum, procedentia ab ipso particulares ecclesias.

Secundo apparet idem, quia nec capella, nec ecclesia parochialis quecumque, debet fundari, nec in ea debet celebrari, nisi de licentia episcopi, et hoc ipsum est ex statuto ecclesie Romane. Ergo eius auctoritate omnes parochie sunt fundate, et per consequens ab ea habent quidquid eis debetur inquantum sunt ecclesie parochiales. Siquidem a principio sine licentia sedis apostolice non licebat basilicam consecrare nec etiam edificare, *De consecratione* d. 1 c. *De locorum*, cum quattuor capitulis sequentibus, postmodum vero ab eadem sede concessum est episcopis ut de licentia ipsorum illa fiant, eadem d. c. *Nemo*, c. *Nullus*, et c. *Clericos*, ex quo apparet quod omnes alie ecclesie auctoritate Romane ecclesie sunt fundate.

Tertio, quia nisi ipsa persone institutio in cura animarum et ipsamet cura et auctoritas rectorie parochialis sint a papa, et similiter ecclesie cathedrales, sequitur inconveniens, scilicet quod papa non poterit episcopatus et parochias dividere nec unire, nec casus absolvendos eis subtrahere, quia fundamentum Dei et potestatem ab eo datam ipse papa

desunt $B^2P^1V^6$

248 Idem θ(-V^2)U$Bm^1\varphi^4P^2$, ibidem V^7B^1 | in^2] *om.* $Bm^1\varphi^2$ | 251 quod φV^7 | 252 total] tunc π(-R) | 257 sole] *add.* et θ(-V^2Sv) | 258 illud] *om.* θ | 260 apparet] patet ρ^1 | idem] illud φ | quod φ | 263 parochie] ecclesie $\theta\rho^1$ | 265 basilicas θ | 266 cum] et [*om.* V^2] in θ | 268 ipsorum] eorum θ, episcoporum $B^1\rho^1$Sr | illa] *om.* θ; ista [ita U] $\varphi\sigma$ | Nemo] *add.* et θ(-V^2) | et] *om.* $\gamma\rho^1$Va | 271 constitutio θ(-V^2) | 272 et^1] aut θ | parochialis] *add.* ecclesie θ

251-252 Matt. 16:18 | 255 Gratian, C.24 q.1 c.18 | 266-267 Gratian, *De cons.* D.1 c.4-8 | 268-269 Gratian, *De cons.* D.1 c.9, D.1 c.15, D.1 c.34

non potest destruere nec diminuere. Si ergo ecclesie parochiales et episcopales sint a Deo fundate, et eis pro suis rectoribus certa potestas data ligandi et solvendi, papa neutrum potest tollere nec mutare. Si dicatur: quamvis matrimonium sit sacramentum et quid divinum, tamen papa potest circa eius materiam aliquid restringere et mutare. Ergo et circa materiam sacramenti penitentie. Dicendum quod non est simile, quia circa id quod non est divinum, licet requisitum sit ad divinum, non est inconveniens papam aliquid posse. Sed id quod in se et de se est divinum, et cum hoc est materia alterius divini, quod papa possit tollere vel mutare non est possibile. Esse autem subditum est materia absolutionis. Sed si subiectio est de iure divino, sicut oportet dicere si prelatio est de iure divino, tunc papa nihil potest circa materiam sicut nec circa formam. Item quod potestas aliarum ecclesiarum sit a Romana patet per Petrum Ravennas, qui sic dicit: *Quod stipiti rami, quod capiti membra, quod soli radii, quod fonti rivuli, hoc apostolice sedis eminentie debent omnes ecclesie quas ubique terrarum religio Christiana fundavit.*

Contra hoc autem arguunt alii sic dicentes. Scriptura sacra statum curatorum dicit esse institutum et ipsos a Christo. Quia accipio tanquam manifestum quod status in quo est potestas et iurisdictio continuatur in diversis temporibus ab illo a quo fuit institutus a principio cum institutus fuit, et conservatur in omnibus temporibus sequentibus, et quod successor alicuius in aliqua dignitate, officio aut statu ab illo eodem instituitur in illo a quo antecessor institutus est, cum in eodem statu succedat quasi eadem persona cum illo, ut patet per inductionem in omnibus baillivis, prepositis, prioribus, magistris ordinum, et sic de aliis, alias successor nullomodo censeretur quasi eadem persona cum antecessore. Sed status et potestas et iurisdictio discipulorum septuaginta duorum continuatur in sacerdotibus curatis, sicut status apostolorum et potestas et iurisdictio in episcopis, et succedunt sacerdotes curati septuaginta duobus discipulis sicut episcopi

desunt $B^2P^1V^6$

276 potest] habet φ | 277 sunt $\rho^1\sigma$ | 278 dicatur] *add.* quod φ | 280 aliquid] *om.* θ^1(-BoV^2)ρ^1 | 282 id] illud θV^7 | sit] *om.* θ | 284 alterius] alicuius φ | quod] *add.* hoc φ | 287 sicut] *om.* θ | 288 Romana] *add.* ecclesia θ | 290 hec θ(-V^2) | 292 sic] *om.* φ | sacra] sancta P^2B^1Barb. | 293 esse] etiam ρ^1 | accipiunt θ | 295-296 cum ... fuit] *om.* [quod Sv] θ(-V^2) | 299 persona] *add.* sit θ(-V^2) | cum illo] *om.* φ; cum antecessore θ, cum eo ψ | ut] sicut [sed φ^3] γ | inductionem] iurisdictionem γ | 301 antecessore] *add.* suo ρ^1

289-291 Cf. Thomas de Hibernia, *Manipulus florum*, fol. 57r | 292-380 Scriptura ... convinceretur: cf. Jean de Pouilly, *Quodlibet* 5, qu. 12, Biblioteca Apostolica Vaticana, MS Vat. lat. 1017, fols. 214r-215r

succedunt apostolis. Ergo sequitur quod ab illo eodem a quo status discipulorum fuit institutus a principio modo est institutus status curatorum, et a quo fuerunt instituti discipuli sunt instituti curati, habentes auctoritatem et iurisdictionem ab illo eodem a quo et discipuli septuaginta duo.

Sed status discipulorum a Christo est institutus, et ipsi ab eo instituti et missi, potestatem ab ipso Christo immediate accipientes, non ab aliquo apostolorum, sicut nec alii apostoli a Petro. Item post resurrectionem apostolis et discipulis simul potestatem predicandi et potestatem clavium contulit utrisque quando dixit: *Sicut misit me pater, et ego mitto vos*, scilicet ad predicandum, et postea: *Quecumque remiseritis* etc., quo ad potestatem ligandi et solvendi. Item Matthei ultimo in fine, dicit Dominus in monte Galilee, parum ante ascensionem: *Euntes ergo, docete omnes gentes* – ecce eis dat officium predicandi – *baptizantes eos in nomine Patris, et Filii, et Spiritus Sancti* – ecce potestatem baptizandi dat eis. Marci ultimo: *Euntes in mundum universum, predicate Evangelium omni creature*. Et sequitur post: *Illi autem profecti predicaverunt ubique, Domino cooperante et sermonem confirmante sequentibus signis*.

Dices quod ibi non fuerunt septuaginta duo quando hoc dixit apostolis. Immo fuerunt, et hoc negare videtur maxime hereticum et contra Scripturam que alias salvari non potest. Quia Actuum 2, quando reversi sunt de monte Oliveti unde Christus ascendit, dixit Petrus: *Oportet ex his viris qui nobiscum sunt congregati omni tempore quo intravit et exivit Dominus Jesus inter nos, incipiens a baptismate Joannis usque in diem qua assumptus est a nobis, testem resurrectionis eius nobiscum fieri unum ex istis*. Et statuerunt duos, Joseph et Mathiam, qui fuerunt de septuaginta duobus discipulis. Ergo ipsi et alii discipuli fuerunt in ascensione Christi cum Christus iterato misit eos ad predicandum et baptizandum. Immo si debeat illa Scriptura verificari, oportet eos, scilicet septuaginta duos, fuisse

desunt $B^2P^1V^6$

305 isto [ipso V^4] φ | 308 illo] *om.* θ | 311 Christo] *om.* π(-R)Barb. | 312-313 a ... et^1] *om.* φ | 313 discipulis] *add.* enim φ | simul] *add.* et apostolis φ | potestatem^2] *add.* iurisdictionis θ | 314 quando dixit] dicens [*om.* S] θ | 315 scilicet] *om.* ρ^1 | 316 dicit [*om.* $V^2\varphi^5$; dixit θ^2BoV^5, dicitur Sψ] in fine α | 318 dat eis θ(-V^2)φ^3WBarb. | 319 eis] *add.* et θ(-V^2S) | 320 predicate] *add.* ubique ρ^1 | 321 post] *om.* θ; postea φ | 321-322 predicaverunt ... signis] etc. θ | 322 et ... signis] etc. ρ^1 | signis] *add.* forte φ | 327-330 omni ... istis] etc. usque ibi [*om.* ρ^2] ρ^1 | 328 in diem] *om.* φ(-Bm^1) | 329 nobiscum] *om.* φ | 331 Ergo] *add.* et φ | 333 illa] *om.* θ

314 Joan. 20:21 | 315 Cf. Joan. 20:23 | 316-319 Matt. 28:19 | 320-321 Marc. 16:15 | 321-322 Marc. 16:20 | 325-330 The reference should be Act. 1:21-22.

semper cum Christo sicut et duodecim. Ergo et apostoli et discipuli omnes immediate sunt a Christo instituti, et ab illo acceperunt sine medio potestatem. Unde et Paulus, 2 ad Corinthios 10, dicit: *Nam et si amplius aliquid gloriatus fuero de potestate nostra quam dedit nobis Dominus*, non alius. Ergo nec Petrus. Item Actuum 9: *Vas electionis* etc. Et Actuum 13: *Segregate mihi Paulum et Barnabam ad opus ad quod assumpsi eos*, et ad Galatas in principio: *Paulus apostolus, non ab homine electus, neque per hominem, sed per Jesum Christum et Deum Patrem*. Et pari ratione vel maiori alii apostoli quos immediate vocavit, ut Matthei 4: Petrum et Andream, Jacobum et Joannem, filios Zebedei, et Matthei 9 et Marci 2: Mattheum. Et ad Galatas 2, super illo verbo: *Cum venisset Petrus Antiochiam, in facie restiti ei*, glossa: *Tanquam par, hoc enim non auderet nisi sciret se non imparem fore*. Non ergo ab ipso potestatem habuit. Ergo a Christo.

Sequitur ergo quod status curatorum et ipsi sint a Deo immediate instituti, et ab ipso habent immediate potestatem. Status enim istorum et illorum non est alius et alius, sicut status isti non sunt alii quam erant ante centum annos. Sed est unus status continuatus a Christo semper, et potestas a Christo data illis continuata in istis. Quare enim potestas a Christo collata Petro continuata est in summo pontifice, et potestas collata aliis apostolis non est continuata in aliis episcopis, et potestas collata discipulis non est continuata in curatis, non potes dicere. Et ideo curati sunt vere ordinarii, habentes iurisdictionem ordinariam, non iure humano sibi datam, sed a Christo immediate, in prima institutione ecclesie, in qua hos duos ordines et solum instituit. Et non sunt vicarii episcoporum, sed

desunt B^{2}P^{1}V^{6}

334 duodecim] *add.* apostoli θ | et^{2}] *om.* θ | 335 accipiunt φ(-U) | 336 et^{1}] *om.* θ(-V^{2}) | Nam θ] *om.* B^{1}ρ^{1}; hec verba [hoc verbo Pr] φ, vera [veris? Sr] ψσ, veni π^{1}Barb. | 337 glorificatus θ | 338 electionis] *add.* mihi iste [*om.* V^{5}] est [*inv.* Bo] θ | Et] item α | 339 ad^{1} ... eos] etc. ρ^{1} | 340 neque] non P^{2}B^{1}Barb. | 341 Deum] Dominum [*add.* nostrum V^{3}] θ(-Bo) | Et^{2}] ex φ | 342 apostoli alii [aliqui V^{2}] α | ut] *om.* ρ^{1}; *add.* habetur θ | 4] *add.* scilicet ρ^{1} | 343 et^{2}] *om.* πρ | Matthei 9] *om.* ρ^{1} | 344 Mattheum] *om.* α | illo verbo] illud θ | 345 faciem θφ(-V^{4})B^{1}Barb. | restitit [resistit V^{4}] Bm^{1}Wφ^{4}π(-R) | glossa] *add.* dicit θ(-V^{2}) | enim] autem [tamen V^{5}] θ | 346 non [*om.* V^{7}Sr] imparem θψπ^{1}σ] parem φB^{1}ρ | 348 sint] fuerunt π(-R)Barb. | Deo] Christo θ | 349-350 et illorum] *om.* φ | 350 est] sunt [*om.* Sv] θ(-V^{2}) | 352 illis] *add.* semper θ, est ψ | continuata] *add.* est θ | 354 collata] *add.* aliis Rρ | 355 potes θ(-Sv)P^{2}Rρ^{1}] potest SvφV^{7}π(-R)Barb.Va, possumus Sr | 356 vere] *om.* Wψ; veri φ(-φ^{5}) | 357 sibi] *om.* ρ^{1} | dato πBarb. | sed] *om.* ρ^{1} | 358 solum] *add.* illos φ(-Bm^{1}) | instituit] *add.* Christus θ(-V^{2})

336-337 2 Cor. 10:8 | 338 Act. 9:15 | 338-339 Act. 13:2 | 339-341 Gal. 1:1 | 342 Matt. 4:18-22 | 343 Matt. 9:9 | Marc. 2:14 | 344-345 Gal. 2:11 | 345-346 *Liber vite. Biblia cum glosis ordinariis et interlinearibus*, Gal. 2:11, 4:1249v

Jesu Christi, ab ipso instituti, inferiores tamen et minores episcopis, nec ab ipsis possunt destitui nisi rationabili causa, sicut nec episcopi a papa, cum non sint eorum vicarii sed Christi. Item episcopi habent inferiorem potestatem a Deo immediate sub papa, sed non a papa. Quia tunc, sede papali vacante, potestas in prelatis inferioribus periret, sicut sensus, absciso capite, deficiunt in ceteris membris. Et si ita esset, adhuc manifestius constat quod episcopus ordinatus, tempore vacationis illius, et consecratus, nullam penitus haberet potestatem. Et cum illa vacatio possit durare multis annis, sequeretur quod potestas ecclesie totaliter periret, quod nepharium est dicere. Consimiliter potest argui quod curati suam potestatem non habent nec a papa nec ab episcopis. Ergo etc. Ex quo patet quod nec papa a prelatis potest potestatem datam a Christo eis auferre et aliis non prelatis dare, nec statum ecclesie a Christo institutum destruere et immutare, cum sit ei data potestas in edificationem et non in destructionem, sicut et apostolo, 2 ad Corinthios 10. Et hoc pulchre dicit Urbanus papa, 25 q. 1 *Sunt quidam*: *Inde novas leges condere potest unde evangeliste aliquid nequaquam dixerunt. Ubi vero Dominus vel eius apostoli et eos sequentes sancti patres finaliter aliquid diffinierunt, ibi nec novam legem Romanus pontifex dare potest, sed potius quod predicatum est usque ad animam et sanguinem confirmare debet. Si enim quod docuerunt apostoli et prophete, quod absit, destruere niteretur, non sententiam dare sed magis errare convinceretur.*

Responsio ad illa per ordinem prout iacent. Dicendum est, quando ergo dicunt statum curatorum esse institutum a Christo, et ipsos etiam curatos esse immediate institutos a Christo, dicendum quod falsum est. Quia Christus per se non fecit nisi unum solum curatum, scilicet Petrum,

desunt $B^2P^1V^6$

359 ipso] eo θ(-V^2) | 360 nisi] *add.* ex φ | sicut] *om.* ρ^1 | 364 deficiunt] desinunt $V^2\theta^4$, desinit θ^2V^5, perit Bo | 365 ordinarius φ | 365-366 illius et consecratus] *om.* φ | 365 illius] papatus θ(-V^2) | 365-366 consecrationis $\psi\pi$Barb. | 366 ista θ | posset θ(-V^5) | 367 ecclesie] *om.* [illa Sv] θ | 368 esset θ(-V^2) | 370 a[1]] *om.* θ | prelatis] *om.* θ(-V^2) | datam a Christo] a Christo prelatis datam θ(-V^2) | 371 statum] statutum π(-P^4)Barb. | 372 cum] *add.* sic φ | eis π(-R) | et] *om.* αB^1 | 374 papa] *om.* θ | Inde] unde $\theta\psi$ | unde] ubi θ(-V^2V^3) | 375 nequaquam aliquid [aliqui V^2, aliud S] α | Ubi vero Dominus] *om.* ρ^1 | 379 niteretur] videretur [videntur St] φ | 380 magis] *om.* ρ^1 | errare] destruere φ | 381 ad illa $\psi\pi^1\rho$] *om.* θ(-V^2); ad ista $V^2\varphi B^1\sigma$ | 382 etiam] *om.* θ | etiam ipsos φ | 383 dicendum] *add.* est θ(-BoV^2) | 384 per se] *om.* θ | solum] *add.* prelatum sive θ

373 2 Cor. 10:8 | 374-380 Gratian, C.25 q.1 c.6

quando ei dixit soli: *Pasce oves meas*, quod prius ei promiserat dicens: *Tibi dabo claves regni celorum* etc., et *Confirma fratres tuos*, et *Si peccaverit in te frater tuus, corripe* etc., que omnia pertinent ad curatum, et soli Petro dicta sunt. Unde sibi soli curam animarum commisit Christus. Sed quia impossibile erat quod per se solum perfecte totius gregis curam gereret, ideo commisit ei per consequens sibi facere alios curatos, quantum ipse pro sui adiutorio et populi salute indigeret. Nec Christus per se instituit nisi unam solam curam totius ecclesie sue. Non enim divisit ipse pastores suos, dicens Petro: Pasce oves circumcisionis, et Paulo: Pasce oves gentium, sed unam curam totius ovilis instituit quam Petro commisit, ut fiat *unum ovile et unus pastor*. Sed postmodum Petrus per se et per alios divisit provincias et dioceses et parochias, 80 d. *In illis*. Unde status curatorum, prout distinguitur a statu episcoporum et pape, non fuit a Christo institutus, qui nullas parochias sub episcopis distinxit, nec ipsi curati sunt a Christo instituti in suis parochiis, sed solus Petrus, ut dictum est.

Quod postea dicitur: status in quo est potestas et iurisdictio continuatur in diversis temporibus ab illo a quo fuit institutus, et conservatur, dicendum quod verum est secundum intentionem constituentis, et non contra eam, et mediate vel immediate. Quod postea dicitur: successor alicuius in aliqua dignitate vel officio ab illo instituitur a quo et antecessor, dicendum quod verum est quando instituens antecessorem retinet sibi institutionem successoris, et potest hoc facere. Secus autem si non sibi retineret, sed alteri committeret. Unde quando papa erigit de novo sedem cathedralem, ipse primum episcopum ibi instituit. Successores autem non sibi instituendos semper reservat, sed electionem illis quos facit canonicos committit, et confirmationem et per consequens institutionem metropolitano cui eam subicit. Sicut in baillivis et prepositis idem est institutor predecessorum et successorum quando rex instituens sibi hoc ipsum reservat, aliter non. In prioribus etiam et abbatibus consuevit communiter

desunt $B^2P^1V^6$

385-386 quod ... etc.] *om.* ρ^1Va | 385 quod] et φ | 388 Sed] *om.* π | 390 sibi] *om.* $B^1\sigma$; soli α | 391 suo φ | 393 dicendo θ(-V^2) | circumcisionis ... oves²] *hom.* ρ^1 | 397 prout] qui φ | 398 qui] quia [quod S] θφ | 399 a] ab ipso θ(-V^2) | sed solus Petrus] *om.* θ | 401 dicitur] *add.* quod πBarb. | potestas] *om.* $V^2\theta^4\varphi$ | et] *om.* φ | 403 instituentis [institutis Bo; *add.* seu constituentis Bm^1] $\theta\varphi^1W\rho^1$Sr | 404 et] *om.* $\theta\psi B^1$ | 405 vel] et φ | et] *om.* φ | 409 episcopum] sedem φ | ibi] *om.* π(-P^4)Barb. | 410 fecit σ | 412 et] *om.* ρ^1 | idem] idem et unus [unus et idem W] φ | 414 etiam] *om.* θV^7

385 Joan. 21:17 | 385-386 Matt. 16:19 | 386 Luc. 22:32 | 386-387 Matt. 18:15 | 395 Joan. 10:16 | 396 Gratian, D.80 c.2

primus institui ab alio, saltem immediate, quam successores. Sicut beatus Bernardus prefectus est in abbatem Clarevallensem ab abbate Cisterciensi, sibi dante subditos et simul utrosque mittente – successores autem facti sunt per electionem – quo etiam modo omnes religiones utuntur in conventibus novis formandis. Nihilominus secundum veritatem semper institutor status et primi prelati in statu est institutor successorum, immediate vel mediate, inquantum eius virtute fit institutio ab alio cui ipse commisit, sicut archiepiscopus, cui papa submittit episcopum quem instituit, ab ipso papa ius instituendi accipit.

Quod dicunt, quod aliter non censeretur eadem persona successor cum predecessore nisi ab eodem institueretur, dicendum quod a quocumque instituatur, dum tamen in idem succedat, quantum ad illud reputatur idem. Sicut fiscus succedens criminoso, vel non habenti alias heredem iure suo, non instituitur ab illo a quo institutus fuerat defunctus. Tamen in hereditate in qua succedit reputatur eadem persona cum defuncto, et dicitur verus successor.

Quod postea dicunt, quod status et potestas discipulorum continuatus est in curatis, sicut status et iurisdictio et potestas apostolorum in episcopis, et succedunt curati discipulis sicut episcopi apostolis, dicendum quod discipuli pro tempore discipulatus Christi, idest usque ad passionem vel ascensionem, non fuerunt sacerdotes nec fuerunt curati, licet post Pentecostem quidam ex eis fuerunt sacerdotes, quidam episcopi et quidam diaconi, non sacerdotes nec curati. Unde non habuerunt pro tempore quo vocati sunt discipuli statum curatorum, nec quantum ad ordinem, nec quantum ad curam determinate parochie. Unde status eorum proprie non est continuatus in curatis. Sed verum est quod status illorum fuit figura status curatorum quo ad potestatem predicandi et temporalia metendi, et quantum ad hoc succedunt eis, idest habent hanc potestatem sicut illi. Et sic intelliguntur omnes auctoritates que hoc sonant. Similiter dicendum de

desunt $B^2P^1V^6$; 440 *post verbum* fuit *des.* V^7

415 alio] aliquo φ | immediatius φ | 416 prefectus] *om.* ρ^1 | 417 sibi] *om.* γ | dante [ante Sv] sibi θ | autem] etiam ρ^1 | 418 religiosi $\theta\pi$Barb. | 420 status] *om.* $\varphi\rho^1$ | et] *om.* φ | est] *add.* etiam φ | 423 accepit π(-R)Barb.Sr | 424 Quod[1]] *add.* autem θ | 425 instituerentur [instituentur W] φV^7 | dicendum] *add.* est $\theta(-V^2)$ | 428 ab illo] *om.* α | 429-430 et ... successor] *om.* $\theta(-V^2)$ | 432 apostolorum] discipulorum ρ^1 | 433 et ... apostolis] *om.* $\theta\psi$ | et] *add.* quod φ | 434 idest] *om.* πBm^2Barb. | 436 fuerunt] fuerunt facti θ^2, facti fuerint Bo, fuerint facti V^5, fuerint facti quidam θ^4, fuerint $StBm^1\varphi^4$ | et] *om.* θ | 437 non[1]] nec θ | pro tempore] ex φ | 439 proprie] *om.* α | 440 istorum [ipsorum UPr, episcoporum W] $\varphi(-V^4)$ | fuit] *add.* vera ρ^1 | 441 potestatem] statum φ | 442 succedit θ | hanc] eandem $\theta(-V^2)$ | 443 dicendum] *add.* est $\theta(-V^3)$

apostolis, quod ante passionem non habuerunt ipsi statum episcoporum nec ordinem.

Dicunt tamen aliqui quod in cena omnes simul facti sunt episcopi sicut et sacerdotes. Primo, quia Dei perfecta sunt opera. Unde instituens sacramentum debuit perfecte ipsum instituere quo ad materiam et ministrum. Unde sicut instituens eucharistiam instituit ministrum, faciens apostolos sacerdotes, ita instituens sacramentum ordinis debuit instituere ministrum, qui est episcopus ordinans sacerdotes.

Secundo, quia omnia sacramenta debuerunt institui ante Christi passionem, inter que consummatio ordinis est episcopatus.

Tertio, quia dicitur ad Ephesios 4: *Dedit quosdam apostolos, quosdam pastores et doctores*. Sed pastor nomen est et officium episcopi. Ergo ipse fecit aliquos episcopos. Sed non nisi apostolos. Ergo etc.

Item 21 d. c. 1, ultra medium, dicitur quod Christus *duodecim apostolos tanquam maiores sacerdotes, septuaginta duos discipulos quasi minores sacerdotes instituit*.

Item Augustinus, *De questionibus Veteris et Novi Testamenti*, dicit apostolos factos a Christo episcopos et antistites.

Paulus etiam episcopus fuit, qui et Timotheum episcopum ordinavit, 1 ad Timotheum 4: *cum impositione manuum presbyteri*, glossa: *idest episcopi*.

Septimo, sic Isidorus, secundo libro *De origine officiorum*: *Episcopi sunt constituti per totum mundum in sedibus apostolorum*. Ex quo habetur quod apostoli fuerunt episcopi, alias non habuissent sedes episcopales, et quod episcopi successerunt eis sicut papa Petro.

Octavo, tertia epistola Anacleti, ubi dicitur sic: *Scimus a Domino apostolos esse electos, et postea per diversas provincias ad predicandum*

desunt $B^2V^7P^1V^6$

445 nec ordinem] *om.* ρ^1 | nec] et φ | 446 simul] *om.* $\theta\varphi$ | episcopi] *add.* simul θ(-V^2) | sicut] *om.* θ(-V^2)B^1Barb. | 447 sacerdotes] *add.* et ratio [*add.* est B^1] π(-R)Barb. | 449 ministrum[1]] *add.* faciens ρ^1 | 452 debuerunt institui] instituit ρ^1 | 454 quosdam[2]] *om.* ρ^1 | 455 et[1]] quosdam φ | est] *om.* ρ^1 | 456 facit ρ^1 | 457 c. 1] *om.* φ | 463 4] *add.* ibi θ(-V^2) | glossa] glossa dicit [*inv.* V^5] ibi [*inv.* Bo] θ(-V^2) | 465 sic] *om.* θ(-V^2) | secundo] in θ | 468 episcopi] ipsi $\pi^1\rho^1$Sr | 469 Octavo] *add.* sic θ(-Sv) | 470 ad predicandum] *om.* πBarb.

454-455 Eph. 4:11 | 457-459 Gratian, D.21 1[a] pars | 460 Cf. Ps.-Augustine, *Quaestiones Veteris et Novi Testamenti* 1.93 (PL 35: 2287; cf. CSEL 50: 163-165) | 462-463 1 Tim. 4:14 | 463-464 *Liber vite. Biblia cum glosis ordinariis et interlinearibus*, 1 Tim. 4:14, 4:1281r | 465-466 Isidore, *De ecclesiasticis officiis* 2.5.6 (PL 83: 782) | 469-471 Ps.-Isidore, *Collectio decretalium* (PL 130: 76), ed. P. Hinschius, *Decretales Pseudo-Isidorianae* (Leipzig, 1863), p. 82

dispersos. Ex quo habetur quod a Domino habuerunt potestatem predicandi, non solum ante passionem sed semper, et quod facti fuerunt a Domino episcopi, quia medium sapit naturam extremorum. Cum ergo inter electionem et dispersionem fuerunt facti episcopi, ex quo electio et dispersio, que fuerunt extrema, facta sunt a Domino, ergo et medium, idest ordinatio episcopalis.

Nono, Dionysius in libro *De ecclesiastica hierarchia* dixit: *Ipse Christus in sacerdotalem consummationem ducens discipulos, subsistens in sanctissimum Patrem suum, retulit hierarchie perfectionem*. Ex quo habetur, cum sacerdotalis consummatio et hierarchica perfectio non sit nisi in episcopatu, quod Christus discipulos, idest apostolos, per seipsum fecit episcopos, alias non duxisset eos in illam consummationem nec perfectionem, sed duci fecisset.

Decimo, Maximus commentator ibidem dicit: *Ipse Dominus Jesus discipulos suos in episcopos consecrans*. Expressa est auctoritas; glossa non indiget.

Undecimo, quia sicut tradunt sancti, et specialiter Isidorus, *De ortu et obitu patrum*, Mathias fuit unus ex septuaginta duobus discipulis, qui tamen non a Petro factus est apostolus sed a Christo. Unde Dionysius, *De ecclesiastica hierarchia*, exponens illud Actuum 1: *Ostende quem elegeris ex his* etc., dicit de Petro sic: *Ipse discipulorum vertex, cum ordinata sibi hierarchia decade, in duodenarii discipulorum veniens sanctificam consummationem, in divinitates electionem timidus reliquit, dicens: "Ostende quem elegeris," et divina sorte divinitus ostensum in sancti duodenarii hierarchicum numerum recepit. De divina autem sorte huic*

desunt $B^2V^7P^1V^6$

471 habetur] patet ρ^1 | Domino] Deo π(-R)Barb. | 477 in libro] *om.* φ | dixit] *add.* sic φ | Christus] Jesus Christus [*inv.* V^5] θ | 478 subsistens] submittens [subiunctos V^2, submittere V^3] θ | 482 eos] illos πBarb. | consummationem illam α | 488 ex] de $B^1\rho^1$ | 489 Dionysius] *add.* in libro θ(-O) | 491 ordinata $V^3\pi$Barb.Va] coordinata α(-V^3)Sr, ordinatas ρ^1 | sibi] *om.* ρ^1 | 492 hierarchica σ | duodenam π(-R)Barb. | sanctificam θ(-V^2V^5)] sanctificavi V^5, sanctificans Barb. *et cet. mss.* | 493 timidius θ(-Bo) | 494 elegeris] *add.* ex his θ(-V^2) | divinitus] *add.* est ρ^1 | 495 hierarchiam π(-R)Barb. | numerum [*add.* alias in sancti duedecenarium V^1] hierarchicum α | sorte] *om.* φ | 495-496 huic Mathie] habuit Mathia φ(-St)

477-479 Ps.-Dionysius, *De ecclesiastica hierarchia*, chap. 5 (*Dionysiaca* 2: 1362) | 484-485 The reference should be to Petrus Hispanus, *Expositio in librum De ecclesiastica hierarchia*, chap. 5, Alonso 208. | 487-488 Cf. Isidore, *De ortu et obitu patrum*, chap. 79 (PL 83: 153) | 489-497 Ps.-Dionysius, *De ecclesiastica hierarchia*, chap. 5 (*Dionysiaca* 2: 1363-1365) | 490-491 Act. 1:24

Mathie data, videtur mihi eloquia sortem nominasse divinum quoddam, declarans illi hierarchico choro a divina electione ostensum. Ubi dicit commentator: *Et beatus Petrus, apostolorum princeps, cum aliis decem completurus duodenarium apostolicum, Deo commisit electionem, dicens: "Ostende quem elegeris." Et divina sorte demonstratum in numerum duodenarii apostolici suscepit.* Et subdit: *De sorte autem illa que cedidit super Mathiam, mihi videtur quod sors ibi dicatur aliquod divinum donum, demonstrans apostolice congregationi quem Deus in apostolum elegisset.* Si autem ceteri apostoli potestatem et consecrationem recepissent a Petro, Mathias eandem ab eo recepisset.

Responsio: sicut supradictum est, non est probabile quod fecerit aliquem de apostolis episcopum nisi Petrum, nec illum ante resurrectionem. De cena autem, quod tunc eos fecerit episcopos est omnino improbabile, quia antequam aliquis sit perfecte et complete sacerdos, et antequam hoc innotescat, non debet fieri episcopus. Sed tunc non fuerunt facti perfecte et complete sacerdotes, si tunc non susceperunt potestatem ligandi et solvendi, vel saltem non innotuit usque ad resurrectionem, quando dixit: *Quorum remiseritis* etc. Unde non debuerunt tunc fieri episcopi, propter etiam alias causas superius memoratas. Item nec in resurrectione quando dixit: *Accipite Spiritum Sanctum* etc., quia per illa verba, que communiter dicuntur cuilibet simplici sacerdoti, non est probabile quod sint facti episcopi, ut supra dictum fuit. Item tunc Thomas, qui erat absens, non fuisset factus episcopus per illa verba, sicut nec recepit Spiritum Sanctum per illam insufflationem, secundum illud 1 Joannis 5: *Spiritus est qui testificatur quoniam Christus est veritas.* Et postea: *Qui credit in Filium Dei habet testimonium Dei in se.* Ergo, per oppositum, quamdiu Thomas respuit credere veritatem resurrectionis

desunt $B^2V^7P^1V^6$

496 videntur φ | mihi] in ρ^1 | eloquia] *add.* divina θ(-V^2Sv) | divinum] donum φ | quod π(-R) | 497 hierarchico choro] decachoro [decathorum U] φ | 498 Et] *om.* φ | decem] *om.* α | 499 expleturus ρ^1 | 505 ab eo] *om.* αB^1Barb. | 506 quod] *om.* ρ^1; *add.* Deus θ(-V^2), Christus φ | fecerit] *om.* ρ^1 | 507 nisi] *add.* unum scilicet θ | 508 De] in θ | tunc] *om.* θ(-V^2) | fecerit episcopos eos θ(-V^2), fecerit [fecit W] eos episcopos γSr | omnino] valde θ(-V^2) | 509 improbabile] *add.* omnino θ(-BoV^2) | quod π(-R) | sit ... complete] digne et perfecte et complete [et complete *om.* θ^2] sit [fit Sv] θ | 511 si] sed $\theta^2\theta^3P^2$, et φ | 514 memoratas] dictas ρ^1 | nec] *om.* θ; non πBarb. | 517 episcopi] sacerdotes $Bm^1\varphi^2$ | 518 fuisset] fuit ρ^1 | 519 illam] *om.* θ | 520 Et] *om.* ρ^1Sr

497-504 Petrus Hispanus, *Expositio in librum De ecclesiastica hierarchia*, chap. 5, Alonso 209 | 513 Joan. 20:23 | 515 Joan. 20:22 | 519-520 1 Joan. 5:6 | 521 1 Joan. 5:10

Christi, non habuit in se Spiritum Sanctum qui testimonium perhibet de Christo.

Ad primum, de institutione sacramenti, dicendum quod Dei perfecta sunt opera, secundum tamen congruentiam et decentiam operis operati et modi operandi. Non decebat autem pro tunc facere episcopos sicut decebat facere sacerdotes. Quia ex quo sacramentum cepit esse in usu, ex tunc semper debuit esse in ecclesia, vel formaliter vel virtute, et maxime sacramentum de quo specialiter verificatur illud: *Ecce ego vobiscum sum omnibus diebus, usque ad consummationem seculi*. Subtracturus igitur sui presentiam palpabilem et visibilem, invisibilem et sacramentalem perpetuam nobis promisit. Unde ex tunc eucharistia debuit esse in ecclesia formaliter vel virtute. Sed formaliter tunc de eucharistia nihil reservatum fuit, sicut nec de agno paschali propter legis prohibitionem, Exodi 12. Ideo sacerdotes debuerunt fieri, in quorum virtute remaneret eucharistia conficienda. Sed sacramentum ordinis, quo ad effectum suum, indelebile remanebat in apostolis. Unde non erat tanta necessitas instituendi eius ministrum. Alia necessitas, propter confessionem apostolorum et discipulorum qui peccaverant, superius tacta fuit.

Ad secundum, dicendum quod omnia sacramenta sunt instituta ante Christi passionem, sed non omnia sunt executa. Verbi gratia, sacramentum penitentie fuit a Christo institutum quando dixit: *Agite penitentiam; appropinquabit regnum celorum*, Matthei 4, sicut sacramentum baptismi quando dixit: *Nisi quis renatus fuerit ex aqua et Spiritu* etc., Joannis 3. Unde sicut Joannes baptizando predicavit baptismum Christi, sic dicendo: *Agite penitentiam*, Matthei 3, predicavit penitentiam Novi Testamenti. Vel quando Christus dixit leprosis: *Ostendite vos sacerdotibus*, Luce 17, vel discipulis: *Solvite eum*, Joannis 11, tunc instituit sacramentum confessionis et absolutionis. Non tamen fuit executum ante passionem, quia nec

desunt $B^2V^7P^1V^6$

525 primam π(-R)Barb.Va | de ... sacramenti] *om.* ρ^1 | 526 operati] operantis [operatis P^4] π(-R)Barb. | 527 pro tunc] *om.* ρ^1 | 528 usum π(-R)Barb. | 529 et maxime] *om.* ρ^1 | 530 verificatur] dictum [*om.* φ^3] est γ | 533 perpetuam] *om.* ρ^1 | 533-534 debuit ... eucharistia] *hom.* ρ^1 | 535 paschali] *om.* π(-R)Barb. | 537 indelebilem [indelebiliter Bo] α(-V^5) | 538 tanta] *om.* φ | 539 ministrum] sacramentum θ; *add.* scilicet [*om.* St; idest U] episcopum φ | 539-540 Alia ... fuit] *om.* α | 539 necessitas $\rho^1\sigma$] auctoritas πBarb. | propter $\rho^1\sigma$] per πBarb. | 540 peccaverant Rρ^1Sr] peccaverunt π(-R)Barb.Va | 542 Christi] *om.* πBarb. | omnia sunt] sunt omnia tunc [*om.* Pr; *inv.* Bm^1] φ | Verbi gratia] ubi ergo φ(-St)B^1 | 545 Spiritu] *add.* Sancto $\theta\varphi^3$WP^2B^1 | 549 eum] *add.* vos θ(-V^2) | 550 et absolutionis] *om.* ρ^1 | fuit] *om.* ρ^1 | quia] *add.* tunc θ | nec] non θ

530-531 Matt. 28:20 | 535 Ex. 12:1-14 | 543-544 Matt. 4:17 | 545 Joan. 3:5 | 547 Matt. 3:2 | 548 Luc. 17:14 | 549 Joan. 11:44

erant ministri instituti, nec claves adhuc date regni celorum, que etiam dari non debuerunt antequam esset apertum regnum celorum, nisi implicite, forte ex naturali concomitantia ad sacerdotium, imminente passione, quia quod parum deest quasi nihil deesse videtur. Unde instituendo sacerdotium, Christus ordinem episcopalem instituit. Sed tamen non tunc dedit, quia non decuit.

Ad tertium, dicendum quod Christus dedit pastores dando primum et universalem immediate, dicendo Petro: *Pasce oves meas*, et per illum alios particulares. Vel pastores dedit immediate quando sacerdotes fecit, qui pane vivo qui de celo descendit pascerent oves suas.

Ad quartum, dicendum quod li "tanquam" solvit argumentum. Christus enim omnes apostolos non fecit episcopos sive maiores sacerdotes, sed in eis significabantur episcopi, ac si essent episcopi propter officium predicandi et visitandi per civitates et castella, et quia erant superiores omnibus aliis, et quia erant futuri episcopi. Et similiter fecit discipulos, non sacerdotes, sed tanquam minores sacerdotes, idest similes in hoc, quod sicut illi sub apostolis predicabant et curabant infirmos, sic et minores sacerdotes sub episcopis predicant et curant infirmos spirituales per administrationem sacramentorum.

Ad quintum de Augustino, supra solutum fuit de episcopo dicendo, quia presbyteri idem sunt qui et sacerdotes, 21 d. *Cleros* § *Presbyter*. Et sicut ibi dicitur, *apud veteres idem episcopi et presbyteri fuerunt*, et olim episcopi dicebantur presbyteri, 95 d. *Olim* et c. sequenti. Et sacerdos quandoque ponitur pro episcopo, *De consecratione* d. 1 *Solemnitates*, 81 d. *Oportet*. Unde ibi accipit Augustinus episcopos pro presbyteris, et similiter antistites, quia *sacerdos antistes dictus est pro eo quod ante stat*, ut dicit Isidorus, et habetur dicto capitulo *Cleros* § *Pontifex ubi antistes*. Et hoc, vel quia stat ante aram, et hoc habet episcopus inquantum sacerdos,

desunt $B^2V^7P^1V^6$

551 ad hoc ρ^1 | 553 forte] *om.* α | 558 universalem] *add.* pastorem φ | Petro] *om.* ρ^1 | istum θ | 559 particulares] titulares π(-R)Barb. | Vel] illis scilicet ovibus φ | mediate φ | 560 vivo] et vino θP^2B^1 | 563 specificabantur [specificabuntur seu specificabantur Bo, specificabuntur P^3] θ | essent] fuissent φ | propter] per α | 564 per] *om.* φ | 565 superiores] *add.* in ρ^1 | 566 non] *add.* quidem φ | 567-568 sic ... infirmos] *hom.* $\theta\varphi^5$ | 570 quintum] *add.* dicendum $\theta(-V^2)$ | dicendum πVa | 571 quia $V^2\theta^4RBm^2$Barb.σ] quod $\theta^2BoV^5\gamma\pi(-R)\rho^2$ | 573 et^1] *om.* ρ^1Va | sacerdotes ρ^1 | 574 ponuntur ρ^1 | 575 accepit $\theta(-V^5V^3)$ | 576 pro] *om.* ρ^1 | 577 dicto] *om.* ρ^1

558 Joan. 21:17 | 571-572 Gratian, D.21 c.1 | 573 Gratian, D.95 c.5-6 | 574 Gratian, *De cons.* D.1 c.16 | 574-575 Gratian, D.81 c.23 | 576-577 Gratian, D.21 c.1

vel quia stat ante alios, primus in ordine ecclesie, ut super se nullum habeat, et sic est episcopus. Unde utroque modo accipitur antistes, sed ibi accipitur pro simplici sacerdote ab Augustino, sicut 2 Paralipomenon 29: *Donec sanctificarentur antistites*, idest sacerdotes. Vel non dicit illud assertive, sed inquisitive.

Ad sextum de Paulo, dicendum quod fuit episcopus factus cum Barnaba ab apostolis cum oratione, sibi manum imponentibus, Actuum 13. Non autem factus est a Christo episcopus, nec pari ratione alii apostoli quibus non fuit indignior, sed solus Petrus, qui fuit princeps apostolorum. Non enim unus sacerdos facit alium, sed episcopus est qui facit alios sacerdotes et episcopos. Ideo simul facti sunt sacerdotes, non unus primus solus qui alios faceret. Sed non simul episcopi, sed primo Petrus solus, qui alios faceret.

Ad septimum, dicendum quod non negatur quin omnes apostoli preter Judam Scariotis fuerint veri episcopi finaliter consecrati. Sed dicitur quod non fuerunt a Christo sine medio consecrati, nisi solus Petrus. Quod vero dicitur episcopos constitutos in sedibus apostolorum, intelligendum est, non eisdem numero, sicut papa in sede Petri, sed in similibus quantum ad hoc, quod sicut illi fuerunt veri episcopi et habuerunt plebem sibi subiectam, sic et isti habent, sed non eandem. Nullus enim forte episcopus modernus habet eandem sedem vel plebem numero cum aliquo alio cpostolo. Nec patriarcha Hierosolimitanus, de quo magis videretur, habet plebem nec sedem Jacobi, quia illic sedes est Sathane non Christi. Unde sedes illa iam non est, nec plebs illa fidelis, sed penitus alia infidelis. Unde non habet esse sed tantum nomen, inquantum ecclesia Romana vult habere illum patriarcham in pari honore ac si haberet populum, propter spem recuperandi terram sanctam, non propter rem quam habeat, nisi forte in quibusdam suffraganeis quos non habuit Jacobus.

Ad octavum, dicendum quod apostoli fuerunt a Domino dispersi ad predicandum per diversas provincias, non quod sine Petro daret eis

desunt $B^2V^7P^1V^6$

582 sanctificantur [sanctificatur V^2V^3] θ | 585 sibi] et θ | 589 et ... sacerdotes[2]] *hom.* ρ^1 | 593 fuerint $\theta^4\gamma(-U\varphi^5)B^1Bm^2$Barb.] fuerunt $\theta^2\theta^3U\varphi^5\pi^1\rho^2$Va | 593-594 Sed ... consecrati] *hom.* θ | 596 non] *add.* in φ | eis γ(-U) | 597 sicut] *om.* θP^2 | illi] alii ρ^1 | veri] *om.* θ | 598 sic] sicut $\theta(-V^2)$ | 598-599 Nullus ... eandem] *hom.* θ | 598 enim] *om.* πBarb. | 599 habet] *om.* π | 600 videtur α | 603 esse] rem $\rho^1\sigma$ | 604 habere $\theta^2U\rho^1$Va] *om.* πBarb.; haberi $\alpha(-\theta^2U)$Sr

581-582 2 Par. 29:34 | 585-586 Act. 13:2-3

auctoritatem predicandi, sed quia dedit eis scientiam et gratiam et facundiam in omni idiomate predicandi, et potestatem per miracula confirmandi. Et inspiravit et revelavit Petro et ecclesie quod mitterent, et ipsis quod obedirent, sicut dixit Spiritus Sanctus: *Segregate mihi Paulum* etc., Actuum 13. Quod postea infertur de medio, dicendum quod non sequitur quod Christus eis dederit potestatem episcopalem presidendi sicut nec predicandi. Sed bene dedit eis interiorem potestatem ordinis, per ministrum tamen alium consecrando.

Ad nonum, dicendum quod Christus discipulos suos duxit ad episcopalem dignitatem per Petrum eos consecrando, sicut duxit populum suum per desertum in manu Moysi et Aaron.

Ad decimum, dicendum quod illud commentum non est authenticum, nec probat dictum suum. Unde eadem facilitate contemnitur qua probatur, sicut dicit Hieronymus. Vel potest dici Christum discipulos suos per Petrum non per se ipsum in episcopos consecrasse, sicut Dominus dicitur consecrasse Aaron et eum induisse vestibus pontificalibus, quamvis hoc totum fecerit per Moysem, Ecclesiastici 45: *Excelsum fecit Aaron* etc. *Dedit illi sacerdotium gentium* etc. *Circumcinxit eum zona iustitie*. Item sicut dictum est Joanni baptiste de Christo: *Hic est qui baptizat*, scilicet principaliter per potestatem auctoritatis secundum quod Deus, et singulariter per potestatem excellentie secundum quod homo, quamvis non baptizaret sine ministro secundum illud: *Quamvis Jesus non baptizaret, sed discipuli eius*, ita Christus consecravit discipulos ministerio Petri.

Ad undecimum, dicendum quod licet Mathias fuerit electus in apostolum a Deo, non tamen fuit consecratus in episcopum a Deo sine

desunt $B^2V^7P^1V^6$

609 eis] *om.* $\theta(-V^2)$ | 611 quod] *add.* eos [eis φ^5] φ | mitterent] mitteret [*add.* et θ^4] ipsos [populos Bo] $\theta(-V^2)$ | 614 dederit eis $\theta(-V^2)\varphi^1P^2B^1$Barb.Va | dedit ρ^1 | 615 eis] *om.* πBarb. | 616 ministerium ρ^1 | alium] *add.* eos φ | 617 dicendum] *om.* π | suos] *om.* φ | ad] *om.* π(-R) | 622 Christum [undecim V^4] θ^2Bo$V^5\varphi B^1$] Christus [Christi P^4] $V^2\theta^4P^2\pi^1\rho\sigma$ | 623 ipsum] *add.* apostolos $\theta(-V^2)$ | 626 eum] illum θ | 627 Item] *om.* ρ^1 | 628 scilicet] *om.* α(-U) | auctoritatem potestatis θ | 630 quamvis[1] ... ministro] *om.* π(-R)Barb. | Quamvis Jesus] licet Christus $\theta(-V^2)$ | 631 ita] item ρ^1 | discipulos] *add.* suos $\theta^1(-V^2)$, suo θ^2 | 633 dicendum] *om.* πBarb. | licet] *om.* θ | fuit θ | 633-634 electus ... fuit] *hom.* φ | 634 Deo[2]] *add.* non tamen φ

612-613 Act. 13:2 | 621-622 Cf. Thomas de Hibernia, *Manipulus florum*, fol. 139r: "Quod de scripturis sacris auctoritatem non habet eadem facilitate contempnitur qua probatur." The statement is attributed to Jerome, *Ad metuadem virginem*. | 625-627 Eccli. 45:7-9 | 627-628 Joan. 1:33 | 630-631 Joan. 4:2

ministro. Immo a Petro, vel ordinatus a Petro, quia probabile est quod fuerit ultimus de duodecim ordinatus, sicut ultimo vocatus. Sicut Paulus non minus quam Mathias electus est a Deo in apostolum, qui tamen factus est episcopus ministerio aliorum. Sicut etiam dicitur: *Nemo assumit sibi honorem nisi qui vocatur a Deo tanquam Aaron*, et tamen Aaron sorte divina, sicut Mathias, electus est, virga sua florente, qui fuit nihilominus per hominem secundum ritum illius temporis consecratus. Sic etiam beatus Nicholaus et multi alii in episcopos divina revelatione promoti sunt et electi, sed ab hominibus consecrati.

Quid ergo dicunt, quod status apostolorum continuatur in episcopis, verum est, et de statu primo quo ad potestatem et auctoritatem predicandi (si illa in eis non fuerit interrupta) et dignitatem super alios, et quo ad statum ultimum, quia finaliter omnes apostoli fuerunt episcopi. Et quod dicit de discipulis, verum est quod quantum ad aliquid et aliquo modo status eorum continuatur in curatis. Quia sicut illi sub apostolis habuerunt potestatem predicandi, sic et curati sub episcopis. Non autem sic quod illi fuerunt primi curati, et isti post illos. Et similiter intelligendum est de successione que est per representationem, non per veram successionem. Non enim est intelligendum quod sicut papa est successor Petri, et ideo habet potestatem Petri, quod eodem modo episcopi sint successores apostolorum, et ideo habeant potestatem eorum, nec quod curati sint successores septuaginta duorum discipulorum, et per hoc habeant potestatem eorum, eodem modo quo episcopus qui nunc est succedit predecessori suo in episcopatu, et curatus qui nunc est in cura curato qui ante se fuit, quia sequerentur multa inconvenientia. Primum quidem, sequeretur quod sicut non fuerunt nisi tredecim apostoli preter Petrum, ita non essent nisi tredecim episcopi cum papa. Et sicut non fuerunt nisi septuaginta duo discipuli, ita non essent nisi totidem curati. Nulla enim ratio est quod Petrus non habeat nisi unum successorem, et quilibet

desunt $B^2V^7P^1V^6$

635 Immo] non ρ^1 | probabile] probatum ρ^1 | 636 fuerit] fuit ρ^1 | 638 est] *om.* π(-R) | Sic $P^2\pi$Va | 639 vocatus est θ | 640 sicut] *add.* et θ(-Bo) | sua] *add.* florida seu θ | 641 Sicut $\alpha\pi^1$SzBarb. | etiam] *om.* Boπ(-R)Barb.; et θ(-BoV^2V^3)R | 643 sed] *om.* π(-R) | 645 et[1]] *om.* $\theta\pi$(-R)Barb. | 646 si] *add.* tamen φ | et[1]] ac ρ^1; *add.* quo ad [*om.* Barb.] θ(-V^2)Barb. | 648 dicunt [debent V^3] θ, dicitur P^2Bm^2Barb., loquitur ρ^2 | quod $\rho^1\sigma$] *om.* Barb. *et cet. mss.* | quantum] quo θ | et] *add.* in ρ^1 | modo] *om.* ρ^1 | 650 sic autem α | 653-654 et ... Petri] *hom.* $\theta P^2\pi$(-R) | 654 quod] *om.* θ(-V^2) | 655 potestates θ | quod] *om.* γ | 657 quo] sicut [*om.* V^2] θ | est] *om.* θ(-Bo) | 659 quidem] *add.* inconveniens θ(-V^2) | 661 episcopi] *add.* vel quattuordecim θ(-V^2V^3) | 663 habet φ

638-639 Heb. 5:4 | 639-641 Cf. Num. 17:1-8, Ex. 29:1ff. | 641-643 Cf. Jacobus a Voragine, *Legenda aurea* 3.2, Graesse 23

aliorum habeat plures. Quia si illorum ecclesie fuerunt a Deo fundate, non potuerunt dividi ab ecclesia sicut nec sedes Petri. Secundo, sequeretur quod multi apostolorum non habuissent successores, quia non habuerunt determinatas sedes, sicut Paulus, qui Rome mortuus, non abstulit Petro sedem suam, nec totam nec partem. Jacobus etiam Zebedei, martirizatus Hierosolimis ubi alius Jacobus sedebat, successorem non habuit. Immo forte preter Petrum et Jacobum Hierosolimorum, de quo infra dicetur, non est proprie et vere alicui alii apostolo assignare successorem, et multo minus septuaginta duobus discipulis, de quibus nec uni potest fingi assignata determinata parochia per Christum.

Quod postea inferunt, quod ab illo eodem a quo fuit institutus status discipulorum, ab illo fuit institutus status curatorum, non sequitur, quia non sunt veri nec proprii successores eorum, ut dictum est. Immo inquantum sacerdotes curati differunt totaliter ab eis, quia nec illi erant sacerdotes, nec illi erant curati, quia non habebant aliquam plebem determinatam sibi commissam sicut curati, nec poterant aliquem solvere nec ligare. Unde est totaliter alius status, licet de illo statu habeant duo, scilicet predicare et temporalia metere.

Quod ulterius concludunt, quod ab eodem instituuntur curati a quo et discipuli, dicendum quod non sequitur etiam si esset idem status ille et ille. Quia Dominus, qui discipulos primos instituit, dato quod fuissent primi curati, sequentes curatos non sibi reservavit instituendos, sed commisit vicario suo generali, cui curam omnium ovium commisit dicens: *Pasce oves meas*. Illas autem oves Petrus pascit quas pascendas committit, quia qui per alium facit, per se ipsum facere videtur. Sed illas Petrus non pascit quas alius pascit non nomine Petri, nec a Petro institutus, sed ab alio. Unde quicumque dicit quod aliqui pastores vel curati in ovili Christi instituuntur, non a Petro, sed immediate a Christo, falsificat verbum a Christo dictum Petro: *Pasce oves meas*. Sed debuit dicere: pasce oves meas

desunt $B^2V^7V^6$; 684 *usque ad verbum* discipulos *deest* P^1

664 Quia si] si enim φ | illorum] istorum [istarum U] φ | 665 ab ecclesia] per ecclesiam [ecclesias St] φ | Secundo] *add.* quia ρ^1 | 667 mortuus] *add.* est αSr | non] nec θ(-V^2) | 669 Jacobus] *add.* Alphei θ | 670 Petrum] *add.* Romanorum φ | Jacobum] *add.* Alphei φ Hierosolimitanorum episcopum θ(-V^2) | 671 et vere] successor [*om.* P^4] et non est π(-R) | alii] *om.* πBarb. | 673 assignata] *add.* et θ | 674 infertur ρ^1 | 678 illi] *om.* θ | erant] *om.* πBarb.; erant similiter [*inv.* Bo] θ | 679 absolvere θ | 680 alius] aliquis π(-R) | 683 quod] *om.* ρ^1 | ille¹] iste $P^2\rho^1$Va | ille²] iste θ | 684 primos θP^2R$Bm^2\sigma$] primo [proprios primo P^1] $\varphi\pi$(-R)ρ(-Bm^2) | 687 pascendas] *add.* ipse [esse W] φ | 689 Petri] suo θ(-V^2)

686-687 Joan. 21:17

una cum pastoribus quos tibi adiungo vel adiungam. Et tunc est satis mirum, si Christus erat immediate instituturus omnes alios pastores, episcopos et curatos per mundum particulariter, sicut successorem Petri universaliter, quare non ita dixit aliis apostolis pro episcopis, et discipulis pro curatis: pascite oves meas et vos cum Petro, sed sub Petro, sicut paterfamilias omnibus operariis quos immediate conduxit dixit: *Ite et vos in vineam meam*, Matthei 20. Si etiam erat eis daturus eque immediate claves iurisdictionis sicut successori Petri, mirum est quare non ita dixit eis aliquando: dabo vobis claves regni celorum cum Petro, sicut hoc dixit Petro. Nam de aliis que dedit eis sicut Petro, puta intellectum Scripturarum, et gratiam predicandi, dixit communiter: *Dabo vobis os et sapientiam cui non poterunt resistere*, et de potestate miraculorum: *Dedi vobis virtutem et potestatem* etc., Luce 10. Unde cum non legatur Christus dedisse nec promisisse claves iurisdictionis nec curam animarum aliis apostolis nec discipulis sicut Petro, dato quod episcopi succedant apostolis et curati discipulis, sicut papa Petro, non sequitur quod habeant curam nec potestatem sicut ipse immediate a Christo.

Quod dicunt postea, sicut apostoli non habuerunt potestatem suam a Petro, nec discipuli ab apostolis, nec etiam a Petro, sed omnes immediate a Christo, sic episcopi et curati non a papa sed a Christo, dicendum quod, sicut supra dictum est, omnes apostoli et omnes discipuli omnem potestatem iurisdictionis acceperunt a Petro. Sed dato quod omnes illi, quasi primi episcopi et primi curati, accepissent immediate a Christo, non tamen sequitur quod successores accipiant immediate ab eo, sed magis a successore suo, quia Christus hoc sibi non retinuit, sed successori suo commisit. Sicut enim se habebant illi predecessores ad Christum per se ipsum ecclesiam regentem, ita eorum successores ad illum qui Christo succedit in regimine universalis ecclesie. Unde sicut illi a Christo sunt instituti, quasi predecessores a predecessore, ita et isti a Petro et

desunt $B^{2}V^{7}V^{6}$

695 episcopos et curatos] *om.* α | 698 ad omnes operarios πBarb. | conduxerat $ρ^{1}$ | dixit] *om.* $π^{2}$Barb. | 699 Matthei 20] *om.* πBarb. | etiam] *om.* α | eis daturus [*add.* est vel V^{3}] erat [esset P^{2}] α(-V^{2}) | 700 sicut] *om.* $ρ^{1}$ | quare] quia $ρ^{1}$ | 701 hoc] *om.* θ(-V^{2}) | 703 communiter] *om.* θ | 704 et] etc. θSr | 705 vobis] *add.* per θ(-BoV^{2}Sv) | Christum $θ^{2}θ^{3}P^{2}$π(-R) | 706 nec^{1}] vel α | 708 non] *add.* tamen θ(-V^{2}) | 712 sic [*om.* Bo; si V^{3}; *corr. ab* sicut B^{1}] $θφ^{3}B^{1}$Rσ] sicut γ(-$φ^{3}$)P^{1}Tρ, sed P^{4} | 713 sicut] *om.* φ(-U) | 714 quasi] qui $P^{4}B^{1}$Barb. | 721-722 ita ... successore] *om.* $ρ^{1}$ | 721 et^{1}] *om.* θ(-V^{2}) | ipsi π(-R)Barb.

698-699 Matt. 20:4 & 7 | 701-702 Cf. Matt. 16:19 | 703-704 Luc. 21:15 | 704-705 Cf. Luc. 10:19

successoribus, quasi successores a successore. Sicut enim dicitur *C. Ad legem Juliam de ambitu* l. una, *lex Julia*, ambitus cessat in urbe, quia ibi dat imperator omnes dignitates quia presens, de quo non est verisimile quod per pecuniam corrumpatur. Sed in provinciis, in quibus dat dignitates et officia per alios propter sui absentiam, ibi locum habere potest. Ex quo habetur quod princeps, ubi presens est, officia distribuit per se ipsum; absens vero aliis committit distribuenda. Sed procuratorem Cesaris vel fisci, qui est immediate loco sui, semper ipse facit per se ipsum. Iuxta quod etiam introductum est quod papa per se ipsum confert beneficia in curia vacantia regulariter. Alibi vero vacantia aliis conferenda dimisit. Ita ergo Christus, dum presens corporaliter et visibiliter ecclesiam instituebat, per seipsum instituit omnes officiales quos oportuit. Sed ex quo ecclesie corporalem presentiam subtraxit, et Petro et suis successoribus regimen commisit. Illum quidem suum vicarium per se semper instituit, idest immediate sibi potestatis plenitudinem tribuit. Ceteras autem dignitates sibi instituendas dimisit.

Quod postea dicunt, quod Christus immediate dedit apostolis potestatem predicandi et baptizandi, etiam post resurrectionem et in die ascensionis, dicendum quod propter hoc non dedit eis potestatem iurisdictionis. Si dicatur quod immo, quia dicitur ad Galatas ultimo: *Communicet autem is qui catechizatur verbo ei qui se catechizat in omnibus bonis*. Ergo qui predicat, vel qui baptizat, potest accipere temporalia. Dicendum quod nec potestas metendi temporalia arguit potestatem iurisdictionis, ut supra dictum est, sed solum potestatem in iudicio agendi, sicut patet in curatis, qui decimas sibi debitas coram superiore in iudicio prosequuntur. Item etiam non sequitur, si Christus adhuc presens corpore per se ipsum dedit apostolis potestatem predicandi et baptizandi vel aliam quamcumque, quod propter hoc det eorum successoribus. Sed magis quod successor Petri det successoribus illorum, maxime quia privilegia paucorum legem communem non faciunt. Unde si illi primi

desunt $B^2V^7V^6$

722 a] *add.* suo φ | 725 corrumpatur] *add.* per seipsum θ(-V^2Sv) | 728 procuratorem USr] procurator Barb. *et cet. mss.* | 729 sui] eius φ | 733 instituebat] regebat θ(-V^2) | 735 regimen] *om.* φ | siquidem θ(-BoV^2) | semper] *om.* π^2Barb.; ipsum $V^2\varphi P^4$Va | 737 institutas ρ^1 | 738 Quod[1]] *add.* autem θ | 739 etiam] *om.* ρ^1 | et[2]] *om.* π(-R)ρ(-Bm^2)Sr | 740 eis] *om.* φ | 742 Communicet] communiter ρ^1 | is] his $\theta^2V^2V^5\rho^1$ | verbo] sive ρ^1 | ei] eius [*om.* V^2] θ(-Bo) | se] *om.* ρ^1 | 748 et] *om.* π(-R)Barb.Sr | 749 quamcumque] *add.* potestatem [vel potestatem S] θ | propter] papa π(-R)Barb. | 750 quod] quia ρ^1 | illorum] *add.* et θ(-V^2)

722-723 *Cod.* 9.26.1(?) | 741-743 Gal. 6:6

propter suam sanctitatem hoc habuissent a Christo, qui confirmati non poterant abuti, non oportet quod ita sit de aliis. Immo in aliis debuit servari communis causa unitatis, quod ab uno capite omnes acciperent suas potestates limitatas.

Item sicut quando rex mittit milites ad pugnam et aciem, licet dicat pluribus simul: ite et pugnate contra hostes, defendite cives, non est propter hoc intentio sua facere quemlibet capitaneum nec ducem; quia cum dispositione itur ad bellum, sed est intentio sua quod omnes sint sub uno duce quem ipsemet constituit, cui omnes obediant, et a quo ordinentur omnes in acie, et fiant tribuni quinquagenarii etc., sicut ei videbitur – ipsius etiam est per se vel per alium acies distinguere, et cuilibet aciei quem volet preficere – ita etiam, licet omnibus apostolis simul dixerit Christus: *Euntes docete omnes gentes, baptizantes* etc., *predicate Evangelium omni creature* etc., non tamen intellexit quod predicarent nec baptizarent, demones et vicia debellando, ecclesiam congregando, nisi prout a Petro capitaneo ordinarentur et mitterentur et preficerentur. Unde per illa verba non dat eis potestatem sed idoneitatem, aperiendo scilicet sensum ut intelligerent Scripturas, et docendo formam baptismi, et dando virtutem per miracula confirmandi. Sed potestatem hoc exequendi Petro tribuendam omnibus dereliquit, ne aliter suam aciem turbaret, plura capita faciendo, ut dicerent: *Ego sum Pauli; ego Apollo* etc., 1 ad Corinthios 1, quod nunquam dicerent, scientes alios missos a Petro et Petrum a Christo.

Quod autem dicunt, datam discipulis in resurrectione potestatem ligandi et solvendi, patet ex precedentibus esse falsum. Quia non erant sacerdotes, nec ibi loquitur nisi de potestate que est in foro conscientie, quando dicit: *Quorum remiseritis peccata*. Et quod dicunt, quando dixit: *Sicut misit me*

desunt $B^2V^7V^6$

752 sui θ | confirmati] *add.* in gratia [curam V^1] θB^1 | 753 oportet] ostenditur π^2Barb. | Immo in aliis] sed φ; *add.* sic π^2Barb. | 754 utilitatis φ | 755 suam potestatem limitatam α | 757 hostes] *add.* et θP^2 | cives] cruces [crucem φ^3] φ | 760 uno] *add.* capite sive θ | instituit ρ^1 | obediant] *add.* tanquam sibi θ | 761 tribuni] *add.* et θB^1 | ei] *om.* ρ^1 | 764 etc.] *add.* et θ(-V^2)ρ^1 | 766 et] etiam θ(-V^2V^3) | debellando] *add.* et θ(-V^2) | ecclesiam] *add.* vero φ | 767 Petro] *add.* eorum θ | et[1]] *om.* ρ^1 | 768 dedit θ | 769 intelligant [intelligunt Sv] θ(-Bo) | 770 dando] docendo π(-R) | hec α(-$\theta^4\varphi^5$)RVa | 771 exequendi] *add.* in φ | ne] nec $OV^2\theta^4$, vel π^2 | 772 ego[2]] *add.* sum θ(-V^2), autem $P^2\rho^1$Va | etc.] ego [*add.* autem Sr] Cephe [Ceste Va] $\rho^1\sigma$ | 774 Christo] *add.* solum θ(-V^2) | 776 falsum] *add.* et θP^2, et maxime φ | 778 Et] ad [*add.* illud θ^2BoV^5] θ

761 Cf. Ex. 18:21 & 25 | 764 Matt. 28:19 | 765 Marc. 16:15 | 772-773 1 Cor. 1:12 | 778 Joan. 20:23 | 778-779 Joan. 20:21

Pater, et ego mitto vos, quod tunc dedit potestatem predicandi discipulis sicut et apostolis, dicendum quod non. Quia ex quo sacramentum ordinis fuit institutum, quod fuit in cena, cum ordo doctorum in ecclesia sit precipuus, ex tunc non licuit nisi ordinato, saltem in diaconum, predicare. Unde etiam post Spiritus Sancti missionem, quando erant sanctiores et doctiores facti, nullus nisi diaconus legitur predicasse. Unde cum tunc non essent discipuli diaconi, sed postmodum fuerunt ordinati, non est verisimile quod Christus eis dederit potestatem predicandi, et quod potestas predicandi quam prius habuerant expiravit, quando scilicet ventum est ad illud tempus quando soli ordinati debebant predicare, quod fuit postquam fuit sacramentum ordinis institutum et post resurrectionem.

Quod postea dicunt, quod discipuli receperunt potestatem predicandi et baptizandi in monte Galilee et in ascensione cum apostolis non est verum dato quod fuissent presentes. Quia scilicet non erant capaces illius potestatis de congruitate et decentia, propter illud quod dictum est de predicatione appropriata ordini sacro. Et idem est de baptismo, quod post institutionem ordinis, cum sit ianua sacramentorum, debetur sacerdotibus qui habent claves, vel eorum immediate ministris, sicut diaconis. Hi enim soli in primitiva ecclesia baptizabant. Tunc enim in baptizando iuvabant levite sacerdotes, sicut Philippus diaconus baptizavit eunuchum et plures alios in Samaria, Actuum 8. Unde cum actus activorum sint in patiente et disposito,et discipuli nondum diaconi non essent per consequens apti nec dispositi secundum exigentiam legis nove ad predicandum nec ad baptizandum, per consequens pro tunc Christus nullam potestatem eis dedit dato quod essent presentes. Unde etiam Mattheus et Marcus, ubi hoc referunt, solum de undecim discipulis, qui intelliguntur apostoli, faciunt mentionem, de aliis discipulis tacentes, quod non est nisi aut quia non

desunt $B^2V^7V^6$

779 predicandi] *om.* θ | 780 et] *om.* φ | non] *add.* est verum θ | 783 sanctiores] *add.* sancti [facti φ^3Pr] φ(-W) | 784 doctores $\theta^1\varphi^1$ | nulli θ | diaconi θ | leguntur θ, legem [*corr. ad* legitur T] π(-P^1)Barb. | 786 dedit ρ^1Sr | 787 habuerunt π^2Barb.Sr | 788 solum π(-P^1)Barb. | 789 et post resurrectionem] *om.* $\alpha\sigma$ | 790-791 et baptizandi] *om.* $\alpha\pi^2$Barb. | 791 non] *om.* π^2 | 792 dato] *add.* etiam φ | 793 propter id σ, et φ | 794 approbata P^4B^1 | Et] etiam $\varphi\pi^2$Barb. | idem] dicendum φ | baptismo] *add.* videlicet φ | post] prius ρ^1 | 795 ordinis] *add.* ipse baptismus φ | 797 in^2] *om.* $P^2P^4B^1$Barb.Sr | 798 sicut] unde θ | 799 et] *om.* θ(-V^2) | 800 diaconi non essent] essent diaconi et φ | consequens] *add.* non essent φ | 802 baptizandum] *add.* et ρ^1 | pro tunc Christus] ideo Christus pro tunc φ | 803 dato] *add.* etiam ρ^1 | hec [hic S] θ(-Bo)π^1Va

799 Act. 8:12-13, 38 | 803-804 Cf. Matt. 28:16-20, Marc. 16:14-20

erant presentes, aut si erant presentes, ad solos apostolos dirigebatur sermo, et illis solis dabatur illa potestas modo supra exposito.

Potestas vero prius data discipulis videtur defecisse in passione, quia non misit eos simpliciter, sed *in omnem civitatem et locum quo erat ipse venturus*. Unde postquam cessavit via Christi, cessavit eorum potestas, sicut cessat virtus legalium adveniente veritate, usque ad cuius adventum erant imposita, ad Hebreos 9, ibi: *usque ad tempus prefinitionis impositum*, ad Galatas 4: *usque ad prefinitum tempus*. Et eadem ratio est de apostolis specialiter, quia in passione, si omnes deviaverunt a fide preter beatam virginem, potestatem et auctoritatem quam habuerunt perdiderunt. Unde post resurrectionem de novo, modo supra exposito, potestatem receperunt etiam contraria continentem. Quia prius dictum est: *In viam gentium ne abieritis, et in civitates Samaritanorum ne intraveritis*. Postea vero dictum est, Matthei ultimo: *Docete omnes gentes*, Marci ultimo: *Euntes in mundum universum* etc., Actuum 1: *Eritis mihi testes in Judea et Samaria et usque ad ultimum terre*.

Quod postea dicunt, esse hereticum dicere quod septuaginta duo discipuli sicut et duodecim apostoli non fuerunt in ascensione et non semper fuerunt cum Christo, dicendum quod immo oppositum dicere est hereticum, quia contra Evangelium in multis locis. Nam Joannis 4 discipuli abierant in civitatem ut cibos emerent, quando inventus est solus cum muliere. Unde mirabantur quod cum muliere loquebatur, scilicet solus, alias non fuissent mirati. Nam aliis presentibus sepe cum mulieribus, etiam extraneis, loquebatur, sicut Chananee, Matthei 15, Magdalene, Luce 7, et sic de aliis. Unde tunc non fuerunt apostoli nec discipuli cum eo. Similiter nec quando pernoctabat in oratione solus, discipulis in mari laborantibus, Matthei 14. Nec in transfiguratione et suscitatione puelle fuerunt secum nisi tres, Matthei 17, Luce 9. Nec in

desunt B^{2}V^{7}V^{6}

806 solos] alios θ | 807 solum [sola St] $\varphi\rho^{1}$ | debetur P^{4}B^{1}Barb. | illa] *om.* θ | 808 Potestas vero] et potestas φ | 811 cuius] eius θ(-V^{2}V^{3}) | 812 erat θ | ibi] *om.* ρ^{1} | prefinitionis impositum] et eadem ratio est π(-R)Barb. | 813 finitum Bm^{1}Wφ^{4} | 814 a fide] *om.* θ | 816 supra] *add.* dicto π(-R)Barb. | potestatem] *add.* iterum θ | 817 etiam] et θP^{2}, et quasi φ | retinentem ρ^{1} | est] *add.* eis θ | 819 est] *add.* eis θ | ultimo^{1}] *add.* euntes θ | gentes] *add.* et θP^{2}B^{1} | 820 etc.] *add.* et θ(-V^{2}V^{3})P^{2}B^{1} | 822 esse] *om.* φ(-Bm^{1}) | 823 et^{1}] *om.* θ | undecim φ | apostoli] *om.* φ | et^{2}] *add.* sic π(-R)Barb. | 826 abierunt γ, iverunt [*om.* V^{2}] $\theta^{2}\theta^{3}$, iverant θ^{4} | 828 solus] *om.* φ | 829 etiam] et θ(-V^{2}) | 831 eo] *add.* et ρ^{1} | nec] *om.* [etiam φ^{3}] φ | solis θ(-Sv)Va

809-810 Luc. 10:1 | 812 Heb. 9:10 | 813 Gal. 4:2 | 817-818 Matt. 10:5 | 819 Matt. 28:19 | 819-820 Marc. 15:15 | 820-821 Act. 1:8 | 825 Joan. 4:5-27 | 829 Matt. 15:21-28 | 830 Luc. 7:36-50 | 832 Matt. 14:22-23 | 833 Matt. 17:1-8 | Luc. 8:49-56, 9:28-36

cena nisi duodecim, Matthei 26, Marci 14, Luce 22, alias frustra illi soli nominarentur. Item in resurrectione, quando ostendit eis manus et latus, Thomas, unus ex duodecim, non erat cum eis quando venit Jesus. Non ergo omnes apostoli, et multo minus omnes septuaginta duo discipuli, semper fuerunt cum Christo. Quod ergo dicit Petrus: *Oportet ex his viris qui nobiscum sunt congregati omni tempore quo intravit et exivit Dominus Jesus, incipiens a baptismate Joannis usque in diem qua assumptus est*, non est intentionis sue quod septuaginta duo, ex quibus unus erat eligendus in apostolum, semper actu fuerunt cum eis et cum Christo in omni loco. Sed quod semper fuerunt de eorum congregatione familiari cum Christo, non abeuntes retro sicut quidam ex toto, nec sicut turba discipulorum communium qui ibant et redibant, quasi dicat: non de communibus discipulis, nec de turba, sed de illis qui erant de familia Christi, qui erant ab ipsomet Christo iam electi et informati ad predicandum consimiliter sicut apostoli, qui modum vivendi consimilem apostolis habebant, de illis inquam, non de aliis erat merito apostolus eligendus. Unde sensus est: *Qui nobiscum sunt congregati omni tempore*, idest qui fuerunt segregati a turba discipulorum, et congregati in ministerium Christi, et perseveraverunt in ea vocatione in qua vocati erant, sicut et nos, non abeuntes retro sicut alii, non prevaricantes statum suum sicut Judas.

Quod postea dicunt de Paulo, de potestate quam dedit Dominus, supra solutum est, quia dedit mediante Petro. Quia non est verisimile quod Christus voluerit scindere ecclesie unitatem, qui propter hoc significandum voluit tunicam suam inconsutilem non scindi. Dictum est autem supra, ex auctoritate Cypriani et aliorum, quod unitas ecclesie rumperetur nisi ab uno capite, scilicet Petro, et eius successoribus, omnis iurisdictio et prelatio ecclesiastica causaretur. Ergo etc. Quod inducunt: *Segregate mihi Saulum*, magis est ad oppositum, quia Deus ipsum segregavit ex utero

desunt $B^2V^7V^6$

835 latus] *add.* et φ | 836 Jesus] *om.* φ(-Bm^1)π^1Barb. | 837 et] ergo P^4B^1 | omnes^2] *om.* α | 838 Quod] quando π(-P^1)Barb. | viris] *om.* ρ^1 | 839-840 qui ... qua] etc. usque [*add.* ad V^5] θ | 842 fuerunt θ(-BoV^5V^3)$UWB^1\rho^1$Sr] fuerint $BoV^5V^3\gamma$(-UW)Va, fuerant π^1Barb., fuissent P^1 | cum eis] *om.* B^1Barb.; cum apostolis φ | 843 familiarius θ(-V^2) | 844 abientes $P^2\pi^2$ | 845 communium] *om.* ρ^1; omnium α | dicat] *add.* Petrus φ | 847 qui erant] *om.* π^2Barb. | iam] *om.* π^2Barb. | 848 qui] in φ | modo φ | consimilem] consimiles φ | 849 habebant] *om.* φ | merito] *om.* θ | 853 retrorsum ρ^1 | 855 dedit] *add.* ei [sibi V^5] $P^2\theta$ | 857 qui] *om.* φ | hoc] quam φ | 857-858 signandum [signanter Sv] θ(-V^3)Barb., signandam [figurandam W, significandam PrV^4] φ | 861 crearetur [creatura Bo] θ | 862 Paulum $\theta\varphi^1W\rho^1$ | quia] quare ρ^1

834 Matt. 26:20 | Marc. 14:17 | Luc. 22:14 | 835 Cf. Joan. 20:19-24 | 838-840 Act. 1:21-22 | 857-858 Cf. Joan. 19:23-24 | 861-862 Act. 13:2

synagoge per electionem gratie, et elegit apostolum. Sed tamen voluit non per se sed per alios segregare a populo, et constituere prelatum principaliter per Petrum. Unde fuit apostolus et doctor per inspirationem et iudex angelorum per Christum. Sed fuit episcopus et iudex aliorum et magister gentium quo ad auctoritatem per Petrum. Quod dicit glossa: *In faciem restiti ei tanquam par*, verum est in cognitione veritatis Evangelii. Unde et de hoc ipsum reprehendit, non correctione prelati sed proximi. Unde de Paulo, quem Christus vas electionis fecit ad portandum nomen suum, et de aliis apostolis quibus prius dixit: *Docete omnes gentes*, et *predicate Evangelium omni creature*, posset imaginari quod, sicut quando datur a papa vel cancellario auctoritate pape alicui licentia ubique terrarum docendi in theologica facultate, non tamen propter hoc debet ipse predicare in ecclesiis parochialibus nisi de licentia curatorum, sic etiam Paulus et alii apostoli, a Christo facti magistri in theologia, non debuerunt predicare in ecclesia specialiter Petro commissa nisi de eius licentia. Unde a Christo habuerunt idoneitatem, a Petro auctoritatem.

Quod postea dicunt, quod status curatorum et status discipulorum sunt unus status, et similiter status apostolorum et episcoporum, sicut status isti non sunt alii quam ante centum annos, dicendum quod quando Christus misit discipulos *in omnem civitatem et locum quo erat ipse venturus*, si et fecisset ipsos curatos in illis civitatibus et locis ad que eos mittebat, dans eis curam animarum ibi, tunc posset dici quod illi qui eis in illis civitatibus et locis successissent in cura et regimine animarum haberent eundem statum, sicut curati moderni in certis parochiis ad predecessores suos in eisdem ante centum vel ducentos annos. Et similiter, si apostoli habuissent certos episcopatus distinctos, sicut habuerunt Petrus et Jacobus minor, tunc episcopi succedentes eis in illis episcopatibus fuissent vere unum cum

desunt $B^2V^7V^6$

863 voluit non] noluit [voluit S] θP^2 | 866 angelorum] aliorum et magister gentium [gentilium π^2] quo ad auctoritatem π(-R)Barb. | 866-867 Christum ... per] *hom.* P^4 | 866 episcopus] electus θ | 866-867 et³ ... auctoritatem] *om.* P^1 | 868 facie θ(-Bo)P^2 | restitit [resisti P^4] π(-R)Barb. | 869 proximi] Christi ρ^1 | 871 et¹] *add.* ita θ | 873 alicui] *om.* π | 876 etiam] nec [ut V^2] θ | et] nec θ | 880 et²] *add.* status $\theta^2V^2\rho^1$ | episcoporum] *add.* status [*om.* θ^2] sunt [sint Sv] unus status θ(-V^2) | 882 discipulos] *add.* binos [bonos Sz] $\rho^1\sigma$ | et²] *om.* $P^2\pi$(-R)Barb.; *add.* ipse θ | 883 ipsos] illos $P^2P^4B^1$, eos θP^1Sr | 884 quod] ut ρ^1 | eis²] *om.* θ(-V^2) | 885 et²] *add.* in π^2Barb.Sr | 887 eisdem] *add.* autem ρ^1 | vel ducentos] *om.* φ | 889 episcopatibus] civitatibus πBarb.

867-868 *Liber vite. Biblia cum glosis ordinariis et interlinearibus*, Gal. 2:11, 4:1249v | 870-871 Cf. Act. 9:15 | 871 Matt. 28:19 | 872 Marc. 16:15 | 882 Luc. 10:1

eis, sicut papa cum Petro et generaliter successor cum predecessore, et esset unus status istorum et illorum. Et bene sequeretur quod status illorum curatorum esset a Christo institutus et continuatus, et similiter status apostolorum et episcoporum, si apostoli fuissent a Christo facti episcopi et in suis sedibus collocati, et in eisdem numero sedibus episcopi nostri temporis successissent. Non tamen propter hoc sequeretur quod isti successores instituerentur a Christo sicut illi, nec quod immediate potestatem haberent a Christo sicut illi, sed successores eorum a successore Christi, sicut predecessores a Christo. Sicut quando aliquis fundat capellam, dato sibi ab episcopo iure patronatus, ipse quidem quamdiu vivit ponit ibi capellanos. Post mortem autem suam successores ponunt, ita quod, licet iura capelle sint a solo primo, tamen successores in iure capelle non habent a solo primo illa iura, sed a successoribus suis a quibus immediate presentantur vel instituuntur, licet ius presentandi vel conferendi habeant successores a predecessore, et totum procedat ex ordinatione primi. Ita etiam, dato quod Christus ante passionem posuisset per totum mundum primos episcopos et primos curatos in locis istis, dans eis immediate omnem potestatem quam nunc habent episcopi et curati, et ordinans quod deinceps usque ad finem mundi sic servaretur, et quod quicumque esset in tali loco haberet talem et talem potestatem, nihilominus tamen ex quo totum ius suum plenum, quantum puro homini dare decuit, dedit Petro, ex quo Petrus hanc potestatem habuit, quando primum vacavit quicumque de prelatis a Christo institutis, Petrus habuit substituere sicut Christus instituit, dans successori potestatem quam Christus dedit predecessori. Et licet in hoc sit dissimile, quod Christus resurgens ex mortuis iam non moritur, sicut moritur fundator capelle, tamen absentia Christi, qua vicario suo commisit potestatis plenitudinem, quantum ad illud de quo queritur equipollet.

Item falsum est quod Christus fecerit discipulos curatos in locis illis, et fantasticum. Unde nunquam in toto Novo Testamento legitur quod discipuli a Christo fuerint facti curati. Similiter nec apostoli facti sunt ab

desunt $B^2V^7V^6$

890 generaliter] *add.* sicut ρ^1 | et²] *om.* P^4B^1 | 891 sequitur $P^2\pi$(-R)Barb.Sr | 892 institutus] constitutus ρ^1 | 895 nostri] nunc σ | 896-897 nec ... illi] *hom.* P^4B^1Barb. | 897 eorum] illorum α | 900 suam] *add.* sui θ(-V^2S) | successores] *add.* sui φ | 902 capelle] *om.* φ | solo] se π^2Barb. | suis] illius primi θ(-V^2) | 903 ius] *add.* primum θ | 908 ordinasset φ | et] *om.* φ | 910 totum] *om.* θ | puto ρ^1 | 911 dare] *om.* $V^2\gamma$ | decuit dare θ(-V^2) | 913-917 potestatem ... equipollet] *om.* φ^3 | 913-914 potestatem ... predecessori] *om.* γ | 915 ex] a φ | sicut moritur] *om.* π(-R)Barb. | 916 presentia θ | 917 illud] id θ | queritur] arguitur ρ^1 | 919 toto] *om.* π^2Barb. | 920 Similiter] sicut [sic V^2] θ

eo episcopi nisi Petrus. Sed a Petro immediate vel mediate facti sunt finaliter omnes alii episcopi. Et quia dicitur de apostolis, Actuum 6: *Orantes*, scilicet apostoli, *imposuerunt eis*, scilicet discipulis ordinando, *manus*, convincitur quod non solus Petrus erat tunc episcopus ordinans, alias dixisset imposuit. Unde tunc Joannes saltem iam erat episcopus; postea vero alii omnes, alias per mundum separati non potuissent alios, sicut oportebat, ordinare presbyteros nec episcopos consecrare. Facti vero a Petro episcopi, omnes fuerunt archiepiscopi, habentes diversas provincias, in eis ponentes episcopos, non habentes ipsi certam sedem, sicut Paulus, discurrens per mundum, auctoritate Petri ubique ponebat episcopos, sicut Titum, Timotheum et Dionysium. Similiter Andreas per Achaiam, Thomas per Indiam, et sic de aliis. Unde cum episcopi constituti per apostolos viventes essent veri episcopi in suis sedibus determinatis sicut illi qui nunc sunt, non tamen erant successores viventium proprie loquendo de successione, que facit identitatem status successoris ad predecessorem et continuationem, unde apostoli alii a Petro et Jacobo magis videntur fuisse patriarche, non habentes tamen aliquam sedem specialem episcopalem, sed unam totam terram, vel quantum poterant Christo lucrari. Quia et sic ordinavit Petrus eos mittens, ut irent quocumque Dominus inspiraret, sicut Paulus a Spiritu Sancto nunc prohibebatur ad aliquos ire, nunc iubebatur, Actuum 17: *Vocati sunt a Spiritu Sancto loqui verbum Dei in Asia*. Et postea statim: *Visio per noctem est Paulo ostensa*, vocans eum ad Macedones. Unde non solum ponebant

desunt $\mathrm{B}^2\mathrm{V}^7\mathrm{V}^6$

921 mediate vel immediate $\rho^1\sigma$ | 922 episcopi] *om.* ρ^1Va | 923 eis] *om.* γ | 924 quod] *add.* tunc $\alpha(-\varphi^5)$ | non] *om.* $\theta\mathrm{P}^2$ | tunc] *om.* α | 925 dixisset] *add.* in singulari sic orans φ | imposuit] *om.* $\theta\mathrm{P}^2$; imposuisset π^2Barb.Va; *add.* manus etc. scilicet Petrus φ | iam] *om.* γ | 926 vero] *om.* $\mathrm{V}^2\varphi\pi$Barb. | alii] *om.* $\gamma(-\mathrm{U}\varphi^5)\pi^1$Barb. | omnes alii $\theta\mathrm{U}\varphi^5\pi^2$ | alias] *om.* $\theta\mathrm{U}\varphi^5\pi^2$ | potuisset $\mathrm{P}^2\rho^1$Va | alios] *om.* $\pi(-\mathrm{P}^1)$Barb.; quilibet $\mathrm{P}^1\rho^1\sigma$ | 927 oportebat] ostendebat B^1, ostendebatur Barb. | consecrare] *add.* nisi essent episcopi $\theta(-\mathrm{V}^2)$ | 931 et] *om.* $\gamma\rho^1\sigma$ | 932 cum] licet φ | constituti] *om.* θ | 933 apostolos] episcopos ρ^1; *add.* sicut $\theta^2\mathrm{BoV}^5$, si V^2, sic θ^4 | viventes] *add.* positi $\theta(-\mathrm{V}^2)$ | sedibus] locis φ | 934 illi] *om.* θ | tamen] *add.* proprie RB^1Barb.Va | erant] *add.* proprie P^1 | successores] *add.* proprie P^4 | 935 identitatem] eundem [idem V^2] θ | statum $\theta(-\mathrm{V}^2)$ | 936 apostoli] episcopi $\theta(-\mathrm{Bo})$ | 937 tamen] *om.* θ; quidem φ | aliquam] *om.* θ | 937-938 specialem [*om.* W] sedem φ | 938 specialem] *add.* sedem V^2, aut aliquam specialem sedem [*inv.* Bo; sedem spiritualem V^3, papalem sedem Sv] $\theta(-\mathrm{V}^2)$ | inquantum π^2Barb. | 939 et] *add.* si $\mathrm{P}^2\pi(-\mathrm{P}^1)$ | 941 ire] *om.* θ | iubebatur] *add.* accedere $\theta(-\mathrm{V}^2)$

922-924 Act. 6:6 | 930-932 Cf. Eusebius, *Historia ecclesiastica* 3.4 (PG 20: 219-222); Isidore, *De ortu et obitu patrum*, chap. 81 (PL 83: 154) | 941-942 The reference should be Act. 16:6. | 942-943 Act. 16:9

curatos in parochiis, sicut dicitur de Paulo et Barnaba, Actuum 14: *Cum constituissent illis per singulas ecclesias presbyteros*, immo etiam episcopos, non utique nisi auctoritate Petri. Unde cum auctoritate episcopali sive patriarchali erant etiam legati beati Petri a latere, habentes plenissimam potestatem, quia bene sciebat eos non abusuros, et sciebat quod hoc erat voluntas Domini. Et quod dicit Paulus: *Pro Christo legatione fungimur*, intelligendum est mediante Petro, eius vicario generali. Unde patriarche magis videntur successores apostolorum, considerato statu quem finaliter habuerunt. Attamen patriarchatus, certum est quod sunt ab ecclesia instituti. Unde et ab ea sunt quandoque variati, 22 d. *Renovantes*. Ergo multo magis episcopatus sunt ab ipsa ecclesia. Unde et secundum Augustinum, ecclesia episcopos tanquam filios genuit loco patrum, idest apostolorum, 68 d. *Quorum*.

Quod postea dicunt, quod non potest dari ratio quare potestas data Petro sit continuata in summo pontifice a Christo, et data apostolis et discipulis non sit continuata in episcopis et curatis ab ipso, dicendum quod immo quintuplex ad presens. Prima quidem, quia summus pontifex in eadem sede numerali succedit Petro, scilicet in ecclesia Romana, in qua Petrus sedit et ultimo resedit. Non est autem dare aliquem alium episcopum qui in eadem sede succedat alicui alii apostolo nisi forte patriarcha Hierosolimitanus, qui succedit Jacobo Alphei. Unde non est simile. Et tamen de hoc de quo magis videretur, si recte consideretur patriarcha Hierosolimitanus, non habet sedem que fuit Jacobi eandem, quia modo illic

desunt $B^2V^7V^6$

944 dicitur] *om.* θ | Barnaba] *add.* legitur θ(-V^2) | 945 instituisset ρ^1 | illis ... ecclesias] alios θ | immo] et θ | etiam] et π(-R)Barb. | 946 nisi] sine [in V^2] θ | Unde cum auctoritate] *om.* πBarb. | 947 patriarche θ(-Bo), parochiali φ | beati] *om.* θ; auctoritate φ | 948 sciebat[1]] *add.* Petrus φ | 948-949 et ... dicit] *om.* φ | 949 hoc] *om.* θ | Domini] Dei $\theta P^2\rho^1$ | 951 videntur] *add.* esse θ(-Bo) | 952 statu] *add.* eorum θ | Attamen] et tamen omnes θ(-V^2), omnes V^2 | 953 et] *om.* φ | 954 Revocantes π^2Barb. | 955 Unde] que [quod W] φ | et] etiam [*om.* U] φ(-St) | secundum Augustinum] sicut Augustinus dicit [*om.* P^1] π^2Barb. | ecclesia[2]] *om.* φ | 956 generavit [ponit Barb.] ρSr | Quorum] quo tamen et cum hoc, *et tunc praeterit verba interiacentia* (Quod ... hoc) *et procedit ad verba* de quo (lineam 965) ρ^1 | 958 et discipulis] *om.* πBarb. | 959 ab ipso] *om.* θ | 960 quintuplex] *add.* ratio BoV^2V^3, est ratio V^5, ratio est St, ratio potest dare θ^2, ratio potest assignari Sv | presens] *add.* assignatur ratio Bm^1, et assignari θ^2, potest assignari θ^3V^3 | Primo γ(-Bm^1)π(-B^1)Barb. | quidem] *om.* [ratio B^1] πBarb. | 961 numerali] materiali α | scilicet] *om.* φ | 964 *Post verbum* simile *praeterit verba interiacentia* (Et ... presentem) *et procedit ad verbum* Secunda (lineam 972) ρ^1 | 964-965 Et ... hoc] *om.* ρ^1 | 964 Et] *om.* θ | tamen] tunc π(-P^1) | 965 videtur θ

944-945 Act. 14:22 | 949-950 2 Cor. 5:20 | 954 Gratian, D.22 c.6 | 956 Gratian, D.68 c.6

sedes est Sathane, nec eandem plebem, quia nunc est alia penitus infidelis. Nec est successor secundum rem illius, sed solum secundum nomen, ex ordinatione ecclesie Romane, ut habeat ex primo suo patriarcha honorem propter spem recuperandi terram sanctam, magis quam propter rem presentem.

Secunda ratio est quia potestas data Petro non potest dari ab homine puro. Unde oportet quod ab illo a quo data est potestas Petro, idest Christo, continuetur sive detur cuilibet successori. Sed potestas data aliis apostolis et discipulis, cum sit limitata et coartata, potest dari ab homine, sicut fit saltem quando papa dat alicui episcopatum vel curam, et de novo instituendo novum episcopatum et novam curam. Quia tunc dat illi quem promovet tantam potestatem quantam habet alius episcopus vel curatus, etiam si esset institutus a Christo.

Tertia ratio est quia statui episcoporum et sacerdotum non est annexa potestas iurisdictionis a Christo sicut est statui papatus. Cuius probatio est, quia illa que sunt annexa de iure divino homo non potest ab invicem separare, secundum illud Matthei 18: *Quod Deus coniunxit homo non separet*. Sed papa potest facere verum episcopum et verum sacerdotem qui nullum habebunt subditum, nec aliquam iurisdictionem in aliquo foro. Nec ex hoc quod aliquis est sacerdos maior, sicut episcopus, vel sacerdos minor, non habet ipse aliquam potestatem iurisdictionis, nisi cum hoc aliunde sibi detur. Nec econtrario ex hoc quod aliquis est electus et etiam confirmatus in episcopum, vel institutus in cura, est ipse episcopus nec sacerdos, licet infra certum tempus debeat esse, sicut electus in episcopum infra tres menses debet consecrari, habens curam animarum infra annum debet ordinari in sacerdotem, 100 d. *Quoniam quidem; De electione, Licet canon, Libro sexto*. Unde apparet quod episcopatui et sacerdotio non est annexa aliqua potestas iurisdictionis, sed papatui, licet similiter potestas ordinis non sit ei annexa nisi ex debito. Tamen potestatis plenitudo est ei annexa. Papatus enim dicit statum prelationis super totam ecclesiam cum

desunt $B^2V^7V^6$

967 alia] *om.* θ | 968 est successor] etiam succedit [successit γ(-Uφ^5)] α | illi γ | 971 *Post verbum* presentem *redit ad verbum* Quod[1] (lineam 957) ρ^1 | 974 sive detur] *om.* φ; et detur θ | 975 sit] *add.* mutata π^2Barb. | limitata] *om.* π^2 | 976 et] vel φ | 978 potestatem] *om.* π(-R)Barb. | 983 Quos θ(-V^2) | 984 et] *om.* π(-P^1) | 986 episcopus] Christus P^4B^1Barb. | 987 non] *om.* θ(-V^2)P^2Barb. | cum] *om.* B^1Barb. | hoc] *om.* π(-R)Barb. | 989 curam θ(-V^2) | est] *praem.* non θ | 995 ei[1]] eo ρ^1 | nisi] quasi φ | ei[2]] eo ρ^1

983-984 The reference should be Matt. 19:6. Cf. Marc. 10:9. | 992 Gratian, D.100 c.1 | 992-993 *Sext.* 1.6.14

plenitudine potestatis. Unde annexa est hec potestas sibi inseparabiliter a Deo. Ideo potestas papalis continuatur a Deo ad successores, quia annexa statui, non autem potestas prelationis a primis episcopis et sacerdotibus ad successores.

Sed verum est quod potestas ordinis annexa essentialiter statui ordinatorum in sacerdotibus et episcopis precedentibus et sequentibus a Deo continuatur, ex nova tamen Dei datione. Quia potestas conficiendi et potestas clavium ordinis, que fuit in primo sacerdote, semper est ab eodem in quolibet sacerdote, licet non eque immediate, quia mediante ministro ordinante est in modernis quam Christus per se immediate contulit primis sacerdotibus, scilicet apostolis. Unde melius dicitur potestas sacerdotum secundi ordinis continuata ab apostolis ad modernos sacerdotes quam a discipulis, quia illi fuerunt vere primi sacerdotes, non isti. Et similiter potestas confirmandi et ordinandi, que est annexa ordini episcopatus essentialiter, continuatur in omnibus episcopis a primo episcopo, qui fuit Petrus, a Christo. Sed proprie loquendo de potestate ordinis, non est continuatio, quia continua sunt quorum ultima sunt unum numero. Non est autem aliqua una numero potestas ordinis in primo sacerdote vel episcopo et in posterioribus, sed solum similis. Ideo non est continuatio, sed assimulatio. Sed papalis potestas, que est annexa statui, illa est una numero, sicut diceretur alta iustitia debita alicui castro continuari in omnibus succedentibus sibi in dominio castri. Nam sicut castrum est unum numero, ita et illa. Sic autem est de potestate papatus que debetur statui, non de aliis, ut visum est. Ideo etc.

Quarta ratio et quarta differentia est quia, licet loquendo de potestate annexa episcopatui certe diocesis, et sacerdotio certe parochie, ab illo tempore a quo ista distinctio fuit, a primo episcopo vel curato ad sequentes hec continuatur una in omnibus, sicut autem et unus episcopatus et una parochia, tamen non est annexio a Deo nec necessaria. Quia potest remanere episcopus vel sacerdos, dato quod non maneat ille populus, vel

desunt $B^2V^7V^6$

998 a Deo] *om.* αP^4B^1Barb. | quia] *add.* est $\theta\varphi$ | 999 potestas] *om.* φ | 1001 annexa] annexa est [*inv.* Bo] $\theta\varphi^1$ | 1002 subsequentibus π(-P^1)Barb. | 1003 Deo] *add.* etiam θ(-V^2) | continuatis P^4B^1 | 1006 quam] quia iam [*om.* Barb.] P^2B^1Barb. | 1010 ordini episcopatus] episcopatui φ | 1012 ordinis] *om.* φ | 1013 unum] *add.* in γ(-Bm^1)πBarb. | 1015 in] *om.* φ | 1016 sed[1]] *add.* est [solum P^4] $\gamma\pi^1$Barb.Sr | 1017 alta] aliqua [*om.* φ^5] φ | 1018 successoribus ρ^1 | 1020 non] *add.* autem ita [ista V^2; *add.* est Sv] θ | 1021 Quarta[1]] *add.* est Bm^1 | ratio] *add.* est θ(-Bo)φ^3Va | 1023 illa φ | distinctio] annexio φ | 1024 hec] *om.* φ; hoc $\theta^4P^2\pi$(-R)Va | continuetur θSr, continuando φ | una[1]] *add.* sit φ | sicut $\rho^1\sigma$] sic Barb. *et cet. mss.* | autem] sunt ρ^1Sr | 1025 non] *om.* ρ^1 | annexa π(-R)Barb.Sr | nec necessaria] nec [sed ab B^1] ecclesia [ecclesie Barb.] π^2Barb. | 1026 maneat] remaneat θP^2

desinat esse subditus per infidelitatem, sicut est nunc episcopus Bethlehemitanus qui nullam habet iurisdictionem, nec est prelatus, quia non habet subditum, quod non contingit de papa. Quia dato quod forte posset perdere populum Romanum, non tamen populum fidelem, quia ecclesia non deficit. Unde hic est semper continuatio et necessaria et a Deo, quod non est in aliis.

Quinta ratio et quinta differentia est quia in papatu successio est ordinata secundum ius divinum. In aliis autem secundum ius humanum. Est enim ius divinum quod ille succedat Petro in quem concurrit consensus ecclesie vel illorum in quos super hoc ecclesia transtulit ius suum, sic quod ad minus maior pars consentiat, nec aliter esse potest. Sed in aliis successio est secundum ius humanum, scilicet vel per electionem inferiorum, vel per provisionem superioris, nisi hoc, quod de iure divino est quod papa omnes inferiores dignitates distribuat per se vel per alium. Unde quod per electionem inferiorum fiat, sicut fit communiter, non est de iure divino, quia tunc papa non posset providere. Ergo est de iure humano, et ex concessione pape.

Quod dicunt postea, quod curati sunt vere ordinarii habentes iurisdictionem ordinariam, concedatur in foro conscientie. Nec tamen propter hoc sequitur quin et status ipsorum et iurisdictio sit a papa, qui potest dare ordinariam iurisdictionem non solum persone, sicut legato, sed etiam ecclesie, sicut monasteriis, etiam monialium quarundam que habent officialem suum, quibus solus papa potest dare claves iurisdictionis, quamvis non claves ordinis.

Quod postea dicunt, quod curati habent iurisdictionem ordinariam non iure humano sibi datam, sed a Christo immediate in prima institutione ecclesie, si loquantur de iurisdictione in foro exteriori, certum est quod hanc non habent curati nisi iure humano, quia nec nisi de consuetudine, de qua in paucis casibus excommunicant, etiam iuris ordine non servato, *De officio <iudicis> ordinarii* c. 2. Nec illa fuit eis data in prima institutione in qua nec discipulis data fuit, ut supra dictum est. Eodem

desunt $B^2V^7V^6$

1027 per] propter ρ^1 | 1029 subditos [subditus R] πBarb. | 1031 deficiet π^2 | hec ρ^1Sr | 1034 ius^2] *om.* $V^2\gamma$(-Bm^1)π^1Sr | humanum ius θ(-V^5) | 1037 sic quod] quod scilicet ρ^1 | 1039 superiorum ρVa | nisi hoc quod] nihilominus etiam φ | 1044 veri φ | 1046 dare] *om.* θ | 1047 persone] pape π(-P^1)Barb. | 1048 quarundam] *add.* dare et dat θ(-V^2) | 1056 ista $\theta\rho^1$ | eis] *om.* σ

1056 X. 1.31.2

modo, de iurisdictione ordinaria in foro conscientie, non potest dici quod eam habeant a Christo in prima institutione, idest in discipulis. Quia nec illam discipuli habuerunt, alias frustra habuissent, quia cum non essent sacerdotes, non poterant in foro conscientie solvere nec ligare.

Quod dicunt, quod Christus hos duos solos ordines instituit, si referatur ad potestatem ordinis verum est. Quia Christus ordinem simplicium sacerdotum instituit in cena, quando per seipsum omnes apostolos sacerdotes fecit. Similiter ordinem episcoporum instituit quando Petrum consecravit, qui in hoc omnibus episcopis par fuit. Non autem instituit ordinem episcoporum in apostolis aliis, sicut in primis episcopis a se factis, quia non sunt ab eo facti episcopi, ut dictum est. Nec similiter instituit ordinem sacerdotum in discipulis, scilicet ipsos faciendo primo sacerdotes, quia nunquam eos fecit sacerdotes. Si autem considerentur isti duo ordines quo ad potestatem iurisdictionis sibi propriam, sicut quod curatus in una parochia sub episcopo habet populum subditum ad forum conscientie, episcopus sub papa per suam diocesim habet potestatem in utroque foro, sic isti duo ordines non sunt a Christo instituti in prima institutione ecclesie, quando predicando elegit apostolos et septuaginta duos discipulos, quasi dederit apostolis pro se et pro omnibus futuris episcopis potestatem iurisdictionis in utroque foro, et discipulis pro se et pro omnibus futuris curatis, sicut dedit Petro pro se et pro successoribus suis, sicut intendunt illi qui sunt contrarie opinionis. Et quod ita non fuerit apparet ex precedentibus, quia nihil iurisdictionis eis contulit. Sed Petro dedit soli pro se et pro successoribus suis totam potestatem iurisdictionis ecclesie distribuendam episcopis et curatis et aliis sicut expediens iudicaret. Apostolus enim, ad Hebreos 1, probans Christum prelatum angelis, inter alia sic arguit: *Cui enim angelorum dixit aliquando: Filius meus es tu?* sicut supple dixit Christo, quasi dicat nulli. Ex quo concludit

desunt $B^2V^7V^6$

1058 nec θ(-V^2) | 1059 habent π(-R) | 1060 illi π^2Barb. | 1061 nec] vel θ(-V^2) | 1062 duos] *om.* φ | solos [solus θ^2] duos θ(-V^2) | referant θ(-BoV^2) | 1063 Quod θ | simplicem θ(-V^2V^3) | 1065 Consimiliter ρ^1 | 1069 scilicet ... sacerdotes] *om.* φ | primos θP^2B^1 | 1070 considerantur φ | 1071 proprie [proprii V^2] θ | 1072 habeat [habeant Bo] θP^2 | populum] *add.* sibi θ(-V^2)φ^5 | 1075 quando] *add.* scilicet αP^1 | 1076 quasi] quando π(-R) | dedit π(-R) | 1078 pro[1]] *om.* θ(-BoV^2V^3) | curatis] *add.* in foro conscientie θ(-V^2) | pro[3]] *add.* omnibus θP^4 | 1078-1079 suis successoribus α(-P^2)Va | 1079 intelligunt θ | fuerint θ(-V^2)B^1, fuerunt P^4, fuerunt instituti Barb. | 1080 ex] in φ | 1081 dedit] *om.* φ | pro[2]] *om.* θ | suis successoribus $\theta\varphi^1$Va | 1083 enim] *om.* θ | 1083-1084 prelatum angelis] angelis [*add.* esse Bm^1] maiorem [*inv.* St] φ | 1084 inter alia] *om.* φ | aliquando] *om.* ρ^1

1083-1085 Heb. 1:5

quod non sic sunt angeli filii Dei per naturam sicut Christus, sed tantum filii per gratiam. Ita etiam licet arguere in proposito, cui apostolorum dixit aliquando: tibi dabo claves regni celorum? Certe nulli nisi Petro. Ergo nulli nisi Petro eas dedit. Nam quando eis dixit: *Quecumque alligaveritis*, vel *Quorum remiseritis*, si etiam intelligeretur de potestate iurisdictionis, adhuc non dedit per hoc eam, nec dixit se eam eis daturum per se ipsum. Sed potest verificari de potestate data per alium, ut sit sensus: quecumque alligaveritis et quorum remiseritis per claves vobis dandas non a me, sed a successore meo etc.

Potest tamen dici status episcoporum et curatorum institutus a Deo dupliciter. Uno modo a Christo implicite et in virtute in Petro, quia Petrus fuit verus curatus et cuiuslibet parochie et cuiuslibet diocesis. Unde sicut in quaternario continetur binarius et ternarius materialiter et si non formaliter, ita in Petro utrumque statum Christus instituit materialiter. Item virtualiter, quia in ipso fuit potestas dioceses et parochias episcopis et presbyteris assignandi. Secundo modo a Spiritu Sancto, a quo inspirati apostoli in primitiva ecclesia per dioceses episcopos, per parochias presbyteros, posuerunt. Et ab illis primis vere et proprie episcopatus et rectorie continuate fuerunt ad succedentes in illis.

Quod dicunt postea, quod curati non possunt ab episcopis destitui nisi ex causa rationabili, sicut nec episcopi a papa, si intelligunt de potentia ordinata, verum est. Quia nec episcopus curatum, nec papa episcopum, sed nec curatum, debent deponere nisi ex causa rationabili. Aliter peccant, sicut et in omnibus in quibus irrationabiliter agunt. Si autem intelligant de potentia absoluta, falsum est in utroque, sed differenter. Quia si episcopus, substantiali iuris ordine non servato, deponat curatum, nihil agit, quia sententia eius, qui iuri subest, prolata contra iuris ordinem essentialem, non tenet, *C. De sententiis et interlocutionibus omnium iudicum* 1. *Prolatam*. Sed si hoc faciat iuris ordine servato, licet sententia sit iniusta ex

desunt B^{2}V^{7}V^6

1086 tantum] tamen φ(-Bm^{1}Pr) | 1087 filii] *om.* $\varphi\rho^1$; *add.* Dei θ | 1089 eas] *om.* φ | 1090 Quorum] *om.* ρ^1 | remiseritis] solveritis [solveris Bm^2] ρ^1 | etiam] *om.* θ | 1091 per hoc] hic πBarb. | 1092 verificari] *add.* etiam $\pi\rho^2$Va | de] ex θ | 1093 ligaveritis V$^2\gamma$(-V^4)π(-B^1)Va | remiseritis] solveritis γ | 1094 meo] *om.* θ | 1095 status] *add.* etiam BoV$^5\theta^4$ | episcoporum et] *om.* θ | curatorum] *add.* etiam θ^2 | 1096 et] *add.* alio π(-P^1) | 1097 et^2] *om.* π(-R) | 1100 ipso] Christo π(-P^1)Barb. | parochie θP$^2\pi\rho^2$ | 1102 episcopos] *add.* et θ | 1103 illis] aliis θP^2 | 1104 rectorie θ(-V^2)φVa] rectoria πBarb.Sr, rectorias V$^2\rho^1$, territoria P^2 | successores ρ^1 | 1105 episcopis] eis θP^4 | 1106 intelligant θP^2 | potestate π^2Barb. | 1108 debet θ(-V^2) | Alias πBarb. | 1109 irrationabiliter] non naturaliter [rationabiliter P^1] π^2Barb. | 1112 que θ(-Bo)P^2

1088 Cf. Matt. 16:19 | 1089-1090 Matt. 18:18 | 1113-1114 *Cod.* 7.45.4

animo vel ex causa, si non appelletur tenet, et transiens in rem iudicatam facit ius. Et desinit iste vere esse curatus, et successor erit verus curatus, quia sententia lata contra ius litigatorum, non contra ius constitutionis, tenet nisi per appellationem rescindatur, *C. Que sententie sine appellatione rescindantur* 1. 2, *Extra De sententia et re iudicata* c. *Cum inter*. Sed episcopus vel curatus, et quicumque alius in dignitate ecclesiastica constitutus, ab ea per papam potest deponi sine causa rationabili et iuris ordine non servato. Et ita tenet sententia ac si esset iusta et debito modo lata, licet papa peccet et tanto gravius quanto est maior. Si autem episcopi et curati essent sic a Deo instituti in particulari quod quilibet diocesanus et curatus potestatem quam habet ratione qua diocesanus vel curatus haberet a Deo eque immediate sicut papa, ipsi a papa non possent deponi plus quam econtrario, licet sint inferiores eo, quia papa non est supra ius divinum ut tollat ipsum vel faciat contra ipsum.

Si dicatur quod de iure divino est, non quod iste sit episcopus nec ille curatus, sed quod ex quo est episcopus vel curatus quod habeat potestatem episcopatui vel cure debitam, et ideo potest destitui et institui, quia institutio et destitutio persone est humana, sed institutio status et per consequens destitutio est divina, adhuc non valet. Quia tunc sequeretur quod, quamdiu esset episcopus vel curatus, non posset per excommunicationem nec per suspensionem impediri ab executione solvendi et ligandi, sicut nec ab executione conficiendi vel confirmandi seu ordinandi. Nec possent ei casus aliqui subtrahi, nec episcopatus seu cura minui vel dividi seu mutari, quia illud quod est de iure divino est immutabile. Item aut isti intelligunt quod status episcoporum et curatorum in communi et potestas eorum in communi sit a Deo, sed status huius episcopatus et illius parochie et cuiuslibet in particulari sit ab homine, aut intelligunt quod status cuiuslibet episcopi et curati et potestas quam habent communiter

desunt B^{2}V^{7}V^6

1115 tenet] *om.* π(-P^1)Barb. | transit θ | iudicatam] *add.* et θ | 1116 et^2 ... curatus^2] *hom.* π(-R)Barb. | erit] *om.* ρ^1 | 1117 institutionis π(-P^4)Barb. | 1119 Extra De sententia] *om.* θ(-V^2) | et] *add.* de θ(-V^2) | 1120 vel] et ρ^1 | 1123 prolata πBarb. | 1124 et^2] vel $\theta\pi$(-RT)Barb. | 1125 potestatem ... curatus^2] *hom.* π(-R)Barb. | curatus^2] *add.* est φ | 1126 papa^1] *add.* et [tunc Sr] $\rho^1\sigma$ | 1127 quia] quod γ(-UBm^1) | est] *om.* σ | 1128 vel] ut [et Sr] φ(-U) | 1129 non quod] quod nec φ | nec] vel ρ | ille] *om.* ρ^1 | 1131 et^1] *om.* π^2Barb. | et^2] vel θ | 1133 adhuc] *add.* autem θ | 1135 per] *om.* θ | et] vel θ | 1136 vel] *om.* [et St] φ | 1137 eis θ | 1139-1140 et^2 ... communi] *hom.* $\theta\pi$(-R)Barb. | 1140 et] *add.* huius [huiusmodi θ^2] cure θ(-BoV^2) | illius] vel [huius BoV^2] θ | 1142 communiter] in communi et in [*om.* V^5] particulari θ; *add.* et [*om.* Sz] in particulari ρ^1

1118-1119 The reference should be *Dig.* 49.8.1. | 1119 X. 2.27.13

sint a Deo, non ab homine, in communi et in particulari. Si primo modo, istud implicat contradictionem, quia nihil est in genere quod non est in aliqua eius specie. Unde impossibile est quod potestas episcoporum et curatorum in communi sit a Deo et non ab homine, et cum hoc quod potestas cuiuslibet episcopi et curati et sue ecclesie in particulari sit ab homine. Quia cum generationes non sint nisi singularium, sicut dicitur primo *Metaphysice*, et probatur septimo, impossibile est quod Deus causet potestatem in communi immediate sine homine, et non causet illo modo aliquam potestatem in particulari. Si secundo modo, quo ad potestatem ordinis verum est et in particulari et in communi. In particulari quidem, quia potestas ordinis in quolibet sacerdote et episcopo est a solo Deo principaliter. Item in communi quo ad potestatem ordinis verum est quod Deus instituit episcopos in Petro et simplices sacerdotes primo in apostolis, et quod Deus ordinavit quod isti duo ordines essent in ecclesia, scilicet maiores et minores sacerdotes, sine quibus non staret ecclesia, aut non staret ordinate. Nam sine episcopis non esset ordo nec confirmatio; sine sacerdotibus non essent alia sacramenta. Sed quod essent alii episcopi a papa hoc Christus per seipsum non fecit, qui unum solum episcopum fecit. Quod vero essent alii sacerdotes ab episcopis bene fecit, qui simplices sacerdotes ordinavit et postea Petrum episcopum seorsum fecit. Sed Christus multa instituit que non per se executus fuit, sicut baptismum et quedam alia, quia ipse non baptizabat. Unde ipse bene instituit, idest voluit et ordinavit, quod esset preter papam alii episcopi, quia ipse solus non sufficeret. Que autem sunt necessaria ecclesie sunt ex institutione Christi. Unde dixit Actuum 13: *Segregate mihi Saulum et Barnabam in opus ad quod assumpsi eos*, idest episcopatum et predicationem Evangelii. Sed quo ad potestatem iurisdictionis non est verum, nec in particulari nec in communi, quia utroque modo ipsa est a Petro, sicut dictum est et adhuc dicetur.

desunt $B^2V^7V^6$

1143 sint] *om.* ρ^1 | in^1 ... particulari] *om.* ρ^1 | et] non π^1, nec B^1Barb. | 1144 istud] *om.* ρ^1 | 1147 sint π^1Barb., sunt B^1 | 1150 isto φ | 1152 et^1] *om.* α | 1153 quia] quod φ(-U) | Deo] *add.* et θ(-V^2) | 1156 et] *add.* verum est φ | illi P^4B^1Barb. | 1157 sacerdotes] ordines sacerdotum π^2Barb. | 1160 non] *om.* α | 1161 episcopis] *add.* Christus θ | 1163 Christus] post ρ^1 | 1164 bene] *om.* ρ^1 | 1167 Paulum θ(-V^2)φ^3WB^1Barb. | in] ad θ | 1168 eos] *om.* φ | idest] scilicet α | episcopatum] episcopum φ(-U); *praem.* ad θ | 1170 Petro] Deo φ

1148-1149 Aristotle, *Metaphysica* A.1 (981a17) | 1149 Aristotle, *Metaphysica* Z.8 | 1167-1168 Act. 13:2

Quod postea dicunt, quod episcopi non sunt vicarii pape, nec curati episcoporum, sed sunt vicarii Jesu Christi, verum est in parte et in parte non. Verum est enim, sicut dicit Ambrosius super primam epistolam ad Corinthios, et habetur 33 q. 5 *Mulier*, quod *episcopus habet personam Christi*. Unde dicit ibi de muliere velanda, quod sicut *ante iudicem Christum, ita ante episcopum sit*. Quilibet etiam sacerdos gerit vicem Christi, conficiendo et absolvendo, *De penitentia* d. 2 *Inter hec*. Sed falsum est quod episcopus et curatus ita proprie sint vicarii Christi sicut papa, quia ipsi non sunt vicarii nisi secundum quid. Papa autem simpliciter et universaliter in omnibus ecclesie communitatibus est vicarius Jesu Christi, *De translatione* c. *Inter corporalia*, c. *Quanto*, c. *Licet*. Item falsum est quod cum hoc episcopus quilibet non sit vicarius pape, quia ecclesia Romana impartitur et largitur omnibus aliis ecclesiis vices suas, 2 q. 6 *Decreto* et c. sequenti. Item curatis quibuslibet in sua ordinatione dicit episcopus: *Quanto fragiliores sumus, tanto amplius his auxiliis indigemus*. Illius vices gerunt ad cuius auxilium assumuntur. Nec obstat quod sunt ordinarii, quia etiam legatus a latere est ordinarius, et tamen pape est vicarius.

Quod postea probant, quod episcopi non habent potestatem suam a papa, nec curati a papa nec ab episcopo, sed ambo immediate a Deo, quia tunc vacante sede periret potestas in inferioribus, et ordinatus sede vacante nullam haberet potestatem, dicendum quod non sequitur. Quia cessante causa in fieri tantum non oportet quod cesset effectus iam factus. Sed solum cessante causa in esse. Non dicitur autem quod papa, ratione persone que corruptibilis est, sit causa in esse potestatum ecclesie, quia

desunt B^{2}V^{7}V^6

1172 curati] *add.* sunt θ(-BoV^2) | 1174 Verum est enim] unde θ, verum et enim [*om.* U] φ, verum etiam ρ^1 | Ambrosius] glossa φ | 1175 quod] *om.* φ | habet] *add.* primam ρ^1 | 1176 dicitur φ | celanda [celande S] θ | 1177 sit V$^5\gamma$(-Bm^1)Sr] fit θ(-BoV^5)ρ^1Va, sic [*om.* P^1] BoBm$^1\pi$Barb. | 1178 conficiendo P^{2}P^{4}Tρ^1Sr] confitendo θB^{1}P^{1}RBarb.Va, confitentes φ | et θ(-V^2)P^1] *om.* Barb. *et cet. mss.* | hec] hoc hircum ρ^1 | 1179 est] *om.* φ(-φ^3) | 1182 translatione] *add.* episcoporum φ | c. Quanto] *om.* θ(-V^2)φ | 1185 et] *om.* ρ^1Va | curatis [curatus S; *corr. a* curati T; *add.* dicit θ^2] αTBarb.] curati π(-T)$\rho^1\sigma$ | quibuslibet [quilibet St, cuiuslibet U] γB^{1}Barb.] quibusdam [*add.* dicit θ^1] θ, quibus π(-B^1)$\rho^1\sigma$ | 1185-1186 dicit episcopus] *om.* θ; *inv.* φ | 1186 his] necessariis α | indigemus] *add.* unde θ(-V^2) | 1187 Illius] *add.* ergo φ | Non ρ^1 | quod] *om.* ρ^1 | sint $\pi^2\rho$(-Bm^2) | 1188 a] de θ(-V^2) | 1191 a papa nec] *om.* θ | 1192 tunc] *om.* π^2Barb. | 1194 tantum] *om.* ρ^1 | iam factus] *om.* ρ^1 | 1195 solum] *om.* θ | ratione] *add.* sue θ | 1196 in esse] *om.* θ | potestatis φ

1174-1177 Gratian, C.33 q.5 c.19 | 1178 Gratian, *De poen.* D.3 c. 35 (?) | 1182 X. 1.7.2-4 | 1184-1185 Gratian, C.2 q.6 c.11-12

tunc bene sequeretur illud quod dicunt, scilicet quod sede papali vacante periret omnis potestas ecclesie, sicut absciso capite pereunt sensus in toto corpore, et eclipsato vel subtracto sole pereunt radii in aere. Sed isto modo sedes papalis que non moritur, *De rescriptis* c. *Si gratiose*, et fundata a Deo non potest destrui, est causa omnium istorum in esse. Persona autem pape non est causa nisi in fieri, quando ipse per se facit aliquem episcopum aut curatum. Et satis apparet consequentia ista derisoria, quia isto modo probaretur quod constitutiones papales non essent a papa, nec haberent vigorem a papa, quia tunc perderent vigorem sede vacante. Eodem modo iudices delegati a papa, lite contestata, et penitentiarii pape dicerentur non habere a papa suam potestatem, quia manet papa mortuo. Unde argumentum concludit quod non sunt a papa sicut a causa in esse, considerata persona, sed solum in fieri. Sed sic sunt a papa, idest a potestate sedis apostolice et ecclesie Romane que semper permanet, fundata supra firmam petram. Sed ratio bene probat quod potestas curatorum non est ab episcopis suis, nec ab earum sedibus, sicut a causa in esse, sed solum sicut a causa in fieri; a sede autem papali sicut a causa in esse. Quia destructa sede pontificali in aliqua civitate, puta propter insecutionem hostilem alicuius cardinalis, *De penis* c. *Felicis, Libro sexto*, nihilominus remanet potestas in curatis. Eodem modo probatur quod potestas episcoporum non est a metropolitanis nec a patriarchis nec a sedibus eorum sicut a causa conservante, quia manet illis etiam destructis. Propter quod oportet omnem aliam potestatem ecclesiasticam esse a sede immobili, scilicet Romana.

Quod postea dicunt, quod papa non potest prelatis auferre potestatem eis datam et non prelatis dare, si intelligant de potestate ordinis, sic verum est quod papa non potest prelatis auferre, quia caracter est indelebilis. Sed quod dicunt, quod illam potestatem non potest dare non prelatis, verum est de potestate sacerdotali, quia illam papa non potest dare non sacerdoti,

desunt B^{2}V^{7}V^{6}

1197 illud] *om.* φ | 1199 modo] *add.* non est P$^{2}\pi^{2}$ | 1201 destitui ρ^{1} | autem] vero θ | 1202 quando] quia θ | 1203 aut] vel [et P^{3}] θ(-V^{2})P$^{2}\rho^{1}$ | Et] *add.* sic [si B^{1}] π(-R)Barb. | 1204-1205 nec ... papa] *hom.* θ | 1207 manent φ(-φ^{5}) | 1211 super π(-P^{1})Barb.Va | Sed] unde φ | ratio] *om.* $\theta\varphi$ | 1213-1214 sed ... esse] *hom.* θ | 1214 pontificali] episcopali [papali W] φ | in] cum P^{4}B^{1}Barb. | 1215 persecutionem B$^{1}\rho$(-Bm^{2}) | 1218 conservativa B^{1}Barb., conservata P^{4} | destitutis π(-P^{1})Barb.Va | 1219 omnem] *om.* θ | aliam] illam θ(-V^{2}) | sede] *add.* immortali et [*om.* Stφ^{2}] φ | 1223 auferre] *add.* potestatem ordinis πBarb. | 1224 istam ρ^{1} | 1225 istam φ | non^{2}] nisi α(-St)

1200 *Sext.* 1.3.5 | 1215 *Sext.* 5.9.5

sicut conficere aut absolvere. De potestate autem pontificali, quo ad confirmationem et minores ordines, non est verum, quia Gregorius confirmationem concessit ad tempus simplicibus sacerdotibus, 95 d. *Pervenit*. Et presbyteri cardinales et aliqui abbates ex privilegio pape conferunt minores ordines. Si autem intelligant de potestate iurisdictionis, quod illam a Christo datam papa non possit auferre, implicatur falsum, scilicet quod potestas iurisdictionis sit a Christo collata alicui prelato nisi pape, ut supra visum est. Et ideo falsum est quod illam potestatem non possit papa dare non prelatis, cum etiam hoc possit facere minimus episcopus in utroque foro, qui dat officiali suo non episcopo potestatem excommunicandi, et penitentiario non episcopo potestatem absolvendi, quod etiam facit minimus curatus suo vicario. Sed verum est quod hanc potestatem, sive sit a Deo, sive non, non potest ipse auferre a prelatis totaliter, licet possit particulariter, quamdiu sunt prelati quo ad essentiam, quia esset contradictio, scilicet quod esset prelatus, et non esset prelatus. Sed executionem actualem iurisdictionis potest eis auferre, remanentibus prelatis, per excommunicationem vel suspensionem et eam diminuere. Et per hoc apparet quod non habent a Deo hanc potestatem, alias non posset in eis suspendi nec mutari.

Quod postea dicunt, quod papa non potest destruere nec immutare statum ecclesie a Christo institutum, verum est. Sed hoc est contra eos qui dicunt quod status episcoporum et curatorum est a Christo in ecclesia institutus, sicut et status papalis. Quia tunc sequeretur quod sicut papa non potest mutare statum papalem, auferendo vel transferendo sedem Romanam, nec potestatem pape suam vel successoris diminuere, vel episcopatum suum dividere, sic non posset sedem episcopalem aliquam amovere ex toto, nec transferre nec dividere, nec potestatem episcoporum nec curatorum diminuere nec restringere, quod est falsum et hereticum

desunt $B^2V^7V^6$

1226 sicut] *add.* est [et U] φ | 1227 quia] *add.* beatus φ | 1231 istam φ | 1233 istam $\varphi\rho^1$ | 1234 papa ... possit²] *hom.* ρ^1 | etiam] *om.* θ(-V^2) | possit²] *add.* dare vel θ(-V^2) | minimus] unus π^1Barb., minor B^1 | 1235 non episcopo] *om.* α | 1236 non episcopo] suo θ | 1237 minimus] minor [unus P^4] π(-R) | 1238 a prelatis] *om.* θ | 1239 essentiam] ecclesiam ρ^1 | 1241 executivam ρ^1 | iurisdictionem ρ^2 | 1243 apparet] patet ρ^1 | aliter π^2Barb. | 1244 nec] vel θ^1(-V^2), et θ^2 | 1245 nec] vel θ(-V^2) | mutare θ | 1248 constitutus θ | 1249 immutare α | 1250 nec ... suam] nec papa [pape P^2] potestatem suam $V^2\theta^4P^2$, nec [ut Bo] potest [posset θ^2Bo] potestatem suam $\theta^2BoV^5\varphi$, nec potestatem suam papalem [papatus sui Barb.] B^1Barb. | 1251 sicut [*corr. ad* sic P^4] π | non $\theta StP^2\rho^1\sigma$] nec φ(-St)πBarb. | potest φ | episcopalem] temporalem P^4B^1 | 1253 nec¹] vel $P^2\pi$Barb. | nec²] vel π^2Barb.

1228-1229 Gratian, D.95 c.1

dicere. Si autem intelligunt quod status episcoporum et curatorum quo ad potestatem iurisdictionis est a Deo non in particulari sed in communi – unde licet papa possit tollere statum huius episcopi vel curati, non solum amovendo personam de statu sed etiam funditus amovendo illum statum particularem, puta privando civitatem aliquam in perpetuum dignitate pontificali, vel parochiam aliquam privando speciali curato, tamen non potest amovere totum statum curatorum universaliter de mundo, nec totum statum episcoporum, faciendo quod ipse sit solus prelatus in mundo, sicut potuit amovere totum statum Templariorum, qui erant ab ipso – adhuc sequitur inconveniens. Primo quidem, quia hoc est impossibile ut supradictum est, quia esset effectus universalis sine particulari. Secundo, quia sequeretur quod papa non posset diminuere potestatem episcoporum nec curatorum in communi, faciendo legem generalem in omnibus, puta quod nullus episcopus possit absolvere patricidam, et quod nullus curatus possit absolvere homicidam. Quia constat, cum dicatur cuilibet curato in sua ordinatione: *Quorum remiseritis peccata* indefinite, et episcopis in apostolis sit dictum: *Quecumque alligaveritis* etc., si hanc potestatem in generali habet status episcoporum et curatorum a Christo, papa non potest eam in generali restringere, nec eis casus aliquos subtrahere. Eodem modo, cum usum potestatis a Deo date non possit ipse impedire per quamcumque excommunicationem vel suspensionem, si potestas ligandi et solvendi quo ad iurisdictionem in utroque foro est a Deo, ipse non potest impedire in generali omnes prelatos per excommunicationem vel suspensionem in aliquo casu ab executione officii, licet possit hunc aut illum. Et per consequens non potest de hoc facere legem communem, quia posset contingere omnes esse excommunicatos, et tunc in omnibus impediretur potestas divina. Unde tunc non valeret constitutio quod omnes curati qui

desunt B^{2}V^{7}V^{6}

1262 statum] *add.* sive ordinem θ(-V^{2}) | 1263 Ad hoc ρ^{1} | sequeretur θ(-V^{2}) | 1264 quia] quasi ρ^{1} | esset] *om.* [est Bm^{1}] φ(-U) | 1265 posset θ^{2}B^{1}ρ^{2}Sr] poterit [poteret U; *corr. a* posset Bm^{2}] α(-θ^{2})Bm^{2}Barb., poterat π(-B^{1})Va | 1268 patricidam ... absolvere] *hom.* θρ^{1} | Quia] quare ρ^{1} | 1269 constat] *add.* quod θ(-V^{2}) | cuilibet curato] *om.* π(-P^{1})Barb. | 1270 indefinite] *om.* ρ^{1} | sit dictum] *om.* φ^{3}; sicut [sic Bm^{2}Br] dictum est φ(-φ^{3})ρ^{1} | 1271 in generali] immediate φ | habent φ | 1271-1272 status ... curatorum] *om.* φ | 1272 Christo] *add.* tunc φ | in generali] immediate [*om.* φ^{3}] φ | 1273 restringere] destruere φ | Eodem] eo α | 1274 ipse] *add.* immediate π(-P^{1})Barb. | impedire] *om.* π^{1}Barb.; tollere B^{1} | 1275 suspensionem] *add.* item adhuc φ | 1277-1278 in aliquo casu] aliquo modo [*om.* UW] α | 1278 posset θ(-V^{5}) | aut] vel θ | 1278-1279 Et ... posset] *om.* ρ^{1} | 1281 tunc] *om.* P^{4}B^{1}, cum P^{1}Barb.

sunt manifesti concubinarii sunt suspensi, *De cohabitatione clericorum et mulierum* c. ultimo, nec quod episcopi in aliquo casu in generali essent excommunicati nec suspensi, cum sint multi tales in iure expressi, sicut de suspensione episcoporum, *De temporibus ordinationum* c. 1; *De usuris* c. 1; *De rebus ecclesie non alienandis* c. 1, *Libro sexto*. Restat igitur quod potestas iurisdictionis in omnibus episcopis et curatis, prout ab eis habetur, et prout suis ecclesiis debetur, in communi et in particulari est a papa immediate, non a Christo nisi papa mediante, idest sede papali sive ecclesia Romana.

Sed utrum papa de potentia absoluta posset destruere funditus ordinem curatorum et episcoporum, faciendo quod non esset in mundo aliquis curatus nec aliquis episcopus nisi ipse, certum est quod non quo ad potestatem ordinis. Quia sic non sunt ab ipso nisi sicut a ministro et causa in fieri, etiam quo ad quosdam tantum, non in esse alicui, nec etiam ipsa sedes Petri, quia antequam Petrus esset factus curatus ecclesie nec prelatus, fuerunt facti sacerdotes, et ipsemet prius intelligitur factus episcopus quam sedes sibi data. Et iterum, si non essent alii episcopi et alii sacerdotes ab ipso, periret ecclesia, et ipso vivente, qui non posset per se nec per non ministros sacramenta ministrare, et ipso mortuo, quia non essent ministri necessarii, nec esset qui faceret eos. Et hoc esset contra ordinationem Christi, qui voluit in ecclesia esse tot ministros quot essent necessarii. Sed quo ad potestatem ordinariam quam habent episcopi et curati in quantum rectores populi Christiani ad vitam suam constituti, videtur quod papa de absoluta et si non de ordinata potentia posset eos amovere quantum est de iure ecclesiastico, quidquid sit de iure patronatus laicorum. Non enim potest papa facere, nec de iure nec de facto, quin ecclesia habeat rectores et sufficientes et necessarios ad salutem. Quia tunc periret ecclesia Dei, et frustraretur predestinatio sanctorum, quod est

desunt $B^2V^7V^6$

1282 manifeste ρ^1 | sunt²] sint θ | 1283 ultimo] finali θ(-V^2) | 1284 cum] *add.* tamen θ(-V^2)ρ^1Sr | expresse πBarb. | 1286 De ... sexto] *om.* ρ | 1287 omnibus] *om.* θ | 1288 in²] *om.* $\theta P^2P^4\sigma$ | 1289 idest] et [vel Sv] θ, scilicet π(-P^1)Barb. | 1291 possit ρ^1 | 1294 sic] sicut πSr | 1295 etiam¹] et $P^2\pi^2\rho$ | quosdam] *add.* scilicet [*om.* W] quos [*add.* tamen St] ipsemet ordinat φ | 1296 quod ρ^1 | 1297 prelatus] *add.* ecclesie θ(-V^2) | 1298 data] *add.* esset θ(-V^2) | 1299 ipso¹] *add.* papa φ | et] etiam P^2B^1 | qui] quia γ | 1300 ministrare] *add.* cum ipse non sufficeret θ(-V^2) | quod ρ^1 | 1301 essent] *add.* in rerum natura φ | 1302 esse] *om.* θ | 1305 de¹] *add.* potentia θ | 1307 enim] tamen θ(-V^2) | 1308 et¹] *om.* α

1282-1283 X. 3.2.10 | 1285 X. 1.11.1 | 1285-1286 X. 5.19.1 | 1286 *Sext.* 3.9.1

impossibile secundum illud ad Romanos 9: *Voluntati autem eius quis resistit?* quasi dicens nullus. Sed bene potest facere, de facto et cum peccato suo, quod ecclesia non habeat ita bonos rectores, nec ita bonum modum regendi sicut deberet et expediret. Si ergo papa statueret quod nulla ecclesia parochialis haberet specialem rectorem ad vitam et ordinarium sicut habet, sed quilibet episcopus poneret et deponeret vicarios tot et tales ad tempus et ad placitum quot et quales populo sufficerent, propter hoc non tolleretur salus parochianorum. Sicut in multis religionibus abbates per priores vel prepositos regunt monachos suos in prioratibus diversis, qui eis ministrant ecclesiastica sacramenta sicut delegati, quos ipsi instituunt et destituunt sicut volunt. Sed forte non ita bene fieret, quia melius solet curari res propria quam aliena, et quanto magis appropriatur tanto magis diligitur. Unde dicit lex: *Commune vicium est negligi quod communiter possidetur, C. Quando et quibus, Quarta pars, Ex bonis decurionum debetis* < l. 2 § *Ita.*> Propter quod a principio sancti patres ordinaverunt presbyteros proprios per singulas ecclesias. Propter quod etiam de novo rationabiliter est statutum quod religiosi non amoveant curatos, qui ad curam populi per eos in eorum ecclesiis presentantur episcopis et instituuntur ab ipsis. Immo nequeunt nisi per episcopos ex causa rationabili amoveri, *De capellis monachorum* c. 1, *Libro sexto.* Eodem modo, de potentia absoluta posset papa ecclesiam regere per episcopos legatos annuales missos ad tempus ad provincias et dioceses, sicut olim imperatores regebant mundum per presides, per consules et legatos. Non tamen est verisimile quod aliquis alius modus sit ita conveniens sicut ille qui nunc est de episcopis et curatis, quem sancti patres, docti a Spiritu Sancto, a principio tradiderunt.

Unde ex illo modo quo papa non potest destruere episcopos et curatos, non sequitur quin potestas iurisdictionis eorum sit a papa. Ergo potestas

desunt B^{2}V^{7}V^6

1311 quasi ... nullus] *om.* α | facere] facere papa [*inv.* Bo] θ(-V^2) | 1313 regendi] *om.* θ | 1314 ad vitam] *om.* πBarb. | 1317 non] *om.* θP^2 | Sicut] *add.* et φ | in] *om.* φ(-St) | 1318 abbates] *add.* primi ρ^1 | vel] et φ | 1322 magis^1] *om.* φ | tanto] *om.* P$^2\pi$(-B^1)Barb. | vicium] ius non ρ^1 | 1323 est] *add.* generaliter θ(-V^2) | C.] *om.* φ; si π^2 | Quando] qui θ(-BoV^2) | et] *add.* a θ(-V^2) | 1323-1324 Quarta ... debetis] l. de legibus θ(-BoV^2) | 1324 Ex] de φ | decurionum] de iure π^2, dotaliter ρ^1 | debeatur $\pi\rho^1$Sr | l ... Ita Barb.] *om.* Va; l. ii li. xi θ(-Bo)φ^5P$^2\rho^1$, li. 10 Bo, l.ii li. ix φ(-φ^5), l. ii li. vi Sr, vii li. xi R, c. vii li. P^1, vii l. quod papa [*om.* P^4] P^{4}B^1 | 1325 proprios] singulos π^2Barb. | 1326 statutum] *om.* θ(-Bo); institutum ρ^1 | 1328 Immo] ideo ρ^1 | 1329 episcopos] ipsos φ | 1331 annuales] et tales φ | provinciam ρ^1 | 1332 presides] *add.* et θ | 1334 iste $\theta\rho^1$Va | 1335 a^1] *om.* ρ^1 | principio] *add.* mundi ρ^1 | 1336 isto α(-SvP^2)

1310-1311 Rom. 9:19 | 1322-1324 *Cod.* 10.35.2 § 1a | 1329-1330 *Sext.* 3.18.1

iurisdictionis in papa est a Christo immediate tribus modis, quorum nullo modo potestas iurisdictionis est in aliis prelatis a Christo, sed ab homine. Primo quidem quo ad potestatem status, quia statui papali et sedi Petri sive ecclesie Romane Christus dedit in perpetuum prelationem super totam ecclesiam et plenitudinem potestatis. Isto autem modo nullus episcopatus mundi habet a Christo prelationem nec iurisdictionem nec fundationem, quia episcopatus a Deo fundatus non potest destrui de iure, nec de facto. Sed non est aliquis alius episcopatus particularis in mundo qui non possit funditus destrui, vel de iure a papa vel de facto. Ergo nullus alius episcopatus habet suam potestatem nec suam fundationem a Christo.

Maior patet Actuum 5: *Si est ex Deo, non poteritis dissolvere eos, quia firmum fundamentum Dei stat.* Nec porte inferi prevalent adversus ecclesiam a Christo fundatam, nec domus fundata a Christo super firmam petram potest aliquo modo corruere. Unde ecclesia universalis et ecclesia Romana, ut est ad minus sedes Petri, nullo modo potest destrui, nec de iure nec de facto. Minor patet, quia omnis alia ecclesia particularis potest perdere statum episcopalem de iure ex statuto pape, sicut probatur *De penis* c. *Felicis*, ubi dicitur quod civitas quevis alia preter urbem, que culpabilis est in insecutione hostili cardinalis, pontificali dignitate perpetuo privatur. Item de facto apparet, etiam in civitatibus quibus apostoli prefuerunt, que maxime viderentur esse fundate a Deo, sicut in Grecia, in quibus Paulus et Joannes apostoli prefuerunt, quia vix est ibi de principalibus ecclesiis aliqua que non sit in heresi et scismate. Similiter sedes Jacobi Hierusalem de facto non habet populum Christianum subditum. Unde episcopi catholici illorum locorum solo nomine sunt episcopi, quo ad potestatem quam non habent in illos qui non sunt de ecclesia. Hoc etiam predixit Christus, dicens Petro: *Ego pro te rogavi, ut non deficiat fides tua; et tu aliquando conversus confirma fratres tuos.* Ex

desunt $B^2V^7V^6$

1343 prelationem] plenitudinem ρ^1 | 1346 vel^1] *om.* α | alius] *om.* P^4B^1Barb. | 1347 habet] *add.* de iure θ | 1348 patet] *add.* quia dicitur [*om.* ρ^2] ρ^1 | 5] *add.* dicitur ρ^2 | ex] a θ | potestis θ | quia] unde ρ^1 | 1349 prevalebunt $\theta P^1\rho$(-Bm^2)Va | 1350 Christo^1] Deo P^4B^1Barb.σ | supra θ | 1352 ad minus] a Domino φ | 1353 alia] *om.* π^2Barb. | particulariter ρ^1, parochialis π(-R)Barb. | 1354 ex] et γ | pape] *om.* θ | 1355 Felicis] *add.* libro [in θ^4] sexto θ(-V^2) | 1357 privetur θ(-V^2)φ | civitatibus] *add.* in $\theta^2V^2SvP^2$ | 1358 viderentur γ(-φ^5)R$\rho^1\sigma$] videntur $\theta\varphi^5\pi$(-R)Barb. | in^1] etiam ρ^1 | in^2] *add.* locis in θ(-V^2) | 1359 fuerunt ρ^1 | 1360 que non] quin P^2B^1Barb. | scismate] *add.* et θ | 1361 Hierosolimis θ, Hierosolimitana φ | de facto] *om.* π^2Barb. | 1362 istorum [ipsorum W] φ(-St) | 1363 illis ρ^1 | 1364 ecclesia] *add.* et θ(-V^2) | Hoc] sic [sicut StBm^1] φ

1348-1349 Act. 5:39; cf. 2 Tim. 2:19 | 1349-1350 Cf. Matt. 16:18 | 1354-1355 *Sext.* 5.9.5 | 1364-1365 Luc. 22:32

quo habetur quod sola ecclesia Petri non potest a fide deficere totaliter. Omnis autem alia ecclesia aliorum apostolorum potest a fide deficere totaliter, indigens ab ecclesia Petri confirmari si vacillet, vel ad fidem reduci si erret. Verbi gratia, sicut exemplificat Gregorius in homilia de septuaginta duobus discipulis: *Andreas post se ducit Achaiam*, ita quod ecclesia Andree fuit tota Achaia. Et illa quasi funditus deficit a fide, et per consequens desinit esse de ecclesia Christi, nec per consequens in ea sunt claves Christi. *Joannes Asiam*, et ecclesia Joannis Asiana tota subversa est a fide. *Thomas Indiam*, Mattheus Ethiopiam, Bartholomeus aliam Indiam, et ille etiam illorum apostolorum ecclesie heresi vel scismate funditus corruerunt. Et sic omnis potestas ecclesie et clavium in omni episcopatu mundi particulari, alio ab episcopatu Romano Petri, potest perire de iure vel de facto vel utroque modo, et hec fuit minor.

Secundo, quia potestas pape sola est a Deo, non ab homine, prout respicit personam pape. Sicut enim cum rex dat alicui castrum cui est annexa ex dono eiusdem regis alta iustitia, et ille donatarius moritur sine herede, ille cui rex dat secundo illud castrum cum pertinentiis habet illam altam iustitiam ex duplici dono regis, uno facto castro prius pro omnibus ad quos pervenerit, alio ex dono facto sibi de castro et pertinentiis. Ita quia hereditate non possidetur sanctuarium Dei, Petrus, cui datus est papatus cum preeminentia universali et plenitudine potestatis, nullum heredem habuit ad quem iure suo papatum transmiserit. Unde is qui dicitur esse successor Petri hanc successionem non habet a Petro, sed a Christo, qui dat sibi illud quod prius dedit Petro. Econtrario autem quicumque succedit alicui alii prelato in ecclesia prelationem illam et potestatem predecessoris habet ab homine, non quidem predecessore, sed a superiore

desunt B^{2}V^{7}V^6

1368 Petri] Romana [*om.* V^2] θ | 1370 Achaiam] *add.* quod φ | ita] *add.* intelligendum est φ | 1371 defecit φ(-UPr) | 1372 desinit ... consequens] *hom.* θ | ea] *add.* non θ(-V^2) | 1373 claves] *add.* ecclesie θ(-V^2) | 1375 iste ρ^1 | ecclesie] *add.* ab φ | funditus] *om.* φ | 1378 hoc P^{2}P^{4}B^{1}Sr | 1379 quod θ(-Bo) | pape] *om.* Uρ^1; papalis [papale Bl] φ(-UV^4) | 1381 eiusdem regis] etiam regio θ | alta] aliqua φ, alia [illa P^4, alius B^1(-T)] π(-P^1)Barb. | ille] iste θφ | 1382 ille] iste [isto U] φ | dat] *om.* V^{2}γ | secundo dat θ(-V^2) | castrum] *add.* dat V^{2}φ | pertinentiis] *add.* concedit P^{2}Barb. | habet] concedit π^2 | 1383 altam] *om.* ρ^1; annexam φ, aliam π(-P^1)Barb. | iustitiam] *om.* ρ^1 | regio π^2 | uno] *add.* videlicet [*praem.* modo Uφ^5] ex dono φ | 1384 ex] *om.* θ | quia] quod ρSr | 1385 Dei] *om.* θ | 1387 quem] *add.* de φ(-W) | suo] *add.* ad ρ^1 | transmiserit θ(-V^{2}S)σ] transmisit [transivit Bm^2] Sφρ^1, transmitteret P^2, transmiserat V^{2}πBarb. | dicitur] debet φ | 1388 hanc] *om.* θ(-V^2) | 1389 illud] illud ius [*inv.* V^5] θ | 1391 quidem] *add.* a [et P^3] θ | a] *om.* π^{2}Bm^{2}Barb.

1369-1374 Gregory the Great, *Quadraginta homiliarum in Evangelia libri duo* 1.17.17 (PL 76: 1148)

se instituente, et sibi illud committente vel conferente, sicut patet ex modo loquendi superiorum, qui in dignitatibus sibi subditos electos vel presentatos sibi instituunt vel confirmant.

Tertio, potestas pape est a Deo per hoc, quod non potest attingi nisi secundum ordinationem Dei, scilicet ex consensu ecclesie vel illorum quibus ecclesia commisit, contra quod nihil potest per ecclesiam ordinari – quamvis cum hoc requiratur consensus liber acceptantis, quem non sequitur vinculum reale divinum, sed solum humanum, ut supra dictum est – supra quod fundatur acquisitio potestatis de iure divino, propter quod papa potest cedere voluntarius, sed non potest deponi invitus. Sed omnis alia dignitas attingitur ex ordinatione humana, circa quam non potest fingi aliquis modus contra quem non possit per papam aliter ordinari, qui potest omnem aliam dignitatem dare et distribuere sicut vult, cum in toto patrimonio Petri habeat plenitudinem potestatis.

Quod postea probant, papam non posse auferre potestatem suam prelatis et dare non prelatis, nec ordinem ecclesie immutare, quia non est sibi data potestas in destructionem sed in edificationem, sciendum quod, cum papa ut papa non habeat potestatem nisi a Christo, in hac potestate est considerare substantiam rei date et finem ad quem datur. Si ergo papa faciat aliquid cuius potestatem faciendi quo ad substantiam non accepit, nihil agit, sicut nec mandatarius excedens fines mandati, *De officio delegati* c. *Cum olim abbas*; *Ff. Mandati* 1. *Diligenter*. Si autem papa faciat aliquid secundum potestatem sibi commissam, licet contrarium fini committentis, ipse quidem peccat, abutens potestate sibi commissa, sed tamen tenet quod facit. Sicut quando fert sententiam iniustam, facit quidem contra intentionem committentis, non contra commissionem. Unde valet, et talis sententia est tenenda et timenda secundum Gregorium. Sic igitur, si papa nitatur auferre potestatem prelatis contra Christi ordinationem, puta potestatem caracteris, nihil agit. Si autem contra Christi intentionem, idest finem intentum, valet sed peccat, quia non est

desunt B^{2}V^{7}V^{6}

1392 vel conferente] *om.* α | 1396 illorum] eorum θ(-V^{2}) | 1397 quod] quam P^{4}B^{1}Barb. | nihil] non [nec Barb.] ρ | 1398 cum hoc] tamen φ | requiritur ρ^{1} | quem] quam π(-P^{1}) | 1399 reale] tale ρ^{1} | 1400 supra] *om.* θ; super ρ^{1} | fundet θ(-V^{2}) | 1407 et ... prelatis^{2}] *hom.* ρ^{1} | mutare $\theta\varphi$ | 1413 1.] *add.* si $\alpha\pi$(-P^{1}) | 1414 fini] sui π(-R) | 1416 quando] qui [*om.* V^{2}] θ | fert] fecit P^{4}, facit B^{1}Barb.

1412-1413 X. 1.29.32 | 1413 *Dig.* 17.1.5 | 1418 Cf. Gregory the Great, *Quadraginta homiliarum in Evangelia libri duo* 2.26.6 (PL 76: 1201) sibi data potestas ad finem destruendi sed edificandi. Sed bene est sibi data potestas qua abutendo potest multa bona destruere et mala facere et deedificare et scandalizare, sicut Deus dedit homini liberum arbitrium non ad peccandum sed ad bene agendum, et tamen liberum arbitrium est potentia qua peccatur secundum Augustinum. Item verum est quod papa non habet potestatem qua possit destruere ecclesiam. Habet tamen potestatem destruendi illa que ipse non Christus fecit in ecclesia.

Quod postea inducunt ad idem, quod papa non potest facere contra leges divinas, verum est, destituendo illud quod leges divine instituunt, vel destruendo illud quod ille construunt, trahendo secum executionem per voluntatem beneplaciti. Sed bene potest facere contra illud quod leges divine prohibent, stando in finibus prohibitionis et voluntate signi. Alias non posset peccare, cum peccatum non sit aliud quam transgressio legis divine et celestium inobedientia preceptorum secundum Ambrosium. Unde potestatem caracteris, quam sacramentum legis divine instrumentaliter imprimit, non potest destruere, nec potestatem iurisdictionis sue, quam etiam lex divina fundavit, non potest ipsemet destruere. Sed omnem potestatem iurisdictionis que est a se potest auferre prelatis et dare non prelatis, quamvis hoc faciendo peccaret contra legem Dei, prohibentem omnem ordinationem indebitam, non solum contra ordinationem Dei, sed etiam contra ordinationem humanam rationabilem, secundum illud: *Omnia honeste et secundum ordinem fiant in vobis*. Posset enim papa destruere omnes ordines approbatos, et revocare omnia privilegia a se vel predecessoribus suis quibuscumque personis vel ecclesiis concessa, et omnia iura a se et suis predecessoribus condita uno verbo evertere. Sed certum est quod irrationabiliter ageret, et peccaret.

desunt $B^2V^7V^6$

1423 multa] *add.* facere ρ^1 | et^1] *add.* multa φ | 1424 et] *om.* ρ^1 | 1429 postea] *add.* dicunt [debent V^3; *add.* quod Bo] sive θ | 1430 leges divinas] legem divinam [*om.* V^2] αB^1 | 1431 construunt] constituunt θB^1Va, instituunt φ | 1433 et] per [pro Bm^1] φ | voluntatem φ(-Bm^1) | Aliter π^2Barb. | 1436 Unde] *add.* secundum ρ^1 | divine] Dei [*om.* U] φ | 1437 nec] *om.* α | potestatem] *add.* etiam φ | 1438 ipse θ | 1441 ordinationem^1] inordinationem $\theta^2V^2\theta^4\varphi RBm^2\sigma$ | 1443 Omnia] *om.* σ | 1445-1446 vel ... predecessoribus] *om.* ρ^1 | 1446 et] vel a φ | 1447 et] *add.* graviter θ | *Post verbum* peccaret *add. sequentia verba* π(-P^1)Barb.: Minor patet, quia nullus potest sedem episcopalem construere [constituere P^4] de novo nisi papa aut eius auctoritate. Tertio patet idem sic. Quia si sedes et potestas et dignitas [dignitas

1426 Cf. Augustine, *De vera religione*, chap. 14 (PL 34: 133-134; CCL 32: 204; CSEL 77: 20) | 1435 Cf. Ambrose, *De paradiso*, chap. 8 (PL 14: 309; CSEL 32: 296) | 1443 1 Cor. 14:40

et potestas P[4]], ubicumque sunt, essent a Deo et non a papa, papa [*om.* P[4]] non posset eas auferre nec transferre nec [transferre nec *om.* Barb.] dividere nec unire. Sed consequens est falsum. Ergo et antecedens. Probatio consequentie [*om.* B[1]], quia papa non potest tollere nec mutare nec [mutare nec *om.* P[4]] minuere ius divinum, quia servus non potest tollere legem domini sui, 25 q. 1 Sunt quidam [quidem B[1]]. Si ergo ubicumque est constitutio [institutio P[4]] ecclesie cathedralis illa dicatur fundata a Deo et non ab homine, et [sed P[4]] de [a P[4]] iure divino et [*om.* P[4]] non humano, papa non potest illam destruere nec mutare. Minor patet, scilicet [sed B[1]] falsitas consequentis [*add.* declaratur B[1], sed Barb.], quia papa multas civitates privavit [premuit P[4]] dignitate pontificali. Est [*om.* P[4]] etiam statutum generale quod civitas culpabilis in [etiam P[4]] hostili [hostii R] persecutione cardinalis eoipso est dignitate pontificali privata, preter Romam, De penis c. Felicis, Libro sexto. Papa etiam potest episcopatus transferre, et non solum personas sed etiam sedes, sicut de facto frequenter apparet et de iure, De translatione episcoporum, per totum. Ipse etiam dividit et unit episcopatus, sicut in eodem titulo [eo libro T] habetur. Et confirmatur per apostolum, qui dicit: Firmum fundamentum [firmamentum P[4]TBarb.] Dei [*om.* B[1]] stat [Dei stat: distat P[4]], 2 ad Timotheum 2. Unde si [*add.* Dei Barb.] alie ecclesie sunt a Deo fundate sicut ecclesia [etiam P[4]] Romana, [*add.* tunc R] sunt immobiles sicut Romana ecclesia [sunt ... ecclesia *om.* P[4]], quam nec papa potest destruere nec dividere nec unire. Et dato [data P[4]] quod papa ex causa rationabili posset [esset P[4]] sedem suam mutare localiter, forte cum concilio generali, tamen sedem papalem non potest ipse destruere, nec dividere, nec diminuere in aliquo sedis apostolice [*add.* dignitatem vel B[1]] potestatem, etiam cum consensu concilii generalis [concilii (concilio T) generalis consensu B[1]]. Si ergo dicamus, gratia exempli, quod sedes Hierosolimitana, que fuit sedes Jacobi apostoli [*om.* P[4]], sit eque fundata [sit eque fundata R: sic fuit fundata B[1], fuit eque fundata P[4], quod fundata sit Barb.] a Christo sicut sedes Petri [Christi π(-P[1])], tunc non poterit papa [*om.* B[1]Barb.] sedem Hierosolimitanam privare episcopo, nec alibi transferre, nec [*add.* mutare nec B[1]] dividere, nec [*om.* P[4]] diminuere eius potestatem, quod est absurdum. Si dicatur: non est simile de aliis ecclesiis super quas est papa, et de Romana in qua ipse est [*om.* B[1]], sed [*add.* non Barb.] super ipsam non est, dicendum quod [quia Barb.] est oppositum [oppositio Barb.] in adiecto [obiecto B[1]], ut supra [*om.* P[4]] dictum est, scilicet quod aliquid [aliquis B[1]] sit de [*des.* T] iure divino [*om.* P[4]] et tamen sit subditum [subiectum P[4]] pape, quia papa non est super ius divinum sed sub ipso. Unde potestas que est de iure divino nullo modo subest [est sub P[4]] pape [papa P[4]], ut possit eam [eum P[4]] in se tollere vel mutare [immutare P[4]Barb.], sicut patet in potestate caracteris.

Epilogus

Tractatus de causa immediata ecclesiastice potestatis Quantum ad Articulos et Conclusiones Principales et Incidentales

Articuli autem sunt sex. Primus articulus, de potestate Petri singulari [**1**: 1-261]. Secundus, de potestate quam a Christo alii apostoli receperunt [**2**: 1-1389]. Tertius, de potestate septuaginta duorum discipulorum Christi quam habuerunt ab eo [**3**: 1-471]. Quartus, de potestate pape [**4**: 1-951]. Quintus de potestate episcoporum [**5**: 1-732]. Sextus, de potestate curatorum [**6**: 1-1447].

I. Primus articulus principalis, de potestate Petri singulari, habet quinque conclusiones principales. Prima de potestate Petri super alios apostolos [**1**: 7-71]. Secunda, de primatia eius super totam ecclesiam [**1**: 72-116]. Tertia, de plenitudine potestatis eius [**1**: 117-165]. Quarta, de potestate episcopali [**1**: 166-196]. Quinta, de tempore collationis istorum [**1**: 197-261].

1. Prima conclusio principalis, de potestate Petri super alios apostolos, est quod Petrus a Christo factus est princeps et vertex et preses apostolorum [**1**: 8-33], et illa continet incidentaliter alias tres conclusiones.

(1) Prima conclusio incidentalis, quod omnes apostoli fuerunt pares quo ad potestatem ordinis sacerdotalem et episcopalem finaliter et substantialiter, sed Petrus superior omnibus quo ad potestatem iurisdictionis [**1**: 34-38].

(2) Secunda, quod Petrus et Paulus fuerunt pares merito passionis in consecrando Romam. Ideo in gestis papalibus coniunguntur.

desunt $V^5V^7B^1V^6$

5 autem] *om.* θB^2 | articulus] *add.* est ρ^1 | singulari] *add.* et continet conclusiones ρ^1 | 6-15 Secundus ... istorum] *om.* ρ^1 | 6 Secundus] *add.* articulus φ | receperunt] habuerunt θ(-V^2) | 7 Tertius] *add.* articulus φ | Christi] *om.* α | 8 eo] ipso [eo $Bo\theta^4$] Christo θ(-V^2) | 11 principalis] *om.* θ | 13 preeminentia θ | 15 episcopali] *add.* eius θ(-V^2) | 17 de ... apostolos] *om.* ρ^1 | 18 est^1] *om.* φB^2 | 19-20 et ... conclusiones] *om.* ρ^1 | 21 Prima ... incidentalis] item ρ^1; *add.* est θ | 22 sacerdotalis $Bo\varphi B^2$ | episcopalis $Bo\varphi B^2$ | 25 Secunda] item *et similiter per Epilogum* ρ^1 | 26 in^1] *om.* θ

Sed Petrus fuit maior eo in potestate prelationis et iurisdictionis [**1**: 39-62].

(3) Tertia, quod Jacobus dedit sententiam de cessatione legalium, non quia esset maior Petro, sed quia erat iudex specialis in loco iudicii [**1**: 63-71].

2. Secunda conclusio principalis, de prelatione Petri super ecclesiam, est quod solus Petrus accepit immediate a solo Christo potestatem super totam ecclesiam [**1**: 73-94]. Habet autem duas incidentales.

(1) Prima, quod apostoli et seniores miserunt Petrum et Joannem, non missione auctoritatis, qua superior mittit inferiorem, quo ad Petrum, sed missione concilii et precum, quibus quandoque inferior movet superiorem ad aliquid faciendum [**1**: 95-104].

(2) Secunda, quod Petrus habuit primatum super alios apostolos et super totam ecclesiam primo et principaliter Dei ordinatione, sed postea etiam concurrente aliorum apostolorum voluntate consequente et acceptante [**1**: 105-116].

3. Tertia conclusio principalis, de plenitudine potestatis in Petro, est quod Petrus habuit plenitudinem potestatis [**1**: 118-143], habens unam conclusionem annexam.

(1) Conclusio annexa est quod soli Petro Christus dedit plenitudinem potestatis et preeminentiam super omnes [**1**: 143-165].

4. Quarta conclusio principalis, de potestate episcopali Petri, est quod Petrus factus est immediate episcopus a Christo [**1**: 167-173], et habet tres annexas.

(1) Prima, quod Christus per se fecit primum episcopum Petrum a quo ceteri episcoparentur [**1**: 173-186].

(2) Secunda, quod quando Christus dixit Petro: *Pasce oves meas*, imposuit sibi officium pastoris et episcopi [**1**: 186-194].

(3) Tertia, quod tunc eum in episcopum consecravit, conferens ei

desunt $V^5V^7B^1V^6$

29 Jacobus] *add.* minor θ | 31 iudicii] illo φB^2 | 32-33 Secunda ... est] item ρ^1 | 33 solo] *om.* θ | 34 totam] *om.* ρ^1 | Habet ... incidentales] *om.* ρ^1 | 40 Dei] de φ(-Pr) | 41-42 consequente θ^1(-Bo)$P^2\pi^1\rho$] consentiente θ^2BoφB^2, consequenter $P^1\sigma$ | 42 et acceptante] *om.* φ | 43 Tertia ... est] item ρ^1 | 44-46 habens ... quod] et ρ^1 | 46 est] *om.* φ(-Bm^1)$B^2\sigma$ | soli Petro] sibi soli ρ^1 | Christus] *add.* hanc ρ^2 | dedit] *add.* hanc Bm^2 | 47 eminentiam ρ^1 | omnes] alios apostolos θ | 48-50 Quarta ... annexas] *om.* $Bm^1\varphi^2B^2$ | 48 Quarta ... est] item ρ^1 | potestate ... Petri] Petri dignitate sive potestate episcopali θ^2, Petri potestate sive dignitate episcopali Boθ^4 | 48-49 Petri ... et] *om.* φ^3 | 49-50 et ... annexas] *om.* ρ^1 | 50 tres] *add.* conclusiones θP^2P^4 | 54 pastoris et] *om.* φB^2

sine sacramento omnem rem sacramenti per potestatem excellentie [**1**: 194-196].

5. Quinta conclusio principalis, de tempore collationis predictarum potestatum, habet septem conclusiones incidentaliter sibi annexas vel explicitas.

(1) Prima, quod Christus non fecit Petrum generalem vicarium suum ante resurrectionem, sed solum imminente ascensione [**1**: 198-209].

(2) Secunda, quod Petrus non est factus pastor ecclesie ante resurrectionem [**1**: 209-214].

(3) Tertia, quod Petro per illa verba: *Tibi dabo claves regni celorum*, non sunt claves tradite sed promisse [**1**: 215-221].

(4) Quarta, quod nullus factus est sacerdos ante cenam, quando primo institutum est sacramentum eucharistie [**1**: 221-225].

(5) Quinta, quod nullus ante cenam habuit claves ligandi et solvendi in foro conscientie [**1**: 225-228].

(6) Sexta, quod Petrus non est factus episcopus nec pastor ecclesie ante et nisi per illa verba: *Pasce oves meas* [**1**: 228-237].

(7) Septima, quod illa verba: *Pasce oves meas*, non sunt promissio de futura datione sicut illa: *Tibi dabo*, sed sunt collatio potestatis in presenti sub hoc sensu: *Pasce*, idest potestatem accipe pascendi per omnium sacramentorum administrationem quibus ecclesia pascitur [**1**: 237-245].

II. Secundus articulus principalis, de potestate apostolorum data eis immediate a Christo, habet octo conclusiones principales. Prima, de potestate miracula faciendi [**2**: 8-25]. Secunda, de potestate predicandi [**2**: 26-80]. Tertia, de potestate metendi temporalia [**2**: 81-126]. Quarta, de potestate baptizandi [**2**: 127-161]. Quinta, de potestate sacerdotali [**2**: 162-198]. Sexta, de potestate ligandi et solvendi [**2**: 199-386]. Septima, de potestate episcopali [**2**: 387-895]. Octava, de potestate iurisdictionis [**2**: 896-1389].

1. Prima conclusio principalis de potestate apostolorum est de potestate miracula faciendi, scilicet quod omnes apostoli acceperunt

desunt $V^5V^7B^1V^6$

56 excellentie] *add.* vel [*add.* per Sv] potestatis excellentiam $\theta(-V^2)$ | 58-60 Quinta ... explicitas] *om.* ρ^1 | 59 potestatum] *add.* et $\theta(-V^2)$ | incidentales $\alpha(-P^2)P^1$ | 62 suum] *om.* α | 69 primum $\theta\rho(-Bm^2)$ | 72 nec pastor ecclesie] *om.* ρ^1 | ecclesie] *om.* φ | 73 ante] *add.* resurrectionem θ | et] *add.* non θ | 74 quod] *add.* per $\theta(-V^2)$ | ista φB^2 | sunt] fuit facta $\theta(-V^2)$ | promissio] *om.* $Bm^1\varphi^2$ | 75 sicut] *add.* per $\theta(-V^2)$, sunt φB^2 | sunt] data $\theta(-V^2)$ | 79 principalis] *add.* est $\theta(-Sv)\rho^1$ | 80 Christo] *add.* et $\theta\rho^1$ | octo] multas ρ^1 | principales] *om.* $\varphi(-U)\rho^1$ | 80-85 Prima ... iurisdictionis] *om.* ρ^1 | 82 temporalia [*om.* B^2; *add.* et O] metendi α | 86 de^1 ... apostolorum] *om.* ρ^1 | 86-87 est de potestate] *om.* θ | de^2 ... scilicet] *om.* ρ^1 | 87 faciendi] *add.* est [per apostolos est V^2] $\theta(-S)$

immediate a Christo potestatem miracula faciendi et nullus a Petro [**2**: 9-10], et continet quattuor conclusiones incidentales.

(1) Prima conclusio incidentalis est quod nullus qui unquam fecit miracula accepit a puro homine hanc potestatem, sed a solo Deo [**2**: 10-12].

(2) Secunda, quod alii apostoli habuerunt minorem potestatem miracula faciendi quam Petrus, et sub eo, et ei deferebant in miraculis faciendis [**2**: 15-18].

(3) Tertia, quod primum miraculum in primitiva ecclesia, scilicet de erectione claudi, factum est per Petrum [**2**: 18-21].

(4) Quarta, quod solius Petri umbra sanabantur infirmi [**2**: 23-25].

2. Secunda conclusio principalis, de potestate predicandi apostolorum, est quod omnes apostoli acceperunt a Christo immediate auctoritatem predicandi, et habet quindecim conclusiones annexas.

(1) Prima, quod apostoli ante passionem acceperunt potestatem predicandi Judeis tantum [**2**: 27-31].

(2) Secunda, quod post resurrectionem acceperunt potestatem predicandi ubique aliquomodo [**2**: 31-34].

(3) Tertia, quod ante passionem alii apostoli non suberant regimini Petri, nec in predicando nec in aliis, sed solius Christi [**2**: 34-36].

(4) Quarta, quod post ascensionem, in predicando et in omnibus aliis, subfuerunt omnes alii apostoli Petro [**2**: 36-40].

(5) Quinta, quod ubicumque Petrus presens erat, omnes alii in predicando sibi deferebant [**2**: 40-41].

(6) Sexta, quod Petrus inter omnes fecit primum sermonem [**2**: 41-43].

(7) Septima, quod in acie ecclesie ordinata Christus fecit Petrum capitaneum, et alios apostolos voluit esse duces post eum, et sub eo et per eum [**2**: 44-53].

(8) Octava, quod a Petro facta est ordinatio et divisio predicationum et predicatorum, licet de consilio aliorum [**2**: 53-55].

desunt $V^5V^7B^1V^6$

88 a Christo immediate $\alpha(-\varphi^3)\rho^1$ | 89 et ... incidentales] *om.* ρ^1 | 90 conclusio ... est] *om.* ρ^1 | 97 electione θP^2R | claudi] Mathie [*om.* V^2] θ | 99-100 Secunda ... est] item ρ^1 | 101 et ... annexas] *om.* ρ^1 | et] *add.* hec [hoc Bo] $\theta(-V^2)$ | quindecim $\theta(-V^2)\varphi^1$Sr] quattuordecim $V^2\varphi^2P^2\pi$Barb.Va, ibi B^2 | 102 receperunt $\theta(-V^2)$ | 104 receperunt $\theta(-V^2)$ | 110 aliis] *om.* φ | 116 eo] *om.* $\varphi(-\varphi^5)B^2$ | 118 a] sub θ | et divisio] *om.* θ

(9) Nona, quod ad Petrum, rectorem totius ecclesie, non ad subditos pertinuit ponere subrectores [**2**: 55-58].

(10) Decima, quod ex quo Petro totius ecclesie cura fuit commissa, nulli licuit sine eius auctoritate pascere nec regere gregem Dei [**2**: 58-62].

(11) Undecima, quod Petri fuit sub se pastores alios ordinare, in partem sollicitudinis eos vocando [**2**: 62-63].

(12) Duodecima, quod solius Petri principaliter fuit ordinare de successore Jude et diaconis ministerio preponendis, licet ipse aliis electionem commiserit, qui solus per se poterat providere [**2**: 63-70].

(13) Tertia decima, quod omnis electio et institutio ad aliquam rectoriam in tota ecclesia Dei ad alium pertinens quam ad papam est collata a Petro vel eius successore [**2**: 70-71].

(14) Quarta decima, quod omnis divisio et institutio provinciarum et diocesum est facta a Petro vel eius auctoritate [**2**: 71-72].

(15) Quinta decima, quod alii apostoli post Pentecostem predicaverunt auctoritate et potestate sibi data a Petro, non immediate a Christo nisi quo ad inspirationem et confirmationem miraculorum [**2**: 72-80].

3. Tertia conclusio principalis, de potestate metendi temporalia, est quod omnes apostoli a Christo immediate acceperunt potestatem necessaria corpori recipiendi ab illis quibus spiritualia seminarent [**2**: 82-88], et habet quattuor incidentales.

(1) Prima, quod hanc potestatem metendi temporalia alii apostoli post Pentecostem habuerunt immediate a Petro [**2**: 88-91].

(2) Secunda, quod Petrus ecclesiam aliis apostolis et successoribus regendam dimisit, metropoles et dioceses dividendo, suam cuique assignando [**2**: 91-95].

(3) Tertia, quod prima divisio predicationum, scilicet in gentes et circumcisionem, facta est auctoritate Petri, licet de consilio et voluntate aliorum [**2**: 95-107].

(4) Quarta, quod primum concilium, de cessatione legalium,

desunt $V^5V^7B^1V^6$

120 ad^2] *om.* ρ^1 | 121 rectores φB^2 | 125 pastores] *om.* ρ^1 | 133 est] erit ρ^1 | 135 vel] aut ρ^1 | 138 et confirmationem] *om.* ρ^1 | 140 Tertia ... est] item ρ^1 | 142 corporis φB^2 | 143 et ... incidentales] *om.* ρ^1 | 145 Petro] Christo φ | 146 ecclesiam] *add.* immediate ρ^1 | 147 commisit θ, divisit φB^2 | dividendo] *add.* et $\theta(-V^2)P^2Sr$ | sua ρ^1 | cuicumque ρ^1 | 149 et] *add.* in θ | 152 Quarta] *add.* conclusio θ(-Sv)Sr | primum] *om.* φ

congregatum et regulatum est auctoritate Petri, licet epistola scripta fuerit sub nomine communi [**2**: 108-125].

4. Quarta conclusio principalis, de potestate baptizandi, est quod omnes apostoli acceperunt immediate a Christo potestatem baptizandi, et habet sex incidentales.

(1) Prima, quod omnes apostoli ante passionem a Christo habuerunt auctoritatem baptizandi [**2**: 128-134].

(2) Secunda, de opinione Joannis Chrysostomi, quod apostoli baptizabant solum baptismo Joannis [**2**: 134-139].

(3) Tertia, de opinione Augustini, quod baptizabant baptismo Christi [**2**: 139-147].

(4) Quarta, quod apostoli fuerunt baptizati baptismo Christi antequam illi baptizarent [**2**: 147-151].

(5) Quinta, quod licebat eis baptizare, sicut nunc layco fideli, deficiente sacerdote [**2**: 151-154].

(6) Sexta, quod post resurrectionem data est eis a Christo auctoritas baptizandi per totum mundum, non quod hoc exequerentur nisi ex ordinatione Petri et commissione [**2**: 154-161].

5. Quinta conclusio principalis, de potestate sacerdotali, est quod omnes apostoli facti sunt immediate a Christo sacerdotes in cena [**2**: 163-165], et habet quinque incidentales.

(1) Prima, quod nullus debuit fieri sacerdos evangelicus ante institutionem sacramenti eucharistie [**2**: 166-171].

(2) Secunda, quod in consummatione Novi Testamenti, que fuit in passione, debuerunt institui ministri eius sacerdotes [**2**: 171-180].

(3) Tertia, quod in passione, cum consummatione legis nove, debuit sacramentorum institutio consummari, et cum sacramentis ministri eorum institui [**2**: 171-180].

(4) Quarta, quod fuerunt facti sacerdotes per illa verba: *Hoc facite in meam commemorationem* [**2**: 180-191].

desunt $V^5V^7B^1V^6$

154 fuerit] *add.* auctoritate communi sive θ | 155 Quarta ... est] item ρ^1 | 156 receperunt θ(-V^2) | 157 et ... incidentales] *om.* ρ^1 | 161 baptismo] baptismate α(-B^2)P^4 | 162 baptismo] baptismate φP^4 | 164 baptismo] baptismate φP^4 | 165 illi πBarb.Sr] ipsi [ipso S] θP^2, alios φ, illo ρ^1Va | 168-169 a ... auctoritas] potestas a Christo et auctoritas [et auctoritas *om.* Sr] αSr | 169 quod] *add.* ex ρ^1 | 172 Quinta ... est] item ρ^1 | 174 et ... incidentales] *om.* ρ^1 | 177 confirmatione φVa | 178 institui ... sacerdotes] ministri eius fieri [*om.* V^2Sv] et [*om.* V^2] institui sacerdotes θ | sacerdotes] *om.* πBarb.Va | 179 nove] veteris θ | 180 consummari] *om.* θ; confirmari [confirmatio Br] ρ^1 | 181 minister πBarb. | 182 quod] *add.* omnes apostoli θ

(5) Quinta, quod Judas cum aliis communicavit, et factus est sacerdos cum eis [**2**: 191-198].

6. Sexta conclusio principalis, de potestate clavium ordinis, est quod eam omnes equaliter a Christo simul et semel acceperunt [**2**: 200-202], et habet decem incidentales.

(1) Prima, quod apostoli ante cenam non habuerunt claves ordinis [**2**: 204-212].

(2) Secunda, quod illa verba dicta omnibus: *Quecumque alligaveritis super terram* etc., fuerunt verba promissionis de futuro, non collationis [**2**: 212-218].

(3) Tertia, quod potestas ligandi et solvendi in foro conscientie fuit data a Christo non soli Petro, sed etiam aliis [**2**: 219-240].

(4) Quarta, de opinione rationabiliori, quod potestas ligandi et solvendi data est in cena omnibus apostolis simul cum potestate conficiendi, et quod per illa verba: *Accipite Spiritum Sanctum*, in resurrectione non dedit eis Christus novam potestatem, nec per sequentia: *Quorum remiseritis* etc., sed declaravit potestatem prius datam ad actum absolvendi [**2**: 241-278].

(5) Quinta, de alia opinione minus probabili inter omnes, quod in cena nullam potestatem receperunt per illa verba: *Hoc facite*, sed per illa verba: *Quorum remiseritis*, facti sunt sacerdotes, de novo accipientes utramque potestatem [**2**: 279-308].

(6) Sexta, de opinione magis communi, quod in cena facti sunt sacerdotes, accipientes solum potestatem consecrandi per illa verba: *Hoc facite*. Sed in resurrectione acceperunt de novo potestatem absolvendi per illa verba: *Quorum remiseritis* [**2**: 309-313].

(7) Septima, quod sicut opinio dicit quod caracter sacerdotalis et episcopalis est unus qui ampliatur per consecrationem episcopalem ad effectum confirmandi et ordinandi, sic est unus et multo fortius ad conficiendum et absolvendum. Sed prius datur ad conficiendum per illa verba: *Accipite potestatem dicendi missas*.

desunt $V^5V^7B^1V^6$

185 cum eis] *om.* φ | 186 Sexta ... potestate] item quod potestatem ρ^1 | 186-187 est ... eam] *om.* ρ^1 | 187 omnes] *add.* apostoli ρ^1 | 188 et ... incidentales] *om.* ρ^1 | 194 et] atque γ(-B^2) | 195 solum $\theta P^2\pi^1$Barb. | 196 rationabili φBarb. | 198 quod] *om.* ρ^1 | 199 eis] *om.* θ | 201 datam] *add.* quantum φB^2 | 202 alia] *om.* θ | 203 potestatem] *add.* habuerunt vel θ | 207 solam θ | 211 quod[2]] *om.* θ^2BoSv; et V^2V^3; *add.* sicut [si φ^5] $\varphi B^2\sigma$ | 213 effectum] officium α | 214 daturus ρ^1 | 215 missas] *add.* et θ

Ampliatur per verba sequentia: *Quorum remiseritis*. Ampliatur ad ligandum et solvendum [**2**: 314-321].

(8) Octava, quod eedem opiniones vendicant sibi locum in qualibet ordinatione sacerdotis, in qua licet non sint intervalla dierum, sicut fuerunt inter verba dicta in cena et in resurrectione, sunt tamen intervalla horarum [**2**: 322-335].

(9) Nona, quod probabilior est opinio que dicit sacerdotes factos in cena non in resurrectione, quia tunc Thomas absens non fuisset factus sacerdos [**2**: 336-343].

(10) Decima, quod per illa verba: *Accipite Spiritum Sanctum*, Thomas non recepit Spiritum Sanctum, non quia absens, sed quia incredulus [**2**: 344-349].

7. Septima conclusio principalis, de potestate episcopali in aliis apostolis, est quod non sunt facti a Christo episcopi sed a Petro, et ipsi et omnes alii immediate vel mediate [**2**: 388-391], et habet triginta una incidentales.

(1) Prima, quod alii non sic sunt facti a Christo episcopi cum Petro sicut sunt facti cum eo sacerdotes [**2**: 391-399].

(2) Secunda, quod Jacobus minor consecratus est vera ordinatione in episcopum a Petro, Jacobo et Joanne [**2**: 400-410].

(3) Tertia, quod illa ordinatio non fuit simulatoria ad effigiendum veram consecrationem [**2**: 411-422].

(4) Quarta, quod non fuit promotio ad archiepiscopatum solum, sed vera episcopalis consecratio [**2**: 423-440].

(5) Quinta, quod non fuit sola intronizatio, sed vera ordinatio [**2**: 441-452].

(6) Sexta, quod nullus alius preter Petrum factus est a Christo episcopus [**2**: 453-463].

(7) Septima, quod apostoli non sunt facti episcopi per illa verba: *Quecumque alligaveritis super terram* [**2**: 464-472].

desunt $V^5V^7B^1V^6$

216 verba] *om.* α | Ampliatur²] *om.* θP^2Barb.; *add.* inquam [quantum UBm^1] φB^2 | 218 eedem] hee φB^2 | 220 dierum] *om.* α | 222 dicit] *add.* omnes θ | 223 Thomas tunc α | 224 factus] *om.* $\theta\pi$Barb. | 228-229 Septima ... est] item ρ^1 | 229 quod] *add.* alii apostoli ρ^1 | et] sed φ; *add.* etiam ρ^1 | ipse φB^2 | 230-232 et² ... Prima] item [quod Br] ρ^1 | 232 Prima] *add.* est θ | alii] *om.* ρ^1; *add.* apostoli $\theta(-V^2)$ | sic] *om.* φB^2 | sint $\varphi^3\varphi^4$ | cum Petro] *om.* ρ^1 | 234 minor] *add.* factus est et θ | est] *om.* θ | vera] *add.* consecratione et $\theta(-V^2)$ | 235 Jacobo] *om.* ρ^1 | 236 ista φB^2 | ordinatio] *om.* θ | similatio [assimilatio φ^5] γ | 238 archiepiscopum φB^2 | 240 ordinatio] consecratio ρ^1 | 244 facti] *add.* a Christo θ

(8) Octava, quod nec per illa verba: *Hoc facite in meam commemorationem* [**2**: 473-482].

(9) Nona, quod nec per illa verba: *Accipite Spiritum Sanctum, quorum remiseritis* etc. [**2**: 483-511].

(10) Decima, quod Deus in principio ecclesie non fecit nisi unum episcopum, scilicet Petrum, qui suffecit ad alios faciendos [**2**: 512-518].

(11) Undecima, quod tres episcopi non requiruntur ad unum episcopum consecrandum de necessitate sacramenti, sed solum de necessitate precepti, ex statuto Petri [**2**: 518-527].

(12) Duodecima, quod Petrus solus fecit Joannem episcopum. Sed cum Joanne fecit Jacobum fratrem eius secundo, cum quibus tertio fecit Jacobum Alphei [**2**: 552-559].

(13) Tertia decima, quod Paulus et alii apostoli non semper servaverunt illam formam de tribus consecrantibus unum episcopum, sed quando potuerunt eos habere [**2**: 559-565].

(14) Quarta decima, quod Jacobus et Joannes erant digniores aliis post Petrum, et Joannes maior fratre meritis, licet minor etate [**2**: 566-586].

(15) Quinta decima, quod falsum est dicere apostolos simplices sacerdotes existentes potuisse episcopos consecrare [**2**: 587-600].

(16) Sexta decima, quod in veteri lege Moyses, non sacerdos consecratus, erat maior sacerdotibus consecratis. Sed in nova lege nullus non sacerdos est dignior sacerdote [**2**: 601-611].

(17) Septima decima, sicut Moyses solum Aaron fecit pontificem, a quo in omnes alios pontificatus derivatus est, sed fecit omnes filios eius sacerdotes, ita Christus solum Petrum fecit episcopum, a quo omnes alii sunt postea facti, sed fecit simul omnes alios apostolos sacerdotes [**2**: 612-633].

(18) Octava decima, quod quia omnes sacerdotes sunt pares, non autem omnes episcopi, ideo simul alii apostoli facti sunt cum Petro sacerdotes, et non simul episcopi [**2**: 637-661].

(19) Nona decima, quod Petrus non fuit maior sacerdos aliis, quia

desunt $V^5V^7B^1V^6$

246 ista φB^2 | verba] *om.* α(-Sφ^3B^2)RP^1Bm^2Barb. | 248 verba] *om.* α(-φ^3B^2)RP^1Bm^2Barb. | 251 sufficit P^4P^1Bm^2Barb.Va, sufficeret ρ^2 | 254 de[1] ... sacramenti] *om.* φB^2 | 260 istam θ | 260-261 unum episcopum] *om.* πBarb. | 261 sed] *add.* solum θ | poterant [poterunt U] φ | 262 erant] fuerunt φB^2 | 263 merito φB^2 | 270 Septima decima] item quod ρ^1 | 271 sed] et ρ^1 | 272 ita] sic [*om.* Bm^2] quod ρ^1 | 273 facti] *add.* episcopi θ | 277 et] *om.* θ(-V^2) | 278 aliis] vel magis θ(-V^2)

non potuit plus quam illi conficere nec absolvere. Sed fuit maior episcopus, quia superintendens toti mundo [**2**: 661-665].

(20) Vicesima, quod verbum Augustini, quod Christus fecit omnes apostolos episcopos, intelligitur uno modo sic, quod fecit immediate Petrum, alios mediante Petro. Alio modo, episcopos, idest presbyteros [**2**: 666-682].

(21) Vicesima prima, quod illud verbum concilii, quod Christus dedit claves ecclesie apostolis eorumque successoribus, probat quod sicut Christus non fecit alios episcopos per se sed per alios, sic nec fecit apostolos alios episcopos nisi per Petrum [**2**: 683-722].

(22) Vicesima secunda, quod plus est promissum Petro soli per illa verba: *Quodcumque ligaveris*, quam aliis per illa verba: *Quecumque alligaveritis* [**2**: 700-709].

(23) Vicesima tertia, quod claves episcopales sunt potestas confirmandi et ordinandi [**2**: 718-719].

(24) Vicesima quarta, quod apostoli fuerunt pares in honore sacerdotii et pontificatus finaliter quo ad potestatem ordinis, sed non quo ad conferentem, nec quo ad potestatem iurisdictionis [**2**: 723-736].

(25) Vicesima quinta, quod apostoli non statim quod fuerunt assumpti in apostolos facti sunt predicatores, nec sacerdotes ante cenam, nec episcopi ante Pentecostem [**2**: 737-756].

(26) Vicesima sexta, quod Petrus non est factus simul sacerdos et episcopus sicut Aaron [**2**: 757-770].

(27) Vicesima septima, quod apostoli non sunt facti episcopi per illa verba: *Accipite Spiritum Sanctum* [**2**: 772-785].

(28) Vicesima octava, quod Judas non fuit episcopus [**2**: 786-807].

(29) Vicesima nona, quod Jacobus Zebedei solium sacerdotale prius conscendit per martyrium [**2**: 808-815].

(30) Tricesima, quod Jacobus minor primus habuit determinatam sedem episcopalem, et quod Hierosolima fuit prima sedes episcopalis in nova lege [**2**: 818-825].

desunt $V^5V^7B^1V^6$

280 superintendens] sicut [semper B^2] intendens φB^2 | 283 alios] *add.* vero θ(-V^2) | 288 apostolos] *om.* ρ^1 | Petrum] *add.* Vicesima secunda [item ρ^1] quod claves episcopales sunt potestas confirmandi et ordinandi $P^1\rho^1\sigma$ | 289 Vicesima tertia $P^1\sigma$, item ρ^1 | 290 Quodcumque θ(-V^2)P^2Barb.Sr] quecumque $V^2\varphi B^2\pi\rho^1$Va | aliis] *om.* φ(-St) | 292-293 Vicesima tertia ... ordinandi] *om.* $P^4P^1\rho\sigma$ | 295 sacerdotali α | 298 quod[1] θ(-V^2)$B^2P^1\rho$] *om.* $V^2\gamma$(-B^2)$\pi^1\sigma$ | quod[2]] cum θ(-V^2)Sr | 299 facti sunt] fuerunt α | 301 quod $\theta B^2P^2P^1\rho^1$] *om.* $\varphi\pi^1$Barb.σ | est] *om.* ρ^1 | 304 illa] *om.* [hec St] φ(-W)B^2 | 308 prius ρ^1 | 309 Hierosolimitana ρ^1Va

(31) Tricesima prima, quod Mathias, Paulus et Barnabas fuerunt veri apostoli, non tamen facti episcopi a Christo, sed ab aliis [**2**: 828-842].

8. Octava conclusio principalis, de potestate iurisdictionis apostolorum, est quod eam non habuerunt immediate a Christo, sed a Petro [**2**: 847-849], et habet quindecim incidentales.

(1) Prima, quod idem est habere potestatem iurisdictionis, sive prelationem, et habere subditum [**2**: 849-864].

(2) Secunda, quod Christus aliis apostolis non dedit immediate aliquos subditos [**2**: 864-876].

(3) Tertia, quod Christus non dedit aliis apostolis per se potestatem iurisdictionis, nec plenam nec semiplenam [**2**: 877-900].

(4) Quarta, quod potestas miraculorum, predicandi, temporalia metendi, conficiendi, absolvendi in foro conscientie nullam iurisdictionem important de se [**2**: 901-962].

(5) Quinta, quod claves ordinis et iurisdictionis differunt realiter [**2**: 984-991].

(6) Sexta, quod per illa verba: *Tibi dabo claves*, Christus Petro promisit utrasque claves. Sed per illa: *Quecumque alligaveritis*, non promisit aliis nisi claves ordinis [**2**: 963-1006].

(7) Septima, quod Christus, dando aliis a Petro claves ordinis, non attenuavit promissionem factam Petro, quam tamen minorasset si dedisset aliis claves iurisdictionis [**2**: 1007-1053].

(8) Octava, quod illa verba: *Quecumque alligaveritis*, et illa: *Quorum remiseritis*, in sensu litterali intelliguntur de clavibus ordinis, non de clavibus iurisdictionis in aliquo foro [**2**: 1080-1172].

(9) Nona, quod omnis potestas iurisdictionis quam habuerunt alii apostoli, specialiter post ascensionem, et qua usi sunt in quocumque foro, fuit eis collata a Petro [**2**: 1172-1223].

(10) Decima, quod unitas ecclesie requirit quod omnis iurisdictio et prelatio in ecclesia procedat et originetur a Petro [**2**: 1224-1254].

desunt $V^5V^7B^1V^6$

311 et] *om.* γ(-B^2)σ | 312 veri] facti πBarb. | alio πBarb. | 314-315 Octava ... est] item ρ^1 | 315 quod] *add.* apostoli ρ^1 | eam] potestatem iurisdictionis ρ^1 | 316 et ... incidentales] *om.* ρ^1 | quindecim [quinque W] φB^2] quattuordecim θ(-V^2), tredecim $V^2P^2\pi$Barb.σ | 317 Prima] *add.* est φ(-φ^5) | 321-323 Christus ... quod] *om.* θ | 321 dedit] *add.* immediate ρ^1 | apostolis] *om.* φB^2 | 323 miracula θ(-V^2) | predicandi] faciendi θ(-V^2) | 324 conficiendi] *add.* et θ(-V^2)ρ^1 | 324-325 iurisdictionis potestatem [*om.* φ^4; *inv.* φ^3] φ(-φ^5) | 326 Quarta θ | et] vel φ | 328 Quinta θ | 329 alligaveris ρ^1 | 330 aliis] *add.* apostolis θ(-V^2) | 331 Sexta θ | 334 Septima θ | 338 Octava θ | habuerunt] *add.* omnes ρ^1 | 341 Nona θ

(11) Undecima, quod tota potestas ecclesie fuit collata Petro. Immo non est collata ecclesie nisi in Petro [**2**: 1255-1272].

(12) Duodecima, quod potestas Pauli excommunicandi fuit a Petro. Sed executio tradens sathane fuit a Christo [**2**: 1273-1292].

(13) Tertia decima, quod aliquis habet iurisdictionem in foro contentioso qui nullam habet in foro conscientie, et econtrario. Sed utrobique nullus potest nisi subditum solvere vel ligare [**2**: 1309-1323].

(14) Quarta decima, quod ad solvendum in foro exteriori una tantum potestas sufficit, scilicet iurisdictionis. Sed ad solvendum et ligandum in foro interiori requiritur duplex, scilicet potestas ordinis et potestas iurisdictionis [**2**: 1346-1353].

(15) Quinta decima, quomodo apostoli constituti sunt a Christo principes super omnem terram ad iudicandum in die iudicii immediate, sed mediante Petro ad iudicandum in hoc mundo [**2**: 1358-1389].

III. Tertius articulus principalis, de potestate discipulorum a Christo, habet tres conclusiones principales. Prima, quod septuaginta duo discipuli acceperunt a Christo potestatem similem apostolis, non equalem [**3**: 7-103]. Secunda, quod a Christo nullam habuerunt ordinis potestatem [**3**: 104-341]. Tertia, quod nec potestatem iurisdictionis in aliquo foro [**3**: 342-471].

1. Prima conclusio principalis, de potestate discipulorum simili apostolis non equali, habet septem explicitas.

(1) Prima, de triplici acceptione discipulorum Christi [**3**: 8-29].

(2) Secunda, quod septuaginta duo discipuli acceperunt a Christo potestatem predicandi sicut et apostoli, sed non tantam nec post resurrectionem [**3**: 30-68].

(3) Tertia, quod habuerunt etiam a Christo potestatem miracula faciendi, sed minorem quam apostoli [**3**: 69-80].

(4) Quarta, quod similiter interdixit eis portare peram et sacculum [**3**: 81-84].

desunt $V^5V^7B^1V^6$

343 Decima θ | 345 Undecima θ | quod] *add.* tota θ | 347 Duodecima θ | habens θ(-BoSv) | 349 vel] et $\theta\varphi$, nec ρ^1 | 351-354 Quarta decima ... iurisdictionis] *om.* Sv | 351 Tertia decima θ | 352 iurisdictio ρ^1 | 352-353 et ligandum] *om.* α | 353 interiori] *add.* scilicet conscientie θ | 354 potestas] *om.* θ | 355 Quarta [Tertia Sv] decima θ | quomodo] quod ρSr | 359 principalis] *add.* est ρ^1 | 359-360 a ... Prima] scilicet ρ^1 | 359 a Christo] *om.* φ; *add.* data θ^2Bo, data et θ^4 | 362-366 Secunda ... explicitas] *om.* ρ^1 | 367 Item primo ρ^1 | acceptatione π | 368 discipuli] *om.* σ | 369 predicandi] *om.* θ | et] *om.* θ(-V^2)P^2 | 371 etiam] *om.* ρ | 373 similiter] *om.* ρ^1 | interdixit] *add.* Jesus θ^4 | eis] *add.* Jesus θ^2Bo

(5) Quinta, quod similiter dedit eis potestatem metendi temporalia [**3**: 84-90].

(6) Sexta, quod discipuli non habuerunt a Christo potestatem baptizandi, nec ante resurrectionem nec post [**3**: 91-98].

(7) Septima, quod discipuli non baptizaverunt quousque per apostolos fuerunt diaconi ordinati [**3**: 98-103].

2. Secunda conclusio principalis, de potestate ordinis in discipulis, est quod eam non habuerunt a Christo [**3**: 105-106], et habet septem incidentales.

(1) Prima, quod discipuli in omnibus et per omnia semper et ubique fuerunt minores et inferiores apostolis [**3**: 107-112].

(2) Secunda, quod septuaginta duo discipuli a Christo nullam acceperunt potestatem ordinis, nec sunt facti ab eo episcopi nec sacerdotes [**3**: 106-145].

(3) Tertia, quod ex septuaginta duobus discipulis Mathias est electus in apostolum et septem diaconi assumpti [**3**: 145-245].

(4) Quarta, quod septuaginta duo discipuli non habuerunt a Christo potestatem ligandi nec solvendi in foro conscientie [**3**: 246-255].

(5) Quinta, de opinione que dicit discipulos fuisse presentes quando dictum est apostolis: *Accipite Spiritum Sanctum* [**3**: 256-320].

(6) Sexta, quod quando dictum est apostolis: *Quorum remiseritis*, discipuli non erant sacerdotes, nec tunc facti sunt [**3**: 290-320].

(7) Septima, quod discipuli figuram gerebant sacerdotum, nec tamen erant sacerdotes, et apostoli episcoporum, nec erant adhuc episcopi, sicut pontifex et sacerdos legalis gerebant typum evangelici episcopi et sacerdotis, nec tamen erant, et Melchisedech typum Christi, nec erat Christus [**3**: 321-341].

3. Tertia conclusio principalis, de potestate iurisdictionis in discipulis, quod septuaginta duo non habuerunt a Christo aliquam potestatem iurisdictionis in aliquo foro [**3**: 343-378], et habet unam incidentalem,

desunt $V^5V^7B^1V^6$

377 a Christo] *om.* θ | 380 ordinati in diaconos θ(-V^2) | 381 Secunda ... principalis] item ρ^1 | est] *om.* ρ^1 | 382-383 et ... incidentales] *om.* ρ^1 | 384 in omnibus] *om.* φ | 386 quod septuaginta duo] *om.* ρ^1 | 387 receperunt θ(-V^2)B^2 | 390 sumpti ρ^1 | 392 nec] et πBarb. | 397 quando] *om.* θ | apostolis] *add.* tantum θ(-V^2) | remiseritis] *add.* quia θ(-V^2) | 398 tunc] tamen ρ^1 | 399-400 nec ... sacerdotes] *om.* θ | 402 erat θ(-Sv)π^1Barb. | 403 typum] *om.* γVa; figuram θ | nec] *add.* tamen θ | 404 Tertia ... discipulis] item ρ^1 | discipulis] *add.* est θB^2 | 406-407 et ... scilicet] item [*om.* Br] ρ^1

scilicet quod illa verba: *Quecumque alligaveritis*, et *Quorum remiseritis*, non sunt dicta discipulis sed tantum apostolis [**3**: 379-428].

IV. Quartus articulus principalis, de potestate pape, habet tres conclusiones principales. Prima, quod potestas papalis non est ab ecclesia [**4**: 7-348]. Secunda, quod est immediate a solo Christo [**4**: 349-585]. Tertia, quod ab ipsa procedit omnis potestas iurisdictionis et prelatio spiritualis in tota ecclesia Dei [**4**: 586-951].

1. Prima conclusio principalis, quod papa non habet potestatem papalem ab ecclesia, nec ab aliquo puro homine, habet duodecim incidentales.

(1) Prima, quod si potestas papalis esset ab ecclesia, ipsa posset destrui et transferri et papa deponi ab ecclesia [**4**: 8-28].

(2) Secunda, quod universalis ecclesia non potest dignitatem papalem amovere, nec a Roma transferre, nec ius eligendi cardinalibus auferre, nec papam deponere [**4**: 29-78].

(3) Tertia, quod electus qui a superiore confirmatur, vel ex eius privilegio pro confirmato habetur, non potest deponi ab electoribus, sed ab illo superiore, vel ex commissione illius superioris [**4**: 108-119].

(4) Quarta, quod electus qui habet superiorem ratione delicti, licet ab illo non confirmetur, potest tamen ab illo non a subditis deponi, et sic papa potest deponere omnem principem secularem qui meruit deponi [**4**: 120-155].

(5) Quinta, quod quando superior habet potestatem solum a subditis, nec habet alium superiorem aliquomodo, aut ad illum non potest haberi recursus, tunc abutens potestate potest deponi a subditis [**4**: 156-163, 230-248].

(6) Sexta, quod habens potestatem a Deo, ab illa quamdiu eam habet a nullo homine potest deponi in aliquo casu [**4**: 163-170, 249-252].

(7) Septima, quod papa propter heresim non deponitur de iure,

desunt $V^5V^7B^1V^6$

408 tantummodo θ | 409 principalis] *om.* θ; *add.* est ρ^1 | 409-414 habet ... principalis] *om.* ρ^1 | 411 Christo] Deo θB^2 | 412 prelationis P^4P^1Barb. | 413 Dei] *om.* θStBm^1PrV^4; tamen UWBlB^2 | 414 principalis] *om.* θ(-Bo) | quod papa] scilicet [*om.* Sz] quod ρ^1 | 415-416 habet ... incidentales] *om.* ρ^1 | 421 cardinalibus] *add.* sine papa ρ^1Va | auferre] auferri ρ^1; *add.* sine papa Sr | 422 quod] *om.* ρ^1 | ex] ab θ | 423 non] nec γ | 424 vel] nisi $\rho^1\sigma$ | illius] *om.* ρ^1 | 426 superiorem] *add.* saltem θ(-V^2) | 427 illo^1] isto θ(-V^2) | confirmatur π^1Sr, sit confirmatus φB^2 | 428 principem] *om.* φ | secularem principem θ(-V^2) | 431 aut] *om.* φ | 434 eam] illam [illa P^4] πBarb. | 437 propter] preter φ(-U)

sed tantum de facto, quia hereticus ipso iure est privatus omni potestate iurisdictionis ecclesiastice a Deo, non ab homine [**4**: 177-190].

(8) Octava, quod licet papa propter peccatum in moribus non possit deponi, potest tamen ei resisti, et est contra eum concilium convocandum, et orandum ut Deus eum corrigat, vel de medio tollat [**4**: 190-229].

(9) Nona, quod potestas pape est maior omni alia potestate totius ecclesie [**4**: 253-258].

(10) Decima, quod infideles et scismatici non habent vocem in electione pape [**4**: 269-273].

(11) Undecima, quod populus potest sibi constituere superiorem quo ad potestatem temporalem, non autem quo ad spiritualem nisi ille eam habeat aliunde [**4**: 274-295].

(12) Duodecima, quod imperator a principio habuit imperium ex consensu populi. Sed papa non habet papatum ex consensu ecclesie sed a Deo [**4**: 310-328].

2. Secunda conclusio principalis, quod papa habet preeminentiam et plenitudinem potestatis in ecclesia immediate a solo Deo [**4**: 350-354], et habet octo incidentales.

(1) Prima, quod Petrus accepit a Christo preeminentiam et plenitudinem potestatis pro se et pro successoribus suis [**4**: 355-372].

(2) Secunda, quod episcopus Romanus, non Antiochenus nec quicumque alius, est proprius successor Petri [**4**: 373-384].

(3) Tertia, quod electus a cardinalibus legitime est verus Petri successor et vicarius Jesu Christi [**4**: 385-413].

(4) Quarta, quod papa non potest transferre sedem Romanam nisi ex voluntate Dei interpretativa, ex causa evidenti, cum assensu concilii generalis [**4**: 434-500].

(5) Quinta, quod papa potest cedere et resignare papatui de consensu cardinalium [**4**: 501-534].

(6) Sexta, quod potestas caracteris adheret persone viventi, morienti et resurgenti. Unde ei renuntiari non potest [**4**: 535-542].

desunt $V^5V^7B^1V^6$

442 possit] potest φB^2 | concilium] *add.* faciendum θ | 448 pape] *om.* θ^2; *add.* et per consequens in dando ius eligendi $\theta(-V^2)$ | 449 potest] habet P^4P^1Barb. | 453 populi] papali $\varphi(-\varphi^3)$Va | 455 Secunda ... principalis] item ρ^1; *add.* est θ | 457 et ... incidentales] *om.* ρ^1 | et] *om.* σ | 459 pro²] *om.* θP^2 | suis successoribus $\theta(-V^2)\varphi\rho^2$Va | 466 consensu ρ^1Va | 470 viventi] *add.* et θP^2 | 471 renuntiare [resignari St] $\alpha(-SvP^2)$

(7) Septima, quod potestas iurisdictionis ordinarie debetur statui, qui ex hominum voluntate acquiritur et perditur [**4**: 542-555].

(8) Octava, quod consensus matrimonii est sacramentum, et ideo causat vinculum insolubile. Sed consensus cardinalium eligentium et pape acceptantis non sunt sacramentum, et per consequens causant effectum dissolubilem, sicut et sponsalia [**4**: 558-585].

3. Tertia conclusio principalis est quod omnis potestas iurisdictionis ecclesiastice et prelatio in ecclesia procedit et derivatur a potestate papali [**4**: 587-614], et habet quinque incidentales.

(1) Prima, quod ecclesia Romana fundavit omnes alias ecclesias et instituit, et non solum personas in eis [**4**: 615-708].

(2) Secunda, quod Petrus dioceses et provincias primus instituit et divisit [**4**: 644-660].

(3) Tertia, quod hereticum est dicere aliam ecclesiam quam Romanam esse fundatam immediate a Christo [**4**: 677-708].

(4) Quarta, quod ecclesia Romana fundavit aliquas ecclesias per se immediate, omnes autem alias mediate [**4**: 709-737].

(5) Quinta, quod ecclesia Romana fundavit ecclesias precedentes, tenendo eas in suis fundamentis, et per Petrum cuius sedes fuit [**4**: 738-775].

V. Quintus articulus principalis, de potestate episcoporum, habet tres conclusiones principales. Prima, de potestate ordinis episcopalis [**5**: 6-116]. Secunda, de potestate iurisdictionis personali [**5**: 117-666]. Tertia, de potestate ecclesiarum cathedralium [**5**: 667-732].

1. Prima conclusio principalis, de potestate ordinis episcoporum, habet septem incidentales.

(1) Prima, quod omnes episcopi habent potestatem ordinis eque immediate a Christo sicut papa [**5**: 7-24].

(2) Secunda, quod Petrus super omnes episcopos in potestate ordinis solus habuit privilegium duplex. Primum, quod ipse sine ministro et sacramento mediis fuit a Christo consecratus.

desunt $V^5V^7B^1V^6$

472 statui] *add.* non persone [pape V^1] θ(-V^2), iurisdictionis V^2 | 473 qui] *add.* status θ(-V^2) | 474 ideo] *om.* φB^2 | et ideo] non ρ^1 | 476 sacramenta P^4P^1Barb. | 477 causant V^2Sv(-S)$P^2R\rho^1$Va] causat [cause Bo] θ(-V^2Sv)$\varphi B^2P^4P^1$Barb.Sr | et] *om.* θ(-V^2)φ | sponsalia] *add.* de futuro [futura θ^2] θ(-V^2) | 478 Tertia ... est] item ρ^1 | 480 et ... incidentales] *om.* ρ^1 | 481 omnes] *om.* θ | 482 personas] *add.* instituit π^1Barb. | 483 prius ρ^1 | 490 petram ρ^1 | 492-497 habet ... incidentales] *om.* ρ^1 | 495 potestate] *add.* iurisdictionis θ(-V^2) | 502 consecratus] *add.* et πBarb.

Secundum, quod ab ipso omnes alii ministerialiter acceperunt potestatem ordinis [**5**: 24-42].

(3) Tertia, quod omnes episcopi habent eque perfectam in essentia potestatem ordinis sicut papa [**5**: 43-49].

(4) Quarta, quod electus in papam est verus papa ante consecrationem, licet electus in episcopum non sit verus episcopus ante consecrationem [**5**: 49-62].

(5) Quinta, quod papa non consecratus potest facere personas habiles et inhabiles ad matrimonium, committere sacramentalia non episcopis, dare indulgentias, et huiusmodi [**5**: 62-67].

(6) Sexta, quod omnes episcopi habent eque virtuosam in effectu proprio potestatem ordinis sicut papa [**5**: 68-80].

(7) Septima, quod papa ante consecrationem non potest committere confirmationem nec minores ordines non episcopis [**5**: 106-116].

2. Secunda conclusio principalis, de potestate iurisdictionis quo ad personas episcoporum, est quod omnis potestas iurisdictionis quam habent episcopi in utroque foro non solum subest pape, immo etiam est a papa [**5**: 118-143], et habet quattuordecim incidentales.

(1) Prima, quod dato quod status episcopalis esset totaliter a Deo, habens ab ipso omnem suam potestatem sibi datam, nihilominus ipse status et eius potestas a quocumque habeatur habetur a papa [**5**: 144-187].

(2) Secunda, quod papa non habet a cardinalibus nec ab homine ius papatus, nec potestatem nec dignitatem papalem, sed a solo Deo [**5**: 188-228].

(3) Tertia, quod omnis potestas limitata in communitate procedit a potestate plena in illa [**5**: 229-258].

(4) Quarta, quod negare se habere potestatem a papa est negare se subditum ei in illa [**5**: 268-277].

(5) Quinta, quod dicere se esse subiectum pape in sua potestate,

desunt $V^5V^7B^1V^6$

503 ipso] eo φB^2 | 508-509 licet ... consecrationem] *hom.* Boρ^1 | 511 matrimonium] *add.* et ρ^1 | 511-512 sacramentalia ... episcopis] non episcopis [episcopus O, episcopi P^3] non sacramentalia θ(-V^2) | 513 omnis episcopus habet φB^2 | 515 papa] *om.* P^4P^1Barb. | consecrationem] confirmationem ρ^1 | 518-519 Secunda ... est] item ρ^1 | 519 personas episcoporum] episcopos θ | 521 et ... incidentales] *om.* ρ^1 | 522 quod[1]] *om.* ρ^1 | 523 omnem] totalem ρ^1 | 526 habet] potest θ(-V^2) | 527 papalem] habere θ(-V^2) | 530 plena] *add.* in ea et [*om.* S] est [et est: vel V^2] θ | in illa] *om.* P^4P^1Barb. | 531 se[2]] *om.* π | 532 ei] *om.* [esse V^2] θ | 533 esse] *om.* $\alpha\rho^2$Va | subiectum] subditum $P^4P^1\rho$(-Bm^2)Sr

sed negare se habere eam ex eius commissione, est negare pape plenitudinem potestatis [**5**: 278-288].

(6) Sexta, quod si papa potest ad libitum ponere et deponere prelatos ecclesie, sequitur quod ab ipso est omnis prelatio [**5**: 289-371].

(7) Septima, quod nisi solus papatus esset a Deo, ceteri prelati non indigerent confirmari postquam sunt electi, sicut nec papa [**5**: 372-395].

(8) Octava, de opinione que imaginatur potestatem iurisdictionis esse a Deo mediante homine eo modo quo potestas ordinis, et non minus [**5**: 396-454].

(9) Nona, quod papatus est immediate a Deo non obstante quod non acquiratur nisi mediante electione cardinalium [**5**: 455-471].

(10) Decima, quod si potestas iurisdictionis in prelatis esset a Deo sicut et potestas caracteris, tunc esset ita determinatus modus a Deo prefixus acquirendi istam sicut illam, et tunc papa non posset istam dare et auferre ad libitum, sicut nec illam [**5**: 472-493].

(11) Undecima, quod in papatu est certus modus acquirendi quem papa non potest mutare [**5**: 494-514].

(12) Duodecima, quod papa non potest auferre cardinalibus ius eligendi nisi consentiente universali ecclesia [**5**: 515-563].

(13) Tertia decima, quod licet omnis prelatio iuste accepta habeatur a Deo tanquam inspirante, non tamen a Deo immediate conferente nisi solus papatus [**5**: 581-610].

(14) Quarta decima, quod papa potest etiam licite prelatos deponere sine culpa, non tamen sine causa. Non sic autem principes seculares [**5**: 611-666].

3. Tertia conclusio principalis, de potestate iurisdictionis episcopalis quo ad ipsas sedes et ecclesias, est quod etiam ipse omnem dignitatem, prelationem et iurisdictionem quam habent habent a papa et ecclesia Romana [**5**: 668-699], et habet duas incidentales.

desunt $V^5V^7B^1V^6$

537 prelatio] *add.* ecclesie θ(-V^2) | 539 papa θ | 540 nec] *om.* [a W] γVa | 546 acquiritur φ | 547 est $P^2P^4P^1$Barb. | 548 et] *om.* θP^2 | 550 istam] illam φB^2 | et] vel θ(-V^2) | 553 posset θ^2BoSvγ(-U) | 556 a[1] ... inspirante] tanquam inspirante Deo θ(-V^2) | 557 papa π^1Va | 558 etiam] et φB^2 | licite] *om.* θ | 561-562 Tertia ... est] item ρ^1 | 562 etiam ipse] *om.* Barb.; ipse θ(-V^2)P^4P^1, omnes ecclesie ρ^1 | dignitatem] *add.* et $P^2\rho^1$Sr | 563 et iurisdictionem] *om.* ρ^1 | quam] etiam θ(-V^2) | habent[1]] *add.* et omnem iurisdictionem ρ^1 | habent[2]] *om.* θ(-V^2)$P^2\sigma$ | 564 Romana] *add.* quam habent ipse ecclesie θ(-V^2) | et ... incidentales] *om.* ρ^1

(1) Prima, quod si alie ecclesie essent a Christo fundate, papa non posset eas destruere nec dividere nec diminuere [**5**: 700-726].

(2) Secunda, quod dicere quod alie ecclesie habeant potestatem a Deo, et tamen quod in ea subsint pape, sic quod ab ipso possit illa potestas diminui vel auferri, est dicere quod papa est supra ius divinum et potest illud destruere ad libitum [**5**: 726-732].

VI. Sextus articulus principalis, de potestate curatorum, habet tres conclusiones principales. Prima, de potestate ordinis sacerdotalis [**6**: 7-23]. Secunda, de potestate iurisdictionis quo ad personas curatorum [**6**: 24-241]. Tertia, quo ad ipsas ecclesias vel curas [**6**: 242-1447].

1. Prima conclusio principalis, de potestate ordinis sacerdotalis, est quod omnis sacerdos habet potestatem conficiendi et absolvendi eque immediate et eque perfectam et virtuosam a Deo sicut episcopus et sicut papa [**6**: 8-19]. Et habet unam incidentalem, scilicet quod in hoc fuit privilegium apostolorum, quod sine alio ministro et sacramento a Christo fuerunt immediate sacerdotes ordinati [**6**: 20-23].

2. Secunda conclusio principalis, de potestate iurisdictionis quo ad curatos, quod eam habent a papa simpliciter et principaliter, licet sub Deo [**6**: 25-33], et hec habet quinque incidentales.

(1) Prima, quod si iurisdictio episcoporum et curatorum non esset a papa, papa non posset ad se trahere causas illorum in foro exteriori, nec in foro conscientie, per se vel per alium absolvendo subditos eorum, quin remitteret ad eos iterum absolvendos [**6**: 33-75].

(2) Secunda, quod si iurisdictio episcoporum et curatorum in utroque foro esset a Deo, papa non posset, eos excommunicando, facere nullam absolutionem illorum a vinculo vel a culpa [**6**: 104-119].

desunt $V^5V^7B^1V^6$

567 ecclesie] *om.* θ | habent $P^4P^1\rho$ | 568 possit] *om.* [potest St] φ | illa] ista [ipsa W] φB^2 | 569 minui $\theta(-V^2)$ | 571 principalis] *add.* et ultimus θ | 571-575 habet ... est] item [*add.* primo Bm^2] ρ^1 | 577 immediatam $\theta(-V^2)$ | et^2] *add.* eque $\alpha(-V^2P^2)\rho^2$ | 578 Et ... scilicet] item ρ^1 | 581-582 Secunda ... curatos] item ρ^1 | 582 curatos] *add.* est $\theta(-V^2)$ | eam] curati omnem potestatem iurisdictionis quam habent ρ^1 | habent [habeant Barb.] eam P^4P^1Barb.Sr | licet] sed P^4P^1Barb.Sr | 583 et ... incidentales] *om.* ρ^1 | hec] *om.* $\alpha(-P^2)$ | 585 papa^2] *om.* ρ | causas] curas ρ^1 | 586 exteriori ... foro] *hom.* ρ^1 | absolvere ρ^1 | 587 ad] *om.* $\varphi B^2\rho^1$ | 590 excommunicando eos $\theta(-V^2)\varphi B^2$ | 591 nullam ... culpa] quod absolutio illorum [eorum θ^2] curatorum et episcoporum [episcoporum et curatorum Bo] sit nulla a vinculo vel [nec Boθ^4(-S)] a culpa. Idest, non potest facere papa per excommunicationem suam in episcopos et curatos, quod non valeat absolutio eorum [illorum Boθ^4] a vinculo vel a culpa [Idest ... culpa *om.* S], quam ipsi aliis impenderent [impenderet Bo, impedirent S] $\theta(-V^2)$ | vel] et ρ^1

(3) Tertia, quod si iurisdictio est de iure divino, per consequens et subiectio. Unde prelato non possunt amoveri subditi, maxime prelatione manente, si illa est de iure divino [**6**: 120-150].

(4) Quarta, quod si potestas episcoporum et curatorum est de iure divino, ex confessione facienda proprio sacerdoti multa inconvenientia sequuntur, que omnia cessant si solus papa est proprius sacerdos de iure divino, alii autem ex eius commissione, sicut est veritas [**6**: 151-229].

(5) Quinta, quod si iurisdictio episcoporum non esset a papa, et illa curatorum non esset ab utroque, nec papa posset mittere legatos per mundum, nec episcopus predicatores et confessores per diocesim, nisi de licentia illorum [**6**: 230-241].

3. Tertia conclusio principalis, de potestate curatorum per comparationem ad ecclesias ipsorum, est quod quidquid iuris et potestatis spiritualis habent ecclesie parochiales inquantum huiusmodi, totum habent a papa et ecclesia Romana [**6**: 243-250], et habet incidentales quadraginta novem.

(1) Prima, quod ecclesie parochiales non essent de ecclesia Dei nisi essent fundate ab ecclesia Petri [**6**: 250-259].

(2) Secunda, quod nulla ecclesia unquam fuit fundata licite, nec fundari potest, nisi de licentia et auctoritate pape seu ecclesie Romane [**6**: 260-270].

(3) Tertia, quod si alie ecclesie essent fundate a Deo et non a papa, papa non posset eas dividere, nec unire, nec auferre, nec transferre, nec earum rectoribus casus absolvendos restringere [**6**: 271-287].

(4) Quarta, de obiectione aliorum qui sunt contrarie opinionis, que multa implicat contraria supradictis [**6**: 292-380].

(5) Quinta, quod Christus non fecit per se et immediate nisi unum curatum, scilicet Petrum, nec instituit nisi unam solam curam,

desunt $V^5V^7B^1V^6$

594 Unde] a φB^2 | prelatis $\theta(\text{-}V^2)Bm^2$, prelatio π^1Va, prelati $V^2\rho^2$ | possunt $U\rho^1$Sr] possent $\theta StBm^1P^2P^1$Barb., posset $\varphi^2B^2\pi^1$Va | subditi subtrahi vel amoveri $\theta(\text{-}V^2)$ | 595 stante prelatione $\theta(\text{-}V^2)$ | 598 sequerentur θ(-Bo), sequantur ρ^1, sequeretur BoSr, sequentur Va | 601 episcoporum] *add.* et curatorum θ | 603 episcopi π^1Barb.Sr | 605-606 Tertia ... est] item ρ^1 | 606 ipsorum] *add.* et curas $\theta(\text{-}V^2)$ | iuris] iurisdictionis $\theta(\text{-}V^2)$ | et potestatis] potestatisque [potestatis quod P^3] $\theta(\text{-}V^2)$ | 607 parochiales] curatorum ρ^1 | 608 et[1]] *add.* ab $\theta(\text{-}V^2)$ | 608-609 et[2] ... novem] *om.* ρ^1 | 609 quadraginta septem Barb. | 610 de] in φB^2 | 612 licite] *om.* φB^2 | 615 et ... papa] *om.* θ | 616 papa] *om.* ρ^1Va | 616-617 nec transferre] *om.* P^4P^1Barb. | 619 aliorum] eorum φ | 620 contradictoria $\theta V^4\rho^1$ | 621 unum] *add.* solum θ

scilicet totius ecclesie, committens Petro alios per se instituere et substituere et illis curas dividere sicut ecclesie expediret [**6**: 381-396].

(6) Sexta, quod status episcoporum et curatorum prout distinguuntur a statu pape in potestate iurisdictionis non fuerunt immediate a Christo instituti, sic quod ipse fecerit primos curatos et primos episcopos alios a Petro, sicut fecit primum papam [**6**: 396-400].

(7) Septima, quod successor non instituitur immediate ab illo a quo predecessor sed ab alio, quando institutor et fundator hoc sibi non retinuit sed alii commisit [**6**: 401-423].

(8) Octava, quod status discipulorum non fuit status curatorum, nec quo ad ordinem nec quo ad curam animarum, sed fuit figura eorum [**6**: 431-445].

(9) Nona, quod alii apostoli non sunt facti episcopi a Christo, nec in cena, nec quando dictum est eis: *Accipite Spiritum Sanctum*, nec alias [**6**: 506-524].

(10) Decima, quod non fuit tanta necessitas instituendi in passione episcopos sicut sacerdotes propter eucharistiam et penitentiam [**6**: 525-540].

(11) Undecima, quod Christus in cena instituit ordinem episcopalem, sed non ipsum dedit nisi in suo fundamento, idest sacerdotio [**6**: 541-556].

(12) Duodecima, quod episcopi non sunt ita proprie successores aliorum apostolorum, nec curati discipulorum, sicut papa est successor Petri [**6**: 644-673].

(13) Tertia decima, quod dato quod Christus instituisset discipulos primos curatos, et quod curati moderni essent veri successores eorum, adhuc non sequitur quod isti instituantur a Christo sicut illi [**6**: 682-687].

(14) Quarta decima, quod Petrus non pasceret oves Christi, nec

desunt $V^5V^7B^1V^6$

624 illas [illa P^4] πBarb. | 626-627 distinguitur θBarb.Va | 627-628 non ... instituti] non immediate a Christo instituti sunt $\theta(-V^2)$, non immediate est [*om.* W] institutus [*inv.* Bm^1] a Christo φB^2 | 628 sic ... fecerit] nam Christus non instituit immediate [*inv.* Bm^1] φB^2 | ipse πBarb.] *om. cet. mss.* | 629 fecit] *add.* ipsum $\theta(-V^2)$ | 631 substituitur $\theta(-V^2)$ | 641 propter eucharistiam] *om.* P^4P^1Barb. | 644 idest sacerdotio] *om.* φ^3 | idest] scilicet [sed W] $\alpha(-\varphi^3)\rho^2$ | sacerdotio] *praem.* in $\alpha(-\varphi^3 W)\rho$ | 647 aliorum] *om.* $\theta(-V^2)$ | 649 discipulos] *om.* φ | 650 primos] *om.* $\varphi\pi$Barb. | 651 sequeretur [sequerentur O] θB^2Barb. | instituerentur θ

per consequens esset verum verbum Christi: *Pasce oves meas*, si aliquis alius pasceret eas non auctoritate Petri [**6**: 687-693].

(15) Quinta decima, quod si episcopi et curati pro eo quod dicuntur succedere apostolis et discipulis haberent a Christo potestatem suam immediate sicut papa, ita dictum fuisset illis pro se et suis successoribus: Vobis dabo claves regni celorum, et Pascite oves meas, sicut Petro, licet forte non eque generaliter [**6**: 693-709].

(16) Sexta decima, quod sicut papa et imperator dignitates vacantes in sua curia dant per se, alias per suos, sed suam vicariam generalem nulli dant nisi per seipsos, sic Christus presens pro tempore sue presentie officia distribuit, et semper suo vicario generali per se ipsum potestatem tribuit. Sed per illum quasi absens cetera distribuit [**6**: 722-737].

(17) Septima decima, quod Christus post resurrectionem, mittens apostolos ad predicandum et baptizandum, intellexit non eis dare auctoritatem et potestatem sine Petro, sed solum idoneitatem et virtutem per miracula confirmandi [**6**: 756-774].

(18) Octava decima, quod discipuli, antequam essent diaconi, non erant in statu congruo recipiendi auctoritatem Evangelium predicandi, nec etiam baptizandi [**6**: 775-807].

(19) Nona decima, quod potestas prius data apostolis et discipulis in passione cessavit [**6**: 808-821].

(20) Vicesima, quod hereticum est dicere apostolos et discipulos semper fuisse cum Domino actu a principio usque ad finem. Dicuntur autem discipuli cum apostolis semper fuisse congregati, quia in sua vocatione permanserunt [**6**: 822-854].

(21) Vicesima prima, quod Paulus a Christo factus est apostolus et doctor Evangelii et iudex angelorum, sed a Petro episcopus et iudex hominum et doctor gentium quo ad auctoritatem [**6**: 855-867].

(22) Vicesima secunda, quod si Christus fecisset apostolos episcopos, assignans eis certas dioceses, et discipulos sacerdotes, assignans eis certas parochias, in quibus eis successissent moderni

desunt $V^5V^7B^1V^6$

654 verbum] *add.* Jesu π^1Barb. | 656 quod[1]] *om.* ρ^1 | 658 sicut] *add.* a φ(-φ^3) | 660 eque generaliter] equaliter φ | 663 se] seipsos θ(-V^2) | alias] *praem.* et α(-V^2) | 666 Sed] et γ | 670 auctoritatem et] *om.* U | et potestatem] *om.* φ(-U) | 672 nec θ | 677 dicere] *add.* omnes θ^2 | apostolos] *add.* omnes Boθ^4 | 678 Domino] Christo [*om.* W] φB^2 | 680 qui $\theta R\sigma$ | convocatione θ | 682 doctus $\theta P^2P^4\rho^1$ | Evangelii [Evangelia B^2] $\varphi B^2P^1Bm^2Sr$] Evangelium $\theta P^2R\rho^2$Va, eorum P^4, earum Barb. | 686 certam diocesim φ

episcopi et curati, tunc vere et proprie esset unus status in illis et in istis continuatus a Christo. Non tamen essent isti in illo statu instituti a Christo sicut illi, sed isti a successore Petro, sicut illi a predecessore Christo [**6**: 879-917].

(23) Vicesima tertia, quod discipuli non fuerunt facti a Christo sacerdotes nec curati, nec apostoli ab eo facti sunt episcopi. Et quando per alios facti sunt episcopi, non habuerunt certas sedes in quibus moderni sint proprie eorum successores [**6**: 918-943].

(24) Vicesima quarta, quod omnes apostoli fuerunt finaliter episcopi, quia constituebant ubique presbyteros, immo archiepiscopi et patriarche, quia et episcopos, sicut in eorum gestis legitur. Et quando ordinaverunt diaconos, tunc iam erant plures ex eis episcopi, saltem Joannes cum Petro [**6**: 922-949].

(25) Vicesima quinta, de quinque rationibus propter quas potius continuatur status et potestas Petri in papa quam apostolorum et discipulorum in episcopis et curatis [**6**: 957-1043].

(26) Vicesima sexta, quod curati sunt ordinarii. Habent tamen iurisdictionem suam a papa [**6**: 1044-1050].

(27) Vicesima septima, quod curati non habent iurisdictionem in aliquo foro ex institutione Christi dantis eam discipulis quasi primis curatis [**6**: 1051-1061].

(28) Vicesima octava, quod ordines episcoporum et curatorum sunt instituti a Christo explicite quo ad potestatem ordinis, curatorum quidem in apostolis non in discipulis, episcoporum in Petro non in aliis. Quo ad potestatem vero iurisdictionis sunt instituti a Christo in Petro materialiter et virtualiter, sed a Petro formaliter [**6**: 1062-1104].

(29) Vicesima nona, quod episcopi et curati non possunt de potentia ordinata deponi nisi ex causa rationabili. Sed de potentia absoluta possunt deponi etiam sine iusta causa, ab episcopo

desunt $V^5V^7B^1V^6$

690 Petro] *om.* θ | 692-693 non ... sacerdotes] non fuerunt a Christo sacerdotes facti θ, non fuerunt a Christo [a Christo non fuerunt St] facti sacerdotes φ(-Bm^1)$B^2\rho^2$ | 693 ab ... sunt] facti sunt ab eo RP^1Barb., sunt facti ab eo ρ^1 | eo] ipso θ | 695 proprii θ | 697 qui φB^2 | immo] *add.* fuerunt φB^2 | 698 et[1]] *om.* $\varphi B^2\pi^1$Barb. | et[2]] etiam ρ^1 | quia et] sed constituebant φB^2 | episcopos] *add.* constituebant θ(-V^2) | 699 diaconos] dioceses $P^4\rho$Va | 702 continuantur π^1Va | quam] *add.* aliorum [in aliorum Sv] θ | 704-708 Vicesima sexta ... curatis] *om.* Barb. | 705 suam] *om.* θ | papa] *add.* tantum φB^2 | 706 habent] *add.* aliquam $\theta^2\varphi B^2$ | 709 Vicesima sexta Barb. | 711 episcoporum] *add.* vero θ(-V^2) | 715 Vicesima septima Barb.

quidem curati, iuris ordine servato, a papa vero omnes alii prelati ecclesie, etiam iuris ordine non servato [**6**: 1105-1123].

(30) Tricesima, quod si episcopi et curati haberent potestatem suam a Deo, non possent deponi, sicut nec papa [**6**: 1123-1128].

(31) Tricesima prima, quod si institutio esset humana et potestas divina, tunc possent quidem ex toto deponi. Sed manentes in statu non possent per excommunicationem ab executione potestatis impediri [**6**: 1129-1138].

(32) Tricesima secunda, quod contradictio est dicere quod status et potestas ecclesiarum vel prelatorum in communi sit a Deo, non ab homine, et in particulari potestas cuiuslibet sit ab homine [**6**: 1138-1151].

(33) Tricesima tertia, quod potestas ordinis in omnibus est a Christo in particulari et in communi. Potestas vero iurisdictionis utroque modo in aliis est a Petro data, licet a Christo aliquo modo instituta et ordinata [**6**: 1151-1171].

(34) Tricesima quarta, quod episcopi et curati sunt vicarii Christi, sed nihilominus etiam pape, et curati episcopi, licet sint ordinarii hi et illi [**6**: 1172-1189].

(35) Tricesima quinta, quod potestas episcoporum et curatorum est a papa sicut a causa in fieri, sed ab ecclesia Romana sicut a causa in esse que semper stat, et sedes ipsa non moritur. Unde manet et viget sede vacante sicut stante. Sedes autem episcopalis alia non est causa curatorum nec parochiarum nisi in fieri, nec similiter sedes patriarchalis nec metropolitana ecclesiarum suffraganeorum et personarum [**6**: 1190-1220].

(36) Tricesima sexta, quod papa potestatem ordinis non potest auferre prelatis nec dare non prelatis simpliciter. Sed secundum quid potestatem ordinis pontificalis quo ad confirmationem et

desunt $V^5V^7B^1V^6$

720 Vicesima octava Barb. | 722 Vicesima nona Barb. | et] sed θ(-V^2) | 723 quidem] *om.* θ | 724 posset [possunt U] φ | excommunicationem] *add.* aut suspensionem deponi θ(-V^2) | ab] *om.* φ; cum P^4P^1Barb. | executio φ | potestatis] *add.* nec θ | 726 secunda] *om.* Barb. | 727 vel] et θ | 728 potestas] *add.* et status θ(-V^2) | 730 Tricesima prima Barb. | 734 Tricesima secunda Barb. | 735 sed] *om.* α(-P^2) | curati] *add.* etiam θ(-V^2) | 736 illi] alii φB^2 | 737 Tricesima tertia Barb. | 740 manet et viget φB^2] manent et fiunt Barb. *et cet. mss.* | sede] *praem.* etiam θ(-V^2) | stante] *add.* sive sedente papa θ(-V^2) | 742 ecclesiarum] est causa [ecclesia V^2] θ | 742-743 suffraganeorum] *add.* ipsorum [ipse U] φ, ipsarum B^2 | 743 et] *om.* φB^2 | personarum] *om.* φ | 744 Tricesima quarta Barb. | 746 quid] *add.* quoniam θ(-V^2)

collationem minorum ordinum potest dare non episcopo sacerdoti [**6**: 1221-1230].

(37) Tricesima septima, quod potestatem iurisdictionis potest papa auferre omnibus prelatis eos deponendo. Sed manentibus prelatis non potest auferre ex toto [**6**: 1230-1244].

(38) Tricesima octava, quod potestatem iurisdictionis prelatorum potest dare ad libitum non prelatis in utroque foro [**6**: 1233-1237].

(39) Tricesima nona, quod quia papa non potest immutare statum ab ecclesia institutum – potest autem mutare statum episcoporum et curatorum, et sedes et potestatem eorum in communi et in particulari – ideo concluditur quod uterque status in communi et in particulari est a papa, non a Christo, nisi inspirante quod tales status instituerentur a Petro in potestate iurisdictionis [**6**: 1245-1290].

(40) Quadragesima, quod papa non posset destruere statum episcoporum et curatorum quo ad officia ordinum [**6**: 1291-1303].

(41) Quadragesima prima, quod papa de potentia absoluta et si non ordinata posset amovere omnes episcopos et curatos de suis ecclesiis, regendo universalem ecclesiam per legatos et commissarios, ordinarios vel delegatos [**6**: 1303-1335].

(42) Quadragesima secunda, quod potestas papalis prout concernit statum sola est a Deo immediate [**6**: 1336-1347].

(43) Quadragesima tertia, quod omnis episcopatus et omnis ecclesia preter Romanam potest destrui de iure et de facto. Ideo nulla alia ecclesia est fundata a Christo [**6**: 1353-1378].

(44) Quadragesima quarta, quod potestas pape, etiam prout

desunt $V^5V^7B^1V^6$

747 sacerdoti] *add.* Tricesima septima, quod papa [*om.* B^2] potestatem iurisdictionis prelatorum potest dare ad libitum non prelatis in utroque foro φ(-V^4)B^2 | 749 Tricesima quinta Barb., Tricesima octava φ(-V^4)B^2 | 750-751 eos ... toto] quo ad executionem ad tempus. Sed non potest eam auferre [quo ... auferre *om.* Sv] ex toto, ita quod [que P^3] remaneant prelati et eam non habeant [habeat Bo] θ(-V^2) | 751 posset [possit P^4] π^1Barb. | 752-753 Tricesima octava ... foro] *om.* φ(-V^4)B^2 | 752 Tricesima sexta Barb. | 754 Tricesima septima Barb. | quia] *om.* θ | non] *om.* Boφ | mutare $P^1\rho$Sr | statum] *add.* ecclesie universalem [universalis θ^2] θ(-V^2) | 755 ab ... statum] *hom.* φ | immutare σ | 757 excluditur ρ^1 | 761 Tricesima octava Barb. | 762 et curatorum] *om.* $\varphi\rho^1$ | 763 Tricesima nona Barb. | potentia] *add.* sua θ | si] *om.* θ | 764 non] *add.* de π^1Barb. | 765 et] *om.* φ | 767 secunda] *om.* Barb. | 768 immediate] *add.* Quadragesima tertia, quod potestas pape, etiam prout respicit personam, est ex dono Dei immediate et nulla alia B^2P^2 | 769 Quadragesima prima Barb., Quadragesima quarta B^2P^2 | 772-773 Quadragesima quarta ... alia] *om.* B^2P^2 | 772 Quadragesima secunda Barb. | etiam] *om.* ρ^1

respicit personam, est ex dono Dei immediate et nulla alia [**6**: 1379-1394].

(45) Quadragesima quinta, quod potestas pape adhuc tertio modo singulariter est ex Deo quo ad modum habendi, quia est ex ordinatione divina, idest electione universalis ecclesie, vel eorum in quos transtulit ius suum [**6**: 1395-1405].

(46) Quadragesima sexta, quod factum pape in quo excedit limites sue potestatis est nullum. Sed factum in quo abutitur potestate est validum, sed peccatum [**6**: 1406-1418].

(47) Quadragesima septima, quod papa non potest prelatis subtrahere potestatem ordinis ad quam non se extendit sua potestas. Sed potest eis auferre potestatem iurisdictionis, in qua habet plenitudinem potestatis [**6**: 1419-1428].

(48) Quadragesima octava, quod papa potest de facto facere contra legem Dei prohibentem que stat in finibus sue prohibitionis. Sed contra legem Dei que secum trahit suam executionem non potest [**6**: 1429-1443].

(49) Quadragesima nona, quod papa posset de potentia absoluta destruere omnes ordines a sede apostolica approbatos, omnia privilegia quibuscumque data revocare, et omnia iura evertere uno verbo. Sed irrationabiliter ageret et peccaret [**6**: 1443-1447].

Hec autem omnia dicta sunt, nihil temere asserendo, sed dando peritioribus materiam cogitandi, et ut per sedem apostolicam in illis que dubia sunt veritas declaretur, aut declarata alias confirmetur.

desunt $V^5V^7B^1V^6$

773 personam] *add.* eius θ(-V^2) | ex] a φ | 775 Quadragesima tertia Barb. | 776 ex^1] a $\theta\varphi^1B^2\rho^2$Va | 777 idest] et [*om.* Bo] ex [*om.* WB^2] BoφB^2 | 779 Quadragesima quarta Barb. | 782 Quadragesima quinta Barb. | 782-783 subtrahere prelatis θ^2Sv$\varphi B^2\rho^2$ | 783 ad quam] quantum enim [*om.* V^2] ad hoc [*om.* V^2] θ | 786 Quadragesima sexta Barb. | 788 consecutionem ρ^1 | 790 Quadragesima septima Barb. | 791 approbatos] *add.* et θ(-V^2) | 792 data revocare] *om.* ρ^1 | 795 et] *om.* ρ^1

Appendix A
A Supplement to Article Two: Version A

The following material, which is included in all the manuscripts with the exception of $B^2V^6Bm^2BrSz$ and Sr, could be inserted above at p. 139, line 636, or more appropriately read as an appendix here. On this question see the discussion in the introduction, pp. 90-92.

Item confirmant aliqui istam opinionem quibusdam auctoritatibus dicentes sic. Quod ceteri apostoli a Petro potestatem receperunt, et quod ab ipso incepit pontificalis ordo, quodque ab eo septuaginta duo discipuli potestatem acceperunt, videtur per auctoritates aliquas Canonis et sanctorum. Paulus enim, qui *non ab hominibus, neque per hominem*, sed a Deo factus est apostolus, qui operatus est ei in apostolatum inter gentes sicut operatus est Petro in apostolatum circumcisionis, sicut habetur ad Galatas 1 et 2, non obstante quod in apostolatu par fuerit aliis, tamen, sicut habetur Actuum 13, ex consilio Spiritus Sancti ipse et Barnabas missi sunt in Hierusalem ad Petrum, Jacobum et Joannem qui erant ibi. Qui, audito consilio Spiritus Sancti, ieiunantes et orantes, imposuerunt Paulo et Barnabe manus in modum ordinandorum, sicut colligitur ex collatione historie cum textu Actuum 13. Si igitur Paulus ordinatus fuit per manuum impositionem et Barnabas cum eo, non obstante quod Paulus fuit immediate vocatus a Deo patre et Jesu Christo, sicut ipse testatur ad Galatas, cum alii apostoli a Petro eo non fuerint superiores, sequitur quod alii receperunt a Petro manuum impositionem et sic consecrationem.

Dicunt aliqui quod manuum impositio, licet eis facta sit in modum ordinandorum vel consecrandorum, non tamen est certum quod tunc

desunt $B^2\rho$Sr

2 acceperunt [ceperunt S] θ | 3 inceperit φ(-StW), cepit Stψ | quodque] et quod φ | 6 in] ad α | 7 sicut[1]] *om.* θ | sicut[2]] ut θ | 8 apostolatum π(-B^1) | fuit φ | 13 manus $\theta\varphi^5$ | 15 et] *add.* Domino φ | 16 eo] et Paulo φ | fuerunt $\theta^2V^2V^5\pi$(-R)Va

5 Gal. 1:1 | 7-8 Gal. 1:1, 2:7-8 | 9 Act. 13:1-3 | 12-13 Cf. Petrus Comestor, *Historia scholastica*, in *Act. Apost.*, chap. 66 (PL 198: 1689)

fuerint ordinati. Immo potius credendum est quod sicut in primitiva ecclesia multi sine ista solemnitate ordinati sunt, ita Barnabas et Paulus, qui consilio Spiritus Sancti ad apostolatum electi sunt, in hoc cum aliis privilegiati sunt, ut talis solemnitas circa eos non fieret, ut dicunt, ordinationis vel consecrationis. De hoc tamen non habetur certitudo, quia nec de ordinatione aut consecratione aliorum apostolorum a Petro aliquid legitur in Scriptura nisi *Hoc facite in meam commemorationem*, quo ad ordinationem, et quod Christus insufflavit et dixit: *Accipite Spiritum Sanctum, quorum remiseritis peccata* etc. Dicunt etiam cum hoc quod multa fiebant in primitiva ecclesia que hodie non fiunt, et aliqua observantur hodie in ecclesia que tunc non fuerunt in omnibus observata, ut quod tunc aliquis sine ceteris ordinibus precedentibus promovebatur ad sacerdotium, quod hodie non observatur, sicut hec in *Scholastica historia* recitantur.

Dicendum quod ista solutio non valet, primo quantum ad hoc quod dicunt, quod per illam manuum impositionem non fuerunt tunc ordinati. Quia manus impositio in modum ordinandorum vel consecrandorum non debet alicui fieri nisi ad ipsum ordinandum et consecrandum, vel simpliciter et pure, quando certum est ipsum non fuisse ordinatum, vel sub conditione, quando est dubium. Alias fieret iniuria et illusio sacramento, et esset mendacium in cultu Christiane religionis, quod est contra doctrinam Augustini, et Pauli, ad Galatas 2, ubi reprehendit Petrum de quadam simulatione qua ipse et quidam alii simulatorie et non recte ibant ad veritatem Evangelii. Unde *De celebratione missarum* c. *De homine*, reprehenditur sacerdos qui exteriori ritu simulabat se hostiam consecrare, nec tamen intendebat consecrare, nec etiam consecrabat, subticendo verba consecrationis. Unde sicut non liceret imponere manum in modum confirmandi nisi confirmando, sic nec in modum ordinandi nisi ordinando, vel supplendo manuum impositionem obmissam alias

desunt B²ρSr

22 cum aliis] *om.* θ| 31 ut quod] et θ| 32 hec [hic S] θ(-V²)ψRVa] hoc [*om.* U; hic T] V²φπ(-R)| historia] *om.* φ²| Historia scholastica θφ³| 33 recitantur θ(-V²)ψRVa] recitatur V²φπ(-R)| 34-35 quod dicunt ψ] *om.* θφ; quod dicit πVa| 37 et consecrandum] *om.* π(-R)| 38 et pure] utpote φVa| fuisse] *add.* alias θR, simul [semel P¹] ψπ²| 39 et] vel θ| 43 ibant] *om.* θ(-V²)| Evangelii] *add.* ambularent [ambularet V³, ambularem P³] θ¹

26 Luc. 22:19| 27-28 Joan. 20:22-23| 32 Petrus Comestor, *Historia scholastica* (PL 198: 1054-1722)| 41 Cf. Augustine, *De mendacio*, chap. 10 (PL 40: 500-501, CSEL 41: 436-437); *Contra mendacium*, chap. 12 (PL 40: 536-537, CSEL 41: 504-507)| Gal. 2:11ff.| 43-44 X. 3.41.7.

ordinando, sicut dicitur *De sacramentis* <*non*> *iterandis* [*vel non*] c. ultimo.

Quod dicunt secundo, quod in primitiva ecclesia multi sunt ordinati sine hac solemnitate, dicendum quod falsum est propter quattuor. Prima quia, cum maior solemnitas soleat adhiberi ex ritu ab apostolis tradito circa ordinationem sacerdotum et episcoporum quam diaconorum, cum in primitiva ecclesia in ordinatione diaconorum fuerit servata solemnitas de impositione manuum cum oratione, ut habetur Actuum 6, multo magis in ordinatione sacerdotum et episcoporum. Secundo, quia solus Christus potuit dare rem sacramenti sine sacramento. Unde apostoli non potuerunt dare rem ordinis sacerdotii nec episcopatus sine vera ordinatione et sacramentali consecratione. Tertio, quia licet apostoli in ritu a se instituto possent dispensare, tamen in substantia ordinationis et consecrationis sacerdotis vel episcopi non potuerunt ipsi dispensare. Unde cum impositio manuum cum oratione sit de substantia ordinis sacerdotalis, propter quod omissa necessario est supplenda, *De sacramentis non iterandis* c. ultimo, et eodem modo ipsa est de substantia ordinis episcopalis, non potuerunt apostoli sine hac solemnitate, idest sine manuum impositione, quemquam ordinare in sacerdotem nec in episcopum. Quarto, quia nunquam aliquis diceret quod apostoli baptizassent in nomine Domini Jesu, non exprimendo explicite nomen trinitatis, nisi quia expresse legitur Actuum 8 et 19, et tunc dicuntur hoc fecisse dispensative, non auctoritate propria, sed Spiritus Sancti volentis nomen Jesu exosum autenticare, ut homines in eo ponerent spem salutis. Unde cum non legantur apostoli quemquam ordinasse sine manuum impositione, que etiam impositio est de substantia ordinum diaconorum, presbyterorum, episcoporum, sicut expressio trinitatis de substantia forme baptismi, non licet fingere quod apostoli ordinaverunt sine manuum impositione. Immo non habemus aliunde quod manus impositio sit de substantia ordinis nisi quia sic ordinabant apostoli.

Quod dicunt tertio, quod credendum est Paulum et Barnabam sine hac solemnitate alias ordinatos, non est verum. Primo, quia Leo papa dicit eos

desunt $B^2\rho$Sr

49 ordinato $\theta^4\varphi$ | 55 observata $\psi\pi^2$Va | 57 quia] *add.* cum φ | 58 potuit] potuerit φ(-W) | 59-60 et ... consecratione] *om.* θ | 64 iterandis vel non π | 67 nec] vel $\theta\varphi^1V^4$ | in²] *om.* θ(-V^3) | 70 hec θ(-BoV^2) | 71 volentes φ

49-50 X. 1.16.3 | 56 Act. 6:6 | 64 X. 1.16.3 | 69-70 Act. 8:16, 19:5

tunc fuisse ordinatos. Unde quia erat dominica, ostendit illo exemplo sacerdotes maiores, idest episcopos, non nisi in dominica consecrandos, 75 d. *Quod die dominico.* Secundo, quia non dicimus quod apostoli confirmarent sine manuum impositione. Immo quia legimus Actuum 8: *Tunc imponebant manus super illos, et accipiebant Spiritum Sanctum*, et similiter Actuum 19, dicimus quod apostoli confirmabant manus imponendo super omnes quos confirmabant. Ita etiam cum legamus manus impositas septem diaconis primis, et dicamus eos tunc ordinatos, et pari ratione omnes alios diaconos sic credimus ordinatos, et legamus Paulo et Barnabe manus cum oratione impositas tunc quando a Domino ad episcopatum et prelationem sunt electi, credendum est magis tunc cum illa solemnitate eos fuisse ordinatos et consecratos quam alias sine illa. Et si in aliis apostolis quorum ordinatio non legitur crederetur hec solemnitas omissa, in istis tamen in quibus legitur hec solemnitas servata non debet fingi fuisse omissa. Immo magis econtrario, ex hoc quod legitur istis apostolis facta fuisse manus impositio, credenda est facta fuisse aliis qualis ad episcopi ordinationem requiritur, nam ordinationem sacerdotalem quam a Domino receperunt in eis non licuit iterare, nec in Petro episcopalem quam a Domino recepit.

Quod dicunt quarto: nihil legi in Scriptura de ordinatione aliorum apostolorum, nec a Petro nec a Christo, nisi illud *Hoc facite*, et *Accipite Spiritum Sanctum* etc., verum est explicite et expresse. Sed quia legitur apostolos confirmasse, diaconos ordinasse, et Paulum et Barnabam presbyteros ordinasse, quod non potest fieri nisi ab episcopo, ideo concluditur apostolos in episcopos ab aliquo ordinatos. Et quia episcopus non potest fieri nisi ab episcopo, necesse fuit saltem unum episcopum fieri a Christo, a quo alii fierent, et probabilius est de Petro, sicut supra dictum est. Et quia petra Christus Petrum sibi assimilare voluit, probabile est quod per ipsum ceteros episcopos fecerit. Per illa autem verba: *Hoc facite*,

desunt B²ρSr

86-87 manus ... confirmabant] *hom.* θ | 87 super π(-R)] *om. cet. mss.* | 89 credamus φ | 90 oratione] *add.* esse ψπ² | 95 econtrario] *add.* et θφ | ex] *om.* θ²θ³φ | 96 credendum ψπ² | 98 quam] qualem θφ | 101 illud] *om.* φ | 104 ordinasse Va] *om.* θ²θ³π; fecisse θ⁴, consecrasse φ | 107 quo] *add.* omnes [primo omnes SvP³, post omnes V³] θφ¹ | dictum] deductum φP²Va | 108 est¹ Bm¹Wπ] fuit θφ(-Bm¹W)P²Va, est vel deductum fuit V⁷ | assimilari θ²θ³π² | 109 Per²] propter φ

83 Gratian, D.75 c.5 | 84-85 Act. 8:17 | 86 Act. 19:6 | 101 Luc. 22:19 | 101-102 Joan. 20:22 | 103 Cf. Act. 8:14-17, 19: 1-7 | Cf. Act. 6:1-6 | 103-104 Cf. Act. 14:23 | 109 Luc. 22:19

facti sunt sacerdotes, sed non episcopi. Per illa: *Accipite* < etc. >, nec sacerdotes nec episcopi, sicut in superioribus est deductum. Specialiter autem quod per illa verba: *Accipite Spiritum Sanctum*, non sint facti episcopi patet, quia verba sacramentalia prolata a ministro tantum operantur quantum prolata a Christo, sicut verba: *Hoc est corpus meum*, ita conficiunt quando proferuntur a sacerdote sicut confecerunt quando fuerunt prolata a Christo. Unde si Christus per illa verba dicta illis qui erant facti sacerdotes quo ad substantiam et actum principalem per verba eis dicta in traditione calicis: *Hoc facite*, fecit eos episcopos, pari ratione episcopus, dicendo illa verba: *Accipite Spiritum Sanctum, quorum remiseritis* etc., illi quem fecit sacerdotem, tradendo calicem cum forma verborum prescripta, si hoc intenderet, faceret eum episcopum. Si dicatur: non est simile, quia Christus non instituit quod per illa verba fierent alii episcopi, licet per illa fecerit episcopos, sicut non instituit quod per illa verba: *Hoc facite*, fierent sacerdotes, quamvis per illa eos fecerit – unde non fiunt sacerdotes per illa verba, etiam ab episcopo prolata, sed per alia; per illa autem verba: *Hoc est corpus meum*, fit sacramentum eucharistie, non quia Christus illis usus fuit conficiendo, sed quia instituit ut illis uterentur ministri – non valet, quia verba quibus fiunt sacerdotes per episcopum equipollent verbis quibus Christus eos fecit in sensu. Cum enim Christus confecisset corpus et sanguinem, quod fuit missam instituere et celebrare, dixit: *Hoc facite*, idest missam celebrate, hoc est celebrandi potestatem accipite, et hoc est quod dicit episcopus: *Accipite potestatem dicendi missas* etc. Unde si Christus per illa verba: *Accipite* < etc. >, fecisset eos episcopos, verisimile est quod illis vel equipollentibus dedisset virtutem quod per ea deinceps episcopi fierent, quod est falsum.

desunt $B^2\rho$Sr

112 sunt [fuerunt P^4] $V^7\pi$(-R) | 113 sacramentaliter φ | 116 verba] *add.* scilicet [*om.* UW] Accipite Spiritum Sanctum φ | 117 erant] *add.* iam φ | et] *add.* quo ad θ | 118-119 fecit ... episcopus] *om.* θ^1 | pari ... episcopus] *om.* θ^2 | 119 illa verba] *om.* π(-R) | 120 etc.] *add.* episcopus V^5, fecit eos episcopos [*add.* pari ratione et Bo] episcopus $BoV^2\theta^4$ | 121 dicant [dicunt BoV^2Sv] θ | 122 non[1]] *praem.* quod α | ista $\theta(-V^5)$ | 125 sacerdotes] *om.* θ | 126 illa] ista φ | 127 fuerit $\theta\varphi^1$ | conficiendo] *om.* α | 128 quia] *add.* illa αP^1 | 132 episcopus] Christus π(-R) | 133 ista φ(-St) | 134 verisimile ... illis] verisimiliter [*add.* illis ψ] $\theta\psi$, verbis similibus [similibusne V^4] φ | 135 eadem α

110 Joan. 20:22 | 112 Joan. 20:22 | 114 Matt. 26:26, Marc. 14:22, Luc. 22:19 | 118 Luc. 22:19 | 124 Luc. 22:19 | 131 Luc. 22:19 | 133-134 Joan. 20:22

Quod dicunt quinto: multa in primitiva ecclesia fieri que nunc non fiunt et econtrario, intelligentes de ritu sacramentorum, dicendum quod multa cerimonialia accidentaliter sunt postea superaddita propter solemnitatem et reverentiam sacramentorum, quia tunc pauca adhibebantur, que non essent de substantia. Sed quantum ad illa que sunt de substantia sacramentorum, credendum est quod nihil tunc fuerit observatum quod non modo observetur, alias moderna ecclesia non haberet vera sacramenta. Similiter econtrario substantialia in sacramentis que nunc sunt tunc fuerunt observata, nisi quantum expresse legitur contrarium, sicut de forma baptismi ad tempus, ut dictum est.

Quod dicunt sexto, quod tunc aliquis sine precedentibus ordinibus promovebatur ad sacerdotium, non oportet hoc dicere, nec videtur rationabile. Quia cum oporteat quandoque sacerdotem exorcisare cathecuminos, qui est proprius actus exorciste, absurdum est esse sacerdotem qui non est exorcista. Immo, cum sit absurdum in ordinatis quod superior non possit illud quod potest inferior, propter quod sacerdos dicit Evangelium et Epistolam, et diaconus Epistolam, nec aliquis possit modo debito et congruo in actum ordinum nisi habeat ordinem, inordinatum est et contra naturam ordinum, etiam prout sunt a Christo instituti, quod aliquis habeat ordinem superiorem et non habeat ordinem inferiorem. Sed quod ordines sacri non dentur simul est a solo statuto ecclesie. Unde rationabilius credi potest quod illi qui ordinabantur in primitiva ecclesia in ordine superiori, si prius non erant in minoribus constituti, quod tunc ordinabantur simul ad omnes illos ordines. Sed tota ordinatio denominabatur a supremo sicut a digniori, sicut modo, quando conferuntur simul quattuor minores ordines, dicitur aliquis in acolitum ordinari, quia ille est ordo superior inter illos, quia immediatior ministerio corporis Christi. Unde tunc dicebantur in diaconos ordinari, quia cum diaconatu recipiebant omnes ordines precedentes, adhibita solemnitate substantialiter debita cuilibet ordinationi per se, quam nec apostolis licuit omittere nec mutare. Similiter dicebantur presbyteri et episcopi ordinari, non quia non recepissent ordines precedentes tunc vel prius, sed quia tota ordinatio, si erat plurium ordinum, denominabatur ab ultimo et supremo.

desunt $B^2\rho$Sr

137 Quod] *add.* autem θ | dicunt quinto] vero dicunt γ | 138 intelligendum est θ | 143 observetur] servetur θ(-Bo) | non[2]] *add.* modo φ | 149 quandoque sacerdotem] quemcumque sacerdotem $\theta^2\theta^3$, quelibet V^3, quemlibet Sv | 150 proprius] primus [prius V^1] $\theta^2\theta^3\psi$, prior θ^4 | 151 in ordinatis] inordinatum π(-R) | 156 ordinem[1]] *om.* $\varphi(-\varphi^5)$ | 157 dantur $\theta^2V^2V^5P^4$, ordinantur π^2 | 160 tota] *add.* illa π(-R) | 165 omnes] *add.* minores $\psi\pi^2$ | 168 quia[1]] qui $\gamma(-\varphi^3)$Va

Item 21 d. § *Decretis* dicitur: *Petrum quasi summum sacerdotem Dominus elegit, dum ei pro omnibus claves regni celorum tribuit, et a se petra Petri sibi nomen imposuit*, ubi habetur quod Petro claves dedit Christus, a quo videntur per subsequentia ibidem claves ad alios derivari. Item eadem d. *In novo*, et secundo libro Isidori, *De origine officiorum*, c. 5, in quibus locis habetur quod *in novo testamento post Christum*, sicut dicit Isidorus, *sacerdotalis ordo a Petro incepit. Ipsi enim primo datus est pontificatus in ecclesia Christi*, ut habetur ibidem. Sed si aliis cum Petro datus est pontificatus, non ipsi primo. Igitur, cum secunda descendant a primo, ab eo tanquam a primo post Christum derivatus est pontificatus in alios. Item Leo papa, in sermone qui incipit: *Quotiens nobis misericordiam Dei*, et intitulatur in aliquibus libris antiquis sermo Gregorii, dicit: *Sicut permanet quod in Christo Petrus credidit, ita permanet quod in Petro Christus instituit.* Et post: *Petrus in accepta fortitudine perseverans, suscepta ecclesie gubernacula non reliquit. Sicut enim est pre ceteris ordinatus, ut dum petra dicitur, dum fundamentum pronuntiatur, dum regni celorum ianitor constituitur, dum ligandorum solvendorumque arbiter, mensura etiam in celis iudiciorum difinitione, preficitur, qualis ipsi cum Christo esset societas, per ipsa appellationum eius ministeria noscimus.* Si igitur Petrus pre ceteris est ordinatus, non ceteri simul cum Petro. Item Leo papa, in alio sermone de apostolis qui incipit: *Gaudeo dilectissimi*: *Quamvis in populo Dei multi sacerdotes sint multique pastores, omnes tamen proprie regit Petrus quos principaliter regit Christus. Magnum et mirabile huic viro consortium potentie sue tribuit divina dignatio, ut si quid cum eo commune esse voluit ceteris principibus, nunquam nisi per ipsum dedit quidquid aliis non negavit.* Igitur ex quo aliis non negavit sed concessit ordinem et potestatem episcopalem et usum

desunt B^{2}ρSr

171 pre φ | 173 per] *om.* α | claves] *om.* φ | 176 primo] Petro θ | 177 aliis] alicui φ | 178 non] tamen θ^1, cum θ^2 | 179 primo^1] prima φ(-U), primis π(-R) | 181 et] *om.* φ | Gregorii] *add.* sic φ | 184 relinquit θ^2V^{5}Svψπ(-R) | Sic φVa | 186 instituitur [construitur Sv] θ(-V^3) | 187 mensura] *add.* que θ | difinitione φP^{4}Va] defunctione [prefunctione V^5; *add.* ac definitione Bo] θR, Dei functione ψπ^2 | 188 ipsa] ipsum φ | appellationis φ, apostolorum θ^1 | eius θ(-BoV^2)Va] *om.* φ; cuius [causa cuius B^1] BoV^{2}ψπ | ministerium φ | 194 volebat [velit P^4] π(-R)

170-172 Gratian, D.21 1ª Pars | 174-177 Gratian, D.21 c.2; Isidore, *De ecclesiasticis officiis* 2.5.5 (PL 83: 781) | 180-189 Leo the Great, *Sermo* 3.2-3 (PL 54: 146, CCL 138: 12) | 190-195 Leo the Great, *Sermo* 4.2 (PL 54: 150, CCL 138: 18)

clavium ecclesie, sequitur quod ceteris per Petrum hoc concessit; et sic alii receperunt a Christo mediante Petro.

Dicunt autem isti quod ad omnia preter quam ad ultimum responsiones ex predictis pro alia parte colligi possunt. Quod autem in ultima auctoritate Leonis dicitur, quod *nunquam nisi per ipsum dedit* etc., dicitur quod hoc intelligitur de firmitate fidei Petri, que eius exemplo transivit ad alios. Unde dicitur ibidem: *Divine gratie ita ordinatur auxilium, ut firmitas, que per Christum Petro tribuitur, per Petrum apostolis conferatur*. De potestate enim clavium dicitur ibidem, ut prius dictum est: *Transivit in alios episcopos ius istius potestatis* etc.

Dicendum quod ista solutio non valet, et primo quod dicunt, quod ex dictis pro alia parte colligi possunt responsiones ad omnia preter ultimum. Non valet, quia ex responsionibus datis ad ea que pro parte opposita isti inducunt apparet quod illa non fulciunt illam partem nec infringunt istam.

Quod dicunt secundo, quod illud verbum: *Nunquam nisi per Petrum dedit*, intelligitur de firmitate fidei per exemplum in alios transferenda, dicendum quod illa expositio est contra textum tripliciter. Primo, illud quod dicit universaliter restringendo ad unum particulariter, sicut si diceretur "omnis homo currit" verum est de Sorte tantum. Hec enim expositio falsificat propositionem simpliciter, quia non omnis homo currit, sed solus Sor currit. Ita cum auctoritas dicat: *Nunquam nisi per Petrum dedit quidquid aliis non negavit*, cum fides sive fidei firmitas sit unum solum de multis que Christus aliis apostolis non negavit sed dedit, ad istud solum auctoritatem universalem restringere est eam simpliciter falsificare.

Secundo, quia li "per" semper dicit habitudinem alicuius cause. Cum autem non sint nisi quattuor cause, ut dicitur 2 *Physicorum*, oportet quod causa exemplaris reducatur ad unam de illis, vel non erit causa. Unde et reducitur ad genus cause efficientis vel finalis, quia exemplar movet agens ad assimulandum sibi exemplatum, que motio, quia non habet locum in

desunt $B^2 \rho$Sr

199 ad[1]] *add.* ista $\psi\pi^2$ | 207 et ... dicunt] *om.* α | 210 illa] ista θ(-V^5)P^2 | 213 illa] ista $\theta\varphi$ | Primo] *add.* quia $\varphi\pi^2$ | 214 dicitur $\theta^2\theta^3 S\varphi^5\pi$(-$P^1$) | universaliter] *add.* intelligendo particulariter vel θ | particulariter] *add.* falsificatur φ | 216 expositio] *om.* φ | falsificat propositionem] falsificatur φ | 217 sed ... currit[2]] *hom.* θ | Sortes π(-P^4)Va | 218 fidei] *om.* φ | 223 oportet] ostenditur [patet P^4] π(-R) | 224 et] *om.* [non V^5] θ(-V^3); vel [illis W] φ

203-205 Leo the Great, *Sermo* 4.3 (PL 54: 151-152, CCL 138: 20) | 206 Leo the Great, *Sermo* 4.3 (PL 54: 151, CCL 138: 19) | 211-212 Leo the Great, *Sermo* 4.2 (PL 54: 150, CCL 138: 18) | 223 Aristotle, *Physica* 2.3 (194b16-195a3)

Deo, qui est movens omnino immobile, oportet quod illud creatum per quod Deus agere dicitur sit movens, non ipsum Deum, sed cum Deo movens et agens in passum ad effectum. Unde Deus non diceretur per Petrum aliquid dare nisi Petrus cum Deo et sub Deo illud daret aliquo modo, et non sic quod solus Deus daret ad exemplar dati, Petro nihil dante. Unde non diceretur Petro: *Confirma fratres tuos*, si ipse ad firmitatem nihil ageret, sed solum ad exemplar eius alii firmarentur, maxime cum ipse tunc dederit peius exemplum firmitatis quam alii, qui ter Deum negavit. Unde magis fuisset hoc dicendum beate virgini, que a fide non fuit infirmata, ad cuius etiam soliditatem pro tunc apostoli sunt firmati. Unde illa verba magis respiciunt auctoritatem et potestatem confirmandi in fide quam solum exemplum firmitatis fidei, sub hoc sensu: *Ego rogavi pro te ut non deficiat fides tua*, scilicet finaliter, *et tu aliquando conversus confirma fratres tuos*, idest post conversionem tuam accipies potestatem et auctoritatem ceteros in fide confirmandi pro te et successoribus tuis. Unde non accepit tunc hanc potestatem, sed postea quando dictum est ei: *Pasce oves meas*.

Tertio, quia illa que magis possunt dari per hominem minus debent negari Petro quam illa que minus. Unde cum consecratio episcopalis et iurisdictio possint dari per hominem et dentur cotidie (quia unus episcopus consecrat alium; quicumque etiam iudex ordinarius dat cui vult suam iurisdictionem), fides autem sit donum Dei per infusionem, et bona qualitas mentis quam Deus in nobis operatur sine nobis, ut dicit Augustinus, absurdum est dicere quod Christus det per Petrum fidem vel fidei firmitatem aliis, et non dederit per Petrum aliis munus consecrationis episcopalis et munus potestatis iurisdictionis. Inter que etiam est gradus, quia potestas consecrationis non potest dari per hominem simpliciter, sed solum secundum quid, scilicet instrumentaliter per potestatem ministerii. Sed potestas iudiciaria potest dari simpliciter per hominem, maxime ab

desunt $B^2\rho$Sr

228 agere dicitur] aggreditur φ | 231 Petro] *add.* Petro [ipso V^3] $\theta^1\psi$RVa | 232 dante] dato φ | Unde ... Petro] *om.* $\theta^2\psi$; item per hoc θ^1, frustra igitur Christus [*om.* φ^5] videretur [videretur (videtur U) Christus φ^1] Petro dixisse φ | ipse] *add.* Petrus φ | ad] *add.* hanc $\psi\pi^2$ | 233 firmarentur] *add.* etiam male diceretur et inaniter et θ^1(-V^5) | 239 te] *add.* Petre $P^2\pi^2$ | finaliter scilicet $\theta\varphi$ | 240 idest] scilicet π | 241 pro te et] etiam pro θ | 246 dantur [datur Bo, dicitur Sv] θ(-V^3) | 248 autem] *add.* cum θStBm^{1}B^1 | 249 nobis^2] verbis θ(-BoSv)ψ | 250 Christus] *om.* φ | 254 instrumenta [*om.* Bo; per instrumenta V^5] θ

232 Luc. 22:32 | 239-240 Luc. 22:32 | 243 Joan. 21:17 | 249-250 Cf. Augustine, *Enchiridion* 9.31 (PL 40:247, CCL 46:66)

illo qui in ea habet plenitudinem potestatis. Est etiam advertendum quod illam gratiam Christus fecit Petro tunc quando Petro consortium sue potentie tribuit, quod quidem consortium promisit quando dixit: *Tu es Petrus et super hanc petram edificabo ecclesiam meam* etc. Non autem dedit quousque dixit ei: *Pasce oves meas*. Unde illa que ante illam collationem apostolis tribuit non tribuit ipse per Petrum, sicut sacerdotium, quod in cena omnibus immediate dedit, non uni per alium.

Item ubi in predicto capitulo, 21 d. *In novo*, dicitur quod *episcoporum ordinatio fieri debet pretaxato ordine et modo*, ille modus non habetur ibi, sed habetur 66 d. § *Porro*, et sumitur de secunda epistola Anacleti, de quo sumitur dictum capitulum *In novo*. In quo capitulo *Porro* dicitur sic: *Porro et Hierosolimitanorum primus archiepiscopus, beatus Jacobus, qui iustus dicebatur, et secundum carnem Domini frater nuncupatus est, a Petro, Jacobo et Joanne apostolis est ordinatus, successoribus dantibus formam videlicet, ut minus quam a tribus episcopis, reliquisque omnibus assensum prebentibus, nullatenus episcopus ordinetur, et communi voto ordinatio celebretur*. Sed consecratio episcopalis non iteratur circa eundem. Igitur Jacobus Alphei prius non fuit consecratus episcopus, sed a Petro recepit consecrationem, et a filiis Zebedei.

Ad istam rationem ponitur una responsio in glossa, c. *Porro*, super verbum "ordinatus," ubi dicitur: *Idest ad certi loci administrationem electus*. Licet hec responsio sit vera, tamen insufficientia ipsius patet ex prima epistola Anacleti pape, ubi dicitur, scribendo episcopis Gallie, sic: *Si non minus quam a tribus apostolis Jacobus fuit ordinatus episcopus, sed profecto eos instituente Domino formam tradidisse non minus quam a tribus episcopis episcopum ordinari debere*, ubi attendat lector quod dicitur: *instituente Domino*. Ex quo habetur quod manuum impositio tunc

desunt B²ρSr

257 fecit] *om.* θ| fecit Christus φ³π| 261 non tribuit] *om.* θ| Petrum] *add.* non dedit θ¹| 262 dedit] *add.* et θ| 264-265 ille ... habetur πVa] modus ipse [*om.* Sv] est ibi et [*om.* Bo] habetur θ¹, ille ibi sed habetur θ², qui non [*om.* Bm¹] ibi [*add.* habetur Bm¹] sed habetur Bm¹φ², qui habetur ψ, que St, qui non U| 271 et] ut θ| 273 prius] *om.* φ(-φ⁵)| recepit] *om.* θ| 274 consecrationem] *add.* habuit θ¹| 276 verbo [vero P³] θ| ordinatur P⁴P¹, ordinatio B¹| 277 sufficientia θ²ψRB¹Va| ipsius] sua θ| 278 Anacleti pape [*om.* B¹] γπ²] Avicen. pape π¹Va, pape [*om.* Bo; ipse V³] θ| sic Si] *om.* φ| 280 profecto] prefecit [perfecit V³, profecit Sv] θ

258-259 Matt. 16:18 | 260 Joan. 21:17 | 263-264 Gratian, D.21 c.2 | 265-272 Gratian, D.66 c.2| 275-277 *Decretum Gratiani* ..., D.66 c.2, fol. 116v| 278-281 The reference should be to Anicitus papa: cf. Ps.-Isidore, *Collectio decretalium* (PL 130: 115), Hinschius 120.

fuit facta Jacobo Alphei, non propter novam consecrationem, sed ad expressionem forme consecrationis prius tradite et institute a Christo, et tamen illud verbum: *instituente Domino*, omisit Gratianus compilator. Si queratur quare Petrus et alii tunc expresserunt formam consecrationis in Jacobo Alphei, dicendum quod hoc factum fuit post lapidationem Stephani, qui fuit quasi primicerius inter septem diaconos, quando Judei ceperunt alios persequi de ecclesia, in tantum quod omnes discipuli preter apostolos, qui ut pastores gregis erant ceteris constantiores, dispersi sunt per regiones Judee et Samarie, fugientes a facie persecutorum iuxta quod preceperat Dominus: *Si vos persecuti fuerint in una civitate, fugite in aliam*. Tunc apostoli, previdentes quod ad gentes in posterum essent transituri, providentes fidelibus qui erant in Hierusalem remansuri, expresserunt formam consecrationis traditam a Christo in Jacobo Alphei, ad instructionem ecclesie et ad determinationem plebis, sicut hec patent ex septimo capitulo et principio octavi capituli Actuum Apostolorum, conferendo glossas et historiam cum textu.

Dicendum quod ista solutio non valet, nec est vera solutio sicut isti dicunt, sed falsa, ut supra multipliciter est ostensum. Quod dicunt ergo primo, quod ex verbo omisso a Gratiano: *instituente Domino*, apparet quod illa manus impositio non fuit ad novam consecrationem sed ad forme expressionem, dicendum quod non est verum. Primo quidem, non dicit auctoritas quod Dominus illam formam instituerit, quia tunc in nulla necessitate licuisset, nec possibile fuisset, episcopum nisi a tribus consecrari, quod non potuissent apostoli observare quando fuerunt ab invicem divisi, non habentes in sua societate alios episcopos. Cum enim Lucas in Actibus diligenter nominet socios Pauli, non omisisset nominare episcopos socios si eos habuisset, sicut nominat se, Silam et alios. Unde cum in naturalibus virtus multiplicata non possit in effectum aliquem in quem non possit virtus sola quantum est de se, nisi forte quod non potest

desunt B^{2}ρSr

285 Si] sed φ(-UV^{4}) | 290 apostolos] quam apostoli φ | 292 fuerint] *add.* homines α | 296 instructionem] institutionem [ministrationem V^{5}; *add.* vel instructionem Bo] θ | 299 sicut] ut θ | 301 Gratiano] *add.* scilicet θ | 303 quidem] *add.* quia φ | 304 istam φ | nulla] missa [missam Sv] θ(-Bo) | 305 necessitate] *add.* non θ^{1}(-Bo) | 306-307 ab invicem] apostoli θ | 308 diligenter] *om.* ψB^{1} | 309 nominat θB^{1}Va] nominavit γ, nominant π(-B^{1}) | se] *om.* φ | 311 quod] *add.* virtus sola φ

292-293 Matt. 10:23 | 297 Act. 7:54-60, 8:1-3 | 298 Cf. Petrus Comestor, *Historia scholastica*, in Act. Apost., chap. 37 (PL 198: 1668) | 301 Cf. Ps.-Isidore, *Collectio decretalium* (PL 130: 115), Hinschius 120

in ita intensum effectum sicut quando est multiplicata, quando scilicet effectus recipit magis et minus (sicut tres candele magis illuminant quam una sola, sed tamen tres candele in illuminando non habent aliquem effectum specie quem non habeat una sola), ita cum ordo episcopalis sit unius rationis in omnibus quantum est de natura ordinis, nullum effectum possunt habere tres episcopi quem non possit habere unus, et equalem, quia non recipit magis nec minus. Unde quantum est de natura sua et primaria institutione, ita potest unus episcopus sine aliis consecrare episcopum, sicut confirmare baptizatum vel ordinare presbyterum. Propter quod non est verisimile quod Christus, tanquam substantiale et de necessitate sacramenti, in ordinatione episcopi instituerit illud quod esset repugnans perfectioni dignitatis episcopalis. Unde non dicit auctoritas: Domino instituente illam formam, sed dicit: *Domino eos instituente*, idest instituente et inspirante quod propter congruitatem et reverentiam et solemnitatem dignitatis episcopalis, quandocumque hoc posset commode servari, episcopus non ordinaretur nisi a tribus, non propter necessitatem sacramenti, quod potest aliter fieri. Unde tunc primo factum est illud statutum verbo et servatum exemplo. Sed exemplum debuit esse verum, non simulatorium. Unde fuit vera consecratio, non simulata, ut dictum est.

Quod autem dicunt: tunc manus impositionem factam Jacobo non ad novam consecrationem, est magis absurdum quam illud quod dixit Gratianus si non fuit vera consecratio. Quia manus impositio in modum ordinandorum, ut dictum est, nullo modo debet fieri nisi illi qui ordinatur, aut in quo suppletur illud quod fuit omissum. Si autem fuisset a Domino ordinatus quomodocumque, certum est quod fuisset perfecte ordinatus, et per consequens nihil erat supplendum. Unde non fuisset sibi aliqua manus impositio facienda.

Quod vero dicunt: illam ordinationem factam esse imminente dispersione, et tunc eis formam traditam istorum et aliorum sacramento-

desunt B$^2\rho$Sr

312 in V$^2\gamma$RVa] *om.* θ(-V^2)π(-R) | 314 tamen] *om.* θ | 317 equalem] *add.* et [*exp.* R] π | 318 nec] et $\theta^1\psi$B^1, neque P^1 | 323 perfectioni] professioni π(-B^1) | 324 dicit ... idest] *om.* π^2 | dicit] *om.* φ | 324-325 idest instituente θ^2Boφ(-φ^5)] *om.* φ^5; instituente V^{2}V^{5}SvB^{1}Va, instruente V$^3\psi\pi$(-B^1) | 325 et^2 γ(-St)RVa] *om.* θStπ(-R) | 326 quandoque π | 327 ordinetur [ordinari P^1] π(-R) | 329 Sed] quod quidem φ | 333 dixit $\theta^4\gamma$(-V^4)RVa] dicit $\theta^2\theta^3$V$^4\pi$(-R) | 340 vero] quinto θ | 341 et^1] *add.* ex $\theta\psi$Va

324 Cf. Ps.-Isidore, *Collectio decretalium* (PL 130: 115), Hinschius 120

rum, satis est probabile. Sed quod datum sit eis exemplum falsum et simulatorium est omnino improbabile, cum de malo exemplo et simulatorio Paulus in faciem Petro restiterit, ad Galatas 2.

Item si omnes apostoli fuerunt facti episcopi immediate per Christum, et post passionem et ascensionem Domini, tota ecclesia fuit Hierosolimis ubi morabantur apostoli. Sequitur quod in eadem diocesi fuerunt plures episcopi, quod est monstruosum quale non debuit esse in factis Christi. Item tunc duodecim episcopi fuissent universales totius ecclesie, et per consequens duodecim vocati in plenitudine potestatis, quod est contra Bernardum in secunda *Ad Eugenium papam*, dicentem: *Et si alii multi vocati sunt in partem sollicitudinis, solus tamen Romanus pontifex habet plenitudinem potestatis*. Idem verbum Bernardi ponitur *Extra*, *De auctoritate et usu pallii, Ad honorem*.

Ad ista respondetur per seriem Evangeliorum, quod in primitiva ecclesia non statim fuit distinctio diocesum, nec statim inter gentes in diocesibus distinctis fuerunt apostoli positi per Christum. Immo sicut dixit Christus, Matthei 15: *Non sum missus nisi ad oves que perierant domus Israel*, ita Christus dixit, sicut habetur Actuum 1: *Eritis mihi testes in Hierusalem et in Judea et Samaria et usque ad ultimum terre*. Voluit enim Christus istum progressum esse antequam transirent ad gentes, ut primo essent testes eius in Hierusalem, deinde, post lapidationem Stephani et mortem Jacobi Zebedei Cessi gladio, quod egrederentur de Hierusalem et predicarent in finibus Judee. Postea transirent ad Samaritanos, et deinde procederent per universum orbem, ita quod non transirent ad gentes quousque Judei redderent se indignos predicatione Evangelii. Et ex illa mora apostolorum simul in Hierusalem multe sunt consecute utilitates in primitiva ecclesia ad informationem totius ecclesie converse ex gentibus et Judeis. Fuerunt enim ibi quasi in loco generalis concilii. Unde et quattuor synodos solemnes legimus in Actibus Apostolorum Hierosolimis: primam, de substitutione Mathie, de qua Actuum 1; secundam, de

desunt $B^2\rho$Sr

343 est ... improbabile] tunc est improbabile $Bm^1\varphi^2$, non est probabile φ^3 | 345 fuerint θ(-BoV^3), fuissent [fuisset Pr] φ | 346 fuerit θ(-V^5Sv), fuerat ψVa | 350 plenitudinem θ^4(-S)φV^7 | 351 secunda $\theta^4\gamma$(-U)RP^1Va] secundo $\theta^2\theta^3 UP^4B^1$ | 353 Idem] istud φ | Bernardi] *om.* θ | 354 Ad honorem] *om.* θ^2; c. 4 θ^1 | 356 inter gentes π^1Va] *om.* φ^3; in gentes $\alpha(-\varphi^3)$, regentes π^2 | 357 dicit φ(-U) | 359 sicut] *om.* θ; et φ | habetur] *om.* θ | 360 in] *add.* omni $\theta^2\psi B^1$ | 367 secute θ | 369 et] *om.* φ | 371 Mathie] *add.* loco [in locum Bo] Jude θ

344 Gal. 2:11ff. | 351-353 Bernard, *De consideratione* 2.8.16 (PL 182: 752), Leclercq and Rochais 424 | 353-354 X. 1.8.4 | 358-359 Matt. 15:24 | 359-360 Act. 1:8 | 371 Act. 1:12-26

electione septem diaconorum, de qua Actuum 6; tertiam, de non imponendo onere legalium conversis ex gentibus, de qua habetur Actuum 15; quartam, in qua statutum est non prohibere Judeos a legalibus observantiis dummodo non ponerent spem in eis, de qua Actuum 21. Non ergo tanquam in una diocesi, vel determinati ad unam diocesim, morabantur apostoli Hierosolimis, sed ad informationem totius universalis ecclesie converse ex Judeis pro parte, et pro parte converse et plenius convertende ex gentibus, sicut patet ex predictis synodis et aliis, que patet legentibus Actus Apostolorum et historias ecclesie primitive. Non ergo fuit hoc monstruosum quod ibidem morabantur, sed utile et necessarium. Postea vero receperunt dioceses et etiam provincias distinctas, sicut patet legenti Isidorum, *De ortu et obitu patrum*, et alias historias. Nec fuerunt duodecim episcopi universales. Solus enim Petrus, qui fuit caput apostolorum, fuit universalis ecclesie episcopus, ex causis tactis a Rabano et glossa super illud Matthei 16: *Tibi dabo claves* etc. Dicit enim Rabanus, dicit etiam glossa: *Specialiter potestatem eam Petro concessit. Ideo enim eum principem apostolorum, et Christi oportuit esse vicarium, ad quem diversa membra ecclesie recurrerent si forte inter se dissentirent. Quod si diversa capita essent in ecclesia, unitatis vinculum rumperetur.* Huic concordat c. 24 q. 1 *Loquitur Dominus*.

Dicendum quod solutio bona est, et ista duo argumenta falsum concludunt quantum ad hoc, quod concludunt apostolos non fuisse episcopos quamdiu simul manserunt in diocesi Hierosolimitana. Quia immo antequam discederent, oportuit eos esse episcopos; alias non habuissent qui eos faceret, nec ipsi alios fecissent. Sed non oportet quod fuerint facti per Christum, sed potuerunt fieri, et facti sunt, per Petrum, ut dictum est. Sicut enim Rome consecrantur omnes electi presentes qui ibi confirmantur, intentione ut aliis diocesibus, non illi, preficiantur, ita tunc

desunt $B^2\rho$Sr

372 electione] *add.* et ordinatione ψB^1 | 374 non prohibere] *om.* α | 375 observantiis] *add.* non prohibendos [prohibens Bm^1, prohibendis W] φ | 377 formationem P^4P^1; reformationem B^1 | 378 pro[1]] ex π | 380 legentibus] *om.* [in Bo] $\theta^2\theta^3$; per θ^4 | 385 episcopus] *add.* et θ | tactis] datis π(-R) | a] ex θ^1(-BoV^3), de θ^2 | 387 eam] hanc φ | enim] *om.* $\psi\pi^2$ | 389 Quod] ne φ | 390 forent capita φ | in ecclesia essent [*om.* θ^2] θ | 391 Loquitur] *om.* $\theta^4\gamma$ | Dominus loquitur $\theta^2\theta^3$ | 395 immo] omnino [omnes U] φ | 396 faceret] facerent $\theta^4\varphi$ | 397 fuerint] fuerunt $Bm^1\varphi^2V^7$ | 399 illi] *add.* scilicet Romane diocesi φ

372 Act. 6:2-7 | 373-374 Act. 15:6-29 | 375 Act. 21:17-25 | 383 Isidore, *De ortu et obitu patrum*, chap. 81 (PL 83: 154) | 385-390 *Cat. aur. in Matt.* 16.3, 1: 252B (1: 274A) | 386 Matt. 16:19 | 391 Gratian, C.24 q.1 c.18

Petrus alios consecravit, assignans eis dioceses, sicut Jacobo Alphei, vel intentione in proximo ad diversas partes eos mittendi, sicut et factum fuit. Simon tamen et Judas simul usque ad martyrium sine divisione leguntur predicasse et officium episcoporum exercuisse. Unde quia Christus diversas terras aliis apostolis non divisit, sed Petro divisionem dimisit, ideo etiam consecrationem eorum ei commisit. Si ergo manserunt in diocesi Hierosolimitana postquam fuit assignata Jacobo, episcopalia exercentes, hoc fuit vel auctoritate Petri, qui cum et ubi voluit legatos misit (unde non ibi fuerunt sicut proprii diocesani; ideo non fuit monstruosum, quamvis Petrus tunc papa in una diocesi potuerit ponere duos vel plures episcopos et quemlibet in solidum vel pro parte sicut voluit), vel fuit de voluntate Jacobi, quia non debet unus episcopus in diocesi alterius sine illius licentia episcopalia exercere, 92 d. *Non liceat* § *De episcopis*, et quinque capitulis sequentibus. Vel Petrus potuit et voluit coadiutores dare Jacobo, qui solus forte non sufficiebat ad episcopalia exercenda circa multitudinem conversorum. Item non fuerunt episcopi universalis ecclesie sicut Petrus, quia fuerunt ab eo instituti, qui non potuit facere alium papam a se, nec alium equalem sibi. Sed si fuissent facti episcopi a Christo cum Petro per illa verba: *Quecumque alligaveritis super terram*, vel per illa: *Quorum remiseritis peccata*, vel per illa: *Euntes docete omnes gentes*, vel per illa: *Euntes in mundum universum, predicate Evangelium omni creature*, tunc cum ibi nulla fiat restrictio, eque facti fuissent episcopi universalis ecclesie sicut Petrus. Unde rationes satis bene concludunt quod non sint facti a Christo episcopi simul cum Petro. Sed non concludunt quin sint facti a Petro post Pentecostem, ante dispersionem.

Item si apostoli a Christo immediate ordinati et consecrati fuerint, tunc sine certis ecclesiis et certis titulis fuerunt episcopi, quod est inconveniens. Dicitur ad hoc rationabiliter, ut dicunt illi, quod sicut quo ad alia in

desunt $B^2\rho$Sr

400 Alphei] *add.* Hierusalem [Hierosolimis θ^3, Hierosolimitanam S] θ | 404 terras] *om.* θ | apostolis] *add.* dioceses $V^5\theta^4$ | divisit] *add.* dioceses BoV^2 | 404-405 ideo ... commisit] *om.* φ^1 | 405 etiam π^2Va] *om.* P^4; ad φ^5, et *cet. mss.* | ei $\theta\varphi^2P^2$] *om.* $V^7\pi$; dictis Va | 406 fuit] fuerunt φ | exercenda [exercencia V^4] φ | 407 ubi] ibi [*om.* Bo] θ^1, illi θ^2 | 408 ibi fuerunt] *inv.* θ; ibi fecerunt moram [mora P^2] $\psi\pi^2$ | 409 diocesi] *add.* tunc θ | 410 vel²] *add.* hoc φ | 411 illius] eius ψB^1 | 412 licet θ | 413 et] si φ | 415 Item] *add.* alii apostoli φ | 418 verba] *om.* π(-B^1) | ligaveritis [ligaveris V^3] θ | 421 ibi] *om.* θ | fiat] sit π | 425 fuerint π(-B^1)] fuerunt αB^1, fuerant Va | 427 quod] *add.* quo ad hoc [hec θ^4, illa $\theta^2\theta^3$] $\theta\varphi$ | quo] *om.* $\theta\varphi$

412-413 Gratian, D.92 c.3-8 | 418 Matt. 18:18 | 418-419 Joan. 20:23 | 419 Matt. 28:19 | 420 Marc. 16:15

primitiva ecclesia aliqua fiebant pro conditione temporis que post fuerunt prohibita – exemplo enim Petri, qui de Antiochia transivit Romam, aliqui de una sede migraverunt ad aliam, quod post, in Niceno concilio, septimo decimo canone eiusdem concilii, fuit prohibitum; in quo canone dicitur sic: *Propter multam turbationem et seditiones que fiunt, placuit consuetudinem omnimode amputare, ita ut de civitate ad civitatem non episcopus, non presbyter, non diaconus transferatur*, scilicet propria auctoritate, ut habetur in eodem canone – consimiliter episcopi sine titulis certis in primitiva ecclesia facti fuerunt, qui tamen post certas parochias et certum populum receperunt. Unde in Antiocheno concilio, c. 16, fit mentio de episcopis vacantibus, quomodo in ecclesiis vacantibus debeant recipi, videlicet non *absque perfecto et integro concilio*, quod tunc est perfectum si sit ibi metropolitanus antistes, ut dicitur ibidem. Hoc tamen post distinctionem diocesum et provinciarum, et fide dilatata in gentibus, prohibitum fuit in concilio Chalcedonensi specialiter quo ad ordinationes, c. 5 eiusdem concilii, et ponitur 70 d. *Neminem*, quod canon diminute compilavit Gratianus. Ubi enim posuit: *Decrevit sancta synodus vacuam habere manus impositionem*, non determinat qualiter vacuam, quod tamen determinat canon dicti concilii. Statim enim subditur in originali: *et nusquam posse ministrare*, ex quo habetur quod manus impositio habetur vacua quantum ad ministerium sive executionem, quod tamen non determinat Gratianus, licet ibidem ponatur in glossa hoc verbum: *quo ad executionem*.

Dicendum quod solutio non valet, quia si in minoribus ordinibus absurdum est quod promoveatur quis ad sacros ordines sine titulo, propter quod ordinator tenetur ei de competenti beneficio providere, ne mendicare cogatur in opprobrium ordinis clericalis, *De prebendis* c. *Cum secundum*, 93 d. *Diaconi*, *De clericis coniugatis* c. *Joannes* in fine, multo magis absurdum videtur aliquem in episcopum ordinari, nisi sit ei

desunt B$^2\rho$Sr

430 transmigrarent θ^2Bo, transmigrarunt [transmigrarens V^5, transmigraverunt S] θ^1(-Bo) | 436 in] *om.* α | 441 distinctionem ... provinciarum] distinctas dioceses et [*om.* V^3] provincias [provincias et dioceses St] α | 442 specialiter] qualiter π(-R) | ordines α | 443 et] ut $\psi\pi^2$ | 445 quod] sed [sic Sv] θ | 452 quis] *om.* θ | 455 Joannes] urbes φ | in fine] *om.* π(-R)

430-434 Cf. Mansi 2: 681-682 | 437-439 Cf. Mansi 2:1325 | 442-450 Cf. Mansi 7:375; Gratian, D.70 c.1; *Decretum Gratiani* ..., D.70 c.1, fol. 119r | 454-455 X. 3.5.16 | 455 Gratian, D.93 c.23 | X. 3.3.7

provisum, aut per ordinatorem provideatur eidem, de titulo competenti. Unde cum Christus per se non providerit de certis titulis nec de certis ecclesiis nisi soli Petro, cui totam ecclesiam commisit, videtur absurdum quod Christus alios apostolos in episcopos ordinaverit, quibus nec de titulis nec de ecclesiis providit.

Si dicatur quod pari ratione non debuit eos facere sacerdotes, quia nec in sacerdotem debet quis sine titulo ordinari, dicendum quod ista prohibitio non sic est ex natura sacramenti sicut illa. Quia potestas episcopi propria et principalis respicit corpus Christi misticum, sicut patet ex eius actibus propriis, qui sunt confirmare et ordinare. Unde frustratur ordinatio episcopalis suo principali fine nisi preficiatur populo. Sed potestas principalis sacerdotis est super corpus Christi verum, ad quod conficiendum non indiget populo, sed solum propter honorem cleri est ab ecclesia statutum quod non ordinetur quis nisi habeat victum. Item apostoli erant religiosi qui propter Christum omnia reliquerunt, quibus Christus promiserat quod hec omnia adicerentur eis. Unde non est simile de ordine presbyteratus et episcopatus propter predicta, et maxime quia ille non requirit populum propter principalem finem sicut iste.

Quod postea dicunt, quod in primitiva ecclesia fiebant multa que modo non fiunt, concedatur. Nihil tamen fiebat de consensu apostolorum quod non esset pro tunc rationabile. Quod dicunt in speciali, quod tunc exemplo Petri, qui de Antiochia transiit, alii sedes suas mutabant, dicendum quod Petrus, qui erat sponsus universalis ecclesie, Christo sibi committente, illi non particulari ecclesie erat astrictus. Unde non tenebatur ipse in Antiochia plus quam in quacumque alia totius orbis residere, sed libere ibi sedit, libere recessit. Sed episcopo, qui certam ecclesiam desponsavit acceptando electionem vel provisionem de se factam, non licet propria auctoritate dimittere, nec unquam istud licuit nisi de voluntate superioris. Nec exemplum Petri profuit, qui illi certe ecclesie astrictus tunc non fuit.

desunt $B^2\rho$Sr

457 provideatur eidem [ei B^1] π] eidem [eiusdem V^5, ei ψ] provideatur [promoveatur φ^5] α | 464 ex] de α | 466 Unde] *add.* et φ | 468 sacerdotalis π | 471 qui] quia θ | reliquerunt [reliquerent P^1] $\theta V^7\pi^2$Va] reliquerant $\gamma(-V^7)\pi^1$ | 475 Quod^1] *add.* autem θ | 479 qui] *om.* θ | illi] nulli $\psi\pi^2$; *add.* scilicet universali ecclesie φ | 480 non^1] *om.* $\theta^1\psi\pi^2$ | ecclesie] *add.* non θ^1 | 482 sedit] *add.* et $\psi\pi^2$ | 485 illi] nulli $\psi\pi^2$ | non] *om.* $\psi\pi^2$ | astrictus ... fuit $Bm^1\pi^1$] non astrictus tunc fuit $\theta^2\theta^3$, non fuit tunc astrictus θ^4, tunc astrictus non fuit $\varphi(-Bm^1)$, sic astrictus non fuit Va

471-472 Cf. Matt. 6:33

Immo sicut Petro non licuit universalem ecclesiam deserere, nisi forte de eiusdem consensu, ita nunquam licuit cuicumque episcopo proprie ecclesie resignare, nec ad aliam se transferre, auctoritate propria, immo nec nisi de licentia pape. Et hoc est etiam aliud signum quod quilibet episcopus tenet suum episcopatum a papa, in cuius solius manibus potest illud resignare. Non enim valet renuntiatio nisi fiat illi cuius est institutio, 17 q. 1 *Consaldus*, *De renuntiatione* c. ultimo. Unde cum nullus episcopus possit renuntiare nisi in manu pape, 7 q. 1 *Quam periculosum*, *De renuntiatione*, *Nisi cum pridem* in fine, inde est quod a papa vel eius virtute procedit omnis episcopalis institutio et iuris acquisitio. Similiter, quia dicit lex, *Auth. De defensore civitatis* § *Iusiurandum*, § *Nisi*, coll. 3, quod preses provincie non potest deponere defensorem civitatis quem non posuit, sed debet renuntiare prefecto qui posuit, ut inde procedat cure privatio unde datur, cum a solo papa episcopus a cura pastorali deponi possit, a papa huius cure datio processit, 3 q. 6 *Accusatus*, 5 q. 4 *Duodecim*, in fine primi responsi ibi: *Finis vero cause eius ad sedem apostolicam deferatur*.

Sed ex hoc videtur quod episcopi non sic habent a papa administrationes ecclesiarum sibi commissas sicut procurator est a domino constitutus. Quia procurator, secundum iura, quamvis per litis contestationem sit factus quasi dominus litis, nihilominus etiam tunc propter egritudinem potest amoveri ab omni prosecutione invitus, et totaliter revocari, *De procuratoribus* c. *Quamvis*, *Libro sexto*. Episcopus autem, pro sola egritudine non debet ab administratione sue ecclesie removeri, nec ei successor dari, licet ei dari valeat coadiutor, 7 q. 1 c. 2 et quinque capitulis sequentibus, c. *Quamvis* et c. *Petisti*; *De clerico egrotante* c. *Ex parte*; c. 1 *Libro sexto*. Unde videtur quod episcopus non sit a papa procurator constitutus.

desunt B^{2}ρSr

491 illud] illum θ(-V^{3})ψ | 492 Consaldus] Consultius θ(-Bo) | 494 Nisi ... fine] in fine cum [cum: *om*. Pr; in ... cum: nisi W] pridem instare φ | 496 quia] *om*. Pr; cum θ, quod St, quid U, qui Bm^{1}φ^{4}, autem W | § Iusiurandum] *om*. α | § Nisi] *om*. πVa | 498 cure] iure [iuris P^{4}] V^{7}π(-R) | 499 datur] *add*. unde φ | 503 habeant φ(-W) | 504 procurator] *add*. qui φ | 505 institutus π | 507 ab omni π^{2}] a omne RVa, attamen P^{4}, a cause [causa S] α | 508 revocari] *om*. α̇ | 511 capitulis] scilicet π(-R) | et] *om*. π | 512 c. 1] *om*. φ

492 Gratian, C.17 q.2 c.1 | X. 1.9.15 | 493 Gratian, C.7 q.1 c.8 | 493-494 X. 1.9.10 | 496 *Auth*. 3.2.1 § 1 = *Nov*. 15.1 § 1 | 500 Gratian, C.3 q.6 c.5 | 500-502 Gratian, C.5 q.4 c.2 | 508 *Sext*. 1.19.2 | 510-511 Gratian, C.7 q.1 c.2-7 | 511 Gratian, C.7 q.1 c.14 | Gratian, C.7 q.1 c.17 | 511-512 X. 3.6.5 | 512 *Sext*. 3.5.1

Dicendum ad hoc quod episcopi non constituuntur sicut nudi procuratores ad tempus certum, sicut procurator ad unam causam, sed sicut summi administratores ad vitam suam, pro communi tamen utilitate non privata. Unde sicut tutor propter longam egritudinem non amovetur, sed datur curator qui potius dicitur administrator, *Ff. De tutelis* 1. *Solent*, sic et episcopo egroto morbo perpetuo datur coadiutor. Et hoc est intelligendum quando per coadiutorem potest sufficienter succurri utilitati publice. Alioquin si necessitas vel utilitas rei publice exposcat episcopum egrotum totaliter amoveri, tunc non propter solam egritudinem, quia afflicto non est danda afflictio secundum illa iura, sed propter suam insufficientiam et inutilitatem et rei publice necessitatem vel utilitatem, que preferenda est private, potest simpliciter amoveri, et alius subrogari, quod probatur dupliciter.

Primo per illud quod habetur 15 q. 6 c. *Alius*, ubi dicitur quod Zacharias papa *regem Francorum non tam pro suis iniquitatibus, quam pro eo quod tante potestati erat inutilis, a regno deposuit, et Pipinum, Karoli imperatoris patrem, in eius locum substituit.* Si igitur principem terrenum papa potuit licite propter eius inutilitatem et rei publice utilitatem, non solum propter culpam, deponere et alium substituere, multo magis prelatum ecclesiasticum. Non obstat quod ibi dicitur in glossa super verbo "inutilis": *Non intelligas inutilis, idest insufficiens, tunc enim debuisset ei dari coadiutor. Sed dissolutus erat cum mulieribus et effeminatus.* Quia licet hoc sit verum in principe seculari, qui propter solam inutilitatem sine culpa provenientem non debet deponi, nec pro sola culpa que eum non reddit inutilem, nisi esset heresis et scisma, tamen in prelato ecclesie est aliter. Quia pro sola culpa que non reddit eum etiam inutilem potest deponi, quia sola culpa mortalis facit eum indignum prelatione ecclesiastica. Non sic autem est de principatu terreno. Similiter ex sola insufficientia sua et inutilitate, licet non proveniat ex culpa, potest licite deponi, quia etiam culpa incipit esse sibi quando tenet et occupat beneficium et non potest impendere officium nec per se nec per alium.

desunt B²ρSr

516 summi θφ] *om.* ψ; legitimi π¹Va, sunt π² | 517 non¹] *add.* omnino θ | 518 potius] post γ | 1.] *add.* 1 φ | 521 publice²] *om.* γ | 523 afflicto] afflictio α(-St) | addenda φ | afflictio] afflicto α(-St) | illa] multa φ | propter] *add.* solam θ(-V³) | 533 Non] nec φB¹ | 535 adiutor φ(-W) | 536 qui] *add.* deponi [*add.* non U] potest φ | 537-538 provenientem ... culpa] *hom.* φ | 540 indignum] *add.* in θ(-Bo) | 543 etiam] in φ | esse] *om.* θψ | sibi] *om.* φ

518 *Dig.* 26.1.13 | 527-530 Gratian, C.15 q.6 c.3 | 533-536 *Decretum Gratiani ...*, C.15 q.6 c.3, fol. 367r

Unde de ficulnea infructuosa dixit Dominus procuratori, Luce 13: *Succide illam: ut quid etiam terram occupat?*

Secundo probatur per illud quod habetur 7 q. 1 *Mutationes*, ubi dicitur quod mutationes episcoporum possunt et debent fieri communi utilitate ac necessitate, et subiungitur ratio, nam plurimorum utilitas unius utilitati vel voluntati preferenda est. Ex quo habetur quod contra voluntatem suam potest episcopus mutari pro communi utilitate, et non solum quando est voluntarius. Unde sequitur ibi expressius: aliud est mutare, aliud est mutari, nam aliud est sponte transire, aliud coacte aut necessitate venire. Unde isti non mutant civitatem sed mutantur, quia non sponte sed coacte hoc agunt. Si igitur episcopus sine culpa sua propter communem utilitatem invitus amovetur ab ecclesia in qua erat inutilis vel minus utilis, substituto sibi utili vel utiliore, et ipse transfertur ad illam in qua erit utilis vel utilior. Ergo si nulli ecclesie est utilis et sue inutilis, et non possit sufficienter per coadiutorem utilitati publice subveniri, debet penitus amoveri et alius substitui. Sed quando inutilitas sine sua culpa contingit, debet ei victus sufficiens ab eadem ecclesia provideri, 7 q. 1 *Quamvis*.

Quod dicunt, quod in primitiva ecclesia ordinabantur episcopi sine certis titulis, dicendum quod nunquam licuit nec decuit episcopum sine certo titulo ordinare, nisi illi qui poterat sibi et in promptu habebat de titulo providere. Sed Petrus, qui de voluntate Domini habebat coapostolos ad diversas mundi partes mittere, ad illos titulos quos erant sortituri, idest populos quos erant Domino lucraturi, eos ordinavit, et etiam potestatem dedit, ut in sui adiutorium alios episcopos ordinarent et eis sicut sibi videretur titulos assignarent, sicut Paulus Titum Cretensibus prefecit, Dionysium Athenis, et sic de aliis. Unde illi episcopi vacantes, de quibus ordinavit concilium Antiochenum, illicite fuerunt ordinati sine titulis nisi hoc fuerit de licentia summi pontificis, qui potest novos episcopatus facere

desunt $B^2\rho$Sr

545 dicit π | 546 Succidite $\theta^4\varphi$ | 547 illud] id π(-B^1) | 548 communi] cum θ^2Bo$V^2\pi$(-R) | ac] et φ^1Wπ(-R) | 552 mutare] *add.* et φ | est[2]] *om.* α | 555 Si igitur] similiter θP^1 | 557 transferatur [transferetur P^4] $\psi\pi$(-R) | 558 et sue] sed est φ | et[2]] *add.* sic π | 559 sufficienter] *add.* pro eo φ | adiutorem φ | utilitati] *add.* rei φ | 560 inutilitas] *add.* est θ | contingit] *om.* θ | 564 sibi] *om.* $\theta P^2\pi^2$ | 566 mittere] *add.* poterat [poterit φ^5Bl] et φ | idest] et θ | 569 Cretensibus] Colossensibus $\psi\pi^2$ | prefecit] *add.* et θ | 570 Atheniensibus θ | 572 episcopos [*om.* S] θ

545-546 Luc. 13:7 | 547 Gratian, C.7 q.1 c.34 | 561 Gratian, C.7 q.1 c.14 | 569-570 Cf. Eusebius, *Historia ecclesiastica* 3.4 (PG 20: 219-222)

et novos titulos creare, vel simpliciter, vel episcopatus dividendo, 16 q. 1 *Precipimus*, sicut potest antiquum titulum delere, unum episcopatum alteri annectendo, eadem questione c. *Postquam*.

Item quod solus Petrus a Christo auctoritatem pastoralem habuit et alii a Petro, Augustinus, in sermone de Pascha, super illud Joannis 21: "Pasce agnos meos": *Confitenti amorem suum, oves suas commendavit, tanquam non esset ubi ostenderet amorem suum in Christum, nisi esset pastor fidelis sub principe omnium pastorum*. Et ibidem in alia glossa, in principio: *Cum ergo prandissent, finito prandio, commissionem omnium ovium mundi Petro commendavit*. Sed si alii apostoli fuissent immediate potestatem a Christo assecuti, videretur, licet sub Petro oves eis fuisse commissas, quare cum hoc non legatur. Sequitur quod immediate a Christo potestatem pastoralem non fuerunt assecuti. Et confirmatur ratio per aliam glossam ibidem: *Quod maxime omnium tribuit nobis eam que desuper est benivolentia est proximorum procuratio. Preteriens autem Dominus alios, a Petro de talibus loquitur. Eximius enim apostolorum erat Petrus, et os discipulorum, et vertex collegii*. Ecce quod dicit: *Preteriens alios* etc. Ergo soli Petro est hoc dictum, quod non esset si auctoritatem pastoralem assecuti fuissent alii apostoli immediate a Christo. Item Origenes, super illud: "Ascendit Simon Petrus, et traxit rete in terram, plenum magnis piscibus": *Petro sancta ecclesia specialiter est commissa. Sibi specialiter dicitur: "Pasce oves meas." Quod ergo postmodum aperitur in voce, hoc nunc significatur in opere*. Item prima canonica Petri, c. 5, super illud: *Seniores qui in vobis sunt*, dicit glossa: *Sicut Dominus Petro totius gregis curam habere iussit, ita Petrus sequentibus ecclesie pastoribus immediate mandat, ut eum quisque qui secum est gregem Dei sollicita*

desunt $B^2\rho$Sr

573 vel[2]] *om.* θ | 574 episcopatum [episcopum V^4] unum $\theta^4\varphi$Va | 578 suas] *om.* φ | commendavit] committit θ | 580 sub] sine [sive BoSv] $\theta\psi$ | 581 prandidissent φ^1W | omnium] *om.* π^2 | ovium] *om.* [*in marg.* V^4] $\varphi\pi^1$Va | 582 immediate] *om.* α | 586 tribuitur θ | nobis] *add.* per θ | 587 benevolentiam $\varphi V^7\pi^2$ | 588 a] *om.* φP^2 | talibus] casibus θ | 592 Origenes] Chrysostomus θ | 594 Sibi] secundo φ | 598 est] *om.* $\psi\pi^2$

573-574 Gratian, C.16 q.1 c.53 | 575 Gratian, C.16 q.1 c.49 | 577-580 *Cat. aur. in Joan.* 21.3, 2: 590A (2: 646B) | 577-578 Joan. 21:15-16 | 580-582 *Cat. aur. in Joan.* 21.3 (Theophylactus), 2: 590A (2: 646B) | 586-589 *Cat. aur. in Joan.* 21.3 (Chrysostomus), 2: 590A (2: 646B) | 592-595 *Cat. aur. in Joan.* 21.1, 2: 588B (2: 644B-645A). The reference should be to Gregory: cf. Gregory the Great, *Quadraginta homiliarum in Evangelia libri duo* 2.24.4 (PL 76: 1185). | 592-593 Joan. 21:11 | 595-599 *Liber vite. Biblia cum glosis ordinariis et interlinearibus*, 1 Pet. 5:1, 4.1357v | 595-596 1 Pet. 5:1

gubernatione tueatur. Item Marcellus papa, epistola sua prima: *Ad sedem Romanam omnes suffugere debent, ut inde accipiant tuitionem unde acceperunt consecrationem*, quod esse non posset, ut videtur, nisi ceteri apostoli, qui in diversis sedibus sederunt per orbem, a Petro, qui sedit Rome, consecrationem habuissent. Item in quadam glossa Exodi 18, super illud: *Fecit Moyses omnia que Jetro suggesserat*, et in *Historia scholastica* super idem capitulum: Sicut Moyses consilio Jetro constituit tribunos et centuriones quinquagenarios et decanos, sic *Romana ecclesia plurimos vocavit in partem sollicitudinis, scilicet primates, archiepiscopos, episcopos, archidiaconos, archipresbyteros et minores sacerdotes*. Si ergo hos vocavit Romana ecclesia, ipsi non sunt immediate instituti a Christo, sed a Petro et successoribus Petri. Item 22 d. *Sacrosancta*, et sumitur ex tertia epistola Anacleti, habetur quod *sacrosancta Romana et apostolica ecclesia non ab apostolis, sed ab ipso Salvatore nostro primatum obtinuit* et constituta fuit. Sed hoc non ob aliud quam propter id quod Petrus, qui immediate potestatem recepit a Christo, ibidem sedit. Petro enim dictum est Matthei 16: *Tu es Petrus* etc. Alie autem ecclesie, ubi sedebant apostoli alii, non dicuntur immediate constitute a Christo, sed ab apostolis. Sed si ceteri apostoli eque immediate cum Petro recepissent potestatem, possent dici cetere ecclesie immediate a Christo institute sicut et Romana ecclesia. Ergo etc. Item patet ex littera dicti capituli et Anacleti: *Petro a Domino est concessum ut reliquis omnibus preesset apostolis, et Cephas, idest caput, et principium teneret apostolatus*. Item Gregorius in homilia super illud Luce: *Arborem fici habebat quidam*, dicit: *Quid per cultores vinee nisi prepositorum ordo exprimitur? Vinee*, que est ecclesia, *primus cultor Petrus fuit*. Sed a primo in unoquoque genere descendunt posteriora. Unde et in auctoritate Anacleti principium non accipitur pro principio dignitatis. Hoc enim premittitur cum dicitur: *ut reliquis omnibus preesset,*

desunt B^2ρSr

610 ex] de π(-R) | 611 habetur] *om.* $\theta^2\gamma$; dicitur θ^1 | 611-612 Romana ... ecclesia] Romana ecclesia [*inv.* St] et apostolica [*add.* ecclesie V^3] θ(-Bo)φ(-PrBl) | 612 nostro] *om.* φ | 613 id π(-B^1)Va] illud $\theta\varphi$B^1, ea ψ | 619 et] *om.* φ | 621 Item $\theta\psi\pi^2$] *om.* φ(-U)π^1Va; sanctus etiam U | 623 Vinee] vinea φV^7 | que] enim φ | 625 et] *om.* α

599-601 Cf. Ps.-Isidore, *Collectio decretalium* (PL 130: 218-219), Hinschius 224 | 603-604 Ex. 18:24 | 604-608 Petrus Comestor, *Historia scholastica*, Exodus, chap. 37 (PL 198: 1162) | 610-612 Gratian, D.22 c.2 | 615 Matt. 16:18 | 619-621 Gratian, D.22 c.2 | 621-624 Gregory the Great, *Quadraginta homiliarum in Evangelia libri duo* 2.31.3 (PL 76: 1229); cf. *Cat. aur. in Luc.* 13.2, 2: 196A (2: 215A) | 622 Luc. 13:6 | 626-627 Gratian, D.22 c.2

et Cephas, idest caput etc. Ideo oportet quod accipiatur pro principio originis, a quo potestas aliorum derivata est. Item ex epistola Clementis secunda Petrus non solum dicitur princeps apostolorum, sed etiam eorum ordinator, idest consecrator. Dicitur enim ibi sic: *Petrus magister, institutor et princeps apostolorum fuit, atque eorum ordinator*. Quare a Petro, tanquam ab ordinatore eorum, derivata est potestas in alios. De auctoritate vero epistolarum Clementis alibi scriptum fuit. Licet multi de earum auctoritate dubitent, certum est enim quod Hieronymus et Isidorus ponunt eas in principio compilationum suarum ante concilium Nicenum et ante canones qui dicuntur apostolorum. Item Zacharias, exponens *Unum de quattuor Evangeliis* compilatum per Eusebium, in fine glosse sue dicit quod Petrus maiori affectu diligitur a Christo, qui plus ceteris dilexit. Sed Joannes magis familiaria signa dilectionis recepit a Christo. Et post subdit, quod sumit ab Augustino: *Petrus a petra nomen accepit. Ecclesia ergo, que fundatur in Christo, claves ab eo regni celorum accepit, idest potestatem ligandi et solvendi peccata. Quod enim est per proprietatem: ecclesia in Christo, hoc est per significationem: Petrus in petra*. Ex quo habetur quod in Petro ecclesia, que est per significationem in eo, sicut est per proprietatem in Christo, recepit potestatem clavium, quod non esset si illam potestatem omnes apostoli et septuaginta duo discipuli eque immediate recepissent a Christo, tunc enim ecclesia in omnibus illis recepisset potestatem. Item ibidem Zacharias, et sumit ex verbis Bede in homilia: *Petrus claves regni celorum et potestatem iudiciarie potestatis specialiter accepit*. Quomodo autem specialiter exprimit idem Zacharias, recitans verbum Hieronymi super epistolam ad Galatas: *Princeps*, inquit, *apostolorum nunc Petrus nunc Cephas dicitur, et secundum metaphoram petre dicitur ei: "Edificabo ecclesiam meam super hanc Petram," hoc est, super hoc fundamentum fidei*. Si igitur in Petro notatur ecclesie fides, dicta specialitas acceptationis clavium importat, ut

desunt $B^2\rho$Sr

627 oportet] dicitur [dicatur U] φ, ostenditur $\psi\pi^2$ | 629 etiam] et φ | 631 fuit] *add.* consecrator [conservator P^1] π(-R) | 637 de] ex $V^7\pi(-P^4)$ | 641 accepit] *add.* accepit θ^1 | 642 idest] enim θ | 647-648 tunc ... potestatem] *om.* θ | 648 potestatem] *om.* γ | ibidem] idem θ | sumitur θ | 651 idem] *om.* α | recitans] *om.* θ^2V^3; per θ^3Sv | 655 notatur] vocatur $\gamma(-\varphi^5)$R | acceptationis $\theta^2V^2RP^1$Va] acceptionis *cet. mss.* | ut] *om.* π

630-631 Cf. Ps.-Isidore, *Collectio decretalium* (PL 130: 42), Hinschius 50 | 634-636 i.e. Ps.-Isidore, *Collectio decretalium* (PL 130: 19-60), Hinschius 30-66 | 636-644 Zacharias Chrysopolitanus, *In unum ex quatuor* 4.180 (PL 186: 613) | 648-654 Zacharias Chrysopolitanus, *In unum ex quatuor* 3.90 (PL 186: 286-287)

videtur, quod soli Petro, in quo fides ecclesie notatur, immediate a Christo data est. Quod videtur confirmari per Augustinum, *De verbis Domini*, que recitat idem Zacharias: *"Pasce, inquit, oves meas," quasi dicens: quid mihi dabis, quia amas me, pasce oves meas.* Et confirmatur per Augustinum, *De verbis Domini*, super illud: "Iussit Jesus ascendere discipulos suos in naviculam": *Petrus in apostolorum ordine primus.* Et post: *Simon antea vocabatur. Ut Petrus appellaretur, hoc nomen impositum est ut significaret ecclesiam. Ideo Petrus a petra sicut a Christo Christianus. "Et super hanc petram edificabo ecclesiam meam": idest super me edificabo te*, et post idem. Ergo a petra cognominatus, ecclesie figuram portans, apostolatus principatum tenens. Si ergo Petrus signat ecclesiam, et in eo dantur ecclesie claves a Christo, ipse, designans ecclesiam, immediate fundatur in Christo. Unde dicitur in auctoritate: *super hanc petram*, idest super me edificabo te. Et per consequens ipse immediate gerens typum ecclesie recepit a Christo, et ceteri tam apostoli quam alii receperunt potestatem ab eo.

Idem: apparere poterit ex collatione textus quattuor Evangeliorum et aliis auctoritatibus sanctorum, que omnia tria evidenter ostendunt: videlicet quod Petro et successoribus eius data est immediate potestas a Christo; item, quod Petro a Christo datum est esse Cephas ecclesie, idest caput, ita quod exercitatio potestatis aliorum dependet a Petro et Petri successoribus; tertio, quod potestas aliis collata per Christum non tollit quin Petrus et papa, successor Petri, sit immediatus prelatus omnium ovium Christi. Quod vero aliis apostolis et successoribus apostolorum sit collata a Petro immediate potestas, et non immediate a Christo, sed a Christo mediante Petro, non videntur auctoritates ita evidenter probare, quod absque assertione dico.

Quod autem dicunt in conclusione, quod potestas aliis collata per Christum non tollit quin Petrus et papa, Petri successor, sit immediatus

desunt $B^2\rho$Sr

656 videtur] dicitur [*add.* vel ut videtur Bo] θV^7 | 660 suos] *om.* θ | 661 antea] *om.* θ | 665 idem] ibidem φ(-W) | ecclesie] idest consecrator [conservator P^1] π(-R) | 666 significat Bo$\theta^4 V^7 \pi$(-B^1) | 672 Idem π^1Va] item *cet. mss.* | 673 auctoritatibus aliis [auctoritate aliorum φ^5] α | 675 a Christo²] *om.* $\varphi^1 V^4$ | esse] *om.* π(-R) | 676 exercitatio $\alpha(-\theta^2)$] exercitatione O, exercitationi V^1, exercitio π(-B^1), exercitium B^1, executio Va | 679 Christi] *add.* Ad predicta respondent alii quod [que B^1] responsiones patent ex predictis $\psi\pi^2$ | vero] non $\psi\pi^2$ | 680 immediate²] *om.* $\psi\pi^2$ | 684 sint θ^1 | immediati θ^3, immediate θ^4

657-659 Cf. Zacharias Chrysopolitanus, *In unum ex quatuor* 4.180 (PL 186: 611): "Quid est aliud: *Pasce agnos meos*, quam si diceret: si me diligis, pasce oves meas?" | 659-664 Augustine, *Sermo* 76.1 (PL 38: 479) | 660-661 Matt. 14:22

prelatus omnium ovium Christi, dicendum quod immo tolleret, si ita esset. Quia ille non est immediatus prelatus per Deum qui sub se habet alios medios inter se et illos a Deo constitutos. Sic autem est in proposito, si alii habent potestatem a Deo. Ergo etc. Maior patet, quia ideo archiepiscopus non est immediatus prelatus subditorum suffraganeorum suorum, quia inter ipsum et illos sunt alii prelati medii constituti, scilicet episcopi suffraganei, et si illa immediatio esset de iure divino, ipse non esset immediatus sed mediatus prelatus de iure divino. Minor patet, quia inter papam et curatos sunt episcopi medii prelati, qui sunt sub papa et sunt super curatos. Ulterius inter episcopum et parochianos sunt curati medii prelati, quia present parochianis et subsunt episcopis. Dicitur enim prelatus immediatus qui preest sine medio, idest qui inter se et subditos non habet aliquem qui sit nisi subditus. Prelatus vero mediatus est qui habet sub se alium prelatum qui sub eo preest similiter subditis. Igitur si episcopi prelationem qua sub papa presunt illis de sua diocesi, et curati prelationem qua sub papa et episcopis presunt parochianis, habent a Deo, tunc per ordinationem divinam papa non erit immediate prelatus nisi episcoporum, inter quos et ipsum de iure divino non est prelatus medius. Non autem erit immediatus prelatus curatorum, sed episcopus, nec episcopus parochianorum, sed curatus, si et ille preest de iure divino. Nunc autem, quia nulla prelatio de iure divino est immediata nisi prelatio pape, ideo de iure divino papa est immediatus prelatus et iudex omnium, licet ipse posuerit sub se alios prelatos, per quos eis immediationem concessit, non in eos transtulit. Unde nihil potestatis perdidit, sed immediatus sicut prius erat remansit, quia spiritualia per sui concessionem et multiplicationem non dividuntur nec minuuntur, sicut per hoc quod papa mittit legatos vel dat delegatos, potestas sua non tollitur nec minoratur sed multiplicatur et manifestatur.

Quod dicunt ultimo, quod auctoritates non videntur ita evidenter probare quod aliis apostolis et successoribus eorum episcopis sit collata potestas immediate a Petro, et non a Christo nisi mediante Petro, si

desunt $B^2\rho$Sr

685 prelatus] *om.* $\theta^2\pi^1$; prelati θ^1, pastor φ | Christi] *om.* $\theta\psi\pi^2$ | ovium Christi StBm[1]Wπ^1Va] *inv.* UPrφ^4 | tolletur θ^1(-Bo), tollit π^2 | 686 iste θ | Deum] *add.* constitutus φ | 688 ideo] *om.* θ | 689-690 suffraganeorum suorum] suffraganeorum $\theta^2\theta^3$, sui suffraganei θ^4 | 691 illa] ista φ | mediatio Boφ(-U)Va | 693 qui] quia θ | sunt[2]] *om.* $\theta\varphi^2\psi$ | 694 sunt[1]] *om.* θ | supra θ | 695 medii] *om.* θ | 697 habet] *add.* medium θVa | sit ... subditus] sit nisi sub [nisi subsit φ^5] φ | 698 Igitur] similiter θ | 701 immediatus θ | 702 de] *om.* θ^1; dedit θ^2 | 703 erit] est θ | 705 immediata π] *om.* θVa; immediate γ | 707 ipse] *om.* α | quod φVa | 711 legatos] *om.* θ

intelligunt absolute, quod scilicet auctoritates non sic evidenter concludunt quod sit credendum sicut articulus fidei de apostolis, verum dicunt. Quia licet oppositum sit probabilius ut visum est, tamen non est articulus fidei. Immo salva fide potest credi eos a Christo factos fuisse episcopos, et recepisse a Christo omnem potestatem quam habuerunt et nihil a Petro, pro personis tamen suis, de gratia speciali, et non pro suis successoribus, sicut Gregorius refert, primo *Dialogorum*, de beato Equitio, qui a Christo per angelum habuit, et non a papa, auctoritatem predicandi. Sed dicere quod omnes episcopi et curati ex hoc ipso quod ad hos status canonice vocantur habeant totam potestatem suam eque a Deo immediate sicut papa, et non habeant aliquid a papa plus quam econtrario, licet quantum ad eius usum subsint pape et non econtrario, non videtur stare cum articulo fidei de unitate ecclesie ex unitate capitis et plenitudine potestatis, ut superius est ostensum. Si vero intelligunt comparative sub hoc sensu, quod evidentiores et expressiores sunt auctoritates pro parte alia quam pro ista, forte est verum quantum ad aliquas auctoritates intellectas secundum superficiem verborum. Sed intelligendo auctoritates secundum rationem per solutiones datas ad auctoritates pro parte contraria adductas, et per reprobationem solutionum datarum ad auctoritates pro ista parte, apparet oppositum. Et licet multe auctoritates adducte ab istis pro ista parte sint solubiles, tamen ille que sunt adducte principaliter ad probandum quod omnes alie ecclesie sunt fundate a Romana ecclesia, et illa a solo Christo, videntur esse insolubiles, nisi vim littere inferendo, quod Hieronymus asserit *viciosissimum dicendi genus. Depravare*, scilicet, *sententias, et ad voluntatem suam Scripturam trahere repugnantem*, 6 c. *Ad Paulinum*. Immo videtur esse hereticum, sicut superius est deductum.

desunt $B^2\rho$Sr

716 scilicet] secundum [ita P^4] π(-R) | sic] ita θ | 716-717 concludant θ | 717 sicut] quod sit [sic S] θ | de apostolis] *om.* φ | 721 tamen] tantum φ(-StW) | 722 Christo] *add.* et [*om.* θ^2] non θ | 725 totam] *om.* θ | eque a Deo immediate π] a Deo eque immediate α(-StBm^1), eque immediate a Deo StBm^1Va | 727 subsint pape] *inv.* ψ; sibi subsint θ^1(-Bo), subsint θ^2Boφ | 728 de] *om.* π(-R) | 730 et expressiores] *om.* π(-R) | parte] *add.* aliqua $Bm^1\varphi^2$ | 732 rationes θ | 735 ab istis] *om.* W; per istum [istam Pr] φ(-W) | 737 ista θ(-V^2) | sola a Christo θ | 739 viciosum θ

722 Gregory the Great, *Dialogorum libri quattuor* 1.4 (PL 77: 169), Moricca 31-32 | 738-740 The reference should be to c.7: Jerome, *Epistola* 53: *Ad Paulinum* 7 (PL 22: 544; CSEL 54: 453-454).

Appendix B
A Supplement to Article Two: Version B

The following is taken from MS Va: Vienna, Österreichische Nationalbibliothek, MS 2168, fols. 92r-101r. It is Va's distinctive version of the passage given in Appendix A. Since the structure of the passage as a whole is substantially different in Va, the Va version is offered here for comparative purposes. In this regard, see the discussion in our introduction. The individual readings distinctive to Va have been preserved as much as possible.

Quod ceteri apostoli a Petro potestatem receperunt, et quod ab ipso incepit pontificalis ordo, quodque ab eo septuaginta duo discipuli potestatem acceperunt, videtur per auctoritates aliquas Canonis et sanctorum. Paulus enim, qui *non ab homine neque per hominem*, sed a Deo factus <est> apostolus, qui operatus est ei in apostolatum inter gentes sicut operatus est Petro in apostolatum circumcisionis, sicut habetur ad Galatas 1 et 2, non obstante quod in apostolatu par fuerit aliis, tamen, sicut habetur Actuum 13, ex consilio Spiritus Sancti ipse et Barnabas missi sunt in Hierusalem ad Petrum, Jacobum et Joannem qui erant ibi. Qui, audito consilio Spiritus Sancti, ieiunantes et orantes, imposuerunt Paulo et Barnabe manus in modum ordinandorum, sicut colligitur ex collatione historie cum textu Actuum 13. Si igitur Paulus ordinatus fuit per manuum impositionem et Barnabas cum eo, non obstante quod Paulus fuit immediate vocatus a Deo patre et Jesu Christo, sicut ipse testatur ad Galatas, cum alii apostoli a Petro eo non fuerint superiores, sequitur quod alii a Petro receperunt manuum impositionem et sic consecrationem.

Dicunt aliqui quod manuum impositio, licet facta sit eis in modum ordinandorum et consecrandorum, non tamen est certum quod tunc fuerint ordinati. Immo potius credendum est quod sicut in primitiva ecclesia multi sine ista solemnitate ordinati sunt, ita Paulus et Barnabas, qui consilio Spiritus Sancti ad apostolatum electi sunt, [et] in hoc cum aliis

5 ei] est Va | 15 fuerunt Va | 16 receperint Va

privilegiati sunt, ut talis solemnitas circa eos non fieret, ut dicunt, consecrationis vel ordinationis. De hoc tamen non habetur certitudo, quia nec de ordinatione aut consecratione aliorum apostolorum a Petro dicunt aliquid legi in Scriptura nisi *Hoc facite in meam commemorationem*, quo ad ordinationem, et quod Christus insufflavit et dixit: *Accipite Spiritum Sanctum, quorum remiseritis peccata* etc. Dicunt etiam cum hoc quod multa fiebant in primitiva ecclesia que hodie non fiunt, et aliqua observantur hodie in ecclesia que tunc non fuerunt in omnibus servata, ut quod tunc aliquis sine ceteris ordinibus precedentibus promovebatur ad sacerdotium, quod hodie non observatur, sicut hec in *Scholastica historia* recitantur.

Item 21 d. § *Decretis* [ubi prius] dicitur: *Petrum quasi summum pontificem Dominus elegit, dum ei pro omnibus claves regni celorum tribuit, et a se petra Petri sibi nomen imposuit*, ubi habetur quod Petro claves dedit Christus, a quo videntur per subsequentia ibidem claves ad alios derivari. Item eadem d. *In novo* [ubi prius], et secundo libro Isidori, *De origine officiorum*, c. 5, in quibus locis habetur quod *in Novo Testamento post Christum*, sicut dicit Isidorus, *sacerdotalis ordo a Petro incepit. Ipsi enim primo datus est pontificatus* [non ipsi primo] *in ecclesia Christi*, ut habetur ibidem. Sed si aliis cum Petro datus est pontificatus, non ipsi primo. [Cum] igitur, cum secunda descendant a primo, ab eo tanquam a primo post Christum derivatus est pontificatus in alios. Item Leo papa, in sermone qui incipit: *Quotiens nobis ministeriam Dei*, et intitulatur in aliquibus libris antiquis sermo Gregorii, dicit: *Sicut permanet quod in Christo Petrus credidit, ita permanet quod in Petro Christus instituit.* Et post: *Beatus Petrus in accepta fortitudine perseverans, suscepta ecclesie gubernacula non reliquit. Sic <ut> enim est pre ceteris ordinatus, ut dum petra dicitur, dum fundamentum pronuntiatur, dum regni celorum ianitor constituitur, dum ligandorum solvendorumque arbitrator, mensura etiam in celis iudiciorum difinitione, preficitur, qualis ipsi cum Christo esset societas, per ipsa appellationum eius ministeria noscimus.* Si igitur Petrus pre ceteris est ordinatus, non ceteri simul cum Petro. Item Leo papa, in alio sermone de apostolis qui incipit: *Gaudeo dilectissimi*: *Quamvis in populo Dei multi sacerdotes sint multique pastores, omnes tamen proprie regit Petrus quos principaliter regit Christus. Magnum et mirabile huic viro consortium potentie sue tribuit divina dignatio, ut si quid cum eo commune esse voluit ceteris principibus,*

38 Item] idem Va | 42 ut] ubi Va | 50 ut] et Va | 52 predicitur Va | 59 principalibus Va

nunquam nisi per ipsum dedit quidquid aliis non negavit. Igitur ex quo aliis non negavit sed concessit ordinem et potestatem episcopalem et usum clavium ecclesie, sequitur quod ceteris per Petrum hoc concessit, et alii receperunt a Christo mediante Petro.

[Ut] dicunt autem isti quod ad omnia preter <quam> ad ultimum responsiones ex predictis pro alia parte colligi possunt. Quod autem in ultima auctoritate Leonis dicitur, quod *nunquam nisi per ipsum dedit* etc., dicitur quod istud intelligitur de firmitate fidei Petri, que eius exemplo transivit ad alios. Unde dicitur ibidem: *Divine gratie ita ordinatur auxilium, ut firmitas, que per Christum Petro tribuitur, per Petrum apostolis conferatur.* De potestate enim clavium dicitur ibidem, ut prius dictum est: *Transivit in alios apostolos ius istius potestatis* etc.

Item ubi in predicto capitulo, 21 d. *In novo*, dicitur quod *episcoporum ordinatio fieri debet pretaxato ordine et modo*, [et] ille modus non habetur ibi, sed habetur 66 d. § *Porro*, et sumitur de secunda epistola Anacleti, de quo sumitur dictum capitulum *In novo.* In quo capitulo *Porro* dicitur sic: *Porro et Hierosolimitanorum primus archiepiscopus, beatus Jacobus, qui iustus dicebatur, et secundum carnem Domini frater nuncupatus est, a Petro, Jacobo et Joanne apostolis est ordinatus, successoribus dantibus formam videlicet, ut minus quam a tribus episcopis, reliquis<que> omnibus assensum prebentibus, nullatenus episcopus ordinetur, et communi rito ordinatio celebretur.* Sed consecratio episcopalis non iteratur circa eundem. Igitur Jacobus Alphei prius non fuit consecratus episcopus, sed a Petro recepit consecrationem, et a filiis Zebedei.

Ad istam rationem ponitur una responsio in glossa, c. *Porro*, super verbum "ordinatus", ubi dicitur: *Idest ad certi loci administrationem electus.* Licet hec responsio sit vera, tamen <in> sufficientia ipsius patet ex prima epistola Anacleti pape, ubi dicitur, scribendo episcopis Gallie, sic: *Si non minus quam a tribus apostolis Jacobus fuit ordinatus episcopus, sed profecto eos instituente Domino formam tradidisse non minus quam a tribus episcopis episcopum ordinari debere*, ubi attendat lector quod dicitur: *instituente Domino.* Ex quo habetur quod manuum impositio tunc fuit facta Jacobo Alphei, non propter novam consecrationem, sed ad expressionem forme consecrationis prius tradite et institute a Christo, et tamen illud verbum: *instituente Domino*, omisit Gratianus compilator. Si queratur quare Petrus et alii expresserunt formam consecrationis in Jacobo Alphei, dicendum est quod hoc factum fuit post lapidationem Stephani, qui fuit quasi primicerius inter septem diaconos, quando Judei

78 est] et Va | 80 presentibus Va | 87 Aniceni papa Va

ceperunt alios persequi de ecclesia, in tantum quod omnes discipuli preter apostolos, qui ut pastores gregis erant ceteris constantiores, dispersi sunt per regiones Judee et Samarie, fugientes a facie persecutorum iuxta quod preceperat Dominus: *Si vos persecuti fuerint in una civitate, fugite in aliam*. Tunc apostoli, previdentes quod ad gentes in posterum essent transituri, providentes fidelibus qui erant in Hierusalem remansuri, expresserunt formam consecrationis tradita<m> a Christo in Jacobo Alphei, ad instructionem ecclesie et ad determinationem plebis, sicut hec patent ex septimo capitulo et principio octavi capituli Actuum Apostolorum, conferendo glossas et historiam cum textu.

Item si omnes apostoli fuerunt facti episcopi immediate per Christum, et post passionem et ascensionem Domini, tota ecclesia fuerat Hierosolimis ubi morabantur apostoli. Sequitur quod in eadem diocesi fuerunt plures episcopi, quod est monstruosum quale esse non potuit in factis Christi. Item tunc duodecim episcopi fuissent universales totius ecclesie, et per consequens duodecim vocati in plenitudine potestatis, quod est contra Bernardum in secunda *Ad Eugenium papam*, dicentem: *Et si multi alii vocati sunt in partem sollicitudinis, solus tamen Romanus pontifex habet plenitudinem potestatis*. Idem verbum Bernardi ponitur *Extra*, *De auctoritate et usu pallii, Ad honorem*.

Ad ista respondetur per seriem Evangeliarum, quod in primitiva ecclesia non fuit distinctio diocesum, nec statim inter gentes in diocesibus distinctis fuerunt apostoli positi per Christum. Immo sicut dixit Christus, Matthei 15: *Non sum missus nisi ad oves que perierant domus Israel*, ita Christus dixit, sicut habetur Actuum 1: *Eritis mihi testes in Hierusalem, in Judea et Samaria, et usque ad ultimum terre*. Voluit enim Christus istum progressum sic esse antequam transirent ad gentes, ut primo essent testes eius in Hierusalem, deinde, post lapidationem Stephani et mortem Jacobi Zebedei Cessi gladio, quod egrederentur de Hierusalem et predicarent in finibus Judee. Postea transirent ad Samaritanos, et deinde procederent per universum orbem, ita quod non transirent ad gentes quousque Judei redderent se indignos predicatione Evangelii. Et ex illa mora apostolorum simul in Hierusalem multe consecute sunt utilitates in primitiva ecclesia, ad informationem totius ecclesie converse ex gentibus et Judeis. Fuerunt enim ibi quasi in loco generalis concilii. Unde et quattuor synodos solemnes legimus in Actibus [in Actibus] Apostolorum Hierosolimis: primam, de substitutione Mathie, de qua Actuum 1; < secundam, de

98 prosequi Va | 100 Judee] Indie Va | 101 nos Va | 116 Item Va | 120 fuerint Va | 121 15] 16 Va

electione septem diaconorum, de qua Actuum 6; > tertia < m >, de non imponendo onere legalium conversis ex gentibus, de qua habetur Actuum 15; quarta < m >, in qua statutum est non prohibere Judeos a legalibus observantiis dummodo non ponerent spem in eis, de qua Actuum 21. Non ergo tanquam in una diocesi, vel tanquam determinati ad unam diocesim, morabantur apostoli Hierosolimis, sed ad informationem totius universalis ecclesie converse ex Judeis pro parte, < et pro parte > converse et plenius convertende ex gentibus, sicut patet ex predictis synodis et aliis, que patent legentibus Actus Apostolorum et historias ecclesie primitive. Non ergo fuit hoc monstruosum quod ibidem morabantur, sed utile et necessarium. Postea vero receperunt dioceses et etiam provincias distinctas, sicut patet legenti Isidorum, *De ortu et obitu patrum*, et alias historias. Nec fuerunt duodecim episcopi universales. Solus enim Petrus, qui fuit caput apostolorum, fuit universalis ecclesie episcopus ex [ex] causis tactis a Rabano et glossa super illud Matthei 16: *Tibi dabo claves* etc. Dicit enim Rabanus, dicit etiam glossa: *Specialiter potestatem eam Petro concessit. Ideo enim eum principem apostolorum, et Christi oportuit esse vicarium, ad quem diversa membra ecclesie recurr< er >ent si forte inter se dissentirent. Quod si diversa capita essent in ecclesia, unitatis vinculum rumperetur*. Huic concordat c. 24 q. 1 *Loquitur Dominus*, ubi dicitur: *ut unitatem manifestaret* etc.

Item si omnes apostoli a Christo immediate ordinati et consecrati fuerint, tunc sine certis ecclesiis et certis titulis fuerunt episcopi, quod est inconveniens. Dicitur ad hoc rationabiliter quod sicut quo ad alia in primitiva ecclesia aliqua fiebant pro conditione temporis que post fuerunt prohibita – exemplo enim Petri, qui de Antiochia transivit usque Romam, aliqui de una sede migraverunt ad aliam, quod post, in Niceno concilio, septimo decimo capitulo eiusdem concilii, fuit prohibitum; in quo capitulo dicitur sic: *Propter multam turbationem et seditiones que fiunt, placuit consuetudinem omnimode amputare, ita ut de civitate ad civitatem non episcopus, non presbyter, non diaconus transferatur*, scilicet propria auctoritate, ut habetur in eodem capitulo – consimiliter episcopi sine titulis certis in primitiva ecclesia facti fuerunt, qui tamen post certas parochias < et > certum populum receperunt. Unde in Antiocheno concilio, c. 16 eiusdem, fit mentio de episcopis vacantibus, quomodo in ecclesiis vacantibus debeant recipi, videlicet non *absque perfecto et integro*

143 legendibus Va | 146 fuerunt] sunt Va | 148 tactis] certis Va | 154 24] 42 Va | 157 fuerint] fuerant Va | 167 fuerant Va | 170 profecto Va

concilio, quod tunc est perfectum si sit ibi metropolitanus antistes, ut dicitur ibidem. Hoc tamen post distinctionem diocesum et provinciarum, et fide dilatata in gentibus, prohibitum fuit in concilio Chalcedonensi specialiter quo ad ordinationes, 5 c. eiusdem concilii, et ponitur 70 d. *Neminem*, quod c. diminute compilavit Gratianus. Ubi enim posuit: *Decrevit sancta synodus vacuam habere manus impositionem*, non determinat qualiter vacuam, quod tamen determinat c. dicti concilii. Statim enim subditur in originali: *et nusquam posse ministrare*, ex quo habetur quod manus impositio habetur vacua quantum ad ministerium sive executionem, quod tamen non determinat Gratianus, licet ibidem ponatur in glossa hoc verbum: *quo ad executionem*.

Item quod solus Petrus a Christo auctoritatem pastoralem habuit et alii a Petro, Augustinus, in sermone de Pascha, super illud Joannis 21: "Pasce agnos meos": *Confitenti amorem suum, oves suas commendavit, tanquam non* [non] *esset ubi ostenderet amorem suum in Christum, nisi esset pastor fidelis sub principe omnium pastorum*. Et ibidem in alia glossa, in principio: *Cum ergo prandissent, finito prandio, commissionem omnium Petro commenda<vi>t*. Sed si alii apostoli fuissent immediate potestatem a Christo assecuti, videre[n]tur, licet sub Petro oves eis fuisse commissas, quare cum hoc non legatur. Sequitur quod immediate a Christo potestatem pastoralem non fuerunt assecuti. Et confirmatur ratio per aliam glossam ibidem: *Quod maxime omnium tribuit nobis eam que desuper est benivolentia est proximorum procuratio. Preteriens autem Dominus alios, a Petro de talibus loquitur. Eximius enim apostolorum erat Petrus, et os discipulorum, et vertex collegii*. Ecce quod dicit: *Preteriens alios* etc. Ergo soli Petro est hoc dictum, quod non esset si auctoritatem pastoralem assecuti fuissent alii apostoli immediate a Christo. Item Origenes, super illud: "Ascendit Simon Petrus, et traxit rete in terram, plenum magnis piscibus": *Petro sancta ecclesia est specialiter commissa. Sibi specialiter dicitur: "Pasce oves meas." Quod ergo postmodum aperitur in voce, hoc nunc significatur in opere*. Item prima canonica Petri, 5 c., super illud: *Seniores qui in vobis sunt*, dicit glossa: *Sicut Dominus Petro totius gregis curam habere iussit, ita Petrus sequentibus ecclesie pastoribus immediate mandat, ut eum quisque qui secum est gregem Dei sollicita gubernatione tueatur*. Item Marcellus papa, epistola sua prima: *Ad sedem Romanam omnes suffugere debent, ut inde accipiant tuitionem unde acceperunt consecrationem*, quod esse non posset, ut videtur, nisi ceteri apostoli, qui

171 profectum Va | sit] fit Va | 187 finito] fruito Va | 191 fuerant Va | 196 hec Va | 203 immediate] in me Va | 206 inde] in die Va | 207 potest Va

in diversis sedibus sederunt per orbem, a Petro, qui sedit Rome, consecrationem habuissent. Item in quadam glossa Exodi 18, super illud: *Fecit Moyses omnia que Jetro suggesserat*, et in *Historia scholastica* super idem capitulum: Sicut Moyses consilio Jetro constituit tribunos et centuriones [et] quinquagenarios et decanos, sic *Romana ecclesia plurimos vocavit in partem sollicitudinis, scilicet primates, archiepiscopos, episcopos, archidiaconos, archipresbyteros et minores sacerdotes*. Si ergo hos vocavit ecclesia Romana, ipsi non sunt immediate instituti a Christo, sed a Petro et successoribus Petri. Item d. 22 *Sacrosancta*, et sumitur ex tertia epistola Anacleti, habetur quod *sacrosancta Romana et apostolica ecclesia non ab apostolis, sed ab ipso Salvatore nostro primatum obtinuit* et constituta fuit. Sed hoc non ob aliud quam propter id quod Petrus, qui immediate potestatem recepit a Christo, ibidem sedit. Petro enim dictum <est> Matthei 16: *Tu es Petrus* etc. Alie autem ecclesie, ubi sedebant alii apostoli, non dicuntur immediate constitute a Christo, sed ab apostolis. Sed si ceteri apostoli eque immediate cum Petro recepissent potestatem, possent dici cetere ecclesie immediate constitute a Christo sic<ut> et Romana. Item patet ex littera dicti capituli et Anacleti: *Petro a Domino est concessum ut reliquis omnibus preesset apostolis, et Cephas, idest caput, et principium teneret apostolatus*. Item Gregorius, in homilia super illud verbum Lucis: *Arborem fici habebat quidam*, dicit: *Quid per cultores vinee nisi prepositorum ordo exprimitur? Vinee,* que est ecclesia, *primus cultor Petrus fuit*. Sed a primo in unoquoque genere descendunt posteriora. Unde et in auctoritate Anacleti principium non accipitur pro principio dignitatis. Hoc enim premittitur cum dicitur: *ut reliquis omnibus preesset, et Cephas, idest caput* etc. Ideo oportet quod accipiatur pro principio originis, a quo potestas aliorum derivata est. Item ex epistola Clementis secunda Petrus non solum dicitur princeps apostolorum, sed etiam eorum ordinator, idest consecrator. Dicitur enim sic: *Petrus magister, institutor et princeps apostolorum fuit, atque eorum ordinator*. Quare a Petro, tanquam ab ordinatore eorum, derivata est potestas in alios. De auctoritate vero epistolarum Clementis alibi scriptum fuit. Licet multi de earum auctoritate dubitent, certum est enim quod Hieronymus et Isidorus ponunt eas in principio compilationum suarum ante concilium Nicenum et ante canones qui dicuntur apostolorum. Item Zacharias, exponens *Unum de quattuor Evangeliis* compilatum [compilatum] per Eusebium, in fine glosse sue dicit quod Petrus maiori affectu diligitur a Christo. Sed plus

208 sederunt] sedent Va | 211-212 centuarios Va | 230 posteriorii Va

ceteris dilexit Joannem; magis familiaria signa dilectionis recepit a Christo. Et post subdit, quod sumit ab Augustino: *Petrus a petra nomen accepit. Ecclesia ergo, que fundatur in Christo, et claves ab eo regni celorum accepit, idest potestatem ligandi et solvendi peccata. Quod enim est per proprietatem: ecclesia in Christo, hoc est per significationem: Petrus in petra.* Ex quo habetur quod in Petro ecclesia, que est per significationem in eo, sicut est per proprietatem in Christo, recepit potestatem clavium, quod non esset si illam potestatem omnes apostoli et septuaginta duo discipuli eque immediate recepissent a Christo, tunc enim ecclesia in omnibus illis recepisset potestatem. Item ibidem Zacharias, et sumit ex verbis Bede in homilia: *Petrus claves regni celorum et potestatem iudiciarie potestatis specialiter accep*[er]*it*. Quomodo autem specialiter exprimit idem Zacharias, recitans verbum Hieronymi super epistolam ad Galatas: *Princeps*, inquit, *apostolorum nunc Petrus nunc Cephas dicitur, et secundum metaphoram petre dicitur ei: "Edificabo ecclesiam meam super hanc petram," hoc est super hoc fundamentum fidei.* Si ergo in Petro notatur ecclesie fides, dicta specialitas acceptationis clavium importat, ut videtur, quod soli Petro, in quo fides ecclesie notatur, immediate a Christo data est. Quod videtur confirmari per Augustinum, *De verbis Domini*, que recitat idem Zacharias: *Pasce, inquit, oves meas, quasi diceret: quid mihi dabis, quia amas me, pasce oves meas.* Et confirmatur hoc per Augustinum, *De verbis Domini*, super illud: "Iussit Jesus ascendere discipulos suos in naviculam": *Petrus in apostolorum ordine primus.* Et post: *Simon antea vocabatur. Ut Petrus appellaretur, hoc nomen impositum est ut significaret ecclesiam. Ideo Petrus* [ideo Petrus] *a petra sicut a Christo Christianus. "Et super hanc petram edificabo ecclesiam meam": idest super me edificabo te*, et <post idem. Ergo a petra cognominatus, ecclesie figuram portans, apostolatus principatum tenens. Si ergo Petrus signat ecclesiam, et in eo dantur ecclesie claves a Christo, ipse, designans ecclesiam, immediate fundatur in Christo. Unde dicitur in auctoritate: *super hanc petram*, idest: super me edificabo te. Et> per consequens ipse immediate gerens typum ecclesie recepit potestatem a Christo, et ceteri tam apostoli quam alii receperunt potestatem ab eo.

Idem: apparere poterit ex collatione textus quattuor Evangeliorum et aliis auctoritatibus sanctorum, que omnia tria evidenter ostendunt: videlicet quod Petro et eius successoribus data est immediate potestas a Christo; item, quod Petro a Christo datum est esse cephas ecclesie, idest caput, ita quod executio potestatis aliorum dependet a Petro et Petri successore; tertio, quod potestas eis collata per Christum non tollit quin

276 recepit] recipit Va

Petrus et papa, successor Petri, sit immediatus prelatus omnium ovium Christi. Quod vero aliis apostolis et successoribus apostolorum sit collata a Petro immediate potestas, et non immediate a Christo, sed a Christo mediante Petro, non videntur auctoritates ita evidenter probare, quod absque assertione dico.

Dicendum quod [ab]solutio data ad primum non valet, primo quantum ad illud quod dicit, quod per illam manuum impositionem non fuerunt tunc ordinati. Quia manus impositio in modum ordinandorum vel consecrandorum non debet alicui fieri nisi ad ipsum ordinandum et consecrandum, vel simpliciter utpote, quando certum est ipsum alias non fuisse ordinatum, vel sub conditione, quando est dubium. Alias fieret iniuria et illusio sacramento, et esset mendacium in cultu Christiane religionis, quod est contra doctrinam Augustini, et Pauli, ad Galatas 2, ubi reprehendit Petrum de quadam simulatione qua ipse et quidam alii simulatorie et non recte ibant ad veritatem Evangelii. Unde *De celebratione missarum* c. *De homine*, reprehenditur sacerdos qui in exteriori ritu simulabat se hostiam consecrare, nec intendebat consecrare, nec etiam consecrabat, verba subiciendo consecrationis. Unde sicut non liceret imponere manum in modum confirmandi nisi confirmando, sic nec in modum ordinandi nisi ordinando, vel supplendo manuum impositionem omissam alias ordinando, sicut dicitur *De sacramentis* <*non*> *iterandis* [vel non] c. ultimo.

Quod dicunt secundo, quod in primitiva ecclesia multi sunt ordinati sine hac solemnitate, dicendum quod falsum est propter quattuor. Primo quia, cum maior solemnitas debeat exhiberi ex ritu ab apostolis tradito circa ordinationem episcoporum et sacerdotum quam diaconorum, cum in primitiva ecclesia in ordinatione diaconorum fuerit observata solemnitas de impositione manuum cum oratione, ut habetur Actuum 6, multo magis in ordinatione episcoporum et sacerdotum. Secundo, quia solus Christus potuit dare rem sacramenti sine sacramento. Unde apostoli non potuerunt dare rem ordinis sacerdotii nec episcopatus sine vera ordinatione et sacramentali consecratione. Tertio, quia licet apostoli in ritu a se instituto possent dispensare, tamen in substantia ordinationis et consecrationis sacerdotis vel episcopi non potuerunt ipsi dispensare. Unde cum impositio manuum cum oratione sit de substantia ordinis sacerdotalis, propter quod omissio necessario est supplenda, *De sacramentis non iterandis* c. ultimo, et eodem modo ipsa sit de substantia ordinis episcopalis, non potuerunt apostoli sine hac solemnitate, idest sine

293 & 294 quando] quin Va | 306 dicant Va

manuum impositione, quemquam ordinare in sacerdotem nec in episcopum. Quarto, quia nunquam aliquis diceret quod apostoli baptizassent in nomine Domini Jesu, non exprimendo explicite nomen trinitatis, nisi quia expresse hoc legitur Actuum 8 et 19, et tunc dicuntur hoc fecisse dispensative, non auctoritate propria, sed Spiritus Sancti volentis nomen Jesu exosum autenticare, ut homines in eo ponerent spem salutis. Unde cum non legantur apostoli quemquam ordinasse sine manuum impositione, que etiam impositio est de substantia ordinum diaconorum, presbyterorum, episcoporum, sicut expressio trinitatis de substantia forme baptismi, non licet fingere quod apostoli ordinaverunt ad hos ordines sine manuum impositione. Immo non habemus aliunde quod manus impositio sit de substantia ordinum istorum nisi quia sic apostoli ordinabant.

Quod dicunt tertio, quod credendum est Paulum et Barnabam sine hac solemnitate alias ordinatos, non est verum. Primo, quia Leo papa dicit eos tunc fuisse ordinatos. Unde quia erat dominica, ostendit illo exemplo sacerdotes maiores, idest episcopos, non nisi in dominica consecrandos, 75 d. *Quod die dominico*. Secundo, quia non dicimus quod apostoli confirmarent sine manus impositione, que tamen confirmatio dabatur omnibus baptizatis. Immo cum legamus Actuum 8: *Tunc imponebant manus super illos, et accipiebant Spiritum Sanctum*, et similiter Actuum 19, dicimus quod apostoli confirmabant manus imponendo <super> omnes quos confirmabant. Ita etiam cum legamus manus impositas septem diaconibus primis – dicimus autem eos tunc ordinatos, et pari ratione omnes alios diaconos sic credimus ordinatos – ergo pari ratione <cum> legamus Paulo et Barnabe manus cum oratione impositas tunc quando a Domino ad episcopatum et prelationem sunt electi, credendum est magis eos tunc cum illa solemnitate ordinatos et consecratos quam alias sine illa. Et si in aliis apostolis quorum ordinatio non legitur crederetur hec solemnitas omissa, in istis tamen in quibus legitur hec solemnitas servata non debet fingi fuisse omissa. Immo magis econtrario, ex hoc quod legitur istis apostolis facta fuisse manus impositio, credenda est facta fuisse aliis qualis in episcopi ordinatione requiritur, nam ordinationem sacerdotalem quam a Domino receperunt eis non licuit iterare, nec in Petro episcopalem quam a Domino recepit.

Quod dicunt quarto: non legi in Scriptura de ordinatione aliorum apostolorum, nec a Petro nec a Christo, nisi illud *Hoc facite*, et *Accipite Spiritum Sanctum* etc., verum est explicite et expresse. Sed quia legitur

327 volentis] voluntatis Va | 339 diximus Va | apostoli] episcopi Va

apostolos confirmasse Actuum 8, 19, diaconos ordinasse Actuum 6, et Paulum et Barnabam presbyteros etiam ordinasse Actuum 14, quod non potest fieri nisi <ab> episcopo, ideo concluditur apostolos in episcopos ab aliquo ordinatos. Et quia episcopus non potest fieri nisi ab episcopo, necesse fuit saltem unum episcopum fieri a Christo a quo alii fierent, et probabilius est de Petro, sicut supra deductum fuit. Et quia petra sibi Petrum assimilare voluit, probabile est quod per ipsum ceteros episcopos fecit. Per illa autem verba: *Hoc facite*, facti sunt sacerdotes, sed non episcopi. Per illa verba: *Accipite* <etc.>, nec sacerdotes nec episcopi, sicut in superioribus est deductum. Specialiter autem quod per illa verba: *Accipite Spiritum Sanctum*, non <sint> facti episcopi patet, quia verba sacramentalia prolata a ministro tantum operantur quantum prolata a Christo, sicut verba: *Hoc est corpus meum*, ita confici<un>t quando proferuntur a sacerdote sicut confecerunt quando fuerunt prolata a Christo. Unde si Christus per illa verba dicta illis qui erant facti sacerdotes quo ad substantiam et actum principalem per verba eis dicta in traditione calicis: *Hoc facite*, fecit eos episcopos, pari ratione episcopus, dicendo illa verba: *Accipite Spiritum Sanctum, quorum remiseritis* etc., illi quem facit sacerdotem, tradendo calicem in forma verborum prescripta, si intenderet, faceret eum episcopum. Si dicatur: non est simile, quia Christus non instituit quod per illa verba fierent episcopi alii, licet per illa fecerit episcopos, sicut non instituit quod per illa verba: *Hoc facite*, fierent sacerdotes, quamvis per illa eos fecerit – unde non fiunt sacerdotes per illa verba, etiam ab episcopo prolata, sed per alia; per illa autem verba: *Hoc est corpus meum*, fit [autem] sacramentum eucharistie, non quia Christus illis usus fuit conficiendo, sed quia instituit ut illis uterentur ministri – non valet, quia verba quibus fiunt sacerdotes per episcopum equipollent verbis quibus Christus eos fecit in sensu. Cum enim Christus confecisset corpus et sanguinem, quod fuit missam instituere et celebrare, dixit: *Hoc facite*, idest missam celebrate, hoc est celebrandi potestatem accipite, et hoc est quod dicit episcopus: *Accipe potestatem dicendi missas* etc. Unde si Christus per illa verba: *Accipite* <etc.>, fecisset eos episcopos, verisimile est quod illis vel equipollentibus dedisset virtutem quod per ea deinceps episcopi fierent, quod falsum est.

Quod dicunt quinto: multa in primitiva ecclesia facta fuisse que nunc non fiunt et econtrario, intelligentes de ritu sacramentorum, dicendum quod multa cerimonialia accidentaliter sunt postea superaddita propter

369 quod] est Va | 371 quantam Va | 378 prescripta] potest poni Va | 389 celebrate] celebrare Va

solemnitatem et reverentiam sacramentorum, quia tunc pauca adhibebantur que non essent de substantia. Sed quantum ad illa que sunt de substantia sacramentorum, credendum est quod nihil tunc fuerit observatum quod modo non observetur, alias moderna ecclesia non haberet vera sacramenta. Similiter econtrario substantialia in sacramentis tunc fuerunt observata, nisi quantum expresse legitur contrarium, sic<ut> de forma baptismi ad tempus, ut dictum est.

Quod dicunt sexto, quod tunc aliquis sine precedentibus ordinibus promove<b>atur ad sacerdot<i>um, non oportet hoc dicere, nec videtur rationabile. Quia cum oporteat quandoque sacerdotem exorcisare cathecuminos, qui est proprius actus exorciste, absurdum est esse sacerdotem qui non <est> exorcista. Immo, cum sit absurdum in ordinatis quod superior non possit illud quod potest inferior, propter quod sacerdos dicit Evangelium [nisi] et Epistolam, et diaconus Epistolam, nec aliquis possit modo debito et congruo in actum ordinis nisi habeat ordinem, inordinatum est et contra naturam ordinum, etiam prout sunt a Christo instituti, quod aliquis habeat ordinem superiorem et non habeat inferiorem. Sed quod ordine[n]s sacr[ament]i non dentur simul est a solo instituto ecclesie. Unde rationabilius credi potest quod illi qui ordinabantur in primitiva ecclesia in ordine superiori, si prius non erant in minoribus constituti, quod tunc ordinabantur simul ad omnes illos ordines. Sed tota ordinatio denominabatur a supremo sicut a digniori, sicut modo, quando conferuntur simul quattuor minores ordines, dicitur aliquis in acolitatum ordinari, quia ille est ordo superior circa illos, quia immediatior ministerio corporis Christi. Ita et tunc dicebantur in diaconos ordinari, quia cum diaconatu accipiebant omnes ordines precedentes, adhibita solemnitate substantialiter debita cuilibet ordinationi per se, quam nec apostolis licuit omittere nec mutare. Similiter dicebantur presbyteri et episcopi ordinari, non qui<a> non recepissent ordines precedentes tunc vel prius, sed quia tota ordinatio, si erat plurium ordinum, denominabatur ab ultimo et supremo.

Item data ad quintum solutio non valet, et primo quod dicunt, quod ex dictis pro illa parte colligi possunt responsiones ad omnia preter ultimum. Non valet, quia ex responsionibus datis ad ea que pro parte opposita isti inducunt apparet quod illa non fulciunt illam partem nec infringunt istam.

Quod dicunt secundo, quod illud verbum: *Nunquam nisi per Petrum dedit*, intelligitur de firmitate fidei per exemplum in alios transferenda, dicendum quod illa expositio est contra textum tripliciter. Primo, illud

407 cathecuminos] eutergimnos Va | 428 quantum Va | 430 ad] ex Va | 432 secundum Va

quod dicit universaliter restringendo ad unum particulariter, sicut si diceretur "omnis homo currit" <verum est de Sorte tantum. Hec enim expositio falsificat propositionem simpliciter, quia non omnis homo currit,> sed solus Sortes currit. Ita cum auctoritas dicat: *Numquam nisi per Petrum dedit quidquid aliis non negavit*, [quia] cum fides sive fidei firmitas sit unum solum de multis que Christus aliis apostolis non negavit sed dedit, ad istud solum auctoritatem universalem restringere est eam simpliciter falsificare.

Secundo, quia "per" dicit habitudinem alicuius cause. Cum enim non sint nisi quattuor cause, ut dicitur 2 *Physicorum*, oportet quod causa exemplaris reducatur ad unam de illis, vel non erit causa. Unde et reducitur ad genus cause efficientis vel finalis, quia exemplar movet agens ad simulandum sibi exemplatum, que motio, quia non habet locum in Deo, qui est movens omnino immobile, oportet quod illud creatum per quod Deus agere dicitur sit movens, non ipsum Deum, sed cum Deo movens et agens in passum ad effectum. Unde Deus non diceretur per Petrum aliquid dare nisi Petrus cum Deo et sub Deo [et dum Deo] illud daret aliquo modo, et non sic quod solus Deus daret ad exemplar dati Petro, Petro nihil dante. Unde non diceretur Petro: *Confirma fratres tuos*, si ipse ad firmitatem nihil ageret, sed solum ad exemplar eius alii firmarentur, maxime cum ipse dederit peius exemplum firmitatis quam omnes alii, qui ter Dominum negavit. Unde magis fuisset hoc dicendum beati virgini, que non fuit a fide infirmata, ad cuius etiam soliditatem pro tunc apostoli sunt firmati. Unde illa verba magis respiciunt auctoritatem et potestatem confirmandi in fide quam solum exemplum firmitatis fidei, sub hoc sensu: *Ego rogavi pro te ut non deficiat fides tua*, scilicet finaliter, *et tu aliquando conversus confirma fratres tuos*, idest post conversionem tuam accipies potestatem et auctoritatem ceteros in fide confirmandi et pro te et successoribus tuis. Unde non accipit tunc hanc potestatem, sed post quando dictum est ei: *Pasce oves meas*.

Tertio, quia illa que magis possunt dari per hominem minus debent negari Petro quam illa que minus. Unde cum consecratio episcopalis et iurisdictio possi<n>t dari per hominem et dentur cotidie (quia unus episcopus consecrat alium; quicumque etiam iudex ordinarius dat cui vult suam iurisdictionem), fides autem sit donum Dei per infusionem, et bona qualitas meritis quam Deus in nobis operatur sine nobis, ut dicit Augustinus, absurdum est dicere quod Christus per Petrum det fidem vel fidei firmitatem aliis, et non dederit per Petrum aliis munus consecrationis episcopalis et munus potestatis iurisdictionis. Inter que etiam est gradus,

472 & 473 munus] minus Va

quia potestas consecrationis non potest dari per hominem simpliciter, sed solum secundum quid, scilicet instrumentaliter per potestatem ministerii. Sed potestas iudiciaria potest dari simpliciter per hominem, maxime ab illo qui in ea habet plenitudinem potestatis. Est etiam advertendum quod illam gratiam Christus fecit Petro tunc quando Petro consortium sue potentie tribuit, quod quidem consortium promisit quando dixit: *Tu es Petrus et super hanc petram edificabo ecclesiam meam* etc. Non autem dedit quousque dixit ei: *Pasce oves meas.* Unde illa que ante illam collationem apostolis tribuit non tribuit ipse per Petrum, sicut sacerdotium, quod in cena omnibus immediate dedit, non uni per alium.

Item solutio data ad sextum non valet, nec est vera solutio sicut isti dicunt, sed falsa, sicut supra multipliciter est ostensum. Quod dicunt ergo primo, etiam hoc quod ex verbo [c]omisso a Gratiano: *instituente Domino*, apparet quod illa manus impositio non fuit ad novam consecrationem sed ad forme expressionem, dicendum quod non est verum. Primo quidem, non dicit auctoritas quod Dominus illam formam instituerit, quia tunc in nulla necessitate licuisset, nec possibile fuisset, episcopum nisi a tribus consecrari, quod non potuissent apostoli observare quando fuerunt ab invicem divisi, non habentes in sua societate alios episcopos. Cum enim Lucas in Actibus diligenter nomine[n]t socios Pauli, non omisisset nominare episcopos socios si eos habuisset, sicut nominat se, Silam et alios. Unde cum in naturalibus virtus multiplicata non possit in effectum aliquem in quem non possit virtus sola quantum est de se, nisi forte quod non potest in ita intensum effectum sicut quando est multiplicata, quando scilicet effectus recipit magis et minus (sicut tres candele magis illuminant quam una sola, sed tamen tres candele in illuminando non habent aliquem effectum specie quem non habeat una sola), ita cum ordo episcopalis sit unius rationis in omnibus quantum est de natura ordinis, nullum effectum possunt habere tres episcopi quem non possit habere unus, et equalem, quia non recipit magis nec minus. Unde quantum est de natura sua ex primaria institutione, ita potest unus episcopus sine aliis consecrare episcopum, sicut confirmare vel ordinare presbyterum. Propter quod non est verisimile quod Christus, tanquam substantiale et de necessitate sacramenti, in ordinatione episcopi constituit illud quod esset repugnans perfectioni dignitatis episcopalis. Unde non dicit auctoritas: Domino instituente illam formam, sed dicit: Domino eos instituente, idest instituente et inspirante quod propter congruitatem et reverentiam et

474 sed] si Va | 491 ab] ad Va | 494 Silam] filiam Va | 502 quem] quod Va | 503 recipit] res potest Va | 508 profectioni Va

solemnitatem dignitatis episcopalis, quandocumque posset hoc commode servari, episcopus non ordinaretur nisi a tribus, non propter necessitatem sacramenti, quod potest aliter fieri. Unde tunc primo factum est illud statu < tu > m verbo et observatum exemplo. Sed exemplum debuit esse verum, non simulatorium. Unde fuit vera non simulatoria consecratio, ut dictum est.

Quod autem dicunt: tunc manus impositionem factam Jacobo non ad novam consecrationem, est magis absurdum quam illud quod dixit Gratianus si non vera consecratio fuit. Quia manus impositio in modum ordinandorum, ut dictum est, nullo modo debet fieri nisi illi qui ordinatur, aut in quo suppletur illud quod fuit omissum. Si autem fuisset a Domino ordinatus quomodocumque, certum est quod fuisset perfecte ordinatus, et per consequens nihil erat supplendum. Unde non fuisset sibi aliqua manus impositio facienda.

Quod vero dicunt: illam ordinationem factam esse imminente dispersione, et tunc eis formam traditam istorum et aliorum sacramentorum, satis est probabile. Sed quod datum sit eis exemplum falsum et simulatorium est omnino improbabile, cum de malo exemplo et simulatorio Paulus in faciem Petro restiterit, ad Galatas 2.

Item solutio data ad septimum et octavum bona est, et ista duo argumenta falsum concludunt quantum ad hoc, quod concludunt apostolos non fuisse episcopos quamdiu simul manserunt in diocesi Hierosolimitana. Quia immo < ante > quam discederent, oportuit eos esse episcopos; alias non habuissent qui eos faceret, nec ipsi alios fecissent. Sed non oportet quod fuerint facti per Christum, sed potuerunt fieri, et facti sunt, per Petrum, ut dictum est. Sicut enim Rome consecrantur omnes electi presentes qui ibi confirmantur, intentione ut aliis diocesibus, non illi, preficiantur, ita tunc Petrus alios consecravit, assignans eis dioceses, sicut Jacobo Alphei, vel intentione in proximo ad diversas partes eos mittendi, sicut et factum fuit. Simon tamen et Judas simul usque ad martyrium sine divisione leguntur predicasse et officium episcoporum exercuisse. Unde quia Christus non eis diversas terras divisit, sed Petro divisionem dimisit, ideo etiam consecrationem eorum[dem dictis] commisit. Si ergo manserunt in diocesi Hierosolimitana postquam fuit assignata Jacobo, episcopalia exercentes, hoc fuit de voluntate Jacobi, quia non debet unus episcopus in diocesi alterius sine illius licentia spiritualia ministrare vel exercere, 92 d. Non liceat § *De episcopis*, et sex capitulis sequentibus. Vel < fuit > auctoritate Petri, qui quo voluit legatos misit.

513 tunc] cum Va | 526 et[1]] ex Va | 534 ipsi] episcopi Va

Unde non ibi fuerunt sicut proprii diocesani; ideo non fuit monstruosum, quamvis Petrus tunc papa in una diocesi potuerit ponere duos vel plures episcopos et quemlibet in solidum vel pro parte sicut voluit, vel coadiutores dare Jacobo, qui solus forte non sufficiebat ad episcopalia exercenda circa multitudinem conversorum. Item non fuerunt episcopi universalis ecclesie sicut Petrus, quia fuerunt ab eo instituti, qui non potuit facere alium papam a se, nec alium equalem sibi. Sed si fuissent facti episcopi a Christo cum Petro per illa verba: *Quecumque alligaveritis super terram*, vel per illa: *Quorum remiseritis peccata*, vel per illa: *Euntes in mundum universum, predicate Evangelium omni creature*, tunc cum ibi nulla fiat restrictio, eque facti fuissent episcopi universalis ecclesie sicut Petrus. Unde rationes satis bene concludunt quod non sint facti a Christo episcopi simul cum Petro. Sed non concludunt quin sint facti a Petro post Pentecostem, ante dispersionem.

Item solutio data ad nonum non valet, quia si in minoribus ordinibus absurdum est quod promoveatur quis ad sacros ordines sine titulo, propter quod ordinator tenetur sibi de competenti beneficio providere, ne[c] mendicare cogatur in opprobrium ordinis clericalis, *De prebendis* c. *Cum secundum*, 93 d. *Diaconi*, *De clericis coniugatis* c. *Joannes* in fine, multo magis absurdum videtur aliquem in episcopum ordinari, nisi sit provisum ante, vel per ordinatorem provideatur de titulo competenti. Unde cum Christus de se non providerit de certis titulis nec de certis ecclesiis nisi soli Petro, cui totam ecclesiam commisit, videtur absurdum quod Christus alios apostolos in episcopos ordinaverat, quibus nec de titulis nec de ecclesiis provisit.

Si dicatur quod pari ratione < non > debuit eos facere sacerdotes, quia nec in sacerdotem debet quis sine titulo ordinari, dicendum quod ista prohibitio non sic est ex natura sacramenti sicut illa. Quia potestas episcopi propria et principalis respicit corpus Christi misticum, sicut patet ex eius actibus propriis, qui sunt confirmare < et > ordinare. Unde frustratur ordinatio episcopalis suo principali fine nisi preficiatur populo. Sed potestas principalis sacerdotis est super corpus Christi verum, ad quod conficiendum non indiget populo, sed solum propter honorem cleri est ab ecclesia statutum quod non ordinetur quis nisi habeat victum. Item apostoli erant religiosi qui propter Christum omnia reliquerunt (unde propter victum non oportebat eis de titulo providere), quibus Christus promiserat quod hec omnia adicerentur eis. Unde non est simile de ordine

553 circa] tunc Va | 556 cum Petro] tunc Petrus Va | 579 fine ... preficiatur] si sive nihil profidiunt Va

presbyteratus et episcopatus, quia ille non requirit populum propter principalem finem sicut iste.

Quod psotea dicunt, quod in primitiva ecclesia multa fiebant que modo non fiunt, concedatur. Nihil tamen fiebat de consensu apostolorum quod non esset pro tunc rationabile. Quod dicunt in speciali, quod tunc exemplo Petri, qui de Antiochia transiit, alii sedes suas mutabant, dicendum quod Petrus, qui erat sponsus universalis ecclesie, Christo sibi committente, illi non particulari ecclesie erat astrictus. Unde non tenebatur ipse in Antiochia plus quam in quacumque alia totius orbis residere, sed libere ibi sedit, libere recessit. Sed episcopo, qui certam ecclesiam desponsavit acceptando electionem vel provisionem de se factam, non licet eam propria auctoritate dimittere, nec [n]unquam istud licuit nisi de voluntate superiorum. Nec exemplum Petri profuit, qui illi certe ecclesie sic astrictus non fuit. Immo sicut Petro non licuit universalem ecclesiam deserere, nisi forte de eiusdem consensu, ita non licuit [n]unquam cuicumque episcopo proprie ecclesie resignare, nec ad aliam se transferre, auctoritate propria, immo nec nisi de licentia pape. Et hoc <est> etiam aliud signum quod quilibet episcopus tenet suum episcopatum a papa, in cuius solius manibus potest illud resignare. Non enim valet renuntiatio nisi fiat illi cuius est institutio, 17 q. 1 *Consaldus*, *De renuntiatione* c. ultimo. Unde cum nullus episcopus possit renuntiare nisi in manu pape, 7 q. 1 *Quam periculosum*, *De renuntiatione*, *Nisi cum pridem* in fine, inde est quod a papa vel eius virtute procedit omnis episcopalis institutio et iuris acquisitio. Similiter, quia dicit *Auth. De defensoribus civitatum* § *Iusiurandum*, coll. 3, quod preses non potest deponere defensorem quem non posuit, sed debet denuntiare ad gloriosissimos prefectos, ut inde eis fiat cure privatio, unde cum a solo papa episcopus a cura pastorali deponi possit, a papa huiusmodi cure datio processit, 3 q. 6 *Accusatus*, 5 q. 4 *Duodecim*, in fine primi responsi ibi: *Finis vero cause eius ad sedem apostolicam deferatur*.

Sed ex hoc videtur quod episcopi non sic habent a papa administrationes ecclesiarum sibi commissas sicut procurator est a domino constitutus. Quia procurator, secundum iura, quamvis per litis contestationem sit factus quasi dominus litis, nihilominus etiam tunc propter egritudinem potest amoveri ab omni prosecutione invitus, et totaliter revocari, *De procuratoribus* c. *Quamvis, Libro sexto.* Episcopus autem, pro sola egritudine, non debet ab administratione sue ecclesie removeri, nec ei

595 disposavit Va | 598 Petri] patrum Va | qui] quin? Va | 614 Finis] furis? Va | cause] omne Va | 620 a omne Va

successor dari, licet ei dari valeat coadiutor, 7 q. 1 c. 2 et quinque capitulis sequentibus, c. *Quamvis* et c. *Petisti*; *De clerico egrotante* c. *Ex parte*; c. 1 *Libro sexto*. Ergo videtur quod episcopus non sit a papa procurator institutus.

Dicendum ad hoc quod episcopi non constituuntur sicut nudi procuratores ad tempus certum, sicut procurator ad unam causam, sed sicut legitimi administratores ad vitam suam, pro communi utilitate non privata. Unde sic <ut> tutor propter longam egritudinem non amovetur, sed datur curator qui potius dicitur administrator, *Ff. De tutelis* 1. *Solent*, sic et episcopo egroto morbo perpetuo datur coadiutor. Et hoc est intelligendum quando per coadiutorem potest sufficienter succurri utilitati publice. Alioquin si necessitas vel utilitas rei publice exposcat episcopum egrotum totaliter amoveri, tunc non propter egritudinem, sed propter suam insufficientiam et inutilitatem et rei publice necessitatem vel utilitatem, que preferenda est private, potest simpliciter amoveri, et alius subrogari, quod probatur dupliciter.

Primo per illud quod habetur 15 q. 6 c. *Alius*, ubi dicitur quod Zacharias papa *regem Francorum non tam pro suis iniquitatibus, quam pro eo quod tante potestati erat inutilis, a regno deposuit, et Pipinum, Karoli imperatoris patrem, in eius locum substituit*. Si igitur principem terrenum papa potuit licite propter eius inutilitatem et rei publice utilitatem, non solum propter culpam, deponere et alium substituere, multo magis prelatum ecclesiasticum. Non obstat quod ibi dicitur in glossa super verbo "inutilis": *non intelligans inutilis, idest insufficiens, tunc enim debuisset ei dari coadiutor. Sed dissolutus erat cum mulieribus et effeminatus*. Quia licet hoc sit verum in principe seculari, qui propter solam inutil<itat>em sine culpa provenientem non debet deponi, nec pro sola culpa que eum non reddat inutilem, < nisi esset heresis et scisma, tamen in prelato ecclesie est aliter. Quia pro sola culpa que non reddit eum inutilem> etiam potest deponi, quia sola culpa mortalis facit eum inutilem et indignum prelatione ecclesiastica. Non sic autem est in principatu terreno. Similiter ex sola insufficientia sua et inutilitate, licet non proveniat ex culpa, potest licite deponi, quia etiam culpa incipit esse sibi quando tenet et occupat beneficium et non potest impendere officium. Unde de ficulnea infructuosa dixit Dominus procuratori, Luce 13: *Succide illam: ut quid etiam terram occupat*?

Secundo probatur per illud quod habetur 7 q. 1 *Mutationes*, ubi dicitur quod mutationes episcoporum possunt et debent fieri communi utilitate ac

623 7] 6 Va | et] ex Va | 635 sed] si Va | 656 impedire Va | 657 ficulnea] si culnea Va

necessitate, et subiungitur ratio, nam plurimorum utilitas unius utilitati vel voluntati preferenda est. Ex quo habetur quod contra voluntatem suam potest episcopus mutari pro communi utilitate, et non solum <quando est> voluntarius. Unde sequitur ibi expressius: aliud est mutare, aliud est mutari, nam aliud est sponte transire, aliud est coacte aut necessitate venire. Unde isti non mutant civitatem sed mutantur, quia non sponte sed coacte hoc agunt. Si igitur episcopus sine culpa propter communem utilitatem invitus amoveatur ab ecclesia in qua erat inutilis vel minus utilis, substituto sibi utili vel utiliore, et ipse transfertur ad illam in qua erit utilis vel utilior. Ergo si nulli ecclesie est utilis et sue inutilis, et non possit sufficienter per coadiutorem utilitati publice subvenire, debet penitus amoveri et alius substitui. Sed quando inutilitas sine sua culpa contingit, debet ei <victus> sufficiens ab eadem ecclesia provideri, 7 q. 1 *Quamvis*.

Quod postea dicunt, quod in primitiva ecclesia ordinabantur episcopi sine certis titulis, dicendum quod nunquam licuit nec decuit episcopum sine certo titulo ordinare, nisi illi qui poterat sibi et in promptu habebat de titulo providere. Sed Petrus, qui de voluntate Domini habebat coapostolos ad diversas mundi provincias mittere, ad illos titulos quos erant sortituri, idest populos quos erant Domino lucraturi, eos ordinavit, et etiam potestatem dedit, ut in sui adiutorium alios episcopos ordinare<n>t et eis sicut sibi videretur titulos assignare<n>t, sicut Paulus Titum Cretensibus prefecit, Dionysium Athenis, et sic de aliis. Unde illi episcopi vacantes, de quibus ordinavit concilium Antiochenum, illicite fuerunt ordinati sine titulis nisi hoc fuerit de licentia summi pontificis, qui potest novos episcopatus facere et novos titulos creare, vel simpliciter, vel episcopatus dividendo, 16 q. 1 *Precipimus*, sicut potest antiquum titulum delere, episcopatum unum alteri annectendo, eadem questione c. *Postquam*.

Quod autem dicunt in conclusione post omnia argumenta, quod potestas aliis collata per Christum non tollit quin Petrus et papa, Petri successor, sit immediatus prelatus omnium ovium Christi, dicendum quod immo <tolleret, si ita esset>. Quia ille non est immediatus prelatus per Christum qui sub se habet alios mediatos inter se et illos a Deo constitutos. Sic autem est in proposito, si alii habent potestatem a Deo. Ergo etc. Maior patet, quia ideo archiepiscopus non est immediatus prelatus subditorum suffraganeorum suorum, quia inter ipsos et illum sunt alii prelati medii constituti, scilicet episcopi suffraganei, et si illa

672 aliis Va | 673 providere Va | 677 coapostolos] capellos Va | 683 vacantes] notantes Va | 686 Precepimus Va

mediatio esset de iure divino, ipse non esset immediatus sed mediatus prelatus de iure divino. Minor patet, quia inter papam et curatos sunt episcopi medii prelati, qui sunt sub papa et sunt super curatos. Ulterius inter episcopum et parochianos sunt curati medii prelati, quia presunt parochianis et subsunt episcopis. Dicitur enim prelatus immediatus qui preest sine medio, idest qui inter se et subditos non habet medium aliquem qui sit nisi subditus. Prelatus vero mediatus est qui habet sub se alium prelatum qui sub eo preest similiter subditis. Igitur si episcopi prelationem qua sub papa presunt illis de sua diocesi, et curati prelationem qua sub papa et episcopis presunt parochianis, habent a Deo, sicut papa prelationem qua omnibus preest habet a Deo, tunc per ordinationem divinam papa non erit immediate prelatus nisi episcoporum, inter quos et ipsum de iure divino non est prelatus et medius. Non autem erit immediatus prelatus curatorum, sed episcopus, nec episcopus parochianorum, sed curatus, si et ille preest de iure divino. Nunc autem, quia nulla prelatio est de iure divino [est] nisi prelatio pape, ideo de iure divino papa est immediatus prelatus et iudex omnium, licet ipse posuerit sub se alios prelatos, per quod eis iurisdictionem concessit, non in eos transtulit. Unde nihil potestatis perdidit, sed immediatus sicut prius erat remansit, quia spiritualia per sui multiplicationem et concessionem non dividuntur nec diminu<u>ntur, sicut per hoc quod papa mittit legatos vel dat delegatos, potestas sua non tollitur nec minoratur sed multiplicatur et manifestatur.

Quod dicunt ultimo, quod auctoritates non videntur ita evidenter probare quod aliis apostolis et successoribus eorum episcopis sit collata potestas immediate a Petro, et non a Christo nisi mediante Petro, si intelligant absolute, quod scilicet auctoritates non sic evidenter concludunt quod sit credendum sicut articuli fidei de apostolis, <verum> dicunt. Quia licet oppositum sit probabilius ut visum est, tamen non est articulus fidei. Immo salva fide potest credi eos a Christo factos fuisse episcopos, et recepisse a Christo omnem potestatem quam habuerunt et nihil a Petro, pro personis tamen suis, de gratia speciali, et non pro suis successoribus, sicut Gregorius refert, primo *Dialogorum*, de beato Equitio, qui a Christo per angelum habuit, et non a papa, auctoritatem predicandi. Sed dicere quod omnes episcopi et curati ex hoc ipso quod ad hos status canonice vocantur habeant totam potestatem suam eque immediate a Deo sicut papa, et non habeant aliquid a papa plus quam econtrario, licet quantum ad eius usum subsint pape et non econtrario, non videtur stare cum articulo fidei de unitate ecclesie ex unitate capitis et plenitudine potestatis,

699 Minor] maior Va | 707 episcopos Va | 712 et] est Va | 713 pape] papa Va

ut superius est ostensum. Si vero intelligunt comparative sub hoc sensu, quod evidentiores et expressiores sunt auctoritates pro parte alia [alia] quam pro ista, forte est verum quantum ad aliquas auctoritates intellecta[n]s secundum superficiem verborum. Sed intelligendo auctoritates secundum rationem per solutiones datas ad auctoritates pro parte contraria adductas, et per reprobationem solutionum datarum ad auctoritates pro ista parte, apparet oppositum. Et licet multe auctoritates adducte ab istis pro ista parte sint solubiles, tamen ille que sunt adducte principaliter ad probandum quod omnes alie ecclesie sunt fundate a Romana ecclesia, et illa a solo Christo, videntur esse insolubiles, nisi vim littere inferendo, quod Hieronymus asserit *viciosissimum dicendi genus. Depravare*, scilicet, *sententias,* <*et*> *ad voluntatem suam Scripturam trahere repugnantem*, 6 c. *Ad Paulinum*. Immo videtur esse hereticum, sicut superius est deductum.

746 Hieronymus] Joannes Va | asserat Va | 748 Paulum Va

Appendix C
The *De causa* and the Great Schism

The following short piece, transcribed here in its entirety, was prepared by some anonymous protagonist for the Roman line of popes during the period of the Great Schism. The author begins by excerpting some passages from the *De causa* which deal with the question of whether or not the pope can be brought to judgment. He then proceeds to apply the doctrine of the *De causa* to the circumstances of the schism. Naturally he is quite favourably impressed with the *De causa*, considering it nothing short of an act of Providence that the treatise should have been preserved for a century or more in order to help him and his contemporaries find the correct solution to their problems. What is particularly significant about this tract is that it provides firm evidence for the suggestion that the *De causa* proved to be useful, particularly for the opponents of conciliarism, during the fifteenth century.

There are several points in the tract where the author suggests that he is writing during the pontificate of Gregory XII, 1406-1415,[1] although not at the very beginning of his reign.[2] This dating is supported by his statement on line 67ff., where he refers to the election of Urban VI, and then maintains that "nos obedivimus per triginta annos et ultra." Since Urban did not reign for anything approaching thirty years, this must be a reference to obedience to the Roman line of popes in general rather than to Urban in particular. However, given the fact that thirty years or more have elapsed since the election of Urban, our author must have been writing sometime after 1408. It is also supported by the argument which follows on line 74ff., where the author maintains that just as God did not wish to take the papal authority away from Urban VI so that he might confer it on Clement VII, so now he does not wish to take it away from Gregory so that he might confer it on Alexander. Since the Alexander here can be none other than the anti-pope Alexander V, this piece must have been written when both Gregory XII and Alexander V were active, and hence in the period 1409-1410.

[1] Cf. lines 65-66: "primo de Urbano, et modo de Gregorio," and lines 75-76: "Et sic nec modo <Deus> vult tollere, nec voluit, a Gregorio ut tradat Alexandro."

[2] Cf. line 96: "Et <Gregorius> exercuit diu officium papatus."

VIENNA, Österreichische Nationalbibliothek,
MS Vindobonensis Palatinus 4947, fols. 319r-320r

PETRUS DE PALUDE.
DICTA IN TRACTATU DE POTESTATE PAPE ADPLICATA AD SCISMA INTER GREGORIUM XII ET ALEXANDRUM V PAPAS

Iste solemnis doctor theologie, magister Petrus de Palude, episcopus Parisiensis et patriarcha, in tractatu suo de potestate pape sic dicit. Potestas pape propria, que preeminens est toti ecclesie, habens in ea plenitudinem potestatis, est a solo Christo immediate et non ab ecclesia. Quia si talis preeminentia pape, quam habet super alios episcopos et totam ecclesiam, esset ex statuto ecclesie, ecclesia posset illam immutare et transferre, et papam a papatu deponere. Sed hoc non potest, quia non potest facere per quod unitas ecclesie destrueretur. Quia hoc esset contra statutum Christi, qui voluit ecclesiam esse unum ovile, Joannis 10. Hoc autem non esset nisi haberet unum caput, sicut ibi dicit: *Fiet unum ovile et unus pastor*. Non ergo ecclesia potest facere quod non sit papa, et quod in ea nullus sit superior, sed sint equales omnes patriarche aut omnes episcopi, quia dicit apostolus: *Non est mihi data potestas in destructionem, sed in edificationem*. Ex quibus sequitur quod papa, quamdiu est papa, propter quodcumque crimen, nec a concilio, nec a tota ecclesia, nec a toto mundo potest deponi proprie, non solum quia est superior, sed quia est a Deo potestas sua, qui sibi Romani presulis iudicium reservavit. Et dico proprie, quia quando labitur in heresim, tunc eo ipso precisus est ab ecclesia et desinit esse caput, et tunc deponitur de facto, non de iure, quia qui non credit iam iudicatus est de iure, et precisus ab ecclesia. Non potest autem caput a corpore precisum, quamdiu est solum, esse caput illius corporis a quo est precisum. Unde papa desinit per hoc esse caput corporis ecclesie, quia ab illo prescinditur per heresim, ipso facto, iuxta illud Deuteronomii 17: *Non potes alterius gentis hominem super te facere regem*. Unde hereticus non potest esse nec manere papa, quia extra ecclesiam existens non potest habere claves ecclesie quamdiu sit extra. Per alia autem peccata est caput languidum, quod non propter hoc desinit esse caput, nec potest a membris per consequens iudicari. Quod ergo Marcellinus papa, qui idolatraverat, non fuit iudicatus de facto, sed dictum est ei: "Tu ipse iudica causam tuam," 21 d. *Nunc autem*, hoc est quia non erat hereticus, quia a

4-9 Potestas ... potest[1]: cf. *De causa* **4**: 8-13 | 9-16 quia ... edificationem: cf. *De causa* **4**: 30-37 | 16-47 papa[1] ... esset: cf. *De causa* **4**: 177-211.

fide nunquam deviaverat animo, sed motu tormentorum sacrificaverat idolis. Unde falsa est glossa dicens de quocumque alio crimine notorio papa, si est incorrigibilis, potest accusari et amoveri, quia contumacia est heresis, et contumax dicitur infidelis. Quia hoc non est proprie sed solum metaphorice, sicut et simonia dicitur heresis. Et ideo quidquid agat papa quamdiu est papa, nunquam iudicari potest nec condemnari, non propter hoc tantum, quia nullus inferior potest iudicare superiorem quamdiu sit superior, de lege communi, sed potissime propter hoc, quod papatus, qui non est ab homine, non potest ab homine iudicari. Unde propter quodcumque crimen quo papa non desinit esse papa, sicut est omne aliud preter heresim proprie dictam, papa ab homine iudicari non potest. Sed reprehendi potest, sicut Paulus in faciem restitit Petro, quia reprehensibilis erat, ita quod in malis non est ei obediendum, sed resistendum. Unde si cogeret gentes iudaizare, non vere quia tunc esset hereticus, sed similitudinarie, sicut Petrus faciebat, resistendum esset. Vel si papa vellet totum thesaurum ecclesie dare parentibus suis, aut ecclesiam sancti Petri destruere, aut patrimonium Petri alienare, vel aliquod huiusmodi, non esset permittendum, sed esset ei resistendum sine eius depositione. Secundum remedium esset exemplo sancti Hylarii, qui contra Leonem papam prevaluit orando. Quia orandum esset pro ipso a tota ecclesia, quod Deus ipsum corrigeret, vel de medio amoveret. Vel esset contra eum concilium convocandum per cardinales, si ipse nollet convocare, ut per illud moveretur ad desistendum, vel Deus imploraretur, et remedium apponeret, ne ecclesia periclitaretur per illa mala. Item aliud exemplum de hoc remedio, nam Anastasius papa periit scelere proprio et iustorum orationibus percussus, 19 d. *Anastasius*.

Hec ille valens doctor, Petrus de Palude, et multa alia ponit pro nostra conclusione. Et revera bene est notandum, et multum ponderandum, quod iste valens doctor, qui composuit hunc tractatum iam forte sunt elapsi centum anni vel ultra, ita clare loquitur de presenti scismate et informat nos ac si esset presens, utique ex inspiratione divina. Quia ante istud scisma non indiguimus hac clara informatione, sed modo maxime. Et determinat satis aperte quam papam debeamus firmiter tenere, primo de Urbano [Urbanus VI, 1378-1389] et modo de Gregorio [Gregorius XII, 1406-1415], cum clarum sit quod ipsi receperunt claves ecclesie a Deo. De Urbano nullus nostrum Theutonicorum, Almannorum, Ytalicorum, Anglicorum etc. debet dubitare, cum patres nostri mortui magnam

67 sit] sunt MS

47-58 Vel ... Anastasius: cf. *De causa* 4: 216-229.

discussionem et consilia super hoc habentes, determinaverunt se ad eum. Et nos obedivimus per triginta annos et ultra. Et de Gregorio patet. Unde et ille claves, seu ista potestas data a Deo ipsis, non potuit tolli ab eis per adversarios postea supervenientes, nec per illos qui elegerunt ipsos, ut patet clare dicta istius doctoris intuenti. Nec Deus voluit eam tollere ab Urbano ut daret Clementi postea intruso [Clementus vii, 1378-1394], et sic nec modo vult tollere, nec voluit, a Gregorio ut tradat Alexandro [Alexander v, 1409-1410], cum ipsius solius Dei sit dare hanc magnam potestatem iurisdictionis rite electo, aut cui vult, et non vult nisi uni dare quamdiu ille vivat, nisi perdiderit voluntarie renuntiando, vel per veram et propriam heresim incurrendo. Et sicut Petro dixit: *Tibi*, scilicet soli, *dabo*, quia dona Dei sunt sine penitentia secundum apostolum, non auferendo dona que dedit, nec vult quod aliquis alius dissolvat, sicut in caractere sacramentorum, et in signo indelebili episcoporum, et in matrimonio, *quod Deus coniunxit homo non separat* etc. Et licet in istis non sit totaliter similitudo, tamen bene quo ad propositum, ut non possint ab homine auferri et sine consensu ipsius. Et sic omnibus obicientibus et obiectis per adversam partem contra dominum Gregorium respondet ac si esset presens, ut ex scriptis eius potest capi responsio clara ad dicta eorum omnium que obiciunt, ut poterit patere diligenter considerenti. Verum hic nihil assero pertinaciter. Si quis efficaciora motiva adducet, stetur illis. Attestatur ille doctor utriusque iuris, vicarius episcopi Florentinensis, magister Robertus de Fronsola, modum electionis sue narrando. Videbitur ibi clare in tractatu suo, dicens quod omnes cardinales Romani habuerunt occulum ad ipsum propter sanctitatem suam, quia totus sanctus reputabatur, et elegerunt eum concorditer, et vocatus est Gregorius xii. Nescio quare modo sibi contrariatur. Et exercuit diu officium papatus, ac omnes cardinales petiverunt gratias ab eo, quia nulli dubitandum quin erat verus papa, sicut Urbanus, Bonifacius [Bonifacius ix, 1389-1404] etc. Ex quibus clare liquet quod nullus purus homo aut concilium hominum, aut concilia, potuerunt dominum Gregorium deponere de papatu.

80 Matt. 16:19 | 81 Cf. Rom. 11:29 | 84 Matt. 19:6; Marc. 10:9

Index auctorum citatorum

The following is an index to the sources of the *De causa*. It includes Appendix A, but omits the Epilogus and Appendices B and C. References are by chapter and line number.

I. *Scriptura sacra*

II. *Scriptores*

III. *Corpus Iuris Canonici*

IV. *Corpus Iuris Civilis*

Index nominum et rerum

The following is an index to the entire book, both the Prolegomena and the text of the *De causa*, although it does not include the Epilogus or Appendix B. References to the Prolegomena and to the introductions to Appendices A and C are by page number and are printed in italics. References to the text of the *De causa* and to the texts of Appendices A and C are by chapter and line number. Classical, patristic and medieval authors are listed by their first names.